The EU, the WTO and China

This book presents a new theoretical framework for understanding the regulation of international trade. For this purpose, it analyses a series of integrated studies of relations between the EU, the WTO and China. It consists of three main parts. Part I introduces the basic concepts. It surveys the literature on law and globalisation, introduces the concept of sites of governance and the theory of global legal pluralism, and sketches the foundations of global legal pluralism. It shows that each site of governance has both a structural dimension, consisting of institutions, norms and dispute resolution processes, and a relational dimension, comprising its relations with other sites of governance. The totality of sites of governance constitutes a new form of global legal pluralism. Part II analyses global legal pluralism in action in relations between the EU, the WTO and China. It examines the construction of relations between sites, ways in which relations between sites give rise to new legal concepts or transform the character of rules, the tension between regionalism and international integration, and the governance of international production networks. It emphasises the reciprocal interaction between the structural features and the relational features of sites. Part III explores new directions in global legal pluralism. It first analyses regional trade agreements as a way of creating new sites of governance, focusing on agreements involving China. Then it considers how to enhance ethical values in international trade regulation. Based on an institutional analysis of relations between the WTO and other sites of governance, it proposes ways in which global legal pluralism can be used to reform the WTO, today the predominant institution in the regulation of international trade, including trade between the EU and China.

The EU, the WTO and China

Legal Pluralism and International Trade Regulation

Francis Snyder

·HART·
PUBLISHING

OXFORD AND PORTLAND, OREGON
2010

Published in the United Kingdom by Hart Publishing Ltd
16C Worcester Place, Oxford, OX1 2JW
Telephone: +44 (0)1865 517530
Fax: +44 (0)1865 510710
E-mail: mail@hartpub.co.uk
Website: http://www.hartpub.co.uk

Published in North America (US and Canada) by
Hart Publishing
c/o International Specialized Book Services
920 NE 58th Avenue, Suite 300
Portland, OR 97213-3786
USA
Tel: +1 503 287 3093 or toll-free: (1) 800 944 6190
Fax: +1 503 280 8832
E-mail: orders@isbs.com
Website: http://www.isbs.com

British Library Cataloguing in Publication Data
Data Available

ISBN: 978-1-84113-704-9

Typeset by Hope Services, Abingdon, Oxford
Printed and bound in Great Britain by
TJ International Ltd, Padstow, Cornwall

For Anne-Lise

Note to the Reader

This book was written and prepared for publication before the entry into force of the Treaty of Lisbon on 11 December 2009. For the sake of clarity, it uses the Treaty article numbering and the legislative nomenclature which applied at the time of the Treaty articles, legislation and judicial decisions analysed in the book. The Treaty of Lisbon amended the Treaty on European Union (TEU) and the Treaty establishing the European Community (TEC). These amendments resulted in a new Treaty on European Union (TEU) and a new Treaty on the Functioning of the European Union (TFEU). It also renumbered Treaty articles. It requires references to the *European Community* to be read as the *European Union*, references to the *European Court of Justice* to be read as the *Court of Justice* and references to the *Court of First Instance* to be read as the *General Court*. These changes do not affect in any material way the analysis in this book.

For convenience, the following table provides equivalences of numbering in relevant articles in the 1957 Treaty establishing the European Economic Community (TEEC) and successive Treaties up to and including the TEU and the TFEU following the entry into force of the Treaty of Lisbon.

European Treaty Article Numbering: Table of Equivalences

Original numbering of the Treaty establishing the European Economic Community (1957)	**Numbering introduced by the Treaty establishing the European Community (1992) [Maastricht Treaty], used until 2/10/1997**	**Numbering of the Treaty of Amsterdam and the Treaty of Nice, used from 2/10/1997 to 1/12/2009**	**Current numbering in the TEU and TFEU (2009) following adoption of the Lisbon Treaty**
2	2	2	repealed
---	4	4	119 TFEU
---	14	14	26 TFEU
	28	26	31 TFEU
85	81	81	101 TFEU
86	82	82	102 TFEU
92	87	87	107 TFEU
93	88	88	108 TFEU
---	100a	95	114 TFEU
110	131	131	206 TFEU
112	repealed	---	---
113	133	133	207 TFEU
114	repealed	---	---
115	134	134	repealed
190	190	253	296 TFEU
169	169	226	258 TFEU
173	173	230	263 TFEU
175	175	232	266 TFEU
177	177	234	267 TFEU
	228	300	218 TFEU
	238	310	217 TFEU

Preface and Acknowledgments

This book presents a new theoretical framework for understanding the regulation of international trade. It focuses on relations between the EU, the WTO and China. It consists of three main parts. Part I introduces the basic concepts and the theoretical framework. It surveys the literature on law and globalisation, introduces the concept of sites of governance and the theory of global legal pluralism and sketches the foundations of global legal pluralism. It shows that each site of governance has both a structural dimension, consisting of institutions, norms and dispute resolution processes, and a relational dimension, comprising its relations with other sites of governance. The totality of sites of governance constitutes a new form of global legal pluralism. Using this theoretical framework, Part II analyses global legal pluralism in action in relations between the EU, the WTO and China. It examines the construction of relations between sites, ways in which relations between sites give rise to new legal concepts or transform the character of rules, the tension between regionalism and international integration and the governance of international production networks. It emphasises the reciprocal interaction between the structural features and the relational features of sites. Looking toward the future, Part III explores new directions in global legal pluralism. It first analyses regional trade agreements as a way of creating new sites of governance, focusing on agreements involving China. Then it considers how to enhance ethical issues in international trade regulation. Based on an institutional analysis of relations between the WTO and other sites of governance, it proposes ways in which global legal pluralism can be used to reform the WTO, today the predominant institution in the regulation of international trade, including trade between the EU and China.

Nourished by teaching and research in Europe, North America, Africa and Asia, in particular China, this book has taken shape over a number of years. I am grateful to many people, institutions and organisations for their help and support. Without their generous help, the book would never have been completed. It is a pleasure to thank them here. I hope that anyone whom I have neglected to mention, or government officials who wished not to be identified specifically, will find in the book itself an expression of my gratitude.

For encouragement, discussion, comments and support, I wish to thank especially (in alphabetical order) George Bermann, Peter Bernholz, Carol Bernstein, Richard Bernstein, Coit Blacker, Paulo Canelas de Castro, Partha Chatterjee, Cui Zhiyuan, Ding Ding, Maria do Ceu Esteves, Cao Ge Feng, Chen Yongquan, Cheng Weidong, Jill Cottrell, Dai Bingran, Candido Garcia Molyneux, Yash Ghai, Christian Joerges, Tom Heller, David Holloway, Hans Henrik Holm, Beate Kohler-Koch, Stephen Krasner, Jacqueline Lastenouse, Li Qiang, Ahmed Mahiou, Sandrine Maljean-Dubois, Rostane Mehdi, Cosimo Monda, Jens Ladefoged Mortensen, the late Emile Noël, the late Michael Oksenberg, Francois Ost, Rao Geping, José Luis de Sales Marques, Marc Pena, Austin Sarat, Shao Jingchun, Song Ying, Georg Sorensen, Patricia Springborg, Anne-Lise Strahtmann, Nicolas Triart, Mark van Hoecke, Kenji Takamiya, Katherine Verdery, Wang Hui, Wang Xiaoye, Andreas Wimmer,

Wu Zhipan, Yang Zugong, Zeng Lingliang, Zhang Naigen, Zhou Hong and the Globalisation Working Group at the Wissenschaftskolleg zu Berlin (Institute for Advanced Study) in 2000–2001.

For research assistance or help with documents, I am grateful to (again in alphabetical order) Stéphane Arnaud, Bao Yongqing, Brice Bussière, Jill Cottrell, Mariona Ferrar-i-Fons, Romain Galante, Candido Garcia Molyneux, Florence Giorgi, Laurence Henry, Hou Fang, Lina Jaubert-Tzankova, Fudia Komba-Kono, Donia Landoulsi-Faure, Emir Lawless, Carole Le Cloierec-Fouret, Li Ming, Jens Ladefoged Mortensen, Frederico Ortino, Frédérique Pellaton-Capitani, Qiao Shitong, Sabrina Regent, Magda Salykova, Magda Tovar Gomis, KL Thiratayakinant, Nadine Thwaites, Nicolas Triart, Eve Truilhé, Wu Qianlan, Gulrez Yazdani, Yin Xiao, Zhang Yuanyuan and Zhu Dingpu. The staff at the libraries of the European University Institute (Florence), the European Commission, the Centre d'Etudes et de Recherches Internationales et Communautaires (CERIC: CNRS UMR 6201) at the Université Paul Cézanne Aix-Marseille III, the London School of Economics, the Institute of Advanced Legal Studies of the University of London and the Wissenschaftskolleg zu Berlin (Institute for Advanced Study) have been unfailingly generous with their assistance. Amélie Caudroy performed sterling service in preparing the manuscript for the publisher. Oleg Vorontzoff provided indispensable help with the copy editor's queries.

Similarly, I am grateful also to officials of the European Commission in Brussels, the Hong Kong Trade Development Council, the Shenzhen Special Economic Zone and the Ministry of Commerce (Mofcom; formerly Ministry of Foreign Trade and Economic Cooperation, Moftec) of the People's Republic of China in Beijing.

For financial or other material support, I wish to thank the Research Council of the European University Institute in Florence; the Centre d'Etudes et de Recherches Internationales et Communautaires (CERIC: CNRS UMR 6201); Université Paul Cézanne Aix-Marseille III; the China Scholarship Council, Ministry of Education, People's Republic of China for granting me a Chinese Culture Research Fellowship (2006–2007); the European Commission Jean Monnet Programme which awarded me a Jean Monnet Chair *ad personam*; the Law Department, London School of Economics; Peking University Law School; Centre for European Studies, Peking University; Tsinghua Law School, Tsinghua University; and the Wissenschaftskolleg zu Berlin (Institute for Advanced Study). I am especially grateful to Wang Chenguang, former Dean of Tsinghua Law School, and to Zhu Suli, Dean of Peking University Law School. Yin Ming provided invaluable help during my stays at Peking University Law School.

Preliminary versions of various chapters were presented at Academy of International Trade and Investment Law (Macau), Centre for European Studies at Peking University, Columbia Law School (New York), College of Europe (Bruges), College of Europe (Natolin, Warsaw), Colloque Aix-en-Provence/Tübingen, EU-China Higher Education Cooperation Programme International Conference, European Academy of Legal Theory, European University Institute, Fudan University (Shanghai), Guangdong International Research Institute for Technology and Economy (Guangzhou, China), Institute of European Studies of the Chinese Academy of Social Sciences (Beijing), Institute of European Studies of Macau, Institute of Law of the Chinese Academy of Social Sciences (Beijing), International Conference on Sociology of Law (Courmayeur Mont Blanc), Joint Meeting of the Law and Society Association and the Research Committee on Sociology of Law (Budapest), London School of Economics, Peking University Law School, Stanford

University, Tsinghua Law School, University College London, University of Macau, Université de Paris I, Université Paul Cézanne Aix-Marseille III, University of Wuhan, Wissenschaftskolleg zu Berlin and the Zentrum für Europäische Sozialforschung of the Universität Mannheim. I am grateful for comments and discussion on these occasions.

As the book gradually took shape as a sustained argument, preliminary versions of various chapters have been published individually. For this book, however, all chapters have been updated as necessary, revised and sometimes completely rewritten.

—Chapter 2 is an updated, completely revised and rewritten version of an article originally published as 'Economic Globalization and the Law in the 21st Century', in Austin Sarat (ed), *The Blackwell Companion to Law and Society* (New York and Oxford, Blackwell Publishers, 2004) 624–40.

—Chapter 3 is a revised, expanded version of an article originally published as 'Governing Economic Globalization: Global Legal Pluralism and European Law', (1999) (5) 4 *European Law Journal* 334–74.

—A very preliminary, shorter version of part of what is now Chapter 4 was published as 'The European Union, Globalisation and China: EC Anti-dumping Law, Legal Strategies and Unintended Consequences', in Wolfgang Graf Vitzthum, Catherine Prieto and Rostane Mehdi (eds), *Europe et Mondialisation / Europa und die Globalisierung* (Actes du Colloque de la Faculté de Droit et de Science Politique d'Aix-Marseille et de la Faculté de Droit de Tübingen, Aix-en-Provence, 21–22 octobre 2004) (Aix-en-Provence, Presses Universitaires d'Aix-Marseille, 2006) 362–81. A preliminary version of other parts of this chapter was published as 'Antidumping Law and Cross-Cultural Encounters: Toward a Legal Anthropology of International Economic Relations', in Christoph Eberhard and Geneviève Vernicos (eds), *La quête anthropologique du droit: Autour de la démarche d'Etienne Le Roy* (Paris, Karthala, 2006) 59–76.

Chapter 5 is an updated, revised and partly rewritten version of an article that was originally published as 'The Gatekeepers: The European Courts and WTO Law' (2003) 40 *Common Market Law Review* 313–67.

—Chapter 6 is a slightly revised version of an article originally published as 'The Origins of the "Nonmarket Economy": Ideas, Pluralism and Power in EC Antidumping Law about China' (2001) 7 4 *European Law Journal* 369–424.

—Chapter 7 is a revised and partly rewritten version of an article published as 'How Does Europe Regulate Trade With China? The Juridification of Individual Treatment in EC Anti-Dumping Law', in Paul Demaret, Inge Govaere and Dominik Hanf (eds), *Thirty Years of European Legal Studies at the College of Europe / Trente ans d'études juridiques européennes au Collège d'Europe, Liber Professorum 1973–74–2003–04* (Presses interuniversitaires européennes / Peter Lang, Bruxelles, 'Studies of the College of Europe', 2004).

—Chapter 8 is an updated, completely revised and rewritten version of an article originally published as 'Europeanisation and Globalisation as Friends and Rivals: European Union Law and Global Economic Networks', in Francis Snyder (ed), *The Europeanisation of Law: Legal Effects of European Integration* (Oxford, Hart Publishing, 2000) 293–320.

—Chapter 9 is an updated and slightly revised version of an article on 'China's Regional Trade Agreements and WTO Law', originally published in (2009) (43) 1

Journal of World Trade 1-57.

—A preliminary version of Chapter 10 was published in French as 'Ethique, OMC et pluralisme juridique mondial: Etat des lieux et propositions', in Jean-Yves Naudet (ed), *Mondialisation et Ethique des Echanges* (Actes du neuvième colloque d'éthique économique, Aix-en-Provence, 4–5 juillet 2002) (Editions de la Libraire Universitaire, Aix-en-Provence, 2003) 117–56.

I am grateful to the following publishers for permission to use material in which they hold copyright: Wiley-Blackwell for material incorporated into chapters 2, 3 and 6 and for table 11 used in chapter 8; Presses Universitaires d'Aix-Marseille for material incorporated into chapter 4; Karthala for material incorporated into chapter 4; Kluwer Law International for material incorporated into chapter 5; P.I.E. Peter Lang S.A. for material incorporated into chapter 7; and Wolters Kluwer Legal for material incorporated into chapter 9. I would also like to thank GU Zhengkun, Peking University Press and China Translation and Publishing Corporation for the use of the poem taken from the translations of Lao Tzu's *The Book of Tao and The*, Richard Baldwin for allowing me to reproduce his figure in chapter 9, and the European Commission for the three figures used in chapter 8. Moreover, while gratefully acknowledging the authors and publishers of extracted material which appears in this book, and while offering assurances that every care has been taken to establish and acknowledge copyright, and to contact copyright owners, the Publisher asks the owner of any copyright who feels that it may have been accidentally used without permission, to contact them at the address found in the front of this work.

My son Jasper made numerous contributions to this book over the years. I am most grateful to him for his help and support.

My biggest debt is to Anne-Lise Strahtmann, to whom I owe more than words can say and to whom this book is dedicated.

I wish to thank especially Richard Hart, Rachel Turner, Mel Hamill, Jo Ledger and their colleagues, including copy editors, at Hart Publishing. As always, it has been a pleasure to benefit from their cooperation, patience and efficiency.

Needless to say, I am solely responsible for any shortcomings of the book. All suggestions for improvement are welcome.

Francis Snyder
Sils im Engadin
Peking University Law School
20 September 2009

Summary Contents

Note to the Reader vi
Acknowledgements vii
Table of Cases xvii
Table of Legislation xxvii
Table of Treaties xxxv
List of Tables xlix
List of Figures li

1 Introduction 1

PART I GLOBALISATION, SITES OF GOVERNANCE AND GLOBAL LEGAL PLURALISM 9

2 Globalisation and the Law 11
3 Governing Economic Globalisation: Sites of Governance and Global Legal Pluralism 42
4 Foundations of Global Legal Pluralism: International Competition, Legal Strategies and Unintended Consequences in the EU *Chinese Bicycles* Anti-dumping Saga 89

PART II GLOBAL LEGAL PLURALISM IN ACTION: THE EU, THE WTO AND CHINA 151

5 The Construction of Relations between Sites of Governance: the European Courts and WTO Law 153
6 Global Legal Pluralism and the Creation of New Legal Concepts: the 'Non-market Economy' in EC Anti-dumping Law 209
7 Relations between Sites of Governance and the Legalisation of Norms: Individual Treatment in EC Anti-dumping Law about China 265
8 Competing Constellations of Sites: EC Customs Law and International Production Networks 285

PART III NEW DIRECTIONS IN GLOBAL LEGAL PLURALISM 321

9 The Creation of New Sites of Governance: China, Regional Trade Agreements and WTO Law 323
10 Social Solidarity Ethics and the WTO: Toward Closer Relations between Sites of Governance 381

Bibliography 425
Index 475

Contents

Note to the Reader vi
Acknowledgements vii
Table of Cases xvii
Table of Legislation xxvii
Table of Treaties xxxv
List of Tables xlix
List of Figures li

1 Introduction 1

PART I GLOBALISATION, SITES OF GOVERNANCE AND GLOBAL LEGAL PLURALISM 9

2 Globalisation and the Law 11

I. Introduction 11
II. Internationalisation of Legal Fields 12
III. New Institutions and New Norms 16
IV. Specific Fields of Research 20
V. Governance of Globalisation 25
A. Contract 26
B. Hierarchy 26
C. Networks 27
D. Global legal pluralism 29
VI. Global Governance 34

3 Governing Economic Globalisation: Sites of Governance and Global Legal Pluralism 42

I. Introduction 42
A. How is Globalisation Governed? 42
B. The Meaning of Globalisation 42
C. An Analytical Strategy 44
II. An International Production Network: the Global Commodity Chain in Toys 44
III. Elements of Global Legal Pluralism 48
IV. The Toy Sector and the Shape of Global Legal Pluralism 54
A. Outline 54
B. Monopoly or Competition 55
C. Geographical Concentration or Dispersal 64
D. Multiple Memberships 69
E. Property 71
F. Labour 72

G. Links Within a Chain 77
H. Connections between Specific Sites and Particular sets of Economic Relations 78
I. Relations between Sites and the Chain as a Whole 82
V. Conclusion 84

4 Foundations of Global Legal Pluralism: International Competition, Legal Strategies and Unintended Consequences in the EC *Chinese Bicycles* Anti-dumping Saga 89

I. Introduction 89
A. Sites of Governance and Global Legal Pluralism 89
B. Four Perspectives on Anti-dumping Law 90
C. Strategic Actors and the World Bicycle Industry 92
D. Organisation of the Chapter 94
II. International Competition and Anti-dumping Law 95
A. EBMA's Search for Protection 95
B. The European Commission's Analysis 97
C. The Commission's Analysis Confirmed 104
D. Shanghai Bicycle Corporation's Strategy of Litigation 106
III. Globalisation, Circumvention and Economic Regulation 109
A. Competing Legal Strategies in a Globalised Industry 109
B. Anti-dumping Law begets Economic Regulation 115
IV. Renewal of Anti-dumping Duties and the Consequences 119
A. A Short-Lived Victory for EBMA and Commission Strategies 119
B. The Successive Phases 123
C. Consequences, Intended and Unintended 130
V. Conclusion 138
Appendix: Chronology of the *Chinese Bicycles* Saga 142

PART II GLOBAL LEGAL PLURALISM IN ACTION: THE EU, THE WTO AND CHINA 151

5 The Construction of Relations Between Sites of Governance: the European Courts and WTO Law 153

I. Introduction 153
II. WTO and the EC Legal Order 155
A. Effects of WTO Law on the EC Legal Order 155
B. Interpretation of WTO Law and EC Law 156
III. WTO Law and the Individual 165
A. WTO Law and Direct Effect 165
B. WTO Law and the Legality of EC Law 178
C. Supervision of EC Breaches of WTO Law 188
IV. Effects of WTO Law on Relations Between the EC and the Member States 191

A. WTO Law and the Distribution of Powers 191
B. WTO Law and European Integration 199
V. Conclusion 203

6 Global Legal Pluralism and the Creation of New Legal Concepts: the 'Non-market Economy' in EC Anti-dumping Law 209

I. Introduction 209
A. Legal Ideas and Legal Practice 209
B. Aims and Scope of the Chapter 211
C. Argument and Organisation 212
II. The Anti-dumping Law Repertoire: Origins and Circulation 214
A. Roots in the Cold War 214
B. The US and GATT during the 1960s' 'Long boom' 224
C. The Beginning of European Community Anti-dumping Law 234
III. Consolidation of the 'Non-market Economy' Concept 242
A. The Interaction of US Law and GATT Law 242
B. The Birth of the 'Non-market Economy' in EC Anti-dumping Law 248
C. Consolidation 256
D. Legal Rule and Administrative Discretion 258
IV. Conclusion 260

7 Relations between Sites and the Legalisation of Norms: Individual Treatment in EC Anti-dumping Law about China 265

I. Introduction 265
II. The Phase of Administrative Practice 268
III. The Phase of Soft Law 274
IV. The Phase of Hard Law 278
V. Conclusion 282

8 Competing Constellations of Sites: EC Customs Law and International Production Networks 285

I. Introduction 285
II. Globalisation, IPNs and the Europeanisation of Regulation 287
A. Globalisation and IPNs 287
B. The Europeanisation of Regulatory Law 288
C. Implications 289
III. International Production Networks in EC Law and International Law 297
A. The EC Legislative Framework 297
B. International Treaties 301
C. International Production Networks in the European Courts 303
D. Customs Procedures and Anti-dumping Law 315
IV. Conclusion 319

PART III NEW DIRECTIONS IN GLOBAL LEGAL PLURALISM 321

9 The Creation of New Sites of Governance: China, Regional Trade Agreements and WTO Law 323

I. Introduction 323
II. China's Regional Trade Agreements in Outline 328
A. Introduction 328
B. Economic Integration Agreements with Hong Kong and Macao and Related Agreements 332
C. Standard RTAs: ASEAN–China Framework Agreement and Related Agreements 337
D. Bilateral RTAs: Free Trade Agreements with Individual Sovereign States 346
III. China's RTAs and WTO Law 353
A. Introduction 353
B. Non-preferential Rules of Origin 354
C. Safeguards 360
D. Dispute Settlement 363
IV. Conclusion 376

10 Social Solidarity Ethics and the WTO: Toward Closer Relations between Sites of Governance 381

I. Theoretical Framework 381
A. Foundations 381
B. The WTO and Ethics 384
C. Relations between Sites of Governance 386
II. Current Relations between the WTO and Other Sites of Governance 388
A. Introduction 388
B. The GATT Legacy: IMF, World Bank and the UN 389
C. 1995–2000: Agreements with WIPO, OIE and ITU 392
D. 2000–present: Agreements with UNCTAD, ITC, FAO and Codex Alimentarius 394
E. 1997–present: Informal Working Arrangements with WHO, ILO and OECD 395
F. The Future: Relations with UNESCO, MEAs, NGOs and Private Standards Bodies 397
III. Developing Social Solidarity Ethics in International Trade Regulation 399
A. The Matrix of Relations between Sites of Governance 399
B. Institutional Relations between Sites 403
C. Increasing Cooperation in Norm Production 408
D. Expanding Observer Status 415
E Dispute Settlement Processes 418
IV. Conclusion 421

Bibliography 425
Index 475

Table of Cases

European Union

Acme Industry Co Ltd v Council, Case T–48/96, [1999] ECR II–3089 ....157, 181
Afrikanische Frucht-Compagnie GmbH v Council, Joined Cases T–64/01 and T–65/01, [2004] ECR II–521 176
Agrover Srl v Agenzia Dogane Circoscrizione Doganale di Genova, Case C–173/06, [2007] ECR I–8783 ....307, 308
Amministrazione delle finanze dello Stato v Italia Chiquita Italia, Case C–469/93, [1995] ECR I–4533..166
Amministrazione delle Finanze dello Stato v Societe Petrolifera Italiana SpA (SPI) and SpA Michelin Italiana (SAMI), Joined Cases 267/81–269/81, [1983] ECR 801 ....157, 166, 238
Anheuser-Busch Inc v Budejovick? Budvar národni podnik, Case C–245/02, [2004] ECR I–10989 197
Anton Dürbeck v Commission, Case T–252/97, [2000] ECR II–3031 175
Arran Aromatics and Others v Commission, Case T–109/03 191
ASM Lithography BV v Inspecteur van de Belastingdienst-Douane Zuid/kantoor Roermond, Case C–100/05, [2006] ECR I–10005..306
Atlanta AG and others v Council and Commission, Case C–104/97P, [1999] ECR 6983 ....175, 176, 181
Atlanta and Others v European Community, Case T–521/93, [1996] ECR II–1707 ....175, 176, 181
Banan-Kompaniet AB and Skandinaviska Banaimporten AB v Council and Commission, Case T–57/00, [2003] ECR II–577 191
Banatrading GmbH v Council of the European Union, Case T–3/99, [2001] ECR II–2123...176, 185
Beamglow Ltd v European Parliament, Council and Commission, Case T–383/00, [2005] ECR II–5459 190
Belgian State v Banque Indosuez and Others, Case C–177/96, [1997] ECR I–5659...156
Biret International SA v Council, Case 93/02P, [2003] ECR I–10497 190
Bocchi Food Trade International GmbH v Commission, Case T–30/99, [2001] ECR I–4619...168, 176, 186, 190
Bresciani v Amministrazione Italiana delle Finanze, Case 87/75, [1976] ECR 129..173
British Horseracing Board and Others, Case C–203/02, [2004] ECR I–10415 160
Brown Boveri, Case C–79/89, [1991] ECR I–1853 198
Büchel & Co Fahrzeugteilefabrik GmbH v Council of the European Union, Büchel & Co Fahrzeugteilefabrik v Commission of the European Communities, Joined Cases T–74/97 and T–75/97, [2000] ECR II–3067 ....118, 146
Bureau Européen des Unions de Consommateurs (BEUC) v Commission, Case T–256/97, [1999] ECR II–169..161

Bureau Européen des Unions de Consommateurs (BEUC) v Commission, Case T–256/97, [2000] ECR II–101 183
Cantina Produttori Cormòns, Luigi Soini v Ministero delle Politiche Agricole, Alimentari e Forestali, Regione Friuli Venezia Giulia, Case C–24/07, [2008] ECR I–4277 165
CD Cartondruck AG v Council and Commission, Case T–320/00, [2005] ECR II–27 190
Chiquita Brands International Inc, Chiquita Banana Co BV and Chiquita Italia SpA v Commission, Case T–19/01, [2005] ECR II–315 186
Climax Paper Converters v Council of the European Union, Case T–155/94, [1996] ECR II–873 276
Comafrica SpA and Dole Fresh Fruit Europe Ltd & Co v Commission, Case T–230/97, [1997] ECR II–3031 175
Comité Européen des Fabricants de Sucre (CEFS) v Council, Case T–229/R, [1997] ECR II–1649 180
Commission of the European Communities v Council of the European Communities, Case 165/87, [1988] ECR 5545 65
Commission of the European Communities v Kingdom of Denmark, Case C–19/05, [2007] ECR I–8597 307
Commission v Council, Case 22/70, [1971] ECR 263 .... 194, 276
Commission v Council, Case 45/86, [1987] ECR 1493 186
Commission v Council, Case 25/94, [1996] ECR I–1469 310
Commission v Council, Case C–94/03, [2006] ECR I–1 192
Commission v European Parliament and Council, Case C–178/03, [2006] ECR I–107 192
Commission v Germany, Case C–61/94 [1996] ECR I–3989 .... 196, 198, 202, 302
Commission v Ireland, Case C–13/00, [2002] ECR I–2943 .... 194, 195, 202
Commission v Italy, Case 10/61, [1962] ECR (Eng Sp Ed) 1 157
Commission v Netherlands, Case 49/82, [1983] ECR 1195 .... 301, 304
Commission v Portugal, Case C–404/97, [2000] ECR I–4897 202
Committee of the Cotton and Allied Textile Industries of the European Union (Eurocoton) and others v Council, Case T–213/97, [1997] ECR II–1609 .... 157, 161
Confcooperativa Friuli Venezia Giulia, Luigi Soini, Azienda Agricola Vivai Pinat Mario e figlio v Ministero delle Politiche Agricole, Alimentari e Forestali, Regione Friuli Venezia Giulia, Case C–23/07, [2008] ECR I–4277 165
Confcooperative Unione regionale della Cooperazione Fvg Federagricole, Fiulvini Soc Coop rl, Cantina Sociale di Ramusscello e S Vito v Ministero delle Politiche Agricole e Forestali, Regione Veneto, Case C–231/04, [2006] ECJ I–61 164
Confederacion Española de Transporte de Mercancias (CETM) v Commission, Case T–55/99, [2000] ECR I–3207 .... 162, 163, 184
Cordis Obst und Gemüse Grosshandel GmbH v Commission, Case T–18/99, [2001] ECR II–913 .... 168, 176, 190
Demirel v Stadt Schwäbish Gmünd, Case 12/86, [1987] ECR 3719 .... 173, 194
Develey Holding GmbH Beteiligungs KG v Office for Harmonisation in the Internal Market (Trade Marks and Designs) (OHIM), Case T–129/04, [2006] ECR II–811 189

Directeur Général des Douanes et Droits Indirects v Eridiania Beghin-Say SA, Case C–103/96, [1997] ECR I–1453 .... 300, 308
Dole Fresh Fruit International v Council and Commission, Case T–56/00, [2003] ECR II–577 190
Douaneagent der NV Nederlandse Spoorwegen v Inspecteur der invoerrechten en accijnzen, Case 38/75, [1975] ECR 1439 238
Dutch Antillian Dairy Industry Inc and Verenigde Douane-Agenten BV v Rijksdienst voor de keuring van Vee en Vlees, Case C–106/97, [1999] ECR I–5983 180
Eichsfelder Schlachtbetrieb GmbH v Hauptzollamt Hamburg-Jonas, Case C–515/03, [2005] ECR I–7355 313
Electroimpex and Others v Council, Case 157/87, [1990] ECR I–3021 210
Emesa Sugar (Free Zone) NV v Aruba, Case C–17/98, [2000] ECR I–675 .... 155, 159
Etablissements Biret SA v Council, Case C–94/02P, [2003] ECR I–10565 190
Euroalliages, Péchiney Électrométallurgie, Vargon Alloys AB and Ferroatlántica SL v Commission, Case T–132/01, [2003] ECR II–2539 162
Euroalliages v Commission, Case T–188/99, [2000] ECR II–1757 183
Euroalliages v Commission, Case T–188/99, [2001] ECR II–1757 156
Eurocoton and Others v Council, Case C–76/01P, [2003] ECR I–10091 158
Extramet Industrie v Council, Case C–358/89R, [1990] ECR I–431 .... 315, 316
Extramet Industrie v Council (Extramet I), Case C–358/89, [1991] ECR 2501 .... 315, 316
Extramet Industrie v Council (Extramet II), Case C–358/89, [1992] ECR I–3813 .... 315, 316
Fabbrica Italiana Accumulatori Motocarri Mentecchio Spa (FIAMM), Fabbrica Italiana Accumulatori Motocarri Montecchio Technologies Inc (FIAMM Technologies) TBA v Council and Commission; Fedon & Figli and Fedon America v Council and others, Joined Cases C–120/06P and C 121/06, [2006] ECR I 6513 .... 177, 190, 191
Fabbrica italiana accumulatori motocarri Metecchio Spa (FIAMM) and Fabbrica italiana accumulatori motocarri Montecchio Technologies Inc (FIAMM Technologies) v Council and Commission, Case T–69/00, [2005] ECR II–5393 .... 190, 191
Fazenda Pública v Fábrica de Queijo Eru Portuguesa Lda, Case C–187/99, [2001] ECR I–1429 307
Fédération de l'industrie de l'huilerie de la CEE (Fédiol) v Commission, Case 70/87, [1989] ECR 1781 .... 171, 181, 182
Fédération des Industries Condimentaires de France and Others v Commission, Case T–90/03, [2007] ECR II–76 191
Fedon & Figli SpA v Council and Commission, Case T–135/01, [2005] ECR II–29 .... 190, 191
FICF v Commission, Case T–317/02, [2004] ECR II–4325 191
Fixtures Marketing, Case C–46/02, [2004] ECR I–10365 160
Fixtures Marketing, Case C–338/02, [2005] ECR I–10497 160
Fixtures Marketing, Case C–444/02, [2004] ECR I–10549 160
France v Commission, Case C–366, [1991] ECR I–3579 276
Franz Ergenberger v Bundesanstalt fuer Landwirtschaft für Ernährung, Case C–313/04, [2006] ECR I–6331 188

Friesland Coberco Dairy Foods BV *trading as* Friesland Supply Point Ede v Inspecteur van de Belastingdienst/Douane Noord/kantoor Groningen, Case C–11/05, [2006] ECR I–4285 .... 309, 310
Fruchthandelsgesellschaft mbH Chemnitz v Commission, Case T–254/97, [1999] ECR II–2743 .... 175, 176, 180
Gebrüder Knauf Westdeutsche Gipswerke v Haupzollamt Hamburg-Jonas, Case 118/79, [1980] ECR 1183 .... 305, 314
Gebrüder Weis GmbH v Hauptzollamt Würzburg, Case C–292/91, [1993] ECR I–2219 306
GEFCO SA v Receveur principal des douanes, Case C–411/01, [2003] ECR I–11547 311
Germany v Commission, Case C–61/94, [1996] ECR I–3989 155
Germany v Council, Case C–280/93, [1994] ECR I–4973 .... 178, 179, 206
Germany v Council, Case C–122/95, [1998] ECR I–973 .... 156, 174
Germany v EP and Council, Case C–233/94, [1997] ECR I–2405 186
Giant (China) v Council, Case T–17/06, [2006] OJ C74/29 .... 125, 148, 154
Groupe Fremaux SA and Palais Royal Inc v Council and Commission, Case T–301/00, [2005] ECR II–25 190
Gul Ahmed Textile Mills Ltd v Council, Case T–199/04, (2004/C217/44), [2004] OJ C217/24 183
H van de Bor BV v her Voedselvoor zieningsin-en verkoopbureau, Case C–428/99, [2002] ECR I–127 .... 163, 164
Hameico Stuttgart and Others v Council, Case T–99/98, [2003] ECR II–2195 191
Hauptzollamt Hamburg-Jonas/Dimex, Case 89/83, [1984] ECR 2815 312
Hauptzollamt Heilbronn v Temic Telefunken, Case C–437/93, [1995] ECR I–1687 299
Hauptzollamt Mainz v CA Kupferberg & Cie, Case 104/81, [1982] ECR 3641 172
Hauptzollamt München v Wacker Werke GmbH & Co KG [Wacker Werke II], Case C–142/96, [1997] ECR IO–4649 .... 311, 314
Hermès International v FHT Marketing Choice BV, Case C–53/96, [1998] ECR I–3603 .... 158, 167, 192, 194, 195, 196
IHW Rebman GmbH v Haupzollamt Weiden, Case C–56/02, [2003] ECR I–5499 312
Ikea Wholesale Ltd v Commissoners of Customs & Excise, Case C–351/04, [2007] ECR I–7723 187
Industrias Quimicas del Vallés v Commission, Case T–158/03, [2005] ECR II–2425 154
Industrie des Poudres Sphériques v Commission of the European Communities, Case T–5/97, [2000] ECR II–3755 317
Industrie des Poudres Sphériques v Council, Case C–458/98P, [2000] ECR I–8147 .... 159, 316
Industrie des Poudres Sphériques v Council of the European Union, Case T–2/95, [1998] ECR II–3939 316
Industrie des Poudres Sphériques v Council of the European Union, Case T–2/95R, [1998] ECR II–485 316
Interfood GmbH v Hauptzollamt Hamburg-Ericus, Case 92/71, [1972] ECR 231 .... 160, 198

International Fruit Company v Produktschap voor Groenten en Fruit, Joined Cases 21–24/74, [1972] ECR 1219 ....157, 166, 237
International Potash Company v Council of the European Union, Case T–87/98, [2000] ECR II–3179 315
Intervet International BV formerly Hoechst Roussel Vet GmbG v Commission, Case T–212/99, [2002] ECR 1445 177
Italian Republic v Commission of the European Communities, Case C–177/00, [2003] ECR I–233 ....307, 312
Italy v Commission, Case T–226/04, [2006] ECR II–29 186
Italy v Council, Case C–352/96, [1998] ECR I–6937 ....157, 184, 186
Jègo Quéré, Case C–263/02P, [2004] ECR I–3425 166
Jègo Quéré v Commission, Case T–77/01, [2002] ECR II–2365 166
Kingdom of Spain v Council of the European Union, Case C–284/94, [1998] ECR I–7309 ....57, 58, 81
Kloosterboer Rotterdam BV v Minister van Landbouw, Natuurbeheer en Visserij, Case C–317/99, [2001] ECR I–9863 ....156, 183
Kziber, Case C–18/90, [1991] ECR I–99 173
Le Laboratoire du Bain v Council and Commission, Case T–151/00, [2005] ECR II–23 190
Leifer, Case C–83/94, [1995] ECR 3231 157
Luxembourg v Berthe Linster, Aloyse Linster and Yvonne Linster, Case C–287/98, [2000] ECR I–6917 196
Maggi GmbH v Hauptzollamt Munster, Case 260/78, [1979] ECR 2693 299
Marleasing SA v La Commercial Internacional de Alimentacion SA, Case C–106/89, [1990] ECR I–4135 197
Medici Grimm KG v Council of the European Union, Case T–7/99, [2000] ECR II–2671 161
Merck Genéricos–Produtos Farmaceuticos Lda v Merck & Co Inc and Merck Sharp & Dohme Lda, Case C 431/05, [2007] ECR I 7001 195
Metronome Musik GmbH v Music Point Hokamp GmbH, Case C–200/96, [1998] ECR I–1953 ....164, 199
Microsoft v Commission, Case T–201/04R, Order of 22/12/2004 154
Miwon Co Ltd v Council, Case T–51/96, [2000] ECR II–1841 162
Nakajima All Precision Co Ltd v Council, Case C–69/89, [1991] ECR I–2069 ....171, 176, 181, 182, 186, 187, 188, 196
Nederlandse Spoorwegen v Inspecteur der Invoerrechten en Accijnzen, Case 38/75, [1975] ECR 1439 ....65, 157
Neotype Techmashexport v Commission and Council, Joined Cases C–305/86 and C–160/87, [1990] ECR I–2945 257
Netherlands v Commission, Case C–156/00, [2003] ECR I–2527 ....300, 307, 312
Netherlands v European Parliament and Council of the European Union, Case C–377/98R, [2000] ECR I–6229 168
Netherlands v European Parliament and Council of the European Union, Case C–377/98, [2001] ECR I–7079 ....160, 184, 200, 201
Nippon Seiko KK v Council, Case 254/84, [1987] ECR 1923 259
Nokia Corp v Joacim Waerdell, Case C–316/05, [2006] ECR I–12083 201
Nölle v Hauptzollamt Bremen-Freihafen, Case C–16/90, [1991] ECR I–5163 ....257, 259

Norddeutsches Vieh- un Fleischkontor GmbH v Hauptzollamt Hamburg-Jonas–Ausfuhrerstattung, Case 14/74, [1974] ECR 899 236
NTN Corporation and Koyo Seiko v Council, Joined Cases T–163/94 and T–165/94, [1995] ECR II–1381 198
NTN Toyo Bearing Company Ltd and Others v Council, Case 240/84, [1987] ECR 1809 259
NV Firma Leon Van Parys v Belgisch Interventie- an Restitutiebureau, Case C–377/02, [2005] ECR I–1465 .... 187, 188
NV Internationale Crediet- en Handelsvereniging 'Rotterdam' and De Coöperatieve Suikerfabrik en Raffinaderij GA 'Puttershoek' v Netherlands Minister of Agriculture and Fisheries, Joined Cases 73/63 and 74/63, [1964] ECR 3 165
OGT Fruchthandelsgesellschaft mbH v Hauptzollamt Hamburg-St Annen, Case C–307/99, [2001] ECR I–3159 168
Opel Austria v Council, Case T–115/94, [1997] ECR II–39 207
Pabst & Richarz, Case 17/81, [1982] ECR 1331 173
Parfums Christian Dior SA v Tuk Consultancy BV; Assco Gerüste GmbH, Rob van Dijk v Wilhelm Layher GmbH & Co KG, Layher BV, Joined Cases C–300/98 and C–392/98, [2000] ECR I–11307 .... 158, 167, 192, 193, 195, 196, 197
Petrotub SA and Republica SA v Council and Commission, Case C–76/00P, [2003] ECR I–79 .... 159, 160, 161, 184
Petrotub SA and Republica SA v Council, Joined Cases T–33/98 and T–34/98, [1999] ECR II–3837 .... 159, 160, 184
Pfizer Animal Health SA v Council, Case T–13/99, [2002] ECR II–1961 177
Polo/Lauren Company LP v PT Dwidua Langgeng Pratama International Freight Forwarders, Case C–383/98, [2000] ECR I–2519 192
Portugal v Commission, Case C–150/95, [1997] ECR I–5863 .... 160, 182
Portugal v Council, Case C–149/96, [1999] ECR I–8395 .... 167, 168, 171, 178, 179, 181, 182, 184, 185, 187, 190
Practiker Bau- und Heimwerkermärkte, Case C–418/02, [2005] ECR I–5873 198
Prefetto Provincia di Cuneo v Silvano Carbone, Case C–296/00, [2002] ECR I–4657 160
Procter & Gamble v Office for Harmonisation in the Internal Market (Trade Marks & Designs), Case C–383/99, [2001] ECR I–6251 162
Queen, The v Secretary of State for the Environment, Transport and the Regions *ex parte* Omega Air Ltd; Omega Air Ltd; Aero Engines Ireland Ltd, Omega Aviation Services Ltd v Irish Aviation Authority, Joined Cases C–27/00 and C–122/00, [2002] ECR I–2569 .... 168, 169, 170, 174, 182, 188, 189
Queen, The v Secretary of State for the Home Department *ex parte* Julius Barkoci and Marcel Malik, Case C–257/99, [2001] ECR I–6557 .... 164, 165
R & V Haegeman v Belgian State, Case 181/73, [1974] ECR 449 .... 155, 157
Regione autonoma FriulI–Venezia Giulia and Agenzia regionale per lo sviluppo rurale (ERSA) v Ministero delle Politiche Agricole e Forestali, Case C–347/03, [2005] ECR I–3785 165
Rewe-Zentralfinanz v Bundesmonopolverwaltung für Branntwein ('Cassis de Dijon'), Case 120/78, [1979] ECR 649 255
Rica Foods (Free Zone) NV, Free Trade Foods NV and Suproco NV v Commission, Joined Cases T–94/00, T–110/00 and T–159/00, [2002] ECR II–4677 157

Rica Foods (Free Zone) NV and Free Trade Foods NV v Commission, Joined Cases T–332/00 and T–350/00, [2002] ECR II–4755 157
Rica Foods (Free Zone) NY v Commission, Case 40/03P, [2005] ECR I–6811 ....156, 157
Rica Foods (Free Zone) v Commission, Case 41/03P, [2005] ECR I–6875 nyr 156, 157
Ritek Corp and Prodisc Technology Inc v Council and Commission, Case T–274/02, [2006] ECR II–4305 ....161, 184
Rizeni Letoveho Provozu, Case C–335/05, [2007] ECR I–4307 ....198, 204
Roquette Frères SA v Office national interprofessionnel des cereals (ONIC), Case C–114/99, [2000] ECR I–8823 ....312, 313
Rothmans v Commission, Case T–188/97, [1999] ECR II–2463 310
SA LTJ Diffusion v SA SADAS, Case C–291/00, [2003] ECR I–2700 162
Schieving-Nijstad vof and Others v Robert Groeneveld, Case C–89/99, [2001] ECR I–5851 ....158, 167, 193, 197
Schlüter v Hauptzollamt Lorach, Case 9/73, [1973] ECR 1135 ....157, 166
Schutzverband gegen Unwesen in der Wirtschaft eV v Warsteiner Brauerei Hans Cramer GmbH & Co KG, Case C–312/98, [2000] ECR I–9187 192
Shanghai Bicycle Corporation (Group) v Council of the European Union, Case C–477/93, [1997] ECR II–1383 ....106, 143
Shanghai Bicycle Corporation (Group) v Council of the European Union, Case T–170/94, [1997] ECR II–1383 ....98, 103, 106, 107, 108, 143, 144, 276
Shanghai Teraoka Electronic Co Ltd v Council, Case T–35/01, [2004] ECR II–3663 198
Silhouette International Schmied GmbH & Co KG v Hartlauer Handelsgesellschaft mbH, Case C–355/96, [1998] ECR I–4799 ....162, 199, 200
Singer and Geigy v Amministrazione delle finanze dello Stato, Joined Cases 290–291/81, [1983] ECR 847 166
SIOT, Case 266/81, [1983] ECR 731 166
Sociedad General de Autores y Editores de España (SGAE) v Rafael Hoteles, Case C–306/05, [2006] ECR I–11519 196
Spain v Commission, Case C–443/97, [2000] ECR I–2415 280
Spain v Commission, Case C–409/00, [2003] ECR I–1487 163
Spain v Council, Case C–342/03, [2005] ECR I–1975 154
Spain v Council, Case C–310/04, [2006] ECR I–7285 154
Starway SA v Council of the European Union, Case T–80/97, [2000] ECR II–3099 ....112, 117, 146
SZ Sevince v Staatsecretaris Van Justitie, Case C–192/89, [1990] ECR I–346 173
T Port, Case T–2/99, [2001] ECR II–2023 185
T Port GmbH & Co KG v Commission, Case T–1/99, [2001] ECR II–465 ....159, 164
T Port GmbH & Co KG v Commission, Case T–52/99, [2001] ECR II–981 ....167, 176, 184, 186, 189
T Port GmbH & Co v Hauptzollamt Hamburg-Jonas, Joined Cases C–364/95 and C–365/95, [1998] ECR I–1023 ....167, 180
Technointorg v Commission and Council, Joined Cases 294/86 and 77/87, [1988] ECR 6077 257
Tyco Toys (UK) Ltd and Others v Commission and Council, Case T–268/94, [1994] OJ C254/14 ....57, 58

United Kingdom v Council, Case C–150/94, [1998] ECR I–7235 ....57, 80, 81, 235
Viz Stal and Duferco Commerciale v Council, Case T–335/04, [2004] OJ C273/34 183
Von Colson and Kamann v Land Nordrhein-Westfalen, Case 14/83, [1984] ECR 1891 197
Wacker Werke GmbH & Co KG v Hauptzollamt München-West (Wacker Werke I), Case C–16/91, [1992] ECR I–6821 ....301, 313, 314

Hong Kong

Attorney General v Hondar Plastic Industries Ltd [1976] HKLR 7630 72
Attorney General v Leung Kin Wai [1996] HKC 588 75
Core Resources (Far East) Ltd v Sky Finders [1992] 1 HKLR 193 72
Galco International Toys NV v Kader Industrial Co Ltd [1996] HKLY 260 75
HKSAR v Wong Ying Yu & Ors [1997] 3 HKC 452 76
Interlego AG v Lego New Enterprises Ltd [1995] 3 HKC 186 72
Kader Industrial Co Ltd v Galco International Toys NV [1992] 1 HKC 36 75
Lanard Toys Ltd v Winner Toys Manufactory Ltd, HCA No A11340 of 1994, 18 November 1994 72
Mattel Inc v Tonka Corp [1991] 2 HKC 411 72
Navystar (Nagai Shing) Industrial Co Ltd v Fairing Industrial Ltd [1994] 3 HKC 670 72
Ocean Plastic Manufactory Ltd v TCA (Hong Kong) Ltd & Anor [1993] 1 HKC 23 72
Toymax (HK) Ltd v Redsmith International Ltd [1994] 1 HKC 714 75
Video Technology Ltd v Ors & Atari Incorporated & Ors [1982] HKC 504 72

Ireland

Allen & Hanbury's Ltd and Glaxo Group v Controller of Patents, Designs and Trademarks and Clonmel Healthcare Ltd [1997] [1996] IEHC 59 (High Court of Ireland, 26 July 1996) 193

United Kingdom

Leopold Lazarus Limited v Secretary of State for Trade and Industry (unreported) 241
R v Comptroller of Patents, Designs and Trade Marks *ex parte* Lenzing AG v Coutauld (Fibres) Ltd and others [1997] Reports of Patent, Design and Trade Mark Case 245 193

United States of America

Georgetown Steel Corp v United States, US Court of Appeals for the Federal Circuit, 18 September 1986, 801 F 2nd 1308 245

WTO AND ANTI-DUMPING CASES

Anti-dumping – European Union

Bicycle Parts from China [1997] OJ L16/55 112
Bicycles from China [general references] 3, 89, 92, 94, 95, 98, 99, 100, 102, 103, 104, 105, 110, 114, 123, 126, 134, 135, 136, 138, 140, 141,142,271, 382
Bicycles from China [1993] OJ L58/12 (provisional) 96
Bicycles from China [1993] OJ L58/12 (provisional) 132, 271, 273, 276
Bicycles from China [1993] OJ L228/9 (definitive) 96, 271, 273, 276
Bicycles from China [2000] OJ L175/39 (definitive, renewal) 3, 30, 89, 96, 111, 119, 121, 122, 135
Bicycles from Indonesia, Malaysia and Thailand [1996] OJ L91/1 119
Bicycles from Taiwan [1999] OJ L49/1 (definitive) 102, 119, 129
Calcium Metal from China (definitive), [1989] OJ L271/1 316
Calcium Metal from China (definitive), [1994] OJ L270/27 316
Calcium Metal from China (provisional) [1994] OJ L104/5 316
Ferro-Silico-Manganese from China (definitive) [1998] OJ L62/1 318
Glyphosate from China [1997] OJ L243/7 (provisional), [1998] OJ L47/1 (definitive) 278
Leather Handbags from China (definitive), [1997] OJ L208/31 319
Magnesium Oxide from China [1992] OJ L282/23 (provisional); [1993] OJ L145/1 (definitive) 270
Magnetic Disks from Japan, Taiwan and China [1993] OJ L95/5 (provisional); [1993] OJ L262/4 (definitive) 270, 271
Photo Albums from China [1993] OJ L228/16 (provisional); [1993] OJ L333/67 (definitive) 271, 272, 273, 276
Plastic and Leather Handbags from China (provisional), [1997] OJ L33/11 318
Polyester Yarns from Taiwan, Indonesia, India, China and Turkey [1991] OJ L276/7 (provisional); [1992] OJ L88/1 (definitive) 270
Silicon Metal from China (definitive), [1997] OJ L345/1 317
Small Colour TVs from Hong Kong and China [1991] OJ L14/31 (provisional ,[1991] OJ L195/1 (definitive) 269, 270
Tungsten Ores from China [1990] OJ L83/23 (provisional), [1990] OJ L2654/1 (definitive) 268
Video Tapes in Cassettes from China [1991] OJ L106/15 (provisional); [1991] OJ L293/2 (definitive) 269

Anti-dumping – United States

Bicycles from Czechoslovakia, 25 Fed Reg 5, 657 (1960) 224, 229, 242, 243
Chrome-plated Lug Nuts and Wheel Locks from the People's Republic of China, 57 Fed Reg 10, 459 (1992) 246
Electric Golf Cars from Poland, 40 Fed Reg 25, 497 (1975), TD 75-288, 19 CFR G153.46 ....229, 242, 243, 246
Fur Felt Hoods, Bodies and Caps from Czechoslovakia, 27 Fed Reg 6, 099 (1962) 224, 225

Jalousie-Louvre-Sized Sheet Glass from Czechoslovaka, 27 Fed Reg 8, 457 (1962) 224
Oscillating and Ceiling Fans from the People's Republic of China, 57 Fed Reg 24, 019 (1992) 246
Portland Hydraulic Cement, Poland, 28 Fed Reg 6660 (1963) 224

WTO

Chile–Measures Affecting the Transit and Importing of Swordfish, WT/DS193/1 419
European Communities–Conditions for the Granting of Tariff Preferences to Developing Countries WT/DES246/R 419
European Communities–Customs Classification of Certain Computer Equipment, WT/DS62/AB/R 419
European Communities–Measures Affecting the Approval and Marketing of Biotech Products, WTO/DS291/AB/R, WTO/DS292/AB/R, WTO/DS293/WTO/R, ...420
European Communities–Measures Affecting Asbestos and Asbestos-Containing Products, WT/DS/135/AB/R, ...409
European Communities–Measures concerning Meat and Meat Products (Hormones), WT/DS26/AB/R 177, 407, 419
India–Quantitative Restrictions on Imports of Agricultural, Textile and Industrial Products, WTO/DS90/AB/R 419
United States–Import Prohibition of Shrimp and Certain Shrimp Products, WT/DS58/AB/R) 407
United States–Measures Affecting the Cross-Border Supply of Gambling and Betting Services, WT/DS285/AB/R 385
US-CVD on Hot rolled Steel, WT/DS138/AB/R (2000) 407

Table of Legislation

Australia

Anti-dumping Act 1921....216

European Union

EEC/EC Directives

Directive 69/73/EEC, art 2....304
Directive 76/119/EEC....289
Directive 86/560/EEC, art 2(2)....204
Directive 88/378/EEC....80
Directive 98/44/EC (Biotechnology)....184, 185, 200, 201
art 4....200
art 4(1)....200
Directive (Trade Marks)....162, 199
arts 5–7....199

EEC/EC Regulations

Anti-circumvention Regulation *see* Regulation (EC) 71/97
Basic Anti-dumping Regulation *see* Regulation (EC) 384/96
Exemption Regulation *see* Regulation (EC) 88/97
Regulation /EEC) 459/68....237, 238, 239, 256
Preamble
Recitals 1–2....237
Recital 6....237
art 2(7)....238
art 3....257
art 3(2)....238
art 3(2)(a)....253
art 3(6)....238
Regulation (EEC) 109/70....235, 249, 250
Regulation (EEC) 1492/70....235
Regulation (EEC) 2567/70....235
Regulation (EEC) 1414/72, Annex....249
Regulation (EEC) 1751/72, Annex....249
Regulation (EEC) 955/73, Annex....249
Regulation (EEC) 956/73, Annex....249
Regulation (EEC) 957/73, Annex....249
Regulation (EEC) 2011/73....250
Regulation (EEC) 112/74, art7(2)....305
Regulation (EEC) 238/74, Annex....249
Regulation (EEC) 958/75....249

Regulation (EEC) 1484/75 183
Regulation (EEC) 2777/75 183
Regulation (EEC) 1411/77 250
Regulation (EEC) 2896/77 235
Annex 249
Regulation (EEC) 2532/78 ....249, 250, 252, 257
Preamble, Recital 3 250
art 14 250
Regulation (EEC) 925/79 ....252, 257
Annex 249
Regulation (EEC) 1681/79 ....252, 253, 256
Preamble, Recitals 2–3 253
art 1 257
Regulation (EEC) 3017/79 ....256, 257, 258
Preamble 257
Recitals 3–5 256
Recital 6 257
art 2(5) 257
art 17 256
Regulation (EEC) 636/82 289
Regulation (EEC) 799/82 250
Regulation (EEC) 1765/82 249
Regulation (EEC) 1766/82 250
Regulation (EEC) 3420/83 ....249, 250
Regulation (EEC) 3421/83 250
Regulation (ECC) 2176/84 257
art 2(5) 257
art 13(10) 109, 283
Regulation (EEC) 2641/84 181
Regulation (EEC) 2473/86 ....289, 313, 314
Regulation (EEC) 1761/87 ....109, 283
Regulation (EEC) 2423/88 ....257, 258
art 2(5) 257
Regulation (EEC) 2432/88, art 13(3) 102
Regulation (EEC) 1193/92 ....108, 142
Regulation (EC) 1765/92 ....160, 161
Regulation (EC) 2081/92 192
Regulation (EC) 2912/92 302
Regulation (EC) 2913/92 ....298, 299, 301, 312
art 86 299
art 114(1) 298
art 114(2)(c)–(d) 298
art 114(2)(e) 299
art 115 298
art 115(1)(a) 299
art 115(1)(b) 300
art 115(2) 300
art 118(3) 300

art 123 299
art 126 300
art 127 299
art 144(2)(c) 301
art 145(1) 301
art 145(3)(b) 301
art 146 301
art 160 301
Regulation (EC) 404/93 (Banana Regulation) 174, 176, 185
Regulation (EC) 550/93 142
art 1(2) 103
Regulation (EC) 1607/93 142
Regulation (EC) 2454/93 ....298, 302
Title III 298
art 502(2) 309
art 502(4) 311
art 536 298
art 536(a) 300
arts 537–538 298
art 539 ....298, 309
art 540 298
art 541 298
art 541(1) 300
arts 542–544 298
art 545 ....298, 299
arts 545–548 ....298, 299
art 549 ....298, 299
art 549(i) 300
art 550 ....298, 299
art 551 299
art 552 ....299, 300
art 561(1)–(2) 300
art 569(1)–(2) 300
art 570(1) 300
art 572(1) 300
art 575(3) 300
art 585 298
art 585(1) 311
arts 586–592 298
arts 600–605 300
art 611(2)(b) 312
art 613 312
Annex 70, Pt B 309
Annex 73 309
Regulation (EC) 2472/93 ....122, 146
Regulation (EC) 2474/93 ....99, 105, 109, 110, 115, 116, 117, 127, 136, 137, 143, 144, 145, 146, 147, 148, 149, 150
Regulation (EC) 2747/93 149

Regulation (EC) 3030/93 56
Regulation (EC) 3448/93 299
Regulation (EC) 3665/93 300
Regulation (EC) 232/94 182
Regulation (EC) 517/94 56
Regulation (EC) 519/94 ....56, 57, 58, 59
Annexes II–III 59, 60, 61, 62, 63
Regulation (EC) 520/94 56
Regulation (EC) 1385/94 301
Regulation (EC) 1921/94 ....57, 58
art 1 58
Regulation (EC) 2193/94 300
Regulation (EC) 3036/94 301
Regulation (EC) 3283/94 ....157, 181
art 9(5) 281
Regulation (EC) 3285/94 192
Regulation (EC) 3290/94 183
Regulation (EC) 538/95, Annex II, art 1 59
Regulation (EC) 905/95 122
Regulation (EC) 1172/95 298
Regulation (EC) 1765/95 182
Regulation (EC) 384/96 (Basic anti-dumping Regulation) 98, 101, 105, 106, 110, 116, 122, 123, 124, 126, 157, 159, 161, 162, 181, 182, 184, 187, 237, 271, 278, 279, 281
art 1(1)–(2) 210
art 1(4) 210
art 2(7)(b)–(c) 122
art 3(5) 198
art 4(1)(a) 99
art 4(2) 99
art 5(10) 183
art 6(7) 183
art 7(1) 210
art 7(2) 258
art 9(4) 102, 210
art 9(5) 281
art 13 115
art 13(1) 110, 114, 159
art 13(2) 110, 117
art 13(3) 106, 110
art 13(4) 115
art 21 ....162, 183
art 21(1) 103
Regulation (EC) 612/96 60
Regulation (EC) 648/96 143
Regulation (EC) 703/96 ....109, 112, 143
Preamble, para 6(a)–(b) 109
para 4 ....110, 111

para 5 ... 110
paras 7–8 ... 111
paras 10–11 ... 111
paras 14–15 ... 111
para 18 ... 111
Regulation (EC) 706/96
art 1 ... 110
art 2(2)–(3) ... 110
Regulation (EC) 752/96
Preamble, Title 6 ... 59
art 1 ... 59
Regulation (EC) 899/96 ... 60
art 1 ... 60
art 3 ... 60
Annex I ... 60
Annex III ... 60
Regulation (EC) 71/97 (Anti-circumvention Regulation) ... 110, 115, 116, 117, 118, 125, 126, 127, 133, 136, 137, 143, 144, 145, 146, 147, 148, 149
arts 1–2 ... 114
art 3 ... 115
Regulation (EC) 88/97 (Exemption Regulation) ... 99, 115, 116, 118, 119, 125, 126, 127, 131, 136, 137, 143, 144, 145, 146, 147, 148, 149, 150
art 1 ... 130
art 2 ... 115
art 3 ... 116
art 4(4) ... 116
art 5 ... 127, 128, 129
art 7 ... 116
art 7(1) ... 127, 128, 129
art 8 ... 116
arts 10–11 ... 116, 127, 128, 129
art 12 ... 116
Annexes I–II ... 116
Regulation (EC) 847/97 ... 60
arts 1–2 ... 61
art 3 ... 62
Annexes I–IV ... 61
Regulation (EC) 2026/97
art 1(1) ... 210
art 12(1) ... 210
art 15(1) ... 210
Regulation (EC) 905/98 ... 210, 211, 278, 279, 280
Regulation (EC) 1138/98 ... 62
Preamble ... 63
Recitals 2–3 ... 63
art 1 ... 62
Annexes I–II ... 62
Regulation (EC) 1637/98 ... 168

Regulation (EC) 2362/98 .... 176, 184
Regulation (EC) 387/99 145
Regulation (EC) 925/1999 188
Regulation (EEC) 459/68 228
Regulation (EC) 1524/2000 .... 123, 124, 125, 133, 146, 147, 148, 149
Regulation (EC) 1917/2000 298
art 2 298
art 6(4) 298
art 32 298
Regulation (EC) 2700/2000 .... 298, 301
Regulation (EC) 993/2001 .... 298, 299, 300, 302, 309
Regulation (EC) 1488/2001 299
Regulation (EC) 1669/2001 298
Regulation (EC) 2080/2001 146
Regulation (EC) 2131/2001 .... 122, 123, 124, 146
Regulation (EC) 1972/2002 .... 281, 283
Preamble, Recital 7 281
art 1(6) 281
art 2 283
Regulation (EC) 806/2003 301
Regulation (EC) 1914/2003 299
Regulation (EC) 2286/2003 298
Regulation (EC) 886/2004 299
Regulation (EC) 179/2005 298
Regulation (EC) 1095/2005 .... 99, 125, 127, 130, 131, 133, 135, 136, 137, 148, 149, 150
Regulation (EC) 1892/2005 .... 125, 148
Regulation (EC) 1949/2005 298
Regulation (EC) 215/2006 298
Regulation (EC) 1651/2006 .... 125, 149
Regulation (EC) 1713/2006 299
Regulation (EC) 88/2007 302
Regulation (EC) 171/2008 .... 125, 126, 133
Regulation (EC) 3286/94, art 7 216

France

Ordonnance N 58–1264 du 20.12.1958, art 2 237

Germany

Decree of 5.12.63 236

Hong Kong

Toys and Children's Products Safety Ordinance 1992 80

Italy

Legge n 39 del 11 Gennaio 1963 237

United Kingdom

Anti-dumping Law 1921 216
Customs Duties (Dumping and Subsidies) Act 1969 241
s 4(4) 241

United States of America

Anti-dumping Act 1921 ....242, 243, 244, 247
§ 205 243
§ 205(b) 243
Clayton Act 1914 215
Emergency Tariff Act 1921 (Anti-dumping Act 1921) 216, 217, 219, 220, 224, 226, 227
Title II 216, 217
§ 202(a) 217
§ 205 217
§ 206 217
Omnibus Trade and Competitiveness Act 1988 ....246, 247, 248
Revenue Act 1916 (Anti-dumping Act 1916) 215, 216, 217
§ 801 215
Sherman Antitrust Act 1890 215
Tariff Act 1894, section 73 215
Tariff Act 1930 ....217, 219, 248
Title VII 247, 248
§ 771(18)(A)–(B) 248
Trade Act 1974 ....242, 243, 244, 247
§ 206 243
Trade Agreements Act 1979 ....214, 247
Title I 247
Trade Expansion Act 1962 221
Treasury Customs Regulation 1968 ....231, 240, 241, 242, 246, 247, 251, 253, 261, 262
Treasury Customs Regulation 1973 ....242, 243, 247

Table of Treaties

European Union and predecessors

EC Treaty ... vi, 153, 188, 209
 art 28 (26 post-Amsterdam) ... 65
 art 92(1) (now 87(1)) ... 163
 art 93(3) (now 88(3) EC) ... 163
 art 100a (now art 95) ... 199, 200
 art 113 (133 post-Amsterdam) ... 65, 192
 art 131 ... 209
 art 133 ... 209
 art 190 (now 253) ... 159
 art 230 (173 EEC, 263 TFEU) ... 166
 art 232 ... 177
 art 234 (177 EEC, 267 TFEU) ... 155, 165, 167, 304
 art 238 ... 206
 art 253 (ex 190) ... 188
 art 300(7) ... 194
 Annex I ... 299, 309
ECSC Treaty ... 252
EEC Treaty ... vi, 237, 252
 art 1 ... 252
 art 112 ... 237
 art 113 ... 237
 art 114 ... 237
 art 115 ... 95, 96, 142
 art 169 (226 EC, 258 TFEU) ... 304
 art 173 (230 EC) ... 57, 182
 art 177 (234 EC) ... 313
Treaty of Amsterdam ... vi, 65, 192
Treaty on European Union ... vi, 153
Treaty on the Functioning of the European Union ... vi
Treaty of Lisbon 2007 ... vi, 153, 209
Treaty of Nice ... 153, 192, 209
 art 4 ... 209
 art 14 ... 209
 arts 81-82 ... 209
 art 87 ... 209
Treaty of Rome 1957, Protocol on German internal trade and connected problems 1957 ... 236

GATT, Uruguay Round and WTO Agreements

Agreement between the World Intellectual Property Organization and the World Trade Organisation (22 December 1995) 393
Agreement on Interpretation and Application of Articles VI, XVI and XXIII of the General Agreement on Tariffs and Trade 244
Anti-dumping Agreement *see* WTO Agreement on the Implementation of Article VI GATT
ASCM *see* WTO Agreement on Subsidies and Countervailing Measures
General Agreement on Tariffs and Trade 1947 ....4, 16, 38, 68, 79, 82, 83, 98, 106, 107, 153, 154, 155, 156, 157, 160, 162, 165, 166, 167, 168, 169, 173, 174, 175, 176, 179, 181, 182, 184, 185, 186, 187, 188, 189, 192, 196, 197, 198, 202, 203, 206, 207, 209, 212, 213, 214, 215, 218, 219, 220, 221, 222, 223, 224, 226, 228, 229, 230, 231, 232, 233, 234, 236, 238, 239, 240, 241, 242, 245, 246, 253, 255, 261, 262, 263, 264, 267, 282, 302, 331, 342, 383, 388, 389, 390, 391, 392, 394, 417, 418, 423
Pt II 225
Pt IV 390
art II:3 390
art III 110, 344, 349
art VI 90, 156, 159, 182, 213, 216, 219, 220, 221, 223, 224, 225, 226, 227, 228, 230, 232, 233, 234, 236, 241, 242, 244, 253, 256, 261, 267, 363, 369
art VI:2 390
art VI:3 390
art VI(1) 220, 222
art VI(1)(a) 228
art VI(1)(b) 220, 222
art VI(1)(b)(i) 221, 225, 226, 228
art VI(1)(b)(ii) 221, 226, 228
art VI(2) 106, 228
art VII 390
art X 344
art XI 83
art XII 391
art XIV 391, 403
art XIX 360, 361, 362, 363, 369
art XV 390, 391
art XV:1 390
art XV:2 390
art XV:9(a) 418
art XVI 234, 256, 390
art XVII 235
art XVIII:B 391
art XX 343, 344, 360, 403, 419
art XX(b) 409
art XX(g) 420

art XXIII 234, 256
art XXIV........329, 330, 331, 333, 346, 353
art XXIV(8)(b) 342
art XXIV(12)........202
art XXVIII 342
art XXXVI:6 390
art XXXVI:7 390
art XXXVIII:2(b)–(c) 390
Sch LXXX........419
Annex I 222
Interpretative Note 1955 ....222, 223, 224, 225, 226, 227, 228, 231, 234, 238, 241, 244, 267
Protocol for the Accession of Hungary 1973 233
Protocol for the Accession of Poland 1967 233
Protocol for the Accession of Romania 1971 233
Protocol amending the Preamble and Parts II and III of GATT 223
General Agreement on Tariffs and Trade 1994 ....160, 167, 172, 182, 344
art I 168
art I(1) 168
art XIII........168
art XV 390
art XX(a)........385
arts XXII–XXIII 362
art XXIV(6)........157
Sch L 159
General Agreement on Trade in Services (GATS) 79, 82, 83, 165, 167, 175, 176, 189, 192, 343, 345, 390, 391, 410
Preamble 345
art I:2 410
art III 345
art III(bis)........345
art V 329, 331, 333, 346, 353
art V(1)(b) 343
art V(6)........334
art VI.4........345
art VIII........345
art XI 391
art XIV(a) 385
International Dairy Agreement........196, 198, 202, 302
Marrakesh Agreement establishing the World Trade Organisation 1994........160, 385
Preamble, Recital 1 385
art III:5 ....389, 390, 391, 406
art V:2........397, 407
art XVI........203
SPS *see* WTO Agreement on Sanitary and Phytosanitary Measures
TBT Agreement *see* WTO Agreement on Technical Barriers to Trade
Uruguay Round Blair House Agreement (BHA) 182, 183
Annex........182

WTO Agreement on Agriculture (Agriculture Agreement) 154, 156, 183
WTO Agreement on the Implementation of Article VI GATT (Anti-dumping Agreement) 90, 99, 134, 156, 157, 159, 161, 162, 181, 183, 184, 186, 187, 244, 267, 363, 369
art 2.2.1 161
art 2.4.2 ....159, 161, 184
art 3.4..........198, 280
art 4..........99
art 6.1 161
art 6.11..........161, 183
art 6.12 161
art 8(3)..........106
WTO Agreement on the Implementation of Article VII GATT 1994....................301
WTO Agreement on Import Licensing Procedures...............................167, 176, 189
WTO Agreement on Rules of Origin 301, 357
art 2(a)..........357
WTO Agreement on Safeguards..........160, 361, 362, 363, 369
art 2(2)..........361
art 3 ....360, 361, 362
art 5..........361
art 5(1)..........362
arts 6–7 361
art 8..........362
art 9 362
art 9(1)..........362
art 9(6)..........362
arts 13–14 362
WTO Agreement on Sanitary and Phytosanitary Measures (SPS) 177, 180, 344, 350, 393, 395, 398, 399, 403, 409, 413
art 1.1 399
art 2..........399
art 3(4)..........393
art 3.3 413
art 3.5 413
art 4 ....413, 414
art 5.1–5.8 413
art 12(3)..........393
art 12.4 413
art 56(1)..........350
Annex A, para 3 413
WTO Agreement on Subsidies and Countervailing Measures (ASCM) 162, 163, 164, 184, 363, 369
art 8.3 163
WTO Agreement on Technical Barriers to Trade (TBT) 77, 78, 82, 169, 170, 182, 185, 188, 189, 200, 344, 350, 398, 399, 403, 409, 413, 414
art 1.1 414
art 2.4 414

art 2.5 350
art 4 398
art 69 350
Annex 1 ....350, 399
Annex 3 350
WTO Agreement on Textiles and Clothing 167
WTO Agreement on Trade-related Aspects of Intellectual Property
(TRIPS) 16, 23, 79, 82, 83, 158, 162, 165, 167, 172, 185, 189, 192, 194, 196, 198, 199, 200, 201, 336, 349, 393, 409, 412, 414
Pt III 193
art 22 192
art 31(bis) 352, 410
art 33 195
art 50 ....158, 167, 189, 193, 196, 197
art 50(1) 193
art 50(6) 167, 193, 194, 197
arts 51–59 349
art 63.2 393
WTO Dispute Settlement Understanding (DSU) 79, 190, 365, 367, 369, 378
art 1 ....371, 418
art 2 371
art 3 371
art 3(7) 376
art 3(10) 378, 379
art 4 372
art 4(2)–(4) 372
art 4(6) 372
art 4(8)–(9) 372
art 4(11) 372
art 5 ....364, 365, 366, 372
art 5(2) 372
art 5(5) 372
art 6 372
art 6(1)–(2) 372
art 7 ....366, 372, 373
art 7(1) 372
art 8 373
art 8(3)(a) 373
art 8(5) 373
art 8(7) 373
art 9 373
art 9(2) 373
art 9(4)–(5) 373
arts 10–11 ....366, 373
art 12 ....366, 373
art 12(4)–(5) 373
art 12(12) 373
art 13 ....373.366

art 14 ... 366, 374
art 14(1)–(2) ... 374
art 15 ... 366, 374
art 15(2) ... 374
art 16 ... 366, 374
art 17 ... 374
art 17.9 ... 407
art 18 ... 374
art 19 ... 366, 374
art 19(2) ... 373
art 20 ... 374
art 21 ... 374
art 21(3) ... 374
art 21(3)(b)–(c) ... 374
art 21(5) ... 374, 375
art 21(6) ... 378
art 22 ... 366, 375
art 22(1)–(2) ... 375
art 22(3)(a)–(b) ... 375
art 22(6) ... 375
arts 23–24 ... 375
art 25 ... 366, 375
arts 26–27 ... 375
art 91(1) ... 374
Annex 1 ... 373
Annex 1(8) ... 373
Annex 3 ... 373
WTO Protocol on Accession of China
s 15 ... 333, 344
s 16 ... 333, 344

Regional Trade Agreements

ACFTA ... 327, 328, 340, 341, 344, 345, 350, 354, 355, 358, 360, 361, 362, 363, 364, 365, 367, 370, 377, 379
ACFTA Agreement on Dispute Settlement Mechanism (ADSM) 2004 ... 340, 365, 366, 367, 368, 369, 371, 378
art 1 ... 371
art 2(1) ... 365, 371
art 2(2)–(3) ... 371
art 2(4) ... 365, 371
art 2(5) ... 365, 366, 371
art 2(6) ... 365, 366, 367, 371
art 2(7) ... 365, 367, 371
art 2(8) ... 367, 371
art 3 ... 371
art 4 ... 372, 376
art 4(1) ... 365, 372

art 4(1)(a) 375
art 4(2)–(9) 372
art 5 ....366, 372, 376
art 5(1)–(2) 366, 372
art 5(3) 372
art 6 ....372, 373
art 6(1) 365, 372
art 6(3)–(5) 373
art 7 373
art 7(1) 365, 373
art 7(3) 365, 373
art 8 373
art 8(1) 366, 373
art 8(2) 366, 372
art 8(3)(a) 366, 376
art 8(3)(b) 366
art 8(4) 366, 374
art 8(5) 366
art 9 366
art 9(1) 374
art 9(4) 374
art 9(7)–(9) 374
art 10 ....366, 373
art 12 378
art 12(1)–(3) 374
art 13 366
art 13(1)–(6) 375
art 14 ....366, 376
ASEAN Charter 340
art 3 340
ASEAN–China Agreement on Goods 2005 ....340, 343, 344, 357, 361, 365
art 2 344
art 4 344
art 5 357
art 7(1) 344
art 8(1) 344
art 9(1)–(5) 361
arts 11–12 344
arts 14–15 344
Annex 1 344
Annex 2, para 6 344
ASEAN–China Agreement on Services 2007 365
art 2(2) 345
arts 3–(4) 345
art 5(4) 345
art 7 345
art 15 345
art 17 345

art 21 ... 345
art 21(1) ... 345
art 22(1)–(2) ... 345
art 28(1) ... 345
art 30 ... 345
ASEAN–China Framework Agreement ... 337, 345, 361, 365, 366
Preamble ... 342, 345
art 1 ... 342
art 3 ... 342
art 3(1) ... 342
art 3(6) ... 342
art 3(8) ... 342
art 4(a)–(b) ... 343
art 6 ... 342
art 6(3)(d) ... 342
art 8(3)(d) ... 361
art 9 ... 343, 361
arts 10–11 ... 343
art 12A ... 343
art 13(2) ... 343
Annexes 1–2 ... 342
Amendment Protocol ... 343
arts 3–4 ... 343
ASEAN–China FTA *see* ACFTA
ASEAN–China RTA ... 328, 329, 330, 331
Asia–Pacific Trade Agreement 1976 ... 339
Asia–Pacific Trade Agreement 2006 (APTA) ... 329, 331
Central American Free Trade Agreement (CAFTA) ... 340
Chile–China RTA 2006 ... 330
China–Australia Trade and Economic Framework Agreement 2003 ... 347
China–Chile FTA ... 327, 346, 349, 350, 351, 352, 353, 354, 355, 358, 360, 362, 363, 364, 368, 369, 370, 377
Preamble ... 349
art 1 ... 349
art 2(1) ... 349
art 2(1)(e) ... 352
art 2(2) ... 349
art 3 ... 349
art 5 ... 371
art 7 ... 349
arts 10–12 ... 349
art 13 ... 350
art 15 ... 358
arts 17–20 ... 358
arts 22–23 ... 358
art 29 ... 371
art 44 ... 362
art 44(2)(b)(ii) ... 362

art 45 362
art 46(1) 362
art 49(1)–(2) 362
art 51(1)–(2) 363
art 58 350
art 63(2) 350
art 65 350
art 69 350
art 71(b) 350
art 79 371
art 80 .... 368, 371
art 80(a) 375
art 81 371
art 81(1)–(2) 369
art 82 .... 368, 372, 376
art 83 368
art 83(1) 372
art 83(2) 368, 372
art 83(3)–(4) 372
art 84 372
art 84(1) 368
art 85 .... 368, 373
art 85(1)–(5) 373
art 85(6) 369, 373
art 85(7) 373
art 85(7)(c) 368
art 85(7)(d) 369
art 85(9) 373
art 86(1)–(3) 369, 372, 373
art 87 373
art 87(1)–(3) 373
art 87(4) 372
arts 88–89 373
arts 90–91 374
art 92 374
art 92(1)–(2) 369, 374
art 92(3)–(4) 374
art 92(5) 369, 374
art 93 375
art 93(1)–(3) 369, 375
art 93(4)–(5) 375
art 93(6) 374, 375
art 94 375
art 95 .... 370, 376
art 96 350
art 97 .... 350, 368, 371, 375
art 98 375
art 98(1) 350

arts 105–110 350
art 111 350
art 111(1)(a)–(c) 352
art 112 350
art 113 350
art 113(1)–(3) 351
art 121 ....349, 376
art 194 350
Annex 3 358
Annex 7 373
China–Hong Kong RTA 2004 329
China–Macao RTA 2004 329
China–New Zealand FTA 2008 347
China–Pakistan FTA 327, 330, 346, 349, 352, 353, 354, 355, 358, 360, 362, 364, 368, 370, 377
art 2(1)(a) 352
art 5 371
art 12 371
art 15 360
art 17 360
art 25(1)–(2) 363
art 26(1)–(2) 363
art 27 363
art 27(3)(i) 363
art 28 371
art 35 371
art 46 371
art 48 352
art 49(1)–(2) 352
art 53 ....370, 371
art 53(1) 371, 376
art 53(2) 370, 371
art 53(3)–(5) 370
art 53(8) 370
art 54 ....370, 371
art 54(1) 371, 376
art 54(2) 371
art 55 370
art 56 ....370, 372
arts 57–58 ....370, 371
art 59 ....370, 372, 376
art 60 ....370, 371
art 60(1)–(2) 371
art 61 ....370, 372, 376
art 62 ....370, 372
art 63 ....370, 372, 373
art 63(1)–(6) 373
art 64 ....370, 372, 373

art 64(1) 372, 373
art 64(2)....372
art 64(3)–(4) 372, 373
art 65....370, 373
art 65(1)–(3)....373
arts 66–67 370
art 68....370, 373
arts 69–71 370
art 72....370, 375
art 72(2)–(4)....375
art 73....370, 375
art 74....370, 376
art 75–77 ....371, 375
art 79–61 ....374, 375
Annex III....373
China–Peru FTA 2009 347
China–Singapore FTA....328, 329, 331, 346
China–Thailand FTA....346
Mainland China–Hong Kong CEPA 2003 ....327, 332, 333, 334, 335, 350, 353, 354, 355, 356, 357, 360, 361, 363, 364, 371, 377
Preamble 333
art 2....333
art 2(2)....361
art 4....333
art 5(1)....333
art 5(2)....334
art 6(1)....334
arts 7–8....334
art 9....360
art 10....355
art 11 334
art 11(2)....334
art 12(2)....334
art 13....334
art 13(3)....334
art 14(1)–(3)....335
art 15(1)....335
art 17....335
art 18....361
art 19(1)–(2) 333, 364
art 19(3) 364, 371
art 19(4)....372
art 19(5) 364, 372
art 20(1)–(2)....361
art 21....333
Annex 1....332, 333
Annexes 2–3 332
Annex 4....332, 334

Annex 5 ... 332, 334
art 3.1.2(1)–(2) ... 334
Annex 6 ... 332, 335
Mainland China–Macao CEPA 2003 ... 332, 333, 335, 353, 354, 355, 357
art 13 ... 335
art 17 ... 335
Annex 2, art 5 ... 357
Supplement II ... 357
North American Free Trade Agreement (NAFTA) ... 27, 370, 378
arts 2003–2004 ... 371
art 2005 ... 371
art 2005(5) ... 371
art 2006 ... 372, 374
art 2006(4) ... 372
art 2007 ... 372
art 2007(1)–(5) ... 372
art 2008 ... 372
art 2008(1)–(3) ... 372
art 2009 ... 373
art 2009(2) ... 373
art 2010 ... 373
art 2012(1)–(2) ... 373
art 2012(3)–(5) ... 372
arts 2013–2015 ... 373
art 2017 ... 374
art 2017(1)–(2) ... 374
art 2018 ... 374
arts 2020–2022 ... 376

Other Treaties

Basel Convention on the Transboundary Movements of Hazardous Waste and their Disposal Basel Convention ... 416
Berne Convention for the Protection of Literary and Artistic Works (Paris Act 1971) ... 194, 195
Chicago Convention, Annexes, Chapter 3 ... 169
Convention on Biological Diversity (CBD) 1992 ... 160, 185, 410, 411, 412, 416
art 1 ... 411
art 3 ... 411
art 15(1) ... 411
art 15(4)–(5) ... 411
art 15(7) ... 411
art 27 ... 411
Annex II ... 411
Convention establishing a Customs Cooperation Council 1950 ... 66, 78
Convention on International Trade in Endangered Species of Wild Fauna and Flora (CITES) ... 416
Convention on the Valuation of Goods for Customs Purposes (Brussels, 1950) ... 66

EC–Hungary Agreement on wines 165
EEA Agreement 194
Protocol 28, art 5 194
EEC–China Trade and Cooperation Agreement 1985 339
EEC–Yugoslavia Cooperation Agreement 1980, art 15 306
EEC–Czech Republic Association Agreement 165
art 59(2) 165
Framework Agreement on Bananas between the EC and the Republics of Colombia, Costa Rica, Nicaragua and Venezuela 1994 ....156, 159, 164, 167, 174, 191
Geneva Convention on the Interpretation of Treaties, art 31 242
International Convention on the Harmonized Commodity Description and Coding System 1983 ....65, 301
Protocol 1986 65
International Treaty on Plant Genetic Resources for Food and Agriculture (ITPGR) 410, 411
Pt III 411
arts 1.1–1.2 411
art 2 411
art 9 411
arts 10.1–10.2 411
art 11 411
art 12 411
art 12.3(a) 411
art 12.3(d) 411
art 12.3(f) 411
art 12.3(h) 411
art 13 ....411, 412
art 13(2)(d)(ii) 412
arts 13.1 411
arts 13.2 411
arts 13.3–13.6 411
art 22 412
Annex II 412
ITPGR *see* International Treaty on Plant Genetic Resources for Food and Agriculture
Kyoto International Convention on the Simplification and Harmonization of Customs Procedures 1973 ....61, 64, 65, 66, 67, 301, 302, 303
Pts I–II 66
art 3 67
art 4 66
art 5(1)–(2) 67
art 6 66
art 11(1)–(2) 67
art 11(4) 67
art 11(7) 67
Annex E.6 ....66, 67, 302
Annex E.8 ....66, 67, 302

Annex F.1 ....66, 67, 302, 303
Annex F.2....302, 303
Protocol of Amendment 1999 ....302, 303
Kyoto International Convention on the Simplification and Harmonization of Customs Procedures (revised 1999) 61, 64, 66, 67, 68
Annex H....66
Montreal Protocol on Substances that deplete the Ozone Layer 416
OECD Convention on Combating Bribery 1997....26
Pan–Pearl River Delta (PPRD) Regional Cooperation Framework Agreement 2004 ....336, 353
Pan–Pearl River Delta (PPRD) Intellectual Property Cooperation Agreement....336
art 2(4)....336
art 4(5)....336
Paris Convention for the Protection of Industrial Property, art 6....393
Refugee Convention....21
Rotterdam Convention on the Prior Informed Consent Procedure for Certain Hazardous Chemicals and Pesticides in International Trade (Rotterdam Convention)....416
Standard Material Transfer Agreement....412
Statute of the IMF 390, 418
Stockholm Convention on Persistent Organic Pollutants (Stockholm Convention)....416
Trade Agreement between the European Economic Community and China [1978] OJ L123/1 250
Trade Agreement between the Government of the People's Republic of China and the Government of the Republic of Chile 1971 350
UNESCO Convention on Cultural Diversity 2005 ....397, 410
art 20....410
art 20(1)(b) 410
art 20(2)....410
United Nations Charter 411
United Nations Convention on the Law of the Sea....419, 420
United Nations Framework Convention on Climate Change (UNFCCC) 416
Universal Declaration on Human Rights 404
USA/Soviet Union Bilateral Trade Agreement 1935....218
Vienna Convention on the Law of Treaties 1969, art XXXI 234
Yaoundé Convention....173

Declarations

Declaration on the TRIPS Agreement on Public Health 351
Joint Declaration of the Government of the People's Republic of China and the Government of the Republic of Portugal on the Question of Macao, Beijing 13 April 1987 332
Joint Declaration of the United Kingdom of Great Britain and Northern Ireland and the Government of the People's Republic of China on the Question of Hong Kong, 19 December 1984 332

List of Tables

Table 1 Sources of Components of the Barbie Doll 45
Table 2 Sites of Governance and Norms relevant to the Global Toy Industry 79
Table 3 Progress and Results of Commission Procedures under the Exemption Regulation (Commission Regulation (EC) No 88/97), 1997–2009 127
Table 4 Effects of Globalisation on Ownership Structure of Exporters 138
Table 5 Effects of Globalisation on Ownership Structure of Importers 139
Table 6 Effects of Globalisation on the Ownership Structure of Producers 139
Table 7 Politicisation of Anti-dumping Law Decision-making in the EU 141
Table 8 Procedural Stages in *Bicycles* and *Photo Albums* 271
Table 9 Legalisation of Individual Treatment 282
Table 10 Inward Processing in the EU 1988–1994 290
Table 11 The Evolution of International Production and the Development of Intra-Firm and Intra-Industry Trade 293
Table 12 Use of Inward Processing by Member State 1988–1994 294
Table 13 Trade between the EU Member States and China, 1995 295]
Table 14 RTAs Notified by China to 10 April 2009 328
Table 15 Summary of Rules of Origin in China's RTAs 355
Tablc 16 Mainland–Hong Kong CEPA ROOs 356
Table 17 ACFTA ROOs 359
Table 18 Comparison of Safeguards in China's RTAs 360
Table 19 Comparison of DSMs in China's RTAs, WTO and NAFTA 371
Table 20 The Corporate Governance Matrix 400
Table 21 Matrix of Selected International Organisations in International Trade Regulation 401

List of Figures

Figure 1	Organisation of the Toy Industry	47
Figure 2	Industry Segments and Material Flows in the Bicycle Industry	113
Figure 3	The East Asian 'Noodle Bowl' Syndrome	379

1

Introduction

Thirty spokes share one hub.
It is just the space (the Nothingness) between them
That makes a cart function as a cart.
Knead clay to make a vessel
And you will find within it the space
That makes a vessel as a vessel.
Within a house built with doors and windows
You will find the space
That makes a house function as a house.
Hence the substance (Being) can provide a condition
Under which usefulness is found,
But the Nothingness (space) is the usefulness itself.[1]

The world is changing, and the law with it. During the past 50 years, people in virtually every country have witnessed a fundamental transformation of many of the basic institutional and normative parameters of social life. Globalisation, the development of novel institutions and different types of rules, the fragmentation of international law, institutions and processes, the rise of new strategic actors on the domestic and international stages, and the creation of novel sets of relations among international organisations, regional bodies, States and private or hybrid organisations are part of this transformation. How can we make sense of these changes in our daily lives? This book seeks to provide an answer to this question. It focuses in particular on the regulation of international trade, which here is understood more accurately as global trade because it involves specific sets of transnational or global economic and legal relations instead of simply relations between States.

The book argues that the most coherent and most convincing theoretical framework for studying and analysing international trade regulation today is a theory of global legal pluralism. With all due modesty in an already crowded field, where numerous perspectives and theories jostle for pre-eminence, it aims to present a new theoretical framework for understanding the regulation of international trade. In order to do this, it analyses selected aspects of relations between the European Union (EU),[2] the World

[1] Lao Tzu, *The Book of Tao and Teh*, 2nd edn (trans Gu Zhengkun) (Peking University Press, Beijing, and China Translation and Publishing Corporation, 2006), ch 11.

[2] For the sake of convenience, the expressions 'European Union' or 'EU' are used throughout the book instead of 'European Community' or 'EC', except in references to Treaty article or specific legislation. During the period of research for this book, the EC had exclusive legal competence for international trade in goods, international trade in most services (except for certain matters for which it shared competence with Member States) and international trade in commercial aspects of intellectual property. With the entry into force of the Treaty of Lisbon on 1 December 2009, the EU replaced the European Community (EC). Then, for example, EC anti-dumping law became EU anti-dumping law.

Trade Organisation (WTO) and the People's Republic of China. The argument is developed by means of a series of interconnected studies of relations between the EU, the WTO and China. The groundwork of these studies has been laid piece by piece during the past 10 years, interspersed and stimulated by research on other topics. The book draws these studies together to provide an integrated, coherent theoretical framework, designed to help us understand international trade regulation, and in particular relations between the EU, the WTO and China, in the context of 21st-century globalisation. The discussion is frequently very detailed, in the manner of anthropological 'thick description' and analysis of case studies. Nevertheless, the reader should constantly bear the general argument in mind: international trade today is regulated by changing relations between a multiplicity of sites of governance, which together constitute a new, global form of legal pluralism.

The present chapter gives a brief exposition of the parts of the book and the individual chapters in order to situate them in relation to each other and to clarify their contribution to the theoretical argument as a whole. Following this introductory chapter, the book consists of three main parts.

Part I of the book introduces the basic concepts: globalisation, sites of governance and global legal pluralism. It also presents selected elements of bilateral trade relations between the EU and China within the multilateral legal framework of the WTO. Consisting of three chapters, it first surveys the literature on law and globalisation, then introduces the concept of sites of governance and the theory of global legal pluralism, and finally sketches the foundations of global legal pluralism. Each of these chapters has its own integrity. Taken together, however, they provide a conceptual and theoretical framework for the book as a whole.

Chapter two provides an overview of the principal intersections of economic globalisation and the law in the 21st century, with special but not exclusive reference to international trade. It emphasises ways in which globalisation and law influence and condition each other, identifies some of the main issues in the field, notes several alternative perspectives for analysing these relationships, and then introduces the concepts of sites of governance and global legal pluralism. It also discusses issues of international trade regulation and global governance, such as transparency, legitimacy and accountability, which the intersection of globalisation and law in the contemporary world raises for international and regional organisations, governments, other groups, civil society and citizens alike. It argues that we live in a world of increasing legal pluralism. We need to focus on achieving basic substantive objectives by means of the structures of and relations among diverse sites of governance. The chapter also identifies different ways of managing these relations.

Chapter three elaborates in more detail the concept of sites of governance and the theory of global legal pluralism. It asks and seeks to answer a specific question: How is economic globalisation governed? To answer this question, the chapter presents a case study of the regulation of international trade between the EU and China. It focuses on a typical example of economic globalisation: the global commodity chain in toys. The international toy industry is governed by a multiplicity of sites of governance—international, transnational, regional, national and infra-national—within the framework of global legal pluralism. Each site of governance has two dimensions: a structural dimension, embracing institutions, norms and dispute resolution processes; and a relational dimension, which refers to relations between the site and other sites of governance. These sites deploy a wide variety of legally binding measures ('hard law'), as well as norms which are not legally binding but which nonetheless have significant practical, and even legal, effects ('soft law').[3] The totality of sites of governance constitutes a new form of global legal pluralism. The chapter uses the case study to develop the concept of sites of governance and the theoretical framework of global legal pluralism. The global commodity chain in toys is a good example of economic globalisation. The chapter does not claim that this or any other international production network (IPN) represents all forms of globalisation. Nonetheless, it suggests that the basic argument that is developed on the basis of this example applies to many organisational forms and types of transnational relations which are characteristic of globalisation today.

Chapter four aims to elucidate the foundations of global legal pluralism. A basic hypothesis is that there is a correlation between international economic integration and trade, the disintegration and fragmentation of production, and the rise of global legal pluralism. In other words, globalisation, international competition, legal strategies and their consequences, both intended and unintended, are among the main foundations of global legal pluralism.

The chapter explores these ideas by examining a single example of relations between the EU and China. It focuses on the long-standing anti-dumping saga concerning *Bicycles from China*. Anti-dumping law is one means of regulating international competition. Relations between sites are dynamic social processes which may both be cooperative and contain the seeds of conflict. We can therefore expect these relations to change over time. As they develop, they may lead to changes in the structural features of one or both sites. In some cases, these processes even demonstrate a lack of agreement on fundamental legal concepts of international trade regulation. They may also undercut the social, political or economic bases of international legal concepts which previously formed an important part of the normative (and other) framework of the relationship between sites. Used by strategic actors, these different concepts and new understandings form part of the types of market competition and the legal strategies which underlie global legal pluralism. The *Bicycles* saga shows that globalisation has undercut the basic assumptions of anti-dumping law.

Part II of the book builds on these basic ideas. It considers relations between the EU, China and the WTO as three distinct but interrelated sites of governance. The four chapters in this Part deal with the ways in which courts construct relations between sites of governance, the translation of international trade law into domestic law, the types of rules which are used to regulate international trade and to manage relations between sites, how relations between sites can result in the creation of an international normative repertoire and of new concepts in the field of international trade law, the 'legalisation' of norms, or their transformation from soft law to hard law, and the governance of global commodity chains or IPNs. These chapters show how the structural characteristics of sites of governance influence, condition or determine relations between sites of governance. Reciprocally, the relations between sites of governance influence, condition or determine the structural features of sites of governance.

Institutions often create relations between sites of governance. These relations, however, stem not only from diplomats, legislators or the executive power in governments;

[3] For this definition of soft law, see F Snyder, 'The Effectiveness of European Community Law: Institutions, Processes, Tools and Techniques' (1993) 56(1) *MLR* 19.

they may also originate from or be organised by courts, especially courts of last instance. Such courts often act as 'gatekeepers' in relations between sites. Chapter five considers the ways in which the European Court of Justice (ECJ) through its judgments has acted as a 'gatekeeper' in relations between the WTO and the EU. It argues that the main effects of WTO law on EU law, as seen in the case law of the European courts, have so far been three-fold, and that these effects have occurred in three overlapping phases.

The law of the WTO has contributed to the expansion of the normative resources, or the normative repertoire, available to EU institutions, notably (but not only) the judiciary, and thus also to the power of these institutions. Though enhancing the power of institutions, the ECJ decisions, with certain limited exceptions, have not led to any corresponding empowerment of individuals. Indeed, it can be argued that increasing normative integration between the WTO and EU has weakened the position of individuals within the EU legal order until recently. In addition, WTO law, as interpreted by the European courts, has tended so far to foster tighter relations between the EU and the Member States, as well as greater integration among the Member States in the substantive areas in which it applies.

The chapter shows that, as seen from the EU perspective, the specific characteristics of the EU have exercised a determining influence on relations between the EU and the WTO. These characteristics have been mediated by courts, notably the ECJ. The chapter also identifies certain critical points in ECJ case law which now require a new direction. It suggests that now it is time for the judiciary, the legislature or the executive of the EU to chart new relations between the EU and the WTO.

Relations between sites of governance may give rise to new legal concepts, which may be common to several sites or may be anchored in only some of them. Chapter six focuses on ways in which relations between sites of governance give rise to new legal concepts. It analyses the ways in which relations between sites of governance generated an international normative repertoire concerning anti-dumping law. It traces the origins and development of the concept of 'non-market economy' in WTO and EU anti-dumping law. In addition to the EU and China, it introduces the United States and the GATT as very important sites of governance. It shows that the legal concept of 'non-market economy' in EU anti-dumping law has been socially constructed, by means of relations among a plurality of sites of governance, as part of a changing configuration of legal ideas in specific historical circumstances, and in contexts of political, economic, social and symbolic power.

The concept of 'non-market economy' in EU anti-dumping law, though drawing on earlier elements, had its main roots in the early Cold War. Starting in the 1960s, the GATT multilateral negotiating rounds began to define more specific international rules of the game, but a variety of more localised processes played essential roles as forces of change. Of special importance were, first, the tension between legislative rules and administrative discretion in the United States, and, secondly, the Europeanisation of foreign trade law in the course of European integration. The EU law concept of 'non-market economy' was born in the late 1970s. The main reasons were changes in the international anti-dumping law repertoire, specific ideas in Europe about comparative economic systems, and the perceived emergence of new economic threats, including imports from China. Today this concept is applied to enterprises involved in EC anti-dumping actions in the terminology of 'market economy treatment' (MET) and 'individual treatment' (IT). It also underlies the terminology of 'market economy status' (MES), a country-level designation that is applied to China as a whole. Though this further analysis lies outside the scope of this book, it is crucial to recognise that, despite profound differences in the contexts of the 1950s and of today, the distinct yet close association between a highly technical, enterprise-level analysis (MET; IT) and a macro-political, country-level analysis (MES) is as characteristic of EU and WTO anti-dumping law today as in the past.

Chapter seven examines the ways in which relations between sites of governance can change the structural features of sites, such as norms. Earlier chapters emphasise the role of 'soft law' in the governance of economic globalisation and the regulation of international trade. 'Soft law' may sometimes become 'hard law', for example by judicial decision or by incorporation into legislation. Chapter seven focuses on the second scenario. It considers the 'legalisation' of an EC anti-dumping concept known as 'individual treatment'. In the EU, the notion of individual treatment began as administrative practice; subsequently it was adopted in the form of 'soft law' and later it was incorporated into legislation.

Anti-dumping law, as is well known, is concerned with price competition. 'Dumping' refers to the sale of a product on an export market at a price lower than the product's domestic market price or 'normal value'. The classification of a country as a 'non-market economy', as shown in chapter six, means that the actual prices of its domestic producers are substituted by prices based on a market-economy third country, or analogue country ('surrogate country' in US terminology). In certain circumstances, however, the export price of an allegedly dumped product from a non-market economy country is calculated according to the exporter's real export price, rather than on the basis of an export price from the analogue country. This exception is called 'individual treatment'. It distinguishes the specific exporter from all other exporters in the 'non-market economy' country. It is based on the idea of 'bubbles of capitalism', which, according to this logic (often difficult to accept today), may exist in an economy in which the government plays a dominant role. Chapter seven argues that the legalisation of individual treatment partly reflected the increasing economic ties between the EU and China, notably through foreign direct investment and cooperation in joint ventures. In other words, increasing relations between sites of governance, notably between the strategic actors which use the law, resulted in changes in the norms within one of the sites of governance.

Global commodity chains, IPNs and foreign direct investment are among the most significant elements of contemporary globalisation. They drive foreign trade relations between the EU and China, and underlie relations among the EU, the WTO and China. Chapter eight considers the basic arrangements in EU law and international trade law which foster, structure and channel these transnational economic relationships. The principal legal devices are the customs law arrangements known as inward processing and outward processing. With some variation, these arrangements are shared by the EU, China, the United States and other trading countries. In other words, similar rules common to numerous sites of governance, including States, regional organisations and international organisations, underpin the development of transnational economic relations. The chapter discusses a selection of trade disputes involving inward processing or outward processing which have come before the ECJ. It also analyses the relationship between these customs arrangements and trade defence measures such as anti-dumping law.

Chapter eight argues that globalisation and regional integration are both friends and rivals, mutually reinforcing but also competing with each other. International integration and regional integration constitute different sets or constellations of relations between sites. In the case of the EU, globalisation and its constellation of relations between sites tend to hinder or block certain lines of structural development. Globalisation, for example in the form of global economic networks, is likely to hinder the development of an EU constitution, at least if we understand the term 'constitution' as being roughly analogous to that of the nation State. In other words, we cannot understand the interests, structures and processes involved in European integration today without taking global economic networks into account. The chapter thus challenges us to imagine new forms of governance which are appropriate to and sustainable in contemporary Europe in its international context.

Part III of the book returns to the broader themes of international trade regulation, regional integration and global governance. It comprises two chapters, one on China and regional integration, and the other on ethics, the WTO and global governance. In contrast to most chapters of the book, which are more sociological than normative in character, the final chapter seeks to deploy the ideas of sites of governance and global legal pluralism in an explicitly normative direction.

In addition to giving rise to new legal concepts, or transforming institutions, norms or dispute resolution processes within a particular site, relations between sites of governance may also stimulate the creation of new sites. Regional trade agreements (RTAs) provide striking examples. Chapter nine analyses China's RTAs and identifies a variety of reasons underlying them. It proposes that China's RTAs can be classified according to a three-fold typology: economic integration agreements, standard regional trade agreements with other countries in the Asia–Pacific region, and bilateral free trade agreements with non-Asian countries. It also assesses China's RTAs in the light of WTO law. For this purpose, it focuses in particular on safeguards, rules of origin and dispute settlement mechanisms.

The chapter argues that an RTA creates a new site of governance if it constitutes a locus of decision-making with the authority to settle disputes, as it inevitably does. The new site results from relations between existing sites. In fact, it usually represents a more highly institutionalised form of selected aspects of these relations. However, while reflecting the structural features of the sites concerned, it also usually embodies new structural features of its own. On this basis, it may enter into its own relations with other sites of governance. An examination of China's RTAs is useful in helping us to understand why and how new sites of governance may be created. The creation of RTAs thus contributes to the development of global legal pluralism.

The last chapter, chapter ten, builds on preceding chapters to explore the role of ethical issues in international trade regulation and global governance. It focuses in particular on development, respect for the environment and social justice. We can call this set of values 'social solidarity ethics', because their effective realisation in practice demands and encourages social solidarity within and across national or regional boundaries. Achieving respect for these values in practice is a major challenge of our time.

Using the concept of sites of governance and the theory of global legal pluralism, chapter ten has both analytical and normative purposes. It adopts an institutional perspective to analyse relations between the WTO and other sites of governance, including partnerships between the WTO and other sites and WTO cooperation with other sites in the production of norms, but leaving aside its relations with individual WTO members. By this approach, the chapter aims to suggest a different way of thinking about the issue of trade linkages and the ethical aspects of international trade regulation. It argues that the WTO can best take account of social solidarity ethics in the governance of international trade by strengthening its relations with other sites of governance. This is a strategy focused on relations between sites, notably on relations between institutions, and aimed at closer coordination between sites. It differs from strategies concerned only with internal structures of sites, or those orientated toward relations but involving only norms or dispute-resolution processes, or those concerned not with coordination but rather with expanding the WTO domains of action (constitutionalisation) or putting the WTO into direct competition with other sites of governance (regulatory competition).

The chapter argues that, despite its many links with other international institutions, the WTO currently has relatively few relations with other sites which are directly concerned with social solidarity ethics. Consequently, the best strategy for increasing the extent to which the WTO takes account of ethical issues is to strengthen its institutional relations with other sites and make use of the increasing significance of relations between sites of governance in the context of global legal pluralism.

This book, viewed as a whole, thus aims to contribute to and to develop our understanding of the roles of sites of governance and of the significance of global legal pluralism in international trade regulation. All of the chapters deal with globalisation, sites of governance and relations between them, in particular the EU, the WTO and China. Though sometimes concerned with highly technical subjects, the argument presented in the following chapters seeks to elucidate aspects of the basic changes in the institutional and normative parameters of social life which have occurred in virtually all countries during the past several decades. It also aims to point our empirical research and theoretical perspectives in a normative direction, in particular by emphasising the interconnections between legal pluralism and the development of social solidarity ethics. This is a significant challenge for the present and the future.

Part I

Globalisation, Sites of Governance and Global Legal Pluralism

2

Globalisation and the Law

I. Introduction

During the past 50 years, globalisation and the development of new legal forms have gone hand-in-hand.[1] The term 'globalisation', and even its existence, is contested.[2] However, globalisation is not new, it cannot be reduced merely to market integration, still less to a neo-liberal political and economic project of free trade and open markets, and its ultimate destination is unknown, depending as much on power and politics as on economics. One commonly used definition takes globalisation to mean

> a process (or set of processes) which embodies a transformation in the spatial organization of social relations and transactions—assessed in terms of their extensity, intensity, velocity and impact—generating transcontinental or interregional flows and networks of activity, interaction, and the exercise of power.[3]

Unlike previous globalisations, however, the contemporary process of globalisation so far involves the dominance of financial markets, unusually powerful, often intrusive technology, and worldwide economic and legal integration.

The main shaping factors of globalisation today have been financial market integration, the tremendous growth of multinational companies and IPNs, new technology,

[1] AJ Arnaud, *Entre modernité et mondialisation. Cinq leçons d'histoire de la philosophie du droit* (Paris, Librairie Générale de Droit et de Jurisprudence, 1998); AJ Arnaud, *Critique de la raison juridique, 2. Gouvernants sans frontières: Entre mondialisation et post-mondialisation* (Paris, Librairie Générale de Droit et de Jurisprudence, 2003); MR Ferrarese, *Le istituzioni della globalizzazione: Diritto et diritti nella società transnazionale* (Bolgogna, Il Mulino, 2000); D Mockle (ed), *Mondialisation et Etat de Droit* (Brussels, Bruylant, 2002); JL Halpérin, *Profils des mondialisations du droit* (Paris, Dalloz-Sirey, 2009); T Anghie, BS Chimni, K Mickelson and O Okafor (eds), *The Third World and International Legal Order: Law, Politics and Globalization* (Kluwer Law International, 2003); P De Senarclens, *La mondialisation: Théories, enjeux et débats*, 3rd edn (Paris, Armand Colin, 2002); GZ Capaldo, *The Pillars of Global Law* (Aldershot, Ashgate, 2008). See also the Series on 'The International Library of Essays on Globalization and Law', series editor Michael K Addo, published by Ashgate, which as of April 2009 included volumes on international investment (ed F Beveridge), international law (ed P Schiff Berman) and intellectual property (ed A George). See also Y Ghai, R Luckham and F Snyder (eds), *The Political Economy of Law: A Third World Reader* (Delhi, Oxford University Press, 1987); LL Martin (ed), *International Institutions in the Global Economy* (Cheltenham, Edward Elgar Publishing, 2005).

[2] Cf R Robertson, *Globalization: Social Theory and Global Culture* (London, Sage, 1992); P Hirst and G Thompson, *Globalization in Question: The International Economy and the Possibilities of Governance* (Cambridge, Polity Press, 1996); A Giddens, *The Consequences of Modernity* (Cambridge, Polity Press, 1990); S Sassen, *Losing Control? Sovereignty in an Age of Globalization* (New York, Columbia University Press, 1996); TL Friedman, *The Lexus and the Olive Tree* (New York, Farrar, Strauss and Griroux, 1999); JF Lechner and J Boli (eds), *The Globalization Reader* (Oxford, Blackwell Publishing, 2003); JN Bhagwati, *In Defense of Globalization* (New York, Oxford University Press, 2004).

[3] D Held, A McGrew, D Goldblatt, and J Perraton, *Global Transformations: Politics, Economics and Culture* (Cambridge, Polity Press, 1999), 16 [original italics removed].

changes in the nature and form of work, and the rise of new actors on the international scene. Associated with this transformation have been numerous legal changes, both on a transnational scale and within countries.[4] The early years of the 21st century witness a startling variety of new legal forms and regimes which sometimes differ substantially in nature, content, scale and operation from the largely State-based system of governance of the past several centuries. A multiplicity of other sites of governance complements, supplements or competes with the State, hence the term 'governance' instead of 'government'. While sometimes eroded or even reconfigured, the State remains powerful, if not predominant, with the relative strength of different institutions, norms and dispute resolution processes depending frequently on the specific context.[5]

Focusing on the relationship between globalisation and law, this chapter lays the foundation for the remainder of the book. While globalisation raises a number of challenges for thinking about law,[6] the sheer volume of published work makes a comprehensive survey impossible here. Instead, the chapter aims to provide a brief guide to the literature, giving a retrospective and a prospective assessment of the field. It deals mainly with the legal effects of economic globalisation, while recognising that globalisation is not simply economic and that many aspects of globalisation have implications for law. It focuses primarily on research within the broad fields of sociology of law, international relations and political economy of law, as these are the main disciplinary touchstones of writing on law and globalisation. It focuses mainly but not only on literature in English; it also takes account of work in French and Italian. Most published work so far has appeared in English, many scholars regardless of mother tongue publish in English, and English-language work has tended to establish and define the field. In the long run, however, it is necessary to transcend this parochial view, and in particular to integrate literature in German and in Chinese, to mention only two. This chapter provides stepping-stones for doing so.

II. Internationalisation of Legal Fields

During the past several decades globalisation has affected many, if not all, areas of law to a striking extent. The first substantial treatment of law and globalisation[7] used

[4] N Blomley, D Delaney and RT Ford, *The Legal Geographies Reader* (Oxford, Blackwell, 2001); PS Berman, 'From International Law to Law and Globalization', *ExpressO Preprint Series*, Working Paper 665, 5 July 2005, http:/law.bepress.com/espresso/eps/665.

[5] K Jayasuriya, 'Globalization, Sovereignty, and the Rule of Law: From Political to Economic Constitutionalism?', (2001) 8 *Constellations* 442; A Coleman and, J Maogoto, 'After the party, is there any cure for the hangover? The challenges of the global economy to Westphalian sovereignty' (2003) 30(1) *Legal Issues of European Integration* 35.

[6] B Stern, 'Vers la mondialisation juridique?', *Revue générale de droit international public* (1996) 979; Arnaud, *Entre modernité et mondialisation*, above n 1; W Twining, *Globalalisation and Legal Theory* (London, Butterworths, 2000); M Delmas-Marty, *Trois defis pour un droit mondial* (Paris, Editions du Seuil, 1998); M Chemillier-Gendreau and Y Moulier Boutang (eds), *Le droit dans la mondialisation* (Actes du congrès Marx International II) (Paris, Presses Universitaires de France, 2001); P Fitzpatrick, *Modernism and the Grounds of Law* (Cambridge, Cambridge University Press, 2001); W Graf Vitzthum, R Mehdi and C Prieto (eds), *Europe et mondialisation—Europa und die Globalisierung* (Aix-en-Provence, Presses Universitaires d'Aix-Marseille, 2006).

[7] DM Trubek, Y Dezalay, R Buchanan and JR Davis, 'Global Restructuring and the Law: Studies of the Internationalization of Legal Fields and the Creation of Transnational Arenas' (1994) 44 *Case Western Reserve Law Review* 407.

Bourdieu's concept of social fields[8] to show how new transnational and global economic and political processes and political trends changed the role of lawyers, the logic of legal practices and the nature of the legal field. National legal fields became more 'internationalised', in two senses. First, legal and political arenas which had previously been mainly national in terms of background assumptions, actors and orientation were increasingly influenced by 'external' factors. Second, purportedly 'domestic' decisions were conditioned, shaped or even actually made elsewhere as transnational legal regimes penetrated national legal fields. These changes enhanced the status and role of actors with international linkages and expertise, as well as the power of certain States relative to others.

Recent research refers to the 'de-nationalisation' of much of contemporary rule-making. Sassen[9] addresses the question of the relationship of 'international' norms to 'domestic' norms in a situation in which the two are so intertwined that it is no longer possible to assert that that one set of norms is international and another set is national. Many so-called 'national' norms have in effect been 'de-nationalised'. Their source, content, logic and even interpretation or application owes much, if not everything, to intergovernmental, transnational or international institutions, norms and dispute resolution processes. This is not a question of extra-territoriality but rather of the extent to which the norms of nation States, or of regional organisations such as the European Union, are based on or impregnated by 'international' norms, including WTO international trade rules, codes of conduct, standards or the results of international dispute settlement processes. Formally speaking, the sources of 'national' and 'international' norms are different, and this difference has its legal doctrinal importance in each of the two institutional and normative settings. However, the traditional distinction between 'domestic' and 'foreign', or between 'national' and 'international', often does not adequately capture the political origins, legal content, cultural understandings, economic assumptions and social practices—for example the need for certain types of specialised legal professionals—of contemporary law.

'Denationalisation' is only part, however, of the current transformation of law. National and local institutions, concepts, norms and processes also affect transnational and international concepts, both in the settings in which they originate and in their application. Merry coined the term 'vernacularisation' to denote the process by which concepts and norms of international origin were rendered into local languages, legal culture and social settings, and thus transformed in different ways in different social contexts.[10] Viewed in a broader perspective, these processes may be envisaged as the translation of concepts and norms from one source into the context of another source. Reflecting these concerns, both Coombe and Snyder have argued in favour of specifically anthropological approaches to law and globalisation.[11] Such work on

[8] P Bourdieu, 'The Force of Law: Toward a Sociology of the Juridical Field' (1987) 38 *The Hastings Law Journal* 814.

[9] S Sassen, 'Opening remarks: Producing the transnational inside the national', in M Likosky (ed), *Transnational Legal Processes: Globalisation and Power Disparities* (London, Butterworths LexisNexis, 2002) 189 at 195.

[10] SE Merry, *Human Rights and Gender Violence: Translating International Law into Local Justice* (Chicago, University of Chicago Press, 2006).

[11] RJ Coombe, 'Anthropological Approaches to Law and Society in Conditions of Globalization' in N Blomley, D Delaney and RT Ford (eds), *The Legal Geographies Reader* (Oxford, Blackwell Publishers, 2001) 298; F Snyder, 'Antidumping Law and Cross-Cultural Encounters: Toward a Legal Anthropology of International Economic Relations' in C Eberhard and G Vernicos (eds), *La quête anthropologique du droit: Autour de la demarche d'Etienne Le Roy* (Paris, Editions Karthala, 2006) 59. See also the papers presented

globalisation and the law is sensitive to regional, national and local contexts, and deserves to be encouraged and developed in many settings.

Some legal fields, including the study of the legal profession,[12] have always been more internationalised than others. Areas of law most closely connected with international trade and multinational companies, such as international business contracts,[13] antitrust law and competition policy,[14] financial markets, intellectual property,[15] the Internet and new technology,[16] cybercrime,[17] national security,[18] labour and social law, labour regulation and new forms of work,[19] and now environmental law and public interest law,[20] have been affected more than family law and property law. But even discounting for our lack of empirical knowledge of the effects of globalisation on many areas of law, it is clear that the internationalised sector has tended to grow, despite national and local diversity.[21] The economic and legal transformation of China since 1979, stimulated by Chinese accession to the WTO in 2001, has provided a fertile field for studies of the internationalisation of law.[22] An increasing number of areas are subject to international agreements.[23] Criminal law has been a particularly dynamic

at the Commission on Legal Pluralism, 2008 Conference, Kunming, China, 15–23 July 2008, at http://www.commission-on-legal-pluralism.ch/List_of_organisational_session.pdf.

[12] RL Abel, 'Transnational Legal Practice' (1994) 44 *Case Western Reserve Law Review* 737. The internationalisation of legal professions remains, however, very uneven.

[13] MJ Bonell, *An International Restatement of Contract Law: The UNIDROIT Principles of International Commercial Contracts* (New York, Transnational Juris Publications Inc, 1994).

[14] EM Graham and JD Richardson (eds), *Global Competition Policy* (Washington, DC, Institute for International Economics, 1997); W Pape, 'Socio-Cultural Differences and International Competition Law' (1999) 5(4) *European Law Journal* 438; W Abdelgawad (ed), *Mondialisation et droit de la concurrence: Les réactions normatives des états face à la mondialisation des pratiques anticoncurrentielles et des opérations de concentration*, Acts du Colloque des 14–15 juin 2007, Université de Bourgogne, CNRS, Travaux du Centre de recherche sur le droit des marchés et des investissements internationaux (Paris, Litec, 2008).

[15] 'Symposium Issue: The Inaugural Engelberg Conference on the Culture and Economics of Participation in an International Intellectual Property Regime' (1996–97) 29 *New York University Journal of International Law and Economics*.

[16] L Lessig, *Code and Other Laws of Cyberspace* (New York, Basic Books, 1999); CT Marsden, 'Cyberlaw and International Political Economy', *Law Review of Michigan State University Detroit College of Law*, Summer 2001, 355.

[17] W Capeller, 'Not such a neat net: Some comments on virtual criminality' (2001) 10 *Social & Legal Studies* 229; F Snyder, 'Sites of Criminality and Sites of Governance' (2001) 10(2) *Social and Legal Studies* 251.

[18] ED Mansfield (ed), *International Conflict and the Global Economy* (Cheltenham, Edward Elgar, 2004).

[19] W Sengenberger, and D Campbell, *International Labour Standards and Economic Interdependence* (Essays in commemoration of the 75th anniversary of the International Labour Organisation and the 50th anniversary of the Declaration of Philadelphia) (Geneva, International Labour Organisation, 1994); HH Drummonds, 'Transnational small and emerging business in a world of Nikes and Microsofts' (2000) 4 *Journal of Small and Emerging Business Law* 249; V Spike Peterson, *A Critical Rewriting of Global Political Economy: Integrating Reproductive, Productive and Virtual Economies* (London, Routledge, 2003); J Conaghan, R Fischl and K Klare, *Labour Law in an Era of Globalization: Transformative Practices and Possibilities* (Oxford, Oxford University Press, 2002); E Benvenisti, and D Barak-Erez, *The Welfare State, Globalization and International Law* (Berlin, Springer, 2003); JM Diller and DA Levy, 'Child Labor, Trade and Investment: Toward the Harmonization of International Law' (1997) 94 *American Journal of Comparative Law* 663.

[20] SL Cummings, 'The Internationalization of Public Interest Law', *UCLA School of Law, UCLA Public Law Series,* Paper 6-11, 13 November 2006.

[21] LM Friedman, 'Erewhon: The coming global legal order' (2001) 37 *Stanford Journal of International Law* 347.

[22] J Leng, 'China's Banking Reform in the Context of Globalization and Transition' (2006) 17(5) *European Business Law Review* 1271; F Snyder (ed), *The European Union and China, 1949–2008: Basic Documents and Commentary* (Oxford, Hart Publishing, 2009).

[23] C Patten, 'Globalisation and the Law' (2004) 1 *European Human Rights Law Review* 6.

growth area for legal scholarship; this includes the globalisation of crime[24] and international criminal tribunals,[25] including for terrorism.[26] Similarly, innovative studies have focused on sex trafficking and prostitution.[27]

In understanding the implications of this trend, however, it is useful to bear in mind Krasner's distinction between four concepts of sovereignty: international legal sovereignty, Westphalian sovereignty, interdependence sovereignty and domestic sovereignty.[28] Quiggin, for example, has contended that the loss of interdependence sovereignty does not necessary mean the erosion of Westphalian sovereignty. Hence, a decline in a State's capacity to control flows of people and goods across its frontiers does not inevitably lead to the adoption of neoliberal economic policies.[29]

The internationalisation of legal fields has usually been viewed in the past as being more or less equivalent to Americanisation.[30] The American way of law, embedded in a particular variety of capitalism,[31] has been exported by multinational business, large law firms, international organisations, development programmes, cultural archetypes, and the reception or imposition of US law in many other countries. Often this amounts merely to 'thin globalisation',[32] in the sense of a thin veneer covering an often quite different social, cultural and legal reality, so that the future social practices, normative content and legal culture of globalised law remain contested.[33] Nevertheless, Shapiro's[34] remark that 'much of the time, the globe will turn out to be the US and Western Europe with shadowy addenda' is significant. Historically, it reflects the fact that, so far, the centre of gravity of the global economy remains in transatlantic relations between the United States and the European Union, notably in foreign direct investment and capital market relations[35]; such a concentration is unfortunate because it testifies to the extremely unequal distribution of wealth in the world today. A similar view is captured in more theoretical terms by Santos' distinction between globalised localism and localised globalism: the former refers to the process by which local

[24] E Rotman, 'The Globalization of Criminal Violence' (2000) 10 *Cornell Journal of Law and Public Policy* 1.

[25] L Arturo, 'The Impact of Globalisation on Law Enforcement Institutions' (2006) 7(1) *Human Rights and UK Practice* 10.

[26] M Delmas-Marty, 'Global Crime Calls for Global Justice' (2002) 10(4) *European Journal of Crime, Criminal Law and Criminal Justice* 286.

[27] See eg E Bernstein, *Temporarily Yours: Intimacy, Authenticity and the Commerce of Sex* (Chicago, University of Chicago Press, 2007); V Von Struensee, 'Sex Trafficking: A Plea for Action' (2002) 6 *European Law Journal* 379.

[28] S Krasner, *Sovereignty: Organized Hypocrisy* (Princeton, Princeton University Press, 1999).

[29] J Quiggin, 'Globalization and Economic Sovereignty' (2001) 9 *The Journal of Political Philosophy* 56.

[30] M Hardt and A Negri, *Empire* (Cambridge, Mass, Harvard University Press, 2000).

[31] PA Hall and D Soskice, *Varieties of Capitalism: The Institutional Foundations of Comparative Advantage* (Oxford, Oxford University Press, 2001).

[32] I am indebted to David Trubek for this expression.

[33] See CAG Jones, 'Capitalism, Globalization and Rule of Law: An Alternative Trajaectory of Legal Change in China' (1994) 3 *Social & Legal Studies* 195; JK Winn, 'Relational Practices and the Marginalization of Law: A Study of the Informal Financial Practices of Small Businesses in Taiwan' (1994) 28 *Law & Society Review* 193; F Upham, 'Speculations on Legal Informality: On Winn's "Relational Practices and the Marginalization of Law"' (1994) 28 *Law & Society Review* 233; RP Appelbaum, 'The Future of Law in a Global Economy' (1998) 7 *Social & Legal Studies* 171; RP Appelbaum, W Felstiner and V Gessner (eds), *Rules and Networks: The Legal Culture of Global Business Transactions* (Oxford, Hart Publishing, 2001).

[34] M Shapiro, 'The Globalization of Law' (1993) 37 *Indiana Journal of Global Legal Studies* 37 at 38.

[35] S Sassen, 'The locational and institutional embeddedness of the global economy', in GA Bermann, M Herdegen and PL Lindseth (eds), *Transatlantic Regulatory Cooperation: Legal Problems and Political Prospects* (New York, Oxford University Press, 2000) 47.

phenomena are successfully globalised, while the latter denotes the impact of transnational practices on local conditions.[36]

In the legal world, given the fact of US hegemony in the international political economy, the localisms which have been most frequently globalised so far are American. Striking examples are the globalisation of American jurisprudence by means of international commercial arbitration or intellectual property protection through the WTO Agreement on Trade-related Aspects of Intellectual Property (TRIPS),[37] even though, as Shaffer shows,[38] the US itself is deeply affected by external pressures and international networks.[39] Whether and how the 2008–09 financial crisis will affect this pattern remains to be seen. However, the world is changing, especially with the rise of the BRICSAM (Brazil, Russia, India, China, South Africa, Mexico) countries. In fact, the re-emergence of China is likely to signal the end of Western dominance of the world and eventually to transform the form and content of the internationalisation of law. The future, as Martin Jacques argues,[40] is likely to be characterised by multiple, contested versions of what it means to be modern, including in the field of law.

III. New Institutions and New Norms

Contemporary globalisation has stimulated and has fed on the development of new institutions and new types of norms. An obvious example is the WTO, which was heir to the General Agreement on Tariffs and Trade (GATT) of 1947 and which began operation on 1 January 1995.[41] Numerous other organisations, public, private or hybrid, have also been created. They include a wide range of international standards organisations and other institutions.[42] The most well-known are probably the International Standards Organisation (ISO), the International Accounting Standards Committee (IASC), and debt security rating agencies such as Moody's and S&P.

[36] B de Sousa Santos, *Toward a New Common Sense: Law, Globalization and Emancipation* (London, Butterworths LexisNexis, 2002), 1st edn published as *Toward a New Common Sense: Law, Science and Politics in the Paradigmatic Transition* (New York, Routledge, 1995). See also E Darian-Smith, 'Power in Paradise: The Political Implications of Santos's Utopia' (Winter 1998) 23 *Law & Social Enquiry* 81; E Darian-Smith, *Bridging Divides: The Channel Tunnel and English Legal Identity in the New Europe* (Berkeley, University of California Press, 1999).

[37] RC Wolf, *Trade, Aid and Arbitrate: The Globalization of Western Law* (Dartmouth, Aldershot, Ashgate, 2004); SK Sell, 'Multinational corporations as agents of change: The globalization of intellectual property rights', in AC Cutler, V Haufler and T Porter (eds), *Private Authority and International Affairs* (Buffalo, State University of New York Press, 1999) 169; CJ Arup, *The New World Trade Organization Agreements: Globalizing Law Through Services and Intellectual Property* (Cambridge, Cambridge University Press, 2000).

[38] G Shaffer, 'Globalization and social protection: The impact of EU and international rules in the ratcheting up of US privacy standards' (2000) 25 *Yale Journal of International Law* 1.

[39] F Macmillan, 'International Economic Law and Public International Law: Strangers in the Night' (2004) 10(6) *International Trade Law and Regulation* 115.

[40] M Jacques, *When China Rules the World: The Rise of the Middle Kingdom and the End of the Western World* (London, Allen Lane, 2009).

[41] Among the vast literature, see PFJ Macrory, AE Appleton and MG Plummer (eds), *The World Trade Organization: Legal, Economic and Political Analysis*, 3 vols (New York, Springer, 2005).

[42] L Salter, 'The Standards Regime for Communication and Information Technologies' in AC Cutler, V Haufler and T Porter (eds), *Private Authority and International Affairs* (Buffalo, State University of New York Press, 1999) 97; see also C Brütsch and D Lehmkuhl (eds), *Law and Legalization in International Relations* (London, Routledge Cavendish, 2007).

For example, the IASC currently includes 153 professional accounting bodies in 112 countries and is responsible for developing and approving international accounting standards. The IASC international accounting standards largely reflect Anglo-American practices.[43] They are not legally binding, so the IASC acts as a 'strategic networker'[44] to convince governmental actors to adopt and give legal force to its voluntary standards. Debt security rating agencies, such as Moody's and S&P, exercise significant powers of 'governance without government': these are non-State institutions which derive their international leverage from their gate-keeping role concerning investment funds sought by companies and governments.[45] Other important international regulatory associations are the Basel Committee for Banking Supervision, the Financial Action Task Force on Money Laundering (FATF), the International Association of Insurance Supervisors (IAIS) and the International Organisation of Securities Commissions (IOSCO).[46] As the recent financial crisis has demonstrated, the norms which they produce are of vital importance to consumers.[47] Just as with legislation, they may also be subject to regulatory capture by specific interests.[48]

Among the most striking developments in recent years is increased attention to norms,[49] in particular the emergence of 'soft law', or rules of conduct which in principle are not legally binding but which nevertheless have practical and even legal effects.[50] Long familiar to international lawyers,[51] soft law gained prominence during the 1970s in the form of international codes of conduct to govern the activities of multinational corporations.[52] During the 1990s, codes of conduct were elaborated increasingly not only by international organisations but also by States or by private actors. Soft law is widely used between States or regional organisations, especially when the adoption of legally binding norms or the conclusion of legally binding agreements may be problematic due to changing priorities among trading partners, uncertain domestic or international legal competence, or lack of clear advantages in having a legally binding agreement.[53]

[43] See H Schepel, *The Constitution of Private Governance: Product Standards in the Regulation of Integrating Markets* (Oxford, Hart Publishing, 2005); I Dewing and PO Russell, 'Financial Integration in the EU: the First Phase of EU Endorsement of International Accounting Standards' (2008) 46(2) *Journal of Common Market Studies* 243.

[44] J Braithwaite and P Drahos, *Global Business Regulation* (Cambridge, Cambridge University Press, 2000) 121.

[45] TJ Sinclair, 'Passing judgment: Credit rating processes as regulatory mechanisms of governance in the emerging world order' (1994) 1 *Review of International Political Economy* 133.

[46] P Neville, 'The Development of International Regulatory Associations' (2005) 12(3) *Journal of Financial Crime* 264.

[47] See also K Dawar, 'Global Governance and Its Implications for Consumers' (2006) 16(1) *Consumer Policy Review* 2–4 (introduction to special issue on international standards and the implications for consumers).

[48] See eg W Mattli and N Woods (eds), *The Politics of Global Regulation* (Princeton, Princeton University Press, 2009).

[49] V Haufler, 'Self-regulation and Business Norms: Political Risk, Political Activism' in Cutler *et al*, above n 42, 199.

[50] F Snyder, 'The Effectiveness of European Community Law: Institutions, Processes, Tools and Techniques' (1993) 56 *MLR* 19.

[51] See D Shelton (ed), *Commitment and Compliance: The Role of Non-binding Norms in the International Legal System* (Oxford, Oxford University Press, 2000).

[52] F Nixon, 'Controlling the Transnationals? The UN Code of Conduct' in Y Ghai, R Luckham and F Snyder (eds), *The Political Economy of Law: A Third World Reader* (Delhi, Oxford University Press, 1987) 416.

[53] For examples, see L Senden, *Soft Law in European Community Law* (Oxford, Hart Publishing, 2004); S Lefevre, *Les actes communautaires atypiques* (Brussels, Bruylant, 2006) (EU law); F Snyder, *The European Union and China, 1949–2008: Basic Documents and Commentary* (Oxford, Hart Publishing, 2009) (EU–China policy dialogues).

Compared to hard law, soft law has the advantages of lower contracting costs and lower sovereignty costs, and is often better adapted to conditions of uncertainty or those requiring compromise.[54] Soft law serves sometimes to govern relations between private actors, and sometimes to govern relations internal to private actors.[55] Sobczak argues that such use represents a new generation of codes of conduct as part of a transformation of global and corporate governance.[56] Many corporate codes of conduct have been internationalised.[57] These so-called 'informal agreements' are often used because the obligations they embody are more equivocal and less visible than those contained in legally binding agreements.[58] In some situations, of course, legally binding measures remain paramount because of the political symbolism of 'law', because existing norms require their use or because of their implications for the allocation of power among various institutions.

To what extent does soft law actually work? This is a question not about the boundaries between politics and law, but rather about the social effectiveness of different types of norms. The basic issue is whether soft law can provide the optimum institutional design for governing sensitive issues on which companies, unions, non-governmental organisations (NGOs) or governments initially do not agree, such as international standards concerning working conditions, human rights or protection of the environment. This question is sometimes interpreted as seeking to reconcile economic interests and ethical considerations, but it is more properly read as referring to a balance between different kinds of economic interests and different kinds of ethical considerations. It is not surprising that the rise of soft law has been reflected in the rise of procedural informalism in the US and Europe, or that the latter has been subject to similar debates about democracy, legitimacy and fairness.[59]

Recently, Abbott and colleagues[60] have proposed the concept of legalisation as a systematic framework for analysing these (and other) new norms and procedures. Legalisation has three dimensions: the existence of legal obligations, the precision with which these obligations are defined, and the extent to which responsibility for dispute resolution is delegated to third parties. Each dimension is a continuum, composed of differences of degree, and each can vary independently of the others. Specific norms or specific procedures may be more or less legalised. Applying these ideas, Keohane *et al*[61] define inter-State dispute resolution and transnational dispute resolution as two ideal types, differing in independence from concrete State interests, access by parties other than States and embeddedness in the sense that decisions can be implemented

[54] KW Abbott and D Snidal, 'Hard law and soft law in international governance' (2000) 54 *International Organization* 421.

[55] B Hepple, 'A Race to the Top? International Investment Guidelines and Corporate Codes of Conduct' (1999) 20 *Comparative Labor Law and Policy Journal* 347.

[56] A Sobczak, *Réseaux de sociétés et codes de conduite: Un nouveau modèle de regulation des relations de travail pour les entreprises européennes*, PhD thesis (Florence, European University Institute, 2001).

[57] AS Reid, 'The Internationalisation of Corporate Codes of Conduct' (2003) 24(10) *Business Law Review* 233.

[58] C Lipson, 'Why are Some International Agreements Informal?' (1991) 45 *International Organization* 495.

[59] See eg W Heydebrand, 'Globalisation and the Rise of Procedural Informalism in American and European Law' in V Gessner and D Nelken (eds), *European Ways of Law: Towards a European Sociology of Law* (Oxford, Hart Publishing, 2007) 93.

[60] KW Abbott, RO Keohane, A Moravcsik, AM Slaughter and D Snidal, 'The concept of legalization' (2000) 54 *International Organization* 401.

[61] RO Keohane, A Moravcsik and AM Slaughter, 'Legalized Dispute Resolution: Interstate and Transnational' (2000) 54 *International Organization* 457.

without governmental action. They argue that the transnational dispute resolution is more successful than inter-State dispute resolution in controlling case loads and ensuring compliance, hence it limits the behaviour of States to a greater extent.

The concept of legalisation is useful in disaggregating the boundary between law and politics in terms of three dimensions. This enables us to recognise that there are different kinds of obligations and also that there are different kinds of legal obligations, not all of which are equally constraining or involve strong commitments to action. Of course, once a norm creates legal obligations, it becomes hard law, even though the obligations may be defined only in general terms, or even though the settlement of disputes may not be delegated to a third party. Whether this makes any difference in social practice is an open question.

In principle at least, the analytical framework does not assume that greater legalisation is inherently superior to less legalisation. Yet it is difficult to escape the conclusion that the concept of legalisation is based implicitly on a dichotomous distinction between legal and non-legal.[62] This is despite the authors' effort to define the concept in terms of three dimensions and to articulate each dimension as a continuum. Indeed, the three dimensions themselves suggest that the authors prefer more legalisation, not less. This is reinforced by the remark that that

> When future international legal scholars look back at . . . the end of the twentieth century, they probably will refer to the enormous expansion of the international judiciary as the single most important development of the post-Cold War age.[63]

In fact, Kahler notes that the demand and supply of legalisation depends heavily on the preferences of powerful States.[64] Unfortunately, the analytical framework gives little weight to the role of power in determining the extent of delegation to third-party dispute mechanisms.[65] Hence it needs to be tempered by more attention to power and the political context in which law operates.

A more damaging criticism that can be leveled at the concept of legalisation is that it implicitly reflects the experience of the development of Western law.[66] The concept thus resembles earlier social theories of law based on an implicit teleology, such as modernisation theory. This is a major shortcoming in a world of increasing normative pluralism, quite apart from the fact that it abstracts completely from the international

[62] For other critiques and ensuing reply, see M Finnemore and SJ Toope, 'Alternatives to "Legalisation": Richer Views of Law and Politics' (2000) 54(3) *International Organization* 385; J Goldstein, M Kahler, RO Keohane and AM Slaughter, 'Response to Finnemore and Toope' (2001) 55(3) *International Organization* 759.

[63] C Romano, 'The proliferation of international judicial bodies: The pieces of the puzzle' (1999) 31(4) *New York University Journal of International Law and Politics* 709 at 709, quoted in Keohane *et al*, above n 61, at 457; see also A Del Vecchio, 'Globalisation and Its Effect on International Courts and Tribunals' (2006) 5(1) *Law and Practice of International Courts and Tribunals* 1; P Schiff Berman, 'The Globalization of Jurisdiction' (2002) 151 *University of Pennsylvania Law Review* 311; P Sands, R Mackenzie, CPR Romano, P Sands and Y Shany, *The Manual of International Courts and Tribunals* 2nd edn (Oxford, Oxford University Press, 2010. See also *The Global Community: Yearbook of International Law and Jurisprudence 2001–Present* (GZ Capaldo, Editor-in-Chief) (Oxford, Oxford University Press, 2002).

[64] M Kahler, 'Conclusion: The Causes and Consequences of Legalization' (2000) 54 *International Organization* 661 at 671; see also MN Barnett and R Duvall (eds), *Power in Global Governance* (Cambridge, Cambridge University Press, 2005).

[65] Keohane *et al*, above n 61, at 459, fn 7.

[66] It echoes some of the features of Western legal culture as analysed by F Wieacker, 'Foundations of European Legal Culture' (1990) 38 *American Journal of Comparative Law* 1.

political context.[67] In sum, further research is required in order to assess this general analytical framework.

IV. Specific Fields of Research

Attention to new institutions and new types of norms has characterised much recent research. The past few years have witnessed a dramatic increase in research in certain established areas and the development of new fields of research. Sometimes they represent the transposition of existing national research fields to the international arena. Frequently such developments are the result of crisis. Here it is possible to give only selected examples.

Human rights is a well-established field of law for which economic globalisation poses new issues. Globalisation has a fundamental impact on the idea of the rule of law,[68] on the definition of human rights and on the implementation of human rights norms.[69] Numerous studies concern the impact of multinational companies on human rights. Teubner argues that a matrix of globalised communicative processes endangers fundamental rights, which consequently need to be categorised as institutional rights, personal rights and human rights.[70] In South Africa, HIV/AIDS patients sue pharmaceutical companies, raising the question whether transnational corporations can be held liable to individuals for violations of fundamental rights. Similarly, Likosky suggests that international businesses participating in the Malaysia Multimedia Super Corridor help to recreate relations similar to those of the colonial period which subvert human rights.[71]

Scholarship on the law and practice of human rights has expanded rapidly in recent years. Alston has pioneered the study of human rights in a variety of fields.[72] Harrison's and Hestermeyer's are among the numerous studies which consider the impact of international trade rules on human rights, including the impact of patents on access to medicines.[73] Lang, for example, urges greater attention to the ways in which international

[67] See also V Gessner and D Nelken (eds), *European Ways of Law: Towards a European Sociology of Law* (Oxford, Hart Publishing, 2007), esp A Garapon, 'La place paradoxale de la culture juridique américaine dans la mondialisation', at 71. See also V Gessner, 'Global Legal Interaction and Legal Cultures' (2007) 7(2) *Ratio Juris* 132.

[68] S Zifcak (ed), *Globalisation and the Rule of Law* (London, Routledge, 2005).

[69] Gowan and Brantner argued that the EU has lost ground to Russia and China in defining human rights policies in the United Nations. In their view, this is due both to geo-political shifts and to intrinsic shortcomings in policy-making and implementation by the EU. See R Gowan and F Brantner, *A Global Force for Human Rights? An Audit of European Power at the UN* (London, European Council on Foreign Relations Policy Paper, 2008).

[70] G Teubner, 'The Anonymous Matrix: Human Rights Violations by "Private" Transnational Actors' (2006) 69(3) *MLR* 327.

[71] M Likosky, *The Silicon Empire. Law, Culture and Commerce* (Aldershot, Ashgate, 2005).

[72] See, among many works, HJ Steiner, P Alston and R Goodman, *International Human Rights in Context: Law, Politics, Morals*, 3rd edn (Oxford, Oxford University Press, 2007); P Alston (ed), *People's Rights (The Collected Courses of the Academy of European Law, vol.9/2)* (Oxford, Oxford University Press, 2001); P Alston (ed), *Labour Rights as Human Rights (Collected Courses of the Academy of European Law)* (Oxford, Oxford University Press, 2005).

[73] J Harrison, *Human Rights Impact of the World Trade Organisation* (Oxford, Hart Publishing, 2007); H Hestermeyer, *Human Rights and the WTO: The Case of Patents and Access to Medicines* (Oxford, Oxford University Press, 2007). See also the debate between Petersmann, Howse and Alston in (2002) 13(3) and (4) *European Journal of International Law*.

actors and international regimes shape the way in which people think; for example, the human rights movement has facilitated policy learning and helped to shape knowledge about trade policy.[74] Merry has been a pioneer in investigating the interaction between international human rights norms and local culture.[75] Szablowski also analyses the regulation of conflicts through transnational, national and local legal processes.[76] David Kennedy reassesses international humanitarianism and human rights activism.[77] The field of human rights has also given rise to methodologically innovative studies, such as Riles's analysis of Fijian preparations and participation in the United Nations Fourth World Conference on Women, held in Beijing in 1995.[78] Kneebone and colleagues analyse the development of the Refugees Convention.[79]

Standards, including labour standards and corporate social responsibility (CSR), have received much attention. Muchlinski among others argues that, due to the work of intergovernmental organisations, international minimum standards are emerging in the field of CSR.[80] This is especially important in the field of labour law.[81] For example, in 2005 the building materials group Lafarge and the steel group Arcelor, respectively, signed worldwide CSR agreements with international trade unions.[82] Bai Lin argues that, in China, it is necessary to take account of relations between standardised model norms and local societal concerns, between the voluntary nature of non-governmental norms and the necessity of official legal guidance and enforcement, and between the interests of the international production chain and those of other stakeholders.[83]

International migration is another field of great significance now and in the future. Rejecting sovereignty-based approaches, Juss argues that all people should be entitled to migrate and sign a type of social contract with their host country.[84] Marchetti

[74] ATF Lang, 'Re-thinking Trade and Human Rights' (2007) 15(2) *Tulane Journal of International and Comparative Law* 335.

[75] See SE Merry, *Human Rights and Gender Violence: Translating International Law into Local Justice* (Chicago, University of Chicago Press, 2006); M Goodale and S Merry, *Practice of Human Rights: Tracking Law between the Global and the Local* (Cambridge, Cambridge University Press, 2007). See also RA Wilson (ed), *Human Rights, Culture and Context: Anthropological Perspectives* (London, Pluto Press, 1997).

[76] D Szablowski, *Transnational Law and Local Struggles: Mining Communities and the World Bank* (Oxford, Hart Publishing, 2007).

[77] D Kennedy, *The Dark Sides of Virtue: Reassessing International Humanitariansim* (Princeton, Princeton University Press, 2005).

[78] A Riles, *The Network Inside Out* (Ann Arbor, University of Michigan Press, 2000).

[79] S Kneebone (ed), *The Refugees Convention 50 Years On: Globalisation and International Law* (London, Sweet & Maxwell, 2004).

[80] P Muchlinski, 'Human Rights, Social Responsibility and the Regulation of International Business: The Development of International Standards by Intergovernmental Organisations' (2003) 3(1) *Non-State Actors in International Law* 123.

[81] See Sir B Hepple, *Labour Laws and Global Trade* (Oxford, Hart Publishing, 2005); B Bercusson and C Estlund, *Regulating Labour in the Wake of Globalisation: New Challenges, New Institutions* (Oxford, Hart Publishing, 2008).

[82] See the Agreement on Corporate Social Responsibility and International Industrial Relations, signed on 12 September 2005 between Lafarge Group, on the one hand, and International Federation of Building and Wood Workers (IFBWW), International Federation of Chemical, Energy, Mine and General Workers' Unions (ICEM) and World Federation of Building and Woodworkers Unions (WFBW), on the other hand, available at http://www.bwint.org/default.asp?index=75, visited 15 April 2009; and the Worldwide Agreement on the Principles of Arcelor's Corporate Social Responsibility, signed on 13 September 2005 between Arcelor SA, on the one hand, and International Metalworkers Federation and European Metalworkers Federation, on the other hand, available at: http://www.arcelor. com/rls/data/pages/49//AccordPrincipesResponsabiliteEN.pdf, visited 15 April 2009.

[83] L Bai, 'Improving the Non-Governmental System of Outsourcing Labour Regulation in China' (2007) 13(6) *European Law Journal* 772.

[84] S Singh Juss, *International Migration and Global Justice* (Aldershot, Ashgate, 2006).

proposes a global migratory regime.[85] Such proposals draw on theories of human rights and ideas of multilayered citizenship and multiple political memberships. Human rights scholarship also contributes to this discussion. For example, Koenig deploys a neo-institutionalist analysis in arguing that the globalisation of human rights has resulted in a new model of multicultural citizenship, characterised by the decoupling of individual rights, State membership and national identity.[86] The wide range of social relationships and legal arrangements used by migrants and the impact of migration on the law are explored in von Benda-Beckman *et al.*[87]

A striking example of a burgeoning new field is international health law. International law has long been an important factor in global surveillance of communicable diseases; this includes 'soft law' regimes involving the World Health Organisation (WHO), the WTO, the Food and Agriculture Organisation (FAO) and the World Organisation for Animal Health (OIE).[88] The WHO's International Health Regulations require each member State to communicate to the WHO important national laws concerning health. As Fidler[89] and Aginam[90] in particular have demonstrated, international health law is now developing rapidly, to the point that many refer to the concepts of 'global health governance',[91] 'world health law'[92] or health as a 'Global Public Good'.[93] It has been spurred on by a variety of factors, including a series of health crises such as avian flu,[94] SARS, HIV/AIDS,[95] malaria and tuberculosis, international migration, and the prospects of the spread of formerly tropical

[85] R Marchetti, 'Toward a World Migratory Regime' (2008) 15(2) *Indiana Journal of Global Legal Studies* 471.

[86] M Koenig, 'Mondialisation des droits de l'homme et transformation de l'État-nation. Une analyse néo-institutionnaliste' (2006) 67 *Droit et Société* 673.

[87] F Von Benda-Beckmann, K Von Benda-Beckmann and A Griffiths (eds), *Mobile People, Mobile Law: Expanding Legal Relations in a Contracting World* (Aldershot, Ashgate, 2005).

[88] A Obijifor, 'International Law and Communicable Diseases' (2002) 80(12) *Bulletin of the World Health Organization* 946; M Sohn, J Sapsin, E Gibson, 'Globalization, Public Health and International Law' (2004) 32(4) *Journal of Law and Medical Ethics* 87. In 2003, the OIE, formerly known as the Organisation internationale des épizooties, changed its name to World Organisation for Animal Health but retained the acronym OIE.

[89] DP Fidler, 'Globalization, International Law and Emerging Infectious Diseases' (1996) 2(2) *Emerging Infectious Diseases* 77; DP Fidler, 'Neither Science Nor Shamans: Globalization of Markets and Health in the Developing World' *Indiana Journal of Global Legal Studies*, 7, 1999, 191; DP Fidler, 'The globalization of public health: Emerging infectious diseases and international relations' (1997) 5 *Indiana Journal of Global Legal Studies* 11; DP Fidler, *International Law and Infectious Diseases* (Oxford, Oxford University Press, 1999); DP Fidler, 'Global Health Governance: Overview of the Role of International Law in Protecting and Promoting Global Public Health', paper written for the WHO Project on 'Key Issues in Global Health Governance' no 3, 2002, summary available at http://www.who.int/trade/GHG/en/index.html; DP Fidler, 'Emerging Trends in International Law concerning Global Infectious Disease Control' (2003) 9(3) *Emerging Infectious Diseases* 285.

[90] O Aginam, *Global Health Governance: International Law and Public Health in a Divided World* (Toronto, University of Toronto Press, 2005).

[91] R Dodgson, K Lee and N Drager, 'Global Health Governance: A Conceptual Review', Discussion Paper No 1, Centre on Global Change & Health, London School of Hygiene and Tropical Medicine, and Department of Health & Development, World Health Organisation, February 2002, available at http://whqlibdoc.who.int/publications/2002/a85727_eng.pdf.

[92] LO Gostin, 'World Health Law: Toward a New Conception of Global Health Law Governance for the 21st Century' (2005) 5(1) *Yale Journal of Health Policy Law* 413.

[93] R Smith, D Woodward, A Acharya, R Beaglehole and N Drager, 'Communicable Disease Control: A "Global Public Good" Perspective' (2004) 19(5) *Health Policy and Planning* 271.

[94] On the link between avian flu and trade, see eg S Foucart, 'Les chemins détournés du H5N10', *Le Monde*, 27 February 2007, 3.

[95] T Barnett and A Whiteside, *AIDS in the Twenty-first Century: Disease and Globalization*, 2nd rev edn (London, St Martins Press, 2006).

diseases to rich countries due to climate change.[96] Analysing the spread of HIV, malaria and tuberculosis, Aginam[97] discerns a 'microbial superhighway' between poor and rich countries, and evaluates the prospects for effective global action. The Centre for Applied Legal Studies (CALS) at the University of the Witwatersrand in South Africa has a research project on AIDS law.[98] Better coordination of national health strategies is an imperative.[99] This might include an international health treaty with legally binding obligations concerning R&D for vaccines.[100] Taylor argues that the WHO should serve as a coordinator and perhaps as a platform for eventual codification of international health law, though full consolidation in a single organisation is undesirable.[101] Revision of the International Health Regulations suggests a shift from traditional international legal approaches toward international trade law and from vertical to horizontal mechanisms of global governance.[102]

Today the WHO is no longer the only international organisation in the field: the WTO, the World Bank and other organisations play an important role in international health cooperation.[103] Access to medicines for HIV/AIDS patients in developing countries was agreed through difficult negotiations in the WTO; this led to an amendment of the WTO TRIPS Agreement.[104] Unfortunately, however, the complex multilateral regulatory scheme thus created has been undercut by a series of bilateral trade agreements, in particular by the United States. Such agreements demonstrate the difficulties of using law as the sole basis for a global public health framework. Martin suggests that a preferable option is a non legally-binding code of public health ethics, based on shared universal values and guiding principles about personal, professional, institutional and public responsibility.[105]

[96] C McMurray and R Smith, *Diseases of Globalisation: Socioeconomic Transitions and Health* (London, Earthscan, 2001); D Bettcher and K Lee, 'Glossary on Globalisation and Public Health' (2002) 56(8) *Journal of Epidemiology and Community Health* 8.

[97] O Aginam, 'Salvaging Our Global Neighbourhood: Critical Reflections on the G8 Summit and Global Health Governance in an Interdependent World' (2004) 1 *Law, Social Justice and Global Development*,]. This issue of *LGD* is a special issue on 'Global Health Law': availale at http://www2.warwick.ac.uk/fac/soc/ law/elj/lgd/2004.

[98] CALS (Centre for Applied Legal Studies, University of the Witwatersrand), website http://www.law.wits.ac.za/cals/.

[99] A Ingram, 'Global Leadership and Global Health: Contending Meta-narratives, Divergent Responses, Fatal Consequences' (2005) 19(4) *International Relations* 381; JF Sepulveda, J Frenk, O Gomez-Dantes, MJ McGuinness and F Knaul, 'The New World Order and International Health' (1997) (May 10) 314 (7091) *British Medical Journal* 1404; D Yach and D Bettcher, 'The Globalization of Public Health, II: The Convergence of Self-interest and Altruism' (1998) 88(5) *American Journal of Public Health* 738.

[100] D Archibugi, 'The Global Governance of Communicable Diseases: The Case for Vaccine R&D' (2005) 27(1) *Law and Policy* 33.

[101] AL Taylor, 'Global Governance, International Health Law and WHO: Looking towards the Future' (2002) 80(12) *Bulletin of the World Health Organization* 975.

[102] DP Fidler, 'Emerging Trends in International Law concerning Global Infectious Disease Control', above n 89; Y Arai-Takahashi, 'The World Health Organisation and the Challenges of Globalisation: A Critical Analysis of the Proposed Revision to the International Health Regulations' (2004) 1 *Law, Social Justice and Global Development*, available at http://www2.warwick.ac.uk/ fac/soc/law/elj/lgd/2004_1/arai/ last accessed 12 March 2010.

[103] G Walt, 'Globalisation of International Health', 7 February 1998, *Lancet*, 434; see also S Maljean-Dubois, R Mehdi et Collectif (eds), *La société internationale et les grandes pandémies: 14ème Rencontres internationales d'Aix-en-Provence, 8 et 9 décembre 2006* (Paris, Pedone, 2007).

[104] See eg FM Abbott, 'The WTO Medicines Decision: World Pharmaceutical Trade and the Protection of Public Health' (2005) 99 *The American Journal of International Law* 317.

[105] R Martin, 'Public Health, Ethics and SARSs: Seeking an Ethical Framework to Global Public Health Policy', (2004) 1 *Law, Social Justice & Global Development Journal (LGD)*, http://www2.warwick.ac.uk/fac/ soc/law/elj/lgd2004_1_martin/>.

Another example is international environmental law, which has expanded dramatically in the past few decades. Globalisation may challenge the role of so-called 'pioneer countries' in setting international regulatory standards.[106] Kiss, Shelton and Ishibashi[107] analyse the relationship between economic globalisation and compliance with international environmental agreements. Smith *et al* focus on labour rights, environmental justice, environmental waste and extended producer responsibility in the networks of the global electronic industry.[108] Research by Falkner and colleagues and by the CERIC in Aix-en-Provence[109] concerns the law and politics of the development of international regimes about the depletion of the ozone layer, climate change and agricultural biotechnology, especially genetically modified organisms.[110] Shaffer shows how the WTO works in practice by providing a detailed empirical study of the WTO Committee on Trade and Environment.[111]

Other areas of great significance now and in the future include food security, access to land and water, gender equality, social justice for poor people especially in developing countries, regulation of biotechnology and new technology such as nanotechnology, cybercrime and access to outer space.[112] In considering these and related issues about globalisation and law, scholars have not given sufficient attention so far to the ideas and analyses of scholars from Africa, Asia and Latin America.[113] Nor has the

[106] M Janicke, 'Trend-setters in Environmental Policy: The Character and Role of Pioneer Countries' (2005) 15(2) *European Environment* 129.

[107] A Kiss, D Shelton and K Ishibashi (eds), *Economic Globalization and Compliance with International Environmental Agreements* (Dordrecht, Kluwer Law International, 2003).

[108] T Smith, DA Sonnenfeld and D Naguib (eds), *Challenging the Chip: Labor Rights and Environmental Justice in the Global Electronic Industry* (Philadelphia, Temple University Press, 2006).

[109] E Brosset and E Truilhé-Marengo (eds), *Les enjeux de la normalisation technique internationale: Entre environnement, santé et commerce international* (Paris, La documentation française, 2006); J Bourrinet and S Maljean-Dubois (eds), *Le commerce international des organismes génétiquement modifiés* (Paris, La documentation française, 2002).

[110] See eg C Bail, R Falkner and H Marquard (eds), *The Cartagena Protocol on Biosafety: Reconciling Trade in Biotechnology with Environment and Development?* (London, Earthscan, 2001); R Falkner (ed), *The International Politics of Genetically Modified Food* (London, Palgrave Macmillan, 2007); R Falkner, *Business Power and Conflict in International Environmental Politics* (London, Palgrave Macmillan, 2008).

[111] GC Shaffer, 'The World Trade Organization under Challenge: Democracy and the Law and Politics of the WTO's Treatment of Trade and Environment Matters' (2001) 25 *Harvard Environmental Law Review* 1.

[112] On food security, see eg A Mahiou and F Snyder (eds), *La sécurité alimentaire/Food Security and Food Safety* (Leiden, Martinus Nijhoff for The Hague Academy of International Law, 2006). On access to water, see eg R Pradhan, F von Benda-Beckmann and K von Benda-Beckmann (eds), *Water, Land and Law: Changing Rights to Land and Water in Nepal*, proceedings of a workshop held in Kathmandu, 18–20 March 1998 (Kathmandu, Wageningen, Rotterdam, Legal Research and Development Forum [FREEDEAL], Wageningen Agricultural University [WAU] and Erasmus University Rotterdam [EUR], 2000); P Canelas de Castro, *Recent Developments in Water Law: Principles and Comparative Cases* (Lisbon, Luso-American Foundation, 2005); International Water Law Project, http://www.internationalwaterlaw.org/, visited 18 April 2009. On new technology, see A Paliwala, 'Free Culture, Global Commons and Social Justice in Information Technology Diffusion', (2007) 1 *Law, Social Justice & Global Development Journal (LGD)*, http://www.go.warwick.ac.uk/elj/lgd/2007_1/paliwala.

[113] Eg, SY Peng, 'The WTO Legalistic Approach and East Asia: From the Legal Culture Perspective', *Asian-Pacfic Law & Policy Journal*, 1, 2000, 13; OC Okafor, *The African Human Rights System, Activisit Forces and International Institutions* (Cambridge, Cambridge University Press, 2007); U Baxi, *Human Rights in a Posthuman World* (New Delhi, Oxford University Press, 2007); Y Ghai (ed), *Autonomy and Ethnicity: Negotiating Competing Claims in Multi-ethnic States* (Cambridge, Cambridge University Press, 2000); Y Ghai and J Cottrell (eds), *Economic, Social and Cultural Rights in Practice: The Role of Judges in Implementing Economic, Social and Cultural Rights* (London, Interights, 2004). See also the Festschrift for Professor Upendra Baxi, (2007) 1 *Law, Social Justice & Global Development Journal*, http://go.warwick.ac.uk/elj/lgd/2007_1, http://www2.warwick.ac.uk/fac/soc/law/elj/lgd/2007_1/. For a pioneering exploration of the lives and work of four 'Southern' jurists, see W Twining, 'Human Rights: Southern Voices—Francis Deng, Abdullahi An-Na'im, Yash Ghai and Upendra Baxi,' (2007) 1 *Law, Social Justice & Global Development Journal (LGD)*, <http://www.go.warwick.ac.uk/elj/lgd/2007_1/twining,

burgeoning literature on feminist approaches to law, including international law,[114] been adequately taken into account in work on globalisation and law. To give but one complex example that raises numerous new issues, governments or private companies in several countries are reported to have bought substantial agricultural land in other countries for reasons of food security and/or financial investment. This foreign direct investment in or outright purchase of land raises complex issues concerning the definition of legal entitlements to land, access to land, food security and economic security for people in the countries where the land is located.[115] For instance, is agricultural land in developing countries a natural resource like any other? How can the food entitlements of people in developing countries be insured, in a situation when access through the market is not available or difficult?[116] How should access to such land be regulated in the case of forced migration, for example due to climate change?[117]

V. Governance of Globalisation

Many scholars and policy-makers have been concerned with the role of new institutions and norms, relations between them and problems of regulation and governance in a wide variety of substantive fields. Different empirical research, theoretical perspectives and normative assessments of the impact of globalisation and of new institutions and norms are reflected, directly or indirectly, in ideas about how globalisation is governed. Four main conceptions have emerged so far:

a) contract;
b) hierarchy;
c) networks; and
d) global legal pluralism.[118]

also substantially published as W Twining, 'Human Rights: Southern Voices—Francis Deng, Abdullahi An-Na'im, Yash Ghai and Upendra Baxi' (2006) 11 *Review of Constitutional Studies* 203.

[114] See eg H Charlesworth, C Chinkin and S Wright, 'Feminist Approaches to International Law' (1991) 85(4) *American Journal of International Law* 613; C Chinkin, S Wright and H Charlesworth, 'Feminist Approaches to International Law: Reflections from Another Century,' available at http://cigj.anu.edu.au/cigj/link_documents/Charlesworthpubs/Charlesworth%20Book%20Chapters/Feminist_Approaches_2005.pdf, visited 4 May 2009; T Lovell, 'Nancy Fraser's Integrated Theory of Justice: A "Sociologically Rich" Model for a Global Capitalist Era?' (2007) 1 *Law, Social Justice & Global Development Journal (LGD)*, <http://www.go.warwick.ac.uk/elj/lgd/2007_1/lovell>.

[115] See A Billette, 'Les terres agricoles, de plus en plus convoitées', *Le Monde*, 15 April 2009, at 4; A Billette, 'Après un offensive discrète au Kazakstan, la Chine lorne les terres russes inexploitées', *Le Monde*, 21 April 2009, at 4. The first article is based partly on a report by the non-governmental organisation GRAIN: 'Briefing: Seized: the 2008 landgrab for food and financial security', available at http://www.grain.org/briefings/?id=212, visited 16 April 2009; a list of countries of origin, purchasers, location of the land and purposes is given in the Annex to the briefing. The second article is based partly on an article in *China Daily*, 2003. See also JY Carfantan, *Le choc alimentaire mondial: ce qui nous attend demain* (Paris, Albin Michel, 2009).

[116] On food entitlements, including the legal frameworks, see A Sen, *Poverty and Famines: An Essay on Entitlement and Deprivation* (Oxford, Oxford University Press, 1981).

[117] Consider the example of the Maldive Islands, whose President announced in October 2008 the creation of a sovereign wealth fund to purchase land in neighbouring countries in order to provide land for eventual Maldivian 'climate change refugees': F Bobin, 'Face à la montée des eaux, les Maldives cherchent des terres d'accueil', *Le Monde*, 17 April 2009, at 4.

[118] G Gereffi, J Humphrey and T Sturgeon, 'The Governance of Global Value Chains' (2005) 12(1) *Review of International Political Economy* 78, provide an interesting parallel at the level of firms.

To some extent these different perspectives overlap, but they differ fundamentally in their starting points, conceptual frameworks and the importance they accord to different factors. Each provides only a partial view, and further work is needed to explore their points of convergence or divergence, as well as possible synergies.[119] The following discussion gives a brief outline of each perspective.

A. Contract

In this view, globalisation is governed essentially by agreements between nominally equal parties. The agreements include, but are not limited to, legally binding contracts. The parties may include States, companies, individuals or other actors. Their agreement may be consecrated in either bilateral or multilateral form. Policy dialogues between the European Union and China are a striking example; they also illustrate the point that numerous agreements may not necessarily be legally binding.[120] Another example is the 1997 OECD Convention on Combating Bribery.[121] The contractual perspective is usually associated with an emphasis on strong State sovereignty in external political and economic relations. It is also frequently underpins the law of international business transactions. In the first case the main actors are States, while in the second they are businesses, usually multinational firms or partners in international production networks.

Though useful from the standpoint of positive law, the contractual perspective is less helpful in analysing the governance of globalisation in practice. It does not take full account of the fact that usually the parties to such agreements are not equal in political or economic power, it may neglect the extent to which agreements are merely a mask for coercion, and it provides little leverage for understanding the dynamics of relations between public and private actors in contexts where these relations cannot in any sense be viewed as based on agreement.[122]

B. Hierarchy

A second perspective, which emerged partly from studies of European integration, focuses on multilevel governance, according to which different levels of governance interact, sometimes with regard to the same subject matter, sometimes with regard to different areas of social life.[123] Coordination is required to ensure the coherence of the

[119] See also L Tsuma, 'Hierarchies and Government versus Networks and Governance: Competing Regulatory Paradigms in Global Economic Regulation' (2000) 1 *Law, Social Justice & Global Development*, Internet.

[120] See Snyder, above n 53.

[121] AD Bontrager Unzicker, 'From corruption to cooperation: Globalization brings a multilateral agreement against foreign bribery' (2000) 7 *Indiana Journal of Global Legal Studies* 655.

[122] An exception is the idea of new social contracts proposed by JN Rosenau, *Distant Proximities: Dynamics Beyond Globalization* (Princeton, Princeton University Press, 2003) 300. These new social contracts do not, however, correspond entirely to contracts in the legal sense. They are discussed in section VI. below.

[123] G Marks, *Multi-level Governance and European Integration* (Boulder, Rowman & Littlefield, 2001).

system. Federal systems, such as the United States, Canada, Australia or Germany, illustrate this scenario. So too, on an international plane, do the North American Free Trade Association (NAFTA), the European Union and relations between the WTO and its members, which of course include unitary States, federal States, customs territories and regional organisations. The Massachustts 'Burma' law illustrates the complexities of multilevel governance.[124] Debates about a possible 'constitutionalisation' of the WTO usually invoke or rely on this essentially Kelsenian perspective. With regard to the governance of globalisation, however, this perspective suffers from the shortcoming that it does not take account of the fact that in the international system, institutions and norms are not necessarily arranged in any hierarchical manner, recognised and accepted by all. On the contrary, it is more likely to witness a variety of different claims to primacy, as the examples of relations between the European Union and its Member States or between the WTO and its members demonstrate.

C. Networks

A third perspective focuses on transnational networks, which may be public, private or a hybrid of the two. Transnational governmental networks have been described as 'offer[ing] the world a blueprint for the international architecture of the 21st century'.[125] Transgovernmental cooperation among judges or national regulators, for example, helps to strengthen the State through external cooperation and allows governments to benefit from the expertise of non-State actors. However, executive agreements and transgovernmental networks involve substantial problems of democracy and accountability.[126] They also embody a creative tension, or perhaps even a fundamental contradiction, between the power of the nation State and further international integration.[127]

Private networks may include production alliances, cartels, business associations and the use of coordination service firms, involving private regimes and informal industry norms and practices.[128] In contrast to intergovernmental and transgovernmental networks, they often rely upon multinational corporations.[129] But this is not always the case. For example, two recent empirical studies focus on the global food and flower sectors. Freidberg compares the conjunction of public and private networks in

[124] JF Hellwig, 'The Retreat of the State? The Massachusetts Burma Law and Local Empowerment in the Context of Globalization(s)' (2000) 18 *Wisconsin International Law Journal* 477.

[125] AM Slaughter, 'The Real New World Order' (1997) 75(5) *Foreign Affairs* 183 at 197; see also AM Slaughter, *A New World Order* (Princeton, Princeton University Press, 2004).

[126] See S Picciotto, 'North Atlantic Cooperation and Democratizing Globalism' in GA Bermann, M Herdegen and PL Lindseth (eds), *Transatlantic Regulatory Cooperation: Legal Problems and Political Prospects* (Oxford, Oxford University Press, 2000) 495; AM Slaughter, 'Agencies on the loose? Holding government networks accountable', *ibid*, 521; see also L Tshuma, 'Hierarchies and Government versus Networks and Governance, Competing Regulatory Paradigms in Global Economic Regulation' (2000) 1 *Law, Social Justice and Global Development (LGD)*. 1 available at http://elj.warwick.ac.uk/global/issue/2000-1/tshuma.html. [VO—http://sls.sagepub.com/cgi/content/ abstract/9/1/115] last accessed 13 March 2010.

[127] S Picciotto, 'Networks in International Economic Integration: Fragmented States and the Dilemmas of Neo-liberalism' (1996–97) 17 *Northwestern Journal of International Law & Business* 1014.

[128] See eg D Robinson and TE Stuart, 'Network Effects in the Governance of Strategic Alliances' (2007) 23(1) *Journal of Law, Economics and Organization* 242.

[129] AC Cutler, V Haufler and T Porter (eds), *Private Authority and International Affairs* (Albany, State University of New York Press, 1999); H Wai-chung Yeung, *Transnational Corporations and Business Networks: Hong Kong Firms in the ASEAN Region* (London, Routledge, 1998).

international food networks involving Britain and Zambia with those between France and Burkina Faso.[130] Ziegler analyses the worldwide production, distribution and informal regulation of free-cut flowers.[131] Private actors have been especially important in the regulation of the clothing industry, sustainable forestry and corporate social responsibility.[132] But private networks are not always based on business organisations. The Forestry Stewardship Council is an example of a partnership between NGOs and private businesses which sets its own standards.[133] The International Social and Environmental Accreditation and Labeling Alliance embraces seven international environmental networks, thus enlisting civil society in the formulation and enforcement of international private standards.[134] Such arrangements raise equally serious problems of transparency, participation and accountability.

While studies of private governance often draw substantially upon previous work on corporate governance,[135] they have gone further to focus on corporate control and accountability,[136] and also to analyse new hybrid forms of international regulation, such as international business taxation.[137]

Hybrid networks play an important role in the governance of transatlantic relations between the US and the European Union,[138] even though the primary architects of these relations appear to have high-level intergovernmental (public) networks.[139] They are also significant in other types of international business regulation. In their important study of the globalisation of regulation, as distinct from the globalisation of firms or the globalisation of markets, Braithwaite and Drahos[140] argue that 'regulatory globalization is a process in which different types of actors use various mechanisms to push for or against principles'. They analyse a wide variety of sectors, such as the environment, food, telecommunications, labour standards, and trade and competition.

[130] S Freidberg, *French Beans and Food Scares: Culture and Commerce in an Anxious Age* (Oxford, Oxford University Press, 2004).

[131] C Ziegler, *Favored Flowers: Culture and Economy in the Global System* (Durham, Duke University Press, 2007).

[132] RD Lipschutz and JK Rowe, *Globalization, Governmentality and Global Politics: Regulation for the Rest of Us?* (London, Routledge, 2005); see also G Gereffi, J Humphrey and T Sturgeon, 'The governance of global value chains' (2005) 12(1) *Review of International Political Economy* 78.

[133] See E Meidinger, 'The Administrative Law of Global Private–Public Regulation: The Case of Forestry' (2006) 17 *European Journal of International Law* 47; Forest Stewardship Council, FSC Principles and Criteria for Forest Stewardship, available at http://www.fsc.org/fileadmin/web-data/public/document_ center/international_FSC_policies/standards/FSC_STD_01_001_V4_0_EN_FSC_Principles_and_Criteria.pdf, visited 15 April 2009.

[134] E Meidinger, 'Emerging Trans-sectoral Regulatory Structures in Global Civil Society: The Case of ISEAL (the International Social and Environmental Accreditation and Labelling Alliance)', paper prepared for the 'Tools for Regulation' Panel, Joint Annual Meetings of the Law and Society Association and the Research Committee for the Sociology of Law, 4–7 July 2001, Budapest, Hungary; revised Draft 1.2 available at http://law.buffalo.edu/homepage/eemeid/scholarship/ISEAL.pdf, visited 29 July 2002.

[135] KJ Hopt, H Kanda, M Roe, E Wymeersch and S Prigge (eds), *Comparative Corporate Governance: The State of the Art and Emerging Research* (Oxford, Clarendon Press, 1998); R Gilson, 'Globalizing Corporate Governance: Convergence of Form or Function', *American Journal of Comparative Law*, 49, 2001, 329.

[136] J McCahery, S Picciotto and C Scott, *Corporate Control and Accountability: Changing Structures and the Dynamics of Regulation* (Oxford, Clarendon Press, 1993).

[137] S Picciotto, *International Business Taxation: A Study in the Internationalization of Business Regulation* (London, Weidenfeld & Nicolson, 1992); see also JC Sharman, *Havens in a Storm: The Struggle for Global Tax Regulation* (Ithaca, Cornell University Press, 2006).

[138] GA Bermann, M Herdegen and PL Lindseth (eds), *Transatlantic Regulatory Cooperation: Legal Problems and Political Prospects* (Oxford, Oxford University Press, 2000); MA Pollack and G Shaffer (eds), *Transatlantic Governance in the Global Economy* (Lanham, Md, Rowman & Littlefield, 2001).

[139] Pollack and Shaffer, above n 138, at 293.

[140] J Braithwaite and P Drahos, *Global Business Regulation* (Cambridge, Cambridge University Press, 2000) 9.

Some scholars have argued that global regulation consists mainly in competitive interaction among different national legal systems, in other words, regulatory competition among public authorities.[141] However, others suggest that, in many fields, the legal framework of regulation takes the form of networks of regulatory agencies, often working together with private actors, thus relying on decentralised enforcement, for example through national agencies, rather than international or transnational enforcement.[142] In either situation transparency, dispute settlement and capacity building may be more effective than coercion in inducing compliance.[143] Such processes deserve more attention in the future.

D. Global legal pluralism

A fourth perspective is global legal pluralism. Legal pluralism, pioneered by Eugen Ehrlich,[144] has been defined as 'the presence in a social field of more than one legal order'.[145] This conception invokes Sally Falk Moore's idea of a semi-autonomous social field, as well as a long tradition of field theory and Bourdieu's conceptions of *habitus* and social field.[146] A basic premise is that the multiplicity of legal orders cuts across the territoriality of law.[147] Contemporary work builds on classic legal, anthropological and sociological research on legal pluralism,[148] including its

[141] W Bratton, J McCahery, S Picciotto and C Scott (eds), *International Regulatory Competition and Coordination: Perspectives on Economic Regulation in Europe and the United States* (Oxford, Clarendon Press, 1996).

[142] K Jayasuriya, 'Globalization, Law and the Transformation of Sovereignty: The Emergence of Global Regulatory Governance' (1999) 6 *Indiana Journal of Global Legal Studies* 425.

[143] A Chayes and AH Chayes, *The New Sovereignty: Compliance with International Regulatory Agreements* (Cambridge, Mass, Harvard University Press, 1995).

[144] E Ehrlich, *Fundamental Principles of the Sociology of Law*, originally published 1936, trans WL Moll (New Brunswick, Transaction Publishers, reprint 2002). See also M Hartogh (ed), *Living Law: Reconsidering Eugen Ehrlich* (Oxford, Hart Publishing, 2008).

[145] J Griffiths, 'What is Legal Pluralism?' (1986) 24 *Journal of Legal Pluralism* 1 at 1.

[146] S Falk Moore, 'Law and Social Change: The Semi-autonomous Social Field as an Appropriate Subject of Study' (1973) 7(4) *Law and Society Review* 719, reprinted in S Falk Moore, *Law as Process: An Anthropological Approach* (London, Routledge & Kegan Paul, 1978). See also P Bourdieu, *Outline of a Theory of Practice*, trans R Nice (Cambridge, Cambridge University Press, 1977; orig pub *Esquisse d'une théorie de la pratique, precede de trios etudes d'ethnologie kabyle* (Geneva, Editions Droz, 1972). On field theory, see K Lewin, *Field Theory in Social Science: Selected Theoretical Papers* (ed D Cartwright) (New York, Harper and Row, 1951), which (at 240) defines a 'field' as 'the totality of coexisting facts that are conceived of as mutually interdependent'. The proximity between field theory and network analysis is demonstrated by the fact that Lewis is often considered to be a principal contributor to the development of network analysis: see Linton C Freeman, *The Development of Social Network Analysis: A Study in the Sociology of Science* (Vancouver, Empirical Press, 2004), at 66–68.

[147] See D Schmidtchen and HJ Schmidt-Trenz, 'Territoriality of Law and the International Trade Game: Towards a New Institutional Economics of International Transactions', *German Working Papers in Law and Economics*, vol 2006, art 25, available at http://www.bepress.com/gwp/default/ vol2006/iss1/art25.

[148] See SE Merry, 'Legal Pluralism' (1987) 14 *Law & Society Review* 869; Masaji Chiba, *Legal Pluralism: Toward a General Theory through Japanese Legal Culture* (Tokyo, Tokai University Press, 1989); F von Benda-Beckmann, 'Who's Afraid of Legal Pluralism?' (2002) 47 *Journal of Legal Pluralism and Unofficial Law* 37; K von Benda-Beckmann, 'Globalisation and Legal Pluralism' (February 2002) 4(1) *International Law Forum* 19; see also, O Perez, 'Normative Creativitiy and Global Legal Pluralism: Reflections on the Democratic Critique of Transnational Law' (2003) 10(2) *Indiana Journal of Global Legal Studies* 25; E Le Roy (ed), *Les pluralismes juridiques, Cahiers d'Anthropologie du Droit* (Paris, Karthala, 2003); G Teubner, 'Global Bukowina: Legal Pluralism in the World Society', in G Teubner (ed), *Global Law Without a State* (Aldershot, Dartmouth, 1997) 3; G Teubner, 'Breaking frames: The global interplay of legal

critics.[149] Recent scholarship on global legal pluralism is composed of two strands, drawing to some extent on the same theoretical sources but concerned with different themes. One strand focuses primarily on private law and international commercial arbitration, while the other strand is concerned mainly with the theory of sites of governance, embracing private, public and hybrid sources of norms.

The first strand concentrates on the *lex mercatoria*, the contemporary analogue of the medieval law merchant which private actors used to organise trade and settle business disputes. Drawing on a longstanding tradition in comparative law,[150] modern writers have focused on the development of a private international trade law, notably contract law, and the growth of international commercial arbitration.[151] The modern law merchant is a complex mix of public and private authority, which though designated as 'private' plays an important role in allocating risks, regulating market access, and linking local and global domains.[152]

Recent research derives from Maturana and Varela's concept of autopoesis,[153] and more proximately from Luhman's adaptation of this concept to a theory of social systems,[154] and Teubner's[155] concept of reflexive law as a self-governing system or form of regulated self-regulation. From this standpoint, *lex mercatoria* can be viewed as paradigm of the new global law, especially for private actors. It consists less of detailed rules than of broad principles, such as good faith. Its boundaries are markets, professional communities or social networks, not territories. Instead of being relatively autonomous from political institutions, it depends heavily on other social fields, thus being especially subject to economic pressures. It is not unified but decentered and non-hierarchical.[156] Stimulated by globalisation, it constantly breaks the hierarchical frame of the national constitution within which private rule-making takes place, resulting in a new heterarchical frame, a characteristic of this new global non-State

and social systems' (1997) XLV *American Journal of Comparative Law* 149; Lauren A Benton, *Law and Colonial Cultures: Legal Regimes in World History, 1400–1900* (Cambridge, Cambridge University Press, 2002). See also GR Woodman, 'Ideological Combat and Social Observation: Recent Debate about Legal Pluralism' (1998) 42 *Journal of Legal Pluralism* 21.

149 S Roberts, 'After Government? On Representing Law Without the State' (2005) 68(1) *MLR* 1; R Michaels, 'The Re-State-ment of Non-State Law: The State, Choice of Law and the Challenge from Global Legal Pluralism', Duke Law School Working Paper Series, Duke Law School Faculty Scholarship Series, Paper 21, 1 October 2005; BZ Tamanaha, 'The Folly of the "Social Scientific" Theory of Legal Pluralism' (Summer 1993) 20(2) *Journal of Law and Society* 192; BZ Tamanaha, 'A Non-essentialist Version of Legal Pluralism' (2000) 27 *Journal of Law and Society* 296; BZ Tamanaha, 'Understanding Legal Pluralism: Past to Present, Local to Global' (2007) 29 *Sydney Law Review* 375. A recent philosophical approach to legal pluralism, arguing that law should be understood in terms of people's normative experiences, is E Melissaris, *Ubiquitous Law: Legal Theory and the Space for Legal Pluralism* (Farnham, Ashgate, 2009). A recent critique of legal pluralism in the field of European Union law is J Baquero Cruz, 'The Legacy of the Maastricht-Urteil and the Pluralist Movement' (2008) 14(4) *European Law Journal* 389.

150 F De Ly, *International Business Law and Lex Mercatoria* (Dordrecht, North Holland, 1992).

151 F Nariman, 'East Meets West: Tradition, Globalization and the Future of Arbitration' (2004) 20(2) *Arbitration International* 123.

152 B Goldmann, 'La lex mercatoria dans les contrats et l'arbitrage international' (1994) *Journal du Droit International*, juillet-août-septembre, 195; AC Cutler, 'Globalization, the rule of law, and the modern law merchant: Medievel or late capitalist associations?' (2001) 8 *Constellations* 480.

153 H Maturana and F Varela, *Autopoesis and Cognition: The Realisation of the Living* (Dordrecht, D Reidel Publishing Co, 1980; 1st edn 1973).

154 See N Luhmann, *Essays on Self-Reference* (New York, Columbia University Press, 1990).

155 G Teubner, 'Substantive and reflexive elements in modern law' (1983) 17 *Law & Society Review* 239; G Teubner, *Law as an Autopoietic System* (Oxford, Blackwell Publishers, 1993; orig pub as *Recht als autopoietisches System* (Frankfurt, 1989)).

156 See G Teubner, 'Global Bukowina: Legal Pluralism in the World Society', in Teubner (ed), above n 148, at 3; Teubner (ed), above n 148.

law.[157] Its main institutional locus is international commercial arbitration,[158] though Ladeur has deployed the concept of autopoesis in the analysis of other legal relationships and networks.[159] Resulting from international coalitions of private agents, it influences the size of markets just as the evolution of markets shapes legal doctrine and recourse to arbitration itself.[160] Garth and Dezalay's important study[161] shows empirically how international commercial arbitration has been socially constructed and how it contributes to the reorganisation of hierarchies, modes of authority and structures of power.

However, international commercial arbitration is not entirely independent of the nation State,[162] either in legal terms or in terms of the questions it raises about the role of law in society. Many of the same political and normative questions which have been posed within the framework of domestic constitutions gain in importance when raised at the international level. An example is the formation of a constitution, not necessarily in the sense of a written document but rather in the sense of continuing processes of constitutionalisation or, in Zumbansen's terms, of 'precipitates of constitutional law'.[163] Another is provided by empirical studies showing that local institutions, interest-specific institutions or even personal relationships may be more effective than universalistic norms in providing legal certainty for cross-border or international transactions.[164]

A second strand in contemporary scholarship is the theory of sites of governance as part of global legal pluralism. It combines public, private and hybrid forms of governance with an emphasis on strategic action: the theory of sites of governance as part of global legal pluralism. This theory is developed throughout this book, so it is introduced here in somewhat more detail. In addition to sources already mentioned, the theory of sites of governance is inspired partly by the work of Michel Foucault on power,

[157] G Teubner, 'Breaking frames: The global interplay of legal and social systems', above n 148.

[158] P Kahn, 'Les principes généraux de droit devant les arbitres du commerce international' (1989) *Journal du droit international* 305, CREDMI [Centre de Recherche sur le Droit des Marchés et des Investissements Internationaux], Université de Grenoble, France, *Soveraineté étatique et marches internationaux à la fin du XXè siècle' Mélanges en honneur de Philippe Kahn* (Paris, Litec, 2000); K Lynch, *The Forces of Economic Globalization: Challenges to the Regime of International Commercial Arbitration* (Dordrecht, Kluwer Law International, 2003); J Jemielniak, 'Legitimization Arguments in the Lex Mercatoria Cases' (2005) 18(2) *International Journal for the Semiotics of Law* 175.

[159] K-H Ladeur, 'The Theory of Autopoesis as an Approach to a Better Understanding of Postmodern Law—From the Hierarchy of Norms to the Heterarchy of Changing Patterns of Legal Relationships', *EUI Working Paper LAW* no 2003/4 (Florence, European University Institute, 2003). See also K-H Ladeur, 'Towards a Legal Theory of Supranationality: The Viability of the Network Concept' (1997) 3(1) *European Law Journal* 33.

[160] A Casella, 'On market integration and the development of institutions: The case of international commercial arbitration' (1996) 40 *European Economic Review* 155.

[161] B Garth and Y Dezalay, *Dealing in Virtue: International Commercial Arbitration and the Construction of a Transnational Legal Order* (Chicago, University of Chicago Press, 1996).

[162] See eg A Redfern and M Hunter, *Law and Practice of International Commercial Arbitration*, 3rd edn (London, Sweet & Maxwell, 1999), 62–64; Weixai Gu and Xianchu Zhang, 'The China Style "Commission-Oriented" Competence on Arbitral Jurisdiction: Analysis of Chinese Adaptation into Globalisation' (2006) 9(6) *International Arbitration Law Review* 185; Jingzhou Tao, *Arbitration Law and Practice in China* (New York, Wolters Kluwer, 2008).

[163] P Zumbansen, 'Piercing the Legal Veil: Commercial Arbitration and Transnational Law' (2002) 8 *European Law Journal* 400.

[164] V Gessner and AC Budak, *Emerging Legal Certainty: Empirical Studies on the Globalization of Law* (Ashgate, Dartmouth, for the Oñati International Institute for the Sociology of Law, 1998); see also V Gessner (ed), *Contractual Certainty in International Trade: Empirical Studies and Theoretical Debates on Institutional Support for Global Economic Exchanges* (Oxford, Hart Publishing, 2009).

biopower and governmentality.[165] It also draws on the subsequent research by Hardt and Negri, who build partly on the work of Foucault in analsying the constitution of a new supranational juridical order, which they call 'empire'.[166] Further, the development of the idea of sites of governance has been stimulated by the process of European integration, involving complex relations between the European Union, the European Communities and the Member States[167]; the development of private forms of transnational regulation[168] and regulatory cooperation[169]; and increasingly complex relations between public and private regulation[170]. It also draws to some extent on recent research in political science. Of particular significance is Rosenau's work on 'spheres of authority', which provides a way of imagining 'the transformative dynamics presently at work in the world as the first traces of new terminal entities that may emerge in the future'.[171]

I have argued elsewhere that globalisation is governed by the totality of strategically determined, situationally specific and often episodic conjunctions of a multiplicity of sites throughout the world. [172] Sites may be public, private or mixed. Some are market-based, while others are polity-based. Each site has a structural dimension and a relational dimension. The structural dimension includes institutions, norms and dispute resolution processes. The relational dimension refers to the relations which a site has with other sites. For instance, sites may be hierarchically organised, autonomous or even independent, mutually constitutive,[173] competing or overlapping, part of the same or different regimes, or converging or diverging in terms of institutions, norms or processes of dispute resolution. Networks are one but not the only possible type of relations between sites. The totality of sites represents a new form of global legal pluralism. These ideas are elaborated in detail through this book.

[165] Esp M Foucault, *The History of Sexuality, Volume I: The Will to Knowledge* (trans R Hurley) (London, Penguin, 1990) (originally published in French as *La Volonté de Savoir* (Paris, Editions Gallimard, 1976), first translated as *The History of Sexuality: Volume I. An Introduction* (New York, Vintage, 1978)), 92–102, 135–45; M Foucault, 'Society Must Be Defended', in P Rabinow and N Rose (eds), *The Essential Foucault: Selections from Essential Works of Foucault 1954–1984* (London, The New Press, 2003), 294–99; M Foucault, *Power* (ed JD Faubion, trans R Hurley *et al*), *Essential Works of Foucault, 1954–1984, Volume 3* (London, Allen Lane, The Penguin Press, 1994); M Foucault, *Power/Knowledge: Selected Interviews and Other Writings, 1972–1977* (ed C Gordon, trans C Gordon *et al*) (New York, Pantheon Books, 1980). See also A Hunt and G Wickham, *Foucault and Law: Towards a Sociology of Law as Governance* (London, Pluto Press, 1994).

[166] M Hardt and A Negri, *Empire* (Cambridge, Mass, Harvard University Press, 2000).

[167] See also, N Walker, 'The Idea of Constitutional Pluralism' (May 2002) 65(3) *MLR* 357; M Poiares Maduro, 'Contrapunctual Law: Europe's Constitutional Pluralism in Action' in N Walker (ed), *Sovereignty in Transition* (Oxford, Hart Publishing, 2003) 501; R Higgott, 'The Theory and Practice of Global and Regional Governance: Accommodating American Exceptionalism and European Pluralism' (2005) 10(4) *European Foreign Affairs Review* 575; see also P Zumbansen, '"New Governance" in European Corporate Law Regulation as Transnational Legal Pluralism' (2009) 15(2) *European Law Journal* 246.

[168] AC Cutler, *Private Power and Global Authority: Transnational Merchant Law in the Global Political Economy* (Cambridge, Cambridge University Press, 2003).

[169] Bermann *et al*, above n 138.

[170] Braithwaite and Drahos, above n 140; KH Ladeur (ed), *Public Governance in the Age of Globalization* (Aldershot, Ashgate, 2004).

[171] JN Rosenau, *Distant Proximities: Dynamics Beyond Globalization* (Princeton, Princeton University Press, 2003) 295. See also JN Rosenau, 'Toward an Ontology for Global Governance' in M Hewson and TJ Sinclair (eds), *Approaches to Global Governance Theory* (Albany, State University of NewYork Press, 1999) 287.

[172] F Snyder, 'Governing economic globalisation: Global legal pluralism and European law' (1999) 5 *European Law Journal* 334; slightly shorter version published in M Likosky (ed), *Transnational Legal Processes: Globalisation and Power Disparities* (London, Butterworths LexisNexis, 2002) 65–97; F Snyder, 'Les sites de gouvernance' in R Mehdi and L Boisson de Chazournes (eds), *Une société internationale en mutation: quels acteurs pour une nouvelle gouvernance* (Brussels, Bruylant, 2005) 299.

[173] See, eg Merry, above n 148; P Fitzpatrick, 'Law and Societies', (1984) 22 *Oxgoode Hall Law Journal* 115

Recent research builds to some extent on this foundation. For example, van der Grijp studies the regulation of pesticides by focusing mainly on specific sites, including multilateral approaches, the EU and non-State actors.[174] However, this thesis also considers the dynamics of legal pluralism. Considerable research has been done on relations between sites, or what Santos calls 'interlegality'.[175] Perhaps the most well-known illustration of the convergence of norms among several sites is the internationalisation of human rights.[176] Another example is the social construction of the concept of 'non-market economy' in the anti-dumping law of the United States, the European Union and the WTO.[177] It formed part of a specific legal discourse that emerged from the gradual elaboration of a handful of basic principles and concepts into an international anti-dumping law repertoire during the Cold War. The relations between sites involved asymmetrical power relations, with the most importance influence being the United States. Walker has used the concept of sites in innovative work on constitutional pluralism in the European Union.[178] Maduro develops the conception of contrapunctual law to analyse EU constitutional law.[179] Krisch focuses on national, international and cosmopolitan constituencies in examining the pluralist structure of accountability in global administrative law.[180] Relations between the European Community courts and international tribunals are explored by Bronckers.[181] A particular form of legal pluralism is the relationship between State and non-State norms, a topic which has long been of interest to lawyers, sociologists of law and legal anthropologists. Perez explores both the WTO and private regimes in rethinking the relationship between trade liberalisation and environmental protection.[182] Analysing the relationship from the standpoint of conflict of law, Michaels shows that it would involve a reconceptualisation of the State.[183] Though employing different concepts, Delmas-Marty discusses how comparative law can contribute to a pluralist conception of international criminal law.[184] Wahab presents a study of online dispute resolution, illuminating a virtual site of governance.[185]

[174] N van Der Grijp, *Regulating Pesticide Risk Reduction: The Practice and Dynamics of Legal Pluralism*, PhD thesis, University of Amsterdam, 2008 (Amsterdam, VU Drukkerij, 2008).

[175] B de Sousa Santos, 'Law: A Map of Misreading. Toward a Post-Modern Conception of Law' (1987) 14(3) *Journal of Law and Society* 279.

[176] T Risse, S Ropp and K Sikkink (eds), *The Power of Human Rights: International Norms and Domestic Change* (Cambridge, Cambridge University Press, 1999); C Scott (ed), *Torture as Tort: Comparative Perspectives on the Development of Transnational Human Rights Litigation* (Oxford, Hart Publishing, 2001); A Riles, 'The virtual sociality of rights: the case of "women's rights are human rights"' in *Transnational Legal Processes: Globalisation and Power Disparties* (London, Butterworths LexisNexis, 2002) 420.

[177] F Snyder, 'The Origins of the "Nonmarket Economy": Ideas, Pluralism and Power in EC Antidumping Law about China' (2001) 7 *European Law Journal* 369. A revised version appears in this book.

[178] N Walker, 'The Idea of Constitutional Pluralism' (2002) 65(3) *MLR* 317.

[179] M Poiares Maduro, 'Contrapunctual Law: Europe's Constitutional Pluralism in Action' in N Walker (ed), *Sovereignty in Transition* (Oxford, Hart Publishing, 2003) 501.

[180] N Krisch, 'The Pluralism of Global Administrative Law' (2006) 17(1) *European Journal of International Law* 247.

[181] M Bronckers, 'The Relationship of the EC Courts with Other International Tribunals: Non-commital, Respectful or Submissive?' (2007) 44 *CML Rev* 610.

[182] O Perez, *Ecological Sensitivity and Global Legal Pluralism: Rethinking the Trade and Environment Conflict* (Oxford, Hart Publishing, 2004).

[183] Michaels, above n 149.

[184] M Delmas-Marty, 'The Contribution of Comparative Law to a Pluralist Conception of International Criminal Law' (2003) 1(1) *Journal of International Crime and Justice* 13.

[185] M Wahab, 'Globalisaton and ODR: Dynamics of Change in E-Commerce Dispute Settlement' (2004) 12(1) *International Journal of Law & Information Technology* 123.

Strategic actors, such as companies, governments, NGOs and others, use the law and are shaped by it.[186] In addition, they are fundamental in determining which sites are created, which survive, and how. They influence the development of sites, so that some take on more or less judicial and legal characteristics, and some do not. For example, the dramatic growth of global economic networks has had contradictory effects on recent attempts to develop constitutional systems based on regional integration. In the European Union, globalisation sustains and creates interests and relationships which tend to undercut traditional constitutionalism as a mode of regional governance[187]. Szablowski refers to the World Bank as a 'site of global norm production' and analyses the role of transnational advocacy networks and other actors in transnational law-making.[188] Not surprising, globalisation has provoked not only demands for the constitutionalisation of global governance but also debates about its feasibility and desirability. Nested and overlapping national, regional and international regimes help to create disputes, offer forum-shopping opportunities for strategic actors and may obstruct the resolution of conflicts.[189]

VI. Global Governance

In 2004 the report of the World Commission on the Social Dimension of Globalisation called for a reform of global governance.[190] But how, if at all, should global governance be organised? At least until the 2008 financial crisis, and perhaps beyond, the principal orientation of economic globalisation had been toward economic liberalisation, the opening of markets, increased privatisation and the development of regulation or re-regulation.[191] One predictable result has been the delegation of considerable decision-making power to the market, or, as Weber remarked, an increase in the 'factual autonomy' and legal empowerment of the propertied classes, leading for many people to an increase in authoritarian coercion.[192] A second, equally predictable result has been the use of the private sector to carry out what previously were public functions,[193] and consequently the blurring of the public–private distinction. It has become more difficult to discern a public interest, to identify any specific institutions which should represent it, and to decide where and how decisions about the production and allocation

[186] LK Mytelka and M Delapierre, 'Strategic partnerships, knowledge-based network oligopolies, and the state' in AC Cutler, V Haufler and T Porter (eds), *Private Authority and International Affairs* (Buffalo, State University of New York Press, 1999) 129.

[187] See F Snyder, 'Europeanisation and globalisation as friends and rivals: European Union law in global economic networks' in *The Europeanisation of Law: The Legal Effects of European Intergration* (Oxford, Hart Publishing, 2000) at 294.

[188] D Szablowski, *Transnational Law and Local Struggles: Mining, Communities and the World Bank* (Oxford, Hart Publishing, 2007) at 87.

[189] See eg KJ Alter and S Meunier, 'Nested and Overlapping Regimes in the Transatlantic Banana Trade Dispute' (2006) 13(3) *Journal of European Public Policy* 362.

[190] The World Commission on the Social Dimension of Globalisation, *A Fair Globalisation: Creating Opportunities for All* (Geneva, ILO, 2004), available at http://www.ilo.org/public/english/wcsdg/docs/report.pdf, visited 10 April 2009.

[191] On re-regulation, see Giandomenico Majone (ed), *Deregulation or Re-regulation? Regulatory Reform in Europe and the United States* (London, Pinter Press, and New York, St Martin's Press, 1990).

[192] Max Weber, *Max Weber on Law in Economy and Society* (ed Max Rheinstein, trans Edward Shils and Max Rheinstein) (Cambridge, Mass, Harvard University Press, 1966), 145–46, 188–91.

[193] KH Ladeur (ed), *Public Governance in the Age of Globalization* (Aldershot, Ashgate, 2004)

of public goods and about the achievement of social justice can best be made. Thirdly, these processes in synergy with globalisation have transformed the level or site of governance for making decisions in many significant areas of life. Regulation by States has frequently been complemented or even replaced by regulation or re-regulation by regional, transnational or international sites of governance.

Globalisation has made substantial demands on traditional international institutions and also been embodied in new legal forms, regimes and institutions, which to the average person seem (and frequently are) remote, fundamentally different from general rules of law made by public authorities, and lacking in legitimacy, transparency and accountability. The WTO was established with a wide mandate, was based on the 'single undertaking principle' and was characterised by binding dispute resolution. It has extended international trade law forcefully into areas which previously were solely under national jurisdiction, thus blurring the traditional distinction between the 'international' and the 'domestic',[194] and in fact redefining the meaning of 'trade' and 'international trade regulation'. Partly as a consequence, and partly as a result of other aspects of globalisation, areas such as the environment,[195] public health,[196] food safety and social welfare systems no longer fall within the province of a single nation State alone and can no longer be dealt with adequately on this basis. Together with the rise of new international or transnational institutions and norms, the partial reconfiguration of the State means that norms 'created somewhere else' affect daily life in ways which were previously inconceivable.[197]

It is not surprising that globalisation and its legal implications have provoked a vigorous, often acrimonious and sometimes violent debate about the organisation, legitimacy and democratisation of global governance.[198] Globalisation produces winners and losers, in rich countries[199] as well as in poor countries.[200] In search of social justice, those disadvantaged by globalisation have rejected loyalty. Since they are denied exit, they have tried to voice their views in a variety of ways, often conditioned but not necessarily constrained by their national political systems. Globalisation itself has provided some of the means for the expression of voice and for the creation of new transnational social movements, for example through the Internet. These movements themselves foster increased globalisation, but with a different political orientation and dynamic.[201]

194 MJ Trebilcock and R Howse, *The Regulation of International Trade*, 2nd edn (New York, Routledge, 1999).

195 G Shaffer, 'The World Trade Organization under challenge: Democracy and the law and politics of the WTO's treatment of trade and environmental matters' (2001) 25 *Harvard Environmental Law Review* 1; JB Wiener, 'Something borrowed or something blue: Legal transplants and the evolution of global environmental law' (2001) 27 *Ecology Law Quarterly* 1295.

196 DP Fidler, *International Law and Infectious Diseases* (Oxford, Oxford University Press, 1999); TS Jost, 'The globalization of health law: The case of permissibility of placebo-based research' (2000) 26 *American Journal of Law and Medicine* 175.

197 JH Jackson, *Sovereignty, the WTO and Changing Fundamentals of International Law* (Cambridge, Cambridge University Press, 2006).

198 M Klein, *No Logo* (London, Flamingo, 2000); H Siebert, *Global Governance: An Architecture for the World Economy* (New York, Springer, 2003).

199 C Thomas, 'Globalization and the Reproduction of Hierarchy' (2000) 33 *University of California at Davis Law Review* 1451.

200 E Darian-Smith, 'Structural Inequalities in the Global Legal System' (Review Essay), (2000) 34 *Law & Society Review* 809.

201 ME Keck and K Sikkink, *Activists Beyond Borders: Advocacy Networks in International Politics* (Ithaca, Cornell University Press, 1998); R O'Brien, AM Goetz, JA Scholte and M Williams, *Contesting Global Governance: Multilateral Economic Institutions and Global Social Movements* (Cambridge, Cambridge University Press, 2000).

These conflicts have stimulated debates about the legitimacy, democracy and accountability of sites of governance. The intensity of the discourse about democracy seems to be correlated with the degree of institutional, normative and social integration of international institutions: in the context of economic globalisation, the key triggering element was the strengthening of the WTO, notably its judicial function.[202] The Washington Consensus of the 1980s and 1990s, based on liberalisation, deregulation and privatisation, has collapsed, at least to the extent that the current Post-Washington Consensus 'has added civil society, social capital, capacity building, governance, transparency, a new international economic architecture, institution building and safety nets'.[203] As Higgott notes, however, the Post-Washington Consensus remains sadly deficient.[204] First, it does not have a sufficient theory of politics. Secondly, it is not underpinned by any ethical theory of justice.[205] Management, not legitimate governance (and legitimacy), remains the predominant vision of global governance.[206]

This perspective is totally inadequate to address the questions in the current debates provoked by globalisation and now the 2008 financial crisis. More broadly, especially among people who never accepted the Washington Consensus in the first place, it has given rise to concerns about the emergence and role of global civil society.[207] The collapse of the WTO ministerial conference in Seattle in 1999 was followed by a series of parallel summits. The most well known was the first World Social Forum (WSF), which began in January 2001 in Porto Alegre, Brazil, and has met annually since then, in 2008 in the form of numerous localised meetings known as the 'Global Call for Action'. So far the development of global civil society has been halting but steady, though this varies enormously from country to country.

A central concern in any international institutional scheme must be social justice, in the sense of distributive justice.[208] How can this be ensured? It needs to be ensured in conjunction with other objectives which have been the focus of recent research, such as environmental protection, respect for human rights, public health and food security, and taking into account the institutional and normative characteristics of global legal pluralism. As early as 1993, the Group of Lisbon published a report on *Limits to Competition*. It concluded that 'competition cannot govern the planet' and called for more effective global governance.[209]

Given the variety and range of sites of governance which are relevant to each of these objectives, and a disagreement on the objectives themselves and the means to achieve

[202] E Stein, 'International integration and democracy: No love at first sight' (2001) 95 *American Journal of International Law* 489; BS Chimni, 'International Institutions Today: An Imperial Global State in the Making' (2004) 15(1) *European Journal of International Law* 1.

[203] R Higgott, 'Contested globalization: The changing context and normative challenges' (2000) 26 *Review of International Studies* 131 at 139–40.

[204] *Ibid*, at 152.

[205] See RL Harris and MJ Seid, *Critical Perspectives on Globalization and Neoliberalism in the Developing Countries* (Leiden, Brill, 2000).

[206] OC Okafor, 'The Global Process of Legitimation and the Legitimacy of Global Governance' (1997) 14 *Arizona Journal of International and Comparative Law* 117; O Yasuaki, 'A Transcivilizational Perspective on Global Legal Order in the Twenty-first Century: A Way to Overcome West-centric and Judiciary-centric Deficits in International Legal Thoughts' (2006) 8(1) *International Community Law Review* 29.

[207] H Anheier, M Glasius and M Kaldor (eds), *Global Civil Society 2001* (Oxford, Oxford University Press, 2001).

[208] On the issue of social justice, see the contrasting views of T Nagel, 'The Problem of Global Justice' (2005) 33 *Philosophy and Public Affairs* 113; and J Cohen and C Sabel, 'Extra Rempublicam Nulla Justitia?' (2006) 34 *Philosophy and Public Affairs* 147.

[209] The Group of Lisbon *Limits to Competition* (Lisbon, Gulbenkian Foundation, 1993).

them, such issues are often phrased in institutional terms as demands for legitimacy, democracy and accountability. What do legitimacy, democracy and accountability mean in the context of the legal forms, regimes and institutions of today? From an international perspective, the development of a concept of individual and international responsibility, the participation of civil society, the social responsibility of enterprises, fair trade and protection of the environment are among the most significant priorities in the reformulation and restructuring of the global legal landscape.[210] It is important to establish basic principles to ensure effective participation in the new global public sphere: they include transparency, accountability, responsibility, and participation and empowerment.[211] To some extent, such principles already form part of national administrative law. Not surprisingly, scholars have called for their embodiment in a global administrative law,[212] including transnational mutual recognition regimes.[213] The Basel Committee on Banking Supervision has previously been proposed as a model for achieving accountability and legitimacy in international regulation.[214] Current research may potentially contribute to the achievement of these objectives. For example, further research is needed on the accountability of polycentric regulatory regimes.[215] Research should also address the issues as to whether and to what extent such administrative law principles represent merely the globalisation of laws and practices specific to certain countries, such as the United States, and whether and, if so, how they can be relevant in very different social, political, economic and legal contexts, for example the contemporary world characterised by the increasing importance of China and the other BRICSAM (Brazil, Russia, India, China, South Africa, Mexico) countries.

Who should participate in decision-making, and how? How should decision-making be structured? One view is articulated by Aman,[216] who argues that, confronted with a globalising State, courts and lawmakers need to recognise the continuing delegation of power to the private sector, and develop new forms of accountability to preserve a public voice. However, the aftermath of the financial crisis may provide a new perspective on such proposals. A crucial issue remains the disparities of political power which inform and shape legal relationships.[217] Arguing that global social exchanges should be named 'postmodern colonialism', Silbey[218] urges further efforts to identify connections between

[210] See C Eberhard (ed), *Traduire nos responsabilités planétaires: Recomposer nos paysages juridiques* (Brussels, Bruylant, 2008).

[211] S Picciotto, 'Democratizing Globalism' in D Drache (ed), *The Market or the Public Domain: Global Governance and the Asymmetry of Power* (London, Routledge, 2001) 335.

[212] B Kingsbury, N Krisch and RB Stewart, 'The Emergence of Global Administrative Law', *New York University School of Law, New York University Public Law and Legal Theory Working Papers*, Paper 17, 1 October 2005, available at http://lsr.nellco.org/nyu/èplltwp/papers/17; N Krisch and B Kingsbury, 'Introduction: Global Governance and Global Administrative Law in the International Legal Order' (2006) 17(1) *European Journal of International Law* 1.

[213] See K Nicolaidis and G Shaffer, 'Transnational Mutual Recognition Regimes: Governance without Global Government' (2005) 68 *Law and Contemporary Problems* 267.

[214] MS Barr and GP Miller, 'Global Administrative Law: The View from Basel' (2006) 17(1) *European Journal of International Law* 15.

[215] A useful starting point is Julia Black, 'Constructing and Contesting Legitimacy and Accountability in Polycentric Regulatory Regimes', IILJ Working Paper 2007/12, Global Administrative Law Series, Institute for International Law and Justice, New York University School of Law, available at http://www.iilj.org.

[216] AC Jr Aman, 'The globalizing state: A future-oriented perspective on the public/private distinction, federalism, and democracy' (1998) 31 *Vanderbilt Journal of Transnational Law* 769.

[217] M Likosky (ed), *Transnational Legal Processes: Globalisation and Power Disparities* (London, Butterworths LexisNexis, 2002).

[218] SS Silbey, '"Let them eat cake": Globalization, Postmodern colonialism, and the possibilities of justice' (1997) 31 *Law and Society Review* 207.

law and power, and thus make justice more probable. The current system is unbalanced in favour of countries, organisations and individuals who can afford technical and in particular legal expertise, even though, as Dezalay and Garth[219] show, imported expertise is profoundly shaped by local power struggles. Law may still play a role in achieving social justice, in particular but not only for low-income countries.[220] For example, in a detailed study of *Doe v Unocal*, Holzmeyer argues that transnational legal mobilisation, inclusion of grassroots activists, and the use of human rights discourse as a common vocabulary and strategic resource can be effective in using litigation to ensure corporate accountability.[221] In creating and sustaining international organisations, networks and sites working in favour of social justice, there is much to be learned from examples of how existing international institutions were created, for example by studies of the GATT[222] or of the role of American and British experts, mainly economists and policy specialists, in the creation of the post-World War II international order.[223]

In this respect, 'public' international law needs serious rethinking.[224] In addition, an important role will be played by NGOs. Often described as the emergence of global civil society, NGOs play such an important role in fields such as development aid, sports, human rights and the environment that they have become a competitor of the State in legal as well as factual terms, and such non-State interests should be recognised in international law.[225] Some scholars argue that NGOs should be granted an international legal status, while at the same time there should be a global legal framework to structure their participation and make them accountable.[226] Others argue that NGOs should also be given an increased role in the legislative, executive and judicial branches of the WTO.[227] In this context, it is useful to recall that the term 'non-governmental organisation' covers a wide variety of organisations, including many in which States and the private sector participate, as well as numerous NGOs which at least indirectly are profit-seeking.[228] Reforms of global governance must go further than simply rebalancing access to expertise and structuring NGO participation in decision-making.[229]

[219] Y Dezalay and BG Garth, *The Internationalization of Palace Wars: Lawyers, Economists, and the Contest to Tranform Latin America* (Chicago, University of Chicago Press, 2002).

[220] B de Sousa Santos and CA Rodríguez-Garavita (eds), *Law and Globalization from Below: Towards a Cosmopolitan Legality* (Cambridge, Cambridge University Press, 2005); SM Murshed, *Globalization, Marginalization and Development* (London, Routledge, 2002); see also J Comaroff and JL Comaroff (eds), *Law and Disorder in the Postcolony* (Chicago, University of Chicago Press, 2006).

[221] Cheryl Holzmeyer, 'Human Rights in an Era of Neoliberal Globalization: The Alien Tort Claims Act and Grassroots Mobilization in *Doe v Unocal*' (2009) 43(2) *Law and Society Review* 271.

[222] See DA Irwin, PC Mavroidis and AO Sykes, *The Genesis of the GATT* (Cambridge, Cambridge University Press, 2008).

[223] J Ickenbery, 'A World Economy Restored: Expert Consensus and the Anglo-American Postwar Settlement' (1992) 46(1) *International Organization* 289.

[224] A Von Bogdandy, 'Globalization and Europe: How to Square Democracy, Globalization and International Law' (2004) 15(5) *European Journal of International Law* 885.

[225] S Hobe, 'Global challenges to statehood: The increasing important role of nongovernmental organizations' (1997) 5 *Indiana Journal of Global Legal Studies* 191.

[226] K Nowrot, 'Legal consequences of globalization: The status of non-governmental organizations under international law' (1999) 6 *Indiana Journal of Global Legal Studies* 579.

[227] S Charnowitz, 'Opening the WTO to nongovernmental interests' (2000) 24 *Fordham International Law Journal* 173.

[228] For examples, see J Ravaloson, 'Les organisations non-gouvernementales et la sécurité alimentaire: vers un modèle de gouvernance globale?' in A Mahiou and F Snyder (eds), *La sécurité alimentaire/Food Security and Food Safety* (Leiden, Martinus Nijhoff for The Hague Academy of International Law, 2006) 546–48.

[229] S Charnowiz, *Trade Law and Global Governance* (London, Cameron May Ltd, 2002); Adaraoegbe, Adebayo, 'Energy, Economic Development, the Environment and Effective Global Governance: An Introduction' (2005) 5 *International Energy Law & Taxation Review* 185.

Whether such forms of global governance should be 'constitutionalised'—and indeed what 'constitutionalisation' means in this context—remains highly controversial.[230] Global constitution-making is a highly political and highly risky exercise in a pluralistic world, not just because it might fail but because, as articulated so far, it often elevates trade over other social values, such as democracy, the realisation of human potential, environmental protection, and combating poverty and hunger.[231] The 'insider' culture of international organisations, including the WTO, remains a major obstacle,[232] though in recent years the WTO has made serious progress toward greater openness. In addition, internal administrative and procedural reforms of the WTO, and perhaps other international institutions, are required.[233]

We need further research on the current and potential role of law in achieving the necessary reforms of global governance. Unfortunately the WTO does not participate in the Global Compact, proposed by UN Secretary-General Kofi Annan and launched in July 2000 to disseminate best practices on human rights, labour and the environment. In 2002, a proposal by Petersmann for an analogous 'Global Compact' between the UN and its specialised agencies and other international public organisations such as the WTO as part of global integration law, provoked strong reactions by Alston and Howse. This exchange showed some of the different political values and economic assumptions underlying many widely-held views on international trade law and international human rights law as they currently stand.[234] Some have argued that the WTO should formulate a worldwide public policy for a wide range of issues.[235]

A better way forward is not only to build on the existing diversity of legal forms, institutions, expertise, different forms of participation and legal cultures,[236] but also to do so with the objective of strengthening coordination among international institutions, institutionally, normatively and in terms of dispute resolution processes. The

[230] EU Petersmann, 'How to constitutionalize international law and foreign policy for the benefit of civil society?' (1998) 20 *Michigan Journal of International Law* 1; R Howse and K Nicolaidis, 'Legitimacy and global governance: Why constitutionalizing the WTO is a step too far' in RB Porter, P Sauvé, A Subramanian and A Beviglia-Zampetti (eds), *Efficiency, Equity, and Legitimacy: The Multilateral Trading System at the Millennium* (Washington, DC, Brookings Institution Press, 2001) 227; see also DZ Cass, *The Constitutionalisation of the WTO: Legitimacy, Democracy and Community in the International Trading System* (Oxford, Oxford University Press, 2005).

[231] On the role of law as a cause of world hunger, and also the potential role of law in helping to resolve such problems, see F Snyder, 'Toward an International Law for Adequate Food' in Mahiou and Snyder (eds), above n 228, 79–163.

[232] R Howse, 'From politics to technocracy—and back again: The fate of the multilateral trading regime' (2002) 96 *American Journal of Comparative Law* 94.

[233] E Stein, 'International integration and democracy: No love at first sight' (2001) 95 *American Journal of International Law* 489 at 531–34; P Van Den Bossche and I Alexovicova, 'Effective Global Economic Governance by the World Trade Organisation' (2005) 8(3) *Journal of International Economic Law* 667.

[234] EU Petersmann, 'Time for a United Nations "Global Compact" for Integrating Human Rights into the Law of Worldwide Organizations: Lessons from European Integration' (2002) 13(3) *European Journal of International Law* 621; R Howse, 'Human Rights in the WTO: Whose Rights? What Humanity? Comment on Petersmann' (2002) 13(3) *European Journal of International Law* 651; P Alston, 'Resisting the Merger and Acquisition of Human Rights by Trade Law: A Reply to Petersmann' (2002) 13(4) *European Journal of International Law* 815; EU Petersmann, 'Taking Human Dignity, Poverty and Empowerment of Individuals More Seriously', Rejoinder to Alston' (2002) 13(4) *European Journal of International Law* 845. See *European Journal of International Law*, Discussion Forum on Trade and Human Rights, http://207.57.19.226/forum_tradehumanrights/t/.

[235] LIEI, 'Globalisation through WTO Integration: Neither Friend nor Foe' (2003) 30(2) *Legal Issues of European Integration* 95.

[236] See also C Eberhard, *Le Droit au miroir des cultures. Pour une autre mondialisation* (Paris, Librairie Générale de Droit et de Jurisprudence, 2006); CH Koch, Jr, 'Envisaging a Global Legal Culture' (2004) 25 *Michigan Journal of International Law* 1.

ideas of global legal pluralism and sites of governance provide useful tools for this endeavour. International lawyers and others have been especially active in recent research on global legal pluralism.[237] David Kennedy argues that what we need is 'conversation, interaction and legal pluralism', processes which cannot be captured adequately by more talk of 'constitutionalism'.[238] As Fischer-Lescano and Teubner suggest, the fragmentation of global law reflects the fragmentation of global society. In the future, greater legal fragmentation is more likely than normative unity, and perhaps law may play only a role of damage limitation.[239] In Walker's view, the extent, scope and depth of legal pluralism and the variety of approaches used in trying to understand it are such that a single dominant order or view is unlikely to emerge; hence we should focus on analysing the terms of accommodation among models and among actors.[240]

The last chapter of this book concerns these questions. In addition, several other writers have proposed ways of doing this. Rosenau advances the idea that current and emerging 'spheres of authority', including States, should conclude 'new social contracts' which specify both benefits and obligations, and contain core norms such as organisational devolution, open membership, humanitarian protections, shared expertise, self-reflexivity, the possible exclusion of territoriality, egalitarianism and accountability.[241] In order to establish a form of ordered pluralism, Delmas-Marty proposes the further development of specific normative instruments such as concepts of regulation, techniques of adjustment, and mechanisms of evaluation and control.[242] Such instruments are quite well known in the USA and to some extent the United Kingdom. The analysis of such constitutional tools is developed further by Rosenfeld.[243] Pauwelyn provides a catalogue of techniques for avoiding or resolving normative conflicts.[244]

A useful starting point, though its author refers only to constitutional systems, is Weiler's principle of constitutional tolerance.[245] Recourse to this principle would appear to be subject, necessarily, to 'systemic compatibility', to use Maduro's terminology.[246]

[237] See eg W Burke-White, 'International Legal Pluralism' (2004) 25 *Michigan Journal of International Law* 963, and other articles in this issue from the 25th Anniversary Symposium of the *Michigan Journal of International Law* on 'Diversity or Cacophony: New Sources of Norms in International Law'.

[238] D Kennedy, 'The Mystery of Global Governance', Kormendy Lecture, Ohio Northern University, Pettit College of Law, 25 January 2008, available at http://www.watsoninstitute.org/blss, visited 3 February 2009.

[239] See A Fischer-Lescano and G Teubner, 'Regime Collisions: The Vain Search for Legal Unity in the Fragmentation of Global Law' (2004) 25(4) *Michigan Journal of International Law* 999.

[240] N Walker, 'Beyond Boundary Disputes and Basic Grids: Mapping the Global Disorder of Normative Orders' (2008) 6 *International Journal of Constitutional Law: I-CON* 373.

[241] JN Rosenau, *Distant Proximities: Dynamics Beyond Globalization* (Princeton, Princeton University Press, 2003) 300–14.

[242] M Delmas-Marty, *Les forces imaginaries du droit (II): Le pluralisme ordonné* (Paris, Editions du Seuil, 2006).

[243] M Rosenfeld, 'Rethinking Constitutional Ordering in an Era of Legal and Ideological Pluralism' (2008) 6(3)–(4) *International Journal of Constitutional Law: I-CON* 415.

[244] J Pauwelyn, *Conflict of Norms in Public International Law: How WTO Law Relates to Other Rules of International Law* (Cambridge, Cambridge University Press, 2003), esp at 237–439.

[245] JHH Weiler, 'In Defence of the Status Quo: Europe's Constitutonal *Sonderweg*' in J Weiler and M Wind (eds), *European Constitutonalism Beyond the State* (Cambridge, Cambridge University Press, 2003).

[246] M Poiares Maduro, 'L'interprétation du droit communautaire: la function juridictionnelle dans le contexte du pluralisme constitutionnel', speech to the French Cour de Cassation, 17 December 2007, available at http://network-presidents.eu/IMG/pdf/conferencia_paris_2_.pdf [VO—last accessed 12 March 2010]; English version in: 'Interpreting European Law: Judicial Adjudication in a Context of Constitutional Pluralism' (2007) 1(2) *European Journal of Legal Studies*, available at http://www.ejls.eu.

Berman adds a number of other concepts and mechanisms for managing legal pluralism. They include the use of margins of appreciation, limited autonomy regimes, subsidiarity principles, jurisdictional redundancies, hybrid participation arrangements, mutual recognition regimes, safe harbour arrangements and a pluralist approach to conflict of laws.[247] We can add not only market competition but also the classic range of legal obligations, such as an obligation to inform, an obligation to consult, coordination, mutual recognition or equivalence, harmonisation and the use of regulatory law, whether hard law, soft law or a combination of the two. Halberstam and Stein show that, in a situation with competing claims of authority, broader mutual engagement between sites can be productive in developing shared norms, such as international human rights.[248] The creation of bridging mechanisms or interface organisations with overlapping membership, such as committees of regulators who belong to both worlds, is another possibility.[249] In even more detail, Walker notes that

> rule-making authorities at the expansion relational edges between sites typically seek to instruct, authorize, shame, persuade, influence, encourage, emulate, improve upon or provide an example to one another, and likewise, the rules that they promulgate typically seek to constrain, qualify, supplement or supplant rules emanating from other sites.[250]

This focuses on norms, but a similar analysis can be made of relations between institutions and between dispute settlement processes.[251]

These suggestions provide useful building blocks for thinking about global governance and potentially for linking together sites of governance in webs of global governance. They should be complemented by contributions from other legal cultures, in particular from Asia, Latin America and Africa. We live in a world of increasing legal pluralism. In this new context, we need to focus on achieving basic substantive objectives by the structures of and relations among sites of governance.

[247] PS Berman, 'Global Legal Pluralism' (2007) 80 *Southern California Law Review* 1155.

[248] D Halberstam and E Stein, 'The United Nations, the European Union, and the King of Sweden: Economic Sanctions and Individual Rights in a Plural World Order' (2009) 46 *CML Rev* 13.

[249] For example, permanent bodies composed of EC Member States' national financial regulatory authorities serve as a bridge between the EC and global financial standard-setting bodies, in which the national authorities also participate: see G Bertezzolo, 'The European Union Facing the Global Arena: Standard-setting Bodies and Financial Regulation' (2009) 34(2) *EL Rev* 247.

[250] Walker, above n 178, at 356.

[251] For example, see also Maduro, above n 246, who refers to legal integration, concurrent interpretation, legal externalities and sympathetic consideration.

3

Governing Economic Globalisation: Sites of Governance and Global Legal Pluralism

I. Introduction

A. How is Globalisation Governed?

How is globalisation governed? As we saw in the preceding chapter, theories of contract, hierarchy, networks and sets of governance provide different answers to this question. Building on that discussion, this chapter develops the theory of sites of governance. It argues that globalisation is governed by the totality of strategically determined, situationally specific and often episodic conjunctions of a multiplicity of sites throughout the world. Each site has institutional, normative and processual characteristics. Each site also has relations with numerous other sites. The totality of these sites of governance represents a new global form of legal pluralism. This chapter aims to explore and, within limits, to substantiate this claim. It invites us to think systematically about how globalisation is governed by global legal pluralism.

Focusing on economic globalisation, the chapter aims to increase our understanding of how globalisation is governed and to improve our capacity to analyse these new forms of governance. It is not intended to promote law reform, or to advance a specific political or institutional agenda. Consequently, its perspective is more sociological than normative. As a useful starting point, it adopts the standpoint of strategic actors. Relations among strategic actors can be envisaged as involving different types of organisations, whether firms, States, or regional or international organisations. Alternatively, we can see them as implicating different structures of governance, whether market-based structures or polity-based structures. From a third perspective, these relationships put into play global economic networks and various sites of global legal pluralism. The chapter is intended to highlight these perspectives.

B. The Meaning of Globalisation

Thinking about how economic globalisation is governed requires a definition of globalisation. By 'globalisation' I mean an aggregate of multifaceted, uneven, often contradictory economic, political, social, cultural and legal processes which are characteristic of our time. This chapter concentrates primarily on the economic and legal aspects, but these need to be set within a more general framework.

In economic terms, the most salient features of globalisation, driven by multinational firms, are for present purposes the interpenetration of international financial markets, the possibility of virtually instananeous worldwide flows of information, the fragmentation of ownership, the development of global value chains including IPNs,[1] dispersion of production facilities among different countries, the technical and functional fragmentation of production, the flexibility of the production process, worldwide sourcing, an increase in intra-firm trade, changes in the nature of employment and the emergence of new forms of work.

Viewed from a political standpoint, globalisation has witnessed the rise of new political actors such as multinational firms, NGOs and social movements. It has tended to weaken, fragment and sometimes even restructure the State, but has not by any means destroyed or replaced it; indeed globalisation has strengthened certain aspects of many States. Globalisation has also altered radically the relationship to which we have become accustomed in recent history between governance and territory. It thus has blurred and splintered the boundaries between the domestic and external spheres of nation States and of regional integration organisations; fostered the articulation of systems of multi-level governance, interlocking politics and numerous policy networks; and helped to render universal the discourse of and claims for human rights. In many political and legal settings, such as the European Union and on the international plane, it has raised serious questions about the nature and appropriate form of contemporary governance.

Among the manifold social processes involved in globalisation are the spread of certain models of production and patterns of consumption from specific geographic/political/national contexts to others. Contradictory tendencies have developed towards internationalisation and localisation within as well as among different regions and countries. We have also witnessed the uneven development of new social movements based on different, if not alternative, forms of community.

Seen as a cultural phenomenon, globalisation has implied the emergence of a new global culture, which is shared to some extent by virtually all elite groups. This has enhanced the globalisation of the imagination and of the imaginable.[2] At the same time it has contributed both to the transformation of many local cultures, sometimes strengthening them, sometimes marginalising them, sometimes having both consequences simultaneously. Consequently, it has sometimes increased the range and depth of international and infranational cultural conflicts, as well as resistance to new forms of cultural imperialism.

From the legal standpoint, globalisation has stimulated the development of new institutions, the use of novel types of norms, renewed concern for the ways in which

[1] See in particular the work of the Berkeley Roundtable on the International Economy, eg M Borrus and J Zysman, 'Globalisation with Borders: The Rise of Wintelism as the Future of Industrial Competition' in J Zysman and A Schwartz (eds), *Enlarging Europe: The Industrial Foundations of a New Political Reality* (University of California at Berkeley, 1998) 27; G Gereffi, J Humphrey and T Sturgeon, 'The Governance of Global Value Chains' (2005) 12(1) *Review of International Political Economy* 78; and the research of the Global Value Chains Initiative, at http://www.globalvaluechains.org, visited 24 April 2009.

[2] For this expression, I am indebted to Prof P Barcellona, oral intervention at the Conference on 'Quelle culture pour l'Europe? Ordres juridiques et cultures dans le processus de globalisation', Réseau Européen de Droit et Société (REDS) and Istituto di Ricerca sui Problemi dello Stato e delle Istitutionzi (IRSI), Rome, 2–3 November 1998.

law can be used to achieve social justice, and increasing demands for legitimacy, democracy and accountability in global governance

C. An Analytical Strategy

The remainder of this chapter is divided into four main sections. Section II. introduces the global commodity chain in toys, an empirical anchor for my theoretical argument.[3] Section III. then sketches what I consider to be the basic elements of global legal pluralism. Section IV. presents in more detail the shape of global legal pluralism, bringing together examples of the segments of the global commodity chain in toys, different sites of governance and global legal pluralism. The conclusion in section V. briefly summarises the argument and proposes hypotheses for further research.

II. An International Production Network: The Global Commodity Chain in Toys

Global commodity chains take various forms. I focus here on the international toy industry. The toy industry's global reach and domestic impact can be illustrated clearly by the Barbie doll.[4] In European countries, imports of toys from Asia previously sometimes provoked reactions bordering on xenophobia. In the United States they triggered outrage against cheap Chinese labour and trade deficits with China, which in the case of the toy trade between China and the USA was claimed by the US to amount to US $5.4 billion.[5] This has not, however, been true by and large of the Barbie doll, which is usually viewed instead as a United States or even global product.[6]

The Barbie doll's label says 'made in China'. This suggests, correctly, that, in the production of Barbie, China provides the factory space, labour and electricity, as well as cotton cloth for the dress. It conceals the facts, however, that Japan supplies the nylon hair, Saudia Arabia provides oil, Taiwan refines oil into ethylene for plastic pellets for the body, Japan, the US and Europe supply almost all the machinery and tools, most

[3] The toy industry represents one among several types of global value chain, to use the terminology of Gereffi *et al*, above n 1. Gereffi *et al* are concerned with firm-level relations. The hypothesis underlying this chapter is that the theories of sites of governance and global legal pluralism apply to all types of global value chains, and also to the governance of other, non-economic forms of globalisation.

[4] The empirical part of this chapter reflects the original publication in 'Governing Economic Globalisation: Global Legal Pluralism and European Law' (1999) 5(4) *European Law Journal* 345 and has not been revised to reflect any changes in the global toy industry since then.

[5] R Tempest, 'Barbie and the World Economy', *Los Angeles Times World Report* (A Special Section Produced in Cooperation with *The Korea Times*), Sunday, 13 October 1996, at 3. There are major differences between US and Chinese estimates of US–PRC trade figures. In 1995 the US Department of Commerce estimated the deficit at US $33.8 billion in China's favour, while China estimated the deficit at only US $8.6 billion: cf *ibid*.

[6] See also D Jaffé, *The History of Toys: From Spinning Tops to Robots* (Stroud, Sutton Publishing Ltd, 2006) 142–43.

of the moulds (the most expensive item) come from the US, Japan or Hong Kong, the United States supplies cardboard packaging, paint pigments and moulds, and Hong Kong supplies the banking and insurance, and carries out the delivery of the raw materials to factories in Guangdong Province in south China, together with the collection of the finished products and shipping.

Two Barbie dolls are marketed every second in 140 countries around the world by Mattel Inc of El Segundo, Callifornia. There is a Barbie doll museum in Palo Alto, California. Barbie celebrated her 40th birthday on 9 March 1999, and the US Post Office released a commemorative US postage stamp in June in her honour.[7] The Barbie doll is quintessentially American in origin, style and culture, and of course is the result of a global commodity chain powered by a US buyer. As Table 1 below shows, however, Barbie is a global product, if by 'global' we refer to the fragmentation of the production process, the dispersion of production facilities among different countries, and the organisation of production within international production networks. From the legal standpoint, this suggests that the most important rules are likely to be intellectual property rights, standards and rules of origin.

Table 1 Sources of Components in the Production of the Barbie Doll (1996)

—Label: 'Made in China'
—Origin of components

- Land and factory: China
- Workers for production: China
- Electricity: China
- Cotton cloth for dress: China
- Nylon for hair: Japan
- Oil: Saudia Arabia
- Refining of oil (for body): Taiwan
- Machinery and tools: USA, EU, Japan
- Moulds: USA, Japan, Hong Kong
- Packaging: USA
- Paint: USA
- Banking services, insurance, delivery of parts to factory, collection of finished products, inspection, export/transport: Hong Kong

—Sales by Mattel, Inc, based in El Segundo, California: 2 Barbie dolls per second in 140 countries around the world

Source: This table is based on R Tempest, 'Barbie and the World Economy', *Los Angeles Times World Report* (A Special Section Produced in Cooperation with *The Korea Times*), Sunday, 13 October 1996.

We can understand this industry most easily by conceiving of it as a global commodity chain. By 'commodity chain' I mean 'a network of labor and production processes whose end result is a finished commodity'.[8] Global commodity chains tend to be

[7] Rapport, 'Barbie at 40', *Sky* (Delta Air Lines), March 1999, 54–57.

[8] T Hopkins and AWallerstein, 'Commodity Chains in the World-Economy Prior to 1800' (1986) 10 *Review* 157 at 159.

strongly connected to specific systems of production and to involve particular patterns of coordinated trade.[9]

Each global commodity chain, if we follow Gereffi's widely accepted schema, has three main dimensions. The first refers to the structure of inputs and outputs: products and services are linked together in a sequence in which each activity adds value to its predecessor. The second concerns territoriality; networks of enterprises may be spatially dispersed or concentrated. The third dimension is the structure of governance: relationships of power and authority determine the flow and allocation of resources (financial, material, human) within the chain.[10] Here we are interested especially in the third dimension, the structure of governance which is internal to the chain. Gereffi previously distinguished two distinct types of governance structures within global commodity chains. On the one hand are producer-driven commodity chains, in which the system of production is controlled by large integrated industrial enterprises. On the other hand are buyer-driven commodity chains, in which production networks are typically decentralised and power rests with large retailers, brand-name merchanisers and trading companies.[11] More recently, Gereffi, Humphrey and Sturgeon have proposed a broader typology of forms of governance within global value chains.[12] The concept of a buyer-driven commodity chain provides a useful point of departure for analysing the global commodity chain in the EU–China toy trade.

The global toy industry is a prime example of an international commodity chain dominated by the buyers. It is hierarchically organised (see Figure 1 below). At the top of the hierarchy are large buyers as well as large retailers. The buyers include several US manufacturers, two Japanese manufacturers, and one European company. The most important buyers are two American companies, Mattel and Hasbro. The key elements in the power of buyers are designs and brands. The large buyers are the node in various networks of inventors and creators of toys. Through contract, they control the access of inventors, intermediaries and factories to the market. The most important retailers include large specialist stores such as Toys 'R' Us, discount houses such as Wal-Mart in the US, and hypermarkets or catalogue stores in the EU. Taking buyers and retailers together, the power of this group lies in its control of design, brands and marketing.

Buyers and retailers compete, however, with regard to access to retail markets. The powerful buyers are dependent to some degree on large retailers, such as Toys 'R' Us and discount stores such as Wal-Mart. As economic downturns reveal, however, the two groups have conflicting interests with regard to the retail market. To maintain market share, and to enhance their dominant position in the global commodity chain, buyers have tried recently to lessen their dependence on retailers. Their strategies for

[9] G Gereffi, 'The Organization of Buyer-Driven Global Commodity Chains: How US Retailers Shape Overseas Production Networks', in G Gereffi and M Korzeniewicz (eds), *Commodity Chains and Global Capitalism* (Westport, Conn, Greenwood, 1994) 95 at 96 (hereafter 'The Organization'). See also G Gereffi, 'New Realities of Industrial Development in East Asia and Latin America: Global, Regional and National Trends' in RP Appelbaum and J Henderson (eds), *States and Development in the Asia Pacific Rim* (Newbury Park, Sage 1992) 85; G Gereffi, 'Global Commodity Chains: New Forms of Coordination and Control among Nations and Firms in International Industries' (1996) 4 *Competition & Change* 427; G Gereffi, 'Commodity Chains and Regional Divisions of Labor in East Asia' (1996) 12 *Journal of Asian Business* 75.

[10] Gereffi, 'The Organization', above n 9, at 96–97.

[11] *Ibid*, at 97.

[12] Gereffi *et al*, above n 1.

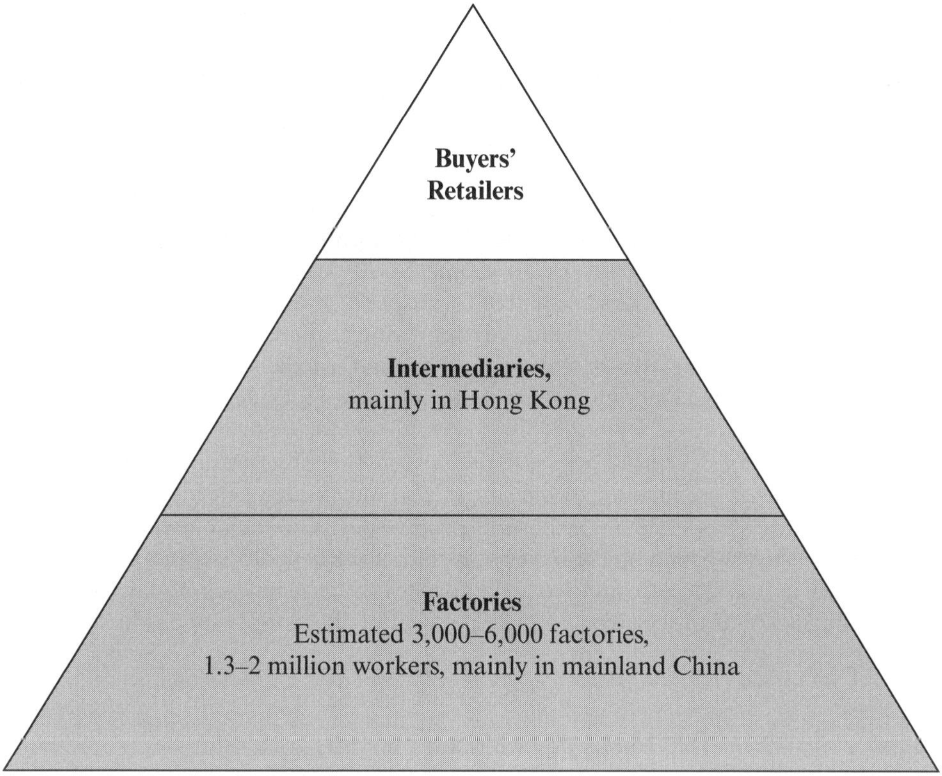

Figure 1 Structure of the Global Toy Industry

doing so include increased direct-to-consumer sales, including catalogues and Internet sales, either from their own website or from online retailers.[13]

The US firms have regional headquarters and a significant share of the toy market in Europe. The European Union toy market is supplied mainly through importer-wholesalers. As of 1995, the EU toy industry comprised about 2,600 firms, producing a great variety of toys and employing just under 100,000 workers, with only 15 firms having more than 500 employees.[14] Each country has its own distinctive retail sector, varying from catalogue stores through hypermarkets to independent retailers.[15] Except for Lego, established in Denmark in 1932 and now one of the world's 10 largest toy manufacturers, there are no large manufacturers or specialist retailers based in Europe similar to those based in the USA. Together with Lego and the Japanese firm Bandai, the US firms dominated the first main peak trade association, Toy Manufacturers of Europe, formed in the early 1990s, and are now the principal players in the current EU peak association, Toy Industries of Europe (TIE).

[13] Cf G Anders and L Bannon, 'Etoys to join web-retailer parade with IPO', *The Wall Street Journal.* Tuesday, 6 April 1999, at B1.

[14] Commission of the European Communities, 'Report from the Commission to the Council on the surveillance measures and quantitative quotas applicable to certain non-textile products originating in the People's Republic of China', COM(95)614 final, Brussels, 6.12.95, 41.

[15] See Hong Kong Trade Development Council, *Practical Guide to Exporting Toys for Hong Kong Traders* (Hong Kong Trade Development Council, Research Department, March 1999) 34–58.

Further down the hierarchy come the Hong Kong companies which act as intermediaries between these multinationals and the toy factories.[16] In East Asia, Hong Kong has been of signal importance in the development of the toy industry. It started in the 1940s as an export platform, then developed in the 1980s as an original equipment manufacturer (OEM) for overseas importers or as an intermediary between local manufacturers and overseas buyers until, starting in the 1990s, Hong Kong became a re-exporter of toys made in China. In 1998, licensing and contract manufacturing for overseas manufacturers, usually to production specifications and product designs provided by the buyers, accounted for an estimated 70 per cent of total domestic toy exports.[17] United States buyers accounted for 51 per cent of Hong Kong's toy exports in the first 10 months of 1995.[18] Today Hong Kong is the location of management, design, R&D, marketing, quality control, finance and usually shipping.[19]

At the bottom of the hierarchy are the factories, most of which are located in China. By 1995 toy production in China involved about 3,000 factories employing more than 1.3 million people.[20] Such factories usually occupy the structural position of OEM, producing to other companies' specifications with machinery provided by the buyer. However, some now operate on the basis of original design manufacturer (ODM), producing to designs supplied by the buyer but sharing the cost of machinery and investment as well as markets according to an agreement with the buyer.[21] Today China and Hong Kong account for between 70 to 90 per cent of the world's toy production.[22]

III. Elements of Global Legal Pluralism

We usually view the legal arrangements which are relevant to such global economic networks in one of three ways. As outlined in the preceding chapter, we often see them essentially in terms of contracts between nominally equal parties, such as individuals, companies or States, whose agreement is consecrated in either bilateral or multilateral form. Alternatively, we conceive of them in hierarchical terms, for example as constituting various regional or international forms of multi-level governance. A further possibility is to conceive of these arrangements in terms of networks. I wish to suggest,

[16] In 1948 Hong Kong had three plastics factories employing 33 people. By 1964 it had 968 factories, including 418 making toys, with a total employment of 31,408 people. See KD Brown, *The British Toy Business: A History Since 1700* (London, The Hambledon Press, 1996) 171.

[17] 'Hong Kong's Toy Industry', *Hong Kong & China Economics*, on the Internet homepage of the Hong Kong Trade Development Council at http://www.tdc.org.hk/main/industries/t2_2_39.htm, last updated 2 July 1998.

[18] *Journal of Commerce*, Friday, 13 January 1995.

[19] See the statement by Dennis Ting, who as of January 1995 was chairman of Kader Industrial Co Ltd, a leading Hong Kong toy firm, as well as of the Hong Kong trading agency's toy advisory committee and of the Hong Kong Toy Council: *ibid*.

[20] J Newton and L Tse, ' 'Kids' Stuff: The Organisation and Politics of the China–EU Trade in Toys', in R Strange, J Slater, and L Wang (eds), *Trade and Investment in China: The European Experience* (London, Routledge, 1998) 147.

[21] Interviews in Hong Kong, Guangzhou, and the Shenzhen Special Economic Zone, China.

[22] Jaffé, above n 6, at 64. This represents a substantial increase since 1998, when Hong Kong and mainland China reportedly accounted for 60% of the world's toy trade: 'Chinese Toy Making: Where the Furbies come from', *The Economist*, 19 December 1998, 95. The book by Jaffé (at 45–65) provides a useful overview of the internationalisation of the toy industry between 1792 and 2006.

however, that all of these conceptions, regardless of their force in normative terms, are descriptively inaccurate and analytically incomplete. There is a fundamental and growing disjunction between our traditional, normative and hierarchical conceptions of the law governing international trade and the shape of the economic networks which are an integral part of economic globalisation. In addition, the concept of networks of relations is useful in specific fields, but it refers only to specific types of relations, not to the elements which are linked by such relations or to other possible types of relations among these elements. In other words, it is too linear and limited in scope to capture the multiplicity of institutions, norms, processes and relations which constitute the governance of economic globalisation today.

We should not necessarily expect the law and economic relations to be isomorphic. But in order to understand how global economic networks are governed in practice, we need to revise many of our basic ideas about the shape of the global legal order. Global economic networks are the product of and a form of strategic behaviour, they usually have a particular locus of power and a specific hierarchy, and often they are governed by a multitude of institutions and norms. Their dramatic growth has placed in question the credibility of lawyers' claims about the hierarchical nature of global economic governance. At the same time it has provoked demands for the constitutionalisation of global governance and debates about its feasibility and desirability. Here we are concerned not with firm-level arrangements or inter-firm linkages. Instead we focus on those arrangements which can be either internal or external to inter-firm relations and which govern global economic networks.

I suggest that the most adequate concept for understanding the global legal (dis)order today is global legal pluralism. By 'global legal pluralism' I mean the totality of strategically determined, situationally specific and often episodic conjunctions of a multiplicity of sites of governance throughout the world. A site of governance is a locus of decision-making with the authority to settle disputes. Each site of governance has two dimensions: a structural dimension, comprising institutions, norms and dispute settlement processes; and a relational dimension, which refers to relations between the site and other sites of governance. Structures affect, condition or determine relations. In turn, relations affect, condition or determine structures.

A contrast with the work of several other writers will illuminate this idea.[23] First, a useful starting point is James Rosenau's concept of 'spheres of authority'. According to Rosenau,

> the world is comprised of spheres of authority (SOAs) that are not necessarily consistent with the division of territorial space and are subject to considerable flux. Such spheres are, in effect, the analytic units of the new ontology. They are distinguished by the presence of actors who can evoke compliance when exercising authority as they engage in the activities that delineate the sphere.[24]

This concept is useful because it pays special attention to social processes and the role of strategic actors. Though focusing on international relations, it is akin to Sally Falk

[23] See also DM Trubek, Y Dezalay, R Buchanan and J Davis, 'Global Restructuring and the Law: Internationalization of Legal Fields and the Creation of Transnational Arenas' (1994) 14 *Case Western Reserve Law Review* 407; B de Sousa Santos, *Toward a New Common Sense: Law, Science and Politics in the Paradigmatic Transition* (New York, Routledge, 1995), esp ch 4, 'Globalization, Nation-States and the Legal Field: From Legal Diaspora to Legal Ecumenism?', at 250–377.

[24] JN Rosenau, 'Toward an Ontology for Global Governance' in M Hewson and TJ Sinclair (eds), *Approaches to Global Governance Theory* (Albany, State University of New York Press, 1999) 287 at 295.

Moore's notion of domestically anchored 'semi-autonomous social fields'[25] in its pluralist conception of normative life. However, the concept of spheres of authority is concerned mainly with political processes. It takes political authority as the main independent variable. For the purpose of this chapter, it does not give sufficient attention to institutions, norms or the settlement of disputes. However, Rosenau also deals with relations between sites. He sets forth in detail the basic assumptions and possible content of new social contracts and other types of relations between spheres of authority.[26]

A second useful contribution is Gunther Teubner's theory of *lex mercatoria* as a paradigm of global law.[27] The principal thesis is that global law develops mainly outside the political structures of nation States and international organisations.[28] The basic device is contract[29] and the paradigm is *lex mercatoria.*[30] From this perspective, global law has several important characteristics. First, its boundaries are not territorial but consist of 'invisible' markets, branches, specialised professional communities, or highly technical social networks, all of which transcend territorial boundaries.[31] Secondly, its sources are not a legislature but rather, according to his theory of autopoiesis,[32] 'self-organizing processes of "structural coupling" of law with ongoing globalized processes of a highly specialized and technical nature'.[33] Thirdly, global law depends closely on various other social fields, instead of being relatively autonomous from political institutions in particular, hence it is subject to economic pressures and so is not strongly institutionalised in the sense of due process or the rule of law.[34] Fourthly, it consists mainly of broad principles, which though not legally binding have the great correlative advantages of flexibility and adaptability.[35] Fifthly, at first it is not politicised, but the gradual juridification of economic relations through contract will lead eventually to the interference of political processes.[36] Sixthly, it is not unified, whether nationally, regionally or on a world scale[37]; instead, due to its dependence on other social processes and its lack of political and institutional support, global law is decentred and non-hierarchical.[38]

This perspective makes several important contributions to advancing our understanding of global legal pluralism. First, it also takes seriously the idea that, apart from nation States, there are other sources of economically and socially significant norms that operate across national borders and to a large extent independently of

[25] S Falk Moore, 'Law and Social Change: The Semi-Autonomous Social Field as an Appropriate Subject of Study' (1973) 7(4) *Law and Society Review* 719, reprinted in S Falk Moore, *Law as Process: An Anthropological Approach* (London, Routledge & Kegan Paul, 1978).

[26] JN Rosenau, *Distant Proximities: Dynamics Beyond Globalisation* (Princeton, Princeton University Press, 2003), esp 300–14, 390–402.

[27] See G Teubner (ed), *Global Law without a State* (Dartmouth, Aldershot, 1997).

[28] See G Teubner, ' "Global Bukowina": Legal Pluralism in the World Society' in Teubner, *ibid*, at 7.

[29] *Ibid*, at 15.

[30] *Ibid*, at 8, 12.

[31] *Ibid*, at 7, 8.

[32] Cf G Teubner (ed), *Autopoietic law: a new approach to law and society* (Berlin, De Gruyter 1988).

[33] Teubner, above n 28, at 8.

[34] *Ibid*, at 8, 19.

[35] *Ibid*, at 21.

[36] *Ibid*, at 21–22; see also G Teubner, 'Foreword: Legal Regimes of Global Non-state Actors' in Teubner, above n 27, xiii–xvii at xiv.

[37] Teubner, above n 28, at 8.

[38] G Teubner, 'Foreword: Legal Regimes of Global Non-state Actors', in Teubner, above n 27, xiii–xvii at xiv.

States. Secondly, it recognises that bundles of these norms may be aggregated in the form of a system, and that there may a plurality of such systems, including norm-generating processes. Indeed, in addition to drawing on the literature on legal pluralism,[39] it expressly uses the term 'global legal pluralism', though in a way different from that being advanced here. Thirdly, it tries to analyse the organisation of these norms and the systems in which they are embedded as part of distinct networks rather than in terms of hierarchy.[40] Fourthly, it gives due weight and attention to the significance of soft law, 'rules of conduct which, in principle, have no legally binding force but which nevertheless may have practical effects'.[41]

For the present purposes, however, this formulation has several shortcomings. First, its starting point, *lex mercatoria*, leads inevitably to an almost exclusive emphasis on contract. It may be true that, in *lex mercatoria*, contract is not only the central legal device but also the primary source of law and means of self-legitimation.[42] Viewed from a different perspective, however, for example that of strategic actors in a global commodity chain, such as multinational firms or that of the regulation of international trade, contract is only one among several legal devices, sources of law and forms of legitimation.

Secondly, this formulation focuses exclusively on non-State actors and intentionally neglects the State. In its context, this methodological choice is useful, if not essential. It is an integral part of the argument that political theories of law are of little relevance to global law.[43] However, it is based on a traditional conception of constitutions as being associated always with the nation State.[44] It also has the necessary consequence, which for the present purposes is unfortunate, that it reveals only part of the picture of global legal pluralism. In particular with regard to international trade, a fundamental role is played by nation States, regional organisations such as the European Union and international organisations such as the WTO, as well as other organisations and networks.

Thirdly, a consequence of focusing on *lex mercatoria* and omitting the State and other political structures is an over emphasis on soft law. In the governance of global economic networks, however, both soft law and legally binding norms, or 'hard law', are important. Indeed, the relationship between hard law and soft law has long been controversial. Today it is one of the most interesting—and difficult—questions currently raised by the governance of globalisation.

Fourthly, the analysis is based a specific conception of legal pluralism. It asks the question, 'Where are concrete norms actually produced?'[45] It then answers this

[39] Cf G Teubner, 'The Two Faces of Janus: Rethinking Legal Pluralism' (1992) 13 *Cardozo Law Review* 1443.

[40] Cf G Teubner, 'The Many-headed Hydras: Networks as Higher-order Collective Actors' in J McCahery, S Picciotto, and C Scott (eds), *Corporate Control and Accountability: Changing Structures and the Dynamics of Regulation* (Oxford, Clarendon Press, 1993) 41.

[41] For this definition, see F Snyder, 'The Effectiveness of European Community Law: Institutions, Processes, Tools and Techniques' (1993) 56(1) *MLR* 19 at 32.

[42] See Teubner, above n 28, at 18.

[43] *Ibid*, at 7.

[44] In fact, Teubner (*ibid*, at 6) quotes N Luhmann, *Das Recht der Gesellschaft* (Frankfurt, Suhrkamp, 1993) at 582, to the effect that 'the structural coupling between law and politics via constitutions has no correspondence on the level of world society.' Cf the different conception of J-P Robé, that the world constitutional structure consists of a global legal order comprised of various territorial and functional legal orders, with different goals and hence problems of coordination: see J-P Robé, 'Multinational Enterprises: The Constitution of a Pluralistic Legal Order' in Teubner, above n 27, 45 at 70.

[45] Teubner, above n 28, 12.

question by defining legal pluralism in terms of discourse, of communicative processes that interpret the world by means of a binary code of legal/illegal.[46] This definition, however, accords relatively little weight to institutions, and it assumes that alternative conceptions of legal pluralism imply 'a set of conflicting social norms'[47] and require 'an implied delegation of state power'.[48] None of these assumptions, as I hope to show, is necessary or indeed helpful in the context of this chapter.

A third author, Nicolien van der Grijp, relies in her PhD thesis partly on Sally Falk Moore's conception of semi-autonomous social fields, as well as on my concept of sites of governance,[49] in trying to specify the concept of 'site of governance' in more detail. In a useful discussion, she identifies a site of governance as comprising

> [a] sphere of territorial, functional or sectoral competence; [a] membership with rights and obligations; [a]n institutional structure to govern internal and external relations; [a]n explicit regulatory discourse and output, and [a] mechanism for stimulating compliance.[50]

These criteria help to elaborate aspects of the structural dimension of sites. However, they are based on an institutionalist conception of social life and are orientated entirely toward the structural aspects of a site of governance. External relations are treated as an aspect of internal institutional structure, in the sense of being a task of institutions. Despite their significance, however, for our purposes these criteria do not give sufficient independent weight to relations between sites. They do not consider relations themselves to be a distinct element of the concept of site of governance. Relations are a crucial, integral part of a site of governance; the relational dimension is inherent to the concept of a site of governance; and relations between sites are a defining characteristic of global legal pluralism.

Fourthly, in research on constitutionalism and law in the European Union, Neil Walker has elaborated, independently from research on international trade, a similar but more detailed conception of the features of 'constitutional sites'.[51] He sets forth a series of criteria for the existence of a constitutional site. They include a claim to autonomy or self-governance, delimitation of competences, autotomy in the interpretation of fundamental rules, institutions, conditions for belonging to the political community in question and means by which that political community can participate in decision-making. He also pays due attention to relations between constitutional sites. In his words,

> constitutionalism in a plural order is necessarily conceived of not only as a property of politics and political processes but as a medium through which they interconnect—as a structural characteristic of the relationship between certain types of political authority or claim to

[46] *Ibid*, 12, 14.

[47] *Ibid*, 14.

[48] *Ibid*, 18. As to other problems with this definition, see PT Muchlinski, '"Global Bukowina" Examined: Viewing the Multinational Enterprise as a Transnational Law-making Community' in Teubner, above n 27, 79 at 85.

[49] As elaborated in an earlier version of this chapter, above n 4; at the 2nd International Workshop for Young Scholars (WISH), Aix-en-Provence, 26–27 September 2002, on which see (2004) 10(5) *European Law Journal* 495, Special Issue, 'Food Safety in European Union Law'; and in F Snyder (ed), *International Food Security and Global Legal Pluralism/Sécurité alimentaire internationale et pluralisme juridique mondial* (Brussels, Bruylant, 2004).

[50] N van der Grijp, *Regulating Pesticide Risk Reduction: The Practice and Dynamics of Legal Pluralism*, PhD thesis, University of Amsterdam (Amsterdam, VU Drukkerij, 2008) 22.

[51] N Walker, 'The Idea of Constitutional Pluralism' (2002) 65(3) *MLR* 317.

> authority situated at different sites or in different processes as well as an internal characteristic of these authoritative claims . . .[52]

Some of these ideas can be translated to the context of international trade regulation, though Walker's research necessarily gives more attention to political communities.

To summarise briefly, 'global legal pluralism', as I use the term, refers to the multiplicity of sites of governance throughout the world. Each side has a structural dimension and a relational dimension. The structural dimension comprises institutions, norms and dispute-settlement processes. The relational dimension encompasses relations between a specific site and all other sites of governance. Global legal pluralism thus involves a variety of institutions, norms and dispute resolution processes located, and produced, at different structured sites around the world.

Legal scholarship has traditionally paid most attention to understanding State, regional and international legal institutions, legally binding norms and dispute resolution processes involving law. Some authors even speak of the 'constitutionalisation' of international trade regulation.[53] In addition, international lawyers and related specialists in international relations have studied international negotiations, norms that at least in principle are not legally binding, global regulatory networks[54] and intergovernmental networks.[55] The analysis of international regimes,[56] multi-level governance and other types of institutional arrangements, such as credit-rating agencies,[57] has largely been the province of political scientists and specialists in international relations. Examples in the field of EU legal and political science scholarship concern multi-level governance,[58] committees[59] and different types of settings, whether highly institutionalised with specified norms, rules and procedures, or non-hierarchical and decentralised.[60] While it is possible to generalise to some extent from this previous work, no one has tried to unite these different elements. Some basic questions therefore remain to be answered. What is included in the concept of a site of governance? States and regional and international organisations are included, but so is a diversity of other

[52] *Ibid,* at 340. As he puts it elsewhere, referring to relations between the EU and the WTO: 'The language of metaconstitutionalism is explicitly relational, capturing the complexly-layered character of the new post-Westphalia pluralism . . . Metaconstitutional sites are defined in relational terms rather than as isolated monads'; see N Walker, 'The EU and the WTO: Constitutionalism in a New Key, in G de Búrca and J Scott (eds), *The EU and the WTO: Legal and Constitutional Issues* (Oxford, Hart Publishing, 2001) at 37.

[53] Cf esp JH Jackson, *The World Trade Organization: Constitution and Jurisprudence* (London, The Royal Institute of International Affairs, 1998); EU Petersmann, 'How to Promote the International Rule of Law? Contributions by the WTO Appellate Review System' in J Cameron and K Campbell (eds), *Dispute Resolution in the World Trade Organisation* (London, Cameron May, 1998) 75; DZ Cass, *The Constitutionalization of the World Trade Organization: Legitimacy, Democracy and Community in the International Trading System* (Oxford, Oxford University Press, 2005).

[54] Cf S Picciotto, 'The Regulatory Criss-cross: Interaction between Jurisdictions and the Construction of Global Regulatory Networks' in W Bratton, J McCahery, S Picciotto, and C Scott (eds), *International Regulatory Competition and Coordination* (Oxford, Clarendon Press, 1996) 89.

[55] Cf A-M Slaughter, 'The Real New World Order' (1997) 76 *Foreign Affairs* 183.

[56] A recent example is M Zacher (with BA Sutton), *Governing Global Networks: International Regimes for Transportation and Communications* (Cambridge, Cambridge University Press, 1996).

[57] Cf T Sinclair, 'Passing Judgment: Credit Rating Processes as Regulatory Mechanisms of Governance in the Emerging World Order' (1994) 1 *Review of International Political Economy* 133.

[58] F Scharpf, *Governing in Europe: Effective and Democratic?* (Oxford, Oxford University Press, 1999).

[59] See C Joerges and E Vos (eds), *EU Committees* (Oxford, Hart Publishing, 1999).

[60] Cf T Risse-Kappen, 'Exploring the Nature of the Beast: International Relations Theory and Comparative Policy Analysis Meet the European Union' (1996) 34 *Journal of Common Market Studies* 51.

institutional, normative and processual sites, such as commercial arbitration,[61] trade associations and so on. How are sites created, and how do they grow, survive or die? How are they structured? What does it mean to say that different structured sites are the anchors of contemporary legal pluralism?

Secondly, the relations among these sites are of many different types. Such relations may involve institutions, norms or dispute-settlement processes, or any combination of these. They may concern structure, process or both. In terms of structural relationships, sites may be autonomous and even independent, part of the same or different regimes, part of a single system of multi-level governance, or otherwise interconnected. In terms of process, they may be distinct and discrete, competing, overlapping or feed into each other, for example in the sense of comprising a 'structural set', 'formed through the mutual convertibility of rules and resources in one domain of action into those pertaining to another'.[62] These relations of structure and process constitute the global legal playing field. They determine the basic characteristics of global legal pluralism, such as equality or hierarchy, dominance or submission, creativity or imitation, convergence or divergence, and so on. They influence profoundly the growth, development and survival of the different sites.

Global legal pluralism is not merely an important part of the context in which global economic networks are constructed, in the sense that it is a factor to be taken into account by strategic actors; it is an integral part of these global economic networks themselves. In other words, global economic networks are constructed on a global playing field, which is organised or structured partly by global legal pluralism. Global legal pluralism does more, however, than simply provide the rules of the game. It also constitutes the game itself, including the players.

IV. The Toy Sector and the Shape of Global Legal Pluralism

A. Outline

We are now in a position to consider in more detail the interconnection between global legal pluralism and the global commodity chain in toys. Instead of starting with norms or a normative system such as a legal system, I propose to begin with social and economic relations. Every global commodity chain has numerous parts. Hopkins and Wallerstein use the term 'boxes' to refer to the separable processes involved in any global commodity chain.[63] I prefer the term 'segment'. This conveys more directly the

[61] See Y Dezalay and BG Garth, *Dealing in Virtue: International Commercial Arbitration and the Construction of a Transnational Legal Order* (Chicago, University of Chicago Press, 1996); see also A Casella, 'On Market Integration and the Development of Institutions: The Case of International Commercial Arbitration' (1996) 40 *European Economic Review* 155. For an example concerning the toy sector, see the 1987 *Award on Dispute over Contract for the Sale of Electric Toys*, in *Selected Works of China International Economic and Trade Arbitration Commission Awards (1963–1988) Updated to 1993* (authorised English version; English version translated by China Law and Culture Publications Limited) (London, Sweet & Maxwell, 1995) at 192–94.

[62] A Giddens, 'A Reply to My Critics' in D Held and JB Thompson (eds), *Social Theory of Modern Societies: Anthony Giddens and His Critics* (Cambridge, Cambridge University Press, 1989) 253 at 299.

[63] TK Hopkins and I Wallerstein, 'Commodity Chains: Construct and Research' in Gereffi and Korzeniewicz, above n 9, at 18.

fact that each part belongs to a larger whole, and it does not necessarily imply that the segment is closed to outside influences. The separable processes or segments may include, for example, invention, production, marketing, distribution and consumption. The boundaries of each segment are socially defined, and so they may also be redefined.[64] Technological and social organisational changes play a role in these processes. So too does law, conceived broadly to encompass the sites of global legal pluralism, with each site comprising its specific institutions, norms and processes. Law helps to construct and to define the segments which make up the global commodity chain in toys.

We can ask a series of questions about the social organisation of the constituent elements of any single segment in the chain. They refer, according to Hopkins and Wallerstein,[65] to:

—the number of components units in each segment (monopoly or competition)
—their geographic concentration or dispersal
—membership in one or more chains
—property arrangements
—modes of labour control
—links within a chain.

I add two further issues:

—connection between economic relations and specific sites
—relations between sites and the chain as a whole.

Thus here I rephrase, elaborate and add to Hopkins' and Wallerstein's questions. I give special emphasis to the institutional, normative and processual components of the sites of global legal pluralism. In the following paragraphs I offer selected examples of the interconnections between these sites and the international commodity chain. The discussion is meant to be illustrative, not exhaustive. It is designed to outline the shape of global legal pluralism.

B. Monopoly or Competition

First, the *number of component units* in the segment. To what degree is a segment monopolised by a small number of production units? What are the main factors determining this structure? What incentives for a particular structure are provided by legal and other institutions, norms and processes? For example, to what extent and how does the law provide or permit barriers to entry? To what extent does it facilitate or require market access, for instance with regard to production and/or distribution? Do different sites of global legal pluralism provide conflicting incentives and, if so, how are these conflicts managed, if not neutralised? If de-monopolisation of any highly profitable segment is an important process in the contemporary world economy, as Hopkins and Wallerstein suggest,[66] what role do the sites of global legal pluralism play

64 *Ibid.*
65 *Ibid*, at 18–19.
66 *Ibid*, at 18.

with regard to this process, for example by encouraging it, by countering it by redefining the boundaries of the segment or by other means, or by creating incentives for shifting capital investment to other segments, or even other chains?

Several sites of global legal pluralism play a role in shaping or determining the number of component units in any given segment in the international commodity chain in toys. Consider some examples.

First, with regard to invention, production and marketing, United States intellectual property law is of crucial significance in determining the number of buyers and maintaining their market power. The highest barriers to entry in buyer-driven commodity chains typically concern product conception, design and marketing. Intellectual property law creates or consolidates barriers to entry.

Secondly, antitrust law has an important impact on production, marketing and distribution. In the United States, Europe or Japan, it helps to define the number of key buyers or manufacturers in the international toy industry. American antitrust law in particular affects the possibility of mergers among buyers. When market leader Mattel Inc acquired the third largest toy manufacturer, Tyco Toys Inc, in 1996, Mattel was quoted in the American media as expressing confidence that the deal would not be blocked by US antitrust law, even though the companies' combined sales represented 19 per cent of the US toy market.[67]

Thirdly, the lack of binding legal regulation of Internet retailing lowers barriers to entry into the retail market in toys. Consequently, when buyers are squeezed by traditional retailers, they turn without great difficulty to the Internet in order to enter the retail sector themselves, either through specialist Internet retailers or by means of the buyers' own websites.

A fourth example, explored in more detail here, concerns EC international trade and customs law concerning the access of importers to the EU toy market.[68] It illustrates clearly the role played by EU legislation and the European Court of Justice in restructuring the EU toy industry. In 1994 the Council of the European Union adopted two major complementary legislative reforms. The first was Council Regulation 519/94 on common rules for imports from certain third countries.[69] It was the general regulation governing imports from non-market economy countries, except for textile products.[70] The second was Council Regulation 520/94 establishing a Community procedure for administrative quantitative quotas.[71] It established a new way of administering quotas, based on a system of licences issued by the Member States according to quan-

[67] J Madore, 'Mattel confident Tyco deal will pass antitrust scrutiny', *The Buffalo News*, Tuesday, 19 November 1996.

[68] Such importers, as shown throughout this book, include both EU and foreign companies, eg in joint ventures in foreign countries, outward processing arrangements or other increasingly complex forms of cooperation which are characteristic of—and indeed create—economic globalization.

[69] [1994] OJ L67/89.

[70] Imports of textiles were governed by one of two other regulations. Council Regulation 3030/93, on common rules for imports of certain textile products from third countries ([1993] OJ L275/1) covered imports of textile products from countries with which the EC has concluded bilateral agreements, protocols or other arrangements. Council Regulation 517/94 on common rules for imports of textile products from certain third countries not covered by bilateral agreements, protocols or other arrangements, or by other specific Community import rules ([1994] OJ L67/1), covered imports of textile products from non-market economy countries with which the Community had not concluded specific arrangements.

[71] Council Regulation 520/94 establishing a Community procedure for administering quantitative quotas, [1991] OJ L66/1.

titative criteria established at Community level.[72] Both were part of a package deal, designed to secure acceptance of the Uruguay Round multilateral trade negotiations, to reinforce existing trade policy instruments and to complete the EC's Common Commercial Policy.

Both the new quota regime and provisions for administering it exemplified the Europeanisation of law. They involved the total or partial replacement of the legislation of the Member States by EC law; EC quotas on seven categories of Chinese products, including toys, replaced approximately 6,417 national quantitative restrictions, including 4,700 on more than 30 Chinese products.[73] Council Regulation 519/94 introduced quotas on seven categories of Chinese products, ranging from gloves to footwear, porcelain tableware, ceramic tableware, glassware, car radios and toys. It imposed separate quotas on product categories SH/NC 9503 41 (stuffed toys, such as teddy bears), SH/NC 9503 49 (non-human toys, such as Ninja Turtles) and SH/NC 9503 90 (other toys, such as die-cast minatures). It did not cover, however, certain other toys such as Barbie dolls.

The adoption of Council Regulation 519/94 inaugurated four years of continuous lobbying, negotiation, litigation, law reform, further litigation and further law reform.[74] The new EC quota regime for toys from China pleased no one, except perhaps the Commission which had brokered the compromise. The United Kingdom, which had opposed the measure in the vote in the Council of Ministers, brought an Article 173 action in the European Court of Justice to annul the Chinese toys quota.[75] It argued that the new Regulation introduced quotas on imports of Chinese toys into the UK market which previously was free of quotas. Subsequently the Council amended the challenged regulation.[76] However, this compromise itself was challenged in the Court by Spain,[77] one of the main initial proponents of quotas on imports of toys from China. Then the European subsidiary of Tyco Toys Inc[78] brought an action in the Court of First Instance to annul the toy quota and to obtain compensation for injury.[79]

The challenge by the United Kingdom to the Chinese toys quota[80] has been ascribed to pressure brought on the UK Government by the largest umbrella trade association,

[72] See F Snyder, *International Trade and Customs Law of the European Union* (London, Butterworths, 1998), 190–202.

[73] *Agence Europe*, no 6272, Wednesday, 13 July 1994, 9.

[74] For further details, see F Snyder, 'Judicial Review in the Age of Globalization: Chinese Toys in the European Court of Justice' in D O'Keefe and A Bavasso (eds), *Liber Amicorum for Gordon Slynn: Judicial Review in European Law* (London, Chancery, 2000) 651.

[75] Case C-150/94 *United Kingdom of Great Britain and Northern Ireland v Council of the European Union* [1998] ECR I-7235.

[76] Council Regulation 1921/94 amending Council Regulation (EC) 519/94 on common rules for imports from certain third countries [1994] OJ L198/1. See also *Agence Europe*, no 6277, Wednesday, 20 July 1994, 13.

[77] Case C-284/94 *Kingdom of Spain v Council of the European Union* [1998] ECR I-7309. The Council was supported by the Commission.

[78] Tyco's trade names include Dr Dreadful, Fashion Magic, Kitchen Littles Cookware, Magna Doodle, Matchbox and View-Master. See its Internet website http://www.matchboxtoys.com. As of February 1999, Tyco Preschool was a Mattel company. See the Internet website of Toy Manufacturers of America at http://www.toy-tma.com/MEMBER/.

[79] Case T-268/94 *Tyco Toys (UK) Ltd and Others v Commission and Council* [1994] OJ C254/14; see also *Agence Europe*, no 6317, Saturday, 17 September 1994, 13. As of 20 April 1999, this case was still pending, but a hearing was expected to be held soon, according to the services of the European Court of Justice. I am grateful to Emir Lawless of the EUI Library for this information. By May 1999, however, the case had been abandoned: interviews in the European Commission.

[80] Case C-150/94 *United Kingdom of Great Britain and Northern Ireland v Council of the European Union* [1998] ECR I-7235.

Toy Manufacturers of Europe (TME). The TME was formed as a political lobbying group in the early 1990s. It brought together European toy manufacturers, except those in France and Spain, together with German producers of plastic toys, which then were grouped instead in a separate organisation, the European Federation of Toy Industries (EFTI), established in 1967.[81] The members of TME accounted for approximately 80 per cent of toy manufacturers and distributors operating in Europe. It was dominated by American toy multinationals, together with the Danish firm Lego and the Japanese firm Bandai. Its members did not manufacture toys in Europe. Their main interest lay in maintaining open markets throughout the world, including the EU, for their main source of production, namely China.[82] They were also concerned to use the EU market and EU law effectively in their strategies for restructuring the international toy sector and ensuring the integration of the EU market into the global commodity chain. The TME had opposed the imposition of quotas from the outset. Its chair, Peter Waterman, considered that the toy industry was being used as a pawn in the debate concerning the accession of China to the WTO.[83] Hong Kong firms accounted for the majority of those affected by the EC toys quota, but they could not seek the help of the Hong Kong Government, at least directly, because their factories were located in China.[84] Toy multinationals therefore lobbied in Europe through the trade association.

Lobbying and litigation were two facets of the same political and legal strategy. They paid off in a series of continual legislative reforms, six in total during a brief four-year period. The first occurred when, five weeks after the UK brought its case, the Commission proposed an increase in the quota, largely because of pressure from the TME.[85] The Member States, however, did not agree.[86] Germany, the UK, The Netherlands and Ireland sought a global solution to the Chinese quota problem, embracing not only toys but also textiles and other products. France, Spain, Portugal and Greece rejected the Commission proposal, both in itself and as a dangerous precedent; they claimed that it favoured traders as against manufacturers. This split between northern and southern countries, between free trade and protectionism, reflected the different Member States' domestic institutional and economic structures.[87] To break the logjam, the Council adopted a compromise solution.[88] It embraced only the toy sector, but it raised the quota for certain toys from China by almost 30 per cent for the period from 15 March to 31 December 1994.[89] This compromise itself, however, provoked further litigation by Spain[90] and the European subsidiary of Tyco Toys Inc.[91]

[81] Known in French as the Fédération Européenne des Industries du Jouet (FEIJ) and in Spanish as the Federacion Europea del Juguete (FEJ). I am grateful to Mr Salvador Miro Sanjuan, President of the Asociacion Española de Fabricantes de Juguetes (AEFJ), for this information.

[82] Newton and Tse, above n 20, at 156.

[83] *Agence Europe*, no 6824, 3 October, 1996, 5.

[84] Cf Newton and Tse, above n 20, at 159.

[85] *Agence Europe*, no 6272, Wednesday, 13 July 1994, 9. Newton and Tse, above n 20, at 159.

[86] *Agence Europe*, no 6275, Saturday, 16 July 1994, 14. For the contrasting viewpoint of traders associations, see *Agence Europe*, no 6289, Saturday, 6 August 1994, 8.

[87] Cf C Garcia Molyneux, *Domestic Structures and International Trade: The Unfair Trade Instruments of the United States and the European Union* (Oxford, Hart Publishing, 2000).

[88] Council Regulation 1921/94 amending Council Regulation 519/94 on common rules for imports from certain third countries [1994] OJ L198/1. See also *Agence Europe*, no 6277, Wednesday, 20 July 1994, 13.

[89] *Ibid*, Art. 1. The toys in question were those falling within Code HS/CN 9503 41 (stuffed toys representing animals or non-human creatures), such as Furbies.

[90] Case C-284/94 *Kingdom of Spain v Council of the European Union* [1998] ECR I-7309. The Council was supported by the Commission.

[91] Case T-268/94 *Tyco Toys (UK) Ltd and Others v Commission and Council* [1994] OJ C254/14, subsequently withdrawn.

The second legislative reform occurred in March 1995, when the Council agreed to raise the toy quota for the year starting 1 January 1995.[92] This was part of a more general revision of quotas on imports from China, in which quotas for some goods were abolished, others increased and others maintained at the then existing level. The quotas for toys were increased by 36.8 per cent for stuffed toys (ECU 274,764,243 for HS/CN code 9503 41), 58.3 per cent for animals (ECU 132,767,177 for HS/CN 9503 49) and 27.8 per cent for other toys (ECU 649,465,212 for HS/CN 90).[93] This included the amounts required to take account of the accession to the EU of Austria, Finland and Sweden. Note that dolls were still free of quotas.

The legislative tinkering continued. In April 1996 the Council adopted a third revision, to take effect as of 1 January 1996.[94] This measure was part of a more general revision of imports on goods from China. Like its predecessor, it benefited importers, distributors and processors of Chinese products, met to some extent the demands of the Chinese Government and conferred new advantages on firms by removing quotas in certain markets. While it did not increase the total quota amount for toys, it fused the three existing quotas into one. This introduced greater flexibility in the implementation of the quotas.[95] Hence it empowered certain firms, notably importers, and increased the free play of the market, while maintaining the overall quota. Arguably, it helped industry to meet changes in consumer demand. As of October 1996 the Tyco Preschool company factory in China was operating six days a week to meet weekly shipments of Tickle Me Elmo, producing 50,000 Elmos a week to sell 1 million by Christmas Eve. [96] It planned to ship 1 million dolls from its five factories in China.[97] In 1997 it imported a supply of 300,000 Sing & Snore Earnie dolls from China by plane instead of container ship, to get them into stores more quickly for the Christmas season.[98]

Fusion of the three quotas into one also created a greater space for restructuring of the toy sector. The EU toy industry at the time was concentrated geographically in the Jura (France), Milan (Italy), Attica (Greece) and Alicante (Spain). These regions accounted for 50 to 60 per cent of toy production in their respective countries, and included both manufacturers and auxiliary industries. The industry comprised about 2,600 firms, producing a great variety of toys, and employing just under 100,000 workers, with only 15 firms having more than 500 employees.[99] Their prices were higher than those of toys from China, quite apart from the possibility of producing counterfeit toys anywhere with computer-assigned design programs.[100] These small EU firms were thus faced with international competition from other producers, as well as being squeezed by the dominant international buyers who controlled the major brands and had easy access to large retailers. They were gradually regrouping and restructuring. The

[92] Council Regulation 538/95 amending Regulation 519/94 on common rules for imports from certain third countries, Art 1, Annex II [1995] OJ L55/1.

[93] Percentage increases are taken from Newton and Tse, above n 20, at 161.

[94] Council Regulation 752/96 amending Annexes II and III of Regulation 519/94 on common rules for imports from certain third countries, art 1 [1996] OJ L103/1.

[95] See *ibid*, preamble, sixth recital.

[96] *USA Today*, Wednesday, 11 December 1996.

[97] D Hoye, 'Tickle-Me Elmo Hottest Yule Toy', *The Arizona Republic*, Wednesday, 4 December 1996.

[98] M Matzer, 'Advertising and Marketing: Holiday '97', *The Los Angeles Times*, Thursday, December 1997, at 4.

[99] Commission of the European Communities, 'Report from the Commission to the Council on the surveillance measures and quantitative quotas applicable to certain non-textile products originating in the People's Republic of China', COM(95)614 final, Brussels, 6.12.95, 41.

[100] *Ibid*, at 44–45.

Commission's original proposal for fusing the three quotas was intended partly to encourage these economic and social processes, even though the Commission recognised that its legislative proposals were based on very incomplete information.[101] As a result, the large trade associations in the sector supported the Commission's proposals.

The Commission took a further step towards an open market in May 1996, when it revised the procedures for allocating quota amounts.[102] It reduced the allocations under import licences for traditional importers by specified percentages, applied to a base equal to average imports for 1992 and 1994.[103] Licence applications by non-traditional importers were to be met in full within the overall quota limits.[104] In addition, a licence issued for a certain category of toys could also be used for the other categories.[105] This revision, as the previous reforms, moved EC law closer to meeting the interests of multinational toy buyers and manufacturers, thus gradually undoing the 1994 compromise. It did so, however, not by increasing or otherwise modifying the quotas themselves, but rather by changing the way they were administered. In particular, it opened more space for new entrants to the import market, while at the same time it increased the flexibility of the administration of licences. In other words, it lowered barriers to entry and the costs of importation, notably for large firms.

In September 1996, litigation in the European Court of Justice bore its first fruit. The Advocate-General gave his Opinion jointly in the two cases brought separately by the UK and Spain. He proposed that the Court should uphold the policy-making and legislative discretion of the Council, and thus reject the claims by the UK and Spain for the annulment of EC legislation. This Opinion was taken by many in the toy sector as a clear signal that the actions brought by the two governments against the Community legislator would ultimately be rejected. At least some academic commentators shared this view.[106] Such a perception neglected the fact that the Advocate-General's Opinion did not state the law, neither was it legally binding on the Court. It captures nicely, however, the real political and symbolic significance of such Opinions, in which, rightly or wrongly, the Advocate-General is often seen to be speaking not merely for the public but also for the Court.

Despite its lack of legal force, the Advocate-General's Opinion would seem to have had a decisive impact on further reform of the quota legislation. It encouraged, if not stimulated, the Member States to adjust further the basic 1994 legislation. The Council, the Community legislator, enacted a subsequent reform in mid-1997.[107]

[101] *Ibid*, at 47. In preparing the Report the Commission sollicited information from a wide variety of producers, importers and traders, either directly or through their trade associations. The response, however, was 'incomplete and rather unsatisfactory': *ibid*, at 3. Nearly all the investigated sectors were composed of numerous small and medium-sized enterprises, 'of which a significant proportion are not even known by the relevant national federations': *ibid*, at 3. Of the importers, the Toy Manufacturers of Europe (TME), Toys Traders of Europe (TTE), the Hong Kong Toys Council, the Japan Toy Association and John Lewis Partnership (UK) submitted remarks: see *ibid*, 45–46.

[102] Commission Regulation 899/96 establishing the quantities to be allocated to importers from the Community quantitative quotas redistributed by Regulation 612/96 [1996] OJ L121/8.

[103] *Ibid*, Art 1 and Annex I.

[104] *Ibid*, Art 3 and Annex III.

[105] *Ibid*, Annex I, note 3, and Annex III, note 2.

[106] Newton and Tse, above n 20, at 161. Doubtless the plaintiff governments and the large trade associations were more aware of the legal status of such an opinion and its relation to the eventual judgment by the ECJ. Small businesses, however, are often much less aware of these crucial legal and institutional distinctions.

[107] Council Regulation 847/97 amending Annexes II and III to Regulation 519/94 on common rules for imports from certain third countries [1997] OJ L122/1.

While maintaining the same overall quota amount for toys, it excluded toy parts and accessories from the quota. It placed these parts and accessories, as well as certain other categories of toys,[108] under Community surveillance, first for the period from publication of the measure on 14 May 1997 until 31 December 1997,[109] and then for the period from 1 January 1998.[110] These changes followed the main conclusions of the Commission's 1996 annual report.[111] The latter, in turn, presented a somewhat simplified version of the recommendations of what were then the two main trade associations, the TME acting on behalf of importers and the Fédération Européenne des Industries du Jouet on behalf of producers. Together these trade associations represented, in the Commission's view, 'almost the entire European toy industry'.[112] The legislative reforms testified to the close coordination between firms, both independently and through trade associations, on the one hand, and Member States and EC institutions, on the other hand. This coordination, in turn, ensured that the adjustments in the law were in step with the changing interests of the EU toy sector, which was then in the process of restructuring within the EU market and of adapting to the new challenges posed by the international market.

The major trade associations had in fact proposed the liberalisation of imports of only 'the components of toys which were meant to be subject to further industrial transformation'.[113] Articulated for political and other reasons in terms of stimulating employment by local assembly and similar processes, this proposal embodied a very clear recognition of the internationalisation of the toy industry and the role of the EU producers in these increasingly global networks. EU producers were to occupy a place in these new networks that was very similar to that of producers in China, except that Chinese factories were engaged in original equipment manufacturing whereas EU producers would involved merely in the final (though industrial) transformation of the toys, albeit with the possibility in some instances of moving into own brand manufacturing. This proposal signaled the eventual transformation of many small and medium-sized EU firms, and to that extent the nation States in which they were situated, into flexible, more precarious world factory sites, dependent, as were Chinese toy factories and their Hong Kong owners, on the multinational firms that occupied the dominant positions and were the key players in the global toy commodity chain. It also implied potentially a shift in legal position. The law governing imports would no longer be the EC quota regulations but rather EC customs regulations on inward processing and potentially (if China were to accept the relevant annexes) the 1973 Kyoto International Convention on the Simplification and Harmonization of Customs Procedures.[114] To return to our model of the international toy commodity

[108] HS/CN code 9503 30 (Other construction sets and construction toys of wood, plastic or other materials).

[109] Council Regulation 847/97, above n 108, Art 1, Annexes I and II.

[110] *Ibid*, Art 2, Annexes III and IV.

[111] Commission of the European Communities, '2nd Report from the Commission to the Council on the surveillance measures and quantitative quotas applicable to certain non-textile products originating in the People's Republic of China', COM(97)11 final, Brussels, 29.1.97, at 45.

[112] *Ibid*, 38.

[113] Quoted in *ibid*, at 38.

[114] [1975] OJ L100/2; Cmnd 5938. The most convenient source is the Internet edition: World Customs Organization, *Handbook of the International Convention on the Simplification and Harmonization of Customs Procedures* (Kyoto, 18 May 1973), 1st edn October 1975, Amending Supplement No 13, January 1993. In June 1999 the 1973 Kyoto Convention was revised, but the revised Convention has not yet been ratified by all parties: see http://www.wcoomd.org/frmpublic.htm. Also available at: http://www.wcoomd.org/home_wco_topics_pfoverviewboxes_tools_and_instruments_pfconventions_instruments.htm], last accessed 4 March 2010.

chain, the legal reforms thus fostered a transformation of the number of production units, an increase in their geographic dispersal, and potentially changes in the property and other arrangements linking various parts of the chain.

A sixth reform followed soon afterwards. Less than a month after the 1997 reform took effect,[115] the Council once again adopted a further regulation.[116] It abolished entirely, with effect as of 1 January 1998, the quotas of toys falling within HS/CN codes 9503 41, 9503 49 and 9503 90.[117] It subjected these products (and continued to subject toys of HS/CN code 9503 30) to prior Community surveillance to ensure adequate monitoring of the volume and prices of imports.[118]

This final step in our saga of legislative reform occurred in the context of—and contributed to—the transformation of the EU toy industry. By definition, therefore, it also affected the gradual restructuring of the global toy commodity chain, including factories in China. By 1996 the EU toy industry had already adapted its production structures and improved production quality to such an extent that, at least from the standpoint of the Commission and most if not all national governments, import quotas were no longer necessary.[119] The EU's restructured toy enterprises imported items that were no longer produced in Europe. As the Commission noted,

> [m]ost manufacturers in Europe are also becoming importers of some items which may be necessary for them to keep their market share both in the EU and on export markets.[120]

EU producers were able to compete in foreign markets: exports of European toys outside the EU grew by a record 16.8 per cent in 1996, while imports in the same year rose by only 3 per cent.[121] The European Commission ascribed this successful adaptation to law. In its view, the temporary protection assured to EU industry by Community quotas permitted the necessary restructuring.[122] It thus also facilitated the redefinition of the role of these EU firms in the global commodity chain.

These changes in the organisation of production and marketing were reflected in the evolution of the organisation of political representation in the EU toy sector. The first major peak association in the EU toy sector was the European Federation of Toy Industries (EFTI), founded in 1967.[123] The EFTI comprised the national associations of the UK, France, The Netherlands, Germany, Italy, Greece and Spain. In the early 1990s the UK national association, the British Toy Manufacturers Association (BTMA), together with the major multinational toy companies (Hasbro, Mattel, Lego, Tomy, Bandai, etc) founded the European Federation of Toy Manufacturers (TME). Greece and Italy also joined the TME, as did the German national association composed of larger companies. However, France, and Spain, and German manufacturers of plastic toys remained in the EFTI. Subsequently, the French and Spanish assoca-

[115] It took effect on the date of publication, 14 May 1997: Council Regulation 847/97, above n 108 art 3.

[116] Council Regulation 1138/98 amending Annexes II and III of Regulation 519/94 on common rules for imports from certain third countries [1998] OJ L159/1.

[117] *Ibid*, art 1 and Annex I.

[118] *Ibid*, art 1 and Annex II.

[119] See Commission of the European Communities, '3rd Report from the Commission on the quantitative quotas and surveillance measures applicable to certain non-textile products originating in the People's Republic of China', COM(1998)128 final, Brussels, 9.3.1998, especially 26–29, 35.

[120] *Ibid*, at 28.

[121] *Ibid*, at 26.

[122] *Ibid*, 27–28.

[123] See n 81 above and accompanying text.

tions began negotiations with the TME to form a single peak association. In 1997, these negotiations culminated in the merger of the TME and the EFTI [124] to form Toy Industries of Europe (TIE). The TIE had essentially the same structure as the TME, with large firms having a major role, but also with representation of industrial unions, except for those of Germany which remained divided. Subsequently, the Greek association and the small associations of the Nordic countries also jointed the TIE.[125] As of February 1999, the co-presidency of TIE was held by the United Kingdom and Spain. The economic changes in the EU toy sector viewed as part of the global commodity chain thus were mirrored, more or less directly, in terms of industrial associations and political representation.

From the time of its formation TIE strongly supported the immediate and total abolition of quotas on toys. In its view, quotas represented an administrative burden, especially for small businesses.[126] In any event they failed to restrict toy imports from China. Rephrasing this view, one might say that quotas were an obstacle to EU firms which sourced partly finished products from abroad, and thus prevented the successful operation of newly articulated global networks. In summary, both the European Commission and the main European trade association agreed by 1997 that toys from China should no longer be subject to quotas. Instead they should be subject merely to surveillance, requiring only an import licence.[127]

The abolition of quotas was, according to the preamble of the 1998 Regulation, neither inconsistent with the objective of taking account of the various interests in play nor liable to disrupt the Community market.[128] In fact, it was the culmination of more than a decade of conflict between Member States and between competing firms. It also represented the temporary conclusion of diverse attempts by EU institutions to manage conflicting interests. These conflicts were inherent in the process of market building and market management in the European Union, partly because of the changes in the way in which the EU market was integrated into the international toy commodity chain. They began with the reform and opening-up of China starting in December 1978, the subsequent restructuring of the international toy industry, and the creation of new economic networks and the thin globalisation of this sector of the Chinese economy. Changes occurred in the domestic and international interests in the sector, and the lines between the domestic and the international were not merely blurred but actually reconfigured. These changes were in turn expressed to some extent in legislative form. Just as the 1994 compromise legislation expressed the balance of interests at the time, changes in the structure of interests led to demands for changes in the law. The gradual legal reforms not only represented these new, changing configurations of

124 According to the Commission Report, note 119 above, it represented national producers, not international buyers. The precise reasons for the merger of EFTI and TME remain unclear to me. One possibility was that, despite quotas, the EFTI alone was too weak to be effective. Another is that Spanish and French producers went international: they linked up successfully with China, HK or other producer firms. A third possibility is that the members of EFTI were integrated in the global commodity chain on some other terms. A fourth, not inconsistent possibility is that the merger resulted from increased US FDI in the toy sector in Spain and France.

125 I am grateful to Mr Salvador Miro Sanjuan, President of the AEFJ, for this information.

126 As to 1996, the EU had 2,000 companies in the toys and games sectors, employing over 100,000 people, of which 55,000 worked in indirect employment: Commission Report, note 120 above, 27.

127 On surveillance, see F Snyder, note 72 above 154, 157.

128 Cf preamble, second and third recitals of Council Regulation 1138/98 amending Annexes II and III of Regulation 519/94 on common rules for imports from certain third countries [1998] OJ L159/1.

interests. They also helped to crystallise and perhaps even to create new interests, especially with regard to the number and nature of units of production.[129]

C. Geographic Concentration or Dispersal

The second question to be addressed concerns *geographic concentration or dispersal*. What is the degree of geographic spread of the units in a specific segment? In other words, are the units in a specific box geographically concentrated, or are they dispersed? For example, are the provision of finance, marketing and retailing geographically concentrated while production is dispersed? Is the prevailing geographic pattern influenced by the sites of global legal pluralism and, if so, how? For example, what incentives do different institutions, norms and processes provide for either concentration or dispersal of the different sites? Do these institutions, norms and processes play a role in the extent to which segments shift from the core to the periphery of the world economy, assuming that, as Hopkins and Wallerstein argue, a box is likely to be relatively geographically concentrated in the core but dispersed on the periphery?

We have already seen that invention, finance, marketing and retailing in the international toy industry are concentrated: the first in the USA, the second and third in the USA and Hong Kong, and the last, so far as control is concerned, in the USA and to lesser extent Europe and Japan. Production has until recently tended to be concentrated mainly in Asia, though it could potentially be much more dispersed.

The geographical separation of production from finance, marketing and retailing is encouraged by international norms concerning the customs operations known in the EU as inward processing and outward processing.[130] It is no exaggeration to describe the existence and increased use of these customs rules as the legal basis for what has been called 'the new international division of labour'.[131]

The overarching international legal framework is provided by the International Convention on the Simplification and Harmonization of Customs Procedures, a veritable international customs code. It was first signed at Kyoto on 18 May 1973 and entered in force on 25 September 1974.[132] An updated version was adopted on 25 June 1999 but has not yet been ratified by all parties.[133] The discussion here is concerned with the 1973 Convention, because it was the normative framework at the time of the empirical research reported in this chapter. The Kyoto Convention is the fruit of

[129] Such a transformation is not unique to the EU. Chinese producers of traditional wooden and other toys are being ousted by international toy companies, such as Lego: cf Turner, 'The Fading Tradition of Tang the Toymaker', *International Herald Tribune*, Friday, 8 January 1999, at 8. For an account of the heterogeneity of toy producers in China, see also the short story by Zhang Xin, 'Where Angels Dare to Tread', trans JA Mathews, in *Contemporary Chinese Women Writers VI: Four Novellas by Zhang Xin* (Plymouth, MI, USA, Panda Books and Beijing, China, Chinese Literature Press, 1998) 97.

[130] On EU law at the time, see F Snyder, above n 72, 83–103.

[131] For case studies from an economic standpoint, see F Froebel, J Heinrichs and O Kreye, *The New International Division of Labour: Structural Unemployment in Industrialised Countries and Industrialisation in Developing Countries* (trans P Burgress) (Cambridge, Cambridge University Press; and Paris, Editions de la Maison des Sciences de l'Homme, 1980).

[132] [1975] OJ L100/2; Cmnd 5938.

[133] The full text is available on the Internet homepage of the World Customs Organisation at http://www.wcoomd.org.

the Customs Cooperation Council (CCC), founded in 1952.[134] Since 1994, the CCC has been known as the World Customs Organisation (WCO). The WCO now oversees the implementation of the Kyoto Convention.[135] Its supervisory functions began with the establishment of the CCC, whose initial *raison d'être* was partly to supervise the application and interpretation of the customs classification system known as either the Brussels Tariff Nomenclature (BTN) or the Customs Cooperation Council Nomenclature.[136]

The WCO as of 1999 had 150 members. The EC Member States have participated since the beginning. However, membership is limited to States and, as a customs union, the EC formally has only observer status, even though the European Court of Justice has taken the view that the Community has replaced the Member States in commitments arising from the Convention.[137] The US joined the CCC in 1970.[138] Hong Kong and China are also members.

The WCO, which is based in Brussels, is virtually the sole international body concerned with the harmonisation of technical customs rules and practices. As currently constituted, its highest body is a Council, composed of the Directors-General of Customs from all Members. The Council is assisted by a Finance Committee of 17 Members and a Policy Commission of 24 Members. In addition, Technical Committees work in the areas of nomenclature and classification, valuation, customs technique and origin. Council bodies at all levels are helped by a General Secretariat, headed by a Secretary-General, assisted by a Deputy Secretary-General and three Directors.[139]

[134] 22 UST 320, TIAS No 7063, 157 UNTS 129. After World War II various European governments, drawing on work previously accomplished under the auspices of the League of Nations, formed in Brussels a European Customs Union Study Group, including a Customs Committee. This led in turn to the Convention establishing a Customs Cooperation Council; the Convention was signed in Brussels on 15 December 1950 and entered into force on 4 November 1952.

[135] The following three paragraphs are based on the WCO Internet home page at http://www.wcoomd.org; E McGovern, *International Trade Regulation: GATT, the United States and the European Community*, 2nd edn (Exeter, Globefield Press, 1986), 45–47, 150–51; JH Jackson, WJ Davey and AO Sykes, *Legal Problems of International Economic Relations: Cases, Materials and Text on the National and International Regulation of Transnational Economic Relations*, 3rd edn (St Paul, Minn, West Publishing Company, 1995), 394; D Lasok, *The Trade and Customs Law of the European Union*, 3rd edn (London, Kluwer, 1998) 237–38, 277–78; and F Snyder, above n 72, 3–9.

[136] The Nomenclature was adopted by the EC Member States and all other major GATT members except the United States and Canada.

[137] Case 38/75 *Nederlandse Spoorwegen v Inspecteur der Invoerrechten en Accijnzen* [1975] ECR 1439. At the time, the Community view was expressed either by the Commission or the Member State holding the Presidency of the Council of Ministers.

[138] Though without adopting the Nomenclature. Together with the EC Member States and other countries, the US participated in the development by the CCC of a new classification system, the Harmonized Commodity Description and Coding System (the Harmonized System), which entered into force on 1 January 1988: see the International Convention on the Harmonized Commodity Description and Coding System, done at Brussels on 14 June 1983, and the Protocol thereto, done at Brussels on 24 June 1986, [1987] OJ L198/3.1035 UNTS 3; KAV 2260. The EC is a party to the International Convention on the Harmonized Commodity Description and Coding System: see Council Decision 87/369 concerning the conclusion of the International Convention on the Harmonized Commodity Description and Coding System and of the Procotol of Amendment thereto [1987] OJ L198/1. Articles 28 and 113 EC (the Amsterdam Treaty has renumbered as Article 26 and Article 133) are the legal bases for the Council's power to conclude the Convention: see Case 165/87 *Commission of the European Communities v Council of the European Communities* [1988] ECR 5545. The EC Combined Nomenclature, which is part of the Common Customs Tariff, follows closely the structure of the Harmonized System. The US adopted the Harmonized System with effect as of 1 January 1989. General similar remarks apply to the 1950 Valuation Convention.

[139] For further details, including a description of the committees, see the WCO website at http://www.wcoomd.org.

The tasks of the WCO are four-fold.[140] First, it drafts and promotes new agreements, mainly concerning customs techniques. Secondly, it makes recommendations to ensure uniform interpretation and application of its existing conventions, notably with regard to the Convention establishing a Customs Cooperation Council,[141] the Nomenclature Convention[142] and the Valuation Convention.[143] The legal status of these recommendations is ambiguous, and probably not very important from the practical standpoint, but it has been suggested that their acceptance by contracting parties 'carries with it an obligation not to arbitrarily resile from the recommendations'.[144] Thirdly, the WCO acts as a conciliator in disputes between contracting parties. Fourthly, it provides information and advice to governments in its fields of activity.

The Kyoto Convention is an unusual international agreement. As mentioned above, here I am concerned with the 1973 Convention, since the 1999 revised Convention has not yet been ratified by all Members.[145] One commentator has described it as 'the equivalent of a whole series of agreements'.[146] The Convention consists of two Parts. Part I contains the Convention itself, including:

a) text and commentary;
b) provisions concerning entry into force;
c) obligations of the contracting parties as regards notification; and
d) provisions concerning extensions.

Part II comprises numerous annexes, including, for example, Annex E.6 concerning temporary admission for inward processing, Annex E.8 concerning temporary exportation for outward processing, and Annex F.1 concerning free zones. The number of annexes is not fixed once-and-for-all. Existing annexes may be amended and new annexes may be added; this was the work of the Council's Permanent Technical Committee.[147]

These annexes contain the basic substantive rules. Each annex usually consists of an introductory summary, definitions of terms, standards, recommended practices and notes. According to the terms of the Convention,[148] standards are those provisions the general application of which is recognised as necessary for the achievement of harmonisation and simplification of customs procedures. Recommended practices are those provisions which are recognised as constituting progress toward the harmonisation and the simplication of customs procedures, the widest possible application of which is considered to be desirable. Notes indicate some of the possible courses of action to be followed in applying the standard or recommended practice concerned.

[140] This paragraph is based on the WCO website at http://www.wcoomd.org and McGovern, above n 135, at 45–48.

[141] Convention establishing a Customs Cooperation Council, Brussels, 15 December 1950, in force 4 November 1952: 157 UNTS 129; TIAS 7063; Cmnd 9232; I Peaslee 374.

[142] International Convention on the Harmonized Commodity Description and Coding System, above n 137.

[143] Convention on the Valuation of Goods for Customs Purposes, Brussels, 15 December 1950, in force 28 July 1953: 171 UNTS 305; Cmd 9233.

[144] McGovern, above n 135, at 48.

[145] References to the Kyoto Convention in the following paragraphs are therefore to the 1973 Convention. The 1999 revised Convention is broadly similar in structure but not identical. The 1999 Convention contains slightly different annexes and adds a new Specific Annex H on Offences.

[146] McGovern, above n 135, at 47.

[147] Kyoto Convention, Art 6.

[148] *Ibid*, Art 4.

The Convention is open to signature by any State Member of the Council and any State Member of the United Nations or its specialised agencies.[149] A State may become a contracting party by signing the Convention without instrument of ratification, by depositing an instrument of ratification after signing it subject to ratification, or by acceding to it.[150] A State which does so must specify which annexes it accepts, and is required to accept at least one annex.[151] A contracting party which accepts an annex is deemed to accept all the standards and recommended practices in it, unless it enters reservations in respect of particular standards or recommended practices, stating the differences between its national legislative provisions and the provisions of the standards or recommended practices in question.[152] States are not permitted to enter reservations against definitions. The Convention does not preclude the application of prohibitions or restrictions imposed under national legislation.[153] At least once every three years, each contracting party bound by an annex is required to review the standards and recommended practices against which it has entered reservations and notify the Secretary-General of the Customs Cooperation Council (now the WCO) of the results of the review.[154]

The 1973 Kyoto Convention on the Simplification and Harmonisation of Customs Procedures had approximately 30 contracting parties; the number has increased to 114 for the 1999 revised Convention. For the present purposes, let us focus on the EC, its Member States, the USA and China in relation to the 1973 Convention, Annex E.6 on inward processing,[155] Annex E.8 on outward processing[156] and Annex F.1 on free zones.[157] As of 1 January 1993, all 15 EC Member States had ratified the Convention, but not all had accepted all of these three annexes.[158] The EC was a contracting party, since a customs union was entitled to be a contracting party if its Member States are also parties. The EC had taken advantage of this provision but it does not have the right to vote.[159] The Convention entered into force for the EC on 26 September 1974. The EC had accepted Annexes E.6, E.8 and F.1; The United States had ratified the Convention and had accepted Annex E.8 on outward processing and Annex F.1 on free zones, but not Annex E.6 on inward processing. China had ratified the Convention

[149] *Ibid*, Art 11(1).

[150] *Ibid*, Art 11(2).

[151] *Ibid*, Art 11(4).

[152] *Ibid*, Art 5(1).

[153] *Ibid*, Art 3. This refers only to provisions of general application enacted either by the legislature or the executive and effective at the national level. However, it includes not only the standard exceptions but also restrictions imposed on economic or any other grounds: see the Commentary on Chapter II, Art 3.

[154] *Ibid*, Art 5(2).

[155] Annex E.6 of the Convention concerns temporary admission for inward processing. It was adopted by the Permanent Technical Committee at its 81st/82nd sessions in October 1973. Subsequently, at its 83rd/84th sessions in March 1974, the Committee added a Note to Recommended Practice 43 (compensating products, or setting-off with equivalent goods). This Annex was incorporated into the Kyoto Convention by decision of the Council at its 43rd/44th Sessions held in Brussels on 10 June 1974. It entered into force on 6 December 1977, and, subject to certain reservations, it entered into force for the EEC on the same date.

[156] Annex E.8 deals with temporary exportation for outward processing. It entered into force for the EEC, with certain reservations, on 20 April 1978.

[157] Annex F.1 concerning free zones entered into force for the EEC on 19 March 1979.

[158] Annex E.6 on inward processing has been accepted by all EC Member States except Greece, Luxembourg, Portugal and Sweden. Annex E.8 on outward processing has been accepted by Denmark, France, Germany, Ireland, Italy, The Netherlands, Spain and the United Kingdom, but not by Austria, Belgium, Finland, Greece, Luxembourg, Portugal and Sweden. Annex F.1 on free zones has been accepted by Austria, Denmark, Finland, France, Ireland, Italy, Luxembourg, The Netherlands, Portugal, Spain and the United Kingdom, but not by Belgium, Germany, Greece and Sweden.

[159] See Kyoto Convention, Art 11(7).

but had not accepted any of these three annexes. Chinese specialists at the time considered Chinese Special Economic Zones (SEZs) as 'not standardized yet, nor [. . .] generally recognised by international laws',[160] and the European Commission considered Chinese legislation concerning SEZs to be incompatible with the GATT.[161] It remains to be seen how the 1999 revised Convention will develop after it has been fully ratified.

These legal provisions have encouraged and facilitated the geographical separation of production from invention, distribution and marketing in the international commodity chain in toys. Since the early 1980s, however, Chinese legislation, both central and local, on SEZs has also had a direct influence on the concentration of production facilities.[162] Chinese laws on foreign direct investment (FDI) and labour are of special importance. Most toy factories in China are located in the Shenzhen SEZ. Shenzhen rules on foreign direct investment (FDI) provide for Chinese–foreign joint ventures, Chinese–foreign contractual joint ventures, wholly foreign-owned enterprises, international leasing, compensation trade, and processing and assembling with materials and parts from foreign suppliers.[163] Recently, however, the fact that labour costs in Shenzhen are higher than in the rest of Guangdong Province, due partly to law, has encouraged toy companies to establish outside the SEZ, though still in Guangdong.[164]

In fact, however, this part of south China belongs to a wider economic area which includes Hong Kong.[165] Toy factories enjoy very close links with entrepreneurs in Hong Kong, and often are part of Hong Kong companies. Production, distribution, quasi-political activities such as participation in trade associations, and often personal or family relations are closely intertwined.[166] Chinese companies, such as Early Light in the Shenzhen SEZ,[167] produce toys on outsourcing contracts for the worlds biggest toy companies, not only Mattel but also Hasbro, Fisher-Price and Ertl from the United States, and Bandai and Tomy from Japan. These contracts are often arranged and

160 See S Xiuping, C Wen and L Xiansheng, *New Progress in China's Special Economic Zones* (Beijing, Foreign Languages Press, 1997) 54.

161 See European Commission, market access database available at http://mkaccdb.eu.int/mkdb/chks.

162 See JD Park, *The Special Economic Zones of China and Their Impact on Its Economic Development* (Westport, Conn, Praeger, 1997).

163 For an introduction, see the Shenzhen SEZ Internet homepage at http://china-window.com/Shenzhen-w/shenzhen.html. On Chinese FDI law generally, see S Lubman, 'The Legal and Policy Environment for Foreign Direct Investment in China: Past Accomplishments, Future Uncertainties', ch 3 in *Publication 662: Private Investments Abroad* (New York, Mathew Bender & Co, 1998); PH Corne, *Foreign Investment in China: The Administrative Legal System* (Hong Kong, Hong Kong University Press, 1997). On European trade and investment in China, see R Strange, J Slater and L Wang (eds), *Trade and Investment in China: The European Experience* (London, Routledge, 1998).

164 Interviews, Guangzhou and Shenzhen. It was reported that as of 1996, the Barbie doll factories in China were the Meitei factory in Dongguan and the Zongmei toy factory in Nanhai, both in Guandgong Province but outside the Shenzhen SEZ: cf Tempest, 'Barbie and the World Economy', *Los Angeles Times World Report* (Special Section Produced in Cooperation with *The Korea Times*), Sunday, 13 October 1996, at 3. In 1998, 800 small toy factories closed in Dongguan: 'Chinese Toy Making', *The Economist*, 19 December 1998, 95 at 98. This did not include Barbie doll factories.

165 See W van Kemenade, *China, Hong Kong, Taiwan, Inc: The Dynamics of a New Empire* (New York, Alfred A Knopf Inc, 1997).

166 See, eg, J Smart and A Smart, 'Personal Relations and Divergent Economies: A Case Study of Hong Kong Investment in South China' (1991) 15 *International Journal of Urban and Regional Research* 216.

167 For a brief historical sketch, see 'The tycoon', *The Economist*, 19 December 1998, at 99. As of 1993, most of the 2,500 registered foreign-funded businesses in the Shenzhen SEZ were small processing and assembly operators from Hong Kong: see GT Crane, 'Reform and Retrenchment in China's Special Economic Zones', in Joint Economic Committee, Congress of the United States (ed), *China's Dilemma's in the 1990s: The Problems of Reforms, Modernization, and Interdependence* (Armonk, NY, ME Sharpe, 1993), 841 at 845.

managed by Hong Kong-based entrepreneurs who, in addition to their role as middlemen, sometimes run their own toy manufacturing company in China and are also prominent in the main Hong Kong sectoral trade association, the Hong Kong Toys Council.[168] More than half of China's toy production is re-exported through Hong Kong.[169] To the extent that power in the toy chain lies in Asia, it is largely still based in Hong Kong.[170] For this reason, as well as to preserve maximum flexibility in a highly innovative and rapidly changing market, the production of toys for the export market previously took place in wholly-owned subsidiaries rather than joint ventures.[171] Today, international companies such as Mattel usually do not own factories or suppliers, though there are exceptions, and they seek to control the quality and other characteristics of the product through standards and intellectual property rights.

D. Multiple Memberships

The third question involves *membership of one or more chains*. Is a segment located in more than one commodity chain? If so, how many? Do specific sites, including institutions, norms and processes, create a structure of incentives so that a particular segment tends to be inserted in more than one commodity chain? To what extent, and how, is this insertion of a particular segment in different commodity chains encouraged or facilitated by the law? What role do law and other types of norms play in the management of relations between the different commodity chains in which a particular segment is located?

Multiple memberships or the arrival into a segment of a new entrant from another commodity chain may often lead to conflicts. For example, Mantua, the celebrated maker of collectors' model electric trains, stemmed from a small manufacturer of electric motors for model boats founded in 1926 by John Tyler, the founder of Tyco Toys Inc. Mantua later merged with the Tyler Manufacturing Company, which was established by John Tyler to sell a new line of electric trains under the name of Tyco Toys. Subsequently it underwent two dramatic changes. First, in 1977, it split off from Tyco when new executives brought in by the company's largest shareholder, the Sara Lee Corporation, imported less expensive, less detailed model trains from Asia. This

168 As of October 1996, the chairman of the Hong Kong Toys Council was Edmund KS Young, executive vice-president of Perfekta Enterprises Ltd, a leading Hong Kong toy manufacturer: Rone Tempest, 'Barbie and the World Economy', *Los Angeles Times World Report*, Sunday, 13 October 1996, at 3. In January 1995, Mr Young was described as chairman of Perfekta and vice-chairman of the Hong Kong Toy Council: see *Journal of Commerce*, Friday, 13 January 1995. As of December 1998, the chairman was TS Wong, head of Jetta, a large toy maker in China: see 'Chinese Toy Making: Where the Furbies come from', *The Economist*, 19 December 1998, 95 at 99. See also Hong Kong Toys Council, Federation of Hong Kong Industries, Members Directory 1999 (Hong Kong Toys Council, 1999).

169 BBC Monitoring Service: Asia Pacific, 14 June 1995, cited in Newton and Tse, above n 20, at 154. See also Hong Kong Trade Development Council, *Practical Guide to Exporting Toys for Hong Kong Traders* (Hong Kong Trade Development Council, Research Department, March 1999).

170 In particular because of the location of branch offices, ownership of local intermediaries and the provision of services.

171 See Newton and Tse, above n 20, at 149–56; E Tsui, 'Marketing Strategies of the Toy Industry in Hong Kong', unpublished MBA dissertation, University of Hong Kong, Hong Kong, 1988. As of 1995, OEM, including products made in mainland China, accounted for 75%–80% of Hong Kong toy sales: see *Journal of Commerce*, Friday, 13 January 1995.

followed the election of a new president and director of Consolidated Foods, the parent company of Sara Lee, who, starting in the mid-1970s, oversaw the globalisation of the company and its early diversification.[172] Secondly, Mantua contined to produce very detailed historical model trains, but by 1997 much of its own manufacturing was also done in China. The number of its employees had shrunk from 400 during World War II to 25 in 1997.[173] The internationalisation of Mantua's own production and changes in its labour force reflected changes in toy production in Hong Kong and China.

A striking contemporary example of multiple memberships is the expansion of major toy companies into other related but potentially or actually distinct sectors, such as television, cinema and the Internet. Mattel, for instance, started in 1945 as a small California toy manufacturer. Its great success, the Barbie doll, was launched in 1959. By 1998 the Barbie doll accounted for 33 per cent of its sales, or a projected US $1.5 billion; preschool and infant toys, such as Fisher Price and Sesame Street, accounted for 33 per cent; and 'Wheels', including Hot Wheels, Matchbox and Disney Entertainment, accounted for another 33 per cent. Recently Mattel has expanded to more high-tech toys and e-commerce.[174] Another example is Tickle Me Elmo, heavily marketed during the 1996 Christmas season by Tyco Toys (since acquired by Mattel). This toy was invented by Ron Dubren of New York and Greg Hyman of Florida. Tyco, who, according to the inventors, recognised the key ingredient and packaging and marketing their product. For their work, the inventors obtained royalties of somewhat less than 5 per cent of the manufacturer's revenue. The largest share of the royalties went to Children's Television Workshop, which owned the licence.[175]

Indeed the major toy companies spread like a web and onto the Web. To lessen its dependence on a few powerful traditional retailers, Mattel linked up with the Internet retailer eToys Inc,[176] from Santa Monica, California. It announced a goal of direct-to-consumer sales of US $1 billion per year, including catalogues and Internet sales, some from Mattel's own website and some from online retailers such as eToys. In 1998 total toy retail sales were US $23 bn, with eToys accounting for only US $23.9 million. Now Toys 'R' Us is also developing Internet sales.[177] Sony recently unveiled robotic dogs, which can be trained either through remote control, or through a computer program.[178]

[172] See the history of the Sara Lee Corporation at http://www.saralee.com/history: http://www.saralee.com/AboutSaraLee/TheSaraLeeHeritage.aspx.

[173] Cf B Kent, 'Maintaining the Model Train Tradition in a Digital World', *The New York Times*, Sunday, 7 December 1997, at 6.

[174] See the outline history of Mattel in M Leibovich and S Stoughton, 'When keeping up isn't child's play; Mattel to acquire Learning Co as industry pursues digitally savvy children', *The Washington Post*, Tuesday, 15 December 1998, at D01.

[175] J Balog, 'The untold toy success story: Elmo's evolution is a surprise to those involved', *USA Today*, Wednesday, 11 December 1996, at 1B.

[176] The web page of eToys Inc is avaialable at http://www.etoys.com.

[177] Cf G Anders and L Bannon, 'Etoys to join web-retailer parade with IPO', *The Wall Street Journal*, Tuesday, 6 April 1999, at B1.

[178] See Agence France-Presse, 'No end of a dog's life for robot pets', *South China Morning Post*, Wednesday, 12 May 1999, at 10.

E. Property

The fourth question concerns *property arrangements*. What property-like arrangements (such as use, ownership, management, control) are associated with the units of a specific segment? Which sites of global legal pluralism are the most relevant to these arrangements? Which specific institutions, norms and processes are determinative with regard to the arrangements in a particular site? Why? If different property-like arrangements prevail among the various units in a segment, what institutions, norms and processes encourage or tolerate diversity? How is such diversity managed?

Intellectual property is crucial to the international toy industry. The importance of brand marketing in the global commodity chain in toys is illustrated by two examples of acquisitions by the leading buyer, Mattel. The first occurred in 1997, when Mattel bought Tyco Toys for US $755 million. According to Mattel, its sales mainly to girls could be complemented by Tyco's 'boy-oriented' products. Previously Mattel led the toy industry in overall sales, and its acquistion of Tyco, previously in third place, gave it a comfortable margin.[179] Mattel considered that its strength lay in brand-building, and that Tyco was under-marketed around the world. Only a quarter of Tyco's sales were then generated outside the United States.[180] As Mattel's then chairman John W Amerman stated, 'The main attraction is Tyco has brands that we can take around the world.' Tyco's Matchbox toys were weaker in the USA than elsewhere, and its Sesame Street toys were beginning to be strong in China. Mattel's aim, according to its then president-to-be Jill Bared, was to turn these products into global power brands.[181] Mattel's second important recent acquistion occurred in 1998, when it announced its plan to buy Pleasant Co, the USA's second largest doll maker, for US $700 million. Mattel's then and current President and Chief Executive Jill Bared announced that 'We have acquired probably one of the blue-chip girls' toy brands of all time'.[182]

Both purchases, as well as its earlier acquisition of Fisher-Price, were consistent with Mattel's strategy of buying companies that were strong in the US domestic market but weak elsewhere. As securities analyst Margaret Whitfield of Tucker Anthony Inc in New York said, 'Mattel has always been looking for strong domestic brands that it can leverage through its global distribution network.' Mattel's aim, in her view, was to increase international sales to more than half of all company sales in an effort to cash in on foreign markets that contain 97 per cent of the world's children.[183] In other words—China.

In order to protect their monopoly over brands, international buyers have brought a number of intellectual property cases in Hong Kong courts. For example, Mattel, the manufacturer of Barbie dolls, sued Tonka Corporation in the Hong Kong High Court in 1991 for infringement of copyright. It alleged that the defendant's Miss America dolls copied the Barbie doll's head sculpture and that its packaging infringed registered

[179] See the Mattel internet home page at http://www.snc.edu/bsad/ba485/apr1998/group8/history.htm.

[180] J Madore, 'Mattel confident Tyco deal will pass antitrust scrutiny', *The Buffalo News*, Tuesday, 19 November 1996, at 3D.

[181] *The Buffalo News*, 19 November 1996. In 1998 Mattel sold Tyco's science and craft lines to Uncle Milton Industries Inc. See 'Former Tyco Toys lines sold to Calif. firm', *Philadelphia Inquirer*, 4 February 1998, at C.1.

[182] S Gregory, 'Mattel plans to buy Pleasant for $700 million: El Segundo firm would acquire the nation's no 2 doll marker as part of a strategy to cash in on foreign markets', *Los Angeles Times*, Tuesday, 16 June 1998, at D.1.

[183] *Ibid.*

trade marks by stating that the Miss America doll's clothes also fit the Barbie doll.[184] Lego brought an action in 1995 against a small Hong Kong company that used the word 'Lego' in its business of publishing entertainment and football magazines. The defendant deleted the word 'Lego' from its name during the course of the court hearing.[185] On the whole, and not surprisingly, the Hong Kong courts have been favourable to such claims.[186]

F. Labour

The fifth question to be addressed involves *modes of labour control*. What modes of labour control are found in each segment? Which sites of global legal pluralism are most relevant, and why? Which specific institutions, norms and processes are significant, and why? To what extent are different modes of labour control encouraged or faciliated by legal or other institutions, norms and processes? Are there conflicts among different sites with regard to modes of labour control? If so, how are these conflicts resolved in institutional, normative and processual terms?

So far as production is concerned, the labour law of nation States is not the only relevant law—or in the case of China even the most important. For example, when Mattel acquired Tyco, analysts said that most of the layoffs would come from outside the United States, where Tyco had most of its operations.[187] The externalities of the acquistion by one US company of another thus occurred mainly in China, where the applicable labour laws for such factories differed radically from those in the US. In fact, one empirical study of factory regimes in Shenzhen and Hong Kong, albeit in the electronics sector rather than the toy sector, concluded that the State was much less significant than the social organisation of the labour market as a factor of control of labour and constraint on management.[188]

The codes of conduct elaborated under the aegis of multinational companies and sector-specific trade associations may be much more important in practice than formal

[184] *Mattel Inc v Tonka Corp* [1991] 2 HKC 411.

[185] *Interlego AG v Lego New Enterprises Ltd* [1995] 3 HKC 186.

[186] See also *Attorney General v Hondar Plastic Industries Ltd* [1976] HKLR 7630 (holding that drawings on which the plaintiff's production of toys was based do not need to have an element of artistry to qualify for copyright protection); *Video Technology Ltd v Ors & Atari Incorporated & Ors* [1982] HKC 504 (allowing an appeal against an interlocutory injunction to restrain the defendants from dealing in any way with certain electronic games similar to Pac-man); *Core Resources (Far East) Ltd v Sky Finders* [1992] 1 HKLR 193 (dismissing appeals against summary judgment for the plaintiff for a sum due in respect of a cheque dishonoured by the defendant after the plaintiff refused to respond to a request regarding its trade mark); *Ocean Plastic Manufactory Ltd v TCA (Hong Kong) Ltd & Anor* [1993] 1 HKC 23 (refusing an application to introduce fresh evidence against a order restraining the defendants from infringing the plaintiff's copyright in a 'baby doll' toy); *Navystar (Nagai Shing) Industrial Co Ltd v Fairing Industrial Ltd* [1994] 3 HKC 670 (dismissing an application to strike out the plaintiff's statement of claim that it owned copyright in drawings of a toy compact disc player and that defendant had infringed the copyright); *Lanard Toys Ltd v Winner Toys Manufactory Ltd*, HCA No A11340 of 1994, 18 November 1994, Cheung J (granting an interlocutory injunction requested by the plaintiff, who, after acquiring the US trade mark from the original owner in about 1982, marketed toy airplanes and helicopters worldwide under the name 'Prop Shots', to prevent the defendant from marketing identical toys bearing the brand name 'Hot Shots').

[187] Madore, above n 180.

[188] C K Lee, 'Factory Regimes of Chinese Capitalism: Different Cultural Logics in Labor Control' in A Ong and DM Nonini (eds), *Ungrounded Empires: The Cultural Politics of Modern Chinese Transnationalism* (London, Routledge, 1997) 115.

national or local legislation. The large toy companies, retailers and trade associations have all adopted sector-specific codes of conduct which are imposed upon or recommended to their factories. Such codes of conduct have been described as 'typically book-sized documents that specify working conditions down to the dimensions of the medical boxes on the wall' and as 'changing China's toy industry more than anything else'.[189] Such claims may be exaggerated, but there is no doubt that codes of conduct may play an important role as a mode of labour control.[190]

One example is the Code of Business Practices of the International Council of Toy Industries (ICTI) which was established in 1974 and incorporated under the law of New York. It is an association of toy associations, embracing manufacturerers and marketers. Its members, as of February 1999, comprised the toy associations of Hong Kong, China, the United States, Japan, Denmark, France, Italy, Spain, Sweden and the United Kingdom, as well as those of Argentina, Australia, Brazil, Canada, Hungary, Korea, Mexico, Philippines, Taiwan and Thailand. The general management functions of ICTI are performed by a president and a secretary, both positions currently held by Toy Manufacturers of America. English is ICTI's official language.

The ICTI Code of Business Practices, which was revised and approved on 1 June 1998, is a voluntary code of conduct containing specific operating conditions which members are expected to meet.Members are expected to obtain agreement of their contractors to these conditions. Supply agreements with firms manufacturing on behalf of ICTI members are expected to provide for adherence. The operating conditions refer to labour practices and the workplace. As with other codes, The ICTI Code borrows from core labour rights set out in International Labour Organisation (ILO) conventions, though it omits certain other rights from other ILO conventions, such as the right to organise and collective bargaining and freedom of association.[191] The purpose of the Code is stated to be to establish a standard of performance, to educate and to encourage commitment, not to punish.

The ICTI Code of Conduct makes elaborate provision for enforcement by the companies through contract. Member companies are expected to evaluate their own facilities, as well as those of their contractors, and request that the latter follow the same procedure with subcontractors. An annual statement of compliance with the Code must be signed by an officer of each manufacturing company or contractor. According to the Code, contracts for toy manufacture should provide that a material failure to comply with the Code, or to implement a corrective action plan on a timely basis, is a breach of contract for which the contract may be cancelled. Annexes to the Code provide guidelines for determining compliance; their applicability is to be determined by a rule of reason.[192]

[189] *The Economist*, 19 December 1998, 95 at 99.

[190] See also Lin Bai, 'Improving the Non-governmental System of Outsourcing Labour Regulation in China' (2007) 13(6) *European Law Journal*, Special Issue on 'The 5th WISH/RIJC: The EU, India and China—Strategic Partners in a Changing World', 772–99.

[191] For a comparison of provisions in four major codes of labour practice with the provisions of ILO conventions, see 'A Comparison of Provisions in Base Codes of Labour Practice', available on the website of the Maquiladora Solidarity Network at http://www.www.web.net/~msn/3codeslg.htm. The four codes in question are the Code of Labour Practices for the Apparel Industry Including Sportswear (The Netherlands), the Ethical Trading Initiative (UK), SA8000 (US and UK), and the Fair Labor Association Workplace Code of Conduct (US).

[192] This description is based on the ICTI Internet home page at http://www.toy-icti.org. The ICTI Code of Business Practices can be found at http://www.toy-icti.org./mission/bizpractice.htm.

These codes have been adopted mainly as a result of pressure from NGOs. For example, the Coalition for the Safe Production of Toys ('Toy Coalition') has been instrumental in getting codes of conduct on labour practices adopted by associations of toy manufacturers and companies. The Toy Coalition was started by several Thai and Hong Kong groups in 1994.[193] It was established in response to fires at a Kader toy factory in Thailand and at a doll factory in Zhili, China, and three other factory accidents in Shenzhen and the nearby area in 1993: 188 people died in the Kader fire, 87 people died and 51 were injured in the Zhili fire, and a total of 71 people died in the Shenzhen accidents.[194] Various officials were sent to prison; and following an inspection tour by President Jiang Zemin and Foreign Minister Qian Qichen, measures were taken to improve working conditions, such as monitoring the payment of the minimum wage. This concerned mainly small and medium-sized Japanese, Taiwanese, Hong Kong and South Korean factories. The workers in Western joint ventures are reported to have had better conditions.[195]

In its campaign the Toy Coalition was joined by other such groups, including the World Development Movement (UK), ICFTU, AFL-CIO (US), Trocaire (Ireland), Italian organisations, the Workers Party (France), Asia Pacific Workers Solidarity Links, PSPD (Korea), Japan Citizens' Liaison Committee for the Safe Production of Toys (Japan), Indonesian groups and the Maquila Solidarity Network (Canada).[196] These NGOs thus constitute worldwide networks linking NGOs in Europe, the United States, Asia and other parts of the world, mirroring, to some extent, multinational corporations and affecting, conditioning and helping to create the norms which are imposed by them.[197]

Despite their political origins, these codes of conduct reflect the organisation of power in the global toy commodity chain in three different respects. Firstly, precisely because they are so few in number, the dominant buyers are unusually susceptible to political pressure. Non-governmental organisations from various countries have successfully put pressure on the small number of powerful American buyers, and the national and international trade associations they control, to elaborate codes of conduct with regard to their mainly Asian workforce. Secondly, the dominant buyers, whose power rests in their control of brands and marketing, are able in effect to determine the content of industry-wide codes of conduct and then to impose them on their suppliers, at least contractually if not always in practice. Codes of conduct thus are analogous to multilaterally negotiated treaties which then are applied as

[193] The reasons for the establishment of the Coalition and its demands for a Charter on the Safe Production of Toys are described in Human Rights for Workers: Special Campaigns, 'Our Children Don't Need Blood-Stained Toys', available at http://www-senser.com/campaign.htm.

[194] In the Zhili case, workers choked to death because all exits were locked to prevent theft by workers. Safety regulations had been ignored, the electrician was not qualified and the factory permit had been issued in exchange for a bribe: see W van Kemenade, *China, Hong Kong, Taiwan, Inc* (trans Diane Webb) (New York, Alfred A Knopf, 1997) at 179.

[195] *Ibid.*

[196] Asian Labour Update, 19 February 1999, home page http://www.amrc.org.hk/asian_labour_update, last accessed 16 February 2010. For example, the Maquila Solidarity Network, based in Toronto, Canada, promotes solidarity with groups in Mexico, Central America and Asia, organising in maquiladora factories and export processing zones to improve working conditions. Its campaigns include the International Toy Campaign. See its website at http://en.maquilasolidarity.org/, last accessed 16 February 2010.

[197] For further discussion, see DM Trubek, J Mosher and JS Rothstein, *Transnationalism in the Regulation of Labor Relations: International Regimes and Transnational Advocacy Networks* (Labor and the Global Economy Research Circle, The International Institute, University of Wisconsin-Madison, January 1999).

standard-form contracts laid down by the leading firms in a particular market.[198] Thirdly, power struggles within the chain occur latently—and sometimes overtly—between buyers and OEMs. The main US buyers use soft law codes, essentially outside the legal system, as a way of ensuring their dominance over the Hong Kong OEM and Chinese producers, while the latter struggle to develop their own ideas and designs in order to break out of their dependence on foreign buyers and foreign market niches.[199]

Based partly on the ICTI example, the Hong Kong Toys Council (HKTC) introduced a Code of Practice for the Toy Industry in July 1997. Although not legally binding, it serves as a reference, an educational and promotional device for its members.[200] In fact, however, it is not clear whether it (or another such code) is widely adopted; if adopted, whether it is enforced; or even what enforcement and compliance might mean given that the Code is not legally binding and sanctions for non-compliance are inadequate. It may be hypothesised that such codes have been adopted by and apply more effectively in practice in joint ventures between Chinese and western companies, or in factories which produce for multinational buyers. It may also be hypothesised that codes of conduct may have little, if any, effect in factories which are wholly locally-owned or produce entirely for local markets. But such a simple hypothesis, that the market for norms reflects the market for toys, is given the lie by the fact that even some companies which produce for multinational buyers evaluate the code of conduct recommended by the HKTC and the US buyer as a cost of doing business and decide not to adopt it. They consider that the items specified in a code of conduct are already dealt with by the US buyer in its specifications to the extent that they are required for marketing the product in the United States.[201] In addition, the rise of NGOs, consumer protection movements and related governmental authority in the domestic Chinese market have also strengthened the salience of codes of conduct in companies producing for the domestic market.

Even if a factory has a code of conduct, effective implementation and monitoring thus remain crucial issues.[202] At least in certain industries, pressure from critics and

[198] PT Muchlinski, '"Global Bukowina" Examined: Viewing the Multinational Enterprise as a Transnational Law-making Community' in G Teubner (ed), *Global Law Without a State* (Dartmouth, Aldershot, 1997) 79 at 86. See also LE Preston, 'The Evolution of Multinational Public Policy towards Business' in CR Lehman and RM Moore (eds), *Multinational Culture: Social Impacts of a Global Economy* (Westport, Conn, Greenwood Press, 1992) 11.

[199] Cf *Journal of Commerce*, Friday, 13 January 1995. Conflicts are inherent in this relationship: see *Kader Industrial Co Ltd v Galco International Toys NV* [1992] 1 HKC 36; *Galco International Toys NV v Kader Industrial Co Ltd* [1996] HKLY 260. Neither is the relationship free from abuse—in 1996 a senior manager with Mattel Toy Vendor Operations Ltd was convicted in Hong Kong for soliciting and accepting rewards based on the value of turnover between his employer and a Taiwan textile manufacturer: see *Attorney General v Leung Kin Wai* [[1996] HKC 588. Even apparently straightforward international transactions are not free from risk: see *Toymax (HK) Ltd v Redsmith International Ltd* [1994] 1 HKC 714 (holding that signing an order form by adding the words 'as agent for overseas buyer' was sufficient to indicate that no personal liability was assumed by the agent and dismissing the plaintiff's claim that the defendant was liable for the contractual default by an associated company).

[200] 'Hong Kong's Toy Industry', *Hong Kong & China Economics*, on the Internet homepage of the Hong Kong Trade Development Council, available at http://www.tdc.org.hk/main/industries/t2-2-39.htm, last updated 2 July 1998.

[201] Interviews, Guangzhou and Shenzhen.

[202] A 1996 case study of a Chinese toy manufacturer's code of conduct concluded that the code did not provide for effective implementation, failed to reflect basic international labour standards, in particular concerning freedom of association, and lacked an independent monitoring device: see J Murray, 'Corporate Codes of Conduct and Labour Standards' (ILO, Bureau for Workers' Activities, Working Paper, 1996) available on the Internet at http://www.ilo.org/public/english/230actra/publ/codes.htm. See also J Porges, 'Codes of Conduct', on the home page of Asian Labour Update, as of 19 February 1999, at

labour rights groups for effective enforcement of codes of conduct can prove effective. The Nike case is instructive. A Vietnam factory of Nike Inc was criticised in 1997 for unsafe working conditions. By 1998 the company had improved its working conditions, and its earlier critic issued a report noting substantial improvements. In March 1999 the chairman of Nike announced that the company, based in Beaverton, Oregon, USA, would disclose the location of all its foreign factories and open them to independent monitors if competitors would agree to do the same. He also sent letters to universities with Nike contracts to enlist them to 'ensure that licensed products bearing the names and logos of schools are manufacturered under fair conditions'.[203] Although the structure of the athletic footwear industry differs somewhat from that of the toy sector, both are buyer-driven commodity chains, so this example may be instructive in demonstrating that action by independent researchers or labour rights groups can have an effect.[204]

It also illustrates the way in which codes of conduct may be enforced through three complementary mechanisms.[205] The first is the market, in which competing firms cooperate in mutually enforcing norms which impose costs on them all, even though one might expect these costs not to be equal and thus not to bear equally on all the affected firms. The second refers to institutions, such as universities, which are linked to manufacturers, by contract or otherwise, thus spreading the costs of effective enforcement to bodies outside the specific economic sector in question. Both of these devices transform an intra-firm code of conduct into multi-lateral sets of norms.[206] Whether such a transformation is necessary depends in part on the structure of the sector concerned, including the buyers as well as the producers.[207] In the toy sector, a

http://www.amrc.org.hk/asian_labour_update, last accessed 16 February 2010. See also various issues of the *Human Rights for Workers Bulletin*, at http://www.senser.com/b21.htm. As of 1998, the Irish NGO Trocaire concluded that child labour was not a significant issue in China, because of the existence of a large pool of unemployed workers and low wages for women. In its view, the main problem was the working conditions of women. See Trocaire, 'Conditions for Toy Workers', available at http://www.trocaire.org/toy3.html. On the extent of child labour in Chinese toy factories in the mid-1990s, see 'By the Sweat and Toil of Children: A Report to Congress' (Bureau of International Affairs, US Dept of Labor, 15 July 1994) (available at http://www.dol.gov/ilab/media/reports/iclp/sweat5/, last accessed 16 February 2010 'Statistics on Child Workers in China', *China Labour Bulletin*, n. 25, April 1996, at http://www.citinv.it/associazioni/CNMS/archivio/paesi/statistisc.html; and Chan Ka Wai, 'Child Labor in China (Change HKCIC-June 1996)', at http://www.citinv.it/associazioni/CNMS/archivio/lavoro/childlab.html, last accessed 16 February 2010.

[203] 'Nike Set to Open Plants to Monitors: Firm's Offer Follows Critic's Report on Safety Gains at Vietnam Site', *International Herald Tribune*, Saturday–Sunday, 13–14 March 1999, at 21.

[204] See also *HKSAR v Wong Ying Yu & Ors* [1997] 3 HKC 452 (dismissing an appeal against conviction for disorderly conduct while staging a protest against the poor working conditions of labourers in the toy industry).

[205] See also Lin Bai, above n 190.

[206] On the distinction between intra-firm and industry-wide codes of conduct, see Muchlinski, above n 198, at 85.

[207] As to the apparel industry, see *The Apparel Industry and Codes of Conduct: A Solution to the International Child Labor Problem?* (US Dept of Labor, Bureau of International Labor Affairs, 1996), also available on the Internet at http://www.dol.gov/ILAB/media/reports/iclp/apparel/overview.htm, last accessed 16 February 2010, See also JP Sajhau, *Business ethics in the textile, clothing and footwear (TCF) industries: Codes of conduct* (ILO, Sectoral Activities Programme, Working Paper SAP 2.60/WP.110 1998), available on the Internet at http://digitalcommons.ilr.cornell.edu/cgi/viewcontent.cgi?article=1008&context=codes, last accessed 16 February 2010 and Benedicto Ernesto R Bitonio, Jr (Director,Bureau of Labour Relations, Department of Labor and Employment, Government of the Philippines), *Toward a Code of Conduct in the Textile, Clothing and Footwear Industries: Laws and Possibilities* (ILO, Sectoral Activities Programme, Workshop Background Paper 1998), available on the Internet at http://www.ilo.org/public/english/dialogue/sector/papers/tcfcode/index.htm,last accessed 16 February 2010 On the apparel industry, see E.Bonacich, L Cheng, N Chinchilla, N Hamilton and P Ong (eds), *Global Production: The Apparel Industry in the Pacific Rim* (Philadelphia, Temple University Press, 1994).

similar multilateralisation may result from the adoption of codes of conduct by international (ICTI) and local (Hong Kong) trade associations, together with effective economic and legal constraints imposed by the buyers on their factories. A third method of enforcement, which might potentially be used in conjunction with the others, is by means of international institutions such as the ILO. The ILO has been quite critical of privately negotiated codes of conduct, and has promoted the complementarity of private initiatives and international labour standards.[208]

G. Links Within a Chain

The sixth question involves *links* between the segments within a commodity chain. How are the segments within a particular commodity chain linked to each other? Which specific institutions, norms and processes create, sustain or transform these links? What role do different sites of global legal pluralism play in linking different segments? Is there any overall coordination of the segments, for example by means of vertical integration, ownership of intellectual property, control of distribution or retail markets, or any other means? How is the discreteness of a particular commodity chain maintained, and what role does global legal pluralism play in this respect?

In buyer-driven commodity chains, such as that for toys, it is the downstream service activities of marketing and distribution which drive the chain.[209] The segments of the chain are coordinated mainly through standards, whether international, regional or national, or a combination of these, concerning product quality, environmental protection and consumer safety.[210] Hence the importance of the Internet and also of standards, both as a tool for managing and coordinating the different sites and also as a form of retailing. Invention, design and marketing tend to be more easily integrated in buyer-driven commodity chains than in producer-driven commodity chains.[211] The conception of toys, intellectual property in brands, and control of marketing and distribution, now particularly via the Internet, are therefore segments of the chain in which competition is most fierce and attention to law most acute.[212] In other words, the international commodity chain in toys, as with other goods, now depends fundamentally on intellectual property, contract and the provision of services, including

[208] See International Labour Office, Working Party on the Social Dimensions of the Liberalization of International Trade, 'Overview of global developments and Office activities concerning codes of conduct, social labelling and other private sector initiatives addressing labour issues' (GB.273/WP/SDL/1(Add.1) and GB.273/WP/SDL/1(Rev.1), both 273rd session, Geneva, November 1998, available on the Internet at http://www.ilo.org/public/english//standards/relm/gb/docs/gb273/sdl-1-a1.htm, and http://www.ilo.org/public/english/standards/relm/gb/docs/gb273/sdl-1.htm, respectively, last accessed 16 Feruary 2010.

[209] E Rabach and EM Kim, 'Where is the Chain in Commodity Chains? The Service Sector Nexus' in Gereffi and Korzeniewicz, above n 9, at 137.

[210] For the present purposes, 'standards' includes both legally binding 'technical regulations' and non-legally binding 'standards' within the meaning of the WTO Agreement on Techical Barriers to Trade.

[211] Rabach and Kim, above n 209.

[212] On the growing importance of the Internet for toy distribution, see eg G Anders and L Bannon, 'EToys to Join Web-retailer Parade with IPO', *The Wall Street Journal*, Tuesday, 6 April 1999, at B1; P Davidson, 'Net retailer eToys faces big risks as its star rises', *USA Today*, Thursday, 8 April 1999, at B.1; A Pollack, 'Makeover at Barbie's: Mattel Sheds Jobs and Looks to the Internet', *International Herald Tribune*, 17–18 April 1999, at 9; A Edgecliffe-Johnson, 'Net gains take precedence over bricks and mortar', *Financial Times*, 28–29 August 1999, at 25.

legal services. The integrity of each segment and coordination among different segments also rests on numerous international, regional and national legally binding technical regulations and non-legally binding standards, which, from the legal standpoint, are framed by the WTO Agreement on Technical Barriers to Trade (TBT Agreement).

H. Connections between Specific Sites and Particular Sets of Economic Relations

A seventh set of questions concerns specifically the *connections between specific sites of global legal pluralism and particular sets of economic relations (segments)*. Do specific sites concern particular aspects of specific segments? For example, do certain sites deal with labour control, others with financial arrangements, others with marketing, others with dispute resolution and so on? How, and why? To what extent are particular sites important in governing the social organisation of the constituent units of a segment even when the sites are not geographically proximate to the segment, in other words when governance, economic processes and territory are not congruent? To what extent do sites have different constituencies, so that they are used by different strategic actors? The last chapter of this book addresses similar questions in considering the extent to which the WTO is concerned with issues of development, environmental protection and social justice. Here we are concerned with the global toy industry.

Table 2 below shows a selection of the sites of governance and the branches of law which are directly relevant to the global commodity chain in toys. The sites include federal States (USA), unitary States (China, Japan), customs territories (Hong Kong, which is a Special Administrative Region of the People's Republic of China), regional integration organisations (European Community, the members of which include both federal States and unitary States), international public organisations (WTO, WCO), international private organisations (International Council of Toy Industries), local private organisations operating under government sponsorship (Hong Kong Toys Council) and the Internet. The types of norms include both legally binding norms (public international law; law of federal States, unitary States, regional integration organisations and customs territories) and norms which are not legally binding (parts of the Kyoto Customs Convention, codes of conduct).

The branches of law shown in Table 2 are merely selected examples. Nonetheless, they suffice to indicate that the sources and types of norms concerning a global commodity chain, even for a relatively simple product such as a toy, can vary enormously. This further suggests the existence of a variety of forms of dispute settlement, such as international commercial arbitration or the WTO dispute settlement system, and the potential for jurisdictional conflicts. It might also suggest the relative advantage of large law firms in dealing with global chains, but this needs to be balanced with the detailed knowledge which local lawyers may have of local law and of the political, economic, social and culture contexts in which it operates.

The lack of congruence between norms, economic processes and territory may be illustrated by three examples. The first concerns EC environmental and health legislation. Greenpeace put pressure on EU institutions and national governments to ban all toys containing phthalates, an additive used to soften PVC products. However, at the time of the empirical research on which this chapter is based, no such EU

Table 2 Sites of Governance and Norms Relevant to the Global Toy Industry

Site of Governance	Examples of Norms Relevant to the Toy Industry
USA	competition law, intellectual property law, environmental law, consumer protection, customs law
China	foreign trade law, customs law, environmental law, labour law, tax law, law of SEZs
Japan	competition law, intellectual property law
Hong Kong	intellectual property law, environmental law, health law, consumer protection, tax, banking law, insurance law, foreign trade law, administrative law
European Community	competition law, intellectual property law, environmental law, consumer protection, customs law
EC Member States	competition law, company law, tax law
World Trade Organisation	GATT, GATS, TRIPS, DSU
World Customs Organisation	Kyoto Customs Convention
ISO and other standardisation organisations	standards
International Council of Toy Industries	Code of Business Practices
Hong Kong Toys Council	Code of Practice for Toy Industry
Internet	Domain names, access protocols, intellectual property, etc

legislation had been enacted. Nevertheless, the risk that such legislation might be enacted in the future had already changed the practices of some toy factories in China. Some factories considered it the major issue confronting Chinese exports of toys to the EU. Their international buyers instructed them to substitute hard plastic for PVC.[213] Some individual EU Member States had already banned imports of toys containing PVC or certain other substances, and these measures had affected toy production in Hong Kong and China.[214] In the United States, the main buyers stopped using phthalates in certain baby products in early 1999, even though, as in the EU, there is no legislation prohibiting it; these business decisions will inevitably affect toy production in China.[215]

A second example refers to toy safety. It exemplifies the interaction and potential incompatibility of norms, institutions and processes from two geographically discrete

213 Interviews in Guangzhou and Shenzhen SEZ, China.

214 See Hong Kong Trade Development Council, *Practical Guide to Exporting Toys for Hong Kong Traders* (Hong Kong Trade Development Council, Research Department, March 1999) 51.

215 See Hong Kong Trade Development Council, Research Department, 'Review and Outlook of Hong Kong's Toy Exports', *Trade Watch*, April 1999, at 6.

sites. The EC 'toys directive'[216] provides that all toys sold in the EU must meet essential safety requirements and bear a 'CE' mark indicating conformity. It was revised in 1996 to be similar to current US requirements,[217] perhaps indicating progress towards mutual recognition and standardisation on toy safety requirements.[218] Such requirements condition Chinese production of toys for export to Europe and the conduct of inspections in Hong Kong. But EU and US safety standards are not the only ones which apply to the marketing of toys produced in Hong Kong and China. In May 1998, the Swedish company Ikea was reported to be facing prosecution in Hong Kong for selling in Hong Kong a toy that caused the death of a boy in Europe; the toy met EU safety requirements but did not meet the more stringent specifications of the Hong Kong Toys and Children's Products Safety Ordinance.[219]

A third example concerns the European Court of Justice. In 1998 the Court decided the cases brought in 1994 by the UK and Spain against quotas on imports of toys from China. I focus here on the United Kingdom case.[220] The point of departure of the Court's analysis was the principle of liberalisation of trade; the introduction of quotas was in its view an exception. The Court noted, however, that the abolition of quotas on imports was 'not a rule of law which the Council is required in principle to observe, but rather the result of a decision made by that institution in the exercise of its discretion'.[221] It remarked that more than 98 per cent of the imports at issue were liberalised before the contested Regulation was adopted,[222] and that the quotas introduced by the Regulation reduced the level of Community trade by almost 50 per cent for some of the toys in question.[223] It followed its previous case law, however, in concluding that when assessing complex economic situations the Council enjoyed substantial discretion, including making findings of fact,[224] and that the exercise of this discretion was subject to only limited judicial review.[225] Similarly, in adopting new Community rules the Council was required to take account only of the general interests of the Community as a whole.[226] The Court also held, following its Advocate-General on this point too, that the Council was entitled to do so by basing its evaluation on 'the mere risk of disturbance', and this could be deduced from the increase in Chinese toy imports.[227] In other words, the judiciary will not substitute its

[216] Council Directive 88/378 [1988] OJ L187/1, as amended.

[217] On harmonised standards under Council Directive 88/378, see Commission Communication in the framework of the implementation of Council Directive 88/378/EEC on the approximation of the laws of the Member States concerning the safety of toys, http://eur-lex.europa.eu/LexUriServ/LexUriServ.do?uri=OJ:C:2009:227:0018:0019:en:PDF, last accessed 16 February 2010. A complete list of European standards concerning toy safety is available at http://ec.europa.eu/enterprise/policies/european-standards/documents/harmonised-standards-legislation/list-references/toys/,last accessed 16 February 2010. For an international overview, see International Council of Toy Industries, 'Toy Safety Standards Around the World,' http://www.toy-icti.org/info/toysafetystandards.html, last accessed 16 February 2010.

[218] See Hong Kong Trade Development Council, above n 214, at 7.

[219] JO Pegg, 'Ikea faces threat of illegal toy charges', *South China Morning Post*, Wednesday, 12 May 1999, at 3. On the Ordinance, enacted in 1992 as 'a substantial departure from the previous reluctance of government to become involved in this area', see J Cottrell, 'Product Liability' in S Nossal (ed), *Law Lectures for Practitioners 1993* (Hong Kong Law Journal Limited, 1993) 72.

[220] Case C-150/94 *United Kingdom v Council* [1998] ECR I-7235.

[221] *Ibid*, para 34.

[222] *Ibid*, para 44.

[223] *Ibid*, para 40.

[224] *Ibid*, paragraph 55.

[225] See *ibid*, para 54.

[226] *Ibid*, para 62.

[227] *Ibid*, para 65.

evaluation of the facts for that of the legislator unless the legislator's assessment appears manifestly incorrect in the light of the information available to it at the time of the adoption of the rules.[228] The European Court of Justice therefore dismissed the UK's application for annulment.

This decision and that in the case brought by Spain were taken more than four years after the cases were brought, and more than two years after the Advocate-General's Opinion in both cases.[229] In accordance with the practice of the European Court of Justice, the judgment was unanimous, but the length of time taken to reach it suggests that the form of unanimity masked the substance of deep disagreement. The judgment of the Court was a delicate compromise, which overlay the compromise crystallised in the Council Regulation that had provoked the litigation.

We can view the judgment of the Court as embodying a two-level compromise. Starting from the level of the ECJ, the first level concerned relations within the Court. The Court was required to reach a unanimous judgment. Thus despite likely disagreements among the judges, there could be no dissenting opinions. The Court practiced judicial restraint. This judicial compromise protected the integrity of a second-level compromise, which concerned market actors, EC institutions and others involved in the EU political process. This second-level compromise was expressed in the form of a complex regulation. The two-level compromise tended to strengthen the EU's relatively open and market-orientated normative order and to insulate and enhance the integrity of the EU political arena.

This two-level compromise was intimately bound up with the definition of EU rules for the globalisation game. Such rules concerned relations between market actors, relations between market actors and governance structures, and relations between different governance structures. But the European Court of Justice did not address these issues directly. Instead, its judgment dealt with them indirectly, by emphasising the importance of judicial restraint in the face of politically sensitive Council legislation. Nevertheless, it had wider consequences. It insulated the EU political process from collateral attack by means of judicial review. It maintained a political arena, structured to some extent by objective interests, populated by conflicts among subjective interests, and involving Member States, firms, trade associations and EU institutions. This arena, at least in the United Kingdom case, was characterised by what Max Weber called the factual 'autonomy' of the propertied classes,[230] that is, an asymmetry of property, information, power and influence upon the Member States and thus the EU legislator.

The judgment of the European Court of Justice thus occurred in a highly political context, and in fact it was highly political in the sense of allocating decision-making power. Its main importance did not lie in a short-term economic impact. A judgment either way would probably have had only marginal financial effects on the distribution of resources among EU importers, producers, retailers or others who gained or lost as a result of the existence of quotas between the adoption of the Regulation and the date

[228] *Ibid*, para 87.

[229] The Opinion of the Advocate-General was heard at the sitting of the Court on 26 September 1996: see Case C-150/94 *United Kingdom of Great Britain and Northern Ireland v Council of the European Union* [1998] ECR I-7235; Case C-284/94 *Kingdom of Spain v Council of the European Union* [1998] ECR I-7309.

[229] Case C-284/94, above n 227. The Council was supported by the Commission.

[230] Max Rheinstein (ed), *Max Weber on Law in Economy and Society* (trans Edward Shils) (Cambridge, Mass, Harvard University Press, 1966) at 146.

of the judgment. The primary significance of the judgment lay in articulating legal principles for the future, in preserving the integrity of the EU political process and in its broader implications for the relationship between EU law and other institutional, normative and processual sites.

The legal principles concerned, firstly, inter-institutional relations within the EU, in particular btween the European Court of Justice and the Council, and, secondly, the role of the EC legislator in dealing with foreign trade. Their broader implications referred to how much impact the international commodity chain could have in influencing EC legislation, both by means of its structural position and by direct and indirect pressure on national governments, the Commission and the Council. They also concerned the role played by EU law as part of global legal pluralism. The judgment of the Court sanctioned the integrity of the EU political process, and thus the political and law-creating salience of market structure. It thus inserted global legal pluralism into EU law and EU law into global legal pluralism. On the one hand, it imported into EU law the institutions, norms and processes of other sites of governance, for example regarding US intellectual property law or the organisation of toy production in the Chinese SEZ of Shenzhen. The latter were incorporated into EU economic, political and legal relations not just as costs of international or local firms in the EU toy sector, but also as elements which contribute to create, consolidate or structure these relations and thus are an integral part of them. The judgment incorporated into the realm of EU law the norms produced by institutions and processes in other sites of global legal pluralism, in the manner of invisible legal transplants. On the other hand, the norms produced by the Council and the European Court of Justice in EU legislative and judicial processes became part of the structure of the global commodity chain in toys. They conditioned, shaped and were integral to the decision-making calculus of strategic actors, including governments and firms, in this specific global economic network.

I. Relations between Sites and the Chain as a Whole

The eighth question concerns relations between *sites and the chain as a whole*. What types of relationships, for example horizontal or vertical, competitive or cooperative, marked-based, State-based or convention-based, exist between the different sites that are relevant to a specific global commodity chain? Does any specific site concern the global commodity chain as a whole? To what extent does the plurality of sites provide an effective way of managing the chain as a whole? Would a single site or a small number of sites be more effective? What does 'effective' mean in this context? In other words, what are our criteria for evaluating the effectiveness of specific sites, and of the totality of sites which we call global legal pluralism, in the organisation and management of the chain as a whole?

Certain sites concern several parts of the chain or the chain as a whole. The most well-known example is the WTO, the institutional anchor of the Uruguay Round Agreements. The latter include the General Agreement on Tariffs and Trade (GATT), the General Agreement on Trade in Services (GATS), the Agreement on Technical Barriers to Trade (TBT Agreement) and the Agreement on Trade-related Aspects of Intellectual Property (TRIPs). For some time they have been important in regard to the international commodity chain in toys, even though the main producer, China, was not a WTO member until 11 December 2001.[231]

The GATT/WTO was a crucial conditioning element in the negotiation of the EU quota on toys from China in 1993–94 and the related litigation between 1994 and 1998.[232] It also cast a long shadow with regard to future disputes, notably by holding out, to China and multinational companies 'located' in mainland China, the promise of new institutions, norms and processes which would be available on Chinese accession. After China joined the WTO, the firms located there were able to benefit from Article XI GATT concerning the general elimination of quantitative restrictions. The provision of services and the protection of intellectual property in brand names were affected by the eventual application of GATS and TRIPs. Even before accession, one could argue that the impact of the GATT on China was already real. Companies were already positioning themselves in anticipation of the further opening up of China's domestic market to imported toys and foreign toy retailers. One has only to note that in 1997, the same year it purchased a major competitor, Tyco, Mattel launched Barbie in China.[233]

These examples show that the WTO affects many aspects of the global commodity chain in toys, perhaps more aspects than any other single site. This, in turn, provides a social, economic, political and cultural basis for the WTO's claim *qua* institution to have the dominant position in international trade law. Viewed from the standpoint of positive law, it may also seem to support the argument that governance of international trade is hierarchical in nature, with the WTO site and WTO law at the top. This positive law perspective differs from a sociological perspective. As this chapter indicates, the WTO is not the only site governing international trade. Viewed from a sociological standpoint, international trade law norms are not necessarily arranged in a hierarchical fashion, and the WTO does not necessarily stand at the apex of a hierarchical of sites of governance. The preceding discussion indicates that the relative positions of different sites of governance are not fixed or indeed hierarchical. Though very important, the WTO is not necessarily dominant among the range of sites of governance which make up global legal pluralism. Seen sociologically, relations between sites of governance are usually in flux. These relations are processes, not yet acquired positions or states of affairs.

[231] Among numerous works on China and the WTO, see S Leonard, *The Dragon Awakes: China's Long March to Geneva* (London, Cameron May 1999); FM Abbott (ed), *China in the World Trading System: Defining the Principles of Engagement* (Cambridge, Kluwer, 1998); Qingjiang Kong, *China and the World Trade Organization: A Legal Perspective* (Singapore, World Scientific, 2002); DZ Cass, BG Williams and G Barker (eds), *China and the World Trading System: Entering the New Millennium* (Cambridge, Cambridge University Press, 2003); Ching Cheong and Ching HungYee, *Handbook on China's WTO Accession and Its Impacts* (London, World Scientific, 2003); H Gao and D Lewis (eds), *China's Participation in the WTO* (London, Cameron May, 2005); Xin Zhang, *Implementation of the WTO Agreements in China* (London, Wildy, Simmons & Hill Publishing, 2005); E Lam, *China and the WTO: A Long March towards the Rule of Law* Alphen aan den Rijn, Wolters Kluwre, 2009). On China's integration into the world system generally, see the dated but still useful E Economy and M Oksenberg (eds), *China Joins the World: Progress and Prospects* (New York, Council on Foreign Relations Press, 1999).

[232] For detailed analysis, see F Snyder, 'Judicial Review in the Age of Globalization: Chinese Toys in the European Court of Justice' in D O'Keefe and A Bavasso (eds), *Liber Amicorum for Gordon Slynn: Judicial Review in European Law* (London, Chancery, 2000) 651.

[233] See the history of Mattel on the company Internet homepage at http://corporate.mattel.com/about-us/history/default.aspx, last accessed 16 February 2010.

V. Conclusion

How is globalisation governed? This chapter has argued, on the basis of an analysis of global economic networks, that globalisation is governed by the totality of strategically determined, situationally specific and often episodic conjunctions of a multiplicity of institutional, normative and processual sites of governance throughout the world. The totality of these sites represents a new global form of legal pluralism.

The development of the global economic relations involved in the international toy industry owes much to corporate strategies. Such a view is consistent with the approach taken here, which privileges the perspective of strategic actors. But these strategies themselves have been pursued taking account of the framework of the law and other normative frameworks, and have been elaborated by using them. They take place, are conditioned by and have contributed to the development of global legal pluralism. To put it more precisely, the development of global networks in the toy industry has occurred in conjunction with the development of a variety of sites of governance throughout the world, each of which comprises institutions, norms and dispute resolution processes, and each of which entertains relations with numerous other sites.

One facet of this argument deserves special emphasis. Not only have strategic actors used the law and been shaped by it; they have been absolutely fundamental in determining which institutional, normative and processual sites have seen the light of day, which have flourished and developed, and which have withered and even died for lack of clients. They have also influenced profoundly the development of sites, so that some have taken on more or less judicial and legal characteristics, while others have not.[234] These strategic actors include governments, businesses and other organisations, and sometimes even individuals. It is surprising, therefore, that the standpoint of strategic actors is often given such short shrift.[235] Legal scholarship often focuses exclusively on institutions and seeks to reconstruct the system, if any, in which these institutions are, or are assumed to be, embedded. Such a perspective is useful in tracing the elaboration of legal doctrine. I would argue, however, that it is not the most fruitful if our aim is to understand how legal institutions and other institutional, normative and processual sites are created, develop and operate in practice.

This scenario embraces but is not limited to EU law. Using the example of the international toy industry, I have attepmpted to show how the EU site, with its own specific characteristics, fits into this broader picture, drawing on and contributing to the life of the other sites of governance within the context of global legal pluralism. Before the more detailed analysis, I sketched the general relationship between global legal pluralism and global economic networks. This order of presentation was intentional: it was intended to jolt us out of our usual way of seeing the EU institutions, including the European Court of Justice, solely in their own terms, in the EU framework and without placing them in any wider context. Our preconceptions, based on previous knowledge

[234] Though of course these strategic actors are not the only cause of judicialisation and legalisation.

[235] Except perhaps in legal anthropology: see F Snyder, 'Anthropology, Dispute Processes and Law: A Critical Introduction' (1981) 8 *British Journal of Law and Society* 141; reprinted in revised and slightly different form in PA Thomas (ed), *Legal Frontiers* (Aldershot, Dartmouth 1996) 135. See also E Le Roy, *Le jeu des lois: Une anthropologie 'dynamique' du Droit* (Paris, LGDJ, 1999).

and limited experience, frequently prevent us from seeing precisely how the EU fits into this broader picture, or from grasping the implications of EU institutions, norms and processes for other parts of a complex system of global legal pluralism. The organization, as well as the content of this chapter, is intended to help to correct our otherwise limited vision. Viewed from the standpoint of economic actors—that is, from the standpoint of decision-makers in economic organisations—EU law appears not as a discrete, bounded and isolated legal system, but rather as a bunch of elements in (or on) the global legal playing field. Consequently, it is not possible any more to grasp how it operates in practice, or to understand it theoretically, without situating it within the sets of relationships among sites of governance that constitute this broader arena.[236]

Taken together, these different but interwoven sets of institutions, norms and dispute settlement processes which comprise global legal pluralism amount to a novel regime for governing global economic networks. They are, however, less a structure of multi-level governance than a conjunction of distinctive institutional and normative sites for the production, implementation and sanctioning of rules, with specific but changing relations with other sites. In the specific case of the toy industry, they testify, in part, to the structure of authority and power within these inter-firm and intra-firm networks, which are characterised by a buyer-driven, rather than a producer-driven, governance structure. These new normative forms for governing global economic networks are among the reasons why the United States, EU and Chinese firms and economies are so intimately linked in the internationalised production and distribution relations which are characteristic of globalisation.

From this discussion we can derive 10 more specific hypotheses. First, global legal pluralism is a way of denoting the structure of sites of governance taken as a whole. Some might suggest that complexity theory provides a means of conceptualising global legal pluralism as a whole. However, as Rosenau has argued, it does not so far seem to take account of power, and thus remains to be developed if this claim is to be more convincing.[237]

Secondly, in this chapter, as in the analysis of other specific situations, we are concerned only with the sites of governance which are pertinent to a particular set of activities, here the global commodity chain in toys. In other words, we can distinguish between sites of governance taken as a whole and those sites which, in specific instances, are brought into play by strategic actors with regard to a specific global commodity chain. Global legal pluralism refers to the former. In contrast, seen from the perspective of a specific global commodity chain, global legal pluralism may be described most accurately as a specific constellation, rather than as a network. The network form is only one possible way of organising relations among sites. I prefer to use the term 'constellation' to refer to the sites of governance which are pertinent to a particular global commodity chain, or other arena, reserving the term 'network' to refer to a specific way of organising relations among sites while recognising that there are other possible forms of organisation.

[236] For an analogous plea with regard to United States law, see AC Aman, 'The Globalizing State: A Future-oriented Perspective on the Public/Private Distinction, Federalism, and Democracy' (1998) 31 *Vanderbilt Journal of Transnational Law* 769.

[237] See DC Earnest and JN Rosenau, 'Signifying Nothing? What Complex Systems Theory Can and Cannot Tell Us About World Politics' in NE Harrison (ed), *Complexity in World Politics: Concepts and Methods of a New Paradigm* (Buffalo, SUNY Press, 2006) 143; JN Rosenau, 'Many Damn Things Simultaneously—At Least for a While: Complexity Theory and World Affairs' in JN Rosenau, *The Study of World Politics: Theoretical and Methodological Challenges* (London, Routledge, 2006) 107.

Thirdly, the two dimensions of each site, namely the structural dimension and the relational dimension, are intimately related. The structural features of a site have an impact on the relations which the site has with other sites. Similarly, the relations which a site has with other sites have an impact on the structural dimensions of the site. Relations between sites may affect institutions, norms and/or dispute settlement processes of the sites involved. We can express these relationships in terms of two hypotheses. First, the structures of a site of governance affect, condition or determine the relations between that site and other sites. Secondly, the relations which a site of governance has with other sites affect, condition or determine the institutions, norms and/or dispute settlement processes of the site. Much depends on the type, intensity and longevity of relations between the sites. These issues are explored in later chapters of the book.

Fourthly, the sites of global legal pluralism may be classified provisionally into two rough categories. Some sites are market-based, being generated by economic actors as part of economic processes. Some are polity-based, in that they form a part of established political structures; this includes sites which are convention-based, deriving from agreements between governments. This classification scheme distinguishes between different types of sites according to their mode of creation. Several questions remain. For example, how are sites created?[238] How are they constituted, developed and legitimated as sites? Which sites have a specific geographical location, and why? What factors (political, social, economic, cultural) account for the specific institutions, norms and dispute resolution processes of a given site of governance? What determines the modes and organisation of dispute resolution? What decision processes are involved?

Fifthly, the various sites differ in decision-making structure, that is, in their institutions, norms and dispute resolution processes. They vary in the extent to which their institutions, norms and processes are inserted in a hierarchy. They may differ in their reliance on case law, the use of precedent, and the binding force of norms and decisions; in other words, in respect of those characteristics which are often associated with State law. These factors affect the outcomes of the various sites, including the different ways in which they allocate risk. At the same time, however, it is important not to overlook the extent to which sites are interrelated, for example in relation to institutional arrangements such as jurisdiction, copying or borrowing of norms, and the interconnection of their dispute-resolution processes. There remain a number of questions for further research. Do sites vary in their resemblance to State law (insertion in a hierarchy, reliance on case law, binding decisions, use of precedent, etc), and why? To what extent do the norms of a particular site combine hard law and soft law?

Sixthly, not all sites of governance are equally vulnerable to economic or political pressures. It is going too far to say that a constellation of sites of governance which is put into play by the economic processes of any specific global commodity chain reflects the structure of authority and power in the global commodity chain in question. Some types of institutions, some types of processes and some types of norms are more permeable to economic processes than others. It should also be noted that in

[238] For example, it has been argued that 'the construction of international issue networks and global policy arenas does not constitute a reduction of the scope of interstate politics but rather its pursuit by other means': S Picciotto, 'Networks in International Economic Integration: Fragmented States and the Dilemmas of Neo-Liberalism' (1996–97) 17 *Northwestern Journal of International Law and Business* 1014 at 1037.

cases of political conflict, for example between NGOs and multinational buyers in the international commodity chain in toys, the struggle between the competing groups is not limited to a single site. Each of the groups may invoke institutions, norms and processes of different sites. This may lead to wider conflicts between different sites, including conflicts of effectiveness and even of legitimacy.

Seventhly, it has been argued recently that the world economic system is entering a new polycentric phase, and that there is no reason to assume that Western business practices and Western law, for example concepts of rule of law, will remain dominant.[239] This contrasts with Garth and Dezalay's view that, while *guanxi* still flourishes, formal law is playing an increasingly important role in Hong Kong and throughout China, especially because trade has fostered more relations between Chinese and non-Chinese.[240] This chapter does not fully support either thesis. Instead, it suggests that the different sites of governance involved in different specific constellations may involve different legal cultures and sets of social relations, sometimes in relative isolation from historically different ones, but sometimes in complex hybrid forms.[241] The same can be said of the different constellations which are at play in different specific situations. Increasing legal pluralism is likely. Time will tell which legal cultures will be dominant in the future.

Eighthly, specific sites are affected by conflicts between economic organisations occupying the same segment in a global commodity chain. For example, conflicts over markets may pit foreign producers, exporters and importers, on the one hand, against domestic producers, on the other hand. Conflicts over markets also occur between companies occupying similar positions in the chain. The occupants of each of these segments try to enlist the norms, institutions and processes of the various sites of governance to improve their position, not only vis-à-vis their direct competitors but also in relation to the occupants of other segments of the global commodity chain. These conflicts involve and have important implications for sites. The most well-known example is the production of case law and the development of legal doctrine. We need to pay more attention to how such conflicts arise, unfold and are resolved, because they are often crucial determinants of the developmental paths of the institutions, norms and processes of various sites.

[239] RP Appelbaum, 'The Future of Law in a Global Economy' (1998) 7(2) *Social and Legal Studies* 171. Appelbaum studied the apparel industry, where at that time 'Even the largest European or North American retailers and manufacturers cannot ordinarily directly access Chinese factories: typically they must work through Hong Kong and Taiwanese intermediaries', *ibid* at 186, citing an interview with SR Walton, Managing Director, Innova Ltd, Hong Kong, 2 May 1993.

[240] Y Dezalay and BG Garth, *Dealing in Virtue: International Commercial Arbitration and the Construction of a Transnational Legal Order* (Chicago, University of Chicago Press, 1996) 261–66.

[241] CAG Jones, 'Capitalism, Globalization and Rule of Law: An Alternative Trajectory of Legal Change in China' (1994) 3 *Social and Legal Studies* 195. For a useful caveat, see DC Clarke, 'Methodologies for Research in Chinese Law' (1996) 30 *University of British Columbia Law Review* 201. Differences in sites are likely to be influenced also by the fact that national structures remain very important for both trade policy and multinational corporate behaviour. On trade policy, see C Garcia Molyneux, *Domestic Structures and International Trade: The Unfair Trade Instruments of the United States and the European Union* (Oxford, Hart Publishing, 2000). On corporate behaviour, see LW Pauly and S Reich, 'National Structures and Multinational Corporate Behaviour: Enduring Differences in the Age of Globalization' (1997) 5 *International Organization* 1. Social and cultural differences will also certainly influence the practical implementation of any international competition rules or conceptions of the rule of law. On the former, cf W Pape, 'Socio-cultural Differences and International Competition Law' (1999) 5(4) *European Law Journal* 438. See also R Peerenboom, *China Modernizes: Threat to the West or Model for the Rest?* (Oxford, Oxford University Press, 2007). On the latter, cf R Peerbenboom (ed), *Judicial Independence in China: Lessons for Global Rule of Law Promotion* (Cambridge, Cambridge University Press, 2009).

Ninthly, taken as a whole, the various sites are not all necessarily hierarchically ordered in relation to each other. Instead, they demonstrate many other types of interrelationships, sometimes hierarchical, sometimes not, sometimes competing, sometimes collaborative. In other words, even when viewed very broadly, they do not make up a legal system. This contrasts strongly with the usual lawyer's view of the multi-level governance of international economic relations. The latter is a normative view. Here I have tried to develop a more sociological perspective. We now need more empirical studies of relations between sites. To what extent are sites interconnected, and how are they connected? How are groups, hierarchies, networks and constellations of sites created, and how, if at all, are such processes connected to economic and political relations?

Tenthly and consequently, these sites are not always, or even usually, alternatives in dispute resolution, as might be expected if one presumes that the norms governing global economic networks are ordered in a hierarchical arrangement. Instead, each site deals with, governs or claims and seeks to govern a discrete part of the global commodity chain. Once a chain is established, its activities are governed by a given set of rules, emanating from a variety of linked sites, except to the extent that normal choice of law rules, for example embodied in contract or in private international law, allow firms a choice of governing legislation or a choice of dispute resolution, or to the extent that other tools, techniques and processes of mediation or adjustment are used to manage relations between sites. More research is required on numerous questions. For example, how do conflicts between sites arise, what are the consequences of such competition, and how are conflicting institutional, normative and processual claims handled? Do certain sites tend to converge or become more uniform in their institutional characteristics, norms or dispute settlement processes, and why?

Lastly, sites of governance use a wide variety of means to manage their relations with each other. As indicated in the preceding chapter, we need further research to explore this hypothesis in more detail. To what extent and why do particular sites use specific normative instruments, such as concepts of regulation, techniques of adjustment and mechanisms of evaluation and control, in managing their relations?[242] To what extent do their institutions and norms give priority to principles and techniques such as the use of margins of appreciation, limited autonomy regimes, subsidiarity principles, jurisdictional redundancies, hybrid participation arrangements, mutual recognition regimes, safe harbour arrangements and a pluralist approach to conflict of laws?[243] Are these normative instruments, principles or techniques universal? Do sites of governance of all kinds tend toward convergence in this respect, and why or why not? What role do public international organisations, such as the WTO and WCO, play in the diffusion or sanctioning of specific normative models?

These broad hypotheses need to be tested. The numerous remaining questions point to directions for future research which can be useful in developing further the theory of sites of governance in the framework of global legal pluralism. They will help us to understand further how economic globalisation is governed. They may also be useful in the analysis of other types of globalisation.

[242] M Delmas-Marty, *Les forces imaginaries du droit (II): Le pluralisme ordonné* (Paris, Editions du Seuil, 2006).

4

Foundations of Global Legal Pluralism: International Competition, Legal Strategies and Unintended Consequences in the EC *Chinese Bicycles* Anti-dumping Saga

I. Introduction

A. Sites of Governance and Global Legal Pluralism

Relations between sites of governance are dynamic social processes which may be cooperative, or marked by conflict or both. As these relations develop, they may lead to changes in the structural dimension of sites, as shown in the preceding chapter. They may also become more complex, bring to the surface implicit conflicts, or undercut basic legal ideas which previously formed part of these relations, and eventually demonstrate the existence of different understandings of fundamental concepts of international trade regulation and the gradual search for the bases of a new relationship. In constructing and transforming relations between sites of governance, strategic actors play a crucial role. Through both intended and unintended consequences, they contribute to changes in institutions, norms and dispute resolution processes, and to the transformation of relations between sites. Today, their legal and other strategies are shaped by the characteristics of contemporary globalisation. A basic hypothesis is that there is a correlation between international economic integration and trade, the disintegration and fragmentation of production, and the rise of global legal pluralism.[1] Globalisation, international competition, legal strategies and their unintended consequences are among the main foundations of global legal pluralism.

This chapter explores these ideas by examining a single (and singular) example of relations between the European Union and China. The EC anti-dumping action often known as *Chinese Bicycles* had its seeds in the late 1980s, and the anti-dumping duties to which it gave rise are still in force today. We can see this saga as a social process, involving EC anti-dumping legislation, litigation, and the elaboration and application of a complex regulatory scheme, reflecting and revealing the crucial role of different strategic actors, and exemplifying and intensifying significant aspects of contemporary globalisation. The saga illustrates the use and abuse of the EC anti-dumping law against China, especially the concept of 'non-market economy'. It reveals a fundamen-

[1] On the first two elements, see R Feenstra, 'Integration of Trade and Disintegration of Production in the Global Economy' (1998) 12(4) *Journal of Economic Perspectives* 31.

tal disagreement between the EU and China about the proper definition of the concept of 'circumvention' in international trade law. But the disagreement was not merely about legal concepts. It also reflected underlying differences of perceptions, expectations and strategies concerning the nature and implications of globalisation. Furthermore, it demonstrates that economic globalisation has undercut the basic assumptions of anti-dumping law. It shows that anti-dumping law is not an adequate way of governing relations between sites of governance today. Lastly, the *Chinese Bicycles* saga underscores the significant role which unintended consequences can play in shaping economic globalisation, relations between sites of governance and global legal pluralism.

B. Four Perspectives on Anti-dumping Law

The *Chinese Bicycles* saga opens up the world of anti-dumping law. Anti-dumping law may be viewed from at least four different perspectives. Each perspective has a distinctive starting point, emphasises contrasting elements and asks different questions.

Firstly, anti-dumping can be seen as an internationally permitted form of continent protection. This perspective sets anti-dumping law firmly in the universe of WTO law. Anti-dumping law contrasts with tariffs and quotas in that it is a form of protection of domestic industry which is contingent, in other words, operated on a one-off or case-by-case basis. It is a form of protectionism that internationally is neither prohibited nor required but permitted. The WTO context also places anti-dumping law in contrast to other international and domestic trade remedies, notably countervailing duties and safeguards. The contrast is sharpened in the WTO framework by the fact that each of the three trade remedies—anti-dumping, countervailing duties and safeguards—is the subject of a different WTO agreement. This perspective asks: Why is anti-dumping law the legal instrument of choice to protect domestic markets today, how is it used and does it need reform?

A second perspective views anti-dumping law as a form of national or regional economic policy instrument subject to multilateral legal supervision. This perspective emphasises anti-dumping law as a policy instrument, either national, for example in China, or regional, for example in the European Union. The use of anti-dumping law is subject to multilateral legal supervision in the form of WTO law, namely Article VI GATT, the Interpretative Note *ad* Article VI GATT and the WTO Agreement on the Implementation of Article VI GATT ('the Anti-dumping Agreement', or ADA). The term 'multilateral' emphasises that each WTO Member has agreed to and participates in the discipline or control of its own policies that is represented in WTO law. In contrast to the first perspective, which stresses a horizontal comparison between different types of trade defence instruments in either the WTO or a national site of governance, this second perspective highlights an apparently vertical dimension. This is the relationship between the WTO and national sites of governance, in which the latter are free to conduct their own affairs in anti-dumping matters so long as they do so in conformity with WTO law. This perspective recalls John Ruggie's concept of 'embedded liberalism',[2] in

[2] JG Ruggie, 'International Regimes, Transactions and Change: Embedded Liberalism in the Postwar Economic Order' in S Krasner (ed), *International Regimes* (Ithaca, Cornell University Press, 1983) 195.

which, under a multilateral umbrella, a country or regional authority (in the case of the EU, for example) is entitled to run its own policies. It asks: How much freedom of manoeuvre do WTO Members have within the WTO framework of international trade regulation, and to what extent are their domestic policies conditioned or shaped by multilateral rules?

A third perspective sees anti-dumping law as a 'buffer' between different economic systems. It views the world of international trade as being composed of different types of economic systems, such as market-based systems and planned economy systems. Trade between these diverse economic systems requires an 'interface mechanism', or 'buffer', which can operate in a way analogous to a lock in a canal in positioning the systems on the same level and thus making possible the flow of goods (and potentially services) between them. This perspective is often associated with the work of Professor John Jackson, one of the founders of the study of modern international trade law, who applied it in particular to relations between the United States and Western Europe, on the one hand, and the former USSR and China, on the other hand.[3] With the break-up of the USSR, economic changes in Russia, and the economic transformation of China since the beginning of opening-up and reform in 1978, whether this perspective is still fruitful is open to question. Among the questions raised by this perspective are: What are its legacies in contemporary anti-dumping law, and to what extent are they still relevant in a world of a variety of competing capitalisms?

The fourth perspective considers anti-dumping law as a means of regulating international competition. Its subject matter is not relations between different means of protecting domestic industry, or relations between different sites of governance presumed to be situated in a hierarchical relationship with each other, or relations between fundamentally different types of economic systems. Instead, it focuses on the international integration of markets, conceptions and definitions of competition, and relations of cooperation or conflict between companies or other types of relationships between other strategic actors, such as governments, consumer groups, downstream users, trade associations or trade unions, which are involved in the struggle for markets, profits and jobs. This perspective expressly contrasts anti-dumping law with other potential means of regulating international competition. These potential means might include, for example, a uniform international competition law, international competition policy guidelines, international cooperation or networks in the area of competition policy, models of international competition law, the development and use of an international competition law and policy repertoire, or the use of sectoral dialogues which may serve as a way of transmitting competition rules, advocacy or concerns from one country to another. This perspective asks: To what extent and how is the contemporary world economy integrated? What does 'international competition' mean? What are the advantages and disadvantages of regulating international competition by means of anti-dumping law? What kinds of regulatory schemes are used? What are the consequences, intended and unintended? What are the alternatives? This chapter adopts the fourth perspective.

[3] For example, see JH Jackson, *The World Trading System: Law and Policy of International Economic Relations*, 2nd edn (Cambridge, Mass, MIT Press, 1997) 248–50.

C. Strategic Actors and the World Bicycle Industry

This chapter seeks to conjoin theory on global legal pluralism and theory on the architecture of markets to explore relations between strategic actors, their legal strategies and the role of anti-dumping law in regulating international competition. It is not concerned to advocate or to assess the development of international competition law as an alternative to anti-dumping law.[4] The theory of global legal pluralism, as elaborated in the preceding chapters, concentrates on the structural and relational dimensions of sites of governance, and on the role of strategic actors in supporting, sustaining and transforming these two dimensions and sustaining global legal pluralism. Research on the architecture of markets, as deployed here, examines the ways in which market actors seek to create and maintain stable markets and to survive as firms. It identifies price undercutting and problems of maintaining the firm as a political coalition as the main sources of market instability.[5] Combining the two strands, this chapter focuses on the ways in which strategic actors use legal rules, institutions and dispute settlement processes. In particular, it analyses how, and with what consequences, strategic actors such as trade associations and governments, as well as companies, use anti-dumping law. It seeks to illuminate what elsewhere I have called 'ideologies of competition'[6] and what Neil Fligstein terms 'conceptions of control'[7]: the forms of knowledge, constructions, understandings and perspectives by which strategic actors seek to encourage, avoid, manage or adjust to competition, and thus to survive the challenges that threaten their positions as governments, companies or other organisations. On this view, law is a significant resource for strategic actors. Their legal strategies are contingent expressions or translations of political and economic strategies, and at the same time they are to some extent relatively autonomous, specific orientations toward legal rules, institutions and dispute settlement processes in their own terms.

The chapter focuses in particular on five strategic actors. The first is the European Bicycle Manufacturers Association (EBMA), based in Brussels. Throughout most of the *Chinese Bicycles* saga, the EBMA was the peak trade association representing European bicycle producers. The second is the Shanghai Bicycle Corporation, a leading company in a large State-owned enterprise (SOE) of Chinese bicycle manufacturers and exporters based in Shanghai. In addition to its intrinsic significance, the Shanghai Bicycle Corporation is used in this chapter as a proxy for Chinese bicycle producers and exporters in general, even though it is not entirely clear from available documents and interviews that this specific company participated in all of the strategies used by Chinese companies; where necessary, this is expressly indicated in the text. A third, sometimes related strategic actor is Giant (China) Co Ltd. A major international producer of bicycles, especially frames, Giant was established in Taiwan in 1972. Its brand was created in 1981. Between 1989 and 1992, it established numerous subsidiaries, in Europe, China and elsewhere. About 1994, it formed a joint venture

[4] For a useful review of anti-dumping law and a critique of the anti-dumping versus competition debate, see G Niels, 'What Is Anti-dumping Policy Really About?' (2000) 14(4) *Journal of Economic Surveys* 467.

[5] N Fligstein, *The Architecture of Markets: An Economic Sociology of Twenty-first Century Capitalist Societies* (Princeton, Princeton University Press, 2001) 70–71.

[6] F Snyder, *New Directions in European Community Law* (London, Weidenfeld & Nicolson, 1990; now published by Cambridge University Press) 63–99.

[7] Fligstein, above n 5, at 70–72.

with the Shanghai Bicycle Corporation to assemble bicycles near Shanghai. A fourth strategic actor is Starway, a small bicycle manufacturer and later assembler, then located near Aix-en-Provence in southern France. Again, in addition to its own intrinsic significance, it stands for a wide range of small and medium-sized EU enterprises in the bicycle industry. The fifth strategic actor is the European Commission, a central institution of the European Union. It formerly was considered to be 'the motor of European integration', and today it seeks to uphold what it or its diverse directorates-general consider, in specific arenas, to be the supranational interest in a wider EU dominated by national governments. It is a relatively small, multinational bureaucracy, which acts as the European Community's anti-dumping authority. Here we are concerned with the legal strategy of the Commission as an organisation, not of different Commissioners, policy analysts or anti-dumping case handlers. These five strategic actors thus exemplify trade associations, Chinese producers and exporters, Chinese SOEs and international companies, small and medium-sized EU producers and EU anti-dumping authorities. They constitute different, overlapping and sometimes competing interests and develop diverse legal strategies in the world bicycle industry.

These five strategic actors, and others, deploy their legal strategies in the context of the highly globalised world bicycle industry. Starting with the post-World War II economic boom in the 1950s, the world bicycle industry began to develop the main features which characterise it today.[8] These include the growth of multinational firms, international production networks (IPNs), worldwide sourcing, and the dispersion and fragmentation of production. In fact, the world bicycle industry today is a dramatic example of these processes. It exemplifies in particularly striking fashion the fragmentation of many goods and services industries. This is true to such an extent that the use of the term 'IPN' to describe it is somewhat misleading, because it concentrates our attention only on production. A more accurate term is 'global value chain', which has been defined as

> the process by which technology is combined with material and labor inputs, and then processed inputs are assembled, marketed and distributed. A single firm may consist of only one link in this process or it may be extensively vertically integrated . . .[9]

'Global value chain' thus includes sourcing, a variety of production processes, assembly, distribution and marketing. Today, according to Galvin and Morkel, 'no firm is integrated enough to the extent that it manufactures an entire bicycle'.[10] A study of Taiwan's bicycle industry showed that more than 90 per cent of bicycle assemblers did not produce any parts except for the frame. Producers were highly specialised: more than 90 per cent produced only one type of part.[11] This was consistent with an earlier, 1990 study of the same industry, which showed that each bicycle producer obtained parts from about 60 suppliers, while each producer of parts supplied as many as

[8] On globalisation of the bicycle industry, see Wan-wen Chu, 'Causes of Growth: A Study of Taiwan's Bicycle Industry' (1997) 21 *Cambridge Journal of Economics* 55; P Galvin and A Morkel, 'The Effect of Product Modularity on Industry Structure: The Case of the World Bicycle Industry' (2001) 8(1) *Industry and Innovation* 31.

[9] B Kogut, 'Designing Global Strategies: Comparative and Competitive Value-added Chains' (1985) 26(4) *Sloan Management Review* 15. On different types of global value chains, see G Gereffi, J Humphrey and T Sturgeon, 'The Governance of Global Value Chains' (2005) 12(1) *Review of International Political Economy* 78.

[10] Galvin and Morkel, above n 8, at 31.

[11] Wan-wen Chu, above n 8, at 63.

20 bicycle assemblers.[12] The Chinese bicycle industry, at least as of 2005, provides a similar example of extreme fragmentation.[13] With the decline of dominant firms, coordination in the industry relies overwhelmingly on international standards, instead of on vertical integration, stable networks or other forms of control. Today the industry is based on modularity, which itself tends to increase the fragmentation of the industry.[14] In this context, the role of strategic actors, relations among them and their legal strategies can be extremely complex.

D. Organisation of the Chapter

The remainder of this chapter consists of four main sections. Section II. looks at the legal origins and initial phase of the *Chinese Bicycles* saga. In this phase, the European Commission, at the request of the EBMA, attempted to regulate international competition between European bicycle manufacturers and Chinese bicycle producers and exporters by means of anti-dumping law. The Shanghai Bicycle Corporation attempted, unsuccessfully, to challenge the resulting anti-dumping duties in the European courts.

Section III. is concerned with the relationship between globalisation, circumvention and economic regulation. It focuses on the transformation of EC anti-dumping law into a form of regulation of both international and domestic competition. It discusses the legal strategies then deployed by Chinese producers and exporters confronted with anti-dumping duties, together with the consequent legal strategies used by the European Commission in an effort to regain control of the European bicycle market, once again on behalf of the EBMA. These competing legal strategies concerned both competition for markets and competition regarding 'ideologies of competition' or 'conceptions of control', as different strategic actors sought to impose their own legal conceptions in defining the situation and avoiding or minimising challenges to their position.

Section IV. goes on to consider the renewal of the anti-dumping duties in 2005, the legal strategies involved, and the intended and unintended consequences. It is sometimes difficult, if not impossible, to untangle intended consequences from unintended consequences. Available documents frequently indicate that a specific actor intended certain consequences, but often it seems clear that other consequences were unexpected, at least by specific actors, or otherwise unintended in the sense that they emerged from the process of increasing globalisation of the bicycle industry without regard to intentions which can be ascribed to individuals or organisations.

In conclusion, section V. summarises the argument. It outlines the effects of increasing globalisation on anti-dumping law, showing in particular that globalisation undercuts the basic assumption of anti-dumping law about the homology between State, territority and economy. It also returns to the implications of globalisation,

[12] W Chu and AC Tung, *The Impact of Currency Appreciation on Taiwan's Industries* (Taipei, Council for Economic Planning and Development, 1990), cited in Wan-wen Chu, above n 8, at 64.

[13] For a clear presentation of the Chinese bicycle industry, which demonstrates the extreme fragmentation, see eg *China Bicycle Yearbook 2005* (Tokyo, Cycle Press, 2004).

[14] Galvin and Morkel, above n 8, at 31.

international competition, legal strategies and unintended consequences for global legal pluralism. In particular, it emphasises the correlation between international economic integration, the fragmentation of production and the rise of global legal pluralism.

II. International Competition and Anti-dumping Law

A. EBMA's Search for Protection

The origins of the *Chinese Bicycles* saga lie in the 1980s.[15] The European Economic Community (EEC) and China established diplomatic relations in 1975. The first trade agreement between the two was concluded in 1978. In December of the same year Chinese President Deng Xiaoping officially launched the 'Four Modernisations', concerning agriculture, industry, science and technology, and national defence.[16] This began Chinese economic reform and 'opening-up' to the outside world. Near the beginning of 1981, Italy requested and obtained from the European Commission a change in EEC import arrangements concerning bicycle tyres and inner tubes from China.[17] Eight years later, on 19 April 1989, the Danish Government applied to the European Commission under Article 115 TEC for authorisation to apply protective measures on bicycle imports from China. Article 115 TEC was a safeguard clause, then designed partly to reconcile the EEC common import policy with national quotas. It provided that the Commission could authorise Member States to take protective measures

> in order to ensure that the execution of measures of commercial policy taken in accordance with this Treaty by any Member State is not obstructed by deflection of trade, or where differences between such measures lead to economic difficulties in one or more of the Member States.

Denmark applied a regime of quotas on bicycles from China, but the quota was exhausted. The Danish Government and industry felt threatened by the possibility that Chinese bicycles imported originally into other EC Member States might appear in great number on the Danish market. The Danes were concerned about the 'announced imminent importation' of 200,000 bicycles originating in China and put into free circulation in another Member State. The prices of these bicycles were about 80 per cent lower than those of bicycles produced in Denmark; at the time, Denmark produced both entire bicycles and bicycle parts. Faced with the request, the Commission considered that Denmark had not met the criteria provided in Article 115 TEC for prohibiting the imports. Only a small share of the Danish market was then held by imports, including imports from China. Consequently, the Commission

[15] A detailed chronology is given in the Appendix to this chapter.

[16] See F Snyder, *The European Union and China, 1949–2008: Basic Documents and Commentary* (Oxford, Hart Publishing, 2009), ch 2.

[17] See Commission Decision of 23 February 1981 changing the import arrangements established by Council Decision 80/1278/EEC and applied in Italy in respect of imports of bicycle tyres and inner tubes from the People's Republic of China [1981] OJ L72/16.

authorised Denmark only to apply intra-Community surveillance until 31 December 1989.[18] Under this procedure, imports were made subject to the issue of an import document, provided by the Member State and requiring detailed information about the imports.[19]

This measure did not stem imports of bicycles from China into the European Community as a whole. Between 1989 and the end of September 1991, imports of bicycles from China had increased from 693,000 units to 2,100,600 units, or more than 200 per cent over a period of two years and nine months. In contrast, EC consumption of bicycles during the period increased only 32.3 per cent.[20] Chinese producers increased their market share from 4.6 per cent in 1989 to 10.5 per cent in 1991. The share of EC industry declined from 33 per cent to 27 per cent during the same period.[21] On average, prices of the allegedly dumped bicycles from China were 43.8 per cent less than those of bicycles produced in the Community.[22] These facts in themselves reflect the internationalisation of the bicycle sector, even in the early 1990s. At that time, Taiwan was the most important exporter to the EU. When, as of 2004, China was the main producer,[23] this included numerous joint ventures, in particular with Taiwan.[24]

In July 1991, the EBMA complained to the European Commission about alleged dumping.[25] This was not directly linked to the Danish request for Article 115 measures, because Article 115 and anti-dumping are dealt with by two entirely different Commission services, with little coordination. The EBMA had a specific 'conception of control'. It presented the sale of bicycles from China at prices lower than EC producer prices as 'dumping'. This legal language situated the imports in a specific legal framework concerning international trade, presented them as potential threats to EC firms and jobs, and advanced EBMA's interests as deserving of protection by the public authorities, namely the European Commission, through law. It was intended to stabilise the market, in the interests of EBMA and its members. It structured perceptions of how the market should work, and allowed actors to interpret their world and to elaborate strategies to deal with changes and potential threats. The main purposes of the EBMA were to protect the interests of its members, which were individual bicycle manufacturing companies, and thus to ensure its own survival and, if possible, its growth.

The EBMA's mission was rendered more complicated by the fact that the Association did not have a monopoly over representation of the extremely fragmented industry. Its interests, certainly with regard to its own survival, were not necessarily the same as those of COLIBI,[26] which is composed of national bicycle manufacturers associations and represents the European bicycle industry as a whole, including

[18] Commission Decision 89/386/EEC of 17 May 1989 authorising the Kingdom of Denmark to apply intra-Community surveillance to imports of certain bicycles originating in the People's Republic of China [1989] OJ L181/53.

[19] See Commission Decision 87/433/EEC of 22 July 1987 on surveillance and protective measures which Member States may be authorised to take pursuant to Article 115 of the EEC Treaty [1987] OJ L238/26.

[20] *Bicycles from China* [1993] OJ L58/12 (provisional), para 38.

[21] *Ibid*, para 39.

[22] *Ibid*, para 44.

[23] For 2004 statistics, see BikeBiz, 'Lies, damn lies and statistics', available at http://bikebiz.co.uk/infozone/stats.php, last visited 18 November 2004.

[24] *Bicycles from China*, para 49, [2000] OJ L175/39 (definitive).

[25] See *Bicycles from China* [1993] OJ L58/12 (provisional), on which the following presentation of facts and procedure is largely based.

[26] Comité de Liaison des fabricants européens de bicyclettes. See http://www.colibi.com.

importers, or of those of other organisations such as suppliers, retailers or cyclists. Indeed, COLIBI and EBMA then were engaged in a power struggle. In July 1992, support for the EBMA's complaint among European Community bicycle producers themselves appears to have been somewhat lukewarm. After the Commission opened an anti-dumping investigation, only 54.3 per cent of all Community producers fully cooperated in the antidumping investigation; a further 10 per cent supplied some basic information on their production and expressed support for the complaint. In the early 1990s, expansion and internationalisation of the bicycle sector was occurring mainly through Chinese exports. This had a direct impact on the EBMA's world view and legal strategy. As we shall see later, EC companies, such as Starway and other small and medium-sized enterprises, were included in the network of Chinese bicycle companies. In October 1991 the Commission published a notice in the EC *Official Journal* announcing the initiation of an anti-dumping investigation concerning imports from Taiwan and China.[27] It advised known importers and exporters, the representatives of the exporting countries and the complainants. Many in these groups presented their views in writing, some Taiwanese and Chinese exporters requested and were granted a hearing, and an association of enterprises with investments in China, in itself a sign of economic globalisation, also requested and was granted a hearing. The Commission then tried to verify the information and carried out investigations at the premises of numerous companies, including Community producers, importers in the Community and producers in Taiwan. No investigation was carried out at the premises of Chinese producers who replied to the Commission's anti-dumping questionnaire because until later reforms of EC anti-dumping law, China was considered simply as a non-market economy, so normal value and export price were determined on the basis of a market economy third country, known as the analogue country. The investigation period was 1 October 1990 to 30 September 1991. Similar investigations or actions were underway during the same period in the United States, Mexico and Argentina.[28]

B. The European Commission's Analysis

Since the beginning of EC anti-dumping law, the Commission has always been the principal EC anti-dumping authority, even if, in various phases of a typical anti-dumping proceeding, it is necessarily accompanied by other institutions. It receives complaints, conducts investigations, imposes provisional anti-dumping duties after consulting an Advisory Committee consisting of Member State representatives and, again after consulting the Advisory Committee, makes proposals to the Council for the imposition of definitive duties. It also conducts reviews, and its Legal Service participates actively in anti-dumping cases before the European courts. The Commission is a reactive rather than proactive institution in the early phases of anti-dumping cases, and also in subsequent requests for extension and reviews. For example, following industry pressure, it

[27] Notice of initiation of an anti-dumping proceeding concerning imports of bicycles originating in Taiwan and the People's Republic of China [1991] OJ C266/6.

[28] See eg Canadian International Trade Tribunal, *Bicycles and Frames Originating in or Exported from Taiwan and the People's Republic of China: Order*, Review No RR-97-003, Ottawa, Wednesday, 10 December 1997.

later withdrew the benefits of the EC's General Scheme of Preferences for bicycles originating in China.[29] In anti-dumping litigation, the Commission also plays a basically reactive role. For example, when the Shanghai Bicycle Corporation brought a case in 1994 to challenge definitive anti-dumping duties, the Commission, through its Legal Service, intervened in support of the Council.[30]

Once it initiates an investigation, however, the Commission can develop its own strategy, within (increasingly narrow) limits. Its Anti-dumping Unit is constrained first by the Commission's own structure, second by the Anti-dumping Advisory Committee and third by the Council; the last two represent the Member States. The proposals made by the Directorate-General External Trade for anti-dumping duties and related legislation must be approved by the college of the Commission. All proposals for anti-dumping duties, as well as the opening of investigations, must be submitted to the Advisory Committee, whose opinion, though not legally binding, is invariably followed by the Commission. While the Commission can enact provisional anti-dumping duties, and can propose definitive anti-dumping duties, its proposals for definitive duties must be approved by the Council. Nevertheless, within these constraints, the Commission aims to preserve its organisational integrity, enhance its regulatory role, maximise its discretion, and promote its vision of effective competition on the EU and international markets. Over the years, it also has developed many official and unofficial contacts with its Chinese counterparts, for example through the Chinese mission in Brussels and EU–China trade dialogue, or directly with the Chinese Ministry of Commerce (Mofcom, formerly the Ministry of Foreign Trade and Economic Cooperation (MOFTEC)).

As the *Chinese Bicycles* saga unfolded, the Commission sought to reconcile three purposes, which proved to be extremely elusive and often contradictory: first, to respond to and if possible meet the demands of the European industry, which constituted its main clients, and before which it hoped to continue to benefit from legitimacy; secondly, to protect small and medium-sized enterprises (SMEs) located in the EU; and, thirdly, to foster the internationalisation of EU industry. This could be traced in the determination of dumping, injury, a causal relationship between the two, and the Community interest, which are the elements required by EC anti-dumping legislation for the imposition of anti-dumping duties. This chapter focuses on two critical phases. This section of the chapter considers the determination of normal value prior to the imposition of anti-dumping duties. The regulation of the bicycle market after the anti-dumping duties were extended to bicycle parts is discussed in section IV.A.

At this point, it is useful to sketch briefly the EC legal framework which supplied the normative resources around which strategic actors clustered, and which they tried to mobilise and deploy for their own purposes. The main legal instrument is the basic EC anti-dumping legislation, Council Regulation (EC) No 384/96 (as amended) ('the basic Regulation').[31] It was based closely on the GATT anti-dumping codes until the end of

[29] Question no 103 de Mme Ernst de la Graete (H-0986/92) (Objet: L'importation de bicycles en provenance de la Chine et des pays bénéficiaires du système de préférences généralisées) and Question no 104 de M Gil-Robles Gil-Delgado (H.1025/92) (Objet: Bicyclettes), Débats du Parlement européen, No 3-423/303, 28.10.92.

[30] Case T-170/94 *Shanghai Bicycle Corporation Group v Council of the European Union* [1997] ECR II-1383.

[31] Council Regulation (EC) No 384/96 of 22 December 1995 on protection against dumped imports from countries not members of the European Community [1996] OJ L56/1; consolidated version available at http://eur-lex.europa.eu/LexUriServ/LexUriServ.do?uri=CONSLEG:1996R0384:20051230:EN:PDF, last accessed 17 February 2010.

1994, and afterwards on the WTO Agreement on the Implementation of Article VI GATT ('the Anti-dumping Agreement'). In principle, it provides for all procedural and substantive aspects of anti-dumping actions. These elements will emerge sufficiently for present purposes if we examine selected aspects of the Commission's analysis. I focus in particular on issues which indicate the extent of globalisation of the international bicycle market.

The first issue concerns the definition of Community industry. The EC anti-dumping law,[32] now following the WTO Anti-dumping Agreement,[33] requires that domestic producers that have substantial links with importers or exporters of the allegedly dumped products may be excluded from the category of domestic (or in this case, Community) industry for the purpose of determining support for potential anti-dumping measures. This is done on a case-by-case basis, considering the effects on EU production and bearing in mind that producer/importers will, *qua* importers, bear the cost of anti-dumping duties.

The Commission's analysis showed that three sources supplied the EC market for bicycles: domestic production, imports through Community importers related to Chinese producers, and allegedly dumped exports from China imported through importers that were not related either to Community producers or to the Chinese producers.[34] Concerning the first source, the Community producers at which the Commission carried out verification visits included major brand names, such as Peugeot and Gitane in France, Kynast, Hercules and Derby in Germany, Batavius and Gazelle in The Netherlands, BH in Spain, and Raleigh and Dawes in the UK. However, one exporter argued that the fully cooperating Community producers were not representative, and that those who received questionnaires later in the proceedings should have been excluded from the definition of Community industry.[35] With regard to the second source, during the Commission's investigation, one exporter requested that Community industry should consist only of producers which did not have business links with Chinese exporters for the purchase of components. Although such links were frequent, the Commission denied the request, concluding that most parts were sourced in the EU, though some came from Japan, Singapore, Taiwan and China.[36] Concerning the third source, a number of Taiwanese and Chinese producers stated that certain Community producers had imported bicycles from Taiwan or China during the investigation period. Though establishing this fact, the Commission concluded that the volume of such imports was insignificant 'in relation to the volume of production of these companies and to the total volume of imports originating in Taiwan and China'.[37] It also found that these imports were a reaction to competition

[32] Now Council Regulation (EC) No 384/96, Art 4((1)(a), (2).

[33] Agreement on the Implementation of Article VI of the General Agreement on Tariffs and Trade 1994, Art 4. Commission Decision 2006/22/EC of 20 January 2006 granting certain parties an exemption from the extension to certain bicycle parts of the anti-dumping duty on bicycles originating in the People's Republic of China imposed by Council Regulation (EEC) No 2474/93, last maintained and amended by Regulation (EC) No 1095/2005, and lifting the suspension of the payment of the anti-dumping duty extended to certain bicycle parts originating in the People's Republic of China granted to certain parties pursuant to Regulation (EC) No 88/97 [2006] OJ L17/16.

[34] On this last point, see *Bicycles from China*, above n 25, para 24.

[35] *Ibid*, para 13.

[36] *Ibid*, paras 10–11.

[37] *Ibid*, para 13. The Commission also drew the more problematic conclusion that the low volume of such imports demonstrated the commitment of EC industry to the production of bicycles.

from lower-priced imports, notably from China; they were a 'measure of legitimate commercial protection' which was necessary in order to remain in the market, for example by maintaining a complete range of models or securing certain market segments.[38]

In practice, defining Community industry proved very complex, first because not all EU producers participated in the proceeding or supported anti-dumping measures and, secondly, because of the (probably related) fact that some EU producers were also importers. These issues, in particular how to distinguish between different groups of EU producers, proved to be at the centre of subsequent developments, mainly involving the European Commission.

Overall, the analysis suggested a relatively low level of globalisation of the EC bicycle market. Perhaps the major indication is the category of importers related to producers. The Commission carried out verification visits at Giant Deutschland, Giant Europe and Giant Holland in The Netherlands, and Giant Manufacturing Taiwan.[39] Established in 1972 in Taiwan as Manufacturing Co Ltd, Giant had the largest bicycle factory plant in Taiwan. The Giant brand was created in 1981. Giant established subsidiaries in Europe in 1986, in the USA in 1987, in France in 1987, and in Canada, Australia, Japan and China between 1989 and 1992. It created a Europe-based factory in The Netherlands in 1996.[40] It also established a joint venture in China between Giant Mfg of Taiwan and Phoenix of China.[41] Giant was then, as today, one of the main producers of bicycles in the world, particularly of bicycle frames. But in the Commission's investigation, it was a rather exceptional example of a highly internationalised company.

A second issue concerns the establishment of dumping. Because of the large number of Chinese companies involved in the case, the Commission used sampling to establish export prices for Chinese products. It identified two types of Chinese companies that were involved in the case: SOEs and joint ventures (JVs). Each category in the sample included two companies. An exporter selling bicycles produced in China via Hong Kong was also included. These five exporters represented more than 85 per cent of all exports to the Community of the companies which replied to the anti-dumping questionnaire.[42] Unfortunately, not all Chinese companies replied to the questionnaire. The Chinese producers which replied accounted for only 73 per cent of total exports from China. The Commission used 'best facts available' to determine the dumping margin for the remaining 27 per cent of exporters.

A third issue concerns the establishment of normal value. Anti-dumping duties are imposed, in theory, on the basis of an analysis of price discrimination, involving a comparison of the price of the product on the producer's domestic market (normal value) and the price of the product on the export market (export price). Dumping denotes the sale of the product on an export market at a price less than the normal value. Hence, price is the essential element in market competition, since, as pointed out

[38] *Ibid.*

[39] *Ibid*, para 5.

[40] See 'Cycles—Profiles—Giant: Dates clés', http://www.giant-bicycle.com/fr/010.000.000/010.020.020.asp, last accessed 16th March 2010 20 October 2004.

[41] Shanghai Giant & Phoenix Bicycle Co Ltd, with a reported annual production capacity of 1.6 million units: see *China Bicycle Yearbook 2005* (Tokyo, Cycle Press, 2004) at 82. On Phoenix Co Ltd, with a reported annual production capacity of 3 million units, see *ibid*, at 85.

[42] *Bicycles from China*, above n 25, para 15.

in another case,[43] the Chinese producers matched domestic producers with regard to quality of the product, reputation and timely delivery.

However, with regard to exports from China, EC anti-dumping law until recently considered China to be a 'non-market economy'.[44] Beginning in the early 1990s, the EC allowed Chinese exporters to prove that they operated on a market basis with regard to exports and thus qualified for 'individual treatment' (IT). Originally introduced to take account of 'bubbles of capitalism' in a socialist economy, this initially relied on administrative discretion, and then on 'soft law' guidelines, and eventually on legislation as discussed in Chapter 7 of the book. In this case, the export price of the individual exporter is taken into account, usually resulting in lower anti-dumping duties. This was the situation until the late 1990s. Starting in 1998, the Commission gave Chinese exporters the opportunity to demonstrate that both domestic and export transactions operated on a market basis, and thus to be granted 'market economy treatment' (MET).[45] This means that the producer/exporter is entirely market-orientated, on both the domestic and the export markets, so that the anti-dumping authority, here the European Commission, takes account of the exporter's own selling price on the domestic market and of its export price in calculating the margin of dumping. This would normally lead to a lower anti-dumping duty. These reforms now form part of the consolidated basic Regulation, but in fact the proportion of claims for individual treatment or market economy treatment which is granted remains relatively limited.[46] The EC anti-dumping law can bear heavily on individual firms and markets. The application of EC anti-dumping law to exports from China has therefore been especially controversial, even to the extent of overshadowing significant international trends such as a shift in the use of anti-dumping law by WTO Members away from 'old users' such as the EC and towards developing countries, and the fact that today most anti-dumping actions against Chinese exports are brought by India.[47]

For the analogue country, at the provisional stage the EBMA suggested Taiwan, whereas the Chinese producers suggested India, Malaysia, Indonesia or Thailand. The Commission contacted producers from the last four countries, but without success: this is not surprising, since there is no reason to expect that competitors of companies being investigated for dumping would willingly give up often confidential business information without a substantial incentive to do so. Hence the Commission selected Taiwan, bearing in mind that Taiwanese producers were already involved in the case and would therefore be more or less required to make the necessary information available in order to support their own arguments. It determined normal value for exports

[43] Canadian International Trade Tribunal, *Bicycles and Frames Originating in or Exported from Taiwan and the People's Republic of China: Order*, above n 28, at 5 (Counsel for the Canadian Bicycle Manufacturers Association), 17 (Findings of the Tribunal).

[44] See chapter six in this book.

[45] See chapter seven in this book.

[46] The distinction is significant in terms of duty levels. One study showed that duties for companies granted MET were about 28% lower than those not granted MET, and duties for companies granted individual treatment were about 15% lower than for those not granted individual treatment: H Detlof and H Fridh, *The EU Treatment of Non-Market Economy Countries in Antidumping Proceedings* (Kommerskollegium/Swedish National Board of Trade, Stockholm, 2006). See also A Polouektov, 'Non-Market Economy Issues in the WTO Anti-dumping Law and Accession Negotiations: Revival of a Two-tier Membership' (2002) 36(1) *Journal of World Trade* 1. See generally Changho Sohn, 'Treatment of Non-Market Economy Countries under the World Trade Organization Anti-dumping Regime' (2005) 39(4) *Journal of World Trade* 763.

[47] See the WTO website at http://www.wto.org.

from China on the basis of market prices in Taiwan.[48] (Note that at the definitive stage, the EBMA suggested Mexico, and this was accepted by the Commission. Taiwan had been the analogue country in the original investigation, but it was involved in a concurrent anti-dumping proceeding[49] and no interested party then proposed it.)

Some Chinese JVs, located in a SEZ, requested individual treatment. The Commission denied individual treatment to all Chinese companies. It stated that individual treatment is appropriate for exporters in centrally-planned economies only in exceptional cases; otherwise, the State authorities could circumvent anti-dumping duties by channelling exports through the exporter with the lowest duty.[50] Individual treatment could be granted when the exporter demonstrated that it operated, and would continue to operate, independently of the State, public bodies and State-controlled corporations in its sales policy, for example by showing that the State or a representative of the State was not in a position to block key decisions of the company. The fact that a company was situated in an SEZ was not sufficient to demonstrate the required degree of autonomy. The Commission concluded that none of the exporters fulfilled these conditions.

A fourth issue is the determination of export price. Here again, I emphasise points which indicate the extent of economic globalisation of the industry. One company was located in Hong Kong. It exported to the EC bicycles produced in a State-owned factory in mainland China. The bicycles were sent to Hong Kong against payment of a manufacturing fee, including labour costs. There was no invoice between the factory in China and the exporter in Hong Kong, which invoiced the sales in the Community. The Commission based its calculation of the export price on the price to the Community as invoiced by the company in Hong Kong.[51]

The fifth issue concerns the dumping margin. The EC law permits the anti-dumping authority to establish the duty at the level of the dumping margin or at the injury margin, whichever is lower.[52] This is called the lesser-duty rule. Pauwels *et al* show that the lesser-duty rule may be manipulated by domestic industry by reducing output to increase prices and hence the injury margin, while the foreign exporter reduces exports to lower the injury margin. The anti-dumping authority may interpret the reduction in domestic production as an indicator of injury.[53] In this case, however, the European Commission fixed the provisional duty at the level of the dumping margin, since the injury margin, caused by price undercutting, was higher.[54] In any event, much depends on the period of investigation chosen by the anti-dumping authority.

A sixth issue is determination of injury. Imports from China, as already noted, substantially undercut Community producer prices and increased in market share. Between 1989 and September 1991, Community industry increased its production capacity from 5,673,000 units to 5,945,000 units, whereas capacity utilisation, having increased from 65 per cent in 1989 to 71 per cent in 1990, dropped to 65.1 per cent by

[48] For details on the calculations, see *Bicycles from China*, above n 25, paras 28–29.

[49] See *Bicycles from Taiwan*, [1999] OJ L49/1 (definitive).

[50] *Bicycles from China*, above n 25, on which this paragraph is largely based.

[51] *Ibid*, para 25.

[52] Then Council Regulation (EEC) No 2432/88, Art 13(3) [1988] OJ L209/1; currently Council Regulation (EC) No 384/96, Art9(4) [1996] OJ L56/1.

[53] W Pauwels, H Vandenbussche and M Weverbergh, 'Strategic Behaviour under European Antidumping Duties' (2001) 8(1) *International Journal of the Economics of Business* 75 at 97.

[54] *Bicycles from China*, above n 25, para 66.

the end of September 1991.[55] Community stocks increased by 26 per cent between 1989 and September 1991.[56] Sales by Community industry stagnated, rising less than 2 per cent per year despite an apparent increase in consumption of 32.3 per cent between 1989 and September 1991.[57] The Commission concluded that although the Community bicycle market increased by 50 per cent during the four years up to 1991, Community industry lost market share to Chinese exporters, who tripled their exports between 1989 and September 1991.[58] It concluded that Community industry suffered material injury.[59]

A final issue concerns the EC's public interest test, known as 'Community interest'. In principle, the Community interest requirement, introduced in 1996, was intended to result in 'an appreciation of all the various interests taken as a whole, including the interests of domestic industry and users and consumers'.[60] In practice, however, up to 2005 the Community interest test proved ineffective, with little analysis of the costs of anti-dumping measures, the real importance of Community industry, the risks associated with continued dumping or the interests of parties who have not contacted the Commission.[61] In this case, the Commission concluded that the adoption of anti-dumping duties was in the interest of the Community. It pointed to the determination of Community industry to remain competitive, while also identifying increasing production capacity in China. The latter included the construction of new plants. It also included the expansion of the Kunshan Development Zone, scheduled to become one of the world's largest bicycle production sites, even compared to Shenzhen, which then had a production capacity of more than 5,000,000 bicycles per year.[62]

Hence the Commission adopted a provisional anti-dumping duty on bicycles from China at a rate of 34.4 per cent, applicable to the net free-at-frontier Community-frontier price, before duty.[63] This vindicated the claims of the EBMA, and in fact the Commission largely accepted the analysis proposed by the EBMA as the representative of Community industry. The legal strategy of the EBMA was successful, although some companies initially opposed its claims or later bolted from the ranks. The (temporary) alliance between EBMA and the EC institutions was signalled later in court. When a Chinese producer and exporter challenged the definitive duties before the Court of First Instance, the EBMA intervened in favour of the Council.[64]

[55] *Ibid*, paras 45–46.
[56] *Ibid*, para 47.
[57] *Ibid*, para 48.
[58] *Ibid*, para 53.
[59] *Ibid*, para 54. Some of these figures were revised slightly at the definitive stage: see *Bicycles from China* [1993] OJ L228/1 (definitive), paras 61–73.
[60] Council Regulation (EC) No 384/96, above n 31, Art 21(1).
[61] See Kommerskollegium/National Board of Trade, 'Treatment of "the Community Interest" in EU Antidumping Investigations', 14 June 2005, Stockholm, Sweden, available at http://www.kommers.se/upload/Analysarkiv/Arbetsomr%E5den/Antidumpning/Antidumpning%20-%20huvudsida/Community_Interest_in_EU_Antidumping_Investigations_-National_Board_of_Trade__SWEDEN.pdf, last accessed 17 February 2010.
[62] *Bicycles from China,* above n 25, para 63.
[63] Commission Regulation (EEC) No 550/93, Art 1(2) [1993] OJ L58/12.
[64] Case T-170/94 *Shanghai Bicycle Corporation Group v Council of the European Union* [1997] ECR II-1383.

C. The Commission's Analysis Confirmed

Following the imposition of provisional duties, a number of Chinese exporters, Community producers, and independent importers and traders submitted comments in writing to the Commission. Some appeared in person before the Commission, and some made representations after the Commission informed them that it intended to propose definitive duties. After consulting the Advisory Committee, the Commission then set the proposal before the Council, composed of the trade ministers of the EC Member States. Selected aspects of the Council's analysis[65] illustrate the conceptions of Chinese companies which were held by the Commission, the Council and many EC Member States at the time. They emphasise the strong economic role of the State, and they give no sign of awareness of the globalisation and fragmentation of the bicycle industry, even by the early 1990s. These views also suffice to suggest the fluidity, indeed ambiguity, of relevant EC anti-dumping law concerning China, and the virtually insurmountable legal and political obstacles faced by Chinese companies seeking to compete in the EC market.

The Council took a very broad view of the role of the Chinese Government in the Chinese economy:

> [I]t is in practice extremely difficult to establish in the case of a country such as the People's Republic of China whether a company really enjoys, both in law and in fact, independence from the State and in particular whether a company has permanent independence where it appears to enjoy independence at a given point in time. The economy of the People's Republic of China is in transition from a fully State controlled economy to a partially market orientated economy. State control subsists in very many aspects of economic life and the law and institutions necessary for the functioning of a market economy are not sufficiently developed and familiar to the economic operators and officials. It is therefore not possible to be certain that contracts and apparent legal guarantees will be effective and the actions of exporters free from governmental interference. Indeed it is clear that the influence of the State on all economic activity in China is still dominant. The State can at any time change the rules applicable to the employment and payment of workers, it controls the supply of energy and can impose limitations on the convertibility and transfer of currency.[66]

We should recall that this was in 1993. It suffices to remark that not all of these elements are strictly relevant to the determination of export prices, the crux of individual treatment, whereas others might also apply to some EU countries and companies. However, the Council noted that, in the case of non-market economy countries, it was especially difficult for the Commission, in the absence of on-site verification, to distinguish between appearance and reality so far as independence from the State in export matters was concerned.

Two Chinese exporters had claimed individual treatment. A Hong Kong company, exporting bicycles produced by a wholly publicly-owned Chinese manufacturer, at first requested and then withdrew its request for individual treatment on behalf of the manufacturer.[67] The Commission had denied individual treatment to another company, a Chinese manufacturer and exporter which claimed to be a joint stock company with

[65] *Bicycles from China* (definitive), above n 59.
[66] *Ibid*, para 19.
[67] *Ibid*, para 24.

only a minority of its shares owned by the State. In the Commission's view, the structure of the new company was not clear, and even a minority shareholding would give the State a significant influence on the company, 'especially when combined with all other means of influence at the disposal of the State in China'.[68] The Council also referred to

> a representative of the Chinese government, who claimed that he represented all bicycle manufacturers with a shareholding of the Chinese State, [and who] declared to the Commission that the Chinese State coordinated the activities of all bicycle manufacturers in China.[69]

Hence the Council denied individual treatment. Its reasons were, first, that this is not required by the EC Anti-dumping Regulation and 'is appropriate only where this gives a more proportionate and effective remedy against injurious dumping than a single country-wide duty'.[70] Secondly, in the Council's view, individual treatment might led to distorted individual results concerning export prices, since it would not take account of efficiency, comparative advantage or product characteristics of individual producers. The argument, as presented in the *Official Journal*, is not very clear, but reading between the lines, it appears to be concerned with the possibility that individual treatment, based solely on export prices, would not take account of other characteristics of individual exporters. It is open to question, however, whether the latter is properly a concern of individual treatment, which by definition is (or should be) concerned only with the determination of an exporter's prices on the export market. The Council also noted that individual treatment might, in certain circumstances, lead to circumvention. Together with the Commission, it concluded that

> departures from the general rule whereby a single anti-dumping duty is established for State trading countries should only be made where they are completely satisfied that [such] difficulties do not arise.[71]

At least one author has argued that, compared to previous cases, the *Bicycles* case represented a regressive change in the application of EC anti-dumping law.[72]

Although revising some of the Commission's provisional stage analysis, the analysis by the Council thus essentially repeated and confirmed the views of the Commission. On 8 September 1993, the Council adopted a Regulation imposing an anti-dumping duty of 30.6 per cent.[73] In an EU of only 12 Member States, it gave little sign that it was composed of the Member States' trade ministers, and therefore potentially embodied a diversity of interests and positions. The Council Regulation consecrated in legally binding form the basic arguments made in July 1991 by the EBMA.

[68] *Ibid*, para 25.
[69] *Ibid*, para 26.
[70] *Ibid*, para 17.
[71] *Ibid*, para 21.
[72] Donghui Fu, 'EC Anti-dumping Law and Individual Treatment Policy in Cases Involving Imports from China' (1997) 31(1) *Journal of World Trade* 73.
[73] *Bicycles from China* (definitive), above n 59. This was Council Regulation (EEC) No 2474/93 of 8 September 1993 imposing a definitive anti-dumping duty on imports into the Community of bicycles originating in the People's Republic of China and collecting definitively the provisional anti-dumping duty [1993] OJ L228/1.

D. Shanghai Bicycle Corporation's Strategy of Litigation

Under EC law, a party which is directly and individually concerned by a decision in the form of a Regulation is entitled to bring a case to annul the legal measure.[74] Litigation was therefore one strategy open to Chinese exporters. A leading Chinese exporter took the case to court. On 23 December 1993, the Shanghai Bicycle Corporation (Group) lodged at the Registry of the European Court of Justice an application for annulment of the Council Regulation imposing the definitive duty.[75] The applicant was the principal company of the Group, an SOE engaged in manufacturing and exporting, composed of 13 production units.[76] By 1994, it had formed a joint venture with the Giant Company and began assembling bicycles near Shanghai; the planned annual capacity by 1996 was to be 1.5 million bicycles.[77]

From all accounts, the Shanghai Bicycle Corporation was not among the companies sampled by the Commission at the provisional stage. After provisional duties were imposed, however, it submitted comments in writing to the Commission, as did a number of other Chinese exporters, Community producers, and independent importers and traders. Some appeared before the Commission to make their submissions orally, though it is not clear whether Shanghai Bicycle Corporation was among them. For the Chinese exporters, as for the European institutions and the EBMA, judicial review was the logical next step, using administrative procedure, legislation and the courts as part of broader competing strategies for the protection or opening of markets.[78] In the case brought by Shanghai Bicycle Corporation, the Council was supported by the Commission and by the EBMA. Since jurisdiction for anti-dumping cases was transferred to the Court of First Instance (CFI) as of 1 January 1994, the CFI assumed jurisdiction.[79] Here I focus only on selected aspects of the case.

The applicant argued that the EC's refusal to grant individual treatment was contrary to the basic EC Anti-dumping Regulation and to the GATT.[80] It also argued that it met fully the conditions for individual treatment set down in a Commission Memorandum of 1 December 1992, which specified the line of conduct that the Commission intended to adopt with regard to JVs in non-market economy countries. It claimed it was entirely free to sell its products abroad, without any State interference, and that it generally sold to unrelated importers in the EU on freely negotiated terms. In its view, it was for the EC institutions to prove State control of exports, not just to assume it and to leave the burden of proving the contrary to the exporters. It also

74 The relevant EC Treaty article today is Art 263 TFEU. I omit discussion of relevant case law concerning direct concern and individual concern.

75 Case C-477/93 *Shanghai Bicycle Corporation Group v Council of the European Union*, subsequently transferred to the Court of First Instance.

76 *Ibid*, paras 24, 26, 29.

77 Wan-wen Chu, above n 8, at 65, fn 2.

78 Litigation in the European courts by Chinese companies remains rare, however. As of 2006, only six Chinese companies, including the Shanghai Bicycle Corporation, had challenged EC anti-dumping determinations in court. See Han Xiaowei, *Study of the Antidumping Cases in the European Court of Justice: the Special Regulations Regarding China 'Non-Market Economy' State*, Working Paper 2006/3, Centre for European Studies, Peking University (in Chinese). This study includes wholly Chinese companies. It does not concern EU companies with a Chinese-invested partner.

79 Case T-170/94 *Shanghai Bicycle Corporation Group v Council of the European Union* [1997] ECR II-1383.

80 Notably Art VI(2) GATT, embodied in Art 8(3) of the Anti-dumping Agreement, in turn incorporated in Art 13(3) of the EC Anti-dumping Regulation.

argued that China was a 'socialist market economy', not a State-trading country, and that companies were responsible for their profits and losses, even though individuals could not own company shares. The first and third arguments were new to the case, or at least there is no indication in the published documents that Chinese exporters had claimed rights based on the GATT or proposed the macro-economic argument about China's economic transformation.

The Council unfortunately, but not surprisingly, took a different view. It noted that neither EC nor GATT law required individual treatment, that the applicant had not demonstrated its freedom to act independently of the State, and that, despite some changes in China, export companies remained subject to State ownership and control. The Council continued:

> In any event, even by conducting an on-the-spot investigation, it is impossible to ascertain the exact degree of State control: on the one hand, some laws are not published and foreigners do not have access to them and, on the other, certain practices take precedence over the law.[81]

Again, this argument was new, so far as one can judge from published documents, but its direct relevance to the case is not clear. It placed the applicant in a double-bind, for if the argument were true, the applicant automatically lost; and if it were false, the applicant failed to satisfy the burden of proof placed upon it.

The CFI, in its judgment of 25 September 1997, agreed with the Council. It demonstrated substantial deference to the EC anti-dumping authorities.[82] It placed the burden of proof squarely on the applicant. It also noted that the applicant

> has not rebutted the argument set out . . . that during the investigation period the People's Republic of China was in transition from a fully State-controlled economy. Nor has it challenged the claim that State control subsisted in many aspects of economic life and that the law and institutions necessary for the functioning of a market economy were not sufficiently developed and familiar to the traders and officials concerned.[83]

It is of considerable importance that, so far as one can ascertain from the case report, the CFI also accepted that statement by the Chinese Government representative that the State coordinated the activities of all bicycle manufacturers. It considered that the fact that the applicant did not deny that this statement had been made to be tantamount to accepting the veracity of the statement,[84] and that this indicated State control over the applicant's exports. The CFI also said that the applicant's statement that China was a 'socialist market economy', 'impliedly acknowledge[s] that it remains a State-trading country'.[85] Regardless of one's view of the concept of a 'socialist market economy', it is difficult to understand how this statement could amount to such an implicit acknowledgement. Most importantly, however, it is difficult to understand how these points about the Chinese economy as a whole are directly relevant to the question at issue, namely, whether the applicant acted on a market economy basis in determining its export prices.

Lastly, the CFI considered the Commission's Memorandum of 11 December 1992 to be a purely internal document, hence the Memorandum could not bind another

[81] *Shanghai Bicycle Corp,* above n 79, para 100.
[82] See *ibid*, paras 101–16.
[83] *Ibid*, para 112.
[84] *Ibid*, para 113.
[85] *Ibid*, para 114.

Community institution and the applicant could not rely on it in court.[86] This was another obstacle to Shanghai Bicycle Corporation's claims that the anti-dumping duty should be annulled, or that it should be granted individual treatment. The CFI judgment consolidated the definitive duties on Chinese bicycles.

One point that does not emerge clearly from the case report deserves to be emphasised. This is the distinction between status as an SOE, on the one hand, and operation on a market basis on the domestic market, the export market or both, on the other hand. The Commission, the Council and the CFI simply presumed that the distinction did not exist. It was up to the Shanghai Bicycle Corporation to prove the contrary. The analysis of the CFI remained very general. It assumed, for example, that State coordination of the industry automatically meant State control of companies on their export markets. The CFI judgment as published does not show that the Shanghai Bicycle Corporation adduced sufficient evidence to demonstrate the contrary. It is not clear why this was so. At the time, EC anti-dumping law concerning individual treatment was in considerable flux, and Chinese companies (and their lawyers) often did not participate so actively and knowledgeably in EC anti-dumping cases as they did in later years. In any event, after 1997, as part of the reform of SOEs in China, the Shanghai Bicycle Corporation (Group) changed its name and business scope. It became a subsidiary of Shanghai Light Industry Holding Company (Group).[87] The Shanghai Bicycle Corporation (Group) was renamed the Shanghai Sheng Long Corporation (Group). In this capacity, its business includes not only bicycle production and distribution, but also plastic accessories to automobiles, foreign trade, real estate and logistics.[88] Clearly, as of the time of the litigation it was an SOE, but this does not necessarily mean that the Chinese Government controlled its strategy and operations on export markets, such as the EU market.

The CFI judgment vindicated the position of the Commission, the Council and hence of the EBMA. Bicycle imports were subject to the conventional EC duty of 6 per cent, and also to the anti-dumping duty of 30.6 per cent.[89] After 1992, they were no longer eligible for the preferential treatment of a 70 per cent reduction of the conventional duty rate under the EC Generalised Scheme of Preferences (GSP) system.[90]

[86] *Ibid*, para 115.

[87] This Group was established in December 1995. Its webpage describes it as follows: 'Shanghai Light Industry Holding Company (Group) was established in December 1995 through the reorganization and change . . . in composition of its founders. Shanghai Light Industry Bureau and Shanghai Second Light Industry Bureau is [*sic*] an organization operating state assets and approved by the Shanghai Municipal Government and authorized by the Shanghai State Assets Administrative Committee. It is a solely state-owned limited liability company with independent legal status.' Its registered capital as of 2004 was 3.8 million RMB. The Group administered 32 companies (groups) and subordinates, including 572 enterprises invested by subordinate holding companies but entrusted to subordinates for management. It also had 179 joint ventures. The Group itself entered into JVs and other cooperative relations with multinational companies, such as the American companies Coca Cola, Alcoa, Gillette and Kodak; the Japanese companies Hitachi, Fuji, Xerox, Daikin, Minolta, Suntory and Kokyo; and the European companies Unilever, Novaritis, Danon and Zwilling JA Henkels. Such JVs and cooperative arrangements accounted for 69% of the gross industry output value of the holding company at the end of 2001. See the website of Shanghai Light Industry Holding Company (Group) at http://www.slihgc.com/qinggong_en/intro.php, last accessed 17 February 2010

[88] I am grateful to Bao Yongqing for help with research on this company. As of 2004, the website of the company was www.sunrise-cn.com, last accessed 17 December 2004, but now it seems no longer available. It is not clear to me whether or not the same company now operates as Shanghai Sunrise Trading Co Ltd, which is listed in *China Bicycle Yearbook 2005* (Tokyo, Cycle Press, 2004), at 90.

[89] See http://www.eurochinabusiness.com/faq/chin.htm, last visited 20 October 2004.

[90] GSP treatment was withdrawn for bicycles from China by Commission Regulation (EEC) No 1193/92 [1992] OJ L124/9.

The judgment shut the door of the European market for direct exports of bicycles by most Chinese exporters, including the Shanghai Bicycle Corporation, at least in the short run. In the medium and longer term, however, this did not prevent Chinese companies from improving their position in the EU market. In fact, despite anti-dumping duties, imports of bicycle parts from China into the EU continued to increase. Chinese exporters simply developed new business and legal strategies.

III. Globalisation, Circumvention and Economic Regulation

A. Competing Legal Strategies in a Globalised Industry

More than two years after definitive duties were imposed, and 18 months before the CFI judgment in the Shanghai Bicycle Corporation annulment action, the EBMA on 7 March 1996 asked the Commission to open another investigation.[91] It claimed that bicycle parts and accessories were being imported from China and used in the assembly of bicycles in the Community. The parts were bicycle frames, forks, rims and hubs.[92] The EBMA evidence indicated that, between 1992 and 1995, imports of bicycles from China into the three main EC importing Member States had decreased by more than 96 per cent, but imports of frames had increased by over 200 per cent.[93] Such parts were not required to pay the 30.6 per cent anti-dumping duty on assembled bicycles. The same evidence also showed that prices for bicycles assembled in the Community from Chinese parts were lower than the non-dumped level of the export price established in the original investigation for bicycles assembled in China.[94] The EBMA claimed that these imports were undermining the effects of the anti-dumping duty. This complaint was to have numerous expected and unexpected consequences, many to the detriment of the EBMA. To paraphrase a European Commission official, in the ensuing debacle the EBMA found out that 'the bicycle world is very small'.[95]

The EBMA complaint framed the issues in terms of circumvention. Circumvention is a hotly contested issue in international trade law.[96] The EC first included anti-circumvention provisions in its anti-dumping law in 1987, originally to deal with the establishment of 'screwdriver factories' in Europe after the imposition of anti-dumping duties.[97] In 1990, a GATT panel in *EEC—Regulation on Imports of Parts and Components*[98] found the application of EC anti-circumvention rules to products from

[91] Commission Regulation (EC) No 703/96 initiating an investigation concerning the circumvention of anti-dumping measures imposed by Council Regulation (EC) No 2474/93 on imports of bicycles originating in the People's Republic of China by assembly operations in the European Community, para 2 [1996] OJ L98/3.

[92] CN codes 8714 91 10, 8714 91 30, 8714 92 10 and 8714 93 10, respectively.

[93] Commission Regulation (EC) No 703/96, above n 91, preamble, para 6(a).

[94] *Ibid*, preamble, para 6(b).

[95] Interview, European Commission, Brussels.

[96] For a more recent example, see *United States—Rules of Origin for Textiles and Apparel Products*, Report of the Panel, 20 June 2003, WT/DS243/R.

[97] Art 13(10) of Council Regulation (EC) No 2176/84, as amended by Council Regulation (EC) No 1761/87, [1987] OJ L167/9.

[98] *EEC—Regulation on Imports of Parts and Components*, Panel Report adopted on 16 May 1990, BISD 375/132 (1991).

Japan to be inconsistent with the Article III GATT non-discrimination principle. However, the EC did not change its law. Current EC anti-dumping legislation provides that anti-dumping duties may be extended to imports when circumvention is taking place. It defines circumvention, in part, as

> a change in the pattern of trade between third countries and the Community or between individual companies in the country subject to the measures and the Community, which stems from a practice, process or work for which there is insufficient due cause or economic justification other than the imposition of the duty . . .[99]

As for assembly operations, the EC basic Regulation today provides that an assembly operation, in the EC or elsewhere, is considered to amount to circumvention when, *inter alia*, the imported parts constitute 60 per cent of more of the total value of the parts of the assembled product, except if the value added to the imported parts during assembly or completion amounts to more than 25 per cent of the total manufacturing cost.[100] Since the beginning of the Uruguay Round negotiations, and until now, GATT/WTO Members have not able to agree on a definition of circumvention or on how to deal with it.[101] Until recently, the EC and the United States argued in favour of the inclusion of anti-circumvention in domestic and international anti-dumping law or other international trade regulation. Asian countries, including China, have taken the opposite position.[102] It is no exaggeration to say that 'One country's circumvention is often another country's globalisation'.

Concluding that the evidence was sufficient to justify the initiation of an investigation under Article 13(3) of the basic Regulation, the Commission opened an investigation.[103] It directed customs authorities to register imports of parts for a period of nine months.[104] It also provided that certificates of non-circumvention could be granted in appropriate cases, thus exempting covered importers from registration or other measures.[105] It sent questionnaires to the Community assemblers, seeking other information and notifying the Chinese authorities.

The investigation covered the period 1 April 1995 to 31 March 1996.[106] Eight of the EC companies mentioned in the complaint or subsequently named sent complete replies to the Commission; two were found to be genuine Community producers, and one was found to be an importer,[107] leaving five assemblers. Ten Community producers

[99] Council Regulation (EC) No 384/96, above n 31, Art 13(1), consolidated version.

[100] *Ibid*, Art 13(2), consolidated version.

[101] See TP Stewart (ed), *The GATT Uruguay Round: A Negotiating History (1986–1992), Volume II: Commentary* (Deventer and Boston, Kluwer, 1993), 1383–1710.

[102] The classic Chinese and Indian position is that circumvention should cover only illegal behaviour, such as the use of false certificates of origin, and that it should not cover delocalisation of factories and shipping parts instead of the entire product. See *United States—Rules of Origin for Textiles and Apparel Products*, above n 96, Panel Report adopted 21 July 2003. However, the Chinese argument in the recent *China—Measures Affecting Imports of Auto Parts*, WT/DS340 (also WT/DS339 and WT/DS342), Appellate Body Report adopted 12 January 2009, is very similar to the EC argument in *Chinese Bicycles*, suggesting that legal positions can change and are often contingent upon political and economic interests.

[103] Commission Regulation (EC) No 706/96, above n 91, Art 1.

[104] *Ibid*, Art 2(2), (3).

[105] *Ibid*, Art 2(3).

[106] Council Regulation (EC) No 71/97 of 10 January 1997 extending the definitive anti-dumping duty imposed by Regulation (EEC) No 2474/93 on bicycles originating in the People's Republic of China to imports of certain bicycle parts from the People's Republic of China, and levying the extended duty on such imports registered under Regulation (EC) No 703/96, para 4 [1997] OJ L16/55; Corrigendum [1997] OJ L95/30; Corrigendum [1997] OJ L179/11.

[107] *Ibid*, para 5.

requested a certificate of non-circumvention within the deadline,[108] and eight others did so after the deadline.[109]

On the whole, investigation showed that, between 1992 and 1996, imports of bicycles from China decreased by more than 98 per cent, or 1.5 million bicycles, but imports of frames increased by almost 140 per cent (in units), or about 450,000 units. The production of bicycles assembled from Chinese parts by the five investigated EU companies increased during this period by 80 per cent, or 110,000 units.[110] All of the parts were consigned from China.[111] Some had Chinese certificates of origin to benefit from preferential treatment under the GSP. Others were declared as of non-Chinese origin so not subject to duty, though the two companies involved were unable to provide sufficient evidence during on-the-spot verifications.[112] For all five companies, the value added to imported parts varied between only 10 per cent and 16 per cent.[113]

The investigation also showed that four assemblers ordered almost complete bicycles in disassembled form from China during the investigation period.[114] As the Commission pointed out, 'parts destined for the same supplier were spread across different containers, sent on different dates and sometimes unloaded at different ports'.[115] This avoided anti-dumping duties which would have been imposed on bicycles or on parts imported together, in which case they would have been classified as complete bicycles. Other Chinese companies moved their production facilities from China to Taiwan and exported assembled bicycles from there. Still others had recourse to false certificates of origin, so that their bicycles, though exported from China, were stated to originate from a country not subject to anti-dumping duties, for example Poland. Again, the evidence demonstrates that some Chinese companies engaged in these activities,[116] but I wish to emphasise that it does not indicate that the Shanghai Bicycle Corporation in particular did so. Nevertheless, it is clear that some EU companies which immediately after the imposition of duties on full bicycles imported most of their bicycles in the form of parts, began to assemble bicycles using a majority of non-Chinese parts. Other producers, which had long imported parts, obtained binding tariff information from national authorities, classifying imported sub-assemblies of parts not as whole bicycles, and thus received official assurance that duties would not be applied to their imports. The situation of Starway illustrates the resulting clash of business and legal strategies. Starway SA was a small company located in Luynes, near Aix-en-Provence in southern France. Established in 1985, it manufactured and sold bicycles. The China Bicycle Company (CBC), one of the largest bicycle manufacturers in China, took over Starway in 1992. From the perspectives of both the CBC and Starway, this represented a legal strategy of international economic and legal integration. Such overseas direct foreign investment (ODFI) as seen from the Chinese viewpoint, ran counter to European expectations at the time concerning the dynamics and direction of globalisation. The CBC was one of the two largest manufacturers of bicycle frames.[117] It

[108] *Ibid*, para 7.
[109] *Ibid*, para 8.
[110] *Ibid*, para 11.
[111] *Ibid*, para 14.
[112] *Ibid*, para 15.
[113] *Ibid*, para 18.
[114] *Ibid*, para 4.
[115] *Ibid*, para 10.
[116] See *Bicycles from China* [2000] OJ L175/39 (definitive, extension), paras 42–48.
[117] The other was Giant: Galvin and Morkel, above n 8, at 42.

brought Starway to the centre of the process of internationalisation which was underway in the world bicycle market. The CBC had production units in mainland China. It purchased bicycles from two CBC companies established in Hong Kong, the Hong Kong (Link) Bicycles Ltd and Regal International Development Ltd.[118] It exported bicycle parts and bicycles to Europe, where Starway and other companies assembled and/or sold them.

In 1996, Starway found itself in the midst of an EC anti-dumping investigation. As already seen, the European Commission, in the early 1990s, had imposed anti-dumping duties on imports of bicycles from China. Chinese producers and exporters reacted by exporting bicycle parts instead of complete bicycles. The Commission then opened an investigation into alleged circumvention.[119] The EC companies mentioned in the original complaint by the EBMA, or subsequently named, sent complete replies to the Commission questionnaire.[120] Two were found to be genuine Community producers, and one was found to be an importer, leaving five assemblers, including Starway.

The Commission sent Starway a questionnaire, which the company completed and returned. The Commission then made an on-site visit at the company headquarters in Luynes. It asked the company to provide documentary evidence proving the origin of parts used. Starway demonstrated the Community origin of parts sourced in the EU, but it was not able to prove to the Commission's satisfaction that any part consigned from China had any other origin than China. Starway claimed that the origin of its parts could be proved using CBC's bills of materials, some of which were available only at CBC headquarters in Hong Kong. It deposited three boxes of documents—'with a total of approximately one cubic metre'—at the Commission's offices in Brussels: six pages of explanations and 82 pages of annexes were required to demonstrate the origin of a single part.[121] Following discussion, it was agreed that the Commission would carry out another on-site investigation. However, Starway also argued that, in the circumstances, the Commission was not legally entitled to insist on certificates of origin. After the second on-site investigation, the Commission concluded that all of Starway's imported parts were of Chinese origin, and that more than 60 per cent of the total value of the parts of the assembled product were Chinese, so anti-dumping duties were extended to the parts imported by Starway. This decision, part of the Commission's legal strategy, foiled the legal strategies so far of both Starway and CBC.

Such business strategies, legal strategies and competing legal perspectives on circumvention and globalisation were facilitated by the context of the world bicycle industry. Producing a bicycle requires more than 100 different parts.[122] Today the bicycle industry is based on product modularity, notably standardisation of the ways in which bicycle components connect and of the spatial location and dimensions of the components, such as tyres, rims, hubs, frames, handlebars, cranks, pedals, saddle, chain and gear cogs, through what Galvin and Morkel call standardised 'attachment and spatial interfaces'.[123] This has implications for both business organisation and legal strategies.

[118] Case T-80/97 *Starway SA v Council of the European Union* [2000] ECR II-3099, para 6.
[119] Commission Regulation (EC) No 703/96, above n 91.
[120] See *Bicycle Parts from China* [1997] OJ L16/55, on which the following paragraph also relies.
[121] *Ibid*, para 25.
[122] Wan-wen Chu, above n 8, at 63.
[123] Galvin and Morkel, above n 8, at 32. Their discussion of interfaces and modularity relies on R Sanchez, 'Towards a Science of Strategic Product Design: System Design, Component Modularity, and

According to Galvin and Morkel, 'the bicycle industry is made up of a number of small and fairly independent industries'.[124] Their analysis indicates that the contemporary bicycle industry may be considered to be four semi-independent industries or industry segments (see Figure 2 below): those producing parts for other industries, such as tyres, cables and ball bearings; those producing mechanical parts of the bicycle, including the drive train, brakes, gears and hubs; those producing non-moving parts of the bicycle, such as saddles, rims and handlebars; and the frame manufacturers, of which the largest are Giant and the CBC.[125]

With regard to legal strategies, such an industrial structure favours contracting rather than vertical integration, outsourcing as a means of maintaining low prices[126] and the use of widely accepted international standards as a means of ensuring quality of products flexibility. Instead of long-term legal arrangements it may also encourage a continuing search for a more favourable position through personal relations, soft norms or short-term law, through personal relationships or both. These causal relations are not one way. Legal strategies, such as contracting, outsourcing and the

Figure 2 Industry Segments and Material Flows in the Bicycle Industry

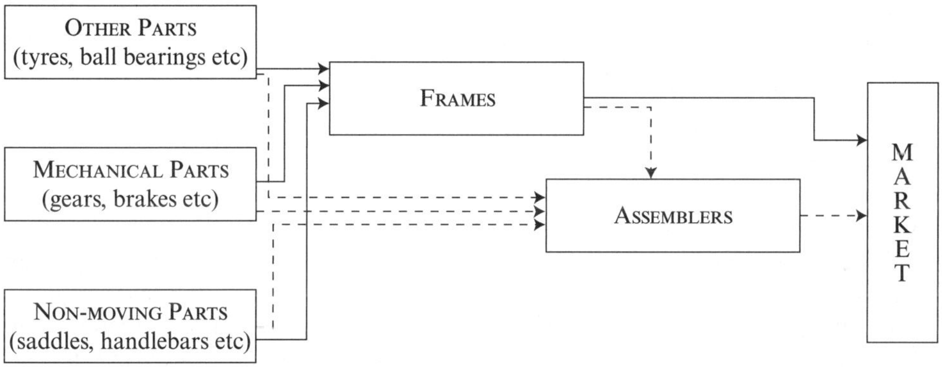

Note: The various parts are sent to firms in the frame manufacturing segment which assemble complete bicycles for the market. These material flows are indicated with the solid lines. The other material flow is all of thebicycle components and frames moving to assemblers that complete the product for distribution to the market. These flows are indicated with dotted lines.

Source: P Galvin and A Morkel, 'The Effect of Product Modularity on Industry Structure: The Case of the World Bicycle Industry' (2001) 8(1) *Industry and Innovation* 31 at 42 [including notes].

Product Leveraging Strategies', *Proceedings of the Second International Product Development Conference on New Approaches to Development and Engineering*, 30–31 May 1994, European Institute for Advanced Studies in Management, Brussels, Belgium, and on R Sanchez and JT Mahoney, 'Modularity and Dynamic Capabilities' in HW Voberda and T Elfring (eds), *Rethinking Strategy* (London, Sage, 2000). See also R Sanchez, 'Product and Process Architectures in the Management of Knowledge Resources' in PI Robertson and NJ Foss (eds), *Resources, Technology and Strategy: Explorations in the Resource-based Perspective* (London, Routledge, 2000) 100; R Sanchez and JT Mahoney, 'Modularity, Flexibility and Knowledge Management in Product and Organisation Design' (1996) 17 (Winter Special Issue) *Strategic Management Journal* 63.

[124] Galvin and Morkel, above n 8, at 39.
[125] *Ibid*, at 41–42.
[126] *Ibid*, at 39.

control through international standards, combine with flexibility and competition to reinforce a fragmented industrial structure. The result is an extremely complex set of legal and economic relationships between companies in the world bicycle industry.

Globalisation of the industry also tended to restructure competitive as well as cooperative relationships. Usually we envisage anti-dumping actions as involving a conflict between domestic producers, on the one hand, and foreign producers, on the other hand. The *Chinese Bicycles* saga revealed, however, a considerably more complex picture. Abstracting from relations involving different types of parts, we can distinguish between several sets of relationships. One set certainly concerned the classic scenario pitting EU producers against Chinese producers and exporters. They were direct competitors. Another set embraced EU producers and EU importers. Though both situated in Europe, they had opposing interests. It is necessary to recognise, however, that their specific interests varied according to what producers produced and what importers imported; for example, if the producer was an assembler of bicycles and relied on the importer for brakes, their interests coincided. A third set concerned EU importers of full bicycles and EU importers of bicycle parts. This distinction gained in salience as the *Chinese Bicycles* saga evolved. A fourth set of competitive relations, which also increased in significance later in the dispute, was between long-standing EU importers and assemblers of bicycle parts from China, on the one hand, and EU importers and assemblers which began to import parts from China after definitive anti-dumping duties were imposed on full bicycles, on the other hand.

Throughout and after the investigation, Chinese companies contested the characterisation of their legal strategies as circumvention. Except for the admittedly illegal use of false certificates of origin, they considered that delocalisation, that is moving production facilities from one country to another, and exporting parts instead of whole bicycles, were normal business strategies in a global economy. On this view, companies confronted with a particular legal arrangement, whether concerning quotas, taxation or anti-dumping duties, should be free to arrange their affairs so as to avoid a negative impact on their business. Such activities were legal, and hence entirely different from the use of false certificates of origin, which all parties condemned, at least in principle. Note, however, that European assemblers, which were governed not by Chinese law but by EC law and the national law of their particular EC Member State, also cooperated in and benefited from these activities. In theory it may be true that 'one country's circumvention is another country's globalisation'; in this case, in practice, the Commission's extension of anti-dumping duties to parts decided the question in favour of the EC position, again consecrating in legal form the strategy of the EBMA. The Commission concluded that the facts satisfied the conditions of Article 13 of the basic Regulation concerning circumvention.[127] It also concluded that the imports of parts had undermined the remedial effects of the duty and that there was evidence of dumping. It extended the 30.6 per cent anti-dumping duty on bicycles to certain essential bicycle parts originating in or consigned from China, with the exception of those parts of proven non-Chinese origin. After consulting the Advisory Committee, it made a proposal to the Council to extend the existing duty on imports of bicycles to imports of bicycle parts. The result was Council Regulation (EC) 71/97, known as 'the Anti-circumvention Regulation'.[128]

[127] Council Regulation (EC) 384/96, above n 31, Art 13(1).

[128] Council Regulation (EC) 71/97, above n 106, Art 2. Essential parts are defined in Art 1 of this Regulation.

B. Anti-dumping Law begets Economic Regulation

In the context of the highly globalised and increasingly competitive bicycle industry, the legal strategy of the European Commission, using EC anti-dumping law, quickly proved less than effective in managing the different sets of cooperative and competitive relations involved in the European bicycle market. A major problem was how to minimise affecting imports of parts which did not constitute circumvention. Long before the imposition of duties on bicycles, an unknown number of EC producers imported bicycle parts from China for assembly and sale on the EC market. Some of the problems faced by these mainly small producers were signalled in a European Parliament written question by Mr Klaus-Heiner Lehne (PPE) in September 1997. Commissioner Sir Leon Brittan defended surveillance under the end-use procedure, but noted that this was the first time an anti-dumping duty had ever been imposed under Article 13 (the anti-circumvention provision) of the basic Regulation.[129] Many Community producers had already requested exemption; most had been part of Community industry in the previous investigations.[130] Other companies subsequently applied for exemption.[131] Attempts to deal with their situation gave birth to a complex regulatory scheme. In addition to limiting the extended duty to essential parts, Council Regulation (EC) 71/97 mandated the establishment of a procedure for adopting measures to authorise the exemption of non-circumventing parts.[132]

In January 1997 the Council adopted a Regulation authorising the exemption of imports of certain parts from the extension of anti-dumping duties ('the Exemption Regulation').[133] It was intended to exempt 'traditional assemblers' and 'new assemblers' which respected the 60 per cent anti-circumvention criterion. It exempted imports of essential parts where:

a) they were declared for free circulation by or on behalf of an exempted party; or
b) they were declared for free circulation under provisions on end-use control.

It also provided for:

c) provisional exemption when the parts were declared for free circulation by, or on behalf of, a party under examination.[134]

A company was entitled to request exemption if it provided evidence that it was using essential bicycle parts for the production or assembly of bicycles above a specified threshold, if it provided prima facie evidence that its assembly operations fell outside

[129] Written Question E-2843/97 by Klaus-Heiner Lehne (PPE) to the Commission (11 September 1997) (Subject: Anti-dumping Regulation as applicable to bicycle parts from China), Answer given by Sir Leon Brittan on behalf of the Commission (28 October 1997) [1998] OJ C134/26.

[130] *Ibid*, para 32.

[131] *Ibid*, para 33.

[132] Council Regulation 71/97, above n 106, Art 3, which provided that the necessary measures were to be adopted by the Commission, after consulting the Advisory Committee. This was based on Art 13(4) of the basic Regulation, which provides that products are to be exempted from anti-dumping duties where they are accompanied by a certificate of non-circumvention.

[133] Commission Regulation (EC) No 88/97 of 20 January 1997 on the authorisation of the exemption of imports of certain bicycle parts originating in the People's Republic of China from the extension by Council Regulation (EC) No 71/97 of the anti-dumping duty imposed by Council Regulation (EEC) No 2474/93 [1997] OJ L17/17; Corrigendum [1997] OJ L97/30.

[134] Commission Regulation (EC) No 88/97, above n 133, Art 2.

the scope of the anti-circumvention provisions of the basis anti-dumping Regulation, and if it had not been refused authorisation of exemption or had an exemption revoked within the preceding 12 months.[135] A detailed questionnaire was sent on request to each company concerned, and the companies were informed that a decision would be based on the information provided in each reply, together with possible on-the-spot visits by the Commission to examine company records and verify information. The Commission was required to consult the Advisory Committee before authorising exemption; if a request for exemption was denied, the rejection was required to be in the form of a Commission Decision.[136] Exempted parties were required to ensure that their assembly operations did not involve circumvention and that the parts they received did not leak to parties not benefiting from an exemption; they were also required to keep records of deliveries and use for at least three years.[137] An exemption could be revoked in case of circumvention, failure to retain records or lack of cooperation.[138]

The procedure was very time-consuming, even though the Commission sought to keep the exemption as 'user-friendly' as possible. It was further complicated by the fact that most assemblers were SMEs. Most, except for a few large assemblers, such as the Dutch company Velteck, did not operate on long-term contracts. In addition, new assemblers were confronted not only with increased imports of parts from China but also with the legal requirement to use non-Chinese parts. Production in the bicycle industry is fragmented, and bicycles are relatively inexpensive to set up and simple to assemble. The EC relies on supplies of parts from other countries, as from Shimano, the world's leading producer of mechanical bicycle parts.[139] At first there were few EU assemblers, but the increase in prices for bicycles, due to anti-dumping duties, the restructuring of EU producers and an increase in sales of high-quality bicycles, stimulated the growth of this sub-sector.

Under the Exemption Regulation itself, the Commission initially exempted 11 companies from the extended duty.[140] It also initiated investigations of the requests by 15 other companies.[141] For these companies, payment of duty was suspended pending receipt of further information; as companies furnished information, they were granted exemption or the suspension was lifted.[142] All in all, 10 Community producers

[135] *Ibid*, Art 3.

[136] *Ibid*, Arts 7 and 4(4), respectively.

[137] *Ibid*, Art 8.

[138] *Ibid*, Art 10.

[139] See www.shimano.com. The Chinese subsidiaries are Shimano (Shanghai) Bicycle Components Co Ltd, located in Shanghai, which reported sales of RMB 350 million in 2003 and an expected increase of 20–30% in 2004: *China Bicycle Yearbook 2005* (Tokyo, Cycle Press, 2004) at 94; and Shimano (Kunshan) Bicycle Components Co Ltd, located in Jiansu Province: *China Bicycle Yearbook 2005* (Tokyo, Cycle Press, 2004) at 143.

[140] Commission Regulation (EC) No 88/97, above n 133, Art 12 and Annex II; Corrigendum, above n 133,

[141] Commission Regulation (EC) No 88/97, Art 11 and Annex I. The list of parties was updated in July 2000, so that a total of 37 companies were under examination, and the suspension from the extended duty was lifted for six other companies: Commission Notice updating the list of parties under examination pursuant to Commission Regulation (EC) No 88/97 on the authorisation of imports of certain bicycle parts originating in the People's Republic of China from the extension by Council Regulation (EC) No 71/97 of the anti-dumping duty imposed by Council Regulation (EEC) No 2474/93 and lifting the suspension of the payment of the extended anti-dumping duty granted to certain parties (2000/C216/07), [2000] OJ L216/8.

[142] For example, a list of applicants for which payment of the extended duty was suspended was published in [1997] OJ C45/3; [1997] OJ C112/9; [1997] OJ C378/2; [1998] OJ C217/9; [1999] OJ C37/3; [1999] OJ C186/6; [2000] OJ C216/8.

requested a certificate of non-circumvention within the deadline, and eight others did so soon afterwards. Starway and a UK company returned completed questionnaires, but neither requested a certificate of non-circumvention. Both claimed that more than 40 per cent of the parts they used originated in countries other than China, but they were unable to provide sufficient evidence. However, the UK company changed its sourcing pattern, so anti-dumping duties were not extended to its imports. Subsequently Starway also changed its sourcing of imports. Instead of importing through a CBC-associated company based in Hong Kong and consigning them via China, it ordered and imported parts directly from, and paid directly to, suppliers established in other Asian countries.[143]

Subsequently, a number of other companies, including Starway, also applied for exemption.[144] In many cases, the Commission investigation showed that the value of parts of Chinese origin used in their assembly operations was lower than 60 per cent of the total value of all parts used, and that in some instances the value added to the parts exceeded 25 per cent of the manufacturing cost of the bicycles.[145] The Commission exempted 18 other companies from the duty.[146] These companies included Starway. Its application was granted, but only with effect from 18 April 1997, the date of its application.[147]

Starway then turned to litigation. It hired a leading Brussels lawyer to bring an action in the CFI to annul the extension of the definitive anti-dumping duty to its imports of parts between 20 April 1996, the date when the Regulation initiating the investigation entered into force, and 18 April 1997, the date when the exemption decision of 28 January 1998 took effect vis-à-vis Starway.[148] The CFI upheld Starway's claim. It concluded that, before the extension of the duty, no specific rules required a trader to obtain certificates of origin to prove non-preferential origin, and in the absence of such a duty it was not customary practice in international trade to do so. The CFI held that to require certificates of origin to the exclusion of other means of proof would infringe Article 13(2) of the basic Regulation, where the EC institutions are aware that some of the traders concerned are unable to produce such certificates for reasons beyond their control.[149] Emphasising 'the exceptional circumstances' of the case, an argument due, no doubt, to Starway's experienced lawyer, the CFI stated that the Commission was required to examine carefully and impartially the documents provided by Starway. It found that the Commission was wrong to reject this evidence because of its volume and complexity. Consequently, it annulled the contested measure.

This victory was sweet but short-lived. The anti-dumping duties imposed by the EC on Chinese exporters led to changes in the international bicycle sector. In addition to stifling direct exports of bicycles from China, they had previously unforeseen and unintended effects on EC importers and non-exempt assemblers. A number of small companies which had originally been exempted from duties stopped assembling

[143] See *Starway SA v Council of the European Union*, above n 118, para 64.

[144] Commission Decision 98/115/EC of 28 January 1998 exempting imports of certain bicycle parts originating in the People's Republic of China from the extension by Council Regulation (EC) No 71/97 of the anti-dumping duty imposed by Council Regulation (EEC) No 2474/93, [1998] OJ L31/25.

[145] *Ibid*, para 3.

[146] *Ibid*, Art 1 and Annex.

[147] *Ibid*.

[148] *Starway SA v Council of the European Union*, above n 118.

[149] *Ibid*, para 112.

bicycles, failed or for other reasons went out of business. One of them, by 2002, was Starway.[150] Its legal strategies to compete and survive failed. Other companies also turned to litigation to defend their interests, but with less success, even in the short term. One example was Büchel & Co, established in Fulda, Germany. An intermediary importer of certain bicycle parts, it mainly produced bicycle parts and marketed them as an ancillary activity. It was a shareholder in Hua Da Plastics Corporation Ltd, which produced bicycle parts and had its registered office in Shanghai. Büchel & Co brought an action to annul both the Anti-circumvention Regulation and the Exemption Regulation, but it was unsuccessful.[151]

Law created law. The Exemption Regulation set up a complex scheme of economic regulation. In effect, under the cover of anti-dumping, it created an intricate system of economic regulation, embracing both international and domestic competition. Unfortunately for the legal strategies of the EBMA and the Commission, subsequent events suggested that, in setting up this regulatory scheme, the Commission underestimated the fragmentation, heterogeneity and complexity of the EU bicycle market, or, due to shortage of resources, simply failed to conduct the necessary market research. From the sociological standpoint, it neglected many of its clients. The task of regulating even a portion of such a highly globalised market proved to be extremely costly in terms of scarce administrative resources. A regulatory scheme designed to distinguish between different types of Community producers using parts imported from China revealed many more varieties of companies in the bicycle sector than one might have imagined simply on the basis of those supporting the EBMA complaints. This was especially true of SMEs.

These events also demonstrated the extent to which the EU bicycle sector had already been internationalised, notably through links with Chinese producers and exporters, even before imposition of anti-dumping duties. The exemption procedure itself revealed numerous examples. Renak International GmbH was a German company which was acquired by a Chinese manufacturer in 1993 and started operations in June 1995, after the original investigation on parts. Its application for exemption was denied in May 1998 on the grounds of circumvention.[152] Euro Cycles in France started operations in 1995, with parts from China making up 65 to 95 per cent of the total value of parts used in its assembly of bicycles. Its application for exemption was rejected in May 1998.[153] Techno Cycles (France) began operation and started to assembly bicycles in March 1996. According to Commission findings, it 'on several occasions ordered almost complete bicycles in disassembled form' from China. Its Chinese suppliers ensured 'that the parts destined for Techno Cycles were spread in different containers sent on different dates and invoiced by different companies in Hong Kong having the same address'. In its assembly operations, the proportion of Chinese parts varied from 64 per cent to 96 per cent, with value added in the EU varying

[150] See Council Decision 2002/606/EC of 16 July 2002, [2002] OJ L195/81.

[151] Joined Cases T-74/97 and T-75/97 *Büchel & Co Fahzeugteilefabrik GmbH v Council of the European Union* (T-74/97) *and Commission of the European Communities* (T-75/97), [2000] ECR II-3067.

[152] Commission Decision 98/299/EC of 24 April 1998 rejecting the application submitted by Renak International GmbH (Germany) for an exemption pursuant to Commission Regulation (EC) No 88/97 from the anti-dumping duty extended to certain bicycle parts originating in the People's Republic of China [1998] OJ L133/23.

[153] Commission Decision 98/323/EC of 29 April 1998 rejecting the application submitted by Eurocycles (France) for an exemption pursuant to Commission Regulation (EC) No 88/97 from the anti-dumping duty extended to certain bicycle parts originating in the People's Republic of China [1998] OJ L141/36.

between 12 per cent and 16 per cent. Its application for exemption was rejected too in May 1998.[154]

The extension of duties to parts reinforced this process of internationalisation, or globalisation with Chinese characteristics. This dramatically weakened the position of the EBMA and threatened its survival strategy. By using anti-dumping law, the Commission went some way toward achieving its objectives, but at considerable cost in terms of relations with both EC importers and assemblers, and Chinese producers and exporters.

IV. Renewal of Anti-dumping Duties and the Consequences

A. A Short-Lived Victory for EBMA and Commission Strategies

Under EC law, as under WTO law, anti-dumping measures last in principle for five years, unless renewed. In early 1998 the Commission published a notice that the duties on imports of bicycles from China, which took effect on 10 September 1993, were due to expire.[155] In June 1998, the EBMA asked the Commission for an expiry review.[156] The Association represented about 58 per cent of total Community production.[157] The EBMA argued that, if the measures expired, dumping would resume and damage to Community industry would result. The Commission initiated an investigation. It received questionnaire replies from 10 Community producers and 14 exporting producers in China, including 11 which had exported bicycles to the Community during the investigation period. It carried out investigations at the premises of three producers in Mexico, the analogue country, and at a sample of Community producers. The investigation period was 1 September 1997 to 31 August 1998.

The Commission's investigation indicated that Community imports of bicycles fell from 2.5 million units in 1991 to fewer than 14,000 units during the investigation period. The Chinese producers which cooperated in the investigation accounted for only 30 per cent of imports during the investigation period.[158] Taiwan had been the analogue country in the original investigation, but it was involved in a concurrent anti-dumping proceeding[159] and no interested party proposed it. Mexico was proposed by the Community producers and chosen by the Commission. Regarding dumping, the Commission observed that dumping had increased since duties were first imposed, notably through circumvention, including the establishment of assembly operations, imports of parts or shipping bicycles with false certificates of origin.[160] It concluded

[154] Commission Decision 98/336/EC of 6 May 1998 rejecting the application submitted by Techno Cycles (France) for an exemption pursuant to Commission Regulation (EC) No 88/97 from the anti-dumping duty extended to certain bicycle parts originating in the People's Republic of China [1998] OJ L148/33. The quotations in the preceding text are from para 6 of the Decision.

[155] [1998] OJ L49/1.

[156] *Bicycles from China* [2000] OJ L175/39 (expiry review), para 7.

[157] *Ibid*, para 71.

[158] *Ibid*, para 21.

[159] See *Bicycles from Taiwan* [1999] OJ L49/1 (definitive). Duties had previously been imposed on imports of bicycles from several other Asian countries: see *Bicycles from Indonesia, Malaysia and Thailand* [1996] OJ L91/1.

[160] See *Bicycles from China* (expiry review), above n 156, paras 42–47.

that 'Chinese exporting producers have made little attempt to compete on the Community market at non-dumped price levels'.[161] It noted that Chinese production capacity was high, an estimated 70 million units, and recently there had been 'considerable investment in joint ventures, in particular from Taiwanese companies, and high tax and duty rebates are granted to export-oriented producers'.[162] However, only about 50 per cent of production capacity was being used.[163] Chinese export prices worldwide had fallen by an average of 17 per cent per unit between 1995 and 1997, with a drop of 27 per cent for exports to the USA.[164] Other countries, such as Canada, the United States, Mexico, South Korea and Vietnam, had imposed anti-dumping duties on imports of bicycles from China, which consequently was under pressure to find alternative markets.[165] The Commission concluded that Chinese exports to the EU would increase considerably if the anti-dumping measures were repealed.[166] Its legal strategy thus mirrored that of the EBMA.

The Commission virtually admitted that, during the investigation period, imports of bicycles from China accounted for less than 1 per cent of total consumption in both volume and value terms.[167] It argued, however, that this did not reflect attempts at circumvention or the imports of parts.[168] With regard to the situation of Community industry, it concluded that EC production fell by at least 25 per cent between 1995 up to the investigation period. Its investigation revealed that

> this decrease was the result of several companies going out of business and reduced production by major Community producers. It should also be mentioned that, in order to survive, some Community producers included in the definition of Community industry in the original investigation switched from the complete cycle of production (ie including manufacture of the frames) to simply assembly or sub-assembly operations using imported parts (frame, forks, complete wheels, crank gears, freewheels, brakes, etc).[169]

Partly as a result, there was a significant drop in Community production capacity, with the actual rate of usage during the investigation period (58 per cent) being substantially less than the rate needed for economic viability in the bicycle industry (70 per cent).[170] Volume sales fell by 24 per cent,[171] and Community industry lost 15 per cent of its market share in volume terms between 1995 and the investigation period.[172]

The Commission's investigation pinpointed another major shift in addition to the switch from complete production to assembly or sub-assembly. During the investigation period, the weighted average price of bicycles sold by Community industry increased by 10 per cent. The investigation revealed that

> the main producers included in the definition of Community industry have changed their product mix and moved to higher-end products. This also required them to concentrate their

[161] *Ibid*, para 48.
[162] *Ibid*, para 49.
[163] *Ibid*, paras 50, 51.
[164] *Ibid*, para 59.
[165] *Ibid*, para 60.
[166] *Ibid*, para 69.
[167] *Ibid*, para 81.
[168] *Ibid*, paras 84–86.
[169] *Ibid*, para 91.
[170] *Ibid*, para 94.
[171] *Ibid*, para 95.
[172] *Ibid*, para 97.

sales activities on dealers/retailers whose resale prices are more stable and more attractive as compared to the other major sales channels such as mass-merchandisers and supermarkets.[173]

This represented a tendency toward a three-fold segmentation of the EU market:

a) Community producers producing more expensive bicycles sold through dealers/retailers;
b) Chinese producers producing more expensive bicycles sold through Community importers and dealers/retailers; and
c) Chinese producers producing less expensive bicycles which reach the EC market through Community importers, or producing parts which are assembled by Community producers, with both categories being sold primarily through mass-merchandisers and supermarkets, such as Decathlon, Carrefour and Wal-Mart.

Chinese producers dominated the third segment. Producers in the EC predominated in the first segment but, given the economic potential of China, especially in any situation approaching open competition, this market position could only be regarded as temporary.

These developments presaged a further restructuring of the internationalised EU bicycle industry. They went far beyond what the Commission might have envisaged in developing its legal strategy for managing the EU market.

According to the Commission, the restructuring also helped to account for (or at least was closely related to) the low level of profitability, ranging from –2.3 per cent to –0.6 per cent, far below the 8 per cent which was considered to be the minimum for the industry in the absence of dumped imports.[174] Investment also dropped,[175] and so did employment: 12 per cent of the workforce in 1995 was laid off during the investigation period.[176] The Commission considered that Community industry had remained in a weak and vulnerable position since anti-dumping duties were first imposed in 1993.[177]

Consequently, the Commission concluded that, unless anti-dumping duties were extended, Chinese exporters would occupy up to 15 per cent of the Community market.[178] Prices for Chinese bicycles were expected to be between 40 to 55 per cent below the Community industry average.[179] This would accentuate the restructuring of Community industry toward production of more expensive bicycles.[180] As economic analysis has shown, if the foreign product is of better quality, anti-dumping policy cannot affect price competition. However, consumers will prefer the domestic, higher-quality product if it sells at the same price as the foreign, lower-quality product due to anti-dumping duties. Anti-dumping duties thus aim to counter foreign price competition.[181] An analysis of the

[173] *Ibid*, para 98.
[174] *Ibid*, paras 101–105.
[175] *Ibid*, para 106.
[176] *Ibid*, para 107.
[177] *Ibid*, para 112.
[178] *Ibid*, para 123.
[179] *Ibid*, para 125. Many product markets in China are characterised by low concentration and low profit margins, As of 2003, see Tianshu Chu and Thomas J Prusa, *The Reasons for and the Impact of Antidumping Protection: The Case of People's Republic of China*, East-West Center Working Papers, University of Hawaii, Economics Series, No 69, April 2004, esp 19–21.
[180] *Bicycles from China* (expiry review), above n 156, para 126.
[181] H Vandenbussche and X Wauthy, 'Inflicting Injury through Product Quality: How European Antidumping Policy Disadvantages European Producers' (2001) 17 *European Journal of Political Economy* 101. On the trade-off between price and quality for recreational bicycles in particular, see Galvin and Morkel, above n 8, at 47.

distribution network indicated that Community industry accounted for between 60 per cent and 65 per cent of total sales in the dealer/retailer sales channel, mainly in the medium and high end of the market. However, some Community producers, mainly in France, Germany and the UK, orientated about 80 per cent of their sales to the lower end of the market, specialising in sales to supermarkets, mass-merchandisers and OEM customers.[182] In the Community bicycles sector as a whole, recent years had witnessed 'the emergence of a few groups which have purchased small, well-known brands and production facilities or merged with other companies in order to restructure and reorganise their activities'.[183] In the view of the Commission, this testified to the capacity of the Community industry to adapt, compete and survive.

In analysing whether it would not be in the Community interest to maintain anti-dumping measures, the Commission placed special emphasis of the interests of Community industry. This in itself is common, but in this case the Commission stressed the importance of maintaining 'effective competition'. Although some parties claimed that Community industry should not be shielded from international competition, especially after five years of duties, the Commission considered that anti-dumping duties were necessary to ensure the viability of the SMEs which comprised the bulk of the Community bicycle sector.[184] Hence it proposed to renew, for another five years, the definitive anti-dumping duty on imports of bicycles from China.[185] On 10 July 2000 the Commission's proposal was adopted by the Council.[186]

Three months later, four large Chinese producer/exporters requested an interim review of the anti-dumping duties imposed on them in 1993 and just renewed.[187] Giant (China) Co Ltd, Guangzhou Viva Bicycle Company Ltd, Merida Bicycle (China) Co Ltd and Kenton Bicycle Group Ltd[188] sought to take advantage of a recent reform of the basic EC anti-dumping Regulation by Council Regulation (EC) No 905/95. This amendment allowed Chinese companies to try to demonstrate that they met the five criteria for market economy treatment (MET). If they were able to show this, the Commission was required to determine the dumping margin using the companies' own data, instead of on the basis of an analogue country or simply limited to individual treatment.[189] Soon afterwards, however, the Chinese companies withdrew the requests, one before providing MET data, two others after the Commission indicated that their MET claim would be rejected, and the other because it had no exports during the selected investigation period.[190]

[182] *Bicycles from China* (expiry review), above n 156, para 127.

[183] *Ibid*, para 138.

[184] See *ibid*, paras 134–39.

[185] *Bicycles from China* [2000] OJ L175/39 (definitive).

[186] *Ibid.*

[187] Notice of initiation of an interim review of the anti-dumping measures applicable to imports of bicycles originating in the People's Republic of China (2000/C278/06), [2000] OJ C278/28.

[188] Giant (China) Co Ltd, located in Kunshan, Jiangsu Province, with an annual production capacity of 3 million units by 2003, reported sales of 2.51 million units in 2003: *China Bicycle Yearbook 2005* (Tokyo, Cycle Press, 2004), at 99. Guangzhou Viva Bicycle Co Ltd, located in Guangzhou, with an annual production capacity of 600,000 units in 2004, reported sales of 260,000 units in 2003: *ibid*, at 221. Merida Bicycle (China) Co Ltd, located in Shenzhen, reported an annual production capacity of 1.8 million units as of 2004: *ibid*, at 201. Kenton Bicycle Group does not seem to be listed in *China Bicycle Yearbook 2005*.

[189] Council Regulation (EC) No 384/96, above n 31, Art 2(7)(b), (c), as amended by Council Regulation (EC) No 905/95 [1998] OJ L128/18.

[190] Council Regulation (EC) No 2131/2001 of 29 October 2001 terminating the review of Council Regulation (EC) No 2472/93 imposing a definitive anti-dumping duty on imports of bicycles originating in the People's Republic of China [2001] OJ L289/8.

B. The Successive Phases

Before examining the consequences, mainly unintended, of the renewal of anti-dumping duties on bicycles in 2000, it is instructive to consider briefly the successive phases of the *Chinese Bicycles* saga. They did not result in any fundamental changes to the stage or to the drama being enacted, but nevertheless they reflected on and amplified what went before, and set it in a slightly different framework. On this basis, we can then consider the consequences of the entire saga as a whole, including the entire period from the early 1990s to the present.

The period after 2000 centred on major procedures and pieces of legislation. The first procedure was an interim review of Council Regulation (EC) No 1524/2000 maintaining the anti-dumping duties on bicycles. On 29 April 2004, the Commission published a Notice announcing the initiation of the review. There were three striking parts of the investigation.

A first unusual part of the investigation was the involvement of the EU Ombudsman in the investigation procedures. On 3 May 2005, a lawyer for a European importer complained to the Ombudsman about the way in which the Commission investigated his or her client. The complaint recited that 'the Commission's case-handlers who carried out the verification . . . were ill-prepared, failed to reply to requests for clarification, were extremely aggressive, and applied an unacceptable verification methodology'. The Ombudsman forwarded the complaint to the Commission for an opinion. Before receiving the opinion, however, the complainant wrote to the Ombudsman to withdraw the complaint. It had already been informed by the Commission that there would be a new investigation, with different case-handlers. The Ombudsman closed the case on 9 December 2005.[191] The incident indicated that how acrimonious the *Chinese Bicycles* saga had become, even in Europe.

The second, most important, unusual aspect of the investigation resulted from the fact that 10 Chinese producers, including Giant (China) Co Ltd, Guangzhou Viva Bicycle Corporation Ltd and Merida Bicycle Co Ltd, applied for MET.[192] None of the requests was granted. The reason given by the Commission was that all Chinese exporters were subject to an export quota system, according to a 2001 Chinese Regulation approved by MOFTEC (now Mofcom) and the Chinese customs authorities. Allocation of quotas was made by a committee consisting of representatives from MOFTEC, the appropriate Chamber of Commerce and the Association of Foreign-funded Enterprises on the basis of criteria established by MOFTEC. This system also included minimum export prices, the establishment of minimum export prices and the establishment of maximum export volumes. MOFTEC and the customs authorities monitored export prices and volumes by the validation of actual export sales contracts. On this basis, the Commission concluded that the applicants for MET were not able to demonstrate that they operated without 'significant' State interference, as required by the MET criteria in the amended basic Regulation. For the same reason, but concerning only the export market, the Commission also denied individual treatment.

[191] Decision of the European Ombudsman 1737/2005/PB on complaint against the European Commission, http://www.ius.info/EUII/EUO/dokumenti/2005/12/European_Ombudsman_Decision_17372005PB_09_12_2005.htm, last accessed 17 February 2010.

[192] This paragraph and the following paragraph are based on Council Regulation (EC) No 2131/2001, above n 190, paras 31–33, 45–47.

This conclusion is difficult to understand, except as a rather rigid application of the letter of the amended basic Regulation. Reflecting what has occurred in cities such as the Municipality of Shanghai, where exports are now carefully monitored so as to prevent anti-dumping problems if possible,[193] the Chinese central government authorities appeared to be taking action to control the prices and volumes of exports. This was done not by setting prices or volumes, but rather by a system of floor prices and volume ceilings. It was a type of administrative guidance, not a manifestation of a complete governmental control of the economy. This effort by MOFTEC to minimise eventual difficulties with China's major trading partners was not recognised formally at all by the Commission. Perhaps not wanting to encourage voluntary export restraints, the Commission appeared to give no credit to its Chinese counterpart, even though the measures were autonomous Chinese measures. Instead, the Commission appeared to focus on the letter rather than the spirit of the law. It also seemed to have lost sight of a central objective of anti-dumping, namely, to protect domestic producers against price competition. Instead, it focused on certain broader objectives, in particular the relation between the State and the market, and an idealistic view of the transformation of the Chinese economy towards a rather rigid characterisation of a market economy, one which hardly exists in any EU Member State or elsewhere. Neither of these objectives is a proper aim of anti-dumping law. Lastly, the Commission's conclusion was not really relevant to whether the Chinese companies operated on a market basis with regard to price competition on the domestic market or on the export market. Again, the Commission seemed to have lost sight of the stated purpose of anti-dumping law. The Commission strategy mirrored that of the EBMA, perhaps in an attempt to reassure this segment of its numerous clients. However, it is open to serious criticism for being extremely short-sighted and for misreading the Chinese Government policy. One might see certain parameters of this lack of understanding in the Explanatory Memorandum by the Commission accompanying its proposal to the Council. The Memorandum recited that the need to ensure consistency with other EU policies and objectives did not apply to anti-dumping measures, external expertise was not needed and the basic anti-dumping Regulation did not foresee a general impact assessment.[194]

A third unusual aspect of the investigation, less damaging to the Commission strategy, was that the investigation uncovered a link between anti-dumping law and competition law.[195] The Dutch competition authorities had imposed a fine on two subsidiaries of the Accell Group NV, a sampled Community producer, for an agreement concerning common minimum prices with two other Community producers and Giant Europe BA, which was related to Giant (China) Co Ltd. Accell had appealed to the Dutch competition authorities. The period of the agreement overlapped with the period of investigation in the anti-dumping proceedings. As a result, the Commission excluded Accell from its analysis of injury, but otherwise concluded that the price-fixing agreement had little, if any, effect on the anti-dumping action. This incident demonstrated, once again, the complexity of relations in the highly globalised bicycle

193 Based on interviews in Shanghai.

194 Commission of the European Communities, Proposal for a Council Regulation imposing a definitive anti-dumping duty on imports of bicycles originating in Vietnam, [and] amending Regulation (EC) No 1524/2000 imposing a definitive anti-dumping duty on imports of bicycles originating in the People's Republic of China, COM(2005) final, Brussels, 9 June 2005, at 2.

195 Council Regulation (EC) No 2131/2001, above n 190, paras 98–102.

industry and the fact that complicated anti-dumping cases may involve numerous aspects of EU law, thus demanding a broad knowledge of EU law on the part of the anti-dumping authority, or at least good coordination among the different parts of the European Commission and its Legal Service.

Following the investigation, the Commission proposed to the Council that the anti-dumping duty of 30.6 per cent originally imposed on imports of bicycles from China in 1993, and maintained in 2000, be replaced by another anti-dumping duty at the level of 48.5 per cent. On 12 July 2005, the amendment was adopted by the Council.[196] In effect, it was an admission of the fact that European bicycle producers were not able to compete directly with Chinese producers on price. As the 1993 duty had previously been extended to imports of parts, the new, higher anti-dumping duty also applied to imports of parts, except for companies exempted under the procedures provided in the Exemption Regulation.[197]

Giant (China) Co Ltd, part of the large multinational group, later requested a partial interim review on the ground that it now met the criteria for MET. The Protocol on the Accession of China to the WTO preserved the use of the EC's non-market economy methodology for 15 years, unless the EU and China agreed on a change in status.[198] In November 2005 the Commission concluded that its findings during the investigation leading up to the July 2005 anti-dumping measure remained valid. Giant (China) Co Ltd was among the companies investigated at that time so, after consulting the Advisory Committee, the Commission denied MET and individual treatment (IT).[199] Giant (China) Co Ltd brought an action for annulment in the CFI,[200] but subsequently it abandoned the case.[201] About a year later, Giant (China) Co Ltd tried again, with a different period of investigation. However, one of Giant's manufacturers did not submit a reply to the MET questionnaire. Commission practice was to examine a group of related companies as a whole. On this ground, the Commission again denied MET and IT.[202] It is difficult to avoid the conclusion that MET and IT, as

[196] Council Regulation (EC) No 1095/2005 of 12 July 2005 imposing a definitive anti-dumping duty on imports of bicycles originating in Vietnam, and amending Regulation (EC) No 1524/2000 imposing a definitive anti-dumping duty on imports of bicycles from China [2005] OJ L183/1.

[197] This does not emerge from Council Regulation (EC) No 1095/2005, above n 196. However, the legal analysis is included in Council Regulation (EC) No 171/2008 of 25 February 2008 maintaining Council Regulation (EC) No 71/97 on the extension of the anti-dumping duty imposed on imports of bicycle originating in the People's Republic of China to imports of certain bicycle parts from the People's Republic of China, paras 1–4, [2008] OJ L55/1.

[198] WTO, *Accession of the People's Republic of China*, Decision of 10 November 2001, Protocol on the Accession of the People's Republic of China, para 15, WT/L/432, 23 November 2010.

[199] Council Regulation (EC) No 1892/2005 of 14 November 2005 terminating the partial interim review of the anti-dumping measures applicable to imports of bicycles originating in the People's Republic of China, [2005] OJ 302/22. Note that both the complainant and the Commission used the term 'market economy status' instead of 'market economy treatment' which had been used before and which was used after this review. 'Market economy treatment' (MET) applies to companies and is usually reserved for anti-dumping investigations, whereas 'market economy status' (MES) is a country-level designation and, despite the assurance of the European Commission in 2004, contains a substantial, macro-political element as part of the broader relations between the EU and China. On the Commission's assurances and criteria concerning MES as of 2004, see European Commission, Trade, 'China—Market economy status in trade defence investigations', Brussels, 28 June 2004, http://trade.ec.europa.eu/doclib/docs/2004/june/tradoc_117795.pdf, last accessed 17 February 2010.

[200] Case T-17/06 *Giant (China) v Council* [2006] OJ C74/29.

[201] Case T-17/06 *Giant (China) v Council*, Order of the President of the Fifth Chamber of the Court of First Instance, 7 July 2006 (Removal from the Register).

[202] Council Regulation (EC) No 1651/2006 terminating the partial interim review of the anti-dumping measures applicable to imports of bicycles originating in the People's Republic of China [2006] OJ L311/6. In this investigation, all parties used the term MET, instead of the country-level designation MES.

elements of EC anti-dumping law, act as partial barriers to market entry, equivalent to non-tariff barriers, serving to protect EC industry against direct price competition by Chinese producers.

The period after 2000 in the *Chinese Bicycles* saga was marked by a second important procedure: the first ever review of an anti-circumvention measure. Council Regulation (EC) No 71/97, the Anti-circumvention Regulation, had extended the 1993 duties on imports of bicycles to imports of parts. Council Regulation (EC) No 88/97 established the procedure for exempting from the duties importers of parts which did not constitute circumvention under the basic EC anti-dumping Regulation. Since then, the Commission had granted exemption to numerous companies. On 28 November 2006 the Commission published a Notice initiating a review of the Anti-circumvention Regulation.[203] It recited that the Commission continued to receive requests for exemption, and in fact the number of companies requested exemption appeared to have increased.[204] This testified to the effects of the Anti-circumvention Regulation and the Exemption Regulation on price competition and market structure. Assemblers in the EU and their Chinese suppliers were, if necessary, reducing the proportion of Chinese parts used in the assembly of bicycles in Europe in order to comply with the Anti-circumvention Regulation and avoid anti-dumping duties on parts in order to compete with EU and Chinese producers of entire bicycles. Curiously, in the light of the eventual conclusion, the Notice also stated that the Commission had at its disposal sufficient prima facie evidence that if the extension of the measures on imports of bicycles to imports of certain bicycle parts were removed, there would be no continuation or recurrence of circumvention practices.[205] After consulting the Advisory Committee, the Commission initiated a review. (The Anti-circumvention Regulation had been in force for 10 years without ever having been reviewed!)

The review dealt only with assemblers. The Commission received completed sampling forms from 158 companies, accounting for virtually all Community production. Eight assemblers, accounting for almost a third of Community production, were selected for the sample as representative of Community industry.[206] All had been exempted from the anti-circumvention measure, so could import and use Chinese parts up to 60 per cent of the total value of the parts of the assembled bicycle.[207] In fact, the review showed that the sampled eight producers used an average proportion of 37 per cent of Chinese parts, while for all cooperating assemblers the proportion was 29 per cent during the review investigation period.[208] The Commission concluded that no circumvention took place during the review investigation period.[209] Concerning the future, however, it considered that the outlook was 'somewhat mixed', especially since

[203] [Commission] Notice 2006/C289/04 of initiation of a review of the extension of the anti-dumping duty imposed on imports of bicycles originating in the People's Republic of China to imports of certain bicycle parts from the People's Republic of China [2006] OJ C289/15.

[204] *Ibid,* para 3.

[205] *Ibid.* The Council Regulation that resulted from the review stated, in somewhat different terms, that the Commission had prima facie evidence that 'if the anti-circumvention measure was removed, there would be no continuation or recurrence of circumvention practices': Council Regulation (EC) No 171/2008 of 25 February 2008 maintaining Council Regulation (EC) No 71/97 on the extension of the anti-dumping duty imposed on imports of bicycles originating in the People's Republic of China to imports of certain bicycle parts from the People's Republic of China, para 6, [2008] OJ L55/1.

[206] Council Regulation (EC) No 171/2008, above n 205, para 14.

[207] *Ibid,* para 23.

[208] *Ibid,* para 24. The review investigation period was 1 October 2005 to 30 September 2006, but the Commission also considered trends from 2003 to the end of the review investigation period: see *ibid,* para 10.

[209] *Ibid,* para 26.

assembly using Chinese parts had increased dramatically between 1993 and 1997, and since Chinese parts remained cheaper than other parts.[210] It admitted, however, that it was impossible to carry out a realistic analysis of price competition, because the Anti-circumvention Regulation and the Exemption Regulation distorted market prices, and because bicycles assembled in the EC during the investigation period consisted of parts from many countries, including the EC, China and others.[211]

With an air of cautious protectionism, the Commission concluded that the risk that circumvention would recur could not be excluded, and that this would undermine the anti-dumping duty on Chinese bicycles.[212] Consequently, it decided to maintain the Anti-circumvention Regulation. This example of 'risk management with a vengeance' preserved existing links between producers in China and assemblers in Europe, and also aimed to preserve the remaining producers in Europe of full bicycles. The Anti-circumvention Regulation and the Exemption Regulation therefore remained in force.

The progress and the results of the Commission procedure under the Exemption Regulation anti-circumvention provisions are given in Table 3 below. As this Table shows, the Commission continued to consider, grant and reject requests for exemption at least as late as January 2009.[213]

Table 3 Progress and Results of Commission Procedures under the Exemption Regulation (Commission Regulation (EC) No 88/97), 1997–2009

ACT	DATE ENACTED	UNDER EXAMINATION (Art 5, Art 11)	EXEMPTED AFTER EXAMINATION (Art 7(1)	EXEMPTION DENIED ie revoked	SUSPENSION LIFTED (Art 10)*
Commission Regulation (EC) No 88/97	20.1.97	15	11	—	—
Commission Notice 97/C 45/03	13.2.97	35	—	—	—
Commission Notice 97/C 112/04	10.4.97	78	—	—	—
Commission Decision 97/447/EC	16.7.97	—	60	—	—

[210] *Ibid*, paras 29–30, 38. The quotation is from para 38.
[211] *Ibid*, para 42.
[212] *Ibid*, para 44.
[213] Commission Decision 2009/48/EC of 22 January 2009 granting certain parties an exemption from the extension to certain bicycle parts of the anti-dumping duty on bicycles originating in the People's Republic of China imposed by Council Regulation (EEC) No 2474/93, last maintained and amended by Regulation (EC) No 1095/2005, and lifting the suspension of the payment of the anti-dumping duty extended to certain bicycle parts originating in the People's Republic of China granted to certain parties pursuant to Commission Regulation (EC) No 88/97 [2009] OJ L19/62. January 2009 was the cut-off date for this chapter, but in fact procedures for change of name and address of exempted parties continued at least until December 2009: see Commission Notice 2009/C291/05, [2009] OJ L291/9.

Table 3 (*cont.*)

ACT	DATE ENACTED	UNDER EXAMINATION (Art 5, Art 11)	EXEMPTED AFTER EXAMINATION (Art 7(1)	EXEMPTION DENIED ie revoked	SUSPENSION LIFTED (Art 10)*
Commission Notice 97/C 220/C	19.7.97	16	—	—	—
Mise à jour 97/C 378/02	13.12.97	28	—	—	—
Commission Decision 97/812/EC	26.11.97	—	—	—	18
Commission Decision 98/115/EC	28.1.98	—	18	—	—
Commission Decision 98/299/EC	24.4.98	—	—	1	—
Commission Decision 98/323/EC	29.4.98	—	—	1	—
Commission Decision 98/336/EC	6.5.98	—	—	1	—
Commission Decision 98/366/EC	9.6.1998	—	6	—	—
Avis de la Commission 98/C 217/05	11.7.98	11	—	—	—
Commission Decision 98/551/EC	21.9.1998	—	—	—	1
Commission Decision 98/684/EC	17.11.1998	—	10	—	—
Avis portent Mise à jour 1999/C37/03	11.2.99	12	—	—	—
Commission Notice 1999/C186/04	2.7.99	17	—	—	—
Commission Notice 2000/C216/07	28.7.2000	38	—	—	6
Commission Decision 2001/108/EC	24.1.2001	—	10	—	3

ACT	DATE ENACTED	UNDER EXAMINATION (Art 5, Art 11)	EXEMPTED AFTER EXAMINATION (Art 7(1)	EXEMPTION DENIED ie revoked	SUSPENSION LIFTED (Art 10)*
Commission Notice 2001/C170/03	14.6.2001	39	—	—	5
Commission Decision 2002/134/EC	11.2.2002	—	18	—	5
Commission Notice 2002/C103/2	30.4.2002	36	—	—	—
Commission Decision 2002/606/EC	16.7.2002	—	31	—	2
Commission Notice 2002/C35/03	14.2.2003	36	—	—	—
Commission Notice 2003/C43/04	22.2.2003	22	—	—	1
Commission Decision 2003/560/EC	22.7.2003	—	—	—	19
Commission Decision 2003/899/EC	28.11.2003		17	—	5
Commission Notice 2004/C54/03	2.3.2004	14	—	—	—
Commission Decision 2006/22/EC	20.1.2006	32	29	5	4
Commission Decision 2006/772/EC	10.11.2006	13	25	3	6
Commission Decision 2008/260/EC	18.3.2006	9	23	4	3
Commission Notice 2008/C310/07	5.12.2008	5			
Commission Decision 2009/48/EC	22.1.2009	1	8	1	1

Source: Calculated from the Commission Notices and Decisions as listed.
Notes: *Duties were suspended temporarily while the companies were under examination. Figures refer to numbers of companies.

C. Consequences, Intended and Unintended

The renewal of anti-dumping duties in 2000 and again in 2005, together with the 2008 decision to maintain the extension of the anti-dumping duty to parts, had several interrelated consequences. We may classify these consequences in three groups. They concerned:

a) the restructuring of the EU bicycle sector as a whole;
b) the fate of trade associations, particularly the EBMA; and
c) the effectiveness of EC anti-dumping duties.

1. The Restructuring of the EU Bicycle Sector

The first group of consequences concerns the restructuring of the EU bicycle sector. In April 2003, *The Wall Street Journal Europe* published an article that illustrated this process. It reported that the imposition of EC anti-dumping duties on bicycle parts stimulated the largest bicycle maker in Poland to restructure its operations. Having previously imported bicycle parts from Asia (including China), Kross Limited began to develop its own production facilities and expand its export markets. After obtaining the ISO 9001 certification, and with the help of engineers from the French sports retailer Decathlon, it produced bicycles under the Decathlon name, shipped other bicycles to well-known UK retailers and opened an office in Germany to market its top-range mountain bike.[214] While it continued to import bicycle parts from China, the value of these imported parts was lower than the threshold established in the EC anti-dumping legislation, so these imports were not considered to amount to circumvention. Kross was therefore eventually exempted from anti-dumping duties on its imported parts.[215] Its integration into this global value chain was a sign of the restructuring of the industry.

In the early 1990s, the Commission found that the bicycles sold by EC producers were 'actually produced in the Community from parts which were sourced mainly in the Community'.[216] As of 2006, the EU industry focused on the assembly of full bicycles, relying mainly on different highly specialised products of parts, either domestic or imported, and there was really no domestic EU industry for production of complete bicycles. The profits were in resale, for example by Decathlon, which sold assembled bicycles under its own brand name in its own retail facilities. From the standpoint of European producers of full bicycles, restructuring meant orientation toward the production of more expensive bicycles and trying to avoid going out of business.

[214] M Strzelecki, 'Bike Maker Shifts Gears to Exports', *The Wall Street Journal Europe*, Friday/Saturday/Sunday, 11–13 April 2003, at A5.

[215] Commission Decision 2006/22/EC of 20 January 2006 granting certain parties an exemption from the extension to certain bicycle parts of the anti-dumping duty on bicycles originating in the People's Republic of China imposed by Council Regulation (EEC) No 2474/93, last maintained and amended by Regulation (EC) No 1095/2005, and lifting the suspension of the payment of the anti-dumping duty extended to certain bicycle parts originating in the People's Republic of China granted to certain parties pursuant to Regulation (EC) No 88/97, Art 1, Table 1, [2006] OJ L17/16.

[216] *Bicycles from China* (definitive), above n 59, para 11.

Among the EU producers sampled in the 2005 investigation, a number, which were already important in the dealer/retailer sub-sector, had expanded sales to mass-merchandisers and supermarkets. In order to maintain the same revenues, they were required to produce in higher volumes to compensate for lower prices, because of the lower prices of mass-merchandisers which had become more important in the bicycle market.[217] Most Chinese producers sold to mass-merchandisers, so EU and Chinese producers competed directly in this market, notably on the basis of price.[218] By 2005, an increasing number of French manufacturers were reported to have stopped doing business with supermarket chains, such as Carrefour, Casino or Intermarché, because they could not compete profitably. The Dutch Access Group announced that Cycles Mercier, its French subsidiary, which previously supplied supermarkets, was going out of business.[219] According to *Bike Europe,* a website for bike professionals, Cycle Europe entered into a sale–leaseback arrangement to finance the dismissal of its 300 workers at two facilities in France.[220]

The Exemption Regulation stimulated many small and medium-sized bicycle assemblers to seek exemption from the duty on the ground that they were not involved in circumvention. Over the years, approximately 266 assemblers were granted exemption from anti-dumping duties on parts (see Table 3 above). In 2003, numerous European assemblers, similar to Starway, went out of business. They included one company in 2003 whose exemption from payment of duties on parts was revoked.[221] However, there remained many small assemblers, for example more than 200 small components factories in Italy, which depended on the continuation of bicycle production in Europe.[222] Others were integrated, or continued to be integrated, as assemblers in global commodity chains starting in China. The EC anti-dumping law encouraged assembly in the EU, using a sufficiently low proportion of Chinese parts (below 60 per cent of total value of parts) to meet the anti-circumvention criteria, and cross-investment between the EU and China in the bicycle industry. Larger Chinese and international companies, such as Giant, benefited from these incentives.

Despite the duties, Chinese companies continued to export bicycles, in particular towards mass-merchandisers and supermarkets, competing directly and successfully with European bicycle producers. They also increasingly exported bicycle parts, took over European companies as they had taken over Starway some years earlier, or created JVs or formed IPNs embracing both EU companies and Chinese companies in increasingly complex production, distribution and marketing arrangements. Chinese exports consisted of parts to assemblers in Europe or otherwise of complete bicycles to supermarkets, the latter because, despite the duties, Chinese bicycles remained less expensive than EC-produced bicycles. As of 2007, China lowered the tax refund on exports on complete bicycles and parts by 4 per cent. This did not of course affect the

[217] Council Regulation (EC) No 1095/2005, above n 196, para 133.

[218] *Ibid*, para 156.

[219] 'EU 2005: Production Shifts from Asia to Eastern Europe', *Bike Europe*, Facts and Figures, Market Reports, EU 2005, published 8 August 2007, available at http://www.bike-eu.com, accessed 22 May 2009.

[220] 'Europe 2006: Shift from Imports to Production in Eastern Europe Continues', *Bike Europe*, Facts and Figures, Market Reports, EU 2006, published 4 January 2008, available at http://www.bike-eu.com, accessed 22 May 2009.

[221] 8 Italian, 4 German, 3 in France, 2 in the UK, 1 in Belgium: Commission Decision 2003/560/EC revoking the exemption from the payment of the anti-dumping duty extended to certain bicycle parts originating in the People's Republic of China granted to certain parties pursuant to Regulation (EC) No 88/97 [2003] OJ L190/10.

[222] Council Regulation (EC) No 1095/2005, above n 196, para 189.

Chinese companies which had already moved part of their production or assembly to the Central and Eastern European countries (CEECs) or to other countries covered by the EC GSP scheme.[223] Chinese bicycles imported into EU declined by 2.3 per cent from 2006 (809,281 units) to 2007 (790,530 units)[224] However, with the 2008–09 financial crisis, China announced a new increase in the export subsidy for bicycles, from 9 per cent to between 11 to 14 per cent, as part of economic rescue plan, reversing the 2007 reduction.[225]

A further aspect was the diversification of sources of imports. As of 2006, eight countries were in the list of the top 10 main suppliers of imports to Europe. At least temporarily, Taiwan gained ground as against China and Vietnam, in particular because Chinese bicycles no longer benefited from the EC GSP system.[226]

Another part of this process was a shift in the sources of supply for complete bicycles after 2004 from China to the Central and Eastern EU Member States. The 2005 EC enlargement and the application of EC anti-dumping duties to imports from China into the new Member States led to a shift in sources of supply of complete bicycles for the EU market from China and Vietnam to the Central and Eastern European countries. In 2005, imports from the CEECs to EU-15 increased by 18.4 per cent, while imports from Asia dropped by 4.8 per cent. Imports from Asia into the CEECs also decreased, for example into Poland by 50 per cent in 2005 as compared to 2004. One report suggested that this indicated that, before the 2005 duties, companies in many CEECs circumvented the previous duties. The same reportedly continued to be true of companies in other countries, such as Belgium, where imports of bicycles rose by 90 per cent in 2005 as compared to 2004, and where Decathlon had built a new 35,000m^2 logistics centre to supply neighbouring countries.[227] This continued in 2006, as complete bicycles were imported from Eastern Europe instead of from Asia.[228]

2. *The Fate of Trade Associations, particularly the EBMA*

A second group of consequences concerns the EBMA. The EBMA was never the sole organisation in the industry. Support in the bicycle industry for complaints by the EBMA steadily declined. In 1993, producers representing 52.2 per cent of total EC production cooperated in the complaint, and a further 10 per cent provided basic information and expressed support.[229] When the EBMA requested an expiry review in 1998, it was reported only to be acting 'on behalf of Community bicycle producers whose collective output constitutes a major proportion of total Community produc-

[223] 'Lowered Export Subsidies Hits Chinese Industry', *Bike Europe*, News, published 10 July 2007, available at http://www.bike-eu.com, accessed 22 May 2009.

[224] Excluding electric bicycles: Eurostat, quoted in 'China 2008: Exports Levelling Off', *Bike Europe*, Facts and Figures, Market Reports, China 2008, published 23 March 2009, available at http://www.bike-eu.com, accessed 22 May 2009.

[225] 'China 2008: Exports Levelling Off', above n 224.

[226] 'Europe 2006: Shift from Imports to Production in Eastern Europe Continues', above n 220.

[227] 'EU 2005: Production Shifts from Asia to Eastern Europe', above n 219.

[228] 'Europe 2006: Shift from Imports to Production in Eastern Europe Continues', above n 220.

[229] *Bicycles from China* (provisional) para 12, above n 20.

tion'.[230] In 2000, the Community producers included as the applicants in 'Community industry' made up about 54 per cent of total EC production and 58 per cent of total Community production during the period of investigation; non-applicants accounted for about 42 per cent of total production.[231] In 2000, the EBMA requested individual duties on each bicycle part, but it withdrew its complaint because of lack of support, in particular because of conflicts between two groups of EU bicycle producers and assemblers.[232] When in 2004 the EBMA complained to the Commission and requested an interim review investigation, it represented only about 35 per cent of total Community production.[233] The complainants plus other Community producers supporting the complaint accounted for more than 80 per cent of total Community production.[234] The 2008 review of the Anti-circumvention Regulation included 158 assemblers, representing almost the totality of EC production. A sample was taken on eight assemblers representing almost one-third of EC production during the review period. The EBMA was not mentioned, but there was no reason why it should be since the review was initiated by the Commission.[235]

As of May 2009, the representation of European bicycle producers and related groups appeared to have fragmented into several more specific sectoral associations. COLIBI represents the European bicycle industry, namely bicycle manufacturers. It includes national associations from 11 countries: Austria, Belgium, Denmark, Finland, France, Germany, Italy, The Netherlands, Portugual, Spain and the United Kingdom.[236] The Association of the European Two-wheeler Parts and Accessories Industry, COLIPED, which was founded in 1960, represents manufacturers of parts and components.[237] It has both effective and associate members. The nine effective members are the national, professional associations of Belgium, Finland, France, Germany, Italy, The Netherlands, Spain and the United Kingdom. The European Twowheel Retailers' Association (ETRA) was founded in 1995, as a complement to ECF/BEUC representing consumers, COLIBI and COLIPED. It is a grouping of national two-wheel retailer organisations in Belgium, The Czech Republic, Denmark, France, Germany, The Netherlands, Sweden, Switzerland, the United Kingdom and, despite the name of the association, even the United States. It represents approximately 5,000 independent retailers of bicycles, mopeds and motorcycles which employ about 11,000 people.[238] Members include independent detailers, national professional associations for retailers, and at least two European branches of companies originating in

[230] Notice of initiation of a review of the anti-dumping measures applicable to imports of bicycles originating in the People's Republic of China (98/C281/06), [1998] OJ C281/8.

[231] Council Regulation (EC) No 1524/2000, paras 70–72, [2000] OJ L175/45.

[232] Commission Decision 2000/316/EC of 2 May 2000 terminating the anti-dumping proceedings concerning imports of bicycle frames originating n the People's Republic of China and Taiwan, bicycle forks originating in the People's Republic of China and Taiwan and complete wheels of bicycles originating in the People's Republic of China, as well as the interim review of the anti-dumping measures extended to imports of, *inter alia*, bicycle frames, bicycle forks and complete wheels of bicycles originating in the People's Republic of China [2000] OJ L105/40.

[233] Council Regulation (EC) No 1095/2005, above n 196, para 4.

[234] *Ibid*, para 104.

[235] See Council Regulation (EC) No 171/2008, above n 206.

[236] See http://www.colibi.com. COLIBI stands for Comité de Liaison des Fabricants Européens de Bicyclettes.

[237] See the COLIPED website http://www.coliped.com, visited 23 May 2009. Its full name was originally Comité de Liaison des Fabricants de Pièces et Equipements de Deux-roues des pays de la C.E.'. It became COLIPED vzw (non-profit association) in 2002.

[238] See the ETRA website at http://www.etra-eu.com, visited 23 May 2009.

Taiwan and Japan respectively, namely Giant Europe BV, originally specialised in frames, and Shimano Europe Holding BV, of which the parent was the famous Japanese bicycle parts manufacturer; both were based in The Netherlands and, in the words of the President of the Giant Group, 'consider [themselves] a retail supporting company'.[239] This statement alone evoked the transformation of the bicycle industry in Europe and the decline of the EBMA.

Two principal factors account for this decline. The first and most important was the restructuring of the European bicycle market. Further internationalisation of the bicycle market meant, in part, the inclusion of EU producers into global commodity chains as assemblers. This signified and also resulted in further fragmentation of the EU industry. As the bicycle sector evolved from an earlier period of vertical integration to a period of fragmented production based on modularity, the rise of specialist firms and coordination through standards and the market became the rule. This undermined the extent to which and the cohesiveness with which the EBMA represented the industry, and it enhanced the power of rival sub-sectoral associations. A second factor which may have contributed to the decline of the EBMA as a peak association and its replacement by intra-sectoral trade associations was the increasing institutionalisation and judicialisation of international trade institutions, which tend to de-link issues and strengthen more specialised trade associations.[240] No cases concerning bicycles from China reached the WTO. However, after the establishment of the WTO in 1995, and especially following Chinese accession to the WTO in 2001, the *Chinese Bicycles* saga unfolded in the shadow of WTO law, notably the Anti-dumping Agreement. But ultimately, it was the restructuring of the market that condemned the EBMA to virtual irrelevance.

3. *The Effectiveness of the Anti-dumping Duties*

A third group of consequences refers to the effectiveness, or otherwise, of the anti-dumping duties. To what extent were the EC anti-dumping duties effective? 'Effectiveness' is a slippery term. We can conceive of it as a social process of achieving social change through law, which is usually gradual and which involves negotiation, compromise, implementation of and compliance with law, and sometimes change in organisations.[241] From this perspective, the *Chinese Bicycles* saga reveals surprising results. We can focus first on competition between European producers and Chinese exporters on the EU bicycle market, and then on the European Commission strategy.

Overall, with regard to the bicycle market, the anti-dumping duties proved to be relatively ineffective in preventing imports of bicycles from China and in this way protecting the European bicycle-producing industry. Between 1998 and 2002, imports into

[239] Mr Tony Lo, President of the Giant Group, quoted at http://www.etra-eu.com/page.asp?id=5622065, last accessed 17 February 2010.

[240] For this argument, I am indebted to D De Bièvre, *International Institutions and Domestic Coalitions: The Differential Effects of Negotiations and Judicialisation in European Trade Policy*, EUI Working Paper SPS No 2003/17, Department of Political and Social Sciences, European University Institute, Florence, 2003.

[241] See generally F Snyder, 'The Effectiveness of European Community Law: Institutions, Processes, Tools and Techniques' (1993) 1 *MLR* 19. This conception of implementation was stimulated partly by WH Clune III and RE Lindquist, 'What "Implementation" Isn't: Toward a General Framework for Implementation Research' (1981) *Wisconsin Law Review* 1044.

the EU of complete bicycles from China increased as follows: 1998: 15,000 units; 1999: 47,000 units; 2000: 141,000 units; 2001: 236,000 units; and 2002: 535,000 units.[242] The World Bicycle Industry Review for January to June 2004 reported that imports of bicycles in the EU had rise by 40 per cent, despite the 30.6 per cent anti-dumping duty.[243] The Chinese share of the EU bicycle market increased from 0.73 per cent in 2000 to 4.08 per cent in 2003.[244] Between 1995 and 31 August 1998, employment in the EC industry fell by 12 per cent or 1,800 people. Between 2000 and 31 March 2004, it declined by another 6 per cent. During the latter period, however, production rose as a result of a 24 per cent increase in productivity, measured by output per worker. Prices for bicycles from China imported into the EU continued to decline, for example by 22 per cent between 2000 and 2003. Even in 2005, they undercut the prices of EU-produced bicycles by 53 per cent without the anti-dumping duty and by 39 per cent with the duty.[245] According to the Commission's investigation leading to an increase in definitive duties in 2005, there were 55 times more imports of bicycles from China as in the previous investigation in 1997–98.[246] In 2005, the EBMA President noted that anti-dumping measures on Chinese bicycles had not prevented imports. With the decline in the value of the dollar, to which the Chinese currency was linked, imports of bicycles from China into the EU increased from 40,000 units each year after 1993 to reach a total of 800,000 in 1994. However, the EBMA President considered that the European bicycle industry would be dead without anti-dumping duties.[247]

As of 2003, Taiwan remained the main source of whole bicycles imported into the EU.[248] But production in Taiwan, Japan, the United States and the EU was already in decline. Since about 1998 China has dominated the global bicycle industry. China now produces about 60 per cent of the world's bicycles. In 2000, the European Commission, relying on EU industry figures, estimated available production capacity in China as about 70 million bicycles per year, with the rate of capacity utilisation at just above 50 per cent. [249] In 2005, it increased the estimate to over 80 million bicycles each year; production then was about 66 million, internal demand was about 22 million, and consequently there was considerable scope for increasing exports to Europe. For comparison, bicycles from China accounted for 96 per cent of the United States consumption.[250]

In fact, the bulk of Chinese production capacity is increasingly destined for export. Chinese government policy, managed by the China Bicycle Association (CBA), part of China Light Industrial, a government ministry, currently favours cars rather than bicycles as a primary mode of domestic transport. Even as early as 2004, commentators noted the irony of China's dominant role in world bicycle production and exports at the same time that Chinese government policy was reducing the number of bicycles used in China, especially in large cities such as Beijing, Shanghai and Guangzhou,

[242] 'Origins of Complete Bicycle Imports into the European Union 1998–2002', in *China Bicycle Yearbook 2005* (Tokyo, Cycle Press, 2004), at 318.

[243] World Bicycle Industry Review 2004 (January–June), *ibid*, at 79.

[244] Council Regulation (EC) No 1095/2005, above n 196, para 120.

[245] *Ibid*, paras 122 (price decline) and 123 (price undercutting).

[246] *Ibid*, paras 118 and 120.

[247] According to Mr Brian Montgomery, President of the EBMA, in 'Des clauses de sauvegarde arrêteront-elles la Chine?' *Usinenouvelle.com*, 28 April 2005, available at http://www.usinenouvelle.com/recherche=EBMA, last accessed 17 Feruary 2010.

[248] *Source*: Eurostat, see http://www.colibi.com/generic.asp?id=56579, visited 18 November 2004.

[249] *Bicycles from China* (definitive, extension), above n 116, paras 49–50.

[250] Council Regulation (EC) No 1095/2005, above n 196 para 157.

where major automobile manufacturers were located.[251] For example, in 2007, the southern city of Guangzhou also banned electric bicycles on municipal roads, including suburban areas. The ban was challenged in court, and municipal authorities were reported to have forbidden local newspapers and some websites from reporting on the lawsuit.[252] The Chinese home market has shrunk to about 22–25 million units, compared to 40 million units a few years earlier. Cycle use in China was reported to have dropped from 33 per cent of all trips in 1995 to 20 per cent of all trips in 2003. According to the Cycling Association of China, bicycle ownership was an average of 142.7 bikes per 100 households in 2002, compared to 182.1 in 1998. In Beijing, only 20 per cent of commuters rode bikes in 2002, compared to 60 per cent in 1998.[253]

These changes in the Chinese domestic market provided strong incentives for Chinese producers and exporters to develop new export and legal strategies. In the *Chinese Bicycles* saga, the legal strategies of CBC and Giant (China) Co Ltd, or their counterparts, were quite successful. To some extent, the success of the legal strategies of SMEs such as Starways was more mitigated. In contrast, the legal strategies of the EBMA failed. The restructuring of the EU bicycle industry testifies to this evaluation.

If we focus on the legal strategies of the European Commission, however, we can draw a more nuanced conclusion concerning the effectiveness of the anti-dumping duties. Consider, on the one hand, the economic regulatory scheme established in detail by the Exemption Regulation. By January 2006, it was evident that the Commission's legal strategy of seeking to regulate the highly globalised EU bicycle market by means of EC anti-dumping law, the Anti-circumvention Regulation and a rigid Exemption Regulation would stretch, if not surpass, its administrative capacity.[254] At least from the outside, the result appeared to be a shambles, made more complex by EU enlargement. Some examples reported by the Commission in January 2006 make the point. As of January 2006, 32 companies were still under investigation, but changes in company structure meant that the Commission could not determine whether the assembly activities of the companies amounted to circumvention or

[251] W Hook, 'China Rocks Global Bike Industry', in Sustainable Transport e-update, *Bulletin of the Institute for Transportation & Development Policy (ITDP)*, No 3, January 2003, available at http://www.itdp.org/index.php/news_events/news_detail/china_global_bike_industry/, 16th March 2010]. According to this commentator, the largest bicycle companies in China were either export-orientated, foreign-owned firms, or firms run by the State, with neither being mainly concerned with the Chinese domestic market. This decline correlated with an increase in folding bikes: see Wu Chong, 'Folding bikes perfect answer to traffic jams', *China Daily*, Saturday, 3 December 2005, 4. The relative and absolute decline of domestic market sales to export sales between 1985 and 2003 emerges clearly from the chart 'China's Bicycle Production and Exports 1985–2003', in *China Bicycle Yearbook 2005* (Tokyo, Cycles Press, 2004), at 68. On the increase, however, are electric bicycles: see E Kurtenbach, 'In the cycling kingdom, ever more two-wheelers are battery-powered', *International Herald Tribune*, Monday, 27 July 2009, 16. For an indication of the changing importance of bicycles in Chinese life since 1983, see Ni Ping and Wang Wenlan, *Life with Bicycles* (Beijing, Zhong Guo Wen Lian [China Association of Artists] Publishers, 2004).

[252] 'Media blackout on bicycle suit', *South China Morning Post* (Hong Kong), Wednesday, 10 January 2007, at A4.

[253] See Hook, above n 251; BikeBiz, 'Lies, damn lies and statistics', above n 23

[254] For an example of the complexity of the analysis being carried out as of November 2006, see the different categories in the analysis in the preamble, which was then boiled down to legally binding categories in the Commission Decision 2006/772/EC granting certain parties an exemption from the extension to certain bicycle parts of the anti-dumping duty on bicycles originating in the People's Republic of China imposed by Council Regulation (EEC) No 2474/93, last maintained and amended by Regulation (EC) No 1095/2005, and lifting the suspension of the payment of the anti-dumping duty extended to certain bicycle parts originating in the People's Republic of China granted to certain parties pursuant to Regulation (EC) No 88/97, [2006] OJ L313/5.

not.[255] In one case, the Commission could not determine whether the company, contrary to its obligations under the Exemption Regulation, used bicycle parts during the period.[256] In another case, the Commission was unable to obtain access to essential company accounting records, because the records were kept by the Settlement Senate of a District Court as part of a compulsory debt settlement plan in bankruptcy proceedings.[257] In yet another case, two parties merged into a new legal entity, and the Commission could not verify whether the assembly operations of the new entity constituted circumvention or not.[258] For three companies, the Commission could not determine the value of the ratio of Chinese parts to the value of total parts used in assembly, 'since the parties used a very large number of parts purchased prior to enlargement in their assembly operations'.[259] As of November 2006, the Commission reported that there were still a large number of companies requesting exemption, and that there was no evidence that removal of the duty on parts would lead to the continuation or recurrence of circumvention.[260] Doubtless, to strategic actors other than the EBMA, and perhaps the Commission—and perhaps even to them—all seemed sometimes to demonstrate that the longer the ill-conceived regulatory scheme remained in force, the less it made sense.

Yet, on the other hand, consider the Commission's legal strategy. The Commission sought to respond to and possibly meet the demands of European industry, to protect SMEs located in the EU and to foster the internationalisation of EU industry. With regard to the EBMA, the Commission supported its claims for much of the period. In its 2007–08 review of the Anti-circumvention Regulation, it responded directly to the needs of European assemblers. With regard to SMEs and the internationalisation of the industry, the Commission's legal strategy, to which it clung tenaciously, appears to have succeeded. Whether the Commission, as an institution or as individuals, intended the specific consequences which resulted from the exemption scheme and the evolution of the market is not so important. The most significant point is that, overall, the Commission's legal strategy concerning the situation of SMEs and the internationalisation of the EU bicycle market, often together, seemed to have more or less achieved its objectives. It is true that numerous SMEs, such as Starway, went out of business. Others did not survive the Exemption Regulation. Many others, however, were integrated into global value chains as assemblers of bicycles, using EU, Chinese or other parts. Producers in the EU of full bicycles orientated these activities increasingly toward the high end of the market. From this standpoint, the Commission legal strategy succeeded.

[255] Commission Decision 2006/22/EC of 20 January 2006 granting certain parties an exemption from the extension to certain bicycle parts of the anti-dumping duty on bicycles originating in the People's Republic of China imposed by Council Regulation (EEC) No 2474/93, last maintained and amended by Regulation (EC) No 1095/2005, and lifting the suspension of the payment of the anti-dumping duty extended to certain bicycle parts originating in the People's Republic of China granted to certain parties pursuant to Republic of China granted to certain parties pursuant to Regulation (EC) No 88/97, para 17, [2006] OJ L17/16.

[256] *Ibid*, para 13.

[257] *Ibid*, para 18.

[258] *Ibid*, para 19.

[259] *Ibid*, para 21.

[260] [Commission] Notice 2006/C289/04 of initiation of a review of the extension of the anti-dumping duty imposed on imports of bicycles originating in the People's Republic of China to imports of certain bicycle parts from the People's Republic of China [2006] OJ C289/15.

V. Conclusion

The *Chinese Bicycles* saga began in the late 1980s and continues today. This chapter has analysed its main phases, the legal and business strategies of the principal actors, the transformation of anti-dumping law into domestic economic regulation and the restructuring of the EC bicycle sector, and intended and unintended consequences. During this long and complex saga, trade associations, EC bicycle manufacturers, the anti-dumping authority, Chinese SOEs, multinational companies or EU small and medium-sized businesses sought to use the law in order to create and maintain stable markets and to survive as organisations. For this purpose, they elaborated forms of knowledge, constructions, understandings and perceptions by which they sought to encourage, avoid, manage or adjust to competition, and thus to overcome challenges that threatened their positions or their survival. For these strategic actors, law was a potentially powerful resource. The European Commission and Chinese producers were the most successful in using legal ideas, institutions and dispute settlement processes in the EU site of governance, and in surviving—indeed benefiting from—the restructuring of the European bicycle industry.

Anti-dumping law is based on the assumption of the coincidence between State, territory and firms. According to a commonly held view, international competition pits foreign producers against domestic producers. Anti-dumping law can provide the latter a period of adjustment if necessary, or, as in *Chinese Bicycles*, more lasting protection. However, globalisation, in the form of global value chains, undermines these basic assumptions of anti-dumping law. It alters the conditions of competition, creates new strategic actors, and renders recourse to anti-dumping law problematic and the use of anti-dumping measures of questionable public interest.

Consider three different transformations of markets under conditions of increasing globalisation, taken here to mean increased foreign direct investment. For convenience, all the examples use China and France as exporting country and importing country, respectively. Table 4 below represents the impact of increasing globalisation on the ownership structure of the exporters, situated in China. In the first situation, the exporting firm is 100 per cent Chinese. In the second, it is 60 per cent Chinese and 40 per cent French. In the third, it is 40 per cent Chinese and 60 per cent French. In the final situation, the exporting firm is 100 per cent French. This transformation potentially has significant implications for anti-dumping law, because it may pit domestically-owned, foreign-based producers against domestically-owned, domestically-based producers.

Table 4 Effects of Globalisation on Ownership Structure of Exporters

SITUATION 1	SITUATION 2	SITUATION 3	SITUATION 4
100% Chinese	60% Chinese 40% Chinese	40% French 60% French	100% French

Now, consider an analogous transformation of the ownership structure of the importers, located in France. Table 5 below shows the transformation from a situation (1) in which the importers are 100 per cent French, through a situation (2) in which the importers are 60 per cent French and 40 per cent Chinese and a situation (3) in which the importers are 40 per cent French and 60 per cent Chinese, to a situation (4) in which the importers, situated in France, are 100 per cent Chinese. The transformation is important for anti-dumping law, because it may affect the determination of domestic industry as well as the results of the Community interest test in EC anti-dumping actions.

Table 5 Effects of Globalisation on Ownership Structure of Importers

SITUATION 1	SITUATION 2	SITUATION 3	SITUATION 4
100% French	40% French 60% Chinese	60% Chinese 40% French	100% Chinese

A third transformation, crucial for anti-dumping law, concerns the producers in the importing country. Table 6 below presents the effects of globalisation, in the form of increased foreign direct investment, on the ownership structure of the producers in the importing country, which here is taken to be France. In the first situation, the producers are 100 per cent French; in the last, they are 100 per cent Chinese. This transformation would radically alter the anti-dumping law calculus. The group that demands protection by public authorities is the producers, and the transformation of ownership structure in this case would mean that domestically-based, foreign-owned producers potentially request protection against foreign-based, domestically-owned firms situated in another country.

Table 6 Effects of Globalisation on the Ownership Structure of Producers

SITUATION 1	SITUATION 2	SITUATION 3	SITUATION 4
100% French	60% French 40% Chinese	40% Chinese 60% French	100% Chinese

These different scenarios represent only individual firms. By combining different situations, however, it would be possible to produce a number of different possibilities, for example a scenario involving a 60 per cent French-owned exporter located in China, a 40 per cent Chinese-owned importer situated in France and a 60 per cent Chinese-owned producer in France. Here it is possible only to evoke such a scenario. In a more complex analysis, which is also not feasible here, it would be necessary to distinguish between the numerous different types of firms within the sector or industry in question. It would also be essential to consider the fact that ownership is only one form of corporate control, as has long been well known. Each of these different situations has important implications for governments and policy makers, in particular because globalisation complicates considerably the choices they must make in anti-dumping actions.

Changes in the nature and interests of exporters in many sectors are already underway. Analogous changes have begun also with regard to importers. This chapter suggests that the transformation of the bicycles sector holds lessons for exporters, importers and producers. These current and future possibilities of foreign direct investment have already resulted in changes in EC anti-dumping law. They are likely to do so even more in the future.

Taken together, these three different sets of possible transformations may be expected to contribute to an increasing politicisation of decision-making on EC anti-dumping measures. This emerges clearly from *Chinese Bicycles*, especially the fate of the EBMA.

Table 7 below presents, in simplified form, a picture of potential conflicts among EC Member States concerning the imposition of anti-dumping measures.[261] The left-hand column shows the exporting country, which for the present purposes is taken to be China. For convenience, the table is based on two elementary assumptions:

a) In each Member State there are only two important interests: producers (P) and importers (I). Their interests conflict with regard to the imposition of anti-dumping measures. It is self-evident that other interests may count in real political life, such as consumers, downstream users or others. However, the purpose of the table is to indicate in outline form the potential for conflicts among EC Member States in anti-dumping matters.
b) Member States of the EC take decisions, by voting or not, in two institutional settings. One institutional setting is the Anti-dumping Advisory Committee, which technically speaking advises the European Commission on a wide range of anti-dumping issues, for example with regard to a proposal to the Council for definitive duties. The other institutional setting is the Council of the European Union, which on a Commission proposal imposes definitive duties. It is assumed here that, in each institutional setting, the Government of the Member State has to choose whether to represent the interests of producers or of importers, assuming that either or both are present in its territory. The Member State will represent the dominant economic interests in its territory, whether domestic or foreign, and whether dominance is assessed in terms of volume or value of production, employment, contribution to national tax revenue or another factor.

Factors such as globalisation and EU enlargement have increased the potential for conflict, further politicising decision-making on anti-dumping measures. As Table 7 suggests, both Government and exporters in the exporting country are likely to, and in fact usually do, seek to build alliances with like-minded interests in various EC Member States. Recall that, today, the EU has 27 Member States.

Globalisation may refer to increased foreign direct investment, or it may take other forms. In *Chinese Bicycles*, globalisation created new relations involving EC producers, longstanding EC assemblers, recent EC assemblers, EC importers and Chinese producers, including both SOEs and multinational companies. It contributed to the increased fragmentation of production, the restructuring of the EU bicycle industry and the transformation of its representation by trade associations. In this new context, the basic presuppositions of anti-dumping did not make sense. Anti-dumping law

[261] Here I rely on lectures and discussions during my course on 'WTO and EC Anti-dumping Law', which has been given at the Academy of International Trade and Investment Law, Macao, China, since 1999. See also SJ Evenett and E Vermulst, *The Politicisation of EC Anti-dumping Policy: Member States, Their Votes and the European Commission*, paper presented at the Symposium on a Centennial of Anti-Dumping Legislation and Implementation, University of Michigan, 12 March 2004.

Table 7 Politicisation of Anti-dumping Law Decision-making in the EC

	Country of Export	**EC Member State 1**	**EC Member State 2**	**EC Member State 3**	**EC Member State 4**	**EC Member State 5**
Balance of Economic Interests	E	P	I	P>I	P<I	P=I
Government outcome in Anti-dumping Advisory Committee and in the Council of the European Union	[Opposes duties but is not involved formally in EC decision-making]	Favours duties	Opposes duties	Favours duties	Opposes duties	? [arbitrage, possibility of alliances with other interests, including country of export and/or exporters]

failed to take account of the complexity of economic relations, or of the multiplicity of different but overlapping interests which are involved.

The *Chinese Bicycles* case provides a microcosm of global legal pluralism, a laboratory in which we can begin to understand its foundations. The foundations of global legal pluralism lie in the fragmentation of production, the creation of global value chains, and the development of new strategic actors and their legal strategies. A basic hypothesis of the chapter was that there is a correlation between the international economic integration through trade, the disintegration and fragmentation of production, and the rise of global legal pluralism. The EC anti-dumping law contributed to the restructuring of the EU bicycle sector. This chapter focused mainly on the EC site of governance, but the legal strategies involved here opened up the space for global legal pluralism.

Appendix

Chronology of the *Chinese Bicycles* Saga

(Corrigenda of minor details omitted.)

February 1981: Change in import arrangements: Commission Decision of 23 February 1981 changing the import arrangements established by Council Decision 80/1278/EEC and applied in Italy in respect of imports of bicycle tyres and inner tubes from the People's Republic of China [1981] OJ L72/16.

July 1987: Surveillance and protective measures: Commission Decision of 22 July 1987 on surveillance and protective measures which Member States may be authorised to take pursuant to Article 115 of the EEC Treaty [1987] OJ L238/26.

May 1989: Intra-Community surveillance: Authorisation for Denmark to apply intra-Community surveillance: Commission Decision 89/386/EEC of 17 May 1989, [1989] OJ L181/53.

October 1991: Complaint by European Bicycle Manufacturers Association: Notice of initiation of an anti-dumping proceeding concerning imports of bicycles originating in Taiwan and the People's Republic of China [1991] OJ C266/6.

1992: Withdrawal of GSP for bicycles from China: Commission Regulation (EEC) No 1193/92 [1992] OJ L124/9.

September 1992: Parliamentary questions: Question no 103 de Mme Ernst de la Graete (H-0986/92) (Objet: L'importation de bicycles en provenance de la Chine et des pays bénéficiaires du système de préférences généralisées) and Question no 104 de M Gil-Robles Gil-Delgado (H.1025/92) (Objet: Bicyclettes), Débats du Parlement européen, No 3-423/303, 28.10.92.

September 1992: Parliamentary question: Question écrite no 2265/92 de Mme Karla Peijs (PPE) à la Commission des Communautés européennes (1er septembre 1992) (93/C 47/55) (Objet: Pratique déloyale de dumping portant sur de grandes quantités de bicyclettes en provence de Chine et de Taiwan), Réponse donnée par M Andriessen au nom de la Commission (19 novembre 1992), [1993] OJ C47/265.

November 1992: Parliamentary question: Question écrite no 2807/92 de M Kenneth Coates (S) à la Commission des Communautés européennes (16 novembre 1992) (93/C 155/31) (Objet: Crise dans l'industrie européenne de la bicyclette et dumping des bicyclettes importées de Chine), Réponse donnée par Sir Leon Brittan au nom de la Commission (16 mars 1993), [1993] OJ C155/17.

March 1993: Provisional anti-dumping duty: Imposition of provisional anti-dumping duty: Commission Regulation (EEC) No 550/93 of 5 March 1993 imposing a provisional anti-dumping duty on imports of bicycles originating in the People's Republic of China [1993] OJ L58/12.

June 1993: Provisional anti-dumping duty extended: Extension of validity of provisional anti-dumping duty: Council Regulation (EEC) No 1607/93 of 24 June 1993 extending the provisional anti-dumping duty on imports of bicycles originating in the People's Republic of China [1993] OJ L155/1.

September 1993: Definitive anti-dumping duty: Imposition of definitive anti-dumping duty: Council Regulation (EEC) No 2474/93 imposing a definitive anti-dumping duty on imports into the Community of bicycles originating in the People's Republic of China and collecting definitively the provisional anti-dumping duty [1993] OJ L228/1.

December 1993: Application lodged against definitive anti-dumping duty: see Case T-170/94 (originally registered as Case C-477/93) *Shanghai Bicycle Corporation (Group) v Council of the European Union* [1997] ECR II-1383, para 12.

September 1993: Parliamentary question: Question écrite E-2357/93 posée par Marco Taradash (NI) à la Commission (1er septembre 1993) (94/C279/48) (Objet: Enquête antidumping relative aux bicyclettes d'origine chinoise), Réponse donnée par Sir Leon Brittan au nom de la Commission (7 février 1994), [1994] OJ C279/23.

February 1994: Parliamentary question: Question écrite E-4109/93 posée par Carlos Robles Piquer (PPE) à la Commission (7 février 1994) (94/C 289/123) (Objet: Droits anti-dumping sur les pièces détachées de bicyclettes en provenance de la Chine) and Question écrite E-33/93 posée par José Gil-Robles Gil-Delgado (PPE) à la Commission (9 février 1994) (94/C 289/124) (Objet: L'industrie communautaire de bicyclettes), Réponse commune aux questions écrites E-4109/93 et E-33/93 donnée par Sir Leon Brittan au nom de la Commission (30 mars 1994).

April 1994: Action for annulment brought by Shanghai Bicycle Corporation (Group): Case T-170/94 *Shanghai Bicycle Corporation (Group) v Council of the European Union* ECR [1997] II-1383.

April 1996: Investigation of circumvention: Commission Regulation (EC) No 703/96 of 18 April 1996 initiating an investigation concerning the circumvention of anti-dumping measures imposed by Council Regulation (EEC) No 2474/93 on imports of bicycles originating in the People's Republic of China by assembly operations in the European Community [1996] OJ L98/3.

April 1996: Definitive anti-dumping duties on bicycles from Indonesia, Malaysia and Thailand: Council Regulation (EC) No 648/96, [1996] OJ L91/1.

January 1997: Definitive anti-dumping duty extended to bicycle parts: Council Regulation (EC) No 71/97 of 10 January 1997 extending the definitive anti-dumping duty imposed by Regulation (EEC) No 2474/93 on bicycles originating in the People's Republic of China to imports of certain bicycle parts from the People's Republic of China, and levying the extended duty on such imports registered under Regulation (EC) No 703/96, [1997] OJ L16/55.

January 1997: Establishment of procedure for exemption of certain parts: Establishment of procedure for authorisation of exemption of bicycle parts: Commission Regulation (EC) No 88/97, [1997] OJ L17/17.

February 1997: Updated list of requests for exemption: Commission Notice 97/C45/03 updating the list of parties under examination pursuant to Commission Regulation (EC) No 88/97 of 20 January 1997 on the authorisation of the exemption of imports of certain bicycle parts originating in the People's Republic of China from the extension imposed by Council Regulation 71/97 of the anti-dumping duty imposed by Regulation (EEC) No 2474/93, [1997] OJ C45/03.

March 1997: Action for annulment brought by Starway SA: Action brought on 28 March 1997 by Starway SA against the Council of the European Union [1997] OJ C212/27.

April 1997: Updated list of requests for exemption: Commission Notice 97/C112/04 updating the list of parties under examination pursuant to Commission Regulation (EC) No 88/97 of 20 January 1997 on the authorisation of the exemption of imports of certain bicycle parts originating in the People's Republic of China from the extension imposed by Council Regulation 71/97 of the anti-dumping duty imposed by Regulation (EEC) No 2474/93, [1997] OJ C112/9.

July 1997: Updated list of requests for exemption: Commission Notice 97/C220/03 updating the list of parties under examination pursuant to Commission Regulation (EC) No 88/97 of 20 January 1997 authorising the exemption of imports of certain bicycle parts originating in the People's Republic of China from the extension imposed by Council Regulation 71/97 of the anti-dumping duty imposed by Regulation (EEC) No 2474, [1997] OJ C220/6.

July 1997: Decision exempting importers of certain bicycle parts: Commission Decision 97/447/EC of 16 July 1997 exempting imports of certain bicycle parts originating in the People's Republic of China from the extension by Council Regulation (EC) No 71/97 of the anti-dumping duty imposed by Regulation (EEC) No 2474/93, [1997] OJ L193/32.

September 1997: Parliamentary question: Written Question E-2843/97 by Klaus-Heiner Lehne (PPE) to the Commission (11 September 1997) (Subject: Anti-dumping Regulation as applicable to bicycle parts from China), Answer given by Sir Leon Brittan on behalf of the Commission (28 October 1997), [1998] OJ C134/26.

September 1997: Dismissal of action for annulment: Case T-170/94 *Shanghai Bicycle Corporation (Group) v Council of the European Union* [1997] ECR II-1383.

December 1997: Updated list of requests for exemption: Mise à jour C1997/378/02 de la liste des parties en cours d'examen en vertu du règlement (CE) no 88/97 de la Commission [1997] OJ C378/2.

December 1997: Decision lifting suspension of payment of anti-dumping duty on certain bicycle parts: Commission Decision 97/812/EC lifting the suspension of the payment of the anti-dumping duty extended to certain bicycle parts originating in the People's Republic of China granted to certain parties pursuant to Commission Regulation (EC) No 88/97, [1997] OJ L334/37.

February 1998: Decision exempting importers of certain bicycle parts: Commission Decision 98/115/EC exempting imports of certain bicycle parts originating in the People's Republic of China from the extension by Council Regulation (EC) No 71/97 of the anti-dumping duty imposed by Council Regulation (EEC) No 2474/93, [1998] OJ L31/25.

May 1998: Decision rejecting application by Renak International GmbH (Germany) for exemption: Commission Decision 98/299/EC of 24 April 1998 rejecting the application submitted by Renak International GmbH (Germany) for an exemption pursuant to Commission Regulation (EC) No 88/97 from the anti-dumping duty extended to certain bicycle parts originating in the People's Republic of China [1998] OJ L133/23.

May 1998: Decision rejecting application by Eurocycles (France) for exemption: Commission Decision 98/323/EC of 29 April 1998 rejecting the application submitted by Eurocycles (France) for an exemption pursuant to Commission Regulation (EC) No 88/97 from the anti-dumping duty extended to certain bicycle parts originating in the People's Republic of China [1998] OJ L141/36.

May 1998: Decision rejecting application by Technocycles (France) for exemption: Commission Decision 98/336/EC of 6 May 1998 rejecting the application submitted by Technocycles (France) for an exemption pursuant to Commission Regulation (EC) No 88/97 from the anti-dumping duty extended to certain bicycle parts originating in the People's Republic of China [1998] OJ L148/33.

May 1998: Decision exempting importers of certain bicycle parts: Commission Decision 98/366/EC of 28 May 1998 exempting imports of certain bicycle parts originating in the People's Republic of China from the extension by Council Regulation (EC) No 71/97 of the anti-dumping duty imposed by Council Regulation (EEC) No 2474/93, [1998] OJ L164/49.

July 1998: Updated list of requests for exemption: Avis de la Commission 98/C217/05 portant mise à jour de la liste des parties en cours d'examen en vertu du règlement (CE) no 88/97 de la Commission [1998] OJ C217/9.

September 1998: Request for expiry review: Notice of initiation of a review of the anti-dumping measures applicable to imports of bicycles originating in the People's Republic of China (98/C 281/06), [1998] OJ C281/8.

September 1998: Decision lifting suspension of payment of anti-dumping duty on certain bicycle parts: Commission Decision 98/551/EC of 21 September 1998 lifting the suspension of the payment of the anti-dumping duty extended to certain bicycle parts originating in China granted to *Société Européenne de Commerce sarl (France)* pursuant to Commission Regulation (EC) No 88/97, [1998] OJ L264/64.

November 1998: Decision exempting importers of certain bicycle parts: Commission Decision 98/684/EC of 17 November 1998 exempting imports of certain bicycle parts originating in the People's Republic of China from the extension by Council Regulation (EC) No 71/98 of the anti-dumping duty imposed by Regulation (EEC) No 2747/93, [1998] OJ L320/60.

February 1999: Updated list of request for exemption: Avis de la Commission portant mise à jour de la liste des parties en cours d'examen en vertu du règlement (CE) no 88/97 de la Commission [1999] OJ C37/3.

February 1999: Definitive anti-dumping duties on bicycles from Taiwan: Council Regulation (EC) No 387/99, [1999] OJ L49/1.

July 1999: Updating list of requests for exemption: Commission Notice 1999/C186/04 updating the list of parties under examination pursuant to Commission Regulation (EC) No 88/97 on the authorisation of the exemption of imports of certain bicycle parts originating in the People's Republic of China from the extension by Council Regulation (EC) No 71/97 of the anti-dumping duty imposed by Council Regulation (EEC) No 2474/93, [1999] OJ C186/6.

October 1999: Notification of change of name of exempted parties: Commission Notice 1999/C294/03 concerning parties exempted, pursuant to Commission Regulation (EC) No 88/97 on the authorisation of the exemption of imports of certain bicycle parts originating in the People's Republic of China, from the extension by Council Regulation (EC) No 71/97 of the anti-dumping duty imposed by Council Regulation (EEC) No 2474/93: modification of the name of two exempted companies [1999] OJ C294/3.

November 1999: Initiation of proceeding concerning bicycle frames: Notice of initiation of an anti-dumping proceeding concerning imports of bicycle frames originating in the People's Republic of China and Taiwan and of the initiation of an interim review of the anti-dumping measures extended to imports of certain bicycle parts originating in the People's Republic of China (1999/C318/07), [1999] OJ C318/9.

November 1999: Initiation of proceeding concerning bicycle wheels: Notice of initiation of an anti-dumping proceeding concerning imports of complete wheels of bicycles originating in the People's Republic of China (1999/C318/08), [1999] OJ C318/12.

May 2000: Withdrawal of complaint concerning bicycle frames from China and Taiwan, bicycle forks from China and Taiwan, and bicycle wheels from China: Commission Decision 2000/316/EC of 2 May 2000 terminating the anti-dumping proceedings concerning imports of bicycle frames originating in the People's Republic of China and Taiwan, bicycle forks originating in the People's Republic of China and Taiwan and complete wheels of bicycles originating in the People's Republic of China, as well as the interim review of the anti-dumping measures extended to imports of, *inter alia*, bicycle frames, bicycle forks and complete wheels of bicycles originating in the People's Republic of China, [2000] OJ L105/40.

July 2000:Definitive antidumping duty renewed: Council Regulation (EC) No 1524/2000 of 10 July 2000 imposing a definitive anti-dumping duty on imports of bicycles originating in the People's Republic of China [2000] OJ L175/39.

July 2000: Updating list of requests for exemption: Commission Notice 2000/C216/07 updating the list of parties under examination pursuant to Commission Regulation (EC) No 88/97 on the authorisation of the exemption of imports of certain bicycle parts originating in the People's Republic of China from the extension by Council Regulation (EC) No 71/97 of the anti-dumping duty imposed by Council Regulation (EEC) No 2472/93 and lifting the suspension of the payment of the extended anti-dumping duty granted to certain parties [2000] OJ C216/8.

September 2000: Annulment of antidumping duty: Case T-80/97 *Starway SA v Council of the European Union* [2000] ECR II-3099.

September 2000: Action for annulment of extension of anti-dumping duty to bicycle parts declared inadmissible: Joined Cases T-74/97 and T-75/97 *Büchel & Co Fahrzeugteilefabrik GmbH v Council of the European Union, Büchel & Co Fahrzeugteilefabrik v Commission of the European Communities* [2000] ECR II-3067.

September 2000: Interim review requested by four Chinese companies: Notice of initiation of an interim review of the anti-dumping measures applicable to imports of bicycles originating in the People's Republic of China (2000/C278/06), [2000] OJ C278/28.

January 2001: Decision exempting importers of certain bicycle parts, and lifting suspension of anti-dumping duty on certain bicycle parts: Commission Decision 2001/108/EC of 24 January 2001 exempting imports of certain bicycle parts originating in the People's Republic of China from the extension by Council Regulation (EC) No 71/97 of the anti-dumping duty imposed by Regulation (EEC) No 2474/93, and maintained by Regulation (EC) No 1524/2000, and lifting the suspension of the payment of the anti-dumping duty extended to certain bicycle parts originating in the People's Republic of China granted to certain parties pursuant to Commission Regulation (EC) No 88/97, [2001] OJ L41/30.

June 2001: Updating list of requests for exemption: Commission Notice 2001/C170/03 upgrading the list of parties under examination pursuant to Commission Regulation (EC) No 88/97 on the exemption from the extended anti-dumping duty on imports of certain bicycle parts originating in the People's Republic of China, and lifting the suspension of payment of the extended duty granted to certain parties [2002] OJ C170/5.

October 2001: Definitive duties on internal gear hubs from Japan: Council Regulation (EC) No 2080/2001 of 23 October 2001 imposing a definitive anti-dumping duty on imports of internal gear hubs for bicycles originating in Japan [2001] OJ L282/1.

October 2001: Conclusion of review requested by four Chinese companies: Council Regulation (EC) No 2131/2001 of 29 October 2001 terminating the review of Council Regulation (EC) No 2472/93 imposing a definitive anti-dumping duty on imports of bicycles originating in the People's Republic of China [2001] OJ L289/8.

February 2002: Decision exempting importers of certain bicycle parts, and lifting suspension of anti-dumping duty on certain bicycle parts: Commission Decision 2002/134/EC of 11 February 2002 exempting imports of certain bicycle parts originating in the People's Republic of China from the extension by Council Regulation (EC) No 71/97 of the anti-dumping duty imposed by Regulation (EEC) No 2474/93, and maintained by Regulation (EC) No 1524/2000, and lifting the suspension of the payment of the anti-dumping duty extended to certain bicycle parts originating in the People's Republic of China granted in *Decision exempting importers of certain bicycle parts, and lifting suspension of anti-dumping duty on certain bicycle parts* to certain parties pursuant to Commission Regulation (EC) No 88/97, [2002] OJ L47/43.

July 2002: Decision exempting imports of essential bicycle parts, and revoking the exemption from payment of duty granted to certain parties: Commission Decision 2002/6076/EC of 16 July 2002 granting certain parties an exemption from the extension to essential bicycle parts, by Council Regulation (EC) No 71/97, of the anti-dumping duty on bicycles originating in the People's Republic of China, imposed by Council Regulation (EEC) No 2474/93, and maintained by Regulation (EC) No 1524/2000 and revoking the exemption from the payment of the anti-dumping duty extended to certain bicycle parts originating in the People's Republic of China granted to certain parties pursuant to Commission Regulation (EC) No 88/97, [2002] OJ L195/81.

April 2002: Updating list of requests for exemption: Commission Notice 2002/C103/02 updating the list of parties under examination pursuant to Commission Regulation (EC) No 88/97 on the exemption from the extended anti-dumping duty on imports of certain bicycle parts originating in the People's Republic of China [2002] OJ C103/2.

February 2003: Updating list of requests for exemption: Commission Notice 2003/C35/03 updating the list of parties under examination pursuant to Commission Regulation (EC) No 88/97 on the exemption from the extended anti-dumping duty on imports of certain bicycle parts originating in the People's Republic of China [2003] OJ C35/3.

February 2003: Updating list of requests for exemption: Commission Notice 2003/C35/03 updating the list of parties under examination pursuant to Commission Regulation (EC) No 88/97 on the exemption from the extended anti-dumping duty on imports of certain bicycle parts originating in the People's Republic of China [2003] OJ C43/5.

April 2003: Modification of names and addresses of exempted parties: Commission Notice 2003/C92/04 concerning parties exempted pursuant to Commission Regulation (EC) No 88/97 on the authorisation of the exemption on imports of certain bicycle parts originating in the People's Republic of China from the extension by Council Regulation (EC) No 71/97 of the anti-dumping duty imposed by Council Regulation (EEC) No 2474/93 and maintained by Council Regulation (EC) No 1524/2000: modification of names and addresses of exempted parties [2003] OJ C92/5.

July 2003: Revocation of exemption from payment of duty: Commission Decision 2003/560/EC revoking the exemption from the payment of the anti-dumping duty extended to certain bicycle parts originating in the People's Republic of China granted to certain parties pursuant to Regulation (EC) No 88/97, [2003] OJ L190/10.

December 2003: Decision exempting importers of certain bicycle parts, and lifting suspension of anti-dumping duty on certain bicycle parts: Commission Decision 223/899/EC of 28 November 2003 granting certain parties an exemption from the extension to certain bicycle parts, by Council Regulation (EC) No 71/97, of the anti-dumping duty on bicycles originating in the People's Republic of China imposed by Council Regulation (EEC) No 2474/93, and maintained by Council Regulation (EC) No 1524/2000, and lifting the suspension of the payment of the anti-dumping duty extended to certain bicycle parts originating in the People's Republic of China granted to certain parties pursuant to Commission Regulation (EC) No 88/97, [2003] OJ L336/101.

March 2004: Updating list of requests for exemption: Commission Notice 2004/C54/03 updating the list of parties under examination pursuant to Commission Regulation (EC) No 88/97 on the exemption from the extended anti-dumping duty on imports of certain bicycle parts originating in the People's Republic of China [2004] OJ C54/2.

April 2004: Changes regarding exempted companies: Commission Notice 2004/C97/08 concerning parties exempted, pursuant to Commission Regulation (EC) No 88/97 on the authorisation of the exemption of imports of certain bicycle parts originating in the People's Republic of

China from the extension by Council Regulation (EC) No 71/97 of the anti-dumping duty imposed by Council Regulation (EEC) No 2474/93, and maintained by Council Regulation (EC) No 1524/2000: changes regarding exempted companies [2004] OJ C97/12.

April 2004: Interim review: Notice of initiation of an interim review of the anti-dumping measures applicable to imports of bicycles originating in the People's Republic of China (2004/C 103/04), [2004] OJ C103/80.

July 2005: Amending and increasing anti-dumping duty on bicycles and bicycle parts: Council Regulation (EC) No 1095/2005 of 12 July 2005 imposing a definitive anti-dumping duty on imports of bicycles originating in Vietnam, and amending Regulation (EC) No 1524/2000 imposing a definitive anti-dumping duty on imports of bicycles originating in the People's Republic of China [2005] OJ L183/1 (following interim review for which notice given in April 2004).

August 2005: Changes in name and registered seat of exempted companies: Commission Notice 2005/C195/06 concerning parties exempted, pursuant to Commission Regulation (EC) No 88/97 on the authorisation of the exemption on imports of certain bicycle parts originating in the People's Republic of China from the extension by Council Regulation (EC) No 71/97 of the anti-dumping duty imposed by Council Regulation (EEC) No 2474/93, and maintained by Council Regulation (EC) No 1524/2000: changes in the company name and registered seat of exempted companies [2005] OJ C195/6.

December 2005: Ombudsman Decision on complaint against European Commission: Decision of the European Ombudsman 1737/2005/PB on complaint against the European Commission, http://www.euro-ombudsman.eu.int/decision/en/051737.htm, last accessed 12 February 2006. http://www.ius.info/EUII/EUO/dokumenti/2005/12/European_Ombudsman_Decision_173720 05PB_09_12_2005.htm, last accessed 17 February 2010.

November 2005: Termination of partial interim review: Council Regulation (EC) No 1892/2005 of 14 November 2005 terminating the partial interim review of the anti-dumping measures applicable to imports of bicycles originating in the People's Republic of China, [2005] OJ L302/22.

January 2006: Decision exempting importers of certain bicycle parts, and lifting suspension of anti-dumping duty on certain bicycle parts: Commission Decision 2006/22/EC of 20 January 2006 granting certain parties an exemption from the extension to certain bicycle parts of the anti-dumping duty on bicycles originating in the People's Republic of China imposed by Council Regulation (EEC) No 2474/93, last maintained and amended by Regulation (EC) No 1095/2005, and lifting the suspension of the payment of the anti-dumping duty extended to certain bicycle parts originating in the People's Republic of China granted to certain parties pursuant to Regulation (EC) No 88/97, [2006] OJ L17/16.

March 2006: Action for annulment of decision terminating partial interim review: Case T-17/06 *Giant (China) v Council* [2006] OJ C74/29.

July 2006: Removal from the Register of action for annulment of decision terminating partial interim review: Case T-17/06 *Giant (China) v Council*, Order of the President of the Fifth Chamber of the Court of First Instance, 7 July 2006 (Removal from the Register).

August 2006: Changes in name and address of certain exempted parties: Commission Notice 2006/C186/07 concerning parties exempted, pursuant to Commission Regulation (EC) No 88/97 on the authorisation of the exemption of imports of certain bicycle parts originating in the People's Republic of China from the extension by Council Regulation (EC) No 71/97 of the anti-dumping duty imposed by Council Regulation (EEC) No 2474/93, maintained by Council Regulation (EC) No 1524/2000 and last amended by Council Regulation (EC) No 1095/2005: changes in the name and address of certain exempted parties [2006] OJ C186/7.

November 2006: Decision exempting importers of certain bicycle parts, and lifting suspension of anti-dumping duty on certain bicycle parts: Commission Decision 2006/772/EC granting certain parties an exemption from the extension to certain bicycle parts of the anti-dumping duty on bicycles originating in the People's Republic of China imposed by Council Regulation (EEC) No 2474/93, last maintained and amended by Regulation (EC) No 1095/2005, and lifting the suspension of the payment of the anti-dumping duty extended to certain bicycle parts originating in the People's Republic of China granted to certain parties pursuant to Regulation (EC) No 88/97, [2006] OJ L313/5.

November 2006: Initiation of review of extension of duty to parts: [Commission] Notice 2006/C289/04 of initiation of a review of the extension of the anti-dumping duty imposed on imports of bicycles originating in the People's Republic of China to imports of certain bicycle parts from the People's Republic of China [2006] OJ C289/15.

November 2006: Termination of partial interim review: Council Regulation (EC) No 1651/2006 terminating the partial interim review of the anti-dumping measures applicable to imports of bicycles originating in the People's Republic of China [2006] OJ L311/6.

July 2007: Changes in the name and address of certain exempted parties: Commission Notice 2007/C158/06 concerning parties exempted, pursuant to Commission Regulation (EC) No 88/97 on the authorisation of the exemption of imports of certain bicycle parts originating in the People's Republic of China from the extension by Council Regulation (EC) No 71/97 of the anti-dumping duty imposed by Council Regulation (EEC) No 2747/93: changes in the name and address of certain exempted parties [2007] OJ C158/6.

February 2008: Maintenance of extension to parts following interim review: Council Regulation (EC) No 171/2008 of 25 February 2008 maintaining Council Regulation (EC) No 71/97 on the extension of the anti-dumping duty imposed on imports of bicycles originating in the People's Republic of China to imports of certain bicycle parts from the People's Republic of China [2008] OJ L55/1.

March 2008: Decision exempting importers of certain bicycle parts, and lifting suspension of anti-dumping duty on certain bicycle parts: Commission Decision 2008/260/EC of 18 March 2008 granting certain parties an exemption from the extension to certain bicycle parts of the anti-dumping duty on bicycles originating in the People's Republic of China imposed by Council Regulation (EEC) No 2474/93, last maintained and amended by Regulation (EC) No 1095/2005, and lifting the suspension of the payment of the anti-dumping duty extended to certain bicycle parts originating in the People's Republic of China granted to certain parties pursuant to Commission Regulation (EC) No 88/97, [2008] OJ L81/73.

June 2008: Changes in name and address of certain exempted parties: Commission Notice 2008/C135/04 concerning parties exempted, pursuant to Commission Regulation (EC) No 88/97 on the authorisation of the exemption of imports of certain bicycle parts originating in the People's Republic of China from the extension by Council Regulation (EC) No 71/97 of the anti-dumping duty imposed by Council Regulation (EEC) No 2474/93, maintained by Council Regulation (EC) No 1524/2000 and last amended by Council Regulation (EC) No 1095/2005: changes in the name and address of certain exempted parties [2008] OJ C135/5.

December 2008: List of parties under examination: Commission Notice 2008/C310/07 updating the list of parties under examination pursuant to Commission Regulation (EC) No 88/97 on the exemption from the extended anti-dumping duty on imports of certain bicycle parts originating in the People's Republic of China [2008] OJ C310/09.

January 2009: Decision exempting importers of certain bicycle parts, and lifting suspension of anti-dumping duty on certain bicycle parts: Commission Decision 2009/48/EC of 22 January 2009 granting certain parties an exemption from the extension to certain bicycle parts of the anti-dumping duty on bicycles originating in the People's Republic of China imposed by Council Regulation (EEC) No 2474/93, last maintained and amended by Regulation (EC) No 1095/2005, and lifting the suspension of the payment of the anti-dumping duty extended to certain bicycle parts originating in the People's Republic of China granted to certain parties pursuant to Commission Regulation (EC) No 88/97, [2009] OJ L19/62.

Part II

Global Legal Pluralism in Action: the EU, the WTO and China

5

Constructing Relations Between Sites of Governance: the European Courts and WTO Law*

I. Introduction

It is common to conceive of relations between sites of governance as the work of diplomats, legislators, the executive power in governments or other strategic actors, such as business organisations or other private actors. International agreements, constitutions or legislation may often lay down the basic normative framework. However, depending on the internal structure of the sites of governance in question and the relative power of the institutions concerned, such relations may also originate from, be structured by or be managed by courts. Courts of last instance in particular may act as 'gatekeepers' in relations between sites of governance. This chapter considers the ways in which the European Union courts have through their case law acted as 'gatekeepers' in relations between the WTO and the EU. Following the entry into force of the Treaty of Lisbon on 1 December 2009, the Court of Justice of the European Union includes the Court of Justice (formerly the European Court of Justice, ECJ), the General Court (formerly the Court of First Instance, CFI) and specialised courts.[1]

The law of the General Agreement on Tariffs and Trade (GATT) and, since 1995, of the World Trade Organisation (WTO) has long been intimately intertwined with European Community (EC) and now European Union (EU) law.[2] Today, however, WTO law affects the EU constitutional order in ways which few observers imagined when the WTO was founded. Nevertheless, these far-reaching effects should not be surprising. The EC, as well as its Member States, joined the WTO, and social action always has unintended as well as intended consequences, as shown in the preceding chapter. Moreover, WTO law is a cause as well as a consequence of globalisation, and

* This chapter is an updated, revised and partly rewritten version of an article that was originally published as 'The Gatekeepers: The European Courts and WTO Law' (2003) 40 *Common Market Law Review* 313–67. The article has been reproduced with the permission of Kluwer Law International.

[1] The chapter is based on cases decided before the Lisbon Treaty entered into force. Consequently, it employs the terms European Court of Justice (ECJ) and Court of First Instance (CFI). Similarly, it refers to articles of the EU and EC Treaties according to the numbering of the Treaty of Nice.

[2] This chapter takes account of all ECJ and CFI judgments mentioning GATT or WTO law between 1973 and the cut-off date of 11 May 2007; some later judgments are also mentioned. For other earlier surveys, see E-U Petersmann, 'Application of GATT by the Court of Justice of the European Communities' (1983) 20 *CML Rev* 409; M Maresceau, 'The GATT in the case-law of the European Court of Justice' in M Hilf, FG Jacobs and E-U Petersmann (eds), *The European Community and GATT* (Deventer, Kluwer, 1983) 107; P Eeckhout, 'The domestic legal status of the WTO Agreement: Interconnecting legal systems' (1997) 34 *CML Rev* 11; PJ Kuijper and M Bronckers, 'WTO Law in the European Court of Justice' (2005) 42 *CML Rev* 1313. A Laget-Annamayer, 'Le statut des accords OMC dans l'ordre juridique communautaire: en attendant la consecration de l'invocabilité' (2006) 42(2) *Revue trimestrielle de droit européen* 249.

it has reinforced aspects of globalisation which already have a profound impact on EU policy and law. Furthermore, the WTO and the EU are two of the most significant institutional and normative sites of governance in the world today, so that an intensification of their interaction is not difficult to predict.

These general observations pinpoint the fact of WTO impact on EU law, but they do not identify its precise effects or try to explain them. What specific impact has WTO law had on EU law? The present chapter seeks to answer this question at least in part. For this purpose, it analyses the judgments concerning GATT/WTO law by the ECJ and the CFI. In the last 10 years, this case law has amounted to a veritable flood, requiring the European courts to deal much more frequently and in more detail with WTO law.[3] Nevertheless, despite the dramatic increase in the number of cases in which GATT or WTO law has been pleaded in the recent years, by and large the European courts so far follow basic principles laid down by 2003, if not before. Consequently, pending any major shift in the case law, only a few recent cases add substantially to the existing stock of legal principles or directions of legal analysis. While the case law does not reflect all the effects of WTO law on EU law,[4] it provides a useful starting point for understanding the impact of the WTO on the EU legal order and EU constitutional and administrative law. It also illuminates the role of the judiciary, particularly the European courts, in governing economic and legal globalisation, and in regulating relations between sites of governance.

The main effects of WTO law on EU law, as seen in the case law of the European courts, have so far been three-fold. They have occurred roughly in three overlapping phases, which in both legal and political terms are logically related. More specifically, WTO law has first contributed enormously to the expansion of the normative repertoire available to (and thus to the power of) EC institutions, notably (but not only) the judiciary (see section II. below). Secondly, with certain limited exceptions, however, there has not been any corresponding empowerment of individuals. Indeed, it can be argued that increasing normative integration between the WTO and the EC has contributed to the relative weakening of the legal position of individuals (see section III.). Thirdly, WTO law, as interpreted by the European courts, has tended so far to foster tighter relations between the EC and the Member States, as well as greater integration

[3] In numerous cases a WTO point has been pleaded but not addressed by the ECJ/CFI, or not otherwise referred to by the ECJ/CFI, thus suggesting the extent to which the ECJ/CFI prefers to resolve cases by recourse to EC law alone to the extent possible. See eg; Case C-310/04 *Spain v Council* [2006] ECR I-7285 (applicant argued that new EC support system for cotton was contrary to WTO Agreement on Agriculture); Case T-17/06 *Giant (China) v Council*, Application OJ 25.03.06 C74/29, removed from the register (applicant argued that application of market economy criteria to Chinese exporters in five EC Member States which did not have such criteria at the time of China's accession to WTO constituted a breach of WTO law); Arguments based on WTO law must be sufficiently developed to permit an informed decision: Case T-201/04R *Microsoft v Commission,* Order of 22/12/2004 (proceedings for interim relief). In other cases, WTO law is mentioned merely as part of the factual framework, the legal context or the international legal framework. Such cases sometimes identify unexpected links between sites of governance: see eg; Case T-158/03 *Industrias Químicas del Vallés v Commission* [2005] ECR II-2425 (reference to Commission argument that non-inclusion of metalaxyl in annex of Council Directive was subject of ongoing procedure involving consultation within the WTO SPS Committee); Case C-342/03 *Spain v Council* [2005] ECR I-1975 (factual connection: contested tariff quota regulation was adopted to implement recommendation of WTO mediator in conflict among WTO Members;

[4] On the implementation and transposition of WTO law in EC law, see P Van den Bossche, 'The European Community and the Uruguay Round Agreements', in JH Jackson and AO Sykes (eds), *Implementing the Uruguay Round* (Oxford, Oxford University Press, 1997) 23; P Didier, *Les principaux accords de l'OMC et leur transposition dans la Communauté européenne* (Bruxelles, Bruylant, 1997); F Snyder, *International Trade and Customs Law of the European Union* (London, Butterworths, 1998).

among the Member States in the substantive areas in which it applies. Although it is too early to foresee all implications of this trend, it is clear already that WTO law is beginning to reshape the distribution of power between the EC and the Member States (see section IV.). These developments raise difficult legal (and political) issues, not only for the European courts but also for other EU institutions, national governments, companies and citizens.

II. WTO Law and the EC Legal Order

A. Effects of WTO Law on the EC Legal Order

The law of the WTO has had significant effects on the EC legal order. In particular, it has contributed to the growth and expansion of EC institutions, especially the courts. This impact can be understood most easily by focusing first on the effects of WTO law on the EC legal order, and then on WTO law and the interpretation of EC law. As a result of judgments of the European courts, WTO law is part of the EC legal order. In addition, EC law is presumed to be compatible with WTO law.

1. WTO Law is Part of the EC Legal Order

The ECJ held long ago that international agreements concluded by the Community, including the GATT, are an integral part of the EC legal order,[5] though it never stated that the GATT was an act of one of the EC institutions within the meaning of Article 234 (ex 177) EC.[6] It also held that GATT 1947 was hierarchically superior to EC secondary legislation.[7] Since then, this view has been maintained and in several recent cases extended to WTO law.

Emesa Sugar[8] concerned the validity of a Council Decision imposing tariff quotas and removing milling from the types of working and processing sufficient to confer origin on sugar imports into the EC from Aruba. Both Emesa and Aruba argued that it was excess EC sugar production and exports, not the negligible imports into the EC of sugar from the Overseas Countries and Territories (OCT) [known as OCT sugar], which *inter alia* affected the EC's fulfilment of its WTO obligations. The ECJ rejected this argument, stating that EC sugar production exceeded consumption, cane sugar was imported from the African, Caribbean and Pacific (ACP) countries, and the EC was obliged to import sugar from non-Member countries under the WTO agreements.

[5] Case 181/73 *R & V Haegeman v Belgian State* [1974] ECR 449.

[6] JHJ Bourgeois, 'The European Court of Justice and the WTO: Problems and Challenges' in JHH Weiler (ed), *The EU, the WTO and the NAFTA: Towards a Common Law of International Trade?* (Oxford, Oxford University Press, 2000) 71 at 84.

[7] Case C-61/94 *Germany v Commission* [1996] ECR I-3989.

[8] Case C-17/98 *Emesa Sugar (Free Zone) NV v Aruba* [2000] ECR I-675.

In addition, the EC 'was also required to subsidise sugar exports by granting export refunds, within the limits laid down in the WTO agreements'.[9] The ECJ considered the WTO Agreements to be part of the normative framework of the EC sugar market. The European courts have taken a similar view concerning sugar quotas in later cases,[10] as well as concerning the WTO Anti-dumping Agreement[11] and the WTO Agreement on Agriculture.[12]

2. *EC Law is Presumed to be Compatible with WTO Law*

Assuming that WTO law is part of the EC legal order, the European courts sometimes state that EC law is compatible with WTO law. Usually, however, they simply presume compatibility. In practice, this means that the judiciary accepts the assertion by the EC legislator that Community legislation is WTO-consistent.

Banque Indosuez[13] concerned a Commission Decision imposing definitive anti-dumping duties on iron or steel products from the former Yugoslavia. The preamble to the Decision stated that the arrangements had been adopted in accordance with existing international obligations, in particular Article VI GATT and the Anti-dumping Agreement. Taking this for granted, the ECJ did not refer to GATT or the Anti-dumping Agreement elsewhere in its judgment. Similarly, the ECJ took the WTO normative framework for granted in annulling part of a Council Decision approving the Framework Agreement on Bananas in Case C-122/95 *Germany v Council.*[14]

B. Interpretation of WTO Law and EC Law

1. *Several EC Institutions Interpret WTO Law in their Daily Practice*

Following these judgments, several EC institutions regularly interpret WTO law in their daily practice. The European courts themselves use WTO law as an aid to interpreting a range of legal instruments.

Among the several EC institutions that interpret WTO law, the European courts have been most in the public eye. However, other EC institutions also interpret WTO law regularly in their work. Though this chapter is concerned mainly with the judiciary, WTO

[9] *Ibid*, para 56.

[10] Joined Cases T-94/00, T-110/00 and T-159/00 *Rica Foods (Free Zone) NV, Free Trade Foods NV and Suproco NV v Commission* [2002] ECR II-4677; Joined Cases T-332/00 and T-350/00 *Rica Foods (Free Zone) NV and Free Trade Foods NV v Commission* [2002] ECR II-4755, appealed as Case 40/03P *Rica Foods (Free Zone) NY v Commission* [2005] ECR I-6811 and Case 41/03P *Rica Foods (Free Zone) v Commission* [2005] ECR I-6875 nyr.

[11] See also Case T-188/99 *Euroalliages v Commission* [2001] ECR II-1757.

[12] Case C-317/99 *Kloosterboer Rotterdam BV v Minister van Landbouw, Natuurbeheer en Visserij* [2001] ECR I-9863.

[13] Case C-177/96 *Belgian State v Banque Indosuez and Others* [1997] ECR I-5659.

[14] [1998] ECR I-973.

law has had a wider impact on EC decision-making.[15] Its effects are felt not only by the courts but also by the legislator and executive.[16] For example, the European Parliament takes account of WTO law in its participation in the legislative process.[17]

i. The European Courts

Since its early, initially controversial case law,[18] the ECJ has consistently claimed the authority to interpret GATT law and now WTO law. While no longer contested in areas of exclusive EC competence, this claim raises difficult issues in areas where the EC shares competence with the Member States.

The EC has exclusive competence with regard to the common commercial policy, including tariff quotas and anti-dumping. In Case C-352/96 *Italy v Council*,[19] Italy sought to annul a Council Regulation providing for tariff quotas on rice and broken rice pursuant to agreements between the EC and Australia, and the EC and Thailand. Rejecting this argument, the ECJ interpreted Article XXIV(6) GATT 1994 to mean that

> The concept of 'mutually satisfactory understanding' does not in itself constitute an objective criterion and the requirement to achieve a mutually satisfactory understanding must be regarded as fulfilled when an agreement embodying a solution is concluded by the parties concerned . . .[20]

Similarly, *Acme*[21] was an action to annul definitive anti-dumping duties on microwave ovens from China. The applicant argued *inter alia* that the Anti-dumping Agreement applied. The CFI interpreted the Anti-dumping Agreement with regard to its temporal scope. It concluded that the legality of the Regulation at issue could not be contested in the light of either Council Regulation 3283/94 or the WTO Anti-dumping Agreement, which came into force only after the start of the procedures in this case, but 'primarily' (para 31) in the light of the basic Regulation, general principles and all relevant rules in force at the time.

The CFI interpreted the Anti-dumping Agreement, though the applicant did not plead it, in *Eurocoton*.[22] On appeal, the Advocate-General also interpreted the Anti-dumping Agreement, distinguishing between the purposes of the Agreement and those of Community law: the former aimed at protecting the interests of exporters, exporting

[15] See G de Búrca and J Scott, 'The Impact of the WTO on EU Decision-making', in G de Búrca and J Scott (eds), *The EU and the WTO: Legal and Constitutional Issues* (Oxford, Hart Publishing, 2001).

[16] See A Antoniadis, 'The European Union and WTO Law: A Nexus of Reactive, Coactive and Proactive Approaches' (2007) 6(1) *World Trade Review* 45.

[17] J Bourgeois and O Lynskey, 'The extent to which the EC legislature takes account of WTO obligations: jousting lessons from the European Parliament' in A Dashwood and M Maresceau (eds), *Law and Practice of EU External Relations: Salient Features of a Changing Landscape* (Cambridge, Cambridge University Press, 2008) 202. See also P Bender, 'The European Parliament and the WTO: Positions and initiatives' (2002) 7 *European Foreign Affairs Review* 193.

[18] Joined Cases 21–24/74 *International Fruit Company v Produktschap voor Groenten en Fruit* [1972] ECR 1219; Case 9/73 *Schlüter v Hauptzollamt Lorach* [1973] ECR 1135; Case 181/73 *R & V Haegeman v Belgian State* [1974] ECR 449: Case 38/75 *Nederlandse Spoorwegern v Inspecteur der Invoerrechten en Accijnzen* [1975] ECR 1439; Joined Cases 267/81, 268/81 and 269/81 *Amministrazione delle Finanze dello Stato v Società Petrolifera Italiana SpA (SPI) and SpA Michelin Italiana (SAMI)* [1983] ECR 801. See also Case 10/61 *Commission v Italy* [1962] ECR (Eng Sp Ed) 1. See also Case C-83/94 *Leifer* [1995] ECR 3231.

[19] Case C-352/96 *Italy v Council* [1998] ECR I-6937.

[20] *Ibid*, para 22.

[21] Case T-48/96 *Acme Industry Co Ltd v Council*, [1999] ECR II-3089.

[22] Case T-213/97 *Committee of the Cotton and Allied Textile Industries of the European Union (Eurocoton) and others v Council* [1997] ECR II-1609.

countries and importers, whereas the interests of domestic-industry complaints were protected by EC law.[23]

In areas of shared competence, European judicial interpretation of WTO law is more controversial. In *Hermès*,[24] the ECJ held that it had jurisdiction to interpret Article 50 TRIPS. It based its analysis on the observation that the WTO Agreement 'was concluded by the Community and ratified by the Member States without any allocation between them of their respective obligations towards the other contracting parties'.[25] Stepping into the breach, it stated that

> where a provision can apply both to situations falling within the scope of national law and to situations falling within the scope of Community law, it is clearly in the Community interest that, in order to forestall future differences of interpretation, that provision should be interpreted uniformly, whatever the circumstances in which it is to apply . . .[26]

The ECJ used the same approach in two later cases involving Article 50 TRIPS, first extending it beyond situations governed by trade mark law in *Dior*,[27] and then applying it in the trade mark case of *Groeneveld*.[28] On the grounds of the uniform interpretation of Community law, the ECJ claimed the power to interpret WTO law throughout areas of shared competence, unfortunately without distinguishing between different types of mixed agreements.[29]

In theory, the ECJ has the last word in interpreting WTO law for the purposes of EC law. In practice, however, the Commission and the Council also give what often amount in practice to definitive interpretations of WTO law.

ii. The Commission

The European Commission regularly interprets WTO law in charting policy, drafting legislation, negotiating 'mutually agreed solutions' with the EC's trading partners[30] and interpreting EC law.[31] Sometimes, as with the draft Cosmetics Directive, its interpretation 'may lead, if not necessarily to over-compliance, at least to results which do not seem to flow inexorably from the text or jurisprudence of the WTO'.[32] Such interpretations are in most instances not challenged in court, so they act as a potentially significant but usually unnoticed influence on EC law and policy.

[23] Case C-76/01 P, *Eurocoton and Others v Council* [2003] ECR I-10091, para 32.

[24] Case C-53/96 *Hermès International v FHT Marketing Choice BV* [1998] ECR I-3603.

[25] *Ibid*, para 24.

[26] *Ibid*, para 32.

[27] Joined Cases C-300/98 *Parfums Christian Dior SA v Tuk Consultancy BV* and C-392/98 *Assco Gerüste GmbH, Rob van Dijk v Wilhelm Layher GmbH & Co KG, Layher BV* [2000] ECR I-11307.

[28] Case C-89/99 *Schieving-Nijstad vof and Others v Robert Groeneveld* [2001] ECR I-5851.

[29] See JHJ Bourgeois, 'The European Court of Justice and the WTO: Problems and challenges' in JHHWeiler (ed), *The EU, the WTO and the NAFTA: Towards a Common Law of International Trade* (Oxford, Oxford University Press, 2000) 71 at 87–88; A Rosas, 'The European Union and Mixed Agreements' in A Dashwood and C Hillion (eds), *The General Law of EC External Relations* (London, Sweet & Maxwell, 2000) 200 at 203–07. This may, however, be regarded as a counterpart to the frequent use of mixed agreements, including circumstances when mixity was legally unnecessary: see P Eeckhout, 'The domestic legal status of the WTO Agreement: Interconnecting legal systems' (2005) 34 *CML Rev*11 at 23.

[30] See E Baroncini, 'The European Community and the diplomatic phase of the WTO Dispute Settlement Understanding' (1998) 18 *Yearbook of European Law* 157.

[31] On Commission work intended to prevent GATT panels against the EC, see PJ Kuijper, 'The new WTO dispute settlement system: The impact on the European Community' (1995) 29 *Journal of World Trade* 49 at 60–61.

[32] de Búrca and Scott, above n 15, at 6–12.

For example, in *Petrotub*,[33] the CFI used the Anti-dumping Agreement as a check on the Commission's interpretation of the basic EC anti-dumping Regulation. On appeal, the ECJ, in annulling the CFI decision, also employed the Anti-dumping Agreement in interpreting the basic Regulation. It noted in particular that the giving of reasons requirement specified in Article 2.4.2 of the Agreement was not reiterated in the basic Regulation, because such a requirement was contained in Article 190 (now 253) TEC.[34] The Commission's interpretation apparently relied partly on the Anti-dumping Agreement, though this is not expressly stated in the judgment, perhaps because the relevant provisions of the EC Regulation and the Anti-dumping Agreement are the same.

Similarly, in *Poudres Sphériques*, the Advocate-General confirmed that, as the Commission had argued, the annulment of an anti-dumping measure cannot cause the measure to be replaced by a new regulation with retroactive effect. Such retroactive imposition of anti-dumping duties was prohibited by Article 13(1) of the basic EC anti-dumping Regulation, and it

> was prohibited in principle by Article 11 of the 1979 Anti-dumping Code—contained in the Agreement on Implementation of Article 6 of the General Agreement on Tariffs and Trade (GATT) which was then in force . . .[35]

In Case T-1/99 *T Port*,[36] the Commission relied expressly on its interpretation of the Framework Agreement on Bananas.[37] The CFI accepted the Commission's argument that the positive measures laid down in the Framework Agreement partly offset disadvantages suffered by the applicant banana importer as a result of the Community's export licence scheme.

iii. The Council

The Commission's right of initiative to propose EC legislation means that, among all non-judicial EC institutions, the Commission is the most likely to interpret WTO law or to use WTO law in interpreting EC legislation. *Emesa Sugar*[38] was one of the rare cases involving the interpretation and use of WTO law by the Council. The ECJ confirmed the broad legislative discretion of the Council with regard to tariff quotas and other measures concerning sugar imports from the OCT. It stated that

> In these circumstances [of the Community's WTO obligations], the Council was entitled to take the view that any additional quantity of sugar reaching the Community market . . . would have obliged the Community institutions to increase the amount of the export subsidies . . .[39]

In principle at least, the Commission and the Council could interpret the same provisions of WTO law differently. Though recent case law does not provide any examples

[33] Joined Cases T-33/98 and T-34/98 *Petrotub SA and Republica SA v Council* [1999] ECR II-3837.

[34] Case C-76/00P *Petrotub SA and Republica SA v Council and Commission* [2003] ECR I-79, para 58.

[35] Case C-458/98P *Industrie des Poudres Sphériques v Council* [2000] ECR I-8147, Opinion of A-G Cosmos, para 77, fn 3.

[36] Case T-1/99 *T Port GmbH & Co KG v Commission* [2001] ECR II-465.

[37] The Framework Agreement on Bananas between the EC and the Republics of Colombia, Costa Rica, Nicaragua and Venezuela was signed on 28 and 29 March 1994. Points 1 and 7 of the Framework Agreement were incorporated in Schedule L to GATT 1994 listing the Community's customs concessions.

[38] Case C-17/98 *Emesa Sugar*, above n 8.

[39] *Ibid*, para 56.

of such conflicts, the ECJ Opinion on the Cartagena Protocol is instructive.[40] This was a request for an Opinion on the legal basis of a Council decision concluding the Convention on Biological Diversity, which is not a WTO agreement. The ECJ rejected the Commission's view that the Protocol was primarily a trade policy measure rather than an environmental measure. It concluded that the Commission's interpretation would have rendered the specifically environmental provisions of the Treaty nugatory, whereas environmental policy as well as the common commercial policy were both referred to expressly in the Treaty. The ECJ thus preferred the Council's interpretation, which put environmental policy virtually on the same footing as trade policy within the framework of the Treaty.

2. The European Courts use WTO Law as an Aid in Interpreting a Range of Legal Instruments

The range of EC legal instruments in which the European courts use WTO law as an aid to interpretation includes both EC domestic law, such as secondary legislation and general principles of law, as well as international agreements to which the EC is a party. In addition, litigants often advance the aid-to-interpretation argument in cases involving claims that WTO law provides criteria for assessing the legality of EC secondary legislation. This section concerns only aid to interpretation.[41]

i. EC Secondary Legislation

It is not surprising that the European courts frequently use WTO law as an aid in interpreting EC secondary legislation regarding foreign trade, notably imports, agriculture, anti-dumping and intellectual property. These matters are at the core of the WTO system, just as customs classification was at the core of the GATT.[42]

For example, in *Carbone*,[43] the ECJ referred to the Agreement establishing the WTO, GATT 1994 and the Agreement on Safeguards in interpreting the EC common rules for imports. In Case C-150/95 *Portugal v Commission*,[44] the ECJ analysed the relevant provisions of the Blair House Agreement and used a reference to the Agreement to support its interpretation of Council Regulation 1765/92, as amended, concerning the oilseeds sector.

Most cases in which the European courts use WTO law as an aid to interpreting EC legislation concern anti-dumping. For example, in *Petrotub*,[45] the applicant sought to annul definitive anti-dumping duties on iron and steel products from Romania. The ECJ

[40] Case C-377/98 *Netherlands v European Parliament and Council of the European Union* [2001] ECR I-7079.

[41] In some cases WTO law is used as an interpretative aid by the A-G but not by the ECJ: see eg Case C-46/02 *Fixtures Marketing* [2004] ECR I-10365; Case C-203/02 *The British Horseracing Board and Others* [2004] ECR I-10415; Case C-338/02 *Fixtures Marketing* [2005] ECR I-10497; Case C-444/02 *Fixtures Marketing* [2004] ECR I-10549.

[42] See Case 92/71 *Interfood GmbH v Hauptzollamt Hamburg-Ericus* [1972] ECR 231.

[43] Case C-296/00 *Prefetto Provincia di Cuneo v Silvano Carbone* [2002] ECR I-4657.

[44] [1997] ECR 5863.

[45] Case C-76/00P *Petrotub*, above n 34, an appeal of the CFI judgments in Joined Cases T-33/98 and T-34/98 *Petrotub*, above n 33.

annulled the EC Regulation imposing the duties because the Regulation did not give adequate reasons for imposing those duties. It concluded that a Council Regulation imposing duties on the basis of the asymmetrical method for calculating the dumping margin 'must in particular contain, as part of the statement of reasons required by Article 190 of the Treaty, the specific explanation provided for in Article 2.4.2 of the 1994 Anti-dumping Code'.[46] However, the CFI stated, first, that the applicant's argument concerning the priority among two ways of determining sales below cost was not compatible with Article 2.2.1 of the Anti-dumping Agreement. Secondly, it concluded that, according to the Anti-dumping Agreement, the EC institutions had discretion to choose either of two normal methods to determine the dumping margin, and the interpretation chosen by the Commission was fully in keeping with Article 2.4.2.

Another example is *Medici Grimm*,[47] an application for partial annulment of a definitive anti-dumping duty on leather handbags from China. The applicant's Hong Kong-based manufacturer and exporter partner, Lucci Creation Ltd, requested reimbursement of duties already paid. It argued that both the Anti-dumping Agreement and the basic EC anti-dumping Regulation provided that anti-dumping duties might be imposed only if three conditions were satisfied: dumping, injury, and the existence of a causal link between them. No duty could be imposed in the absence of dumping, and EC institutions were obliged to comply with the Anti-dumping Agreement. The CFI did not mention the Anti-dumping Agreement in its judgment, except in restating the arguments of the parties, but it did hold that no duty could be imposed in the absence of the three conditions, and any finding that one of the conditions was not satisfied must be given retroactive effect. Similarly, in *Eurocoton*,[48] the CFI found that the Anti-dumping Agreement did not require parties to impose anti-dumping duties but simply fixed restrictive conditions. Consequently the applicant could not rely on 'a right to the adoption by the Council of a proposal for a regulation imposing definitive anti-dumping duties submitted to it by the Commission'.[49]

The CFI interpreted the Anti-dumping Agreement and also used it as an aid to interpret EC law in *BEUC*.[50] The Anti dumping Agreement provides that 'interested parties' must be given notice of an anti-dumping investigation and an opportunity to provide relevant information (Article 6.1). It does not include consumer organisations in the definition of 'interested parties', but neither does it preclude WTO Members from including parties not listed (Article 6.11). It further requires investigating authorities to provide opportunities for industrial users of the product under investigation, and for representative consumer organisations in cases where the product is commonly sold at the retail level, to provide relevant information (Article 6.12). The EC decided not to adopt the distinction between retail and non-retail levels. The CFI therefore concluded that

> the Commission does not have grounds for automatically excluding consumer organisations from the circle of interested parties by applying a general criterion such as the distinction between products sold at the retail level and other products. The Commission must decide on a case-by-case basis whether a party should be considered an interested party in the light of the particular circumstances of each case . . .[51]

[46] Case C-76/00P *Petrotub*, above n 34, para 60. See also Case T-274/02 *Ritek Corp and Prodisc Technology Inc v Council and Commission* [2006] ECR II-4305, para 66.

[47] Case T-7/99 *Medici Grimm KG v Council of the European Union* [2000] ECR II-2671.

[48] Case T-213/97 *Eurocoton*, above n 22.

[49] *Ibid*, para 52.

[50] Case T-256/97 *Bureau Européen des Unions de Consommateurs (BEUC) v Commission* [1999] ECR II-169.

[51] *Ibid*, para 76.

Interpreting EC law in the light of the Anti-dumping Agreement, it concluded that

> the Commission cannot exclude consumer organisations from an anti-dumping proceeding without giving them an opportunity to show their interest in the product in question . . .[52]

In *Euroalliages*,[53] the CFI used the Anti-dumping Agreement to interpret Article 21 of the basic EC anti-dumping Regulation concerning the Community interest. It noted that the Agrement and the EC Regulation contained similar requirements to provide meetings for an exchange of views with regard to dumping and injury. It stated, however, that the Anti-dumping Agreement did not contain a similar requirement for meetings to evaluate the Community interest. On this basis, the CFI concluded that the EC law did not require any such meetings. Unfortunately, in this case, in contrast to *BEUC*, the use of the Anti-dumping Agreement to interpret EC law thus did not result in stricter delimitation of administrative discretion, or an enhancement of procedural rights.

The European courts' use of the Anti-dumping Agreement to interpret EC anti-dumping law is to be expected, because EC anti-dumping legislation has since its origins closely followed GATT law. The TRIPS, however, with the exception of its provisions on counterfeit goods,[54] never served as a model for EC law. Nevertheless, in *Silhouette*,[55] Advocate-General Jacobs did use TRIPS as an aid in interpreting EC law. The Advocate-General concluded that the EC Trade Marks Directive precluded Member States from adopting the principle of international exhaustion of trademarks. He recalled that some Member States, and some third countries, do not practise international exhaustion, and 'that has not been held to be contrary' to the GATT.[56] He added that this was not changed by the WTO, because TRIPS expressly excludes the issue of international exhaustion, leaving the EC free to regulate the matter by harmonisation directives applicable to all Member States. The ECJ reached the same result on the merits, but without referring to TRIPS. Advocate-General Jacobs also used TRIPS as an aid to interpretation in *Procter & Gamble*[57] and *LTJ Diffusion*[58]; in the former case the ECJ did not refer to TRIPS, though it reached the same decision on the merits.

Outside the field of foreign trade, arguments by litigants that the courts should use WTO law as an aid to interpret EC law have been less successful. With regard to State aids, for example, the European courts have rejected WTO law as an aid to interpretation and sought to preserve the integrity of EC law in isolation from potentially relevant WTO law. The applicant in *CETM*[59] had received a subsidy under a Spanish Government system of aid for the purchase of commercial vehicles. When the Commission tried to recover the funds, the applicant argued that the aid was not a specific subsidy within the meaning of the WTO Agreement on Subsidies and

[52] *Ibid*, para 77. Cf Case T-51/96 *Miwon Co Ltd v Council* [2000] ECR II-1841, in which the CFI discounted the applicant's reference to the 1960 Second Report of the GATT Group of Experts on Anti-dumping and Countervailing Duties as irrelevant in the light of its finding of the facts.

[53] Case T-132/01 *Euroalliages, Péchiney électrométallurgie, Vargon Alloys AB and Ferroatlántica SL v Commission* [2003] ECR II-2539.

[54] See F Snyder, *International Trade and Customs Law of the European Union* (London, Butterworths, 1998) 270–71.

[55] Case C-355/96 *Silhouette International Schmied GmbH & Co KG v Hartlauer Handeslsgesellschaft mbH* [1998] ECR I-4799.

[56] *Ibid*, para 54.

[57] Case C-383/99 *Procter & Gamble v Office for Harmonisation in the Internal Market (Trade Marks & Designs)* [2001] ECR I-6251, Opinion of A-G Jacobs, paras 12, 15.

[58] Case C-291/00 *SA LTJ Diffusion v SA SADAS* [2003] ECR I-2700, Opinion of A-G Jacobs, paras 36, 39.

[59] Case T-55/99 *Confederacion Española de Transporte de Mercancias (CETM) v Commission* [2000] ECR I-3207.

Countervailing Measures (ASCM). The CFI classified the subsidy as State aid within the meaning of Article 92(1) (now 87(1)) EC. It concluded that

> The reference to the concept of 'subsidy' within the meaning of the WTO Agreement on Subsidies and Countervailing Duties [*sic*] has, as the Commission submits, no relevance whatsoever to the classification of the measure in question as State aid within the meaning of Community law . . .[60]

The purpose of textual interpretation here was conceptual classification. In fact, the applicant's argument about interpretation sought to convince the CFI to use WTO law as a criterion for assessing the validity of EC law, which has been consistently rejected by the European courts. In Case C-409/00 *Spain v Commission*,[61] the ECJ confirmed that the Community could classify an aid as State aid under EC rules even though it was not a subsidy under the WTO Subsidies Agreement. It thus permitted the application of stricter standards within the Community than are applied in international trade. This view is entirely consistent with the European courts' position of emphasising the relative autonomy of the Community within the framework of international (including WTO) law.

Institutions of the EC, such as the Commission, employ the possibility that WTO law can be as an aid to interpretation as part of their negotiating tactics. In *CETM*[62] the Commission considered the ASCM to be irrelevant to the classification of a national measure as a State aid under EC law. In *van de Bor*,[63] however, it referred to the same WTO Agreement as if it had both legal relevance and normative force with regard to EC law on State aids. The case was a preliminary ruling about the powers of Member States to take measures to prevent the spread of bovine spongiform encephalopathy (BSE). The Netherlands had ordered the slaughter of British-born calves and provided for compensation to farmers. Subsequent EC legislation retroactively changed the basis for calculating compensation. A farmer whose compensation was assessed on the first basis objected to reassessment. The national court asked whether The Netherlands was entitled to adopt the original national rules and, if not, whether EC law precluded payment on that basis, especially in the light of possible legitimate expectations based on the initial assessment. On the second point, the Commission argued *inter alia* that the Dutch scheme was not properly notified as a State aid, because the Dutch Government's letter was not contained

> in any format approved by the Commission, such as that set out in Annex II to its letter to Member States of 2 August 1995, which contained the Format for Standardised Notification under Article 93(3) EC and under Article 8.3 of the WTO ASCM . . .[64]

Rejecting this argument, the Advocate-General treated the Commission's letter and the Format for Standardised Notification as not legally binding, even though the essential normative content was necessarily drawn from Article 8.3 ASCM.[65] He concluded that the ECJ did not have enough evidence to conclude that the Dutch scheme was not adequately notified. While reaching the same conclusion on the merits, the

[60] *Ibid*, para 50.

[61] Case C-409/00 *Spain v Commission* [2003] ECR I-1487.

[62] Above n 59.

[63] Case C-428/99 *H van de Bor BV v her Voedselvoor zieningsin-en verkoopbureau* [2002] ECR I-127.

[64] *Ibid*, Opinion of A-G Jacobs, note 25.

[65] Because Article 93(3) EC (now Article 88(3) EC) does not provide any specific guidance about how notification is to be made.

ECJ did not mention the ASCM in its judgment.[66] The outcome gave priority to national health and environmental measures over agricultural market regulation.

In other cases, the European courts have used WTO law more as a general normative element to be taken into account in applying EC secondary legislation. Case T-1/99 *T Port*[67] was an application for compensation for loss allegedly suffered because of the introduction of the EC export licence scheme for bananas. The Commission argued *inter alia* that the disadvantage constituted by the obligation on certain traders to acquire export licences was partly offset by two other accompanying measures in the Framework Agreement on Bananas, namely, an increase in tariff quota and a reduction of customs duty. The CFI stated that this argument 'would not seem to be groundless'.[68] It concluded that

> It follows that the mere fact, assuming it to have been proved, that an operator has borne additional costs connected with its business dealings does not necessarily imply it suffered a corresponding loss . . .[69]

It took benefits conferred by WTO law into account in applying EC law on damages.

ii. General Principles of EC Law and Fundamental Rights

The European courts' use of WTO law as an aid to interpretation of EC domestic law is not limited to secondary legislation. In at least one case, the ECJ used WTO law as an aid in interpreting general principles of law and fundamental rights. *Metronome*[70] concerned a conflict between the exclusive right of a producer of phonograms to authorise or prohibit the renting and lending of its works, on the one hand, and the principle of free enterprise in the German federal constitution, on the other hand. Following the Advocate-General's Opinion, the ECJ affirmed that WTO law was to be used as an aid to interpretation in the sense that

> the general principle of freedom to pursue a trade or profession cannot be interpreted in isolation from the general principles relating to protection of intellectual property rights and international obligations entered into in that sphere by the Community and by the Member States . . .[71]

iii. EC International Agreements

In using WTO law as an aid to interpreting EC secondary legislation, the Advocates-General have gone much farther than the judges. In addition, an Advocate-General has in at least one instance used WTO law as an aid in interpreting another international agreement to which the EC is a party. *Barkoci and Malik*[72] concerned the freedom of establishment of a Czech national wishing to establish himself in a Member

[66] Case C-428/99 *van de Bor*, above n 63.
[67] Case T-1/99 *T Port*, above n 36.
[68] *Ibid*, para 66.
[69] *Ibid*, para 67.
[70] Case C-200/96 *Metronome Musik GmbH v Music Point Hokamp GmbH* [1998] ECR I-1953.
[71] *Ibid*, para 26.
[72] Case C-257/99 *The Queen v Secretary of State for the Home Department, ex parte Julius Barkoci and Marcel Malik* [2001] ECR I-6557.

State as a self-employed worker under the EE–Czech Republic Association Agreement. Rejecting the interpretation advanced by the worker, the Advocate-General cited Article 59(2) of the Agreement which stated that the relevant provisions of the Agreement shall be adjusted by decision of the Association Council to ensure 'a treatment no less favourable than that accorded under the provisions of a future' GATS.[73] He concluded that

> If the parties contemplated that the agreements being negotiated in the context of the General Agreement on Tariffs and Trade ('GATT') might possibly go beyond what is provided in the Agreement so far as concerns freedom of establishment, it was because they were perfectly aware that the Agreement gave that freedom only a limited scope, with no relation to the scope that it has in the context of the Treaty . . .[74]

He used a reference to a future GATS then being negotiated, not yet in force, as an aid to interpretation. However, the ECJ in its judgment did not refer to WTO law.[75]

In the two geographical indication cases, the ECJ followed the Advocates-General in distinguishing between the Hungarian name 'Tokaj' and the Italian names 'Tocai friulano' and 'Tocai italico' as appellations of a vine or a vine variety; the latter were names of a vine or a vine variety, while only the former constituted a geographical indication under the TRIPS and the EC–Hungary Agreement on wines.[76]

III. WTO Law and the Individual

A. WTO Law and Direct Effect

If the WTO has expanded the normative repertoire and thereby increased the power of EC institutions, what implications has it had for the individual?[77] Individuals have argued most frequently that WTO law has direct effect or, more recently, that it provides criteria for evaluating the legality or validity of EC law.[78] They have also

[73] *Ibid*, Opinion of A-G Mischo, para 54.

[74] *Ibid*, para 55.

[75] *Ibid.*

[76] See Case C-347/03 *Regione autonoma Friuli-Venezia Giulia and Agenzia regionale per lo sviluppo rurale (ERSA) v Ministero delle Politiche Agricole e Forestali* [2005] ECR I-3785; Case C-231/04 *Confcooperative, Unione regionale della Cooperazione Fvg Federagricole, Fiulvini Soc Coop rl, Cantina Sociale di Ramusscello e S Vito v Ministero delle Politiche Agricole e Forestali, Regione Veneto*, [2006] ECJ I –61 See also Case C-23/07 *Confcooperativa Friuli Venezia Giulia, Luigi Soini, Azienda Agricola Vivai Pinat Mario e figlio v Ministero delle Politiche Agricole, Alimentari e Forestali, Regione Friuli Venezia Giulia* [2008] ECR I-4277, and Case C-24/07 *Cantina Produttori Cormòns, Luigi Soini v Ministero delle Politiche Agricole, Alimentari e Forestali, Regione Friuli Venezia Giulia* [2008] ECR I-4277.

[77] See M Lukas, 'The role of private parties in the enforcement of the Uruguay Round Agreements' (1995) 29 *Journal of World Trade* 181; B Killmann, 'The access of individuals to international trade dispute settlement' (1996)13 *Journal of International Arbitration* 143; and esp G Shaffer, 'The blurring of the intergovernmental: Public–private partnerships behind US and EC trade claims' in M Pollack and G Shaffer (eds), *Transatlantic Governance in the Global Economy* (Lanham, Md, Rowman and Littlefield 2001) 97.

[78] Throughout the remainder of the chapter, 'legality' will be used instead of 'validity', because most of the cases have been based on Art 230 (ex 173) EC [now Art 263 TFEU] rather than on Art 234 (ex 177) EC [now Art 267 TFEU]. Note, however, that the ECJ rejected a strong distinction between the two in Joined Cases 73 and 74/63 *NV Internationale Crediet- en Handelsvereniging 'Rotterdam' and De Coöperatieve Suikerfabrik en Raffinaderij GA 'Puttershoek' v Netherlands Minister of Agriculture and Fisheries* [1964] ECR 3.

sought to use WTO law to control EC breaches of WTO law. Until recently, however, the increasing normative integration of WTO law into EC law has not resulted in a great empowerment of individuals. It may even have weakened the position of individuals relative to EC institutions, taking into account that the increase in the range of norms which have an impact on individuals has not been matched by an increase in individual access to courts. There are two exceptions, however, and they are likely to increase in salience, and hence importance, in the future.

Private parties are non-privileged applicants in actions for annulment under Article 230 (ex 173) EC.[79] Given difficult access to the European courts, they have long sought to rely on GATT 1947, subsequently on the WTO Agreements, and more recently on the outcomes of WTO dispute settlement procedures, as having direct effect in order to challenge Community secondary legislation in the national courts. On references for a preliminary ruling, the European courts have then had to consider the potential direct effect of the WTO Agreements and the reports of WTO dispute settlement bodies.

1. WTO Agreements do not have Direct Effect in EC Law

Since its early case law, the ECJ has steadfastly maintained that WTO Agreements do not have direct effect in EC law.[80] No legal action has ever been successful on this ground. The European courts have consistently decided that the issue of direct effect has not been relevant to the case before them, or have expressly rejected the direct effect of WTO Agreements. Until recently the case law has remained controversial.[81] Now the ECJ has tried to elaborate a more convincing, coherent justification of this long-standing position.

[79] But see Case T-77/01 *Jégo Quéré v Commission* [2002] ECR II-2365; Case C-263/02P *Jègo Quéré*, [2004] ECR I-3425.

[80] Joined Cases *International Fruit Company NV and others v Produktschap voor Groenten en Fruit* [1972] ECR 1219; Case 9/73 *Schlüter v Hauptzollamt Lörrach* [1973] ECR 1135; Joined Cases 267–269/81 *SPI/SAMI* [1983] ECR 801; Case 266/81 *SIOT* [1983] ECR 731; Joined Cases 290–291/81 *Singer and Geigy v Amministrazione delle finanze dello Stato* [1983] ECR 847; Case C-469/93 *Amministrazione delle finanze dello Stato v Italia Chiquita Italia* [1995] ECR I-4533. The most consistent critic has been E-U Petersmann, who sees the GATT/WTO as the 'third line of constitutional entrenchment' in the EU system: see his *Constitutional Functions and Problems of International Economic Law* (Fribourg, University of Fribourg Press, 1991). This Kantian position adapts the formula of the German Ordoliberal scholar Jan Tumlir, according to whom 'the international economic order can be seen as the second line of national constitutional entrenchment': J Tumlir, 'International economic order and democratic constitutionalism' (1983) 34 *ORDO* 71 at 80. In numerous publications Petersmann has consistently argued that 'the most effective and most democratic means of constitutionalizing discretionary trade policy powers is to incorporate international prohibitions of trade barriers into domestic laws and to enable private traders, producers and consumers to enforce these rules through domestic courts': see E-U Petersmann, 'National constitutions and international economic law' in M Hilf and E-U Petersmann (eds), *National Constitutions and International Economic Law* (Deventer, Kluwer 1993) 3 at 49. For an extended, similar critique of ECJ case law, see KJ Kuilwijk, *The European Court of Justice and the GATT Dilemma: Public Interest v Individual Rights* (Beuningen, The Netherlands, Nexed Editions, 1996). For a reply, see JO Berkey, 'The European Court of Justice and Direct Effect for the GATT: A Question Worth Revisiting' (1998) 9 *European Journal of International Law* 626. See also H Tagaras, 'L'effet direct des accords internationaux de la Communauté' (1984) 19 *Cahiers de Droit Européen* 15. A very useful review is T Cottier and KN Schefer, 'The relationship between World Trade Organization, national and regional law' (1998) 1 *Journal of International Economic Law* 83.

[81] See S Griller, 'Judicial enforceability of WTO law in the European Union: Annotation to Case C-149/96, *Portugal v Council*' (2000) 3(3) *Journal of International Economic Law* 441–472; P Eeckhout, 'Judicial Enforcement of WTO Law in the European Union—Some Further Reflections' (2002) 5(1) *Journal of International Economic Law* 91.

i. The Jurisprudence Constante

In two cases the ECJ dismissed as irrelevant the argument that a WTO Agreement had direct effect. *T Port*[82] concerned post-clearance recovery of customs duties payable on bananas imported from Ecuador in 1995.The applicant relied on the Framework Agreement on Bananas. However, Ecuador was not a contracting party to GATT 1947 and did not become a member of the WTO, and therefore a party to GATT 1994, until 1996. Consequently, the ECJ concluded that Article 234 EC did not apply to cases involving imports of bananas from a third country that was not a party to an international agreement concluded by the Member States before the entry into force of the Treaty. Similarly, the ECJ, in *Hermès*,[83] recognised that the direct effect of Article 50 TRIPs had been argued. However, it stated that it

> was not required to give a ruling on that question, but only to answer the question of interpretation submitted to it by the national court so as to enable that court to interpret Netherlands procedural rules in the light of that article . . .[84]

Forcefully but indirectly, the ECJ affirmed this position, against the Opinion of its Advocate-General, in the leading Case C-149/96 *Portugal v Council.*[85] This was an action for annulment of a Council Decision concerning the conclusion of Memoranda of Understanding between the EC and Pakistan and the EC and India on market access for textile products. Portugal argued that the Council Decision was in breach of the WTO, especially GATT 1994, the Agreement on Textiles and Clothing, and the Agreement on Import Licensing Procedures. Its argument was not based on the claim that the WTO Agreements had direct effect. In fact, it sought to distinguish the issue of direct effect from its main point, namely, that a Member State should be permitted to assert WTO law as a criterion for evaluating the validity of EC law. Rejecting this argument, the ECJ did not state expressly that WTO law did not have direct effect in EC law. However, this conclusion emerges very clearly, albeit implicitly, from the way in which the ECJ uses the same or similar language as in its previous judgments concerning direct effect, as well as from the grounds on which it rejects WTO law as a criterion of validity.

The European courts have expressly rejected the direct effect of TRIPS. In *Dior*,[86] the ECJ stated that TRIPS does not have direct effect in Community law. Similarly, in *Groeneveld*,[87] the ECJ followed its long-standing case law and its Advocate-General[88] by holding that

> the procedural requirements of Article 50 of TRIPS, and in particular Article 50(6), are not such as to create rights upon which individuals may rely directly before the Community courts and the courts of the Member States . . .[89]

Case T-52/99 *T Port*[90] concerned the potential direct effect of GATT, GATS and the Agreement on Import Licensing Procedures. One of the many banana cases, and one

[82] Joined Cases C-364/95 and C-365/95 *T Port GmbH & Co v Hauptzollamt Hamburg-Jonas* [1998] ECR I-1023.
[83] Case C-53/96 *Hermès International v FHT Marketing Choice BV* [1998] ECR I-3603.
[84] *Ibid*, para 35.
[85] [1999] ECR I-8395.
[86] Joined Cases C-300/98 and C-392/98, above n 27.
[87] Case C-89/99 *Schieving-Nijstad vof and Others v Robert Groeneveld* [2001] ECR I-5831.
[88] See Opinion of A-G Jacobs, 15 February 2001, *ibid,* para 41, following *Dior.*
[89] *Ibid*, para 55.
[90] Case T-52/99 *T Port GmbH & Co KG v Commission* [2001] ECR II-981.

of several brought by T Port, it was an action for damages allegedly resulting from the allocation of annual import quantities. The CFI rejected the argument that WTO rules were directly effective. It reached the same result in *Bocchi*[91] and *Cordis*,[92] two other cases decided the same day. *OGT*[93] was another banana case decided less than two months later. A reference for a preliminary ruling, it concerned the interpretation of Articles I and XIII GATT concerning the levy of customs duty on the importation of bananas from Ecuador. A WTO Panel set up at the request of Ecuador had already found that the new system of trade with third countries under EC Regulation 1637/98 continued to infringe Articles I(1) and XIII GATT 1994.[94] The ECJ held that Articles I and XIII GATT were not directly effective.

ii. Toward a Coherent Justification

Recently the European courts have begun to articulate a more coherent, more convincing rationale for their position that, as a matter of principle, the WTO Agreements do not have direct effect in EC law. *Portugal v Council*[95] was a deeply unsatisfactory judgment, because of the inconsistency of argument, gaps in reasoning and the ECJ's failure to come to grips with a strong Opinion by the Advocate-General. Nevertheless, compared to previous cases, it articulated a view of the relationship between WTO law and EC law which was less legalistic, more politically cognisant and hence more realistic in the current international setting. It began to point the way toward a much more coherent conception of the relation between the two sites of governance, notably with regard to who should make the basic decisions about the impact of WTO law in the EC legal order and how such decisions should be made.

Leading cases have been more an *approfondissement* or a reorientation than a revolution compared to long-standing case law. Making use of their special role in the EC judicial system, the Advocates-General have taken the initiative. Three examples will suffice. In *Portugal v Council*,[96] Advocate-General Saggio provided a stimulating analysis of direct effect and criterion of legality, though the ECJ did not follow his Opinion on either point. In *Netherlands v European Parliament and Council*,[97] Advocate-General Jacobs argued that, as a matter of policy, it was desirable for the ECJ to review the legality of Community secondary legislation in the light of the WTO law, a view that is likely to become increasingly salient in the future. In *Omega*,[98] Advocate-General Alber placed the earlier case law about the direct effect of GATT and WTO

[91] Case T-30/99 *Bocchi Food Trade International GmbH v Commission* [2001] ECR I-4619.

[92] Case T-18/99 *Cordis Obst und Gemüse Grosshandel GmbH v Commission* [2001] ECR II-913.

[93] Case C-307/99 *OGT Fruchthandelsgesellschaft mbH v Hauptzollamt Hamburg-St Annen* [2001] ECR I-3159.

[94] European Communities—Regime for the Importation, Sale and Distribution of Bananas (Recourse to Article 21.5 by Ecuador), Report of the Panel, WT/DS27/RW/ECU, Circulated to Members on 6.5.99, DSR 1999: II at 803.

[95] Case C-149/96 *Portugal v Council*, above n 85.

[96] *Ibid*, Opinion of A-G Saggio.

[97] Case C-377/98 *Netherlands v European Parliament and Council of the European Union* [2000] ECR I-6229, Opinion of A-G Jacobs, para 147.

[98] Joined Cases C-27/00 and C-122/00 *The Queen v Secretary of State for the Environment, Transport and the Regions, ex parte Omega Air Ltd; Omega Air Ltd, Aero Engines Ireland Ltd, Omega Aviation Services Ltd v Irish Aviation Authority* [2002] ECR I-2569, Opinion of A-G Alber.

law in a new context. In the long run, his Opinion in *Omega* is likely to be regarded as having altered the terms of the debate and deserves more detailed analysis.

Omega was a reference for a preliminary ruling on an EC Regulation concerning noise emissions from airplanes. Omega claimed that the Regulation was invalid, *inter alia* because, contrary to the WTO Agreement on Technical Barriers to Trade ('TBT Agreement'), it replaced existing international standards (Chapter 3 of the Annexes to the Chicago Convention) with a new criterion. It argued that the ECJ, even excluding direct effect in principle, should review specific provisions of WTO law to see if they met the EC law tests for direct effect. This argument was not entirely clear, but it seems to be based on a distinction between the general principle that WTO law does not usually have direct effect and the possibility that specific WTO law provisions may exceptionally be recognised as having direct effect on a case-by-case basis.

Rejecting this argument, the Advocate-General stated that 'The decisive point is that legal disputes on the content of WTO law are based on negotiations between the Governments'.[99] In his view, 'The Community's position in those negotiations would be seriously affected if Community law recognised a unilateral direct effect of obligations under WTO law'.[100] Thus he drew on two strands in the analysis of GATT/WTO law in previous ECJ case law: first, the importance of negotiation and reciprocity in GATT/WTO dispute settlement; and, secondly, ideas about how to maintain the balance among EC institutions so as to preserve and possibly strengthen the role of the EU on the international stage, especially concerning foreign trade.

But the Advocate-General went further. He made two more original contributions to the direct effect debate. First, he broadened the terms of the debate beyond the ambit of the EC by expressly taking account of the standpoint of the WTO. He argued that

> Direct reliance on rules of WTO law as against measures taken by WTO Members appears inappropriate from the point of view of WTO law as well, however. Regardless of their wording, all provisions of WTO law are subject to a general reservation which accords the States concerned various possibilities of reacting to a breach . . .[101]

The substantive point is not new; it merely repeats the long-standing ECJ view about the flexibility of the GATT/WTO system. What is important is that, in analysing the relation between the EU and the WTO, the Advocate-General purports to express the perspective from the other site. Whether his conception of the WTO perspective is accurate, whether there is in fact any single WTO perspective, or whether the perspectives of the two sites are commensurate, is beside the point here. The views of highly respected scholars in the field of international trade, as seen below, replicate the same controversy.

Secondly, the Advocate-General suggested that the basic decision about the possible direct effect of WTO law in the legal systems of WTO Members should be taken on a multilateral basis, not by each WTO member acting unilaterally. He argued that

> It is therefore not for the Court but for the WTO, or the members of the WTO, to ensure that WTO law is observed in the legal systems concerned. Direct effect of WTO rules is clearly not part of their legislative content. Such content may not be ascribed, at Community law, to WTO law in its original form but at most in the form of transposition measures. In that context WTO law may be (indirectly) significant . . .[102]

[99] *Ibid*, para 92.
[100] *Ibid*, para 93.
[101] *Ibid*, para 94.
[102] *Ibid*, para 95.

The Advocate-General stated that

> Direct effect of WTO law in the legal systems of the WTO members cannot . . . sensibly be brought about unilaterally by individual legal systems, but only at WTO level . . .[103]

He admitted that the relevant provisions of the TBT Agreement were 'perhaps sufficiently precise and unconditional in their wording to be amenable to direct application'.[104] However, this did not mean that they were directly effective, or that they provided criteria for evaluating the legality of Community law. On the contrary, the Advocate-General argued that

> They are subject to the general condition of WTO law that the Members of the WTO are to comply with their obligations not by direct effect of WTO law in their legal systems but exclusively by specific transposition of those obligations . . .[105]

The Advocate-General's Opinion places the issue of institutional choice on another plane by focusing not merely on EC institutions *inter se* but also on relations between sites. It identifies the key issue of whether a single site or legal system, acting unilaterally, or the totality of WTO Members acting on a multilateral basis, should decide whether WTO law has direct effect. The Advocate-General's Opinion represents a plea for multilateralism, instead of unilateralism or even bilateralism, as, for example, if the EU and the United States, or the EU and China, or the United States and China, were to decide on a bilateral basis that they would recognise WTO law as having direct effect in their respective legal orders.

This represents an important clarification of the view of the European courts in four different respects, even though it is not always reflected directly in judicial decisions. For one thing, it expressly recognises the international political and economic context, in which the United States[106] and China[107] in particular do not recognise WTO law as having direct effect. EC law operates in this context, which informs the judgments of the European courts. While it is true that EC law also helps to shape the international setting, and potentially change it, an ECJ judgment recognising the direct effect of WTO law in EC law might have unpredictable and unintended consequences, both within the EU and outside it.

[103] *Ibid.*

[104] *Ibid*, para 96.

[105] *Ibid.*

[106] The US implementing legislation is 19 USC §102(c), which provides that 'No person other than the United States (A) shall have any cause of action or defense under any of the Uruguay Round Agreements or by virtue of congressional approval of such agreement, or (B) may challenge, in any action brought under any provision of law, any action or inaction by any department, agency, or other instrumentality of the United States, any State or political subdivision of a State on the ground that such action or inaction is inconsistent with such agreement.' See also D Leebron, 'Implementation of the Uruguay Round results in the United States' in JH Jackson and AO Sykes (eds), *Implementing the Uruguay Round* (Oxford, Oxford University Press, 1997) 175; Cottier and Schefer, above n 80; RA Brand, 'Direct effect of international economic law in the United States and the European Union' (1996–97) 17 *Northwestern Journal of International Law and Business* 556; RH Steinberg, 'Direct Application of Multilateral Trade Agreements in the United States' in P Demaret, JF Bellis and G García Jiménez (eds), *Regionalism and Multilateralism after the Uruguay Round: Convergence, Divergence and Interaction* (Brussels, European Interuniversity Press, 1997) 715; RE Hudec, 'The legal status of GATT in the domestic law of the United States' in M Hilf, FG Jacobs and E-U Petersmann (eds), *The European Community and GATT* (Deventer, Kluwer, 1986) 188.

[107] See X Zhang, *Implementation of the WTO Agreements in China* (London, Wildy, Simmons & Hill Publishing, 2005), 89–103.

For another thing, it recognises that the consequences for the EC's institutional balance, and thus balance of powers,[108] constitute one of the criteria for deciding whether WTO law has direct effect in EC law. Akin to a political questions doctrine,[109] it is based on the premise that the executive and the legislator, not the judiciary, must play the dominant roles in the field of international trade. Direct effect empowers courts, the administration and private actors. The basic strategy of the EU, as of its main trading partners, is one of

> combining the utmost effect of WTO law abroad with a view to foster market access rights while leaving traditional constitutional allocations of power at home as unimpaired as possible.[110]

This concern is explicit in the Advocate-General's discussion of the importance of maintaining the EC's position in international negotiations. It is implicit in his concern for who should decide whether WTO law has direct effect in EC law.[111] Both of these issues embody important constitutional arrangements. Seen from this standpoint, the Advocate-General's Opinion is a plea for judicial restraint. Accordingly, the issue of the possible direct effect of WTO law in EC law is a matter for the legislative and executive powers, as well as for the courts.[112]

Lastly, the Opinion of the Advocate-General contributes to changing the terms of the debate about what impact WTO law should have in EC law, and how. More specifically, by referring to transposition measures, it aims to pose the basic issue in terms of the *Fediol*[113] clear reference exception, the *Nakajima*[114] transposition exception and indirect effect or consistent interpretation (*interpretation conforme*), instead of in terms of direct effect. In a word, various types of indirect effect are to be more important than direct effect.

This analysis is a real contribution to a clear articulation of European judicial policy. But the Advocate-General's conclusions are not legally binding, and unfortunately the ECJ in its judgment did not expressly address these points. Instead, it simply reiterated its views from *Portugal v Council*.[115] Several questions thus remain.

First, why should the ECJ deny direct effect to WTO law when it already ensures that WTO law is observed in the Community legal system in some other ways? Two answers may be advanced.[116] On the one hand, direct effect would empower individual litigants, most notably multinational companies. It is a potential open door, offering litigants a

[108] This has long been recognised: see eg I Cheyne, 'International agreements and the European Community legal system' (1994) 19 *EL Rev* 581.

[109] For a thoughtful analysis of the ECJ's Opinion 1/94 *WTO* along these lines, see J Bacquero Cruz, 'Disintegration of the law of integration in the external economic relations of the European Community' (1997) 3 *Columbia Journal of European Law* 257.

[110] Cottier and Schefer, above n 80, at 111.

[111] As distinct from the explicit discussion of this point by the ECJ in Case C-149/96 *Portugal v Council* [1999] ECR I-8395.

[112] See also PJ Kuijper and M Bronckers, 'WTO Law in the European Court of Justice' (2005) 42 *CML Rev* 1313 at 1320–21.

[113] Case 70/87 *Fédiol v Commission* [1989] ECR 1781.

[114] Case C-69/89 *Nakajima All Precision Co Ltd v Council* [1991] ECR I-2069.

[115] Case C-149/96 *Portugal v Council*, above n 85.

[116] The classic analysis of the question in general is JH Jackson, 'Status of treaties in domestic legal systems: A policy analysis' (1992) 86 *American Journal of International Law* 310 at 315–19. For synopses of the arguments, see Cottier and Schefer, above n 80, Appendix at 120–22; M Hilf, 'The application of GATT within the Member States of the European Community, with special reference to the Federal Republic of Germany' in Hilf *et al*, above n 106, at 173–82.

virtually limitless possibility of trumping EC law on an *ad hoc* basis.[117] On the other hand, the use of exceptions rather than a general rule enhances the continued power of the European courts as gatekeepers. The clear reference and the transposition exceptions are more limited in their import, are subject to restricted interpretation and cover situations where the EC legislator has clearly signalled in advance its intention to implement WTO law within the EC legal order. They actually satisfy the tests identified by Advocate-General Alber concerning transposition measures.

Secondly, why should the European courts treat WTO law differently from other international agreements? In my view, the answers lie in its complexity, unpredictability, degree of penetration into domestic law and context:

a) The law of the WTO is multilateral rather than bilateral, thus it involves a different set of institutional choices, requires a more intricate balance of powers among EC institutions, and is based on more complex bargains. It also deals with an expanding, more unpredictable agenda, especially because of the relatively autonomous decision-making power of the WTO Panels and Appellate Body. Hence it potentially resembles the phenomena of judicial self-empowerment and 'creeping competence', with which the EC is all too familiar, and with regard to which the EC legislator and executive are more institutionally equipped and endowed with greater legitimacy to confront.[118]
b) Compared to most other international agreements, the WTO touches more areas of so-called 'domestic' law, such that its impact in practice is best left to majoritarian institutions rather than being dependent on individual *ad hoc* claims.[119] But this is not only an issue of institutional choice. If WTO law were directly effective, plaintiffs would be able to use the court to attack EC secondary legislation orientated toward the harmonisation of national law and regional economic integration.[120]
c) Lastly, the differences in context. The international agreements to which the ECJ has granted direct effect concerned trading partners with which the EC had close historical ties, such as an applicant for EC membership (Portugal in *Kupferberg*[121]),

[117] For the argument that one should not automatically assume that GATT 1994 confers individual rights, see Berkey, above n 80, at 656.

[118] Indeed, it has been argued that, if or as the Community's competence with regard to TRIPS expands, the ECJ may find it necessary to 'take back' the power of national courts to grant direct effect to TRIPS which it recognised in *Dior*: see G Bontinck, *The TRIPS Agreement and the ECJ: A New Dawn? Some Comments about Joined Cases C-300/98 and C-392/98* Parfums Dior *and* Assco Gerüste, Jean Monnet Working Paper 16/01, Jean Monnet Program, New York University School of Law, available at http://www.jeanmonnetprogram.org/papers/01/013901.html, visited 4 October 2002.

[119] Eeckhout argues cogently that the constitutional concern for the potential impact of direct effect on the EU's political institutions was the main reason why the ECJ denied direct effect in the *Portugal* case: Eeckhout, above n 81, 96–97.

[120] On the political considerations concerning direct effect, see G Pischel, 'Trade, Treaties and Treason: Some Underlying Aspects of the Difficult Relationship between the EU and the WTO' (2001) 6 *European Foreign Affairs Review* 103; J Klabbers, 'International Law in Community Law: The Law and Politics of Direct Effect' (2002) 21 *Yearbook of European Law* 262. A controversial example is EC agricultural legislation, concerning which it has been argued that 'it would be absurd to have ceded control over all our domestic agricultural measures in deference to strict adherence to the provisions of the GATT. Such issues are of a fundamental importance to the Community, and a careful balancing exercise is required to protect both EC producers' and consumers' interests': P Lee and B Kennedy, 'The Potential Direct Effect of GATT 1994 in European Community Law' (1996) 30 *Journal of World Trade* 67 at 88. The conflict between direct effect of WTO law in EC law and EU regional economic integration is also emphasised by T Einhorn, 'The Impact of the WTO Agreement on TRIPS (Trade-related Aspects of Intellectual Property Rights) on EC Law: A Challenge to Regionalism' (1998) 35 *CML Rev* 1069.

[121] Case 104/81 *Hauptzollamt Mainz v CA Kupferberg & Cie* [1982] ECR 3641.

a party to an Association Agreement (Greece in *Pabst & Richarz*[122], Turkey in *Demirel*[123] and *Sevince*,[124] Morocco in *Kziber*[125]) or parties to the Yaoundé Convention (ACP countries in *Bresciani*[126]). In contrast to the GATT/WTO, these other international agreements also involved parties in a weaker bargaining position than the Community, so the Community could use the threat of exit from the agreement as a way of enforcing compliance.[127] While it is regrettable that the European courts have not articulated clear reasons for their policy, nevertheless it is understandable that they might be reluctant to open the Pandora's box of direct effect.[128]

Thirdly, does WTO law, as seen from the WTO standpoint, actually correspond to the Advocate-General's conception? Scholars differ in their views about the nature of WTO obligations.[129] Some hold that WTO law is to be enforced by specific performance—in other words, that it is intended to be directly applicable (and also sometimes directly effective) in the legal systems of WTO members[130]—others consider that the implementation of WTO law continues to be based to a significant degree on negotiation.[131] Either view has significant normative, institutional and political consequences.[132] The idea that WTO law should have direct effect was proposed by Switzerland during the Uruguay Round negotiations but soundly rejected by other WTO Members.[133] A WTO Panel recently expressed a view similar to that of these other WTO Members. In *United States—Sections 301–310 of the Trade Act of 1994*, the Panel concluded that

> Neither the GATT nor the WTO has so far been interpreted as creating legally enforceable rights and obligations for individuals. Following this approach, the GATT/WTO did not create a new legal order the subjects of which comprise both contracting parties or Members and their nationals . . .[134]

[122] Case 17/81 *Pabst & Richarz* [1982] ECR 1331.

[123] Case 12/86 *Demirel v Stadt Schwäbish Gmünd* [1987] ECR 3719.

[124] Case C-192/89 *SZ Sevince v Staatsecretaris Van Justitie* [1990] ECR I-346.

[125] Case C-18/90 *Kziber* [1991] ECR I-99.

[126] Case 87/75 *Bresciani v Amministrazione Italiana delle Finanze* [1976] ECR 129.

[127] See Berkey, above n 80, 631–32.

[128] See also S Dillon, *International Trade and Economic Law and the European Union* (Oxford, Hart Publishing, 2002) 355–56, 384.

[129] See JH Jackson, 'International Law Status of WTO Dispute Settlement Reports: Obligation to Comply or Option to "Buy Out"?' (2004) 98(1) *The American Journal of International Law* 109, who argues that the result of a WTO dispute creates an international law obligation to comply with the report once adopted. This does not of course determine the issue of direct effect.

[130] See, eg, JH Jackson, 'The legal meaning of a GATT Dispute Settlement report: Some reflections' and 'The WTO Dispute Settlement Understanding: misunderstandings on the nature of legal obligation', both in JH Jackson, *The Jurisprudence of GATT and the WTO: Insights into Treaty Law and Economic Relations* (Cambridge, Cambridge University Press, 2000), 118–32 and 162–67, respectively.

[131] See S Hippler Bello, 'The WTO Dispute Settlement Understanding: Less is more' (1996) 90 *American Journal of International Law* 416 at 417.

[132] See further Berkey, above n 80, at 642–47. On WTO obligations generally, see J Pauwelyn, *The nature of WTO obligations*, Jean Monnet Working Paper 1/02, Jean Monnet Program, New York University Law School, available at http://www.jeanmonnetprogram.org/papers/02/020101.rtf, visited 29 January 2003.

[133] PJ Kuyper, 'The new WTO Dispute Settlement system: The impact on the Community' in JHJ Bourgeois, F Berrod and E Gippini Fournier (eds), *The Uruguay Round Results: A European Lawyer's Perspective* (Brussels, European Interuniversity Press, 1997) 87 at 106.

[134] *United States—Sections 301–310 of the Trade Act of 1974*, WT/DS152/R, para 7.72. See also Espósito, 'International trade and national legal orders: The problem of direct applicability of WTO law' in P Mengozzi (ed), *International Trade Law on the 50th Anniversary of the Multilateral Trade System* (Milan, A. Giuffrè Editore, 1999), 429 at 466–67.

It is noteworthy that a former member of the WTO Appellate Body argued recently that recognising direct effect of WTO law would not only strengthen courts as opposed to governments and parliaments; it would also damage the WTO itself, by leading to increasingly aggressive complaints by Members to compensate for having granted direct effect, thus strengthening further Panels and the Appellate Body in comparison to the political organs of the WTO.[135] In relations between sites of governance, clarity of analysis and full understanding require us to take account of the perspective of the different sites. Here the analogy of the relationship between EC law and national law is helpful. It tells us that two sites of governance can co-exist more or less easily, even though each has a somewhat different view of the relationship.

2. Outcomes of WTO Dispute Settlement Processes do not have Direct Effect in EC Law

Among the main reasons why the European courts have denied direct effect to WTO Agreements, even when the provisions in question are clear, precise and unconditional,[136] lie the characteristics of WTO dispute settlement. More controversially, the European courts have extended this conclusion to encompass the outcomes of WTO dispute settlement processes, namely Panel reports and Appellate Body reports as adopted by the WTO Dispute Settlement Body (DSB).

i. Panel Reports

In the diplomatically-based system of GATT 1947, unadopted Panel reports had no legally binding effects upon the parties to the dispute. In practice, the failure to adopt a Panel report was usually due to the opposition of the losing party. In these circumstances, it would be anomalous for the European courts to hold that the reports had any effects in EC law.

The sole recent case on GATT 1947 is Case C-122/95 *Germany v Council*.[137] A GATT Panel set up on 18 January 1994 concluded that the import regime introduced by the EC Banana Regulation, Council Regulation 404/93, was incompatible with GATT. Due to EC opposition, however, the report was not adopted. Subsequently the EC concluded the Framework Agreement on Bananas, which was incorporated into the EC's Uruguay Round schedules. Germany brought an action to annul the Council Decision concerning the conclusion on behalf of the Community of the Uruguay Round agreements to the extent that the Council thereby approved the Framework Agreement. The ECJ accepted this argument and annulled the provision in question. But it did so on the ground of the Community law principle of non-discrimination, without referring further to the Framework Agreement on Bananas or to the unadopted GATT 1947 Panel report.

[135] CD Ehlermann, *Some personal experiences as member of the Appellate Body of the WTO*, Policy Paper RSC No 02/9, Robert Schuman Centre for Advanced Studies, European University Institute, Florence, at 41–42.

[136] See *Omega*, above n 98, para 89.

[137] [1998] ECR I-973.

Adopted WTO Panel reports have no direct effect either. In *Comafrica*,[138] two members of the Dole group brought an action for interim measures concerning the reduction coefficient on their imports of third-country and non-traditional ACP bananas. They pleaded *inter alia* that a WTO Panel had ruled that the Category B licensing system was not compatible with the GATT, that activity function rules were not compatible with the GATS, and that if this finding was upheld by the WTO DSB, their only alternative source of supply would dry up. Rejecting this claim, the ECJ concluded that the plaintiffs' argument concerning the WTO DSB was irrelevant, because

> any final ruling by the WTO will leave open the possibility for the Commission to pay compensation or will entail modification of the system now in force, which does not rule out that the applicants could derive advantages in future marketing years . . .[139]

The ECJ reduced any discussion of the effect of the adopted Panel report to the issue of direct effect alone. While it did not state specifically that approved Panel reports did not have direct effect in the EC legal order, its emphasis on the different options for implementing the WTO ruling clearly implied its rejection of this argument.[140]

ii. Appellate Body Reports

In *Chemnitz*,[141] the applicant invoked a WTO Appellate Body report, without making specific arguments, so the CFI found no reason to address the issue of its potential direct effect. It did, however, suggest that, absent very specific circumstances, adopted WTO Appellate Body reports have no effect in EC law.[142] In Case C 104/97P *Atlanta*,[143] though, the ECJ reiterated its view that WTO law does not have direct effect. This was an appeal against the CFI judgment in Case T-521/93 *Atlanta*.[144] The appellant companies argued *inter alia* that the WTO DSB decision of 25 September 1997 established that the EC common organisation of the market in bananas was incompatible with WTO law. The ECJ held, however, that

> Such a decision [by the WTO DSB] could only be taken into consideration if the Court of Justice had found GATT to have direct effect in the context of a plea alleging the invalidity of the common organisation of the market . . .[145]

In the Court's view, the applicant should have argued the direct effect point when it first applied to the ECJ, not at the reply stage of the proceedings. It considered the

[138] Case T-230/97 *Comafrica SpA and Dole Fresh Fruit Europe Ltd & Co v Commission* [1997] ECR II-3031.
[139] *Ibid*, para 40.
[140] See also Case T-252/97 *Anton Dürbeck v Commission* [2000] ECR II-3031. It has been argued, however, that direct effect should be granted to an adopted Panel report where the EC has tried to implement the report but where WTO authorities find that the attempt to do so is contrary to WTO law. On this view, direct effect should not be granted where the EC purports to implement a Panel report and WTO authorities find that the implementation is correct, or where the EC attempt to implement the report is challenged in the WTO and the EC seeks to defend itself. The basic distinction between the first situation and the other two is that that to recognise direct effect in the last two situations 'would be invading the jurisdiction of the WTO dispute settlement system to determine when breaches of the WTO rules have ceased or the ability of WTO members to settle disputes as provide for in the WTO agreements'. See S Peers, 'Fundamental right or political whim? WTO law and the European Court of Justice' in de Búrca and Scott, above n 15, at 117–18 (the quotation is from p 118).
[141] Case T-254/97 *Fruchthandelsgesellschaft mbH Chemnitz v Commission* [1999] ECR II-2743.
[142] See *ibid*, paras 26 and 27.
[143] Case C-104/97P *Atlanta AG and others v Council and Commission* [1999] ECR 6983.
[144] Case T-521/93 *Atlanta and Others v European Community* [1996] ECR II-1707.
[145] Case C-104/97P *Atlanta*, above n 143, para 20.

appellant's attempt to plead that the DSB decision was a new matter to be an indirect way of obtaining the principle that the WTO DSB decisions had direct effect, and the ECJ rejected this avenue.[146]

In Case T-52/99 *T Port*,[147] an action for damages, the CFI made a more damaging reference to an adopted WTO Panel and Appellate Body report. The applicant importer argued *inter alia* that, after the WTO DSB declared the EC banana regime to be incompatible with WTO law, the Commission gave an undertaking to the WTO DSB to repeal the conflicting provisions, but its new proposals also infringed the GATT, the GATS and the WTO Agreement on Import Licensing Procedures. The CFI stated that

> Neither the reports of the WTO Panel of 22 May 1997 nor the report of the WTO Standing Appellate Body of 9 September 1997 which was adopted by the Dispute Settlement Body on 25 September 1997 included any special obligations which the Commission intended to implement, within the meaning of the case-law, in Regulation No 2362/98 . . .[148]

Taken at face value, this is a startling statement, because it implies that an adopted WTO Panel report or Appellate Body report does not impose any legal obligations on the Community. Read in context, however, the CFI's conclusion emphasises the Commission's intention to translate any such 'special' obligations into Community legislation, not the legal effect of WTO obligations per se. In other words, its main concern was the *Nakajima* exception (discussed in Section III.B.2) l). Unfortunately, however, the judgment gives the distinct impression that WTO Appellate Body reports do not have any effect in EC law unless they result in special obligations as determined by EC law, in particular by the European courts. The same holds for *Bocchi*[149] and *Cordis*,[150] two other banana cases decided the same day. A similar result was reached in another banana case, *Afrikanische Frucht*.[151]

In *Banatrading*[152] the CFI treated the principle that WTO Appellate Body reports do not have direct effect in EC law as being well established. Bringing an action for damages, the applicant pleaded that Council Regulation 404/93 was incompatible with GATT, as was apparent from the previously rendered WTO Appellate Body report and the WTO Dispute Settlement Body (DSB) decision.[153] Justifying its view that WTO law did not provide criteria for evaluating the validity of EC law, the CFI stated 'Those [WTO law] texts are not such as to create rights upon which individuals may rely directly before the courts by virtue of Community law'.[154] The same result was reached the same day in Case T-2/99 *T Port*.[155]

A series of later cases indicate somewhat more circumspection, subtlety and cunning on the part of the European courts (and other EC institutions) concerning WTO DSB

[146] Several writers have argued that the ECJ should be bound by adopted Panel or Appellate Body reports; see eg G Zonnekeyn, 'The legal status of WTO panel reports in the EC legal order: Some reflections on the Opinion of Advocate General Mischo in the Atlanta case' (1999) 2(4) *Journal of International Economic Law* 713.

[147] Above n 90.

[148] *Ibid*, para 59.

[149] Above n 91.

[150] Above n 92.

[151] Joined Cases T-64/01 and T-65/01 *Afrikanische Frucht-Compagnie GmbH v Council* [2004] ECR II-521.

[152] Case T-3/99 *Banatrading GmbH v Council of the European Union* [2001] ECR II-2123.

[153] Of 9 September 1997 and 25 September 1997, respectively, the same reports which were at issue in *Chemnitz* and the *Atlanta* cases.

[154] *Banatrading*, above n 152, para 43.

[155] [2001] ECR II-2023.

reports. Doubtless this is due partly to the fact that these cases were not concerned with the potential direct effect of DSB reports. In the *Hormones* case,[156] the Appellate Body concluded that EC measures prohibiting the import of meat treated with growth hormones violated the WTO Agreement on Sanitary and Phytosanitary Measures (SPS Agreement), because they were not based on a sufficiently specific and detailed risk assessment. Subsequently, in *Pfizer*,[157] the applicant pharmaceutical company sought to annul an EC Regulation withdrawing authorisation of certain antibiotic growth-promoters in feed stuffs. The ban did not apply to imports of meat produced in third countries in which the use of the growth promoter was authorised. While upholding the ban, the CFI concluded that the fact that it did not apply to such imports did not affect its validity.[158] *Intervet*[159] was an action for failure to act or, in the alternative, for annulment of a Commission letter informing the applicant of its refusal to establish a provisional maximum residue limit for a hormonal substance.[160] The Commission had informed the European Agency for the Evaluation of Medicinal Products (EMEA) [now the European Medicines Agency, EMA] of recent scientific developments, including the WTO report in the *Hormones* case. It did not propose that the WTO Appellate Body report was legally binding, but it concluded that, until scientific evidence was available, it would be appropriate for the Committee for Veterinary Medicinal Products (CVMP) to suspend re-evaluation of the product.[161]

These cases demonstrated judicial deference to the EC legislator in politically sensitive matters. They also appeared to show how EU institutions, notably the European courts and the Commission, were developing a differentiated institutional practice which took account of WTO law.

Nevertheless, with regard to the invocation of DSB reports in the Community courts, the ECJ in effect has shut the door in *FIAMM and Fedon.*[162] It rejected the distinction proposed by the appellants between the direct effect of WTO substantive rules and the direct effect of DSB reports. According to the ECJ, a DSB report cannot be distinguished from WTO substantive rules, because its purpose is to rule on the consistency of a Member's conduct with its WTO obligations. Regardless of their precise legal effect, such reports cannot confer on individuals any more rights than do WTO substantive rules to invoke them in EC courts to challenge the legality of the conduct of EC institutions. They do not add to or subtract from the rights and obligations of WTO Members provided in the WTO Agreements.[163]

With respect, this conclusion is not entirely convincing. The reasons concern the nature of institutions, the necessary role of interpretation in clarifying treaty obligations and relations between the European courts and the WTO dispute settlement

[156] *European Communities—Measures concerning meat and meat products (Hormones)*, Complaint by the United States, Report of the Appellate Body, AB-1997-4, WT/DS48/AB/R.

[157] Case T-13/99 *Pfizer Animal Health SA v Council* [2002] ECR II-1961.

[158] *Ibid*, para 433.

[159] Case T-212/99 *Intervet International BV formerly Hoechst Roussel Vet GmbG v Commission* [2002] ECR 1445.

[160] See R Ancuceanu, 'MRLs of veterinary medicinal products and their regulation in European Community law' (2003) 9 *European Law Journal* 215.

[161] *Intervet*, above n 159, para 26. The CFI held that the Commission letter informing the applicant of its opinion did not constitute a decision which could be the subject of an action for annulment or a 'definition of position' for the purposes of Art 232 EC.

[162] Joined Cases C-120/06P and C-121/06 *Fabbrica Italiana Accumulatori Motocarri Mentecchio Spa (FIAMM), Fabbrica Italiana Accumulatori Motocarri Montecchio Technologies Inc (FIAMM Technologies) TBA v Council and Commission; Fedon & Figli and Fedon America v Council and others* [2006] ECR I-6513

[163] *Ibid*, paras 125–31.

institutions. First, the conclusion appears to neglect any differences between the institutional arrangements involved in adoption of a treaty, on the one hand, and those for settling disputes within the treaty framework, on the other hand. The Parties to the WTO Agreements agreed to establish specific institutions to settle disputes, instead of settling the disputes themselves. The WTO dispute settlement institutions have their own integrity, distinct from that of the WTO Members and the WTO Agreements. From an institutional perspective, a DSB report is necessarily (and intentionally) different from WTO substantive rules. Secondly, the Court's conclusion does not take account of the inevitable differences between the provisions of a general rule and the way in which it is interpreted. The interpretation of a WTO agreement is intended to clarify the rights and obligations of WTO Members. If we consider that interpretation is illegitimate because it necessarily adds to or subtracts from those rights and obligations in ways not intended by the Parties, we deny any possibility of interpretation of the WTO Agreements. In any event, the determination of the proper nature and function of WTO dispute settlement institutions in the interpretation of the WTO Agreements is primarily a matter for the Members of the WTO. Finally, it is unfortunate that the Court did not seize the opportunity to develop a more analytical and elaborate conception of the appropriate relations between the DSB and the European courts. Such a conception is badly needed in the context of globalisation and global legal pluralism,

B. WTO law and the legality of EC law

1. The General Principle: WTO Law does not Provide Criteria for Assessing the Legality of EC Legislation

Faced with the ECJ case law on the direct effect of WTO law, litigants have increasingly argued that WTO law provides criteria for assessing the legality of EC law. However, the European courts have consistently rejected this claim except in specific circumstances. The general principle is that WTO law does not provide criteria for assessing the legality of EC legislation. Nevertheless, the European courts have not addressed this issue unless absolutely necessary.

i. The General Principle

A litigant cannot normally challenge the legality of Community legislation on the ground that it is contrary to WTO law.[164] The most important recent case is Case C-149/96 *Portugal v Council*.[165] Rejecting Portugal's claim, the ECJ held *inter alia* that, having regard to their nature and structure, the WTO Agreements are not in principle among the rules in the light of which the Court is to review the legality of measures adopted by the Community institutions.[166]

[164] This was first established in Case C-280/93 *Germany v Council* [1994] ECR I-4973.
[165] Above n 85.
[166] *Ibid*, para 47.

The ECJ stated that:

a) the WTO system is based mainly on negotiation[167];
b) consequently

> to require the judicial organs to refrain from applying the rules of domestic law which are inconsistent with the WTO agreements would have the consequence of depriving the legislative or executive organs of the contracting parties of the possibility afforded by Article 22 of that memorandum of entering into negotiated arrangements even on a temporary basis . . .[168]

; and

c) 'the lack of reciprocity in that regard on the part of the Community's trading partners . . . may lead to disuniform application of the WTO rules'.[169]

In other words:

> To accept that the role of ensuring that those rules comply with Community law [sic] devolves directly on the Community judicature would deprive the legislature or executive organs of the Community of the scope for manoeuvre enjoyed by their counterparts in the Community's trading partners . . .[170]

The lack of clear reasoning in the judgment, and the sharp difference between the judgment and the Advocate-General's Opinion, suggest the existence of differences of opinion within the Court. But the basic reasons for the ECJ's conclusion were, in legal terms, the idea of reciprocity and the EC constitutional principle of institutional balance; and in political terms, the policy of protecting the position of the Community in international trade negotiations.

In this case, the ECJ clearly reaffirmed its earlier position with regard to GATT 1947, specifically concerning the two instances in which GATT/WTO law could be used as a criterion for evaluating the legality of EC law. Reiterating the view expressed in the 1994 *Germany v Council* judgment,[171] the ECJ stated that

> It is only where the Community intended to implement a particular obligation assumed in the context of the WTO, or where the Community measure refers expressly to the precise provisions of the WTO agreements, that it is for the Court to review the legality of the Community measures in question in the light of the WTO rules . . .[172]

More importantly, however, the ECJ in this case took a judicial *realpolitik* approach to the relationship between WTO law and EC law.[173] More directly than ever before, it confronted the international political context, in which WTO law potentially has a wide variety of effects within Members' legal systems. From this perspective, the criterion of legality involves, simultaneously, the normative relation between EC law and WTO law, the institutional balance within the Community, and the relation between the EU and its major trading partners.

[167] *Ibid*, paras 36, 42.
[168] *Ibid*, para 40.
[169] *Ibid*, para 45.
[170] *Ibid*, para 46.
[171] Case 280/93 *Germany v Council* [1994] ECR I-4973.
[172] *Portugal v Council*, above n 85, para 49.
[173] The same observation is made by Peers, above n 140, at 123.

The judgment can easily be criticised on logical positivist grounds, in particular because it failed to distinguish clearly between direct effect and invocability,[174] or between an action brought by an individual and one brought by a Member State, especially given that the concept of direct effect refers to the invocability of EC law by individuals, not by (and in fact usually against) Member States, and that the EC Member States themselves are WTO Members.[175] Nonetheless, it represents a salutary effort on the part of the European courts to balance the requirement of deciding individual cases with the necessity of taking account of the wider context in which the European courts operate.

ii. The Issue is Addressed only When Absolutely Necessary

The European courts address the issue of legality only when absolutely necessary. This stems partly from the practice of economy in judicial decision-making. It also forms part of a sensible judicial strategy, which signals to potential litigants that arguments about legality must be solidly based and essential to the case if they are to be taken seriously. In this way, the courts can concentrate on cases where the point is of fundamental importance, both in articulating the basic principle and in dealing with its exceptions.

In preliminary rulings the European courts do not address the issue of legality, even when it is pleaded in the main action, if it is not referred to Luxembourg by a national court. In *DADI*,[176] the plaintiff argued that certain provisions of an EC Directive laying down health rules for milk products were contrary to the WTO Agreement on Sanitary and Phytosanitary Measures (SPS Agreement). However, the national court did not refer the issue to the ECJ, which then concluded that there was no need to examine the validity of the EC legislation in the light of the Agreement on Sanitary and Phytosanitary Measures.[177]

Further, the European courts do not address the issue of legality if there has not been any breach of WTO law. For example, in *CEFS*,[178] the applicant sought interim measures in an action for annulment and suspension of Council Regulation fixing intervention prices and compensation for storage costs in the sugar sector. The CFI found that there was no evidence of a breach of the EC's WTO obligations and the sugar export ceiling had not been reached. A similar finding resulted in *Chemnitz*.[179]

A third situation in which the European courts do not address the issue of legality concerns the effects of time. Joined Cases C-364/95 and C-365/95 *T Port*[180] were actions for post-clearance recovery of customs duties payable on bananas imported

[174] See P Manin, 'A propos de l'invocabilité de l'accord instituant l'Organisation mondiale du commerce et de l'accord sur les marches publics: la question de l'invocabilité des accords internationaux conclus par la Communauté européenne' (1997) 33 *Revue Trimestrielle de Droit Européen* 399; G Zonnekeyn, 'The status of WTO law in the EC legal order: The final curtain?' (2000) 34 *Journal of World Trade* 111 at 120 and sources cited there.

[175] See N van de Broek, 'Legal persuasion, political realism, and legitimacy: The European Court's recent treatment of the effect of WTO Agreements in the EC legal order' (2001) 4(2) *Journal of International Economic Law* 411. For well-founded criticism, see PJ Kuijper and M Bronckers, 'WTO Law in the European Court of Justice' (2005) 42 *CML Rev* 1313 at 1342–55 (section by M Bronckers).

[176] Case C-106/97 *Dutch Antillian Dairy Industry Inc and Verenigde Douane-Agenten BV v Rijksdienst voor de keuring van Vee en Vlees* [1999] ECR I-5983.

[177] *Ibid*, paras 57, 58.

[178] Case T-229/R *Comité Européen des Fabricants de Sucre (CEFS) v Council* [1997] ECR II-1649.

[179] Case T-254/97 *Chemnitz*, above n 141.

[180] Above n 82.

from Ecuador in 1995, before Ecuador, which was not a party to GATT 1947, joined the WTO. The applicants pleaded the issue of legality, but the ECJ decided the case solely on the basis of the EC legal principle of non-discrimination. Similarly, in *Acme*,[181] an action for annulment of definitive anti-dumping duties on microwave ovens from China, the CFI held that the legality of the Regulation at issue could not be contested in the light of either Council Regulation 3283/94 or the WTO Anti-dumping Agreement, but 'primarily' in the light of the basic Regulation, general principles and all relevant rules in force at the time.[182] In Case C-104/97 *Atlanta*,[183] the ECJ excluded a plea of invalidity on the ground that

> to admit the plea based on the WTO decision would be tantamount to allowing the appellant to challenge for the first time at the stage of the reply the dismissal by the Court of First Instance of a plea which it had raised before that court, whereas nothing prevented it from submitting such a plea at the time of its application to the Court of Justice . . .[184]

2. *The Exceptions*

The European courts have recognised two exceptions to the principle that WTO law does not provide criteria for assessing the legality of EC law. One is based on the *Fédiol* case,[185] the other on the *Nakajima* case.[186] Since both involve the implementation of WTO law in EC law, they are sometimes are called the 'implementation exceptions'.[187] In fact, however, they originated in very different types of implementation, so I propose to use the terms 'clear reference exception' and 'transposition exception' respectively. In both groups of cases, in contrast to Case 149/96 *Portugal v Council*, the applicants have usually, though not always, been private parties.

i. The Clear Reference Exception

In *Fédiol*, a European trade association sought to annul a Commission Decision refusing to examine certain Argentinean commercial practices to see if they were contrary to the EC's 'New Commercial Policy Instrument' (NCPI).[188] The NCPI was designed to deal with illicit commercial practices other than dumping and subsidies. Its Article 2(1) defined 'illicit commercial practices' as 'any international trade practices attributable to third countries which are incompatible with international law or with generally accepted rules'. The plaintiff argued that this included the GATT. The ECJ held that, while not directly effective in EC law, the GATT formed part of the rules of international law referred to in the EC Regulation. Though the GATT was flexible, the

[181] Case T-48/96 *Acme Industry Co Ltd v Council* [1999] ECR II-3089.
[182] *Ibid*, para 32.
[183] Above n 142. This was an appeal against the CFI judgment in Case T-521/93 *Atlanta*, above n 143.
[184] Case C-104/97 *Atlanta*, above n 143, para 22.
[185] Case 70/87 *Fédération de l'industrie de l'huilerie de la CEE (Fédiol) v Commission* [1989] ECR 1781.
[186] Case 69/89 *Nakajima All Precision Co Ltd v Conseil* [1991] ECR I-2069.
[187] See P Eeckhout, 'The domestic legal status of the WTO Agreement: Interconnecting legal systems' (1997) 34 *CML Rev* 11 at 56. In fact, Eeckhout distinguishes the two exceptions but refers to them as a single category: *ibid*, at 42–47.
[188] Council Regulation 2641/84 of 17 September 1984, [1984] OJ L252/1.

Court could interpret and apply its rules in a specific case, 'in order to establish whether certain specific commercial practices should be considered incompatible with those rules'.[189] It thus could use the GATT to assess the legality of foreign legislation and, by extension, EC legislation. In contrast to direct effect, which would have empowered litigants to invoke and apply GATT provisions more or less directly, the necessary interpretation exception enabled the litigant to invoke the GATT, but ensured that the ECJ controlled whether and how it was applied.

This case involved GATT 1947, but since then the clear reference exception has been applied to GATT 1994 and other WTO Agreements. In recent cases, however, the ECJ has rejected arguments that WTO law should be used to assess the legality of EC legislation. For example, the plaintiffs in *Omega*[190] sought to use the GATT and the Agreement on Technical Barriers to Trade (TBT Agreement) as criteria for assessing a Council Regulation prohibiting the use of modified airplanes at EC airports unless they had been modified by complete re-engining with engines having a by-pass ratio of three or more. The Advocate-General concluded that the case did not involve either exception to the general rule that WTO law does not provide criteria for assessing the legality of EC law. The ECJ, following *Portugal v Council*, rejected the plaintiff's argument.

ii. The Transposition Exception

The second exception to the general rule originated in *Nakajima*.[191] A Japanese printer manufacturer brought an objection of illegality and an action for annulment to contest the imposition of definitive anti-dumping duties. It argued that the EC anti-dumping Regulation was in breach of the GATT Anti-dumping Code. It claimed that the GATT and the Code were included within 'any rule of law' relating to the application of the Treaty, which formed one of the grounds for the review of legality of EC law under Article 173 (now 230) EC. The ECJ noted that the GATT and the Code implementing Article VI GATT 'had the effect of binding the Community'.[192] It held that the EC anti-dumping Regulation

> was adopted in order to comply with the international obligations of the Community, which . . . is therefore under an obligation to ensure compliance with the General Agreement and its implementing measures . . .[193]

In such circumstances, GATT law supplied criteria for assessing the legality of EC law. In this case, however, the ECJ concluded that the EC Regulation was not in breach of the Anti-dumping Code.

The European courts have used this 'transposition exception' in more recent cases. Case C-150/95 *Portugal v Commission*[194] concerned the Uruguay Round Blair House Agreement (BHA), setting a maximum guaranteed area for the production of oilseeds. The EC implemented the BHA by Council Regulation 232/94, which amended Council Regulation 1765/95 on oil seeds, in part by adopting the area figures in the BHA Annex. Portugal sought to annul a Commission implementing Regulation, which had

189 *Fédiol*, above n 185, para 20.
190 Joined Cases C-27/00 and C-122/00 *Omega*, above n 98.
191 Above n 186.
192 *Ibid*, para 29.
193 *Ibid*, para 31.
194 [1997] ECR I-5863.

the effect of reducing the final regional reference amounts for oil seeds. The ECJ used the BHA to assess and confirm the legality of the Commission Regulation.

In *BEUC*,[195] a consumer association invoked the WTO Anti-dumping Agreement to annul a Commission Decision refusing to recognise it as an interested party in an anti-dumping proceeding. Article 6.11 of the Agreement sets out a non-exhaustive list of interested parties for the purposes of that Agreement. In adopting Articles 5(10), 6(7) and 21 of the basic EC anti-dumping Regulation, the EC legislature made open to WTO Members use of the possibility to recognise consumer associations as interested parties. The CFI found that

> These articles correctly implement WTO rules, which allow consumer organisations access to non-confidential information in relation to all elements of the proceeding, including dumping, injury and causality . . . [196]

It annulled the Commission Decision.

The transposition exception is often used in cases about anti-dumping and agriculture.[197] In *Euroalliages*,[198] the applicant sought annulment of a Commission decision terminating anti-dumping duties following an expiry review. It argued that the basic EC anti-dumping Regulation required the retention of duties, on expiry of the original period, where it was shown that injurious dumping was likely to recur. Whereas the applicant did not plead WTO law, the CFI used the WTO Anti-dumping Agreement as a criterion to assess and invalidate the EC Regulation. The applicant lost.

In contrast, in *Kloosterboer*,[199] the applicant relied successfully on WTO law. The WTO Agreement on Agriculture ('Agriculture Agreement') provided for the imposition of additional duties on imports in certain specified conditions. The amended version of the EC poultry meat regime, Council Regulation 2777/75, reiterated this provision. EC Regulation 1484/75 imposed such additional duties. Challenging the duties by means of a preliminary reference, the plaintiff in the main action argued that the duties infringed both the Agriculture Agreement and the EC implementing Regulation. The ECJ referred to Council Regulation 3290/94, which was adopted to implement the Uruguay Round agreements, including the Agriculture Agreement, in Community law. It also referred to the conditions for imposition of duties as allowed by the Agriculture Agreement. However, it conducted the bulk of its analysis with reference only to the EC implementing Regulation. It concluded that, viewed in this light, the Commission had no power to impose duties in this case.

At first sight, it may seem strange that the ECJ did not assess the legality of EC Regulation 1484/75 using the Agriculture Agreement directly as a criterion. However, this case is an ideal exemplification of the 'transposition exemption'. The additional duties were imposed on the basis of the EC poultry regime, which was a direct copy of the relevant provisions of the Agriculture Agreement. In this area of law, as in anti-dumping, EC law is for the most part simply a 'copy-out' transposition of WTO

[195] Case T-256/97 *Bureau Européen des Unions de Consommateurs (BEUC) v Commission* [2000] ECR II-101.

[196] *Ibid*, para 58.

[197] See also Case T-335/04 *Viz Stal and Duferco Commerciale v Council* [2004] OJ C273/34, removed from the Register; and, most recently, Case T-199/04 *Gul Ahmed Textile Mills Ltd v Council* (2004/C217/44), [2004] OJ C217/24.

[198] Case T-188/99 *Euroalliages v Commission* [2000] ECR II-1757.

[199] Case C-317/99 *Kloosterboer Rotterdam BV v Minister van Landbouw, Natuurbeheer en Visserij* [2001] ECR I-9863.

law. Similarly, in *Petrotub*,[200] the ECJ concluded that the EC in 1996 amended its basic anti-dumping Regulation in order to transpose into Community law the WTO Anti-dumping Code. The ECJ therefore reviewed the legality of a Regulation imposing anti-dumping duties in the light of Article 2.4.2 of the Anti-dumping Agreement on the requirement to give reasons for anti-dumping decisions.

Even within the areas of anti-dumping and agriculture, however, the European courts frequently recognise the *Nakajima* exception, but obviate the need to apply it by their interpretation of WTO law. For example, while granting the applicant's argument that the EC anti-dumping Regulation was introduced to implement the Anti-dumping Agreement, the CFI in *Petrotub*[201] considered that the applicant had misinterpreted the relevant Anti-dumping Agreement provisions. Similarly, recognising that the Council Regulation being challenged sought to implement a particular obligation within the GATT framework, the ECJ in Case C-352/96 *Italy v Council*[202] concluded that it was required to review the legality of the Regulation in the light of GATT rules. As a result of its own interpretation of WTO law, however, the ECJ did not actually find it necessary to use WTO law as a criterion for evaluating the legality of EC law. Lastly, in *CETM*[203] the CFI concluded that the concept of 'subsidy' within the meaning of the ASCM was irrelevant to the classification of the measure as a State aid under EC law. It thus rejected the argument by a recipient of State aid that the aid in question was not a specific subsidy within the meaning of the WTO ASCM, so that its classification of the aid as State aid would be incompatible with WTO law.

In numerous cases, the criterion of legality argument has failed. In Case T-52/99 *T Port*,[204] an importer of bananas sought damages for harm allegedly suffered as a result of the Commission's allocation of import quotas. The CFI rejected its argument

> that the Community was guilty of misuse of powers in adopting a regulation containing infringements of the WTO rules, or by continuing infringements already established, when it had undertaken to comply with them . . .[205]

Citing *Portugal v Council*, it reiterated the two exceptions to its general rule that WTO law cannot be as a criterion for evaluating the legality of EC law. But it concluded that the WTO Panel and Appellate Body reports did not include

> any special obligations which the Commission intended to implement, within the meaning of the case-law, in Regulation No 2362/98 . . . The regulation does not make express reference either to any specific obligations arising out of the reports of WTO bodies, or to specific provisions of the agreements contained in the annexes to the WTO Agreement . . .[206]

Bocchi[207] and *Cordis*[208] were decided the same way on the same day.

Case C-377/98 *Netherlands v European Parliament and Council*[209] was an action for the annulment of Directive 98/44 on the legal protection of biotechnological inven-

[200] Case C-76/00, above n 34.

[201] Joined Cases T-33/98 and T-34/98, above n 33. See also Case T-274/02 *Ritek Corp and Prodisc Technology Inc v Council and Commission* [2006] ECR II-4305, paras 98–106.

[202] [1998] ECR I-6937.

[203] Case T-55/99, above n 59.

[204] Above n 90.

[205] *Ibid*, para 57.

[206] *Ibid*, para 59.

[207] Case T-30/99, above n 91.

[208] Case T-18/99, above n 92.

[209] Case C-377/98 *Netherlands v European Parliament and Council of the European Union* [2001] ECR I-7079.

tions. The Netherlands argued that the Directive infringed the EC's international obligations, including TRIPS, the ATBT and the Convention on Biological Diversity (CBD). The Advocate-General stated that while TRIPS, the ATBT and the CBD do not have direct effect,

> More generally, it might be thought that it is in any event desirable as a matter of policy for the Court to be able to review the legality of Community legislation in the light of treaties binding the Community. There is no other court which is in a position to review Community legislation; thus if this Court is denied competence, Member States may be subject to conflicting obligations with no means of resolving them.[210]

The ECJ, citing Case C-149/96 *Portugal v Council*, simply reiterated its view that, 'having regard to their nature and structure', the WTO Agreements, including TRIPS and the ATBT, could not be used as criteria to review the legality of EC law'.[211] With regard to the CBD, however, the ECJ stated that the exclusion applied to the WTO Agreements could not be applied to the CBD, 'which, unlike the WTO agreement, is not strictly based on reciprocal and mutually advantageous arrangements'.[212] Consequently, even if the CBD does not have direct effect, it could be considered as a criterion for reviewing the legality of EC measures. Nevertheless, the ECJ did not change its basic position concerning the WTO Agreements.

In *Banatrading*,[213] the applicant pleaded that the EC Banana Regulation, Council Regulation 404/93, was incompatible with GATT, as was apparent from the Appellate Body report of 9 July 1997 and the DSB decision of 25 September 1997. The CFI rejected this claim on two grounds. First:

> It is settled Community case-law that, having regard to their nature and structure, the WTO Agreement and its annexes are not in principle among the rules in the light of which the Court is to review the legality of measures of the Community institutions . . .[214]

Secondly, the applicant could not now advance a new argument based on the *Fédiol* or *Nakajima* exceptions, because 'those two exceptions [to the general rule that WTO law may not be pleaded by private parties] form the subject-matter of settled case law'.[215] The CFI considered that

> It is clear from the case-law that a judgment which merely confirms law which ought to have been known to the applicant when it brought an action cannot be regarded as a new matter allowing a fresh plea to be raised . . .[216]

The same result was reached in Case T-2/99 *T Port*,[217] another banana case, an annulment action, decided on the same day,

These cases demonstrate that the transposition exception, as currently articulated, has several shortcomings. First, even though the legal import of WTO dispute settlement processes in EC law may not be entirely free from dispute, it is anomalous, to say the least, to maintain that Panel and Appellate Body reports and DSB findings do not

210 *Ibid*, Opinion of A-G Jacobs, para 147.
211 *Ibid*, para 52.
212 *Ibid*, para 53.
213 Case T-3/99, above n 152.
214 *Ibid*, para 43.
215 *Ibid*, para 49.
216 *Ibid*.
217 Above n 155.

comport any legal obligations. Secondly, the meaning of 'any special obligations'[218] or 'particular obligation'[219] is ambiguous, so it is not clear precisely what obligations must be imposed on the EC by WTO law, and how, in order for the exception to apply. Thirdly, the meaning of 'intended to implement, within the meaning of the case-law' has two unfortunate consequences: it appears to give overriding emphasis to the *intentions* of the EC institutions, notably the Commission, rather than to any legal obligations which the Community might have, that is, it emphasises subjective rather than objective factors; and it suggests that 'implementation' as defined in the case law might have a different meaning from the commonsense or generally accepted meaning. Fourthly, one wonders whether the Community can avoid meeting its WTO obligations by avoiding any express reference to WTO law in Community legislation, which surely cannot be the case[220]; and indeed, in the light of the European courts' case law on the duty to state reasons,[221] why an express reference to WTO obligations is required, if this is clear from the context.

In the *Chiquita Brands* case,[222] the CFI reviewed and clarified the transposition exception. It held that the *Nakajima* rule 'is designed, exceptionally, to allow individuals, in an indirect manner, to plead infringement by the Community or its institutions, of GATT rules or WTO agreements'.[223] As an exception, it was to be interpreted strictly. So far, it has been limited primarily to anti-dumping cases, though it could also be applied in other areas.[224] The basic pre-condition is that the Community measure being challenged must

> have been adopted for the purpose of implementing a particular obligation assumed in the context of the WTO Agreements, in other words usually but not always for the purpose of 'specifically transpos[ing] prescriptions arising from the WTO Agreements into Community law.'[225]

To determine whether this is the case, it is necessary to examine separately the specific characteristics of the EC measure and those of the relevant WTO Agreements.[226] The CFI then distinguished between the provisions in relevant WTO Agreements and the DSB conclusions. It considered that the former did not impose any 'particular obligations', while the latter imposed merely 'general obligations'; both differed from the 'particular obligations' imposed by the Anti-dumping Agreement.[227] In addition, the WTO dispute settlement mechanism B was not a judicial system but instead left open wide scope for negotiation.[228] The applicant lost.

[218] In the sense of Case T-52/99 *T Port*, above n 90.

[219] Case T-30/99 *Bocchi*, above n 91, para 63.

[220] See also G Zonnekeyn, 'The latest on indirect effect of WTO law in the EC legal order: The Nakajima case law misjudged?' (2001) 4(3) *Journal of International Economic Law* 597 at 602.

[221] See Case 45/86 *Commission* v *Council* [1987] ECR 1493; Case C-233/94 *Germany v EP and Council* [1997] ECR I-2405.

[222] Case T-19/01 *Chiquita Brands International, Inc, Chiquita Banana Co, BV and Chiquita Italia, SpA v Commission* [2005] ECR II-315; followed in Case T-226/04 *Italy v Commission* [2006] ECR II-29.

[223] Case T-19/01 *Chiquita Brands*, above n 221, para 117.

[224] *Ibid*, para 124.

[225] *Ibid*, para 125. This formulation also includes the situation in C-352/96 *Italy v Council (Rice)* [1998] ECR I-6937, which concerned the transposition into Community law of bilateral agreements concluded following negotiation in the context of the GATT, rather than the transposition of prescriptions in GATT or the WTO Agreements.

[226] Case T-19/01 *Chiquita Brands*, above n 221, para 156.

[227] *Ibid*, paras 158–61.

[228] *Ibid*, para 164.

Leaving aside the CFI's characterisation of the dispute settlement mechanism, there remains one outstanding question which the Court did not analyse, that is, the difference between:

a) transposing WTO agreements; or
b) enacting into EC law rules arising from bilateral agreements following negotiations in GATT, on the one hand; and
c) enacting into EC law the results of WTO dispute settlement, on the other hand.

If one searches for a 'particular obligation' to implement WTO law, the logical order in terms of the strength of the WTO legal obligation would appear to be a), b) and then c). In *Van Parys*,[229] decided by the ECJ a month later, the ECJ did not offer any real analysis of these issues. It is disappointing that the ECJ did not heed the Advocate-General's clear call for 'a specific analysis' of the issues raised by the adoption by the DSB of a decision confirming the incompatibility of an EC measure with WTO law.[230] Instead the ECJ simply referred to its previous case law, notably *Portugal v Council*, despite the fundamental difference in the legal context.[231] It concluded that the EC did not intend to implement a 'particular' WTO obligation. In this case, however, the EC had intentionally changed its legislation to comply with and thus implement a DSB decision. With all due respect, it is difficult to understand how the general characteristics of the WTO dispute settlement mechanism, or the fact that enforcement of WTO DSB decisions may be based on reciprocity, are relevant to the analysis; these phases of the WTO dispute settlement process were no longer at issue.

A more radical view was proposed by the Advocate-General in *Ikea*.[232] The plaintiff sought repayment of anti-dumping duties which the WTO DSB found contrary to the Anti-dumping Agreement. The Advocate-General concluded, for two reasons, that 'to acknowledge that the Court could be bound by the interpretation of the DSB would jeopardise the autonomy of the Community legal order'.[233] First, he drew a sharp distinction between the nature and objectives of the WTO, and those of the EC. Consequently, the fact that EC legislation and WTO Agreements shared the same wording did not mean that they were to be interpreted as meaning the same. Secondly, he also considered that DSB reports do not constitute judicial acts, since the WTO General Council 'even though it rules as a dispute settlement body, none the less constitutes a political body'.[234] In my view, this argument about the effects of WTO DSB decisions in EC law goes too far in minimising the EC's WTO obligations. In terms of the relevant WTO Agreements the case concerns the application of the *Nakajima* exception, However, the basic issue in practice is not simply the comparison of the WTO Anti-dumping Agreement and the basic EC anti-dumping Regulation, but rather whether a WTO DSB decision can be used to interpret and evaluate the legality of a specific EC Regulation imposing anti-dumping duties. With respect, it is therefore difficult to understand how or why the latter operation would undermine the autonomy of the EC legal order, in particular in the field of anti-dumping. Neither is the formal and substantive legitimacy of the basic EC anti-dumping Regulation at all in

[229] Case C-377/02 *NV Firma Leon Van Parys v Belgisch Interventie- an Restitutiebureau* [2005] ECR I-1465.
[230] *Ibid*, Opinion of A-G Tizzano.
[231] *Ibid*, para 164.
[232] Case C-351/04 *Ikea Wholesale Ltd v Commissoners of Customs & Excise* [2007] ECR I-7723.
[233] *Ibid,* Opinion of A-G Léger, para 87.
[234] *Ibid*, para 94.

question. The evaluation concerns an administrative measure taken in an individual case rather than general framework legislation.

The scope of the *Nakajima* exception was at least potentially at issue in *Franz Ergenberger*.[235] It was discussed by the Advocate-General but not by the ECJ. The *Nakajima* exception, as defined by the European courts, applies when an EC measure implements a 'particular' WTO obligation. Noting that the case law was very ambiguous, the Advocate-General proposed that *Nakajima* should apply when two conditions are satisfied:

a) an EC measure implements either a specific WTO provision or a specific group of WTO (GATT) provisions; and
b) an objective comparison of the content of the EC provision and the WTO obligation shows that the provision 'effectively results in the implementation or incorporation of the WTO obligation into Community law'.[236]

It is regrettable that the Advocate-General's helpful analysis, though referring to *Van Parys* in general terms, did not treat in more detail the difficult issue of the implementation of DSB decisions. The ECJ found for the complainant on the basis of the EC Treaty alone.[237]

C. Supervision of EC Breaches of WTO Law

1. *The Duty to State Reasons does not include Compatibility with WTO Law*

In other ways too, litigants have tried to use WTO law to force the European courts to supervise EC breaches of WTO law. Recent cases involve the duty to state reasons and non-contractual liability. Concerning the duty to state reasons, Article 253 (ex 190) EC provides that Regulations, Directives and Decisions adopted jointly by the European Parliament and the Council, and such acts adopted by the Council and the Commission, shall *inter alia* state the reasons on which they are based. The reasons include not only substantive or material reasons, but also the legal basis of the act. However, the substantive reasons do not need to include a statement that the act is compatible with WTO law.

In *Omega*,[238] the plaintiffs in the main action argued that EC Regulation 925/1999 was defective, partly because the statement of reasons did not refer to the GATT and/or the ATBT. The Advocate-General stated, however, that

> As regards the alleged departure from international standards and from the WTO Agreement on Technical Barriers to Trade, the duty in Community law to state reasons cannot extend to showing that every provision is consistent with such international rules or giving reasons for any divergence. The latter would even contain an implied admission of a breach of international law . . .[239]

[235] Case C-313/04 *Franz Ergenberger v Bundesanstalt fuer Landwirtschaft fir Ernäahrung* [2006] ECR I-6331.
[236] *Ibid*, Opinion of A-G Geelhoed, paras 72–76; the quotation is from para 76.
[237] *Ibid.*
[238] Joined Cases C-27/00 and C-122/00, above n 98.
[239] *Ibid*, Opinion of A-G Alber, para 45.

The last point may seem exaggerated, partly there is no reason to suspect that a divergence in itself would constitute 'an implied admission of a breach', and partly because the European courts would be likely to apply to this aspect of the giving-reasons requirement the same principles which they apply concerning legal basis or subsidiarity, namely, that an express statement is not necessary if consistency is sufficiently clear from the context. The latter was in fact the position taken by the ECJ in *Omega*.[240] However, the ECJ did not distinguish the WTO-based normative argument from the technical argument concerning factors about noise and other pollution. Indeed it did not mention WTO law at all except in so far as one can read a reference to WTO law into the statement that 'it is not necessary for details of all relevant factual and legal aspects to be given'.[241] Consequently, it is difficult to draw any conclusions at all about the ECJ view of WTO law in this context, except that the duty to state reasons does not require any reference to WTO law.

On its face, however, it is not at all unreasonable to extend the duty to state reasons to encompass consistency with WTO law. This might impose additional burdens on the EU institutions, both administrative and judicial, not only with regard to WTO law but also potentially concerning other international agreements. It would also go some way toward admitting that consistency with WTO law was a criterion for assessing the legality of EC law, not just exceptionally but as a matter of principle. In fact, it might trigger the clear reference exception, a factor which may partly account for the reluctance of the European courts to interpret the giving-reasons requirement to encompass WTO law. But even if judicial review were limited, it would signal that the EC institutions, including the European courts, take WTO law seriously. Drawing an analogy with the conclusion of the ECJ in its Opinion 2/00 *Cartagena Protocol*,[242] it would be a further step in the direction of recognising that WTO law has real and public constitutional significance in EC law. This is a step, however, which so far the European courts seem determined to avoid. Apart from the EC giving-reasons requirement, the CFI has stated that TRIPS does not contain an obligation to give reasons for decisions.[243]

2. *The EC does not Incur Non-contractual Liability for Breach of WTO Law*

Consistently with this position, the European courts have affirmed in several cases that infringement of WTO law by the EC does not provide grounds for a claim against the EC for damages based on non-contractual liability. Case T-52/99 *T Port*[244] concerned the calculation of annual import quantities. The applicant importer argued that the Commission infringed the GATT, GATS and the Agreement on Import Licensing Procedures by maintaining certain EC rules on the common organisation of the market in bananas after the WTO DSB had declared them incompatible with WTO law. The ECJ held that, as the WTO rules are not in principle intended to confer rights on individuals, the Community cannot incur non-contractual liability as a result of

240 *Ibid*, paras 46–47.

241 *Ibid*, para 46.

242 'The choice of the appropriate legal basis has constitutional significance': Opinion 2/00 (*Cartagena Protocol*) [2001] ECR I-9713, para 5.

243 See Case T-129/04 *Develey Holding GmbH Beteiligungs KG v Office for Harmonisation in the Internal Market (Trade Marks and Designs) (OHIM)* [2006] ECR II-811.

244 Above n 90.

infringement of them.[245] The ECJ reached the same result in other 'banana cases: *Bocchi*,[246] *Cordis*[247] and *Dole*.[248]

Biret, in fact involving two actions,[249] was a landmark case. It concerned the potential non-contractual liability of the EC for damage suffered as a result of EC law which the WTO DSB determined to be contrary to WTO law. In the *Biret* cases[250] the ECJ did not change its earlier position. However, it seemed to indicate that, in appropriate circumstances, it might be prepared to decide that an adopted WTO Appellate Body report could serve as a basis for a challenge to the legality of Community acts and be invoked in support of a claim for compensation.

The Biret companies imported beef from the United States into the Community. They brought an action for compensation for damages suffered as a result of the adoption and retention of the EC Directives banning the importation from the US of meat and meat products treated with growth hormones. The ECJ rejected the claim. It held that, for the period prior to the end of the reasonable time of 15 months given to the EC to comply with the DSB ruling that the hormones ban was incompatible with WTO law, the ECJ could not review the legality of EC measures without 'rendering ineffective' the grant of a reasonable time provided in the WTO Dispute Settlement Understandng (DSU) for WTO compliance.[251] It also stated that no claim could be sustained for damages during the period after 13 February 1998, the date of the DSB decision, and particularly for the period after 13 May 1999, the date when the 15-month period expired, because the Tribunal de commerce de Paris opened judicial liquidation proceedings on 7 December 1995 and provisionally set the date of cession of payments at 28 February 1995.[252] The applicant suffered no damage after 13 May 1999, so the EC could not incur any liability.[253] The ECJ thus left open the possibility for other subsequent claims if the timing were right.

However, in the Joined Cases *FIAMM and Fedon*,[254] the ECJ appears to have closed the door on this possibility. In several preceding 'banana cases', the CFI had rejected claims for damages. It referred to the ECJ's judgment in *Portugal v Council* and concluded that, in the circumstances, the plaintiffs could not rely on WTO law and the EC did not intend to implement any 'particular' WTO obligation. These cases all concerned damage allegedly suffered as a result of increased United States retaliatory customs duties authorised by the DSB, following a finding that the EC's banana import regime was incompatible with WTO law.[255] A similar action concerning other

[245] *Ibid*, para 51.
[246] Above n 91.
[247] Above n 92.
[248] Case T-56/00 *Dole Fresh Fruit International v Council and Commission* [2003] ECR II-577.
[249] Case 93/02 P *Biret International SA v Council* 2003] ECR I-10497; Case C-94/02 P *Etablissements Biret et SA v Council* [2003] ECRI-10565.
[250] *Ibid.*
[251] Case C-93/02 P *Biret International*, above n 248, para 52; Case C-94/02 P *Etablissements Biret*, above n 248, para 55.
[252] *Ibid*, para 53; *ibid*, para 56.
[253] *Ibid*, para 54; *ibid*, para 57.
[254] Joined Cases C-120/06P and C-121/06, above n 162.
[255] See Case T-69/00 *Fabbrica italiana accumulatori motocarri Metecchio Spa (FIAMM) and Fabbrica italiana accumulatori motocarri Montecchio Technologies, Inc (FIAMM Technologies) v Council and Commission* [2005] ECR II-5393; Case T-151/00 *Le Laboratoire du Bain v Council and Commission* [2005] ECR II-23; Case T-301/00 *Groupe Fremaux SA and Palais Royal Inc v Council and Commission* [2005] ECR II-25; Case T-320/00 *CD Cartondruck AG v Council and Commission* [2005] ECR II-27; Case T-383/00 *Beamglow Ltd v European Parliament, Council and Commission* [2005] ECR II-5459; Case T-135/01 *Fedon & Figli SpA v Council and Commission* [2005] ECR II-29.

products subject to the US retaliation also failed.[256] In *Banan-Kompaniet* the CFI also rejected another action for damages concerning bananas, here allegedly caused by the introduction of the EC export licence scheme under the Framework Agreement.[257] Subsequently, *FIAMM* and *Fedon*, two of these numerous similar cases, were appealed and were joined on appeal.[258] The ECJ concluded that the EC cannot incur liability for breach of WTO law due to conduct within its competence, so long as litigants in the EC courts cannot rely on the failure of EC conduct to comply with WTO agreements, even if such a failure is determined by the WTO DSB.[259] The ECJ did not accept the appellants' argument that compensation for damage should be recognised as a third case in which EC breach of WTO Agreements could be pleaded in the EC courts, in addition to the clear reference and the transposition exceptions. Consequently, under current EC law, litigants cannot invoke DSB rulings against the EC in an action for non-contractual liability for breach of WTO law.

IV. Effects of WTO Law on Relations Between the EC and the Member States

A. WTO Law and the Distribution of Powers

While WTO law is by no means external to the EC legal order, the European courts have sharply limited its impact on EC law, especially concerning individuals. The law of the WTO imposes obligations on the EC, but it does not confer rights upon individuals, and individuals cannot enforce the EC's WTO obligations in national or EC courts, except in limited circumstances. The European courts have taken another direction, however, in recent cases about the impact of WTO law on relations between the EC and the Member States. It is premature to describe this impact as a kind of structural reform, in the sense of the 'reshaping of legal, economic and political structures'[260] that has occurred as a result of the impact of EC law on and in the Member States. In the long run, however, this impact of WTO law is likely to be among the most significant, both for Member States and for individuals, though currently it is gradual, uneven and often unnoticed. The main strands of the case law so far concern the impact of WTO law on the distribution of powers between the EC and the Member States, and on increasing integration among the Member States themselves (see section IV.B. below).

[256] Case T-90/03 *Fédération des Industries Condimentaires de France and Others v Commission* [2007] ECR II-76; Case T-317/02 *FICF v Commission* [2004] ECR II-4325; Case T-109/03 *Arran Aromatics and Others v Commission*, Order of 13 July 2006, removed from the Register.

[257] Case T-57/00 *Banan-Kompaniet AB and Skandinaviska Banaimporten AB v Council and Commission* [2003] ECR II-577. In Case T-99/98 *Hameico Stuttgart and Others v Council* [2003] ECR II-2195, the CFI concluded that the applicants did not establish that they had suffered damage, so it was not necessary to consider the arguments concerning WTO law.

[258] Case T-69/00 *Fabbrica italiana accumulatori motocarri Metecchio Spa (FIAMM) and Fabbrica italiana accumulatori motocarri Montecchio Technologies, Inc (FIAMM Technologies) v Council and Commission* [2005] ECR II-5393, and Case T-90/03 *Fédération des Industries Condimentaires de France and Others v Commission* [2005] ECR II-29; appealed as Joined Cases C-120/06P and C-121/06, above n 162.

[259] Joined Cases C-120/06P and C-121/06, above n 162, para 176.

[260] F Snyder, 'The effectiveness of European Community law: Institutions, processes, tools and techniques' (1993) 56 *MLR* 19 at 36.

With regard to the distribution of powers, the European courts have interpreted WTO law as requiring a more precise definition of the distribution of powers between the EC and the Member States. In specifying the powers of the EC, they have also elaborated a principle of the indirect effect of WTO law, subject to certain conditions, with regard to national courts.

1. The Impact of WTO Law Requires more Precise Definition of the Respective Powers of the EC and the Member States

In Opinion 1/94[261] the ECJ held that, while the Community had exclusive competence with regard to matters covered by GATT, it shared with the Member States the competence to act with regard to most matters covered by GATS and TRIPS, with the exception of cross-border supply of services under GATS and counterfeit goods under TRIPs. Since then, subject to the changes introduced by the Treaties of Amsterdam and Nice, the European courts have reaffirmed this earlier conception.

Council Regulation 3285/94 prohibited the release for free circulation, export, re-export or entry for a suspensive procedure of counterfeit and pirated goods. The issue in *Polo/Lauren*[262] was whether it applied to goods in external transit, namely, alleged counterfeit T-shirts en route from Indonesia to Poland. The ECJ reiterated the view it expressed in Opinion 1/94 that 'measures at border crossing points intended to enforce intellectual property rights could be adopted autonomously by the Community institutions on the basis of Article 113 of the Treaty'.[263]

Following *Hermès*, the European courts have begun to trace a more intricate pattern of the distribution of competencies in a series of cases concerning TRIPS. In *Brauerei Hans Cramer*,[264] the German and Austrian Governments argued, in support of the plaintiff trade mark association, that Council Regulation 2081/92 on designations of origin and geographical indications did not preclude national legislation protecting other types of geographical indications. Both referred to Article 22 TRIPS, which requires parties, including both the EC and the Member States, to protect 'geographical indications'. Their argument was that TRIPS allows Member States to adopt protective legislation in areas not specifically covered by EC legislation, or in areas complementing EC legislation. The ECJ accepted the defendant's argument on the basis of EC law alone. Neither the Advocate-General (except in recounting the arguments) nor the ECJ mentioned TRIPS.

Dior[265] was a reference for a preliminary ruling on the interpretation of Article 50 TRIPS. Concerning fields where TRIPS applies, the ECJ distinguished between areas

[261] Opinion 1/94 [1994] ECR I-5267. In Case C-178/03 *Commission v European Parliament and Council* [2006] ECR I-107, note to para 29, and Case C-94/03 *Commission v Council* [2006] ECR I-1, A-G Kokott referred to this case as exemplifying the importance of the choice of the correct legal basis for EC legislation, notably in determining whether the EC's legislation competence is exclusive or shared.

[262] Case C-383/98 *The Polo/Lauren Company, LP v PT Dwidua Langgeng Pratama International Freight Forwarders* [2000] ECR I-2519.

[263] *Ibid*, para 32.

[264] Case C-312/98 *Schutzverband gegen Unwesen in der Wirtschaft eV v Warsteiner Brauerei Hans Cramer GmbH & Co KG* [2000] ECR I-9187.

[265] Joined Cases C-300/98 and C-392/98, above n 27.

in which the Community has legislated and those where it has not. The former fall within the scope of Community law, and national courts must interpret national law in this light. However, the latter fall within the scope of national law:

> Accordingly, Community law neither requests nor forbids that the legal order of a Member State should accord to individuals the right to rely directly on the rule laid down by Article 50(6) of TRIPS or that it should oblige the courts to apply that rule of their own motion . . .[266]

The ECJ also held that

> Article 50 of TRIPS leaves to the Contracting Parties, within the framework of their own legal systems, the task of specifying whether the right to sue under general provisions of national law concerning wrongful acts, in particular unlawful competition, in order to protect an industrial design against copying is to be classified as an 'intellectual property right' within the meaning of Article 50(1) of TRIPS . . .[267]

Here the ECJ did not analyse the resulting configuration of competences to identify possible problems or eventual solutions.[268]

It did not do so in *Groeneveld*[269] either, a case which concerned the power to fix time limits for the purposes of Article 50(6) TRIPS. The Advocate-General concluded that the fixing of time limits is 'in principle' up to national law, though this would appear to apply in his view only to 'procedural rules which vary slightly in detail'; other national alternatives, such as the Netherlands provisions involved in the case, may not 'fully reflect . . . the wording and purpose of Article 50(6)'.[270] The ECJ followed this analysis. It stated that

> Article 50(6) TRIPS is a procedural provision intended to be applied by Community and national courts in accordance with the obligations assumed both by the Community and by the Member States . . .[271]

[266] *Ibid*, para 49. This position is entirely consistent with that of the WTO Panel in *United States—Sections 301–310 of the Trade Act of 1974*, WT/DS152/R, Report of the Panel, 22 December 1999, para 7.72, fn 661.

[267] *Dior*, above n 27, para 63.

[268] So far, national practices vary. Germany partly acknowledged direct effect of substantive standards of TRIPS, except for Part III on enforcement: see Bundesregierung, *Entwurf eines Gesetzes zu den Uebereinkommen vom 15.4.1994 zur Errichtung einer Welthandelsorganisation*, Deutscher Bundestag, Drucksache 12/7655 (neu) 1994 S 335, 337, 344, 347, cited in Cottier and Schefer, above n 80, at 104, fn 78. An Irish court held that TRIPS required the Controller to refuse a grant of a licence pursuant to domestic law: *Allen & Hanbury's Ltd and Glaxo Group v Controller of Patents, Designs and Trademarks and Clonmel Healthcare Ltd* [1997] [1996] IEHC 59 (High Court of Ireland; 26 July 1996);. M Miller, 'The TRIPS Agreement and direct effect in European Community law: You can look . . . but can you touch?' (1999) 74 *Notre Dame Law Review* 597 at 617, argues that the case is not authority to the effect that TRIPS provisions have direct effect in EC law. In *Azrak-Hamway International Inc's Licence of Right (Design Right and Copyright) Application* [1997] *Reports of Patent, Design and Trade Mark Cases* 134 (Ch D), J Dennehey concluded that TRIPS was not part of EC law and therefore could not have direct effect. The UK courts denied direct effect to TRIPS in *R v Comptroller of Patents, Designs and Trade Marks, ex parte Lenzing AG v Coutauld (Fibres) Ltd and others* [1997] *Reports of Patent, Design and Trade Mark Case* 245. For comment on the last two cases, see also P Ruttley, 'The effect of WTO Agreements in EC law: How private parties can use WTO Agreements in litigation before the EC courts and the national courts of EC member states' in P Ruttley, I Macvay and C George (eds), *The WTO and International Trade Regulation* (London, Cameron May, 1998). Given these differences between countries, it is difficult to accept the argument that *Lenzing* sets a EC-wide precedent that TRIPS and the WTO Agreement do not have direct effect: see W Cook, 'Judicial review of the EPO and the direct effect of TRIPS in the European Community' (1997) 7 *European Intellectual Property Review* 367 at 373.

[269] Case C-89/99, above n 28.

[270] *Ibid*, Opinion of A-G Jacobs, paras 58, 56, 57.

[271] *Ibid*, para 41.

In the absence of provisions in TRIPS about when a time limit is to start,

> it is for each contracting party to determine when that period is to start, provided always that it is reasonable having regard to the circumstances of each case and taking into account the balance to be struck between the competing rights and obligations of the intellectual property right holder and of the defendant . . .[272]

The Court held that

> Article 50(6) of TRIPS neither requires nor forbids the Member States to provide, where appropriate, that its judicial authorities are to determine of their own motion the period within which substantive proceedings are to be instituted. Since the provision in question is silent on that point, the scope of the powers conferred on appellate courts in that regard falls within the competence of each Member State . . .[273]

These cases tend to preserve the respective domains of competence of the EC and the Member States.

In contrast, the ECJ in Case C-13/00 *Commission v Ireland*,[274] though not concerned with WTO law, indicated that, in the context of mixed agreements, the EC may enforce international obligations across both domains. The case was an infringement action against Ireland for its failure to adhere to the Berne Convention for the Protection of Literary and Artistic Works (Paris Act 1971) within the prescribed period. In the Commission's view, Ireland thus breached Community law obligations under Article 300(7) EC in conjunction with Article 5 of Protocol 28 annexed to the EEA Agreement. Supporting Ireland, the United Kingdom argued that neither the Paris Act nor the obligation to adhere to it fell wholly within EC competence.

Distinguishing the Opinion of the Advocate-General and the ECJ judgment in *Hermès*,[275] the Advocate-General stated that

> It does not appear certain to me, however, that the simple fact that the respective obligations of the Community and the Member States to the other Contracting Parties [to the EEA Agreement] have not been defined enables the latter to infer that the Community assumes responsibility for fulfilment of the whole of the agreement in question, including those provisions which do not fall within its competence. On the contrary, the very fact that the Community and its Member States had recourse to the formula of a mixed agreement announces to non-member countries that the agreement does not fall wholly within the competence of the Community and that, consequently, the Community is, *a priori*, only assuming responsibility for those parts falling within its competence . . .[276]

However, on the basis of *ERTA*,[277] he concluded that the obligation to adhere to the Paris Act 'should be regarded as an indivisible obligation to adhere to an agreement, various provisions of which affect Community rules'.[278] He thus granted the Commission's argument.

The ECJ followed this conclusion, but on the basis of its judgment in *Demirel*.[279] It considered that

272 *Ibid*, para 66.
273 *Ibid*, para 73.
274 Case C-13/00 *Commission v Ireland* [2002] ECR I-2943.
275 Case C-53/96, above n 24 and accompanying text.
276 *Commission v Ireland*, above n 274, Opinion of A-G Mischo, para 30.
277 Case 22/70 *Commission v Council* [1971] ECR 263.
278 *Commission v Ireland*, above n 274, Opinion of A-G Mischo, para 50.
279 Case 12/86 *Demirel* [1987] ECR 3719.

> mixed agreements . . . have the same status in the Community legal order as purely Community agreements, as these are provisions coming with the scope of Community competence . . .[280]

With regard to such agreements:

> [T]he Member States fulfil, within the Community system, an obligation in relation to the Community, which has assumed responsibility for the due performance of the agreement . . .[281]

The subject-matter of the Berne Convention was 'to a very great extent' governed by Community law,[282] so there was a 'Community interest' in ensuring adherence.[283] Hence 'the requirement of adherence' came 'within the Community framework', with the result that, subject to judicial review, the Commission was competent to ensure compliance.[284] This conclusion goes some way to meet the demands of third countries for greater transparency in the enforcement of the international obligations of the EC and its Member States in mixed agreements.

The more recent *Merck Genéricos* case[285] is consistent with the basic principles articulated by the European courts in earlier cases such as *Hermès* and *Dior*, though its implications are potentially more radical. The applicable Portuguese law provided for a 15-year patent period, while Article 33 TRIPS specified a period of 20 years. The plaintiff in the main action argued that Portuguese law applied; the defendants argued, in essence, that Article 33 TRIPS had direct effect, so trumped Portuguese law. Following earlier principles, the ECJ held that, in view of the Community interest in uniform interpretation, it had jurisdiction to interpret Article 33 TRIPS, a mixed agreement. Again following its previous logic, it found that there was little EC law on patents, and consequently the Member States remained mainly competent in this domain. Hence the Member States were free to choose whether or not to give direct effect to Article 33 TRIPS. The ECJ thus has mandated the decentralisation of decision-making about Article 33 TRIPS to national courts. It remains to be seen whether the result will be greater diversity of application of Article 33 (or other articles) of TRIPS within the EU of 27 Member States.

2. *WTO Law forms Part of the Interpretative Obligation Imposed by EC law on National Courts*

In defining more precisely the respective powers of the EC and the Member States concerning WTO law, always as part of the EC legal order, the European courts have interpreted WTO law as forming part of EC law for the purposes of the obligation of consistent interpretation. Well-established concerning the interpretation of EC

280 *Commission v Ireland*, above n 274, para 14.
281 *Ibid*, para 15.
282 *Ibid*, para 17.
283 *Ibid*, para 19.
284 *Ibid*, para 20.
285 Case C-431/05 *Merck Genéricos—Produtos Farmaceuticos Lda v Merck & Co Inc and Merck Sharp & Dohme Lda* [2007] ECR I-7001.

secondary legislation in the light of GATT/WTO law,[286] it also applies to the interpretation of national legislation in the light of WTO law, as part of the obligations of the Member States under EC law. This is a matter of Community law, which is distinct from, and perhaps even in contradiction to, such effects as WTO law may have on national courts according to WTO law itself, national constitutions or the case law of the national courts.

In its 1998 *Hermès* judgment,[287] the ECJ stated that

> where a provision can apply both to situations falling within the scope of national law and to situations falling within the scope of Community law, it is clearly in the Community interest that, in order to forestall future differences of interpretation, that provision should be interpreted uniformly, whatever the circumstances in which it is to apply . . .[288]

From this observation, the Court drew two conclusions. First, where courts of a Member State are

> called upon to apply national rules with a view to ordering provisional measures for the protection of rights arising under a Community trade mark, [they] are required to do so, as far as possible, in the light of the wording and purpose of Article 50 of the TRIPS Agreement . . .[289]

Though presented in the judgment as part of the reasoning to justify the conclusion that the ECJ had power to interpret TRIPS, this interpretative obligation also follows logically from the principle of uniform interpretation. Secondly, the ECJ itself had jurisdiction to interpret Article 50 TRIPS. The ECJ thus sought to pre-empt national courts from giving different interpretations to WTO law that applies to situations falling within the scope of EC competence or of shared competence. It applied the same logic in subsequent cases.

Linster[290] was a preliminary ruling on an EC Directive which had not been fully transposed into national law within the specified time limit. The Luxembourg Court in its request referred to the distinction in *Nakajima* between direct effect and collateral review of legality (see section III.B.2.ii. above). Referring to its long-standing case law on EC Directives, but without needing to refer to *Nakajima*, the ECJ stated that

> the provisions of the Directive may be taken into account by national courts in order to review whether the national legislature has kept within the limits of the discretion set by it . . .[291]

The ECJ couched its decision solely in terms of EC law, whereas the normative paradigm proposed by the national court was based on the relation of EC law to WTO law.

Following *Hermès*, *Dior*[292] was the first case in which the European courts posited a full-fledged interpretative obligation for national courts involving WTO law. The ECJ drew a bright line between the areas where the EC had legislated and where it had not. Concerning the former, it held that

[286] See, eg, Case C-61/94 *Commission v Germany* [1996] ECR I-3989 (International Dairy Arrangement) and Case C-53/96 *Hermès*, above n 24; Case C-306/05 *Sociedad General de Autores y Editores de España (SGAE) v Rafael Hoteles* [2006] ECR I-11519.

[287] Case C-53/96, above n 24.

[288] *Ibid*, para 32.

[289] *Ibid*, para 28.

[290] Case C-287/98 *Luxembourg v Berthe Linster, Aloyse Linster and Yvonne Linster* [2000] ECR I-6917.

[291] *Ibid*, para 38.

[292] Joined Cases C-300/98 and C-392/98, above n 27.

> the judicial authorities of the Member States are required by virtue of Community law, when called upon to apply national rules with a view to ordering provisional measures for the protection of rights falling within such a field, to do so as far as possible in the light of the wording and purpose of Article 50 of TRIPS . . .[293]

Viewed as judicial technique, the obligation of consistent interpretation may be assimilated to the interpretative obligation imposed by the European courts on national courts, which are required to interpret national law in the light of EC secondary legislation.[294] However, in substantive terms the normative referent is WTO law. In procedural terms, however, the reference is not WTO law per se but instead WTO law as part of the EC legal order, and the obligation of consistent interpretation stems not from WTO law but rather from EC law.

In *Groeneveld*,[295] the ECJ reiterated and to some extent clarified the indirect effect of WTO law. The case concerned the application and interpretation of Article 50(6) TRIPS in the context of trade mark proceedings. The Advocate-General observed that, while Article 50 TRIPS does not have direct effect,

> the lack of direct effect is less significant than it might have been, given that—in the field of trade-mark law—courts must in so far as possible interpret their national law consistently with Article 50. That principle reflects the Court's earlier approach to the effect of GATT 1947, where it stated for example that 'it is important that the provisions of GATT should, like the provisions of all other agreements binding the Community, receive uniform interpretation throughout the Community.'[296]

Amplifying this view, the ECJ held that

> where the judicial authorities are called upon to apply national rules with a view to ordering provisional measures for the protection of intellectual property rights falling within a field to which TRIPS applies and in respect of which the Community has already legislated, they are required to do so as far as possible in the light of the wording and purpose of Article 50(6) of TRIPS, taking account, more particularly, of all the circumstances of the case before them, so as to ensure that a balance is struck between the competing rights and obligations of the right holder and the defendant.[297]

While appearing to be a logical development of previous judgments, the above cases mark a significant development in the position of the European courts concerning the effects of WTO law in EC law. Consider three situations, taking into account that both the EC and the Member States are WTO Members: in situation a) there is a risk of different interpretations of the same EC norm by different national courts; in situation b) there is a risk of different interpretations of the same WTO norm by different national courts; in situation c), there is a risk of different interpretations of the same WTO norm by the European courts and a national court. The recent cases extend earlier ECJ earlier case law about situation a) to situations b) and c). But situations b) and

[293] *Ibid*, para 49.

[294] The principle was established by the ECJ concerning the relationship between EC law and national law in Case 14/83 *Von Colson and Kamann v Land Nordrhein-Westfalen* [1984] ECR 1891 and Case C-106/89 *Marleasing SA v La Commercial Internacional de Alimentacion SA* [1990] ECR I-4135. See also P Mengozzi, 'La Cour de justice et l'applicabilité des règles de l'OMC en droit communautaire à la lumière de l'affaire Portugal c. Conseil' (2000) 3 *Revue du Droit de l'Union Européenne* 509 at 515.

[295] Case C-89/99, above n 28.

[296] *Ibid*, Opinion of A-G Jacobs, para 42.

[297] *Ibid*, para 55, see also paras 35, 36 and 38. See also Case C-245/02 *Anheuser-Busch Inc v Budějovický Budvar, národní podnik* [2004] ECR I-10989.

c) differ from situation a) in two important respects. First, the norm in situation a) is a product of the EC institutions, whereas the norms in situations b) and c) are the product of WTO institutions, even though the European courts have reinterpreted them as being part of the EC legal order. Secondly, the norm in situation a) operates in a context in which other norms originating from the same site are recognised by the European courts as having direct effect. Consistent interpretation, or indirect effect, is a complement to, not a replacement of, direct effect.[298] In contrast, the norms in situations b) and c) operate in a context in which other norms originating from the same site are not recognised by the European courts as having direct effect. The indirect effect of WTO law is a replacement of direct effect, not merely a complement to it.

The principle of indirect effect of GATT law originated in the 1972 *Interfood* judgment,[299] though this case demonstrated that only a very thin line separates the use of international norms as an aid to interpretation, on the one hand, and the principle of consistent interpretation, on the other hand. In 1996 the ECJ held that the interpretative obligation applied 'as far as possible'.[300] However, the idea of consistent interpretation remained largely dormant until recently, when it was extended to the WTO Agreement. More recent cases refer mainly to TRIPS[301] and, within the TRIPS, only to those areas where the EC has competence and where it has legislated. This is not surprising because TRIPS, of all WTO Agreements, requires the most wide-ranging changes in WTO Members' domestic legislation.[302] But the basic principle may have wider implications. Will the principle of indirect effect lead to fewer claims that WTO law, notably TRIPS, should have direct effect? Will the European courts extend it to other areas of shared competence? Will it apply to adopted Panel or Appellate Body reports?[303] Will they extend it beyond the limiting conditions of EC competence and EC legislation? Will it actually give individual litigants greater access to the European courts? Which litigants are most likely to benefit?

An instructive example is *Shanghai Teraoka Electronic.*[304] In this anti-dumping case, the applicants contested definitive anti-dumping duties by arguing that the EC failed to take account of all relevant factors in determining the impact of dumped imports on Community industry. Article 3(5) of the basic EC Regulation was essentially the same as Article 3.4 of the WTO Anti-dumping Agreement, which had been interpreted by the Appellate Body as requiring that all listed factors must be taken into account. Blurring any distinction between the principle of consistent interpretation and the use of WTO law to assess the legality of EC law, namely the EC Regulation imposing

[298] See, eg, the Opinion of the A-G in Case C-418/02 *Practiker Bau- une Heimwerkermärkte* [2005] ECR I-5873.

[299] Case 92/71 *Interfood v Hauptzollamt Hamburg* [1972] ECR 231, para 6. See also Case C-79/89 *Brown Boveri* [1991] ECR I-1853, paras 15–19; Joined Cases T-163/94 and T-165/94 *NTN Corporation and Koyo Seiko v Council* [1995] ECR II-1381, para 65; Case 61-94 *Commission v Germany* [1996] ECR I-3989, para 52.

[300] Case C-61/94 *Commission v Germany*, above n 286, para 52.

[301] An exception is Case C-335/05 *Rizeni Letoveho Provozu* [2007] ECR I-4307; see esp the Opinion of A-G Mengozzi, paras 57–60.

[302] See generally S Dillon, *International Trade and Economic Law and the European Union* (Oxford, Hart Publishing, 2002). See also J Drexl, 'The TRIPS Agreement and the EC: What comes next after joint competence?' in FK Beier and GSchricker (eds), *From GATT to TRIPS—The Agreement on Trade-related Aspects of Intellectual Property Rights* (, Weinheim, 1996).

[303] As Peers argues with regard to Panel reports, once the principle is recognised, there is no reason to exclude adopted Panel or AB reports from its scope: see S Peers, 'Fundamental right or political whim? WTO Law and the European Court of Justice', in de Búrca and Scott, above n 15, 111 at 118.

[304] Case T-35/01 *Shanghai Teraoka Electronic Co Ltd v Council* [2004] ECR II-3663.

anti-dumping duties, the CFI concluded that it should consider whether the EC institutions had evaluated all factors, and decided that they had done so. Numerous other questions, however, remain to be answered.

B. WTO law and European Integration

1. WTO Law Provides a Basis for EC Harmonisation of National Law

The law of the WTO has also influenced the nature and form of European integration, though this aspect of the impact of WTO law has been explored relatively little. The European courts have recently promoted WTO law as a new basis for the harmonisation of national legislation. At the same time, they are laying the groundwork for stricter monitoring by the EC of the WTO law obligations of the Member States *qua* Member States.

Often following the Advocates-General, the European courts have suggested that WTO law supplies a rationale for, or provides a basis for, the harmonisation by the EC of the law of the Member States. *Metronome*[305] concerned an EC Directive providing for an exclusive rental and lending right for phonograms. The Advocate-General observed that

> it is significant that in the preamble to the Directive reference was made to the need for the legislation of the Member States to be approximated 'in such a way as not to conflict with the international conventions.'[306]

Upholding the Directive, the ECJ stated that the obligation to establish an exclusive right was in conformity with the TRIPS.

In *Silhouette*,[307] the Advocate-General concluded that, in the absence of negotiations with third countries to deal with international exhaustion of trade marks,

> a measure based on Article 100a [now Article 95] deals with the internal market and cannot be construed as having dealt with international exhaustion, so the Community can regulate under Article 100a the rights of trade mark owners within the EC concerning goods bearing their mark marketed inside or outside the Community.[308]

This interpretation was possible because, as the Advocate-General pointed out, TRIPS expressly excluded the issue of international exhaustion, leaving the EC free to regulate the matter by harmonisation directives applicable to all Member States. Once the EC had done so, the EC Trade Marks Directive precluded the Member States from adopting the principle of international exhaustion. The ECJ did not mention TRIPS, though it stated that 'Articles 5 to 7 of the Directive must be construed as embodying a complete harmonisation of the rules relating to the rights conferred by a trade mark'.[309] The fact that the Member States, as well as the EC, were party to TRIPS did

[305] Case C-200/96 *Metronome Musik GmbH v Music Point Hokamp GmbH* [1998] ECR I-1953.
[306] *Ibid*, Opinion of A-G Tesauro, para 32.
[307] Case C-355/96 *Silhouette International Schmied GmbH & Co KG v Hartlauer Handelsgesellschaft mbH* [1998] ECR I-4799.
[308] *Ibid*, Opinion of A-G Jacobs, para 47.
[309] *Ibid*, para 25.

not prevent the EC from adopting harmonisation directives in a field of shared competence. In effect, WTO law created a normative space, which the EC could fill by harmonising national law.

The WTO law in *Silhouette* offered WTO Members a single possibility, which the EC used as a basis for harmonising national law. In contrast, Case C-377/98 *Netherlands*[310] involved a situation in which WTO law offered Members a choice among different possibilities. The EC made its choice and harmonised national legislation accordingly. The Netherlands brought an action to annul Directive 98/44 on the legal protection of biotechnological inventions on the ground that it infringed the EC's international obligations, including TRIPS and the ATBT. Rejecting this argument, the Advocate-General observed that TRIPS allows Members to exclude a wide range of subject-matter from patentability, and the EC had exercised this option by excluding only part of that range. He concluded that

> The fact that that option is no longer available to the Netherlands is a consequence not of any infringement of the TRIPS Agreement but of the harmonising effect of the Directive . . .[311]

According to the Advocate-General, this does not mean that the Member States' obligations under TRIPS are affected by Article 4(1) of the Directive, because the latter 'simply exercises a right (of option) and does not affect such obligations'.[312]

Following this view, the ECJ held that

> while the Directive does deprive the Member States of the choice which the TRIPS Agreement offers the parties to that agreement as regards the patentability of plants and animals, the option taken in Article 4 of the Directive is in itself compatible with the Agreement, which, moreover, does not prevent certain party States adopting a common position with a view to its application. The joint selection of an option offered by an international instrument to which the Member States are parties is an act that falls within the approximation of laws provided for by Article 100a of the EC Treaty . . .[313]

According to the European courts, therefore, when the EC chooses among several policy options open to WTO Members, and enacts its choice in the form of an EC Directive, it prevents individual EC Member States from exercising their option in a different way. The EC policy decision binds the Member States *qua* EC Member States. Though WTO Members in their own right, the latter cannot seek to annul an EC Directive implementing the option thus exercised, on the ground that the Directive is incompatible with WTO law.[314] In terms of EC law, the status of EC Member State takes precedence over the status of WTO Member. In addition, an attempt by a Member State to exercise an option first in similar circumstances, that is to engage in regulatory competition, would almost certainly to fall foul of its EC law duty of loyalty.[315] The *Netherlands* judgment leaves Member States some room for manoeuvre, since a 'common position' may embrace different views and 'with a view to its application' is not defined in detail. But WTO law now provides a normative space and a legal

[310] Case C-377/98 *The Netherlands v European Parliament and Council of the European Union* [2001] ECR I-7079.

[311] *Ibid*, Opinion of A-G Jacobs, para 154.

[312] *Ibid*, para 155.

[313] *Ibid*, para 58.

[314] For a critique, see M Bronckers, 'Editorial: La jurisprudence des jurisdictions communautaires relatives à l'OMC demande reparation: plaidoyer pour les droits des Etats membres' (2001) 37 *Cahiers de Droit Européen* 3.

[315] See also Bourgeois, above n 6, at 122.

mechanism for the harmonisation of national law. It thus also reinforces the transfer of authority from the Member States to the Community.[316] This suggests that, within domains of shared EC and Member State competence, as defined by EC law, Member States are likely to find their options within the framework of WTO law limited by EC law, and possibly subject to harmonisation by the EC.[317]

2. EC Monitoring and enforcement of the WTO Obligations of EC Member States qua *Member States*

According to the European courts, the Community can supervise the fulfilment of the WTO obligations of Member States *qua* Member States. This can be done by the European courts, the national courts or the Community administration.

For example, in Case C-377/98 *Netherlands*,[318] the Advocate-General suggested that the ECJ should be able to review the legality of EC legislation in the light of international treaties, 'otherwise Member States may be subject to conflicting obligations with no means of resolving them'.[319] Though not following this suggestion, the ECJ authorised the harmonising effect on national legislation of the EC Biotechnology Directive, which encapsulated the exercise of the Community's option within the framework of TRIPS. In addition, the principle of consistent interpretation provides a means by which national courts, as well as the European courts, supervise Member States' fulfilment of their WTO obligations. Finally, in cases such as *Nokia*,[320] the ECJ underscored the TRIPS obligations of the Member States. It held that because TRIPS requires Member States to provide civil and criminal remedies for trade mark infringement, the existence of such remedies under national law cannot constitute a 'special reason' for a trade mark court to refuse to prohibit a defendant from proceeding with acts which infringe or would infringe the EC trade mark.

Twenty-five years ago, Jacques Bourgeois argued that Commission enforcement of Member States' obligations under EC law also applied to international agreements which had become part of EC law, though he further noted that there had been practically no such proceedings up to that time.[321] As early as 1994, the ECJ held that the European Commission was entitled to bring an action against a Member State for

[316] See also RA Brand, 'Direct effect of international economic law in the United States and the European Union' (1996–97) 17 *Northwestern Journal of International Law and Business* 556 at 603.

[317] For a forceful statement that this position is legally correct, see CA Timmermans, 'The implementation of the Uruguay Round by the EC' in JHJ Bourgeois, F Berrod and E Gippini Fournier (eds), *The Uruguay Round Results: A European Lawyers' Perspective* (Brussels, European Interuniversity Presss, 1995) 501 at 507.

[318] *The Netherlands v European Parliament and Council,* above n 310,

[319] *Ibid*, Opinion of A-G Jacobs, para 147.

[320] Case C-316/05 *Nokia Corp v Joacim Waerdell* [2006] ECR I-12083.

[321] JHJ Bourgeois, 'Effects of international agreements in European Community law: Are the dice cast?' (1984) 82 *Michigan Law Review* 1250 at 1261, 1273. See also M Maresceau, 'The GATT in the case-law of the European Court of Justice' in Hilf *et al*, above n 106, at 110. It has also been argued that *Frankovich* principles on State liability might conceivably apply to non-compliance by Member States with their WTO obligations: see K Govaere, 'The reception of the WTO Agreement in the European Union: The legacy of GATT' in P Demaret, JF Bellis and G García Jimenéz (eds), *Regionalism and Multilateralism after the Uruguay Round: Convergence, Divergence and Interaction* (Brussels, European Interuniversity Press 1997), 703 at 712.

infringement of EC rules implementing rules of GATT 1947.[322] In Case C-13/00 *Commission v Ireland*,[323] the ECJ concluded that the Commission was entitled to assess compliance with the requirement to adhere to an international agreement which created rights and obligations in areas covered partly by Community law. Though not directly concerned with WTO law, the case suggests that the Commission will continue to play this supervisory role. Such monitoring is likely to be more effective if it is pro-active in nature,[324] assuming sufficient resources are available, instead of being reactive and requiring recourse to courts.

These Community powers apply both to domains of exclusive EC competence and to domains of shared competence. The basic mechanism in the former consists of defining an EC Member State's breach of WTO law as a breach of EC law. In the more controversial areas of shared competence in EC law, it would consist of two steps. The first is to categorise a breach of WTO law not as a breach by the Member State *qua* WTO Member, but as a breach by the Member State *qua* EC Member State. The second is to define the breach as a breach of EC law. The first is premised on the duty of loyalty, and the latter on the idea that WTO law is part of the EC legal order. When these principles were first articulated, it is unlikely that many people foresaw these far-reaching implications. Neither could they have foreseen the Uruguay Round results and the subsequent development of WTO law, which have exercised a profound influence on Community law.

As with respect to purely internal Community law, however, the powers of the Commission are likely to remain secondary in importance to decentralised enforcement in ensuring the effectiveness of Community law of WTO origin. Hence the importance of the controversy concerning the potential direct effect of WTO law, and also the significance of recent case law on the transposition exception and the principle of consistent interpretation. From the standpoint of the EU legal order as a whole, as distinct from the standpoint of individual litigants, this

> compensates for the Commission's weak supervisory powers and helps to avoid national acts which violate international law, and which could be attributed to the Union.[325]

This may go some way toward resolving problems which might be analogous, in the EU context, to those addressed by the WTO's 'federal clause', namely Article XXIV:12 GATT, which provides that each contracting party shall take such reasonable measures as may constitutionally be available to it in order to ensure observance of the provisions of the WTO Agreement by the regional and local governments and authorities within its territory.[326] It would not, however, resolve the more difficult issue posed by the fact that, according to the case law of the European courts, the European courts can ensure that the EC Member States comply with their WTO law obligations, but

[322] See Case C-61/94 *Commission v Germany*, above n 298. However, Member States are not entitled to use the WTO to challenge the validity of EC acts as a defence to such an action: Case C-404/97 *Commission v Portugal* [2000] ECR I-4897.

[323] Above n 274.

[324] See PJ Kuijper, 'The new WTO dispute settlement system: The impact on the European Community' (1995) 29 *Journal of World Trade* 49 at 69.

[325] A von Bogdandy and T Makatsch, 'Collision, Co-existence or Co-operation? Prospects for the Relationship between WTO Law and European Union Law' in de Búrca and Scott, above n 15, 131 at 149.

[326] For discussion of this issue in terms of WTO law, see T Cottier and C Germann, 'The WTO and EU distributive policy: the case of regional promotion and assistance', in de Búrca and Scott, above n 15, 185 at 205–07.

neither the European courts nor the Member States can ensure that the European Community itself does so.[327]

V. Conclusion

The EU and the WTO are among the most important sites governing (and driving) globalisation today. This chapter has sought to illuminate certain relations between them, in particular the impact of WTO law on EC law. A review of European court judgments about WTO law helps us to decipher some crucial questions. Which institutions act as gatekeepers in relations between sites? How do they control and shape the form and pace of deeper integration? What strategies do they use, within the framework of their legal, institutional and political roles? What barriers do they create to prevent submersion or takeover? What are the consequences for individuals, whether citizens, residents or legal persons, as well as for Member States? To what extent do increased relations between sites tend to restructure the organisation of power, notably existing institutions, hierarchies and processes? What impact do they have on constitutional principles, constitutional processes and constitutional culture?

Article XVI of the Marrakech Agreement establishing the WTO requires each WTO Member to ensure the conformity of its laws, regulations and administrative procedures with its obligations as provided in the Uruguay Round agreements. In practice, as the EU example demonstrates, 'conformity' can have many meanings. The European courts act as gatekeepers in determining the specific effects of WTO law on EC law.

Since the mid-1990s, the trickle of cases on GATT/WTO law in the European courts has turned into a flood. As a result, we can now discern a specific conceptual framework or lens through which the European courts view WTO law and filter its impact. It has developed in three overlapping but distinct phases, each focused primarily on a different set of issues: first, the effects of the WTO on the EC legal order; secondly, WTO law and the individual; and thirdly, relations between the EC and Member States. Of course, each phase also had wider implications, so that, for example, ECJ judgments concerning relations between the EC and Member States also had significant consequences for the EC legal order and for individuals. Nonetheless, the three phases are sufficiently distinct that we may describe them as the three generations of relations between the GATT/WTO and the EC/EU sites.

For many years the principal debates in the EU about relations between EC law and GATT /WTO law concerned the potential direct effect of GATT and then WTO law in the EC legal order. Now, however, the debate about the potential direct effect of WTO law in the EC legal order appears to be more or less exhausted. The development of global legal pluralism inevitably implies increasing relations between sites of governance. In this new international context, the decision to recognise the direct effect of WTO law is best taken multilaterally or at least in conjunction with other trading partners. Short of granting direct effect, each site of governance must decide on the mechanisms and extent of the domestic effects of WTO law.

[327] The most well-known critique of this position is still that by U Everling, 'Will Europe slip on bananas? The Bananas Judgment of the Court of Justice and national courts' (1996) 33 *CML Rev* 401.

As this chapter indicates, direct effect is not the only way of creating relations between sites of governance. In the context of WTO–EC relations, it is not as good as a conjunction of clear reference, transposition and consistent interpretation. This is not to advocate a 'new legal protectionism',[328] but rather to argue in favour of an appropriate balancing of constitutional values. As Professor John Jackson has reminded us, the question of domestic treaty application is a set of policy issues, not primarily a juridical issue.[329] The effectiveness of WTO law in the EC legal order needs to be assessed on the basis of its cumulative effects, not on the basis of direct effect alone.[330] This includes basic EU constitutional principles, such as democracy, legal certainty and legal equality.[331] Such an approach recognises that the notion of direct effect is 'inherently political'.[332] Consequently, clear reference, transposition and consistent interpretation together are preferable to direct effect, and may prove nearly as effective as direct effect in integrating WTO law into EC law.[333] Their limitations are more than outweighed by their merits.

The limitations of consistent interpretation are well known. The relevant EC or national legislation must exist and be sufficiently flexible to be interpreted,[334] there must not be a manifest conflict between WTO law and the legislation to be interpreted, case-by-case interpretation cannot resolve all problems, and consistent interpretation is less effective than direct effect in establishing legal certainty and hence creating

[328] To conjoin the language of G Beber, 'Agreements concluded by the Community and their possible direct effect: From *International Fruit* to *Kupferberg*' (1983) 20 *CML Rev* 35 at 73, and D Chalmers, 'New protectionism and the European Communities—A question of constitutionality?' in B Jackson and D McGoldrick (eds), *Legal Visions of the New Europe* (London, Graham and Trotman, 1993) 259.

[329] JH Jackson, 'Direct Effect of Treaties in the US and the EU, the Case of the WTO: Some Perceptions and Proposals' in A Arnull, P Eeckhout and T Tridimas (eds), *Change and Continuity in EU Law: Essays in Honour of Sir Francis Jacobs* (Oxford, Oxford University Press, 2008), 361 at 379–80. He argues that an Act of Transformation bringing treaties into domestic law is far preferable to direct effect, including in the sense of a principle of invocability by individuals of the treaty in question. I agree with this argument. Recently, Triart has proposed the introduction of a judicial filtering mechanism. Based on the principle of complete invocability of the EC's international agreements, including the WTO Agreements, it would nevertheless permit the ECJ to suspend invocability in the case of agreements which threatened EC institutional balance, basic values or protection of fundamental rights recognised by EC law. See N Triart, *Le role de la CJCE dans les relations entre l'ordre juridique communautaire et les traits internationaux, entre préservation de l'autonomie et respect de la communauté de droit*, PhD thesis, Faculté de Droit et de Science Politique, Université Paul Cézanne Aix-Marseille III, 21 January 2009, 448–63.

[330] See also P Koutrakos, *EU International Relations Law* (Hart Publishing, Oxford, 2006) 299.

[331] See A von Bogdandy, 'Pluralism, direct effect and the ultimate say: On the relationship between international and domestic constitutional law' (2008) 6(3)–(4) *International Journal of Constitutional Law* 397.

[332] See Klabbers, above n 120, at 264.

[333] See also Griller, above n 81, at 468, who concludes that 'WTO-consistent interpretation could result in the most effective means of judicially enforcing, in the absence of specific measures of transformation, WTO law within the Community legal order'. See also Eeckhout, above n 81, who suggests (at 105) that 'the principle of implementation may well reflect some type of compromise reached within the Court'. As Alan Dashwood remarked, '[I] am beginning to wonder whether it is worth spilling so much learned ink over the WTO's direct effect. The lesson might be drawn from the International Dairy Agreement case and from *Hermès* that the duty of consistent interpretation can do pretty much the same job, while sparing the Court intellectual acrobatics': A Dashwood, *Treatment of Public International Law by European Community Law*, paper presented on 21 October 1999 at the Jean Monnet Symposium on the *Fundamental principles as inspiration and as source of law in the systems of the European Union and the WTO*, quoted in G Zonnekeyn, 'The status of WTO law in the EC legal order: The final curtain?' (2000) 34 *Journal of World Trade* 111 at 124.

[334] For example, in Case C-335/05 *Rizeni Letoveho Provozu* [2007] ECR I-4307, A-G Mengozzi (at paras 58–60) concluded that the wording of Art 2(2) of the Thirteenth Council Directive 86/560/EC on the harmonisation of VAT refunds to taxable persons not established in the Community was unambiguous so the principle of consistent interpretation did not apply.

confidence among the EU's trading partners.[335] Judicial interpretation of EC and national law in the light of WTO law is also likely to be influenced by recent developments in the ECJ's treatment of 'indirect effect' in relations between EC law and national law,[336] though in the WTO–EC context the issues are even more complex and the implications highly uncertain. But it could conceivably lead to the changes in the meaning of EC and national law in theory and practice. Consistent interpretation also has the advantage of flexibility and sensitivity to context. Indirect effect is not only a 'political filter'; it may serve as a mechanism for reinforcing the EU's democratic legitimacy.[337] It is also better suited than direct effect to the changing political, social, economic, cultural and legal contexts which are characteristic of contemporary globalisation.[338]

Recent case law suggests that use of the clear reference exception is in decline, whereas recourse to the transposition exception is on the increase. Though this may be temporary, the two exceptions differ in purpose, and recourse to them reflects changes in relations between WTO law and EC law. Clear reference, as originally conceived, is triggered by a reference, either express or implicit, to WTO law in the preamble or text of EC legislation. It represents a minimal attempt to ensure that interpretation of EC law and determination of its validity take account of WTO law. It operates in a situation of weak normative integration between the two sites. In contrast, transposition is triggered when EC law seeks to transpose WTO law, which originally meant virtually 'copy-out' transposition. It is meant to ensure that EC law is consistent with, or at least compatible with, WTO law. It signals deeper normative integration between the two sites.

If the scope of WTO law were to expand, we might expect even greater recourse to transposition, though not necessarily in 'copy-out' fashion. Deeper and more differentiated integration of the two sites is likely to result, in particular, from adopted WTO Panel and Appellate Body reports. Then we can expect a blurring in practice of the original distinction between clear reference and transposition. 'Implementation' would no longer be an exception but simply an indication that the EC/EU intends to implement WTO law in the EU legal order. With this in mind, the European courts should elaborate more clearly the bases and contours of clear reference and transposition, for example by means of an objective test based on the nature and scope of the EC measure when it does not refer expressly to WTO law.[339]

335 See N Neuwahl, 'Individuals and the GATT: Direct effect and the General Agreement on Tariffs and Trade in Community Law' in N Emiliou and D O'Keeffe (eds), *The European Union and World Trade Law After the Uruguay Round* (Chichester, John Wiley & Sons, 1996), 313 at 322–23; T Einhorn, 'The Impact of the WTO Agreement on TRIPS (Trade-related Aspects of Intellectual Property Rights) on EC Law: A challenge to regionalism' (1998) 35 *CML Rev* 1069 at 1098–99; F Berrod, 'La Cour de Justice refuse l'invocabilité des accords OMC: essai de régulation de la mondialisation—A propos de l'arrêt de la Cour de Justrice du 23 novembre 1999, *Portugal c/ Conseil* (accords textiles avec le Pakistan et l'Inde), (2000) 36(3) *Revue Trimestriel de Droit Européen* 419 at 445–49; Bontinck, above n 118.

336 See G de Búrca and P Craig (eds), *EU Law: Text, Cases, and Materials*, 2nd edn (Oxford, Oxford University Press, 1998), 198–206.

337 I borrow the notion of 'political filter' and the idea that indirect effect may serve as a mechanism for enhancing democratic legitimacy from J Trachtman, 'Bananas, Direct Effect and Compliance' (1999) 10 *European Journal of International Law* 655, esp 660, 677.

338 On the insensitivity of direct effect to different contexts, see JH Jackson, 'Status of Treaties in Domestic Legal Systems: A Policy Analysis' (1992) 86 *AJIL* 310. Cottier and Schefer argue that the consistent interpretation should be 'the prime inroad' of WTO law in national and regional law: see Cottier and Schefer, above n 80, at 89–91.

339 See also P Egli and J Kokott, 'International Decision: *Portuguese Republic v Council of the European Union*' (2000) 94 *American Journal of International Law* 740 at 744.

These means of enforcing WTO law in EC law are consistent with what appears to be emerging as the WTO's own conception of itself. This was described by a WTO Panel in terms 'not of the principle of direct effect but of the principle of indirect effect'.[340] Together with clear reference and transposition, it thus better expresses the complex 'package deal' represented by WTO law, which Montaña I Mora dubs the 'principle of equilibrium'.[341] This calls on the European legislator and executive, as well as the courts, to clarify the meaning and implications of these concepts in this new context. A major gap exists with regard to judicial articulation of the position in EC law of adopted WTO Panel and Appellate Body reports. It is likely that in the future the European courts will find it necessary to grant them greater legal effects in EC law, or at least to articulate a more coherent and convincing position than is the case now.[342] The rapidly increasing number of Panel reports will also provide European and national courts with substantial material for consistent interpretation.[343] In addition, breaches of WTO law by the Member States can be challenged within EC law, but breaches of WTO law by the EC itself cannot, except within the limited scope of the clear reference exception, the transposition exception and the principle of consistent interpretation. Hence a second gap in EC law concerns claims for compensation in cases of non-contractual liability for EC breach of its WTO law obligations. Here again, in the absence of an agreed legislative policy, the European courts should articulate a more logical, more coherent position.

The case law of the European courts concerning WTO law is a microcosm of international integration.[344] Within the constraints (and opportunities) of their judicial role, the European courts play a crucial part in balancing conflicting interests in an increasing complex configuration of overlapping fields of governance, cutting across the local, national, European, transnational and international arenas.[345] It is widely accepted that trade protectionism has redistributive effects. It is also the case that privileging free trade over other, equally—if not more—important values has equally

[340] *United States—Sections 301–310 of the Trade Act of 1974*, Report of the Panel, WT/DS152/R, 22 December 1999, para 7.78. The Panel stated that this view 'represents a GATT/WTO orthodoxy confirmed in a variety of ways over the years including panel and Appellate Body reports as well as the practice of Members' (para 7.79).

[341] M Montaña-Mora, 'Equilibrium: A rediscovered basis for the Court of Justice of the European Communities to refuse direct effect to the Uruguay Round Agreements?' (1966) 30 *Journal of World Trade* 43.

[342] It has been argued that this is a minimum requirement of the Rule of Law: see P Eeckhout, 'The domestic legal status of the WTO Agreement: Interconnecting legal systems' (1997) 34 *CML Rev* 11 at 53; M Hilf, 'The role of national courts in international trade relations' (1997) 18 *Michigan Journal of International Law* 324 at 341–42; C Schmid, *A theoretical reconstruction of WTO constitutionalism and its implications for the relationship with the EU*, EUI Working Paper No 2001/5, Department of Law, European University Institute, Florence, at 27. See also P Eeckhout, *External Relations of the European Union: Legal and Constitutional Foundations* (Oxford, Oxford University Press, 2004) 344. Zonnekeyn argues, however, that the EC should be liable in damages under Art 228 EC for failure to comply with an adopted WTO Panel or Appellate Body ruling: see G Zonnekeyn, 'The status of adopted panel and Appellate Body reports in the European Court of Justice and the Court of First Instance' (2000) 34 *Journal of World Trade* 93 at 106.

[343] See T Cottier, 'Dispute Settlement in the World Trade Organization: Characteristics and Structural Implications for the European Union' (1998) 35 *CML Rev* 325 at 369.

[344] To paraphrase Alter's conclusion about national judges in the process of European integration: see K Alter, *Establishing the Supremacy of European Law: The Making of an International Rule of Law in Europe* (Oxford, Oxford University Press, 2001), esp 231.

[345] See, eg, Case 280/93 *Germany v Council* [1994] ECR I-4973, in which the ECJ (at para 74), refusing Germany's GATT-based challenge to the EC banana regime, stated that 'such difference in treatment appears to be inherent in the objective of integrating previously compartmentalised markets, bearing in mind the different situations of the various categories of economic operators before the establishment of the common organisation of the market'.

significant, though different, redistributive effects. The rules of the WTO potentially play a constitutional role in the EU of protecting certain rights and structuring legislative and administrative decision-making, but they need to be balanced against other emerging EC constitutional values.[346] There may not necessarily be any correlation between economic policy choices, on the one hand, and institutional choices, on the other hand.[347] But the strategy of the European courts as gatekeepers is an attempt to maintain jurisdictional boundaries, a form of subsidiarity in global governance which aims to preserve the remaining shreds of the post-World War II compromise known as embedded liberalism.[348] It is entirely consistent with an overall EC strategy of multilateral governance through the coordination of international institutions in the context of global legal pluralism.

Relations between the WTO and the EC resemble continuing relations between the EC and the Member States. Naturally, there are profound differences between the objectives, means and activities of these two systems of economic and legal (and, for the EU, political) integration. As WTO law expands, the range of application of what are currently exceptions within the framework of EC law is also likely to expand. This process is likely to be less dramatic than changing relations between the EC and Member States, because the WTO is more narrow in substantive scope and likely to remain so for the foreseeable future. It is unlikely that the WTO law, though dominant in some domains, would be the source of 70 per cent of all EU law. In addition, the process is likely to occur mainly through case law, namely Panel and Appellate Body reports and judgments of the European courts, instead of through a combination of case law and legislation. For those concerned with the impact of WTO law on EC law, the Appellate Body and the European courts are therefore crucial institutions.

From another perspective, in assessing the future impact of litigation involving WTO law on EC law, it is of crucial importance to pay attention to the nature of the litigants. In other words, who uses WTO law in court? If individual litigants are mainly large companies,[349] there is a danger that it may prove increasingly difficult for the European courts, within their judicial role, to take account of other interests in European society. Further integration of WTO law into EC law may risk accentuating trends toward greater inequality of life chances and the distribution of wealth, as well as giving priority to neo-liberal globalisation over the protection of the environment and human health. The judicial techniques of clear reference, transposition and consistent interpretation help to tie the hands of courts against taking these risks, and call for the assignment of such political decision-making to other institutions, namely the EU legislator. This is a plea for a clear agreed policy on behalf of the EU Member States and the EC institutions as a whole.

Relations between the WTO and the EC have had a deep impact on EC institutions, norms and dispute resolution processes. Such relations greatly empower EC institutions,

[346] See also J Scott, 'GATT and Community law: rethinking the "regulatory gap"' in J Shaw and G More (eds), *New Legal Dynamics of the European Union* (Oxford, Clarendon Press, 1995) 147.

[347] See Hilf, above n 342, at 351.

[348] See J Ruggie, 'International Regimes, Transactions, and Change: Embedded Liberalism in the Postwar Economic Order' in SD Krasner (ed), *International Regimes* (Ithaca, Cornell University Press 1983) 195.

[349] This is reinforced by legal costs, so much so that the CFI recognised that high lawyers' fees currently reflect the complexity of cases due partly to the impact of the GATT on EC law: see Case T-115/94 *Opel Austria GmbH v Council*, Order of the CFI 15 July 1998, para 29 (application for taxation of costs following judgment in Case T-115/94 *Opel Austria v Council* [1997] ECR II-39).

notably the courts. They have already begun to reshape relations between the EC and Member States. Until recently, they did not substantially expand the normative repertoire of individuals, but this may change due to an increasing number of cases involving clear reference, transposition and consistent interpretation. Consequently, in EU constitutional terms, WTO law has contributed to institutional growth and expansion, fostered policy integration and reinforced the development of a legal culture orientated to legal pluralism in the shape of a multiplicity of sites of governance. However, so far it has contributed little to individual access to justice. Whether relations between the WTO and the EC do so in the future is subject partly to the dynamics of EU law and politics in relations between legislator, executive and judiciary, partly to the *ad hoc* nature of judicial decision-making and the cases brought before the European courts, and partly to the eventual changes in WTO law.

6

Global Legal Pluralism and the Creation of New Legal Concepts: The Concept of 'Non-market Economy' in EC Anti-dumping Law

I. Introduction

A. Legal Ideas and Legal Practice

Relations between sites of governance have frequently given rise to new legal concepts. Among numerous examples, one could refer to multiple instances of the reception of law, the creation of so-called 'customary' law during the colonial period and many instances of the imposition of law. This chapter analyses the ways in which such relations generated an international normative repertoire concerning anti-dumping law. It traces the origins and development of the concept of 'non-market economy' in WTO and EC anti-dumping law, and identifies the United States, the GATT and the European Economic Community (EEC, then European Community (EC), now EU) as important sites of governance.

'Market' and 'market economy' exercise a powerful, even magnetic, grip on our collective imagination. These two ideas are intimately related in popular discourse, politics and law. In the EU they occupy a similar, and indeed constitutional, place. Within the EU, they constitute fundamental legal principles of the internal market and competition law.[1] In EU external relations, they are also extremely significant, for example concerning international trade and anti-dumping law.[2] But what do we mean by 'market' and 'market economy'? When is an economy a 'market economy', and when is it not? Does it make sense to speak of a 'non-market economy' and, if so, what does it mean? How are the ideas of 'market economy' and 'non-market economy' related? This chapter, focusing on EC anti-dumping law, seeks to answer these questions.

The distinction between 'market economy' and 'non-market economy' is part of the received wisdom of contemporary EC anti-dumping law. It runs like a red thread through EC anti-dumping actions against China and other so-called State-trading

[1] See eg Arts 4, 14, 81, 82, 87 EC (Treaty of Nice). References in this chapter to the EC Treaty are to the consolidated version following the Treaty of Nice.

[2] See eg Arts 131, 133 EC. Until the entry into force of the Lisbon Treaty, the EC had exclusive competence in the field of anti-dumping. As a result of the Lisbon Treaty, the EU replaced the EC. This change has not had any impact on anti-dumping law, at least so far.

countries. Its significance stems from the very concept of dumping. In legal terms, dumping is based on the notion of price discrimination on two different markets.[3] To adopt anti-dumping measures, the EC authorities must make an affirmative determination that dumping exists, that it has caused injury and that the adoption of anti-dumping measures is not against the EU interest.[4] A determination of dumping consists of a comparison between the price of the product exported to the EU and the 'normal value' of the identical or like product.[5] The concept of 'normal value' is premised on the existence of a market. However, in the past (and in some rare cases today) the international economy included countries where the economy was controlled by the State, and where by definition the 'market' did not exist. How was 'normal value', or market price, to be determined for exports from such countries? This dilemma, discounting possible protectionism, posed a host of economic and legal problems. Historically, the classification of an exporting country as a 'non-market economy', rather than as a 'market economy', provided one possible solution to the dilemma. Its implications still cloud EU–China relations today.

Since 1979 the EC has initiated more than 100 anti-dumping actions against China.[6] The number has grown in conjunction with China's opening up and marketisation. In fact, the increase has tended to correspond statistically with the main periods of Chinese economic reform. Until 1998, EC anti-dumping law always treated China as a 'non-market economy'.[7] This followed from a long line of EC anti-dumping legislation.

The classification of China as a 'non-market economy' in EC anti-dumping law has two important consequences. First, as we saw in Chapter 4, the normal value of exports from China is usually calculated according to the so-called analogue or surrogate market economy method. This means that normal value (or 'fair value' in United States terminology) is not calculated on the basic of domestic information available in China concerning either prices or costs of production, because these are considered not to reflect supply and demand. Instead, normal value is established by reference to

[3] See J Viner, *Dumping: A Problem in International Trade* (Chicago, Chicago University Press, 1923) at 3; JH Jackson, 'Dumping in International Trade: Its Meaning and Context' in JH Jackson and EA Vermulst (eds), *Anti-dumping Law and Practice: A Comparative Study* (London, Harvester Wheatsheaf, 1990) 1 at 2–3. See also Case 157/87, *Electroimpex and Others v Council* [1990] ECR I- 3021. It is therefore often argued that competition law should replace anti-dumping law. See, eg, RW Bierwagen, *GATT Article VI and the Protectionist Bias in Anti-Dumping Laws* (Deventer, Kluwer, 1990); BM Hoekman and PC Mavroidis, 'Dumping, Anti-dumping and Antitrust' (1996) 30 *Journal of World Trade* 27. For a contrary view, see F Weiss, 'From World Trade Law to World Competition Law' (2000) 23 *Fordham International Law Journal* S250–S273. For the middle group, see MJ Trebilcock, 'Competition Policy and Trade Policy: Mediating the Interface' (1996) 30 *Journal of World Trade* 71.

[4] Arts 1(1), 7(1) and 9(4) Council Regulation (EC) 384/96, [1996] OJ L56/1; see also Arts 1(1), 12(1) and 15(1) of Council Regulation (EC) 2026/97, [1997] OJ L288/1.

[5] Art 1(2) and (4) Council Regulation (EC) 384/96, [1996] OJ L56/1.

[6] For two articles which together provide a survey up to 2000, see E Vermulst and F Graafsma, 'A Decade of European Community Anti-dumping Law and Practice Applicable to Imports from China' (1992) 26 *Journal of World Trade* 5; and Liu Xiang and H Vandenbussche, 'European Union Antidumping Cases against China: An Overview and Future Prospects with Respect to China's World Trade Organisation Membership' (2002) 36 6 *Journal of World Trade* 1125. See also Hu Yuanxiang, *Legal and Policy Issues of the Trade and Economic Relations between China and the EEC: A Comparative Study* (Deventer and Boston, Kluwer, 1991) 231–89. For criticisms of EC law and practice, see eg Lei Wang, 'China's Difficulties and Concerns as a Respondent to Anti-dumping Proceedings', (1996) 19 *World Competition*, 55; Jianyu Wang, 'A Critique of the Application to China of the Non-market Economy Rules of Anti-dumping Legislation and Practice of the European Union', (1999) 33(3) *Journal of World Trade*, 117–45.

[7] The 1998 reform of EC anti-dumping law allowed Chinese companies to try to prove that they operated on a market economy basis. See Council Regulation 905/98, [1998] OJ L128/18. See also F Snyder, *International Trade and Customs Law of the European Union* (London, Butterworths, 1998) 221–22.

prices and production costs in a comparable market economy third country. The sole exception occurs when, under the 1998 reforms, exporters are able to demonstrate that they meet the market economy criteria. In such cases normal value is calculated on the basis of the market price in China. Secondly, all export transactions of the same product by all exporters from China during the investigation period are considered together, and a single anti-dumping margin is calculated. This is the 'single duty rule'. Hence, a single anti-dumping duty applies to all exports of the same product from China.[8] The sole exception is the case in which an exporter is granted individual treatment. Then the dumping margin is calculated using normal value from a surrogate country but the exporter's own export prices to the EU. This usually results in a lower dumping margin, and hence lower anti-dumping duty. In legal terms, the use of an analogue country and the single duty rule follow from the fact that, until the partial legislative reform in 1998, EC anti-dumping law had always classified China as a 'non-market economy'.[9]

B. Aims and Scope of the Chapter

This chapter analyses the development of the idea of 'non-market economy' in EC anti-dumping law.[10] It focuses on two questions. First, where did this idea come from? Secondly, how have relations between legal rules and administrative discretion influenced its development? To answer the first question, the article analyses the origins, emergence and development of the EC law concept of 'non-market economy', mainly between the late 1940s and the early 1980s. This historical discussion necessarily focuses primarily on United States and EC relations with Central and Eastern Europe and the Soviet Union, but its main purpose is to shed light on the development of EC anti-dumping law about China.

With regard to the second question, the relationship between legal rules and administrative discretion has long been a crucial aspect of the normative development of EC anti-dumping law, as well as its implementation in practice. This chapter concentrates principally on the development of legal ideas; chapters 4 and 7 analyse their operation in practice. The chapter thus is a study of legal discourse. It considers the sites involved in the creation of legal ideas, the construction of a normative repertoire, the asymmetrical power relations among sites, the emergence of the concept of 'non-market economy', and some of its implications.

The chapter thus has two general objectives. On the one hand, it aims to elucidate the origins, assumptions and development of the idea of 'non-market economy' in EC anti-dumping law. Inspired by research on translingual practice, it seeks to deconstruct the binary opposition between 'market economy' and 'non-market economy' by 'pinpoint[ing] . . . those historical moments in which the usage of [these] ideas becomes contextually meaningful and acquires legitimacy in a given [legal] language'.[11] It

[8] See W Müller, N Khan and H-A Neumann, *EC Anti-dumping Law—A Commentary on Regulation 384/96* (New York, John Wiley & Sons, 1998) at 152; Snyder, above n 7, at 219, 228.

[9] See Council Regulation 905/98, [1998] OJ L128/18.

[10] See M Foucault, *The Archaeology of Knowledge* (trans AM Sheridan Smith) (London, Routledge, 1972).

[11] LH Liu, *Translingual Practice: Literature, National Culture and Translated Modernity—China, 1900–1937* (Stanford, Stanford University Press, 1995) at xviii.

concentrates mainly on three institutional and normative sites, the United States, the GATT and the EC. This is not, however, a matter simply of 'travelling theory', in the sense of 'a cultural or literary practice that emphasises creative borrowing, appropriation, and the movement of ideas from place to place in an international environment'.[12] Instead, while paying close attention to the sources and circulation of legal ideas, and to the economic and other assumptions underlying them, the chapter it presumes that

> power and knowledge directly imply one another; that there is no power relation without the correlative constitution of a field of knowledge, nor any knowledge that does not presuppose and constitute at the same time power relations . . .[13]

It is based on the assumption that we can grasp the significance of legal ideas and legal discourse best if we understand the assumptions and power relationships that underlie them, shape their development and inform the way they are used in practice.[14] We can thus understand how new legal concepts can result from relations between sites of governance.

On the other hand, the chapter seeks to contribute to the reform of EC anti-dumping law. The concept of 'non-market economy' has had—and continues to have—significant negative consequences for international trade relations between the EU and China. Increasingly, its costs outweigh any benefits. At best it is misleading, and at worst it is a serious obstacle to any real understanding of how best to manage the developing trade relations between the EU and China. We need different analytical tools, especially now that China is a member of the WTO. To find them, we need to escape the conceptual straitjacket imposed by path dependence on outdated paradigms. A new way of thinking must take account of legitimate concerns underlying anti-dumping law, notably unemployment and its social consequences. But it should also be based on common interests and mutual respect, and focused on the harmonious management of trade relations. This in turn requires an understanding of the historical development of the legal concept of 'non-market economy' and the conceptual framework of which it is a part. This chapter is designed to provide a foundation for this task. It thus examines the old to build the new.

C. Argument and Organisation

At first glance the ideas of 'market economy' and 'non-market economy' might seem to be opposites. A 'non-market economy' may appear to be merely the negative side of the market economy coin. Often the distinction between them is used in a dichotomous legal logic with this implication. Yet a moment's reflection tells us that, in reality, things are not so simple. The commonplace distinction between 'market economy' and 'non-

[12] The quotation is from Liu, *ibid*, at 20. It refers to the work of Edward Said, who developed the idea of 'travelling theory': see E Said, *The World, the Text and the Critic* (Cambridge, Mass, Harvard University Press, 1983) at 226–27. See also LH Liu, 'Translingual Practice: The Discourse of Individualism between China and the West' (1993) 1 *Positions* 160.

[13] M Foucault, *Discipline and Punish: The Birth of the Prison* (trans A Sheridan) (London, Penguin Books, 1979) at 27.

[14] See F Snyder, *New Directions in European Community Law* (Cambridge, Cambridge University Press, 1990).

market economy' in EC anti-dumping law gives rise to fundamental questions. For one thing, if the distinction between 'market economy' is based on the presence or absence of State intervention in the economy, it simply does not make historical or contemporary sense. For another, many social scientists and other observers tell us that there are different types of market economies. If this is the case, it follows that it is unlikely that 'non-market economy' would be a uniform category or set of categories. It is also very improbable that 'non-market economy' could be merely a mirror image of 'market economy'.[15] A more basic question is whether 'non-market economy' means simply that certain essential features of a 'market economy' are absent, or whether on the contrary a 'non-market economy' has its own distinctive, even positive, features. Lastly, even if we define 'non-market economy' by reference to a 'market economy', the relation between them may not be simply one of negation or opposition. In sum, the distinction between 'market economy' and 'non-market economy' needs to be historically unpacked and conceptually deconstructed. Once the elements of this conceptual repertoire are displayed, we can understand the real social meaning of these legal concepts.

This chapter argues that the legal concept of 'non-market economy' in EC anti-dumping law was socially constructed, by means of relations among a plurality of institutional and normative sites, as part of a changing configuration of legal ideas in specific historical circumstances, and in contexts of political, economic, social and symbolic power.

This argument is articulated in two main sections. Each section pays close attention to legal texts in order to trace the emergence of the idea of 'non-market economy'. Section II. traces the origins and circulation of an international anti-dumping law repertoire from the early 20th century to the early1970s. It gives special emphasis to early anti-dumping legislation, notably in the United States, the foundation of the GATT in the late 1940s, the American origins of the anti-dumping provisions in Article VI GATT and the crucial interpretative role of a GATT Working Party in the mid-1950s. It argues that, while drawing on earlier elements, the concept of 'non-market economy' in EC anti-dumping law had its origins in the early period of the Cold War. It also examines the crystallisation of certain basic elements of the anti-dumping law repertoire during the 1960s. It considers the reports of early 1960s GATT experts, the normative innovations of the US Treasury Department, the Kennedy Round Anti-dumping Code, the role of GATT Working Parties in the late 1960s and early 1970s, and the hesitant establishment of the EC's common commercial policy, including anti-dumping. It argues that the GATT multilateral negotiating rounds began during this period to define more specific international rules of the game, but a variety of more localised processes played an essential role as forces of change. Of special importance were, first, the tension between legislative rules and administrative discretion in the United States, and, secondly, the Europeanisation of foreign trade law in the course of European integration.

Section III. focuses on the birth of the EC law concept of 'non-market economy' during the 1970s recession. It discusses the tug-of-war between US executive and legislature on anti-dumping law, the elaboration of the EC's common commercial

[15] Consider two very different examples: the Casamance area of Senegal until the mid-20th century and the People's Republic of China until at least the mid-1980s. On the former, see FG Snyder, *Capitalism and Legal Change: An African Transformation* (New York, Academic Press, 1981); on the latter, see eg NR Lardy, *Foreign Trade and Economic Reform in China, 1978–1990* (Cambridge, Cambridge University Press, 1992).

policy, including a distinctive regime for China, the Tokyo Round Anti-dumping and Subsidies Codes, the US Trade Agreements Act of 1979, the EC's innovative but protectionist 1979 anti-dumping legislation, the post-Tokyo Round legislative consolidation and the implications for the exercise of administrative discretion. It argues that the main factors in the creation of the concept of 'non-market economy' in EC anti-dumping law were changes in the international anti-dumping repertoire, specific ideas in Europe about comparative economic systems, and the perceived emergence of new economic threats.

A conclusion in section IV. summarises the detailed argument and its implications.

II. The Anti-dumping Law Repertoire: Origins and Circulation

A. Roots in the Cold War

1. Sites of Global Legal Pluralism

The concept of 'non-market economy' in EC anti-dumping law developed partly through relations among different sites in a world of global legal pluralism. To recap, by 'global legal pluralism', I mean the totality of strategically determined, situationally specific and open episodic conjunctions of a multiplicity of sites throughout the world. The most important sites were the United States, the GATT, the EC, the Soviet bloc of Central and Eastern European countries (with the Soviet Union in the background), and China. Each site has both structural aspects and relational aspects. The structural aspects refer to institutions, norms and dispute resolution processes.[16] The relational aspects of sites refer to the different types of relations that the sites have with each other.[17] The formation of the concept of 'non-market economy' involved both structural features of individual sites as well as the relations between different sites.

Global legal pluralism is a useful frame within which to develop a pluralistic, historical and contextual analysis. From the legal standpoint, the GATT is the normative basis of contemporary EC anti-dumping law. But if our purpose is to understand the origins of the concept of 'non-market economy' in EC anti-dumping law, it is not sufficient simply to trace a straight line directly from GATT law to EC law. In the origins of legal concepts, legal doctrine is often—if not usually—less important than economics or politics, while logic is frequently subservient to or deployed instrumentally by power. Not only is the historical picture thus much more complex than straightforward

[16] Examples of institutional features are the separation of powers between executive and legislature in the United States, the division of competences between the EC and its Member States, the functional separation of powers between Commission, Council, European Parliament and the European courts in the EC, and the capacity of institutions such as the GATT to produce legally binding norms. Normative features refer, eg, to the presence within a site of norms from different sources, the extent to which such norms have legal force, and whether or not they are organised by means of a doctrine of precedent or *jurisprudence constante*. Dispute resolution processes may include settlement by the parties, conciliation or mediation, arbitration and adjudication.

[17] For example, as shown in other chapters of the book, such relations may be hierarchical or egalitarian, competitive or cooperative, or involve mutual awareness, neglect or ignorance, or divergence or convergence of institutions, norms or dispute resolution processes.

transplantation or borrowing. The origins of the EC law concept are also both more diffuse and more political than might appear at first sight. The anti-dumping provisions of the GATT were elaborated in a kind of continuing conversation between the GATT signatories, based on asymmetric power relations, with the United States playing the dominant role, and vis-à-vis (and sometimes involving) other countries. From the 1960s onwards, the EC was a *de facto* party to this conversation. All these voices, sometimes in cooperation, sometimes in competition, had a profound influence on the evolution of EC anti-dumping law.

2. *Foundations of Modern Anti-dumping Law*

The first modern anti-dumping legislation was enacted in Canada in 1904, largely to satisfy manufacturers' demands for protection without increasing tariffs and thus antagonising farmers, though it appears that similar practices were used in the absence of legislation in the late 19th century. As slightly redrafted in 1907, the Canadian legislation provided for the imposition of a special (anti-dumping) duty when

> the export or actual selling price to an importer in Canada is less than the fair market value of the same article when sold for home consumption in the usual and ordinary course in the country whence exported to Canada . . .[18]

Anti-dumping legislation was enacted in New Zealand in 1905 and Australia in 1906. In 1914 South Africa followed the early Canadian model. A broadly similar measure, providing that normal value should be determined on the basis of the price of the product in the exporting country, was proposed in France in 1908. However, this was rejected by the Government, partly because of the practical difficulty of determining normal value in this way.[19] A Japanese law of 1920 imposed additional duties on foreign goods sold in Japan at unreasonably low prices.[20]

In the United States, the Sherman Antitrust Act of 1890 did not clearly apply to anti-dumping, but the Wilson Tariff Act 1894 (§73, Tariff Act of 1894) applied to predatory pricing in certain circumstances. The first US anti-dumping act was the 1916 Anti-dumping Act, known officially as 'Section 801 of the Revenue Act of 1916'.[21] It was basically an antitrust statute, which extended the 1914 Clayton Act provisions on price discrimination to foreign trade.[22] It targeted intentional predatory dumping, defined as systematic selling of goods in the US market at

> a price substantially less than the actual market value of such articles at the time of exportation to the United States in the principal markets of the country of production or of other foreign countries to which they were commonly exported . . .[23]

[18] Viner, above n 3, at 193.

[19] *Ibid*, at 204–15.

[20] *Ibid*, at 274.

[21] Act of Sept 8, 1916, ch 463, §801, 39 Stat 798 (1916), § 801; see JH Jackson, *World Trade and the Law of GATT* (New York, Bobbs-Merrill, 1969), 403, fn 4. See also PM Richards, *Political Primacy in Economic Laws: A Comparison of British and American Anti-dumping Legislation, 1921*, Working Paper No 13/93, Department of Economic History, London School of Economics, July 1993, at 4.

[22] See JJ Barceló, 'A History of GATT Unfair Trade Remedy Law—Confusion of Purposes' (1991) 14 *The World Economy* 311 at 314.

[23] Viner, above n 3, at 243.

Previous anti-dumping legislation referred only to market prices in the country of exportation. This 1916 US statute introduced another comparator, namely, the price of a product on the market of other countries to which it was exported. Like the earlier tests, however, this assumed the existence of a price system in the country of exportation.[24]

After World War I, anti-dumping legislation was targeted mainly at German firms, particularly because of alleged predatory pricing before the War and so-called 'economic aggression during the War.[25] In 1921, Canada amended its anti-dumping law. This changed the definition of 'fair market value' by adding the provision that 'the value of the duty of new or unused goods shall in no case be less than the actual cost of production of similar goods at date of shipment to Canada'.[26] In 1921 Newfoundland enacted legislation similar to the Canadian law. The United Kingdom 1921 Anti-dumping Law rejected the use of domestic price for determining normal value and instead adopted a statutorily defined cost of production.[27] Viner noted, however, that the expression 'cost of production' was used in this case mainly for political reasons.[28] In contrast, the Australian 1921 Anti-dumping Act used the term 'reasonable selling price', defined to refer to either the fair market value or the cost of production plus 5 per cent.[29] However, New Zealand in 1921 enacted legislation similar to the 1921 Canadian law.[30]

The 1921 Canadian law was the model for the US 1921 Anti-dumping Act (Title II of the Emergency Tariff Act 1921).[31] Under the 1916 US Act, petitioners were required to prove that the foreign company intentionally dumped its products. The 1921 Act was adopted to cure this procedural defect and facilitate complaints.[32] The purpose of both statutes was ostensibly to control predatory dumping, not all price

[24] On the 1916 Act, see MA Neville, 'The Anti-dumping Act of 1916: A War-Time Legacy' (1981) 26 *New York Law School Law Review* 535; JL Kessler, 'The Anti-dumping Act of 1916: Antitrust Analogue or Anathema?' 35th Annual Meeting, Section of Antitrust Law, American Bar Association, San Francisco, California, 10–12 August 1987, in (1987) 56 *Antitrust Law Journal* 485. However conceived, the 1916 Act is nevertheless within the scope of application of Art VI GATT: see *United States— Anti-Dumping Act of 1916*, Report of the Appellate Body (AB-200-5, AB-2000-6), WTO, WT/DS136/AB/R, WT/DS162/AB/R, 20 August 2000. For the European Commission's analysis, see European Commission, 'Report to the Committee established under Article 7 of Council Regulation (EC) No 3286/94 (The "Trade Barriers Regulation")—Trade Barriers Regulation Examination Procedure concerning the United States Anti-dumping Act of 1916' (non-confidential version of the report transmitted to the Member States on 17.10.97), DGIE3/EMD(97), Brussels, 7 May 1998.

[25] For an assessment of these claims, see AO Hirshmann, *National Power and the Structure of Foreign Trade* (Berkeley, University of California Press, 1945, expanded edn 1980), 53–70.

[26] Viner, above n 3, at 199.

[27] The UK legislation defined the cost of production as the current sterling equivalent of 95% of the wholesale price charged at the factory to purchasers for domestic consumption less taxes: see *ibid*, at 219.

[28] 'In reality, however, the Act has nothing to do with the cost of production and is directed against imports sold in the United Kingdom at prices below the foreign market price by more than 5 per cent, regardless of whether these prices are below the cost of production': *ibid*, at 222.

[29] *Ibid*, at 229.

[30] *Ibid*, at 231–34.

[31] The 1916 and 1921 statutes are compared in Congress of the United States, Congressional Budget Office, *How the GATT Affects US Anti-dumping and Countervailing Duty Policy*, at 21 (Washington, DC, Congressional Budget Office, September 1994); see also JJ Barceló III, 'A History of GATT Unfair Trade Remedy Law—Confusion of Purposes' (1991) 14 *The World Economy* 311 at 314.

[32] See R Dale, *Anti-dumping Law in a Liberal Trade Order* (London, Macmillan for the Trade Policy Research Centre, 1980) at 12; RH Lantz, 'The Search for Consistency: Treatment of Nonmarket Economies in Transition under United States Anti-dumping and Countervailing Duty Laws' (1995) 10 *American University Journal of International Law and Policy* 993 at 999–1000; Raj Bhala, *International Trade Law: Cases and Materials* (Charlottesville, Va, Michie Law Publishers, 1996) 683–84.

discrimination.[33] The 1921 US Act provided for the imposition of a special anti-dumping duty 'if the purchase price or the exporter's sales price is less than the foreign market value (or, in the absence of such value, than the cost of production)'.[34] It defined 'foreign market value' as

> the price at which such or similar merchandise is sold or freely offered for sale . . . for home consumption (or, if not so sold or offered for home consumption, then for exportation to countries other than the United States . . .[35]

All together, this articulated three different tests:

a) the price on the domestic market of the exporting country;
b) the price for exportation to other countries, not including the importing country (the US); and
c) the cost of production.

The first two tests followed the 1916 US Act, while the third was new. However, all three assumed that the exporting country had a market-based price system.

By the mid-1920s, therefore, certain basic tests for determining normal value in anti-dumping actions had already been established. They included:

a) price on the home market of the country of exportation;
b) price of the product when exported to other countries; and
c) cost of production in the country of exportation.

Not all of the countries that had anti-dumping laws by that time used all three elements, though by 1921 all were part of United States law. Nevertheless, all of them were based on the assumption that the country of exportation had a market-based price system, in other words that it was a market economy. The US 1930 Tariff Act as originally enacted made the same assumption. It did not provide expressly for non-market economy countries, either in these terms or even in terms such as 'State-controlled economy' or 'controlled economy country'.[36]

All these anti-dumping laws raised difficult issues about the scope of administrative discretion in the management of foreign trade, though details varied according to specific domestic structures.[37] Writing in 1923, Viner, the world's leading anti-dumping authority at the time, pinpointed the determination of foreign market values as the main problem in the administration of anti-dumping laws.[38] He considered that the determination of foreign costs of production posed 'almost insuperable' administrative problems.[39] In his opinion:

[33] See JE Pattison, *Anti-dumping and Countervailing Duty Laws*, International Business and Law Series, vol 3 (New York, Clark Boardman Company Ltd, 1984) at §103[2], 1-8–1-10, esp at 1-9, n 10. For a contrary view, see Barceló, above n 31, at 314–15. On the 1921 Act, see PM Richards, *Political Primacy in Economic Laws: A Comparison of British and American Anti-dumping Legislation, 1921*, Working Paper No 13/93, Department of Economic History, London School of Economics, July 1993.

[34] Anti-dumping Act, 1921, §202(a), Title II, Chap 14, Sixty-Seventh Congress, Sess I, 1921. See also Viner, above n 3, at 258–65.

[35] Anti-dumping Act, 1921, §205, Title II, Chap 14, Sixty-Seventh Congress, Sess I, 1921. 'Cost of production' was defined in §206 of the Act.

[36] DL Cuneo and CB Manuel, Jr, 'Roadblock to Trade: The State-controlled Economy Issue in Anti-dumping Law Administration' (1982) 5 *Fordham International Law Journal* 277 at 290.

[37] On Canada and the US, see Viner, above n 3, at 200.

[38] *Ibid*, at 266.

[39] *Ibid*, at 292.

> [t]he development of comprehensive tariff legislation dependent upon the accurate determination of costs of production, whether foreign or domestic, for its administration is a dream incapable of even partial realization . . .[40]

3. *The GATT and Article VI GATT*

These ideas informed post-World War II discussions about anti-dumping law. Following the work of US interdepartmental committees between 1943 and 1945, the United States in 1946 made the initial proposals for the creation of an International Trade Organisation (ITO).[41] The 'Suggested Charter for an International Trade Organisation' that was proposed by the United States contained a section on State-trading, including an article on 'Expansion of Trade by Complete State Monopolies of Export Trade'.[42] The US proposed that countries with a State monopoly of foreign trade should undertake to import an agreed amount, over a specified period, from other ITO members, without any reciprocal undertaking on the part of the non State-trading countries except for tariff concessions.[43] This was based on the 1935 US bilateral trade agreement with the Soviet Union.[44] The US was the leader in 1946–47 in the negotiation and agreement of the GATT, and the political and intellectual origins of the GATT also lay in the United States.[45] When the ITO failed to see the light of day, the GATT began to be applied provisionally on 1 January 1948.[46]

The Cold War following World War II divided the world between two big powers, the United States and the Soviet Union.[47] In this bipolar world, the Soviet bloc included the so-called State-trading countries, then mainly in Central and Eastern Europe.[48] Czechoslovakia, Poland and Yugoslavia were then not State-trading countries. But the

[40] *Ibid*, at 293.

[41] 'From the first, the ITO was primarily an American idea': W Diebold, 'The End of the ITO', *Essays in International Finance*, No 16, October 1952 (Princeton, NJ, Princeton University, International Finance Section, Department of Economics and Social Institutions), at 2. This is reiterated by JS Odell, *Negotiating the World Economy* (Ithaca, Cornell University Press, 2001) 162.

[42] A Polouektov, 'Non-market Economy Issues in the WTO Anti-dumping Law and Accession Negotiations: Revival of a Two-tier Membership' (2002) 36(1) *Journal of World Trade* 1 at 5–6.

[43] J Viner, 'Conflicts of Principle in Drafting a Trade Charter' (1947) 25 *Foreign Affairs* 612 at 624, who states that 'this limitation . . . may perhaps largely explain the apparent coldness of Soviet Russia to the original American proposals'.

[44] Polouektov, above n 42, at 6.

[45] See J Goldstein, 'Creating the GATT Rules: Politics, Institutions, and American Policy' in J Ruggie (ed), *Multilateralism Matters: The Theory and Praxis of an Institutional Form* (New York, Columbia University Press, 1993) 201. On the post-World War II regimes as the internationalisation of the US liberal conceptions, essentially a projection of the US domestic regulatory system onto the world, see AM Burley-Slaughter, 'Regulating the World: Multilateralism, International Law, and the Projection of the New Deal Regulatory State' in Ruggie, *ibid*, at 125. See also JA Finlayson and MW Zacher, 'The GATT and the Regulation of Trade Barriers: Regime Dynamics and Functions' in SD Krasner (ed), *International Regimes* (Ithaca, Cornell University Press, 1983) 273.

[46] See *GATT Analytical Index: Guide to GATT Law and Practice*, updated 6th edn, vol 1 (Geneva, WTO; Lanham, Md, Bernan Press, 1995) 3–6.

[47] For a survey of the period, see JPD Dunbabin, *The Cold War: The Great Powers and Their Allies* (London and New York, Longman, 1994).

[48] For a detailed analysis of relations between the Eastern European countries and the GATT from 1945 to the late 1970s, see MM Kostecki, *East–West Trade and the GATT System* (St Martin's Press New York, for the Trade Policy Research Centre, London, 1978). For the subsequent period, see the articles by John Maslen in *The Yearbook of European Law* reviewing the EC's relations with the State-trading countries of Europe.

Soviet Union declined to participate in the 1946 London Conference, the Havana Conference, and the Geneva negotiations that led to the ill-fated ITO Charter and the GATT. More generally, the US and the Soviet Union held very different concepts of international trade organisation and had different geopolitical interests. This 'rendered impossible any constructive discussion of the place of state-trading monopolies in the multilateral trading system'.[49]

The main concerns of the US at the time were the gradual reduction of trade barriers and non-discrimination. This did not necessarily mean completely free trade. In 1947, Jacob Viner wrote that 'there are few free traders in the present-day world, no one pays any attention to their views, and no person in authority anywhere advocates free trade'.[50] With all due respect, one might therefore be surprised to read in late 20th-century works that the GATT 'is based on principles of free trade in free markets'.[51] Or that GATT is often described as presuming 'the existence of free and open markets where prices are determined by supply and demand under normal competitive conditions.'[52] What is clear is that the GATT assumed 'essentially private-enterprise economies'.[53] Its founders considered State trading to be an aberration, and they presumed that GATT members would not practise State trading on any significant scale. GATT rules in such matters 'were drafted essentially with state trading by *market* economies in mind'.[54]

Consistently with this standpoint, the basic rationale of the GATT was viewed as being to 'de-politicise' international trade by removing politics from economics. It was simply assumed that these could be distinguished as separate spheres, or, more fundamentally, that a capitalist market economy was essentially apolitical, not in the sense that macroeconomic management and industrial structure had no implications for political power, or vice versa, but rather in the sense that the economy was best left in the hands of private enterprise and removed as much as possible from the reach of the State. The anti-dumping provisions of the GATT must be seen in this light.[55]

The United States proposals for an ITO charter included a draft article on anti-dumping law. The 1921 US Anti-dumping Act,[56] though subsequently amended in part by the Tariff Act of 1930, served as the basis for the draft. Following revision, this became the framework of the eventual Article VI GATT 1947.[57] Commentators agree that the US Anti-dumping Act of 1921 was the basis for Article VI GATT 1947,[58] but this was as much in a political and an institutional sense as in an intellectual sense,

[49] Kostecki, above n 48, at 2, see also at 3–9.

[50] Viner, above n 43, at 613.

[51] JH Jackson, WJ Davey and AO Sykes, *Legal Problems of International Economic Relations*, 3rd edn (St Paul, Minn, West Publishing Co, 1995), 1140. See also JH Jackson, 'State Trading and Nonmarket Economies' (1989) 23 *The International Lawyer* 891.

[52] JF Beseler and AN Williams, *Anti-dumping and Anti-subsidy Law: The European Communities* (London, Sweet & Maxwell, 1986) 64.

[53] Kostecki, above n 48, at 35.

[54] EM Ianni, 'The International Treatment of State Trading' (1982) 16(6) *Journal of World Trade Law* 480 at 487 (emphasis in original]).The quotation is taken by Ianni from VS Muhammed, *The Legal Framework of World Trade* (London, Stevens for the London Institute of World Affairs,1958) at 227 (emphasis added by Ianni).

[55] Here we are not concerned with whether these assumptions corresponded to the real world.

[56] 42 Stat 11 (1921), as amended, 129 USC §§160–173 (1964).

[57] See JH Jackson, *World Trade and the Law of GATT* (New York, Bobbs-Merrill, 1969) 403–06; TP Stewart (ed), *The GATT Uruguay Round: A Negotiating History (1986–1992)*, vol II, 1390–1410 (Deventer and Boston, Kluwer, 1993). See also *GATT Analytical Index*, above n 46, at 255.

[58] See Richards, above n 33, at 41. 'With respect to the United States, commercial policy regarding dumping is in substantial agreement with the GATT Code, partly because Article VI was based on the American

because the 1921 US Act itself drew on previous and concurrent elements of the international anti-dumping repertoire.

Article VI GATT provided for the imposition of anti-dumping and countervailing duties.[59] It defined 'dumping' as the introduction of products of one country into the commerce of another country at less than the normal value of the products. In the terms of the Article,

> a product is to be considered as being introduced into the commerce of an importing country at less than its normal value, if the price of the product exported from one country to another
>
> (a) is less than the comparable price, in the ordinary course of trade, for the like product
>
> when destined for consumption in the exporting country, or,
>
> (b) in the absence of such domestic price, is less than either
>
> (i) the highest comparable price for the like product for export to any third country in the ordinary course of trade, or
> (ii) the cost of production of the product in the country of origin plus a reasonable addition for selling cost and profit.[60]

These three comparators for determining normal value all presumed, as already noted, that the country of exportation had market prices and a market economy.

4. *The 1955 Interpretative Note*

With the benefit of hindsight, it might be thought that, all other things being equal, the general formula contained in Article VI(1)(b) GATT would have been sufficient to deal with the issue of price comparability in countries that did not fit into the economic pattern conceived on the basis of the original core signatories of the GATT.[61] The

Anti-dumping Act, partly because the negotiators of the Code tried to avoid conflicts with the Act, and partly because of adjustments in Treasury Department policy since 1967': WA Wares, *The Theory and Practice of American Commercial Policy* (Lexington, Mass, Lexington Books, 1977) at 2. See also JA Laroski, Jr, 'NMEs: A Love Story—Nonmarket and Market Economy Status under US Anti-dumping Law' (1999) 30 *Law and Policy in International Business* 369 at 373: 'The 1921 Act, moreover, served as the basis for Article VI of the General Agreement on Tariffs and Trade (GATT)' (citing Staff of House Comm on Ways and Means, 105th Cong 1st Session, *Overview and Compilation of US Trade Statutes* (Comm Print 1997) at 66').

[59] See GATT 1947, Art VI Anti-dumping and Countervailing Duties, in WTO, *The Results of the Uruguay Round of Multilateral Trade Negotiations: The Legal Texts* (Geneva, WTO, 1995) 493.

[60] Art VI(1) GATT 1947.

[61] Two examples of State-trading countries are relevant, though not determinative. First, in *Swedish Anti-dumping Duties*, the Panel 'was of the opinion that if the Swedish authorities considered that it was not possible to find "a comparable price in the ordinary course of trade for the like product when destined for consumption in the exporting country", no provision in the General Agreement would prevent them from using one of the other two criteria laid down in Article VI': see *Swedish Anti-dumping Duties*, Report adopted on 26 February 1955, para 28, BISD 3S/81; also in P Pescatore, WJ Davey and A Lowenfeld (eds), *Handbook of GATT Dispute Settlement*, vol 2, at 51 (DD14/1); see also *GATT, Analytical Index of the General Agreement (Revised)* (Geneva, The Contracting Parties to the GATT, April 1959) at 32. Secondly, in 1975 the United States representative on the Committee on Anti-dumping Practices 'recalled that the [Kennedy Round] Anti-dumping Code authorized the use of either method [the use of production cost information or third market export prices] if there was no domestic market sales': Seventh Report by the Committee on Anti-dumping Practices adopted on 21 November 1975 (L/4241), GATT, BISD, 22nd Supplement (Geneva, February 1976) 21 at 23.

pattern itself was admitted to be flexible.[62] For example, Article VI GATT did not prohibit the use of domestic prices from any exporting countries; subparagraph (b)(i) did not require that the export price be that from the country of origin; and subparagraph (b)(ii) did not close off the option of using cost of production in specific countries of origin. But all other things were not equal. Politics, as well as economics, influenced the selection and deployment of elements from the existing legal repertoire, and the later formation of new legal concepts.[63]

In 1949 the Coordinating Committee for Multilateral Export Controls (COCOM) was established to restrict the supply to the Soviet Union and its allies of goods and technology that could be converted to military use. Early in the McCarthy era, the United States Congress in 1951 enacted a law that required the United States to withdraw most-favoured-nation (MFN) status from all countries dominated or controlled by the world Communist movement. This presaged subsequent US legislation in 1962 requiring that MFN status be denied to all countries controlled or dominated by Communism.[64]

As seen from the United States and Western Europe, the fact that most of the then Communist countries were not members of GATT had two implications. On the one hand, they were not bound by GATT rules. On the other hand, they as outsiders were less likely to abide by them.[65] In these countries, the price mechanism did not operate as it was assumed to do in liberal, competitive market economy countries. Prices were not determined by the interaction of supply and demand. Foreign trade was determined mainly by the State plan. The currencies of these countries were usually not convertible.[66] Consequently, during the early 1950s the GATT Contracting Parties considered that the conception of dumping expressed in Article VI GATT did not apply to Soviet bloc countries. This political setting placed a premium on administrative discretion.[67] It also presaged that fact that, in addition to its technical legal and economic elements, the concept of 'non-market economy' in anti-dumping law has always embodied a significant component of high politics.

[62] The US draft charter for the ITO had included an article on the expansion of trade by any member country with a complete or substantially complete monopoly of its import trade. The article was subsequently deleted. However, the report from the 1947 Geneva Conference stated that the revised text was sufficiently flexible to allow negotiations with such countries. See *GATT Analytical Index*, above n 46, at 478.

[63] Describing US policy towards China before the early 1980s, Ianni wrote that 'the bias of economic theory against state trading and the United States' ideological opposition to communism converged in a foreign trade policy which rejected state trading': Ianni, above n 54, at 493.

[64] The legislation in question was Pub L No 49, CH 139, §5, 65 Stat 73(1951) and the Trade Expansion Act of 1962, Pub L No 87-794, §231, 76 Stat 876 (1962), both cited in Jackson *et al*, above n 51, at 1156.

[65] J Wilcynski, 'Dumping and Central Planning' (1996) 74 *Political Economy* 250 at 261. See however SS Brown, 'The People's Republic of China and the US Unfair Trade Laws' (1988) 22 *Journal of World Trade* 79 (arguing that as of 1988 there was no empirical evidence that central planning (or other factors) caused China's apparel export prices to be generally lower than those of market economies).

[66] Ianni summarises the conventional wisdom (of the time) as follows: 'There are usually four basic differences between a "non-market economy" (particularly a "centrally planned economy") and a "market economy." Unlike the latter, the former usually involves: (1) a national economic plan of the state which determines resource allocation; (2) the determination of imports and exports by national economic planning; (3) the state's fixing domestic prices which therefore do not fluctuate freely in response to supply and demand; and (4) nonconvertible currencies which may neither be transferred outside the country nor freely converted into any Western currency': Ianni, above n 54, at 482, fn 18, referring to K Dam, *The GATT—Law and International Economic Organization* (Chicago, University of Chicago Press, 1970) at 318 and Comptroller General, US General Accounting Office, Report to Congress: *US Laws and Regulations Applicable to Imports from Nonmarket Economies Could be Improved* (1981) at 2.

[67] I am grateful to Stephen Krasner for this point.

The question of how to ensure price comparability concerning exports from State-trading countries came prominently to the fore in the mid-1950s. This was mainly because of the increasing trade between Eastern European countries, on the one hand, and Western European countries and the United States, on the other hand.[68] The issue of how imports from Eastern European countries should be dealt with in the GATT seems to have been raised first by Czechoslovakia. The country was a market economy when the GATT was drafted, and its later incorporation into the Soviet bloc did not affect its status as a GATT member.

Each year the GATT held a Review Session. In the 1954–55 Review Session, Czechoslovakia proposed to the Review Working Party on 'Other Barriers to Trade' that subparagraph 1(b) of Article VI GATT be amended

> to deal with the special problem of finding comparable prices for the application of that subparagraph to the case of a country all, or substantially all, of whose trade was operated by a state monopoly. The Working Party was not prepared to recommend the amendment of this Article in this respect, but agreed to an interpretative note to meet the case.[69]

This solution was undoubtedly a compromise between different views, though it is also likely that the US voice carried the most weight. This was consistent with the regular practice of GATT working parties at the time. Even in 1979, it was officially reported, with regard to GATT working parties, that 'Since the tendency is to strive for consensus, there is generally some measure of negotiation and compromise in the formulation of the Working Party's report'.[70]

The 1955 Interpretative Note stated that:

> It is recognised that, in the case of imports from a country which has a complete or substantially complete monopoly of its trade and all domestic prices are fixed by the State, special difficulties may exist in determining price comparability for the purposes of paragraph I, and in such cases importing contracting parties may find it necessary to take into account the possibility that a strict comparison with domestic prices in such a country may not always be appropriate.[71]

This Note contained two parts: a definition of a State-controlled economy; and a prescription to GATT contracting parties that they could deviate from the terms of Article VI GATT. The first part constituted a pre-condition for the legal consequences contained in the second part. It is possible, though not certain, that this simply put in formal legal terms what some anti-dumping authorities were already doing in practice,

[68] See Kostecki, above n 48, at 10–11. The 1959 Declaration on relations between the GATT contracting parties and Poland stimulated increased trade, and also encouraged further discussions on how to manage the expanding trade relations: see 'Reports Adopted by the Contracting Parties, Accession, Special Relations, Etc, Relations with Poland, Report on First Annual Review,' adopted on 7 November 1962 (L/1785), in *General Agreement on Tariffs and Trade, Basic Instruments and Selected Documents*, Eleventh Supplement (Decisions, Reports, etc, of the Twentieth Session) (Geneva, The Contracting Parties to the GATT, March 1963) 72 at 73. On Russia and China, see Cheng Yuan, *East–West Trade: Changing Patterns in Chinese Foreign Trade Law and Institutions* (New York, Oceana, 1991) 1–72.

[69] GATT Working Party on 'Other Barriers to Trade', Document L/334, adopted 3 March 1955, 3S/222, 223 para 6; see also proposals at W.9/86, Spec/93/55; both cited in *GATT Analytical Index*, above n 46, at 228.

[70] Annex to the Understanding Regarding Notification, Consultation, Dispute Settlement and Surveillance, para 6 (adopted 28 November 1979), quoted in *GATT Analytical Index*, above n 46, vol 2, at 1111.

[71] Second Supplementary Provision to para 1 of Art VI in Annex I to GATT 1947, in WTO, *The Results of the Uruguay Round of Multilateral Trade Negotiations: The Legal Texts* (Geneva, WTO, 1995) 545–46 (emphasis added); GATT BID 1978–1979 Suppl Anti-dumping Code, 71; *GATT Analytical Index*, above n 46, at 221.

even though it is open to question whether most of the exporting countries really met these strict criteria. It is unlikely, however, that its authors suspected that this would open a veritable Pandora's box with regard to non-market economy dumping and remain a significant part of GATT law for more than 50 years.

What was (and is) the legal status of the 1955 Interpretative Note? The GATT was then a basically diplomatic organisation. Its most inclusive institution at the time was the Intersessional Committee; the Council of Representatives was not established until 1960.[72] Nevertheless, the GATT's 'collection of ad hoc arrangements had grown together into a loose, informal, but clearly functioning international organization'.[73] Working parties were created at the request of one or more contracting parties to deal with specific matters. Until the mid-1950s these matters also included the hearing of disputes, with the working parties consisting of nation States as members who designated their representatives.[74] Their reports were considered to be advisory opinions, on the basis of which the contracting parties could take a final decision.[75] All this might suggest that the Note had no legal force, but the Report of the 1954–55 Working Party on 'Other Barriers to Trade' accepted two amendments to Article VI GATT, including the Interpretative Note. They were both brought into effect by means of a Protocol Amending the Preamble and Parts II and III of the GATT. The Protocol entered into force on 7 October 1957.[76] The 1955 Interpretative Note thus was binding on all GATT contracting parties.

The 1955 Interpretative Note did not formally amend Article VI GATT. Instead it concerned how Article VI GATT should be interpreted. It confirmed existing doubts about the universal applicability of Article VI GATT. It did not exclude the possibility of strict price comparisons; instead, it simply acknowledged that they might not always be feasible.[77] But it did not propose specific alternatives.[78] Indeed, it left entirely open the question as to which norms should be applied when Article VI required interpretation or did not apply. Consequently, it also raised questions about the appropriate balance to be achieved between GATT norms, national law and national interpretative discretion. Yet it did not give any guidelines about how to resolve this dilemma. In the short run, its principal effect was to produce considerable normative ambiguity, or, put positively, to give even greater scope for creative normative interpretation and administrative practice. In the longer term, it opened the door to alternatives other than the specific language of Article VI GATT itself.

[72] *GATT Analytical Index*, above n 46, vol 2, at 1100.

[73] R Hudec, *Adjudication of International Trade Disputes*, Thames Essay No 16 (London, Trade Policy Research Centre, 1978) 3.

[74] JH Jackson, 'The Legal Meaning of a GATT Dispute Settlement Report: Some Reflections' in JH Jackson, *The Jurisprudence of GATT and the WTO: Insights on Treaty Law and Economic Relations* (Cambridge, Cambridge University Press, 2000) 118 at 121.

[75] On the establishment and operation of working parties, see *GATT Analytical Index*, above n 46, vol 2, 1111–13.

[76] *Ibid*, vol 1, 255–56.

[77] For example, according to GATT experts at the time, the prices of a product in a State-trading country might be higher or lower than prices for the product in a market economy country, but from an economic standpoint the former might not necessarily indicate dumping and the latter might not necessarily indicate a lack of dumping: see GATT, *Anti-dumping and Countervailing Duties* (Geneva, GATT, July 1958, GATT Sales No GATT/1958-2) 15. J Boudant, *L'Anti-Dumping communautaire* (Paris, Economica, 1991) 35, refers to the same source at p 16 and ascribes this to a 'Memorandum présenté par la Tchécoslovakie'.

[78] See also Beseler and Williams, above n 52, at 65; Hu Yuanxiang, *Legal and Policy Issues of the Trade and Economic Relations between China and the EEC: A Comparative Study* (Deventer and Boston, Kluwer, 1991) 234.

In practice, as a 1958 GATT study found, importing countries often dealt with these problems in different ways. These strategies included consultations with the exporting country, bilateral agreements about import quantities, the use of prices in comparable third countries, or even, in the case of Belgium, reliance on countervailing duties rather than anti-dumping duties but using a price comparison centred on third-country markets as a basis for calculating the subsidy.[79] These practices were localised in different sites. Viewed in aggregate, though, they represented the seeds of the analogue country method, not yet in terms of legal norms but rather in terms of administrative practice.[80]

B. The US and GATT During the 1960s' 'Long boom'

1. The US Treasury Department and Normative Innovation

At the end of the 1950s, the international normative repertoire used by national anti-dumping authorities thus consisted of Article VI GATT and the 1955 Interpretative Note; these supplemented and perhaps replaced national law. The anti-dumping authorities of the major trading powers were aware of GATT working parties and expert reports, to which they contributed. They also knew of the practices adopted by other GATT contracting parties to deal with dumping by State-trading countries. But national laws, such as the US Anti-dumping Act of 1921,[81] did not deal with the issue of dumping from State-trading countries; then the Soviet Union was the only Communist country, and its foreign trade was insignificant.[82] In this context, it has been suggested that the US Treasury's earliest decisions concerning non-market economy dumping 'seemed to consider, to some extent, the use of home market prices.'[83] This would have been entirely consistent with Article VI GATT and the 1955 Interpretative Note.

The first real break from the specific terms of Article VI GATT came in 1960. Two years after the Kruschchev Ultimatum, and a year before the building of the Berlin Wall, the US Treasury Department dealt with *Bicycles from Czechoslovakia.*[84] It used the prevailing domestic or export prices of similar articles manufactured in a market economy country as the best evidence of fair (normal) value of articles manufactured

[79] GATT, above n 77, 15. On Belgium, see also A Mastropasqua, *Le Marché commun et la défense contre le dumping: De la nécessité d'une législation anti-dumping communautaire* (Rome, Guido Pastena Editore, 1965) 23.

[80] This method was consolidated in further GATT reports. See also ER Patterson, 'Improving GATT Rules for Nonmarket Economies' (1986) 20 *Journal of World Trade Law* 185 at 197.

[81] 19 USC §§160 *et seq* (1976).

[82] R Dale, *Anti-dumping Law in a Liberal Trade Order* (London, Macmillan for the Trade Policy Research Centre, 1980) at 174; Cuneo and Manuel, above n 36, at 282; RH Lantz, 'The Search for Consistency: Treatment of Nonmarket Economies in Transition under United States Anti-dumping and Countervailing Duty Laws' (1995) 10 *American University Journal of International Law and Policy* 993 at 1002.

[83] Cuneo and Manuel, above n 36, at 284. The 1958 Report by GATT anti-dumping experts noted that 'Australia, New Zealand, Sweden and the United States have thus far applied anti-dumping and similar duties only in instances of commercial (price) dumping. It seems that these countries could apply their provisions to imports from state-trading countries, a fact which is stated by some of them'. The names of the specific countries in question are not given. See GATT, above n 77, at 13.

[84] *Bicycles from Czechoslovakia,* 25 *Federal Register* (1960) 6657.

in a State-trading country. In US law, the statutory authority for this practice was questionable at the time.[85] Be that as it may, the case was the first express statement by the US of special criteria for determining normal value in dumping by State-trading countries.[86] Later, in *Fur Felt Hoods, Bodies and Caps from Czechoslovakia*,[87] the Treasury Department in 1962 again rejected the use of prices on the exporter's home market and used the price at which similar merchandise was sold to the US from other third countries. In 1963 it concluded that home-market sales of non-market economy producers were to be considered as not having been made in the ordinary course of trade.[88] According to one writer, this decision was the sole authority for the proposition that prices on the non-market economy domestic market should not be used in determining normal/fair value, and hence for resorting to an analogue (surrogate) country.[89]

It can be argued that this was a permissible interpretation of Article VI GATT, given the normative ambiguity created by the 1955 Interpretative Note. Although the Treasury did not use either the export price in the State-trading country or the cost of production, its rulings could be considered to be an expansive interpretation of 'price . . . for export to any third country' in Article VI(b)(i) GATT. Yet this was certainly not the same as earlier understandings of this provision; these concerned only export prices from the country of exportation (eg, the State-trading country) when, for

[85] See A Downey and J Graham, 'The Regulation of Dumping from State-controlled Economics: Where Next?' in D Wallace and DA Flores (eds), *Interface Two: Conference Proceedings on the Legal Framework of East–West Trade* (Washington, DC, The International Law Institute, Georgetown University Law Center, 1982), 435 at 472, fn 33, referring to PB Feller, 'The Anti-dumping Act and the Future of East–West Trade' (1967) 66 *Michigan Law Review* 115 at 128 and RA Anthony, 'The American Response to Dumping from Capitalist and Socialist Economies—Substantive Premises and Restructured Procedures after the 1967 GATT Code' (1969) 54 *Cornell Law Review* 159 at 212.

[86] GN Horlick, 'The United States Anti-dumping System' in JH Jackson and EA Vermulst (eds), *Anti-dumping Law and Practice: A Comparative Study* (New York and London, Harvester Wheatsheaf, 1990) at 140. Horlick reviews the various criteria used by the US up to 1990, and, having concluded that the search for normal value in a NME is fruitless, suggests that instead the US should implement various market disruption clauses in its bilateral agreements with NME countries: see *ibid*, at 143. For other surveys of the evolution of US law and practice, see JH Bello, AF Holmer and JO Preiss, 'Searching for "Bubbles of Capitalism": Application of the US Anti-dumping and Countervailing Duty Laws to Reforming Nonmarket Economies' (1992) 25 *George Washington Journal of International Law and Economics* 665; RH Lantz, 'The Search for Consistency: Treatment of Nonmarket Economies in Transition under United States Anti-dumping and Countervailing Duty Laws' (1995) 10 *American University Journal of International Law and Policy* 993; JA Laroski, 'NMEs: A Love Story—Nonmarket and Market Economy Status under US Anti-dumping Law' (1999) 30 *Law and Policy in International Business* 369.

[87] 27 Fed Reg 6,099 (1962), discussed in Cuneo and Manuel, above n 36, at 284–85. The same procedure was followed in *Jalousie-Louvre-Sized Sheet Glass from Czechoslovaka*, 27 Fed Reg 8,457 (1962).

[88] *Portland Hydraulic Cement, Poland*, 28 FR 6660 (1963): see GN Horlick and SS Shuman, 'Non-market Economy Trade and US Anti-dumping/Countervailing Duty Laws' (1984) 18 *The International Lawyer* 807 at 808.

[89] RA Anthony, 'The American Response to Dumping from Capitalist and Socialist Economies—Substantive Premises, and Restuctured Procedures after the 1967 GATT Code' (1969) 54 *Cornell Law Review* 159 at 202. See also *ibid*: 'This rationale [for the third-country price test] evidently derives from a statutory provision'. This author thus seeks a statutory basis in US law alone and does not refer to Art VI GATT. This is understandable in that, seen from the perspective of US constitutional law, the GATT is an executive agreement that has no domestic legal effect in the US until it has been proclaimed. Part II GATT, including Art VI, is also inferior to any inconsistent federal legislation. It is curious, however, because Art VI GATT provided the international normative framework within which US anti-dumping authorities took decisions, even though the precise relation between Art VI GATT and US law was very complex, especially in matters of interpretation of GATT provisions couched in very general terms. On GATT law, including Art VI GATT, and US law, see Jackson, *The Jurisprudence of GATT and the WTO*, above n 74, ch 14,'The General Agreement on Tariffs and Trade in United States Domestic Law', esp at 255–56. On the WTO and US law, see D Leebron, 'Implementation of the Uruguay Round Results in the United States' in JH Jackson and AO Sykes (eds), *Implementing the Uruguay Round* (Oxford, Clarendon Press, 1997) 175.

example, domestic sales did not exist or were insufficient in number. For this reason perhaps, the Treasury often used the term 'constructed value' to refer to what was actually a third-country price. But the term 'constructed value' did not reflect US statutes or GATT law at the time. In any event, the Treasury usually did not state the reasons for choosing a specific means of calculating fair (normal) value. It is more likely that the Treasury knew of the practice of other GATT contracting parties. In the context of the Cold War, it developed its own way of dealing with the situation. These decisions were the result of administrative discretion, not mandated by Congressional legislation. Nevertheless, they created new norms that had a crucial influence on later developments, notably in laying the basis for later legislation that used a constructed value based on third-country prices to determine normal value in State-trading countries dumping.[90]

2. *The 1961 GATT Experts Report*

In the late 1950s the GATT contracting parties sponsored several studies of anti-dumping law.[91] These studies culminated in the early 1960s in the first comprehensive report on the operation of Article VI GATT.[92] With regard to the determination of normal value generally, the Report concluded that, in the absence of a normal market value in the exporting country, 'the highest comparable price for the like product for export to any third country in the ordinary course of trade' and 'the cost of production of the product in the country of origin plus a reasonable addition for selling cost and profit' provided 'equal and alternative criteria to be used at the discretion of the importing country'.[93] This reiterated the 1921 US Anti-dumping Act. In terms of GATT law, it simply fell back on paragraph 1(b)(i) and paragraph 1(b)(ii) of Article VI GATT.

The GATT Experts Report did not refer to State-trading countries. This is curious because the administrative problems to which they gave rise in anti-dumping actions were already well known. Neither did the Report mention the 1955 Interpretative Note, or the practices adopted by national anti-dumping authorities. This may have been intentional, and the experts who prepared the Report might have wished to reassert and reinforce the normative primacy of Article VI GATT. But they may also have simply assumed that Article VI GATT could embrace all situations, at least with an ingenious combination of normative interpretation and administrative practice. Either of these strategies, it may be hypothesised, was a way of trying to hold the GATT fort in the face of diverging US Treasury practice. In any event, this approach became part of the cultural baggage of anti-dumping authorities in the US and Europe. It meant, in particular, trying in the first instance to work with these two ways of determining normal value when there was no domestic price in the terms of the first paragraph of Article VI GATT.

[90] Cuneo and Manuel, above n 36, at 286–87.
[91] See, eg, GATT, above n 77.
[92] GATT, *Anti-dumping and Countervailing Duties, Report of Group of Experts*, GATT Sales No GATT/1961–62 (1961).
[93] *Ibid*, at 9.

3. The Kennedy Round Anti-dumping Code

Given the differing interpretations of key terms of Article VI GATT, national administration of anti-dumping laws then constituted a major non-tariff barrier to trade.[94] In this context, the 1961 GATT Experts Report was extremely significant. Though without legal force, it was an important link of the genealogical chain of the first GATT Anti-dumping Code.[95] Known formally as the Agreement on the Implementation of Article VI of the General Agreement on Tariffs and Trade, the Anti-dumping Code was agreed during the Kennedy Round of multilateral tariff negotiations between 1963 and 1968. It was concluded on 30 June 1967 and entered into force on 1 July 1968.[96]

The Kennedy Round Anti-dumping Code was intended to supply a uniform basis for the application of Article VI GATT.[97] This was important, especially for the major trading countries. The purpose of the Code was to elaborate Article VI GATT, not amend it. In fact, however, it embodied a subtle, yet significant reconfiguration of the anti-dumping repertoire.

Article 2(d) of the Code provided that:

> When there are no sales of the like product in the ordinary course of trade in the domestic market of the exporting country or when, because of the *particular market situation*, such sales do not permit a *proper comparison*, the margin of dumping *shall* be determined by comparison with a *comparable price of the like product when exported to any third country* which may be the highest such export price but should be a representative price, or with the *cost of production* in the country of origin plus a reasonable amount for administrative, selling and any other costs and for profits . . .[98]

In addition, the Code stated explicitly that this provision was without prejudice to the 1955 Interpretative Note.[99]

With regard to State-trading country dumping, Article 2(d) was an innovation in three crucial respects. First, it made the State-trading country a normal scenario under GATT anti-dumping law. The main clause of Article 2(d) reiterated Article VI GATT, which was the same as the terms of the US 1921 Anti-dumping Act. However, the subordinate clause ('When . . . situation') assimilated two different scenarios into a single category. The first scenario was 'no sales . . . in the domestic market of the exporting country'; the second was 'the particular market situation', language that clearly echoed the 'special difficulties' referred to in the 1955 Interpretative Note. The device for assimilating these into a single category was the use of the expression 'proper comparison' to cover both scenarios, even though the expression derived originally from the expression 'strict comparison' in the 1955 Interpretative Note, which referred only to the 'particular market situation' of State-trading country dumping. This process of

[94] EA Verlmust, *Anti-dumping Law and Practice in the United States and the European Communities* (Amsterdam, Elsevier North Holland, 1987) 510–11.

[95] Stewart, above n 57, at 1417; Verlmust, above n 94, at 509–10.

[96] Agreement on Implementation of Article VI of the General Agreement on Tariffs and Trade (1968) ('Anti-dumping Code'), reprinted in GATT, *BISD*, 15th Supp at 26. See also GATT, Legal Instruments Embodying the Results of the 1964–67 Trade Conference, vol V at 3453–3707 (Geneva, GATT, 30 June 1967). On the negotiations, see Stewart, above n 57, at 1417–31.

[97] Anti-dumping Code, Art 1.

[98] *Ibid*, Art 2(d), emphasis added.

[99] *Ibid*, Art 2(g). The Interpretative Note, para 2 Ad Art VI, was included in the 'Notes and Supplementary Provisions' to the Agreement.

'normalisation' integrated the 'particular market situation' into the normative mainstream of the GATT, not only by treating it as analogous to, if not a variant of, a scenario that had long been well known, but also by transposing it from the Interpretative Note into an Anti-dumping Code.

Secondly, Article 2(d) took an 'administrative turn' that shifted the frame of reference for dealing with State-trading country dumping. From the technical legal standpoint, the importance of the Article for State-trading country dumping lay in the fact that it consecrated new ways of establishing the dumping margin. The dumping margin is the difference between normal value and export price.[100] It was the crucial element for State-trading country dumping, where normal value was problematic. Henceforth it was to be determined in such cases by reference to the export price or the cost of production. Usually, normal value and dumping margin are intimately related: normal value is one of two elements in determining dumping margin; the other is export price. This is the market economy pattern, which had characterised all anti-dumping discourse up to then. Article 2(d), however, short-circuited this method of analysis.[101] Drawing on well-known GATT concepts, it spelled out ways of determining dumping margin for State-trading country dumping without referring to normal value at all. It thus shifted the frame of reference from the determination of normal value to the calculation of dumping margin, from a general legal concept that was presumed to be universal to a specific, localised administrative task.

Thirdly, Article 2(d) abandoned the search for a market price in a non-market economy. In its place, the Article provided two substitutes for normal value in the case of State-trading country dumping. For the main Western trading countries, these substitutes were not entirely satisfactory, because, read literally, they were still based on the State-trading country's domestic economy. Hence they remained impregnated by the traditional market economy pattern of analysis. Nevertheless, they added some flesh to the 1955 Interpretative Note. More importantly, Article 2(d) thus excluded the use of the domestic price in the State-trading country of exportation. In this respect, it set aside the formal provisions of Article VI GATT so far as State-trading country dumping was concerned.[102] This move, so crucial during the following decades, was expressed in familiar terms. It represented a giant step in the direction of legislative norms providing for the analogue country method of determining normal value, a step that had already been taken by anti-dumping authorities exercising their administrative discretion.

[100] Art VI(2) GATT defines dumping margin as 'the price difference determined in accordance with the provisions of [Article VI] paragraph 1 [GATT]'. The latter, as already seen, provides for three possible methods. First, the price on the export market can be compared with the normal value of the product on the domestic market of the exporting country: Art VI(1)(a) GATT. When this is impossible, a second method is to compare the export price with the highest comparable price for the like product for export to any third country in the ordinary course of trade: Art VI(1)(b)(i) GATT. A third method, which is an alternative to the second method, is to compare the export price with the cost of production in the country of origin plus a reasonable addition for selling cost and profit: Art VI(1)(b)(ii) GATT.

[101] Curiously, one expert described the Kennedy Round Code as laying down two alternative methods for determining normal value: see R Denton, 'The Non-market Economy Rules of the European Community's Anti-dumping and Countervailing Duties Legislation' (1987) 36 *International and Comparative Law Quarterly* 198 at 206. In contrast, two experienced practitioners of EC anti-dumping law concluded that these provisions contained no express rule about the determination of normal value for State-trading country exports: see I Van Bael and J-F Bellis, *Anti-dumping and Other Trade Protection Laws of the EC*, 3rd edn (Bicester, CCH Editions, 1996) at 93, writing about the first EC anti-dumping legislation, Council Regulation 459/68, which enacted these provisions of the Kennedy Round Anti-dumping Code virtually verbatim (see section II.C.3 below). Both were correct, and why this is so is the key to the puzzle.

[102] See also Hu Yuanxing, above n 78, at 234–35.

Article 2(d) of the Kennedy Round Anti-dumping Code showed all the signs of being the result of negotiations in which the US had the upper hand. Its language represented a compromise between the norms generated by US Treasury practice and the 1961 GATT Experts Report. This was enhanced by the fact that US trade negotiations were carried out by the executive. The pragmatic orientation of Article 2(d) reflected the fact that the US, and certainly other anti-dumping authorities too, had by then developed more or less routinised, administrative practices to deal with State-trading country dumping. The reference to export prices in Article 2(d) could conceivably be interpreted to mean the price of a like product when exported from a country other than the State-trading country—in other words, the price in a market economy country. Already well known in US anti-dumping practice, this was the same method used by the Treasury in *Bicycles from Czechoslovakia*.[103] 'Cost of production', left to a lawyer's imagination, might mean either the actual cost in the State-trading country of exportation, or a cost of production 'constructed' on some other basis. The 'construction' of substitutes for normal value was already used in US anti-dumping practice, and later the Treasury constructed the cost of production in the famous 1977 *Polish Golf Car* case.[104] Both methods employed a surrogate or analogue country as a substitute for the State-trading country of exportation. In effect, Article 2(d) of the Code seems to have consolidated in GATT form the norms already developed by the US Treasury Department.

The Kennedy Round Code was the first international dumping code. It entered into force during a period of détente in US–Soviet relations, following the Tet offensive that changed the course of the Vietnam War, and at the time of the signature of the Nuclear Non-proliferation Treaty in July 1968.[105] With regard to State-trading country dumping, it was the first fully-fledged regime, in the sense of a set of 'implicit or explicit principles, norms, rules, and decision-making procedures around which actors' expectations converge in a given area of international relations'.[106] Seen in historical perspective, especially today with Chinese participation in the WTO, it is striking that the actors amounted only to a relative handful of countries, led by a single superpower or hegemon, the United States. The legal rules were an expression of power relations: the basic norms and fundamental understandings came from the dominant power.[107]

The State-trading country dumping provisions of the Code were couched in an apparently pragmatic, non-confrontational mode. The Code expressed dumping by State-trading countries as a technical issue, not as a potential confrontation of economic and political systems. The new international anti-dumping discourse thus appeared to reorientate the role of national anti-dumping authorities away from the comparison of economic systems (and by extension, political systems) and toward quasi-mathematical, administrative functions. In other words, they were in theory no

[103] 25 Fed Reg 5, 657 (1960).

[104] *Electric Golf Cars from Poland; Anti-dumping*, 40 Fed Reg 25, 497 (1975), TD 75-288, 19 CFR G153.46; see section III.A.1 below.

[105] See JPD Dunabin, *The Cold War: The Great Powers and Their Allies* (London, Longman, 1994), esp 167–69, 255–59, 300–306.

[106] S Krasner (ed), *International Regimes* (Ithaca and London, Cornell University Press, 1983) at 2. It is also possible, of course, to view this as a development or interpretation of the existing GATT regime.

[107] '[T]he objectives of international trade organizations are set by the most powerful state in the group or on the basis of a bargain between two or more powerful states': S Strange, *States and Markets*, 2nd edn (London, Pinter, 1988) at 186; see also JS Odell, *Negotiating the World Economy* (Ithaca, Cornell University Press, 2000) 162.

longer called upon to play a political role. It was not that the issue of State-trading country anti-dumping had become entirely apolitical, but rather that politics were now embodied in specific administrative practices, and therefore less visible except to specialists or other close observers. These administrative practices themselves took place within national political contexts. In the US, for example, Treasury made its anti-dumping determinations, in a space of some administrative discretion, within the framework of overtly politically-based legislation adopted by the Congress. Often political and policy differences were apparent in the tug-of-war between Treasury and Congress concerning US anti-dumping law. On the international level, however, the pragmatic, administrative orientation of the Kennedy Round Code may have tended to mask the broader political elements. Partly for these reasons, it had an enormous influence on future law and practice.

4. *The Kennedy Round Code and the United States*

Article 14 of the Kennedy Round Code required

> Each party to this Agreement . . . [to] take all necessary steps, of a general or particular character, to ensure . . . the conformity of its laws, regulations and administrative procedures with the provisions of this Agreement . . .[108]

The Code purported to 'govern the application of Article VI [GATT], in so far as action is taken under anti-dumping legislation or regulations'.[109] But the Anti-dumping Code was binding only on those GATT contracting parties that signed it.[110] A plurilateral agreement, the Code was a separate document from the GATT, and contracting parties were free to sign it or not.[111] The original signatories were Belgium, Canada, Czechoslovakia, Denmark, the European Economic Community (EEC),[112] Finland, France, the Federal Republic of Germany, Greece, Italy, Japan, Luxembourg, The Netherlands, Norway, Sweden, Switzerland, the United Kingdom, the United States and Yugoslavia.[113] By 1976 the list had expanded to include Austria, Hungary, Malta, Portugal and Spain.[114]

In the United States, however, the Kennedy Round Code proved to be deeply problematic. It was quickly caught up in the continuing, often conflictual relations between

[108] Anti-dumping Code, Art 14.

[109] See Anti-dumping Code, Art 1.

[110] It has been suggested therefore that the Code differed from Art VI GATT in that the Code imposed directly binding obligations on its signatories. Van Bael and Bellis, above n 101, at 28. See also 'Final Act authenticating the Results of the 1964–67 Trade Conference held under the auspices of the Contracting Parties to the General Agreement on Tariffs and Trade', in GATT, *Legal Instruments Embodying the Results of the 1964–67 Trade Conference*, vol I (Geneva, 30 June 1967) at 6–7. Paragraph 4 of the Act states that 'The signature of this Final Act evidences the intention of each signatory to take, subject to its constitutional procedures, such steps as are considered appropriate to give effect to those instruments in the negotiation of which it has participated'.

[111] Stewart, above n 57, at 1431.

[112] Then not a contracting party to the GATT: see Anti-dumping Code, Art 13.

[113] *Report by the Committee on Anti-dumping Practices adopted on 12 February 1970*, GATT Doc No. L/3333, Art 2, reprinted in GATT, *BISD*, 17th Supp at 43 (1970).

[114] 'Seventh Report by the Committee on Anti-dumping Practices adopted on 21 November 1975' (L/4241), GATT, *BISD*, 22nd Supplement (Geneva, February 1976), 21 at 21–22.

the Treasury and Congress. The US adhered to the Code under the President's power to enter into executive agreements. The Treasury Department modified its procedures with regard to the determination of dumping. But the same was not true of the Tariff Commission, which was responsible for the determination of injury.[115] Furthermore, the US Congress did not adopt the Code. Consequently, the United States never ratified the Kennedy Round Anti-dumping Code.

Nevertheless, the US Treasury in 1968 adopted a new regulation dealing explicitly with dumping by State-trading countries. It provided as follows:

> *Merchandise from controlled economy country. Ordinarily*, if the information available indicates that the economy of the country from which the merchandise is exported is controlled to an extent that sales or offers of sales of such or similar merchandise in that country in to countries other than the United States do not permit a determination of fair value under §53.3 or §53.4, the Secretary *will determine* fair value on the basis of the *constructed value* of the merchandise determined on the normal costs, expenses and profits as reflected by the prices at which such or similar merchandise is sold by a *non-state-controlled economy country* either (1) for *consumption in its own market;* or (2) to *other countries*, including the *United States*.[116]

A national administrative measure, this was based on previous Treasury practice. However, it lacked any statutory basis in US law.[117]

The 1968 Treasury Regulation differed from the multilateral Kennedy Round Code in three significant respects. First, it introduced a new label of 'controlled-economy countries' for State-trading countries. Its single criterion was the role of the State in the domestic economy, embracing the two GATT criteria of the State's foreign trade monopoly and fixing of domestic prices.[118] Secondly, the conjunction of 'ordinarily' and 'will determine' created a presumption or line of conduct against the use of domestic prices in the State-trading country of exportation; this was stronger than the more conditional terms of the Code. Thirdly, the Regulation provided expressly for the use of an analogue country price, either on its own market or on export markets, including the US, instead of the State-trading country's price for exports to a third country. Compared to the Code, the Treasury Regulation contained numerous new elements: constructed value, use of the surrogate country market, use of surrogate country sales to other countries, and inclusion of the importing country market. This was the first time that a major trading power had ever formally approved the analogue country method in its own administrative regulations or legislation.[119] Overall, this was more protectionist than the Kennedy Round Code.

[115] See JJ Barceló III, 'Anti-dumping Laws as Barriers to Trade—The United States and the International Anti-dumping Code' (1972) 57 *Cornell Law Review* 491 at 532–58.

[116] 19 CFR §53.5(b) (1969), quoted in Cuneo and Manuel, above n 36, at 290–91 (emphasis added). Part 53 of 19 CFR was redesignated Part 153, with no change in the text, in 1970. Horlick and Shuman describe the same provision as 19 CFR §153.5(b) (1973): see Horlick and Schuman, above n 88, at 808–809.

[117] Cuneo and Manuel, above n 36, at 290–91.

[118] The 1955 Interpretative Note referred to 'a country which has a complete or substantially complete monopoly of its trade and all domestic prices are fixed by the State'.

[119] It was re-enacted in 1973: CFR §153.5(b) (1973).

5. GATT Working Parties, 1967–73

The issue of the application of Article VI GATT to State-trading countries was posed directly at the same time as the Kennedy Round Anti-dumping Code was being agreed. Several Central and Eastern European countries, apart from Czechoslovakia, sought to accede to the GATT. This was part of the gradual process of détente, including the development of increasing institutional ties between the US and the Soviet blocs. It also reflected the strategy of Eastern European countries, except the German Democratic Republic, to strengthen their position vis-à-vis the Soviet Union.[120] The respective working parties established to prepare the accession of Poland, Romania and Hungary proposed different ways of dealing with State-trading country dumping.

The Working Party on the Accession of Poland was appointed in 1959.[121] Its Report, adopted on 26 June 1967, recorded the understanding that the Interpretative Note to Article VI GATT would apply. This has been interpreted as suggesting that the strict requirements for the application of the non-market economy exception contained in the Note need not be taken at face value, because, strictly speaking, Poland did not meet these tests.[122] But the Working Party went further and recognised that a contracting party may use as the normal value for a product imported from Poland the prices which prevail generally in its markets for the same or like products or a value for that product constructed on the basis of the price for a like product originating in another country, as long as the method used for determining normal value in any particular case is appropriate and not unreasonable.[123]

Poland thus relinquished any use of its domestic prices. In turn, it achieved:

a) the use of 'may' rather than 'shall';
b) the 'appropriate and not unreasonable' standard; and
c) its main objective, GATT membership.

According to Kostecki, this 'followed the standard of dumping as already practised in relations between the GATT countries and Czechoslovakia'.[124] But it was essentially the US Treasury practice. Though couched in more conditional terms, it further

[120] M Baumer and HD Jacobsen, 'Institutional Aspects of East–West Economic Relations' (1976) 10 *Journal of World Trade* 434 at 436. On phases in East–West security relations, see V Rittberger and M Zürn, 'Towards Regulated Anarchy in East–West Relations: Causes and Consequences of East–West Regimes' in V Rittberger (ed), *International Regimes in East–West Politics* (London and New York, Pinter Publishers, 1990) at 10–11.

[121] See 'Relations with Poland, Report adopted on 9 November 1959 (L(1037/Rev1), GATT, *BISD*, 8th Supplement General Agreement on Tariffs and Trade, Basic Instruments and Selected Documents, 8th Supplement, February 1960), 61 at 61.

[122] Horlick and Schuman, above n 88, at 834.

[123] 'Accession of Poland, Report of the Working Party adopted on 26 June 1967' (L/2806), in GATT, *BISD*, 15th Supplement (Geneva, April 1968), 109 at 111, para 13 (emphasis added); see also GATT, *Analytical Index: Notes on the drafting, interpretation and application of the Articles of the General Agreement*, 3rd rev (Geneva, GATT, 1970) at 40; GATT, *Analytical Index: Notes on the drafting, interpretation and application of the General Agreement*, 'Article VI-16 (m) Additional criteria for price comparisons in the case of imports from Poland, Romania and Hungary', 4th rev (Geneva, GATT, 1989); *Analytical Index: Guide to GATT Law and Practice on CD-ROM*, Part II, Article VI Anti-dumping and Countervailing Duties, II. Interpretation and Application of Article VI, A. Scope and Application of Article VI., 3. Paragraph 1 (3) "normal value", (e) Note 2 Ad Paragraph 1 "imports from a country which has a complete or substantially complete monopoly of its trade and where all domestic prices are fixed by the State" (WTO and Vista Intermedia Corporation, 1997), text at fn 27.

[124] Kostecki, above n 48, at 106.

consolidated the analogue market economy country approach. It was the first time that a State-trading country expressly accepted this approach, though to be sure in the relatively coercive context of GATT accession negotiations. More generally, the agreement formed part of the process of institutionalisation of the analogue country method, in the sense that it was internalised by GATT contracting parties.

This arrangement diverged in several ways from the Kennedy Round Anti-dumping Code, which was adopted only four days later though it did not come into effect until the following year. First, it referred expressly to normal value, not dumping margin, thus further entrenching the analogue country method. Secondly, it offered importing countries the possibility of not using prices in the State-trading country of exportation. Thirdly, in fact it did not mention the State-trading country domestic economy at all. Instead, it provided two other comparators, including the importing country. Fourthly, it permitted the construction of normal value, though how this was to be done left much to administrative discretion. Fifthly, drawing on classic legal language, it added the conditions of appropriateness and reasonableness. In general, much of this formulation greatly increased the scope for administrative discretion, while the two conditions were intended to constrain its exercise within certain general but judicially ascertainable bounds. Taken together, these elements posited a more or less coherent set of norms for determining normal value in cases of non-market economy dumping. They also purported to articulate a shared conception, albeit one achieved by a process of asymmetrical negotiations, that Article VI GATT did not apply.

Strictly speaking, these provisions applied only between Poland and the GATT contracting parties that were signatories to the Protocol for the Accession of Poland.[125] As in the case of previous GATT instruments, however, their actual significance was much wider. The solution established by the Working Party on Poland was followed by other working parties. The Report of the Working Party on 'Accession of Romania' was adopted on 6 October 1971. It used the same normative language as that of the Working Party on Poland.[126] The Report of the Working Party on 'Accession of Hungary', adopted on 30 July 1973, employed similar words.[127] In general, these Reports departed from the original text of Article VI GATT much more than the 1955 Czechoslovakia Working Party compromise.

[125] The Protocol was signed in Geneva on 30 June 1967 and entered into force on 18 October 1967. It did not refer to anti-dumping. See 'Protocol for the Accession of Poland', in GATT, BISD, 15th Supplement (Geneva, April 1968) at 111. The signatory States and dates of signature as of August 1968 were Austria (subject to ratification), Czechoslovakia, Denmark, France, India, Malawi, Kingdom of the Netherlands, New Zealand, Norway, Poland, Portugal, South Africa, Spain, Sweden, Turkey, United Kingdom, United States and Yugoslavia: see 'LXXIX. Protocol for the Accession of Poland to the General Agreement on Tariffs and Trade', in GATT, *Status of Multilateral Protocols of which the Director-General Acts as Depositary* (Geneva, The Contracting Parties to the GATT, July 1969) at 79/Rev1. As of 1993, Austria had ratified the Protocol, and Belgium and Luxembourg had accepted the Protocol: see GATT, *Status of Legal Instruments* (Geneva, The Contracting Parties to the GATT, GATT/LEG/1, Supp No 15, December 1993) at 3–15.2.

[126] L/3557, adopted on 6 October 1971, 18S/94, 96 para 13, in *Analytical Index: Guide to GATT Law and Practice on CD-ROM,* above n 124, text at fn 28. As in the case of Poland, the Protocol of Accession did not refer to dumping: see 'Protocol for the Accession of Romania to the General Agreement on Tariffs and Trade', GATT, *BISD*, 18th Supp (Geneva, April 1972) at 5–10. For the signatories as of 1993, see GATT, *Status of Legal Instruments*, above n 126, at 3–18.1.

[127] L/3889, adopted on 30 July 1973, 20S/34, 37, para 18, in *Analytical Index*, *Analytical Index: Guide to GATT Law and Practice on CD-ROM*, above n 124. The Accession Protocol, as in the case of Poland and Romania, was silent as regards anti-dumping: see 'Protocol for the Accession of Hungary to the General Agreement on Tariffs and Trade', GATT, *BISD*, 20th Supp (Geneva, January 1974) at 3–8. As to signatories as of 1993, see GATT, *Status of Legal Instruments*, above n 126, at 3–20.2.

Poland became a full member of the GATT in October 1967, Romania in November 1971 and Hungary in September 1973.[128] Czechoslovakia was an original member of the Code, and Hungary joined in November 1974.[129] Poland and Romania did not join the 1967 GATT Anti-dumping Code.[130] Other countries, such as the USSR and China, remained outside the GATT. For all these (and other) countries, the meaning of Article VI GATT was being reinterpreted in different sites and by virtue of relations between them, even though not always in exactly the same terms. The 1955 Interpretative Note continued to be preserved with regard to all GATT signatories, whether or not they accepted the Code.[131] Strictly speaking, the world comprised GATT signatories who accepted the Code, GATT signatories who did not accept the Code, and countries that were not signatories of GATT. Except for the first group, however, these normative arrangements were always to some degree equivalent to a cartel. All countries involved in dumping were affected in practice by these developments in the GATT system. But the real distinction lay between importing countries. With regard to anti-dumping, all exporters were in the same position of being bound by a specific importing country's norms. This gave special prominence to the evolving practice and norms of anti-dumping authorities in the main trading partners, particularly the United States and, after 1969, the European Community.

C. The Beginning of European Community Anti-dumping Law

1. The Europeanisation of Law on Foreign Trade in Goods

The late 1960s marked the end of the 'golden age' or foundational period of EC law. By then, the ECJ had laid down basic constitutional principles, the main institutions of the three legally distinct Communities were unified, the 'empty chair' crisis had been resolved, though with the debilitating yet symptomatic Luxembourg Compromise, the

[128] Kostecki, above n 48, at 11, Table 1.1 'Chronology of Relations between East European Countries and the GATT'.

[129] *Ibid*, at 112, fn 55.

[130] Both joined the 1979 Agreement on Implementation of Article VI ('1979 Anti-dumping Code').

[131] Arts 2(g) and 2:7 of the 1967 and 1979 Agreements on the Implementation of Article VI GATT both provide that 'This Article is without prejudice to the Second Supplementary Provision to paragraph 1 of Article VI in Annex I of the General Agreement': 15S/24, 26; 26S/171, 173. See also Art 15 of the 1979 Agreement on Interpretation and Application of Articles VI, XVI and XXIII of the General Agreement: 26S/56, 74–75. See *GATT Analytical Index*, above n 46, vol 1, at 228. Such a provision was necessary because, prior to the WTO agreements, the relation between the GATT and the Code was not settled. For example, the 1990 GATT Panel report on the EEC's anti-circumvention duties on imports of parts and components left open the question whether it was competent to construe Art VI of the GATT in the light of the 1979 Anti-dumping Code: see *BISD* 375/132 (L/6657). Petersmann argues that, in a case in which both parties to the dispute are parties to the Code, it would not make practical sense to invoke only Art XXIII GATT. As he points out, Art XXXI of the1969 Vienna Convention on the Law of Treaties requires that 'there shall be taken into account, together with the context, any subsequent agreement between the parties regarding the interpretation of the treaty or the application of its provisions'. In addition, though the GATT Council was not competent to give authoritative interpretations of Code provisions and the Committee on Anti-dumping Practices was not competent to give authoritative interpretations of GATT provisions, each was competent to take the other set of norms into account, either as part of the rights and obligations to be interpreted or as part of the context. See EU Petersmann, 'GATT Dispute Settlement Proceedings in the Field of Anti-dumping Law' (1991) 28(1) *CML Rev* 69 at 105–06.

common agricultural policy was essentially in place, fundamental integration of the market in goods had been achieved and, before the end of the 1 July 1968 transitional period, the common customs tariff came into effect. The next step in European integration was the development of a common commercial policy.[132]

An important aspect of this development was the Europeanisation of law on foreign trade in goods. 'Europeanisation' entailed, in particular, a shift in the locus of decision-making and a change in the interests to be taken into account.[133] In fact, it began soon after the establishment of the EC. Starting as early as 1960, the Council of Ministers (now Council of the European Union) laid down a Community legal framework orientating and limiting the Member States' trade agreements with third countries, with the exception in practice, in the short run, of Eastern European countries.[134]

In late 1969, the EC enacted a series of Regulations concerning imports from State-trading countries. The first was Council Regulation 109/70, which came into force one month after the end of the transitional period.[135] It applied to imports from all State-trading countries; the term 'State-trading' was already in Article XVII GATT 1947. The countries, all from Central and Eastern Europe plus the Soviet Union, were listed in the Annex.[136] This was not an exclusive list; for example, it did not include Cuba.[137]

The grouping of State-trading countries in EC law thus originated in 1970: they were listed for the purposes of differential treatment concerning imports.[138] This grouping has been traced back to the institutional structure of international trade negotiations during the 1950s. Negotiations took place within the OEEC (later OECD) to abolish many of the quantitative restrictions in international trade between Western industrialised countries. But they did not deal with (nor were there analogous

[132] For a Polish perspective on the intergovernmental character of EEC trade policy at the time, see H de Fiumel, 'Problems of Implementing EEC General Trade Policy toward Socialist Countries' (1981–82) 17 *Soviet and Eastern European Foreign Trade* 50. On problems of establishing a common EEC policy concerning Eastern Europe, see EP Wellenstein, 'The Relations of the European Communities with Eastern Europe', in D O'Keeffe and HG Schermers (eds), *Essays in European Law and Integration* (Deventer, Kluwer, 1982) 197.

[133] See Case C-150/94 *United Kingdom of Great Britain and Northern Ireland v Council of the European Union* [1998] ECR I-7235, Opinion of A-G Léger. See also F Snyder, 'Judicial Review in the Age of Globalization: Chinese Toys in the European Court of Justice' in D O'Keeffe and A Bavasso (eds), *Liber Amicorum for Gordon Slynn: Judicial Review in European Law* (London, Chancery, 2000) 651.

[134] Council Decision of 20 June 1960, JO p 1965/1960 [renegotiations]; Council Decision of 9 October 1961 on standardisation of the duration of trade agreements with third countries, JO p 1274/1961, OJ Sp Ed 1961, p 86 [validity]; Council Decision of 9 October 1961 concerning a consultation procedure in respect of the negotiation of agreements concerning commercial relations between Member States and third countries and in respect of changes in the state of liberalisation in relation to third countries, JO p 1273/1961, OJ Sp Ed 1961, p 84 [pre-consultation]. On the development of common EC rules concerning State-trading countries, see ELM Völker, 'Importing from East-Bloc Countries: Common Rules and Remedies for the Parties Concerned' (1985) 1 *Legal Issues of European Integration* 99.

[135] Council Regulation No 109/70 of 19 December 1969 establishing common rules for imports from the State-trading countries [1970] OJ L19/1, OJ Eng Sp Ed 1970, p 23. This Regulation was later extended to other products by Council Regulation 2896/77, [1977] OJ L338/1. See also Völker, above n 134.

[136] The countries were Bulgaria, Hungary, Poland, Romania, Czechoslovakia and the USSR: Council Regulation No 109/70, above n 135. Further legislation later the same year expanded the list of liberalised products but retained the same list of countries. See Council Regulation 1492/70, OJ [1970] L166/1; Council Regulation 2567/70, OJ [1970] L276/1.

[137] See eg Beseler and Williams, above n 52, at 54; Van Bael and Bellis, above n 101, at 93, fn 152.

[138] The list of individual countries was consistent with, but not necessarily required by, the EC's policy towards Eastern European countries of treating each country individually for purposes of trade relations, instead of dealing with them as single bloc organised with the then extant Council for Mutual Economic Assistance (CMEA): see J Maslen, 'The European Community's Relations with the State-trading Countries of Europe 1984–1986' (1986) 6 *Yearbook of European Law* 335, *passim*, esp 340.

negotiations elsewhere concerning) such restrictions in trade with Eastern European countries or Japan. The political role of foreign trade with the then Communist countries and the benefits of quantitative restrictions in terms of protection for EC producers reinforced, and gradually 'hardened' into law, this initially 'soft' distinction between two groups of trading partners.[139]

2. *The Europeanisation of Anti-dumping Law*

The EC Member States dealt with anti-dumping from the founding of the EC in 1957 until 1 July 1968.[140] Their legislation concerning dumping from State-trading countries was generally consistent with the GATT, though it did not always use the same terms. For example, German anti-dumping law provided for the use of the domestic market price, or, if absent, the price of exports to third countries or, if this was not available, the domestic cost of production.[141] Anti-dumping laws did not apply to intra-German trade—in other words, trade between the German Democratic Republic (GDR) and the Federal Republic of Germany—which the latter considered to be not foreign trade but rather trade of a special kind.[142] France employed the price on the domestic market, or in a transit country or in the country of origin if different from

[139] See Völker, above n 134, at 101–102.

[140] For a brief summary, see J Boudant, *L'Anti-Dumping communautaire* (Paris, Economica, 1991) at 47–49; A Mastropasqua, above n 79, 47–73, 93.

[141] Decree of 5.12.63, sec 2(4), BGB1-II du 12.12.1963: French translation in Mastropasqua, above n 79, at 100.

[142] The special status of intra-German trade (*Innerdeutscher Handel*) was preserved when the Federal Republic acceded to the GATT and later by a protocol to the 1957 Treaty of Rome. For the 1957 Protocol on German internal trade and connected problems, see http://www.ena.lu/treaty_establishing_protocol_german_internal_trade_connected_problems_rome_march_1957-020302331.html, last accessed 18 February 2010. Under the Protocol, Member States were required to ensure that their bilateral agreements with the GDR did not conflict with the principles of the common market and to take appropriate measures to avoid harming the economies of other Member States. Member States were also permitted to take appropriate measures to prevent any difficulties that they might suffer from trade between other Member States and the GDR. It follows that such measures included national measures to counteract dumping by the GDR in Member States other than the Federal Republic of Germany. The 'Berlin Agreement', Military Government Law No 53 of 1949, provided for a series of import quotas limiting the volume or value of GDR deliveries to West Germany: see G Leptin, 'Economic Relations between the Federal Republic of Germany and the German Democratic Republic' in K Dalchoong and G Werner (eds), *New Directions in East–West Relations: German and Korean Perspectives* (Seoul, Korea, Institute of East and West Studies, Yonsei University, 1987) 137 at 146–47 and 149–68. In Case 14/74 *Norddeutsches Vieh- un Fleischkontor GmbH v Hauptzollamt Hamburg-Jonas—Ausfuhrerstattung* [1974] ECR 899, the ECJ held that the transfer of goods from the GDR to the Federal Republic could not be regarded as importation from third countries. On intra-German trade, see M Zürn, 'Intra-German Trade: An Early East–West Regime' in Rittberger, above n 120, at 151–88; M Zürn, *Interessen und Institutionen in der internationalen Politik: Grundlegung und Anwendungen des situationsstrukturellen Ansatzes* (Opladen, Leske & Budrich, 1992) 249–305; C-D Ehlermann, S Kupper, H Lambrecht and G Ollig, *Handelspartner DDR: Innerdeutsche Wittschaftsbeziehungen* (Baden Baden, Nomos Verlag, 1975); Bundesrepublik Deutschland, Presse- Und Informatinsamt der Bundesregierng (ed), *Dokumentation zu den innerdeutschen Beziehungen: Abmachungen und Erklärungen* (Leck, Clausen & Bosse, 1989). On trade volumes, see Leptin, 'Economic Relations between the Federal Republic of Germany and the German Democratic Republic' in Dalchoong and Werner above, at 164–68; J Nitz, 'Probleme und Perspektiven der Wirtschaftsbeziehungen DDR-BRD' (1989) 10 *IPW* Berichte [Institut für Internationale Politik und Wirtschaft der DDR, Berlin] 8 at 9; J Lisiecki, 'Financial and Material Transfers between East and West Germany' (1990) 42 *Soviet Studies* 513 at 523–26.

the exporting country; or, in absence of these, used the price of exports to a third country, or the cost of production.[143] The Italian law was essentially the same.[144]

In 1968 the EC adopted its first anti-dumping legislation, Council Regulation 459/68.[145] This was a central part of the EC's new common commercial policy.[146] The EC formally replaced the Member States with regard to enacting anti-dumping legislation, initiating anti-dumping cases and interpreting anti-dumping law. United States law, policy and pressure all influenced the EC's 1968 anti-dumping Regulation.[147] But the new Regulation also implemented the GATT Anti-dumping Code,[148] of which the EC had been one of the principal promoters and which the EC had recently accepted.[149]

The EC was a signatory of the Kennedy Round Anti-dumping Code, but it was not a member of GATT. Not until the 1972 *International Fruit Company* case did the ECJ assert that

> the Community has assumed the functions inherent in the tariff and trade policy, progressively during the transitional period and in their entirety on the expiry of that period, by virtue of Articles 112 and 113 of the Treaty . . .[150]

It also recognised that

> since that time, the Community, acting through its institutions, has appeared as a partner in the tariff negotiations and as a party to the agreement of all types concluded within the framework of the General Agreement, in accordance with the provisions of Article 114 of the EEC Treaty . . .[151]

Even then, however, it still used cautious language to the effect that

> It therefore appears that, in so far as under the EEC Treaty the Community has assumed the powers previously exercised by Member States in the area covered by the General Agreement, the provisions of that Agreement have the effect of binding the Community.[152]

[143] Ordonnance N 58-1264 du 20.12.1958 relative aux pouvoirs du gouvernement en matière de droits compensateurs and de droit anti-dumping, Art 2 inserting new Art 19*bis*, JO n 298 du 12.12.1958; Mastropasqua, above n 79, at 107–08.

[144] Italian law Loi n 39 du 11 janvier 1963, GU n 40 12.2.1963 p 761; Mastropasqua, above n 79, at 109.

[145] Council Regulation 459/68, [1968] OJ L93/1; OJ Eng Sp Ed Series I 68(I) p 80.

[146] See *ibid*, Preamble, 1st and 2nd recitals. These recitals state: 'Whereas, after the transitional period has ended, the common commercial policy must be based on uniform principles; where implementation of this policy necessarily involves its progressive introduction during the transitional period . . .' [1st recital], and 'Whereas protective measures against dumping . . . by countries which are not members of the EEC are an important aspect of the common commercial policy' [2nd recital].

[147] 'The United States . . . sought to influence the shape of the [then] pending European Economic Community anti-dumping legislation': RA Anthony, 'The American Response to Dumping from Capitalist and Socialist Economies—Substantive Premises, and Restructured Procedures after the 1967 GATT Code' (1969) 54 *Cornell Law Review* 159 at 179, fn 56.

[148] GATT, *BISD*, 15th Supp, 24 (Geneva, April 1968).

[149] The Kennedy Round Anti-dumping Code was incorporated into EC law by Council Decision 68/411, [1968] OJ L305/1. The 6th recital of the Preamble to Council Regulation 459/68, above n 146, states: 'Whereas, in view of the international obligations of the Community and its Member States, this regulation must be drawn up with due regard for the obligations laid down in Article VI of the General Agreement on Tariffs and Trade and in the Agreement on implementation of that Article.'

[150] Joined Cases 21-24/72 *International Fruit Company NV and others v Produktschap voor Groenten en Fruit* [1972] ECR 1219 at 1227, para 14.

[151] *Ibid.*

[152] *Ibid*, para 18.

Only in 1975 did the ECJ affirm that 'so far as fulfillment of the commitments provided for by GATT is concerned, the Community has replaced the Member States'.[153] Not until 1983 did the ECJ state explicitly that

> as regards fulfillment of the commitments laid down in GATT the Community has been substituted for the Member States with effect from 1 July 1968, the date on which the common customs tariff was brought into force . . .[154]

In practice, however, consistently with this process of institutional empowerment through the creative use of legal concepts, the EC already substituted for the Member States within the GATT.[155] This was notably the case in trade policy, in particular anti-dumping, which formed part of the EC's express power and exclusive competence, and with regard to which the Member States as such[156] had little, if any, formal role after 1 July 1968. Both the EC and its Member States had a stake in a coherent EC position about the GATT.

3. *The First EC Anti-dumping Legislation*

Council Regulation 459/68 followed the Kennedy Round Anti-dumping Code closely. On State-trading country dumping, it contained essentially two provisions. Article 3(2) reiterated Article 2(d) of the Code more or less verbatim.[157] It stated that:

> When there are no sales of the like product in the ordinary course of trade in the domestic market of the exporting country, or when, because of the particular market situation, such sales do not permit a proper comparison, a product shall be considered to be dumped if the price of the product when exported to the Community is less than:
>
> —the comparable price of the like product, when exported to any third country . . .; or
>
> —the cost of production in the country of origin . . .[158]

The two comparators were the same as those in the Code. Article 2(7) of the Regulation made it clear that these concerned the dumping margin.

In addition, Article 3(6) of the EC Regulation provided that:

> In the case of imports from countries where trade is on a basis of near or total monopoly and where domestic prices are fixed by the state, account may be taken of the fact that an *exact comparison* between the export price or a product to the Community and the domestic prices in that country *may not always be appropriate*, since in such cases, *special difficulties* may arise in determining the comparability of prices.[159]

This restated the 1955 Interpretative Note in similar terms.

[153] Case 38/75 *Douaneagent der NV Nederlandse Spoorwegen v Inspecteur der invoerrechten en accijnzen* [1975] ECR 1439 at 1450, para 16.

[154] Joined Cases 267/81, 268/81 and 269/81 *Amministrazione delle Finanze dello Stato v Società Petrolifera Italiana SpA (SPI) and SpA Michelin Italiana (SAMI)* [1983] ECR 801 at 829, para 19.

[155] On the role of the ECJ, see K Jan Kuilwijk, *The European Court of Justice and the GATT Dilemma: Public Interest versus Individual Rights?* (Beuningen, Netherlands, Nexed Editions Academic Publishers, 1996) 91–103.

[156] That is, outside the EC, and thus distinguished from the role of Member States in the Council and various committees, such as the Anti-dumping Committee and the Article 113 Committee.

[157] Except that it used the words 'a product shall be considered to have been dumped', rather than 'the margin of dumping shall be determined by . . .'.

[158] Council Regulation 459/68, Art 3(2), [1968] OJ L93/1.

[159] *Ibid*, Art 3(6), emphasis added.

As in the analogous and identical measure concerning coal and steel products,[160] these were the only provisions dealing specifically with dumping by State-trading countries. They potentially overlapped but did not really resolve the difficult problem of how to calculate the dumping margin for exports from State-trading countries. They provided sufficient guidance to distinguish State-trading countries from other exporting countries. They also excluded the use of State-trading country domestic prices. In other respects, however, they were no more specific than the Kennedy Round Code. In particular, they did not take account of US Treasury decisions or regulations, on the one hand, or of the Report of the GATT Working Party on Poland, on the other hand.

It thus may seem that the EC failed to base its new legislation on 'the state of the art', though it could also be argued that there was no special reason why it should follow other examples. From another perspective, however, the juxtaposition of these two provisions and the fact that neither contained clear guidelines created substantial room for administrative discretion. This left the anti-dumping authority, the Commission, the task of sorting out investigations, using the unsatisfactory provisions on 'special difficulties' and 'particular market situation'. As a result, whether by design or as an unintended consequence, administrative practice took precedence over legislative norms in the development of EC anti-dumping law.

4. *Normative Mistranslation and Administrative Discretion*

Lawyers practising in the specialist field of EC anti-dumping law disagreed about whether the 1968 EC anti-dumping legislation contained rules for determining normal value for State-trading country exports.[161] However, the EEC Commission confirmed at the time that Council Regulation 459/68 could be invoked against imports from Eastern European countries.[162] The Commission followed its US analogue, the Treasury Department. It adopted the analogue market economy approach in its anti-dumping practice.[163] In other words, it used its discretion within an ambiguous legislative framework.

Several factors converged to enhance Commission discretion. First, the Europeanisation of anti-dumping law in the late 1960s granted to the Commission a central role and broad discretion. It had sole power, accompanied by the Anti-dumping Advisory Committee, to initiate and investigate anti-dumping actions, to determine both dumping and injury, to impose provisional anti-dumping duties and to propose definitive duties. Secondly, this occurred within an ambiguous and incomplete legislative framework: EEC law followed GATT law, but the Kennedy Round Code was poorly drafted, conceptually ambiguous and relatively open-ended. Moreover, the

160 Commission Recommendation 77/329/ECSC, [1977] OJ L114/6.

161 Cf Van Bael and Bellis, above n 101, at 93, with R Denton, above n 101, at 206.

162 Réponse de la Commission de la CEE à la question écrite no 50/68, JO des Communautés européennes, no C 68, 9 juillet 1968, 8–9, cited in B Tomsa, *La politique commerciale commune de la CEE et les pays de l'Europe de l'Est* (Brussels, Etablissements Emile Bruylant, 1977) at 152. The same applied to anti-dumping in the coal and steel sector: see Commission Recommendation 77/329, above n 162.

163 This was approved by Tomsa, above n 162, at 152.

EC legislation did not incorporate the Report of the GATT Working Party on Poland or the 1968 US Treasury Regulation. By virtue of their greater specificity, these more recent normative developments might have imposed greater constraints on the exercise of administrative discretion. Thirdly, the US failed to implement fully the results of the Kennedy Round. This fell foul of the tug-of-war between the Treasury and Congress, and it deprived the new EC anti-dumping authorities of a clear normative model. It was only natural that the Commission tended to follow the example of its US administrative counterpart.

To some extent, the role of the EEC Commission thus resembled that of the US Treasury Department. But the Commission's use of Treasury practice and norms as a model was inherently paradoxical. This was because the two anti-dumping authorities operated in profoundly different political and institutional contexts. First, the US was a superpower, with a unified foreign and defence policy, while the European Economic Community comprised a small regional organisation of (then) six Member States with different visions of European integration. This was notably true concerning foreign policy and defence. Each EEC Member State had its own specific policies, which at the time were entirely outside the Treaty umbrella. Hence, quite apart from its legal aspects, Cold War domestic politics in the US differed fundamentally from those in Western Europe. This inevitably affected the more specific context of anti-dumping actions.

Secondly, the US anti-dumping system was embedded in an institutional separation of powers. Congress enacted anti-dumping legislation, while the executive administered it, though it could also adopt interpretative regulations. In contrast, the EC had only a functional separation of powers. Legislative and executive powers were shared between several institutions. The Commission had sole right of legislative initiative. The Commission, after consulting an Advisory Committee composed of representatives of the Member States, enacted provisional anti-dumping measures. It drafted and, again after consulting the Advisory Committee, it proposed EC anti-dumping legislation, but the Council enacted the final, definitive measures. The results of Commission administrative practice were usually included in legislative proposals and later adopted as Council Regulations. The European Parliament played no role. The US system was characterised instead by a continuing tug-of-war between executive and legislature.

Thirdly, the Treasury and the Commission worked within different normative frameworks as regards substantive anti-dumping law. United States anti-dumping laws dated from the early 20th century; they underpinned the GATT. In addition, the US Treasury made its own administrative regulations, sometimes substantially different from Congressional legislation. By contrast, the first EC anti-dumping law was enacted at the end of the 1960s. It was an early step in the Europeanisation of foreign trade law. Partly as a result of their historical development, the relevant laws differed, notably concerning the determination of normal value for imports from State-trading countries.

Fourthly, the Treasury and the Commission played different procedural roles in their respective anti-dumping systems. In the US, the Treasury was responsible (until 1979, when it was replaced by the Department of Commerce) only for the determination of dumping, while the Tariff Commission (or after 1980 the International Trade Commission) was in charge of determining injury. In the EC anti-dumping system, however, both tasks fell to the Commission.

The use of the Treasury model for EC anti-dumping law thus was an example of mistranslation. It could not produce in EC law a real echo of the original.[164] In addition, the transposition of norms and practices from one site to another often has unintended consequences. Intentionally or not, the use of the Treasury model in EC anti-dumping actions tended to reinforce the role of administrative discretion.

5. *The Spread of the Analogue Country Approach*

The EC was not the only GATT contracting party to make use of the wide interpretation of Article VI GATT, a possibility opened up by the 1955 Interpretative Note and then the Kennedy Round Anti-dumping Code. Some importing States simply chose to use consultation and compromise if at all possible to settle disputes.[165] Others, however, in addition to the EC, enacted domestic anti-dumping legislation consistently with the terms of the Anti-dumping Code, making use, implicitly or explicitly, of the Interpretative Note.

One example was the United Kingdom. The UK was not then a member of the EC, which it joined in 1973, so until then it was not bound by EC anti-dumping law. The UK Customs Duties (Dumping and Subsidies) Act 1969 referred explicitly to the use of another market economy country to establish fair market price (normal value) for dumped imports from non-market economy countries. It provided that:

> If it appears to the Board of Trade that the system of trading in the country is such, as a result of government monopoly and control, that the fair market price there *cannot appropriately be determined* in accordance [with the other methods prescribed by the section] then there shall be taken as representing the fair market price *such price as the Board may determine* by reference to any price obtained for goods of that description *when exported to the United Kingdom from another country*, with adjustments made to ensure comparability . . .[166]

This provision drew not only on GATT law but also on the 1968 US Treasury Regulation.

Both the UK legislation and the 1968 EC anti-dumping legislation have rightly been criticised for deviating from Article VI GATT.[167] But so too did the 1968 US Treasury Regulation. By the late 1960s, it could be argued that the conjunction of the 1955 Interpretative Note and the Kennedy Round Anti-dumping Code had actually changed the law. From this standpoint, the use of an analogue country to determine normal value for State-trading country exports might appear to be consistent with

[164] 'The task of the translator consists in finding that intended effect [*Intention*] upon the language into which he is translating which produces in it the echo of the original': W Benjamin, 'The Task of the Translator: An Introduction to the Translation of Baudelaire's *Tableaux Parisiens*' in W Benjamin, *Illuminations* (ed H Arendt; trans H Zohn) (New York, Schocken Books, 1985) 69 at 76. I am grateful to Carol Bernstein for bringing this article to my attention.

[165] See Boudant, above n 140, at 35.

[166] Customs Duties (Dumping and Subsidies) Act 1969, s 4(4), emphasis added. This method was followed, eg, in 1973 by Ackner J in *Leopold Lazarus Limited v Secretary of State for Trade and Industry* (unreported; quoted in F Jacobs, 'Anti-dumping Procedures with regard to Imports from Eastern Europe' in M Maresceau (ed), *The Political and Legal Framework of Trade Relations between the European Community and Eastern Europe* (Dordrecht, Kluwer, 1989) at 304). See also R Dale, *Anti-dumping Law in a Liberal Trade Order* (London, Macmillan for the Trade Policy Research Centre, 1980) at 180–81.

[167] See eg Hu Yuanxiang, above n 78, 233–35.

Article VI GATT, as long as the Note and the Code are taken into account. The 1967 Report of the GATT Working Party on Poland opened up additional space for creative interpretation. But this argument neglects two points. First, even when read in conjunction, these legal instruments did not offer importing countries the possibility of not using prices in the State-trading country of exportation. Secondly, the Poland Working Party Report did not change GATT law, in the sense of providing an interpretation of Article VI GATT that might trump the Kennedy Round Code. Certainly, these legal texts, taken together, did not in any way require such a result, even when interpreted with the aid of Article 31 of the Geneva Convention in the Interpretation of Treaties. But in the anti-dumping practice of the US[168] and the EC, this legal interpretation in favour of the use of an analogue country occurred mainly as in the course of administrative practice. The result was virtually to displace Article VI GATT with respect to dumping from State-trading countries.

III. Consolidation of the 'Non-market Economy' Concept

A. The Interaction of US Law and GATT Law

1. Treasury and Congress in the United States

The tug-of-war between Treasury and Congress was a recurrent theme in the development of US anti-dumping law. This was also true of the 1970s. The 1968 US Treasury Regulation provided for the determination of fair value for State-trading country dumping by the use of constructed value, as reflected by prices of a market economy country for the product, either on its own market or in other countries, including the US.[169] In 1973 this was formally adopted again in United States law in the form of a Treasury Customs Regulation.[170] The measure was of special significance to Poland and Yugoslavia, which alone among central and eastern European countries then had MFN status with the United States.[171]

In 1974 the United States Trade Act[172] incorporated the 1973 (previously 1968) Customs Regulation more or less verbatim into the Anti-dumping Act. This, as Horlick and Schuman point out, transformed 'into a statutory instrument that which had been an interpretative regulation issued as an act of administrative discretion.'[173] Congress intervened in this way because, in the post-Vietnam War period, it was concerned about the potential implications of Nixon's policy of détente and the beginning of MFN negotiations with the Soviet Union. In substance, the 1974 Trade Act merely ratified the Treasury's previous anti-dumping practice. The change of legal form, however, virtually excluded any possibility of adopting an alternative anti-dumping

[168] For more detailed analysis of US practice, see Horlick and Schuman, above n 88, 807–40.

[169] 19 CFR §53.5(b) (1969), quoted in Cuneo and Manuel, above n 36, at 290–91. See also n 116 above on the redesignation of §53 of 19 CFR.

[170] CFR §153.5(b) (1973).

[171] See Kostecki, above n 48, at 98.

[172] Trade Act of 1974, Pub L No 93-618, §406, 88 Stat 2062 (1978) (codified at 19 USC §2436 (1976)).

[173] Horlick and Schuman, above n 88, at 810.

methodology.[174] The initial Treasury practice had been announced in the 1960 *Bicycles from Czechoslovakia* case, but it was first put in legislation form in the 1974 Trade Act. This Act also was the first to use the term 'State-controlled economy', which was inserted in an amendment to the 1921 Anti-dumping Act.[175] The same label of 'State-controlled economy', without any elaborated concept or criteria, was still in use in US law as late as 1979.[176]

Subsequently, in the 1977 *Polish Golf Car* case,[177] the US Treasury Department proposed to use a constructed value based on the calculation of the cost of the actual physical inputs, valued not in the State-trading country but instead on the basis of their costs in a market-economy country.[178] This was a second type of 'analogue country' approach. It differed from the Treasury's earlier practice, encapsulated in the 1974 Trade Act. Both used a market economy surrogate for the State-trading country. However, the 'import values' approach used a surrogate at the same level of economic development as the State-trading country. Domestic or export sale prices were based on the surrogate. This took as given the factor mix of the product being sold. In contrast, the 'factors of production' approach employed the surrogate as a means of valuing the inputs actually used in the non-market economy country. Viewed historically, it derived from the cost of production method familiar to the 1921 US Anti-dumping Act. In principle at least, this second method took the State-trading country's comparative advantages more fully into account.

Then, in 1978, the US Treasury adopted the second test in its anti-dumping practice. Amending the Customs Regulations, it provided for the use of a market economy surrogate in calculating the constructed value of allegedly dumped products when the

174 *Ibid.* The 1974 Trade Act also permitted the Treasury to consider 'the constructed value of such or similar merchandise in a non-state-controlled economy country or countries as determined under section [206 of the Act]'. Notwithstanding House and Senate reports to the contrary, existing Treasury regulations did not include the use of a constructed value. In any event, this provision was not used. See Cuneo and Manuel, above n 36, at 292, fn 82 and fn 83; the quotation is from the text at 292.

175 See 19 USC §1303, amending §205 of the Anti-dumping Act 1921 (19 USC §164). The new §205(b) provided that 'If available information indicates to the Secretary that the economy of the country from which the merchandise is exported is state-controlled to an extent that sales or offers of sales of such or similar merchandise in that country or to countries other than the United States do not permit a determination of foreign market value under subsection (a), the Secretary shall determine the foreign market value of the merchandise on the basis of the normal costs, expenses, and profits as reflected by either (1) the prices . . . at which such or similar merchandise of a non-state-controlled-economy country or countries is sold either (A) for consumption in the home market of that country or countries, or (B) to other countries, including the United States; or (2) the constructed value of such or similar merchandise in a non-state-controlled economy country or countries . . .' See also RH Lantz, 'The Search for Consistency: Treatment of Nonmarket Economies in Transition under United States Anti-dumping and Countervailing Duty Laws' (1995) 10(3) *American University Journal of International Law and Policy* 993 at 1002–03.

176 See RL Meuser, 'Note: Dumping from "Controlled Economy" Countries: The Polish Golf Cart Case' (1979) 11 *Law and Policy in International Business* 777.

177 *Electric Golf Cars from Poland; Anti-dumping*, 40 Fed Reg 25, 497 (1975) TD 75-288, 19 CFR G153.46; see also Meuser, above n 178. See also Cuneo and Manuel, above n 36, at 293–95; Horlick and Schuman, above n 88, at 811–13.

178 The idea was proposed by PD Ehrenhaft, then of the Treasury Department, in a speech entitled 'The Treasury's Approach to Imports for State-controlled Economy Countries under the Anti-dumping and Countervailing Duty Laws' in D Wallace, GC Spina, RM Rawson and B McGill (eds), *Interface One: Conference Proceedings on the Application of US Anti-dumping and Countervailing Duty Laws to Imports from State-controlled Economies and State-owned Enterprises* (Washington, DC, The Institute for International and Foreign Trade Law, Georgetown University Law Center, 1980) 78–85; see also PD Ehrenhaft, 'US Policy on Imports from Economies in Transition' in PD Ehrenhaft, B Vernon Hindley, C Michalopoulos, and LA Winters, *Policies on Imports from Economies in Transition: Two Case Studies* (Washington, DC, The World Bank, 1997) 15 at 23–24.

same or similar products were not produced in any market economy country other than the United States. [179] It sought to value the actual physical inputs used in the production of the goods.[180] This did not follow the approach of the US Congress as expressed in the 1974 Trade Act. Both were consistent, however, with the Tokyo Round Codes.

2. The Tokyo Round Codes

The Tokyo Round of multilateral tariff negotiations began in 1973 and ended in 1979.[181] So far as anti-dumping was concerned, it culminated in two related Codes. The first was the Agreement on Implementation of Article VI of the General Agreement on Tariffs and Trade, known as the 1979 Anti-dumping Code.[182] The second was the Agreement on Interpretation and Application of Articles VI, XVI and XXIII of the General Agreement on Tariffs and Trade, better known as the Code on Subsidies and Countervailing Duties or the 1979 Subsidies Code.[183] Both Codes exercised a powerful influence on the new EC legislation that was then being drafted, so they are discussed before the EC law reforms.

So far as State-trading country dumping was concerned, the 1979 Anti-dumping Code reiterated the provisions of the 1967 Code. This was true both with regard to the determination of the dumping margin when the 'particular market situation' did not permit a proper comparison,[184] and also with regard to the 'without prejudice' clause concerning the 1955 Interpretative Note.[185] The 1955 Note, as before, was appended to the Code.[186]

Nevertheless, the Tokyo Round as a whole went much farther than the Kennedy Round concerning dumping by State-trading countries. The innovations took an unusual legal form. The most important principles on State-trading country dumping were expressed in the Code on Subsidies and Countervailing Duties. The Subsidies Code was agreed before the Anti-dumping Code and was more significant. Not only was there cross-fertilisation between the two negotiating teams, but also both drew on the experience of the Committee on Anti-Dumping Practices in its periodic reviews of

[179] Anti-dumping Investigation Procedures Under Anti-dumping Act, 1921, 43 Fed Reg 35, 262, 35, 265 (1978).

[180] For an analysis, see A Downey and J Graham, 'The Regulation of Dumping from State-controlled Economics: Where Next?' in D Wallace and DA Flores (eds), *Interface Two: Conference Proceedings on the Legal Framework of East–West Trade* (Washington, DC, The International Law Institute, Georgetown University Law Center, 1982) 435.

[181] On the negotiatons, see Stewart, above n 57, at 1435–61.

[182] Agreement on the Implementation of Article VI of the General Agreement on Tariffs and Trade (Geneva, GATT, 1979), GATT, *BISD*, 26th Supp, at 171 (1980).

[183] GATT Code on Subsidies and Countervailing Duties (Agreement on Interpretation and Application of Articles VI, XVI and XXIII of the General Agreement on Tariffs and Trade), in Beseler and Williams, above n 52, App 8, at 352.

[184] Art 2(4) of the Tokyo Round Code repeats verbatim Art 2(d) of the Kennedy Round Code. See 1967 Anti-dumping Code, Art 2(d), and 1979 Anti-dumping Code, above n 184, Art 2(4).

[185] Art 2(7) of the Tokyo Round Code repeats verbatim Art 2(g) of the Kennedy Round Code. See 1967 Anti-dumping Code, Art 2(g), and 1979 Anti-dumping Code, above n 184, Art 2(7).

[186] Note to Art VI, para 1(2), 1979 Anti-dumping Code.

the first Anti-dumping Code since 1968.[187] The political importance of subsidies and countervailing duties in US trade policy accounted for the prominence of the Subsidies Code.[188] As with the Kennedy Round Codes, both Tokyo Round Codes applied not to all GATT contracting parties but only to those that accepted them.

The key article for the present purposes was Article 15 of the Subsidies Code. It dealt with 'special situations', echoing references in previous legal instruments to the 'particular market situation'. It provided as follows:

> 1. In cases of alleged injury caused by imports from a country described in NOTES AND SUPPLEMENTAL PROVISIONS to the General Agreement (Annex I, Article VI, paragraph 1, point 2 [ie a country which has a complete or substantially complete monopoly of its trade and where all domestic prices are fixed by the State] the importing signatory *may* base its procedures and measures either
>
>   (a) on this Agreement, or, alternatively
>   (b) on the Agreement on Implementation of Article VI of the General Agreement on Tariffs and Trade.
>
> 2. It is understood that in both cases (a) and (b) above the calculation of the margin of dumping or of the amount of the estimated subsidy can be made by comparison of the export price with
>
>   (a) the price at which a like product of a country other than the importing signatory or those mentioned above is sold, or
>   (b) the constructed value of a like product in a country other than the importing signatory or those mentioned above.
>
> 3. If neither prices nor constructed value as established under (a) or (b) of paragraph 2 above provide an adequate basis for determination of dumping or subsidization then the *price in the importing signatory*, if necessary duly adjusted to reflect reasonable profits, may be used . . .[189]

In effect, this codified the US and EC practices and drew upon their laws.

Article 15(1) of the Subsidies Code referred across to the Anti-dumping Code. It stated expressly that its own provisions could be applied within the framework of the Anti-dumping Code. This allowed importing countries to use either anti-dumping duties or countervailing duties, but not both, to take action against State-trading country exports. In fact, the US Court of Appeals held in 1986 that countervailing duty law did not apply to imports from State-trading countries.[190] In 1992, however, the Department of Commerce found that this decision was not an absolute bar, and countervailing duties could be imposed on products of a particular industry in a

[187] See Beseler and Williams, above n 52, at 17–18. Established in accordance with Art 17 of the Agreement on the Implementation of Article VI GATT; the Committee consisted of representatives of the parties to the Agreement and normally met once a year: see 'Anti-dumping: Establishment of Committee on Anti-Dumping Practices', GATT, *BISD*, 16th Supp (Geneva, April 1969) at 12.

[188] See Beseler and Williams, above n 52, at 11-18, esp at 15–16. For a comparison of US and EU trade policy instruments, see C Garcia Molyneux, *Domestic Structures and International Trade: The Unfair Trade Policy Instruments of the United States and the European Union* (Oxford, Hart Publishing, 2001).

[189] GATT Code on Subsidies and Countervailing Duties, in Beseler and Williams, above n 52, App 8, at 352, emphasis added.

[190] *Georgetown Steel Corp v United States*, US Court of Appeals for the Federal Circuit, 18 September 1986; 801 F 2nd 1308.

non-market economy if the industry itself was market orientated.[191] At least until 1989 the EC had never imposed countervailing duties on such imports.[192]

More importantly, Article 15(2) of the Subsidies Code provided a clear set of criteria for calculating the dumping margin for State-trading company exports. First, it made perfectly clear that the dumping margin in such cases could be determined on the basis of a surrogate or an analogue country, using real prices or constructed values, or, if neither was possible, on the basis of the price in the importing country.[193] This was merely permissible, however, not legally required. Nevertheless, the 1979 Subsidies Code amounted to a substantial clarification of the ambiguous, confusing language of earlier GATT texts, as well as the 1979 Anti-dumping Code. Secondly, the Subsidies Code not only permitted but also gave a high priority to the use of a constructed value as a means of determining the dumping margin.[194] By contrast, the use of a constructed value was not an option under the Anti-dumping Codes. Thirdly, the Code specified that, if other means were not adequate, the price in the importing country's market could be used. This provision was never in the Anti-dumping Code, but its pedigree went at least as back as far as the 1968 US Treasury Regulation.[195] Lastly, the 1979 Subsidies Code established a new hierarchy between different ways of ascertaining the dumping margin, and hence of determining at least a substitute for normal value. The analogue country price, or a constructed price in an analogue country, took precedence over the use of the price on the importing country's market. In contrast, Article 2(4) of the Anti-dumping Code had placed its two alternative tests on an equal footing.

The Tokyo Round Subsidies Code thus went far beyond any previous or contemporaneous anti-dumping code. It codified most of the basic rules on the determination of dumping margin, or a substitute for normal value, in State-trading country dumping. It was therefore not simply a mere reinterpretation of the Kennedy Round Anti-dumping Code.[196] The only lacuna was that it did not specify how the analogue country was to be chosen. Following past practice, this was left to the discretion of the importing countries.

[191] JA Laroski, Jr, 'NMEs: A Love Story—Nonmarket and Market Economy Status under US Anti-dumping Law' (1999) 30 *Law and Policy in International Business* at 376–77 (citing *Oscillating and Ceiling Fans from the People's Republic of China*, 57 Fed Reg 24,019 (Dep't Commerce, 1992) and *Chrome-plated Lug Nuts and Wheel Locks from the People's Republic of China*, 57 Fed Reg 10,459 (Dep't Commerce, 1992). On the argument that the Tokyo Round Subsidies Code was ambiguous and its implications for the relation between anti-dumping law and countervailing duty law, see DR Phelan, *The Application of United States and European Community Domestic Trade Laws to the Imports of Non-market economy GATT Contracting Parties—A Time for Change*, EUI Working Paper LAW No 92/28 (Department of Law, European University Institute, Florence), 26–63.

[192] Jacobs, above n 166, at 293.

[193] Beseler and Williams, above n 52, at 66, described this as 'an important advance'.

[194] Notably, the creator of the *Polish Golf Car* rule described the Subsidies Code as incorporating this rule, which was then used by US anti-dumping authorities, even though it was not included in the Tokyo Round Anti-dumping Code and was not even part of US legislation until the Omnibus Trade and Competitiveness Act of 1988. PD Ehrenhaft, 'US Policy on Imports from Economies in Transition', in Ehrenhaft *et al*, above n 178, at 24

[195] 19 CFR §53.5(b) (1969), quoted in Cuneo and Manuel, above n 36, at 290–91.

[196] See also Beseler and Williams, above n 52, at 66.

3. The US Trade Agreements Act of 1979 and Aftermath

One result of the Tokyo Round was the enactment of the United States Trade Agreements Act of 1979.[197] Title I of this Act repealed the 1921 Anti-dumping Act and added a new Title VII to the 1930 Tariff Act that implemented the provisions of the Tokyo Round.[198] The term 'State-controlled economy' continued to be used. In another seesaw for power with the executive, Congress re-enacted the 'import values' approach in place of the 'factors of production' approach. The former had previously been the method specified in the Treasury's 1968 (and 1973) Customs Regulation, and had been given a Congressional straitjacket in the 1974 Trade Act. In 1978, however, the Treasury adopted the 'factors of production' approach. In seeking to reverse this position, the Trade Agreements Act of 1979 was entirely consistent with Article 15 of the Tokyo Round Subsidies Code.[199]

This US statute[200] was refined by Department of Commerce Regulations that established no fewer than 10 approaches for calculating foreign market price (normal value) for non-market economy imports.[201] As summarised by Vermulst, these were:

> (1) the price at which such or similar merchandise, produced in a *comparable* market economy country, is sold for consumption (a) in the home market of that market economy or (b) to other countries, (c) including the United States; (2)(d) the constructed value of such or similar merchandise in a *comparable* market economy; (3) the 'simulated' constructed value; (4)(f–g) prices or (h) constructed value from market economy country, other than the United States; (5)(i) prices or (j) constructed value of the sales or production of such or similar merchandise in the United States.[202]

Subsequently, the 1988 Omnibus Trade and Competitiveness Act consecrated the 'factors of production' approach as the method to be preferred in calculating normal value.[203]

The multiplicity of options gave great discretion to the anti-dumping authority. In addition, the same statute has been interpreted as having a certain flexibility in another sense, namely, in implying that

[197] Trade Agreements Act of 1979, Pub L No 96-39, 1979 US Code Cong & Admin News) 93 Stat) 144, codfiied at 19 USC §1677b(c) (1982). See Horlick and Schuman, above n 88, at 812–13. A slightly different interpretation of the relationship between Treasury and Congress is presented in JS Neeley, 'Non-market Economy Import Regulation: From Bad to Worse' (1989) 20 *Law & Policy in International Business* 529 at 532.

[198] Raj Bhala, *International Trade Law: Cases and Materials* (Charlottesville, Va, Michie Law Publishers, 1996) 685.

[199] In 1979 Congress also transferred responsibility for dumping investigations from the Treasury to the Department of Commerce: see GN Horlick, 'The United States Anti-dumping System' in JH Jackson and EA Vermulst (eds), *Anti-dumping Law and Practice: A Comparative Study* (New York and London, Harvester Wheatsheaf, 1990) at 105.

[200] 19 CFR §353.8. See EA Vermulst, *Anti-dumping Law and Practice in the United States and the European Communities: A Comparative Analysis* (Elsevier North Holland, Amsterdam, 1987) 359, fn 97.

[201] The 1979 Act also removed responsibility for making sales at less than fair value determinations from the Treasury and turned it over to the Department of Commerce.

[202] Vermulst, above n 200, at 359–60. As to US practice at the time, see Cuneo and Manuel, above n 36, at 295–307.

[203] The Omnibus Trade and Competitiveness Act of 1988, HR 4848, 100th Congress, 2nd session (1988), Pub L 100-418, 102 Stat 1107, quoted in PD Ehrenhaft, 'The Application of Anti-dumping Duties to Imports from "Non-market Economies', in Jackson and Vermulst, above n 199, at 305.

> some industries within a state-controlled country may be entitled to a 'normal' dumping methodology because they are market-oriented, while other 'nonmarket' industries will have the surrogate country methodology applied . . .[204]

This second position was later to have very far-reaching implications for both US and EC anti-dumping law.

In 1988, the Omnibus Trade and Competitiveness Act, amending the Tariff Act of 1930, replaced the term 'State-controlled economy' with the term 'non-market economy'.[205] It defined 'non-market economy' as

> any foreign country that the administering authority [the Department of Commerce] determines does not operate on market principles of cost or pricing structures, so that sales of merchandise in such country do not reflect the fair value of the merchandise . . .[206]

The factors to be considered in making this determination were:

> (i) the extent to which the currency of the foreign country is convertible into the currency of other countries,
> (ii) the extent to which wage rates are determined by free bargaining between labor and management,
> (iii) the extent to which joint ventures or other investments by firms of other foreign countries are permitted in the foreign country,
> (iv) the extent of government ownership or control of the means of production,
> (v) the extent of government control over the allocation of resources and over the price and output decisions of enterprises, and
> (vi) such other factors as the administering authority considers appropriate . . .[207]

These factors were echoed in subsequent EC anti-dumping law.

B. The Birth of the 'Non-market economy' in EC Anti-dumping Law

1. Consolidation of 'State-trading countries' as a Legal Category

During the 1970s the EC renewed its distinction between imports from State-trading countries and all other imports. In June 1972, a Council Regulation expanded the list of products liberalised at Community level, that is, products in respect of which quantitative restrictions had been removed in all Member States. In doing so, however, it extended the reach of EC law further by adding Albania, China, North Vietnam, North Korea and Mongolia to the Community's formal list of State-trading

[204] Neeley, above n 197, at 533.

[205] 19 USC §1677b, amendments (1988), summary available athttp://codes.lp.findlaw.com/uscode/19/4/IV/IV/1677b/notes, last accessed 18 February 2010; current version available at http://codes.lp.findlaw.com/uscode/19/4/IV/IV/1677b, last accessed 18 February 2010.

[206] Section 771(18)(A) to Title VII of the Tariff Act of 1930, 19 USC §1677(18)(A)(1994), quoted in Laroski, above n 193, at 382.

[207] Section 771(18)(B) to Title VII of the Tariff Act of 1930, 19 USC §1677(18)(B), (1994), quoted in Laroski, above n 191, at 382. This article examines the subsequent application of these criteria by US anti-dumping authorities.

countries.[208] In March 1975 another Council Regulation extended the list of products further, brought the list of liberalised products and State-trading countries up to date, and at the same time added the German Democratic Republic to the EC list of State-trading countries.[209] In 1979 the Community promulgated new common rules for imports from State-trading countries, repealing Council Regulation 109/70 and setting down uniform principles for the common commercial policy. It consolidated the same list of State-trading countries, except for the omission of China[210]; imports from China were governed by separate legislation.[211] Council Regulation 1765/82 covered the same countries, except that Albania did not figure on the list.[212] However, Albania and the same other countries were included in the list of State-trading countries in Council Regulation 3420/83 on import arrangements for products from State-trading countries, not liberalised at Community level.[213]

When the EEC's common commercial policy began, China was in the midst of the Cultural Revolution. Changes in EC trade policy toward China ran roughly in parallel with changes in US China policy. The US embargo on trade with China was lifted in 1972, though restrictions on strategic goods through COCOM continued.[214] This followed the new pattern of American diplomacy, including the secret Kissinger trip to China in July 1971, his official trip in October 1971, Nixon's February 1972 visit to Beijing, and the subsequent establishment of 'liaison offices' in Beijing and Washington, all intended by the US and China to counteract the power of the Soviet Union.[215] The People's Republic of China was not on the initial EEC/ECSC lists of State-trading countries. As early as 1972, however, relations between the Community and China improved.[216] China had entered into diplomatic relations with the United Kingdom in 1949, France in 1964 and then Germany in 1972,[217] but even before 1972 China had an active trade with Germany.[218] Starting in 1972, EC import legislation included China in the list of State-trading countries.[219] Though containment of the

[208] Council Regulation 1414/72, Annex [1972] OJ L151/1. Later in the year the list of products was further extended, but the list of State-trading countries remained the same: Council Regulation 1751/72, Annex [1972] OJ L184/1. The list of products and countries was consolidated in August 1972 by Commission Decision 72/322, Annex [1972] OJ L208/1. Legislation in 1973 and 1974 on common rules for imports for State-trading countries also maintained the same list of countries: see Council Regulation 955/73, Annex [1973] OJ L98/14; Council Regulation 956/73, Annex [1973] OJ L98/21; Council Regulation 957/73, Annex [1973] OJ L98/26; and Council Regulation 238/74, Annex [1974] OJ L27/1.

[209] Council Regulation 958/75, [1975] OJ L99/1. A further extension of liberalised products in 1977 contained the same list: Council Regulation 2896/77, Annex [1977] OJ L338/1.

[210] Council Regulation 925/79, Annex [1979] OJ L131/1.

[211] See Council Regulation 2532/78 on common rules for imports from the People's Republic of China [1978] OJ L306/1.

[212] Council Regulation 1765/82 on common rules for imports from State-trading countries [1982] OJ L195/1.

[213] [1983] OJ L346/6.

[214] FC Schroeder, 'The Two Legal Levels of East–West Trade' in Dalchoong and Werner, above n 142, at 110–11, who also describes the similar measures that applied to East Bloc Countries.

[215] See J Mann, *About Face: A History of America's Curious Relationship with China, from Nixon to Clinton* (New York, Knopf, 1999); JPD Dunbabin, *The Cold War: The Great Powers and Their Allies* (London and New York, Longman, 1994) 282–99.

[216] See Harish Kapur, *China and the European Economic Community: The New Connection* (Dordrecht, Martinus Nijhoff, 1986) 22–30.

[217] See F Snyder (ed), *The European Union and China, 1949–2008: Basic Documents and Commentary* (Oxford, Hart Publishing, 2009), ch 1.

[218] See R Audouard, 'Trade without Diplomatic Relations—The Experience of the Federal Republic of Germany' in Dalchoong and Werner, above n 142, at 174–77.

[219] China was first included in the list of State-trading countries in Council Regulation 14514/72, Annex [1972] OJ L151/1.

Soviet Union was not necessarily the European objective, diplomatic relations between the EC and China were established in 1975.[220] The first trade agreement between the EC and China was signed in 1978.[221] It was followed by a substantial increase in imports from China into the EC. This in turn led the EC to treat imports from China separately from those from other State-trading countries, at least with regard to certain products.

In October 1978, Council Regulation 2532/78 laid down the first common rules for imports from China.[222] As a rationale, it referred simply to 'the economic structure of China'.[223] It excluded China from the scope of application of Council Regulation 109/70, the common rules on imports from State-trading countries.[224] In 1982 the Community enacted new common rules on imports from China.[225] As of 1983, imports from China into the Community were subject to two main Regulations.[226] But so far as general import rules were concerned, the EC continued to treat China separately from the listed State-trading countries. China and listed State-trading countries were grouped together, however, for the purposes of the administration of EC anti-dumping law.

The political dynamic underlying this legislation thus consisted of a two-fold Europeanisation of EC foreign trade law. On the one hand, EC legislation recognised the liberalisation by Member States of trade in an increasing number of products, and then it assumed for itself this trade management function. On the other hand, it gradually extended the list of countries officially recognised for the purpose of EC import legislation as State-trading countries. From the standpoint of EC anti-dumping law, three different processes went hand in hand: the Europeanisation of foreign trade law; the expansion of Community powers; and an expansion of the group of countries designated as State-trading countries.

2. *The Landmark Regulation and its Predecessor*

In 1979, even before the Tokyo Round was concluded, the EC made decisive changes in its anti-dumping law concerning State-trading country exports.[227] The first EC legislative reforms occurred in the shadow of the Tokyo Round Codes. The first concerned coal and steel products. Commission Recommendation 158/79/ECSC[228]

[220] See Kapur, above n 216. 26–38, 56–57.

[221] Trade Agreement between the European Economic Community and China [1978] OJ L123/1, reproduced in Snyder, above n 217, 62—66, 76. . Implementing rules for this Agreement were not laid down until 1983: see Council Regulation 3421/83 laying down certain detailed rules for the implementation of the Trade Agreement between the Community and China, [1983] OJ L346/91.

[222] [1978] OJ L306/1. Additional products were added by Council Regulation 799/82, [1982] OJ L92/1.

[223] Council Regulation 2532/78, Preamble, 3rd Recital [1978] OJ L306/1.

[224] *Ibid*, Art 14.

[225] [1982] OJ L195/21.

[226] Council Regulation 1766/82, [1982] OJ L195/1, for products liberalised at Community level, and Council Regulation 3420/83, [1983] OJ L346/6 for other products. See generally Hu Yuanxiang, above n 6, at 291–340; F Snyder, 'Legal Aspects of Trade between the European Union and China: Preliminary Reflections' in N Emiliou and D O'Keeffe (eds), *The European Union and World Trade Law after the GATT Uruguay Round* (Chichester, John Wiley & Sons, 1996) 369–72; and Snyder, above n 7, at 156–58, 595–600.

[227] Certain procedural amendments were made in the interim. See Council Regulation 2011/73, [1973] OJ L206/3; Council Regulation 1411/77, [1977] OJ L160/4.

[228] [1979] OJ L21/14.

was published on 29 January 1979 and entered into force the following day.[229] It amended Article 3(6) of Recommendation 77/329 on non-market economy dumping and aimed to clarify the method of calculating normal value for non-market economy exports.[230] It provided that

> In the case of imports from countries where trade is on a basis of near or total monopoly and where domestic prices are fixed by the State, account *may* be taken of the fact that an exact comparison between the export price of a product to the Community and the domestic price in that country *is not normally appropriate*. In such cases normal value *shall* be determined on the basis of either:
>
> (a) the prices at which a like *product of a market-economy country* or countries is sold either
>
> (i) for consumption in the *domestic market of that country* or
> (ii) to *other countries*, including the *Community*; or
>
> (b) the *constructed value* of a like product in a market-economy country or countries.
>
> If neither prices nor constructed value as established under (a) or (b) above provide an adequate basis for determination of normal value, then the prices or constructed value as determined from the *sales or production in the Community* shall be used . . .[231]

This ambiguous wording ('may', 'is not normally appropriate', 'shall') and awkward construction were the result either of sloppy drafting or political compromise. But the legislation marked a break with its predecessor in several important respects. First, it appeared to establish a presumption that prices on the non-market economy domestic market would not be used. Such was the sense of the words 'is not normally appropriate'. If this were a presumption, it would have represented the first steps in EC anti-dumping legislation toward the analogue country approach.

Secondly, however, in the case of State-trading country dumping, the Recommendation actually required that normal value be established on the basis of an analogue country. This requirement superseded the presumption apparently created by the preceding sentence. The ECSC Recommendation thus was the first Community legislation to consolidate the analogue country approach. It was limited, however, to coal and steel (ECSC) products.

Thirdly, it set down the various comparators or prices to be used to determine normal value of State-trading country exports. The first group ((a)) basically followed the 1968 US Treasury Regulation. The second group ((b)) conformed to the Report of the 1967 GATT Working Party on Poland. In fact, the Recommendation followed closely the Tokyo Round Subsidies Code. However, like the earlier legal instruments, but unlike the Subsidies Code, the ECSC Recommendation actually used the term 'normal value', not 'dumping margin'. It thus was the first Community measure to articulate clearly a range of substitutes for State-trading country domestic prices and to refer expressly to the determination of normal value of State-trading country exports.

Judged according to the principle of legal certainty, especially from a practical administrative standpoint, the Recommendation represented a substantial improvement in Community anti-dumping law. But it was seriously marred by poor drafting, ambiguous construction and even mistakes of law. It referred to practical experience in the application of GATT anti-dumping rules generally since their adoption and to

229 Commission Recommendation 158/79/ECSC, Art 2, [1979] OJ L21/14.
230 See *ibid*, Preamble, 5th Recital.
231 *Ibid*, Art 1(2), emphasis added.

the need to take account of the established practice of the Community's major trading partners.[232] In addition, the Recitals in the Preamble referred in general terms to the GATT anti-dumping code, stating simply that 'these Community rules are, in large measure, transposed from the . . . Anti-dumping Code'.[233] But they did not refer expressly to the Kennedy Round Anti-dumping Code that was then in force. More importantly, they did not contain a single reference to the Tokyo Round Subsidies Code. This was so even though the Recommendation was drafted during the Tokyo Round, and even though the rules in the Recommendation for determining normal value for State-trading country exports were clearly based on the discussions leading to Tokyo Round Subsidies Code or the Code itself. This suggests that, in adopting the measure, the Commission sought to express its own administrative practices in legislative form, to remain consistent with US anti-dumping law, and to anticipate, so far as possible, the main lines of the results of the Tokyo Round. It also suggests, however, that the drafters were not overly concerned with what non-lawyers might view merely as legal niceties but what lawyers consider to be essential to the rule of law and judicial protection.

In August 1979, Council Regulation 1681/79/EC extended the same substantive norms to other economic sectors. [234] Adopted on 1 August, it was published the following day and entered into force three days later.[235] It concerned products covered by the European Economic Community (EEC) Treaty, not coal and steel products covered by the ECSC Treaty. Its Article 1 provided:

> In the case of imports from non-market economy countries and, in particular, those to which Regulations (EEC) No 2532/78 and (EEC) No 925/79 apply, normal value *shall* be determined in an appropriate and not unreasonable manner on the basis of one of the following criteria:
>
> (aa) the price at which the *like product of a market economy third country* is actually sold;
>
> (i) for consumption on the *domestic market of that country*, or
> (ii) to *other countries*, including the *Community*;
>
> (bb) the constructed value of the like product in a market economy third country; or
> (cc) if neither price nor constructed value as established under (aa) or (bb) above provides an adequate basis, the price actually paid or payable in the Community for the like product, duly adjusted, if necessary, to include a reasonable profit margin . . .[236]

This followed the Commission's ECSC Recommendation very closely, both in the Recitals and in the definition of normal value. Though also the product of the Commission, it represented a marked improvement in terms of legal drafting.

Council Regulation 1681/79 was a legislative landmark. It symbolised the birth of the idea of the 'non-market economy' in EC anti-dumping law. First, it used 'non-market economy' as a legal category. Secondly, it abandoned the search for an adequate substantive definition of the category, and instead defined the category by referring to the basic regulations on imports from State-trading countries and China. Thirdly, the countries in the non-market economy category were legally contraposed to market economy countries, not only in anti-dumping law but also by virtue of the fact of being treated in separate import regulations. Fourthly, the Regulation definitively set aside the domestic

[232] *Ibid*, Preamble, 3rd Recital.
[233] *Ibid*, Preamble, 2nd Recital.
[234] [1979] OJ L196/1.
[235] *Ibid*, Art 9.
[236] *Ibid*, Art 1 (footnotes omitted).

price of the non-market economies in the determination of normal value. Indeed, it was the first EC (as distinct from ECSC) legislation to define the concept of 'normal value' and introduce it into the detailed rules on the determination of dumping.[237] Fifthly, it provided in unmistakable terms that, in the case of non-market economy dumping, normal value was to be determined on the basis of an analogue country. Sixthly, it represented a definite break with the plain language of Article VI GATT, though using the same structure. It fused the terms of the 1968 US Treasury Regulation and the Tokyo Round Subsidies Code. Council Regulation 1681/79 crystallised the 'non-market economy' into a distinct legal category.

3. *Explaining Legislative Innovation*

How can we explain this legislative innovation? Three factors seem the most important:

a) changes in the international anti-dumping repertoire;
b) specific ideas in Europe about comparative economic systems; and
c) the perceived emergence of new economic threats.

First, the Regulation was adopted in the shadow of the Tokyo Round Codes. It represented an effort to synthesise logically, in a single sentence and paragraph,[238] a multiplicity of normative elements concerning the determination of normal value in cases of State-trading country dumping. These elements had emerged historically in various sites. In marking a clean break with the terms of Article VI GATT, however, the Community Regulation abandoned certain older elements of the international anti-dumping repertoire. It was based mainly on more recent elements, usually sanctioned by multilateral agreement within the GATT, which took account of administrative practice regarding State-trading country dumping. Indeed, it referred directly (as had its predecessor) to the importance of taking account of the established practices of the EC's main trading partners.[239] It drew especially on US Treasury Regulations and on the Tokyo Round Subsidies Code.

Secondly, while taking account of norms from other sites, the Regulation was an autonomous (or unilateral) measure in terms of Community law. In its treatment of State-trading country dumping, it was harsher than any previous legislation. It failed to follow the Tokyo Round's permissive approach concerning the analogue country method. More precisely, it took advantage of the freedom of interpretation offered by the word 'can', and instead of reading it as 'may', the EC choose to read it as 'shall'. With regard to the analogue country method, there were no conditional clauses or room for discretion. The Regulation established a new principle that was absolutely clear: in determining normal value for non-market economy exports, the price to be compared with the export price was henceforth always a price on the market of another market economy country. This excluded totally the use of the non-market

[237] See *ibid*, Preamble, 3rd Recital, and Art 1 (replacing Art 3(2)(a) of Regulation 459/68).

[238] Indicating that it was probably originally drafted in French.

[239] See Council Regulation 1681/79, Preamble, 2nd Recital [1979] OJ L196/1. As already seen, the US is the main exemplar. For a systematic comparison, focusing in particular on the period between 1980 and 1986, see Vermulst, above n 200.

economy domestic price. Market economies and non-market economies represented two different types of economic systems and should be kept distinct.

While the use of the analogue country method was required, normal value had to be determined in an appropriate and not unreasonable manner. This was a new norm in EC anti-dumping law. The formula was already part of the international anti-dumping law repertoire. It was embodied in the 1967 Report of the GATT Working Party on Poland. Translated into the EC context, it was designed to structure the exercise of the Commission's administrative discretion. It resonated directly with Community administrative law, notably the principle of proportionality developed in EC law by the ECJ.

While drawing on the international anti-dumping law repertoire, the sharp distinction between two types of economic systems in EC anti-dumping law stemmed primarily from the German Ordoliberal school of economic thought. Known also as the Freiburg School, this group was founded in the 1930s, as an opponent of the Nazi regime, by Franz Böhm and Walter Eucken. The Ordoliberals, and Eucken in particular, held that there were two elemental economic forms: exchange or 'transaction economy' (*Verkehrswirtschaft*), and planning or 'centrally administered economy' (*Zentralverwaltungswirtschaft*). These types were distinguished by two criteria: first, a primary criterion, whether the State or private enterprise dominated the economy; and then a secondary criterion, the system of ownership.[240] These economic types constituted the only alternative principles for economic organisation. The two systems were incompatible, and the importation of elements from one to the other harmed the operation of the system.[241] For the functioning of the 'transaction economy' system, the Ordoliberals placed great emphasis on 'economic constitutionalism', namely, the importance of legal constraints on governmental, including administrative, action. They considered that decision-making should be subject to legal principles and clear legal rules. The conjunction of general concepts, such as reasonableness, and detailed rules guiding administrative action was entirely consistent with their ideas.[242] The German Ordoliberals played a central role in the development of EC competition law

[240] N Kloten, 'Zur Typenlehre der Wirtschafts—und Gesellschaftsordnungen' (1955) 7 *Ordo* 123, cited in K Schmidt, 'The Public Sector in a Market Economy' in A Peacock and H Willgerodt, *Germany's Social Market Economy: Origins and Evolution* (Macmillan for the Trade Policy Research Centre, London, 1989) at 195. The Ordoliberals recognised that, in reality, the two types could be mixed. Indeed, one member of the group, A Müller-Armack, invented the term 'social market economy' (*Soziale Marktwirtschaft*) and was a principal architect of the post-World War II German economic model.

[241] See W Eucken, *The Foundations of Economics* (Chicago, University of Chicago Press, 1951) at 109, 118, cited in H Peukert, 'W Eucken (1891–1950) and the Historical School' in P Koslowski (ed), *The Theory of Capitalism in the German Economic Tradition: Historicism, Ordo-Liberalism, Critical Theory, Solidarism* (Berlin, Springer-Verlag, 2000) at 108, 111; R Wagner, 'ORDO Liberalism and the Social Market Economy' in HG Berman and AMC Waterman (eds), *Economics and Religion: Are They Distinct?* (Dordrecht, Kluwer, 1994) 121 at 129, 133, referring to W Eucken, *Grundsätze der Wirtschaftspolitik* (Tıbingen, JB Mohr, 1952) 270–85; T Riha, 'Ordo—The German Neoliberal Model of Economic Order' (1986) 39 *Economia Internazionale* 31 at 35–36. See also KW Nörr, 'Franz Böhm and the Theory of the Private Law Society' in P Koslowski (ed), *The Theory of Capitalism in the German Economic Tradition: Historicism, Ordo-Liberalism, Critical Theory, Solidarism* (Berlin, Springer-Verlag, 2000) 148; E Tuchtfeldt, 'Will Communism and Capitalism Become Similar Economic Systems?' in A Peacock and H Willgerodt (eds), *Germany's Social Market Economy: Origins and Evolution* (London, Macmillan for the Trade Policy Research Centre, 1989) 87.

[242] See also M Streit, 'Economic Order, Private Law and Public Policy: The Freiburg School of Law and Economics in Perspective' (1992) 148 *Zeitschrift für die gesamten Staatswissenschaften / Journal of Theoretical and Institutional Economics* 675.

and to some extent trade law,[243] as well as in EC private law.[244] It may be hypothesised that they also played a leading role in shaping the basic assumptions of Community anti-dumping law.[245]

The third factor that shaped the creation of the concept of 'non-market economy' in EC anti-dumping law was the existence of a new international context and what the EC considered to be new economic threats. Following the oil crisis, the 1970s was a period of recession. United States hegemony declined, and the GATT regime was supported principally by a congruence of purpose among the main trading powers,[246] sometimes described in terms of a club.[247] Within the EC, growing protectionism prevailed, both generally in internal and external trade, and specifically in terms of anti-dumping law. Internally, the increased power of the individual Member States was also evident in the breakdown of the model of European integration based on harmonisation, culminating in the 1979 *Cassis de Dijon* case and the resulting principle of mutual recognition.[248] Externally, this was a period of increased imports into the EC from Eastern European countries, as well as an increasing number of anti-dumping

[243] See also DJ Gerber, 'Competition Law and International Trade: The European Union and the Neo-Liberal Factor' (1995) *Pacific Rim Law & Policy Journal* 37; DJ Gerber, 'Constitutionalizing the Economy: German Neo-liberalism, Competition Law and the "New" Europe' (1994) 42 *American Journal of Comparative Law* 25.

[244] See C Joerges, 'The Science of Private Law and the Nation State' in F Snyder (ed), *The Europeanisation of Law: Legal Effects of European Integration* (Oxford, Hart Publishing, 2000) 47 at (eg) 57 (on the Frankfurt rectorial address of Walter Hallstein, later first President of the European Commission).

[245] The career of A Müller-Armack illustrates the point, without establishing directly that he personally influenced EC anti-dumping policy. Shortly before the end of World War II, he wrote *Wirtschaftslenkung and Marktwirtschaft* (*Planned Economy and Market Economy*) (1946), in which he made proposals to reform the centrally planned economy of the National Socialist period. In 1952 he was appointed by Ludwig Erhard to be Head of the Central Policy Unit at the German Federal Economics Ministry. In this capacity, he 'was involved with all aspects of German, European and international economic policy during the reconstruction phase of the German economy and the re-establishment of the German economic order, based on the principles of the Social Market Economy.' The many matters he dealt with included the liberalisation of foreign trade as well as the Treaty of Rome. In 1958 he was appointed Under-Secretary of State for European Affairs and often served as German representative to the Council of Ministers. (See Watrin, 'Alfred Mıller-Armack—Economic Policy Market and Sociologist of Relıgion' in Koslowskı, above n 241, at 193–94.) He died in 1978, just before the Tokoyo Round Codes were agreed, but his ideas and those of other Ordoliberals, notably Franz Böhm's collaborator Ernst-Joachim Mestmäcker, had a lasting influence on EC law. See generally A Peacock and H Willgerodt (eds), *German Neo-Liberals and the Social Market Economy* (Macmillan for the Trade Policy Research Centre, London, 1989); Peacock and Willgerodt, above n 241. Joerges points out the turn in the early 1970s to a Hayek-inspired Ordnungstheory: see Joerges, above n 244, at 69–70. See also M Streit and M Wohlgemuth, 'The Market Economy and the State: Hayekian and Ordoliberal Conceptions' in Koslowski, above n 241, at 225–69.

[246] See J Ruggie, 'International Regimes, Transactions, and Change: Embedded Liberalism in the Postwar Economic Order', in SD Krasner (ed), *International Regimes* (Ithaca, Cornell University Press, 1983) 195 at 200; C Lipson, 'The Transformation of Trade: The Source and Effects of Regime Change' in Krasner, *ibid*, 233 at 236, 268–70. See also RO Keohane, 'The Theory of Hegemonic Stability and Changes in International Economic Regimes, 1967–1977' in OR Holsti, RM Siverson and AL George (eds), *Change in the International System* (Boulder, Westview Press, 1980) 131 (arguing that, in addition to hegemonic stability theory, domestic political and economic patterns and the strategies of domestic political actors must be taken into account to explain changes in international trade regimes). On the importance of the distribution of power in regime dynamics generally, see S Krasner, 'Global Communications and National Power: Life on the Pareto Frontier' (1991) 43 *World Politics* 336. For an earlier view, giving somewhat more emphasis to the role of catalytic external events, see S Krasner, 'State Power and the Structure of International Trade' (1976) 28 *World Politics* 317.

[247] On the different case in which coalitions of like-minded States, or clubs, form regimes in the absence of a hegemon, see L Eden and FO Hampson, 'Clubs are Trump: The Formation of International Regimes in the Absence of a Hegemon' in J Rogers Hollingsworth and R Boyer (eds), *Contemporary Capitalism: The Embeddedness of Institutions* (Cambridge, Cambridge University Press, 1997) 361.

[248] Case 120/78 *Rewe-Zentralfinanz v Bundesmonopolverwaltung fir Branntwein* ('*Cassis de Dijon*') [1979] ECR 649.

actions against State-trading countries.[249] Moreover, it coincided with the beginning of Chinese 'opening up' and domestic economic changes beginning in December 1978.

In these circumstances, it might be suggested that the concept of 'non-market economy' was a projection of the kind of unity the EC Member States sometimes wished they had.[250] From the standpoint of trade policy, it also tended to invalidate any comparative advantage that might otherwise be enjoyed by 'non-market economy' countries. With the benefit of hindsight, however, it is especially striking to note that the birth of the 'non-market economy' in EC anti-dumping law coincided with the beginning of economic transformation in China and increased Chinese foreign trade. In many ways, of which chronology was merely the most obvious marker, the two were closely entangled, even though each had its own dynamic,[251] and even though EC anti-dumping also drew on an international repertoire of concepts, principles and rules elaborated over the previous half century.

C. Consolidation

Concurrently with the entry into force of the Tokyo Round Codes on Anti-dumping and on Subsidies and Countervailing Duties, the EC replaced its existing anti-dumping legislation.[252] The new legislation, Council Regulation 3017/79,[253] repealed Council Regulation 459/68 and consolidated EC anti-dumping law.[254] It was intended expressly to implement the 1979 GATT Codes on Anti-dumping, on the one hand, and on Subsidies and Countervailing Duties, on the other hand.[255]

The new legislation stated explicitly that

> in implementing these rules it is essential, in order to maintain the balance of rights and obligations which these agreements sought to establish, that the Community take account of their interpretation by the Community's trading partners, as reflected in legislation or established practice . . .[256]

This language signalled the continuing relationship of mutual consultation, selective borrowing and normative translation between the EC and other sites, particularly the

[249] See J Maslen, 'The European Community's Relations with the State-trading Countries of Europe 1984–1986' (1986) 6 *Yearbook of European Law* 335at 345–46; Jacobs, above n 166, at 291–92. For the preceding period, see J Maslen, 'The European Community's Relations with the State-trading Countries 1981–1983' (1983) 3 *Yearbook of European Law* 323.

[250] I am grateful to Katherine Verdery for this point.

[251] For a broad historical perspective, see K Pomerantz, *The Great Divergence: China, Europe, and the Making of the Modern World Economy* (Princeton, Princeton University Press, 2000).

[252] Council Regulation 1681/79, [1979] OJ L196/1, had amended but not abrogated the first EC anti-dumping regulation, Council Regulation 459/68, [1968] OJ L93/1.

[253] Council Regulation 3017/79, [1979] OJ L339/1.

[254] *Ibid*, Art 17.

[255] The 3rd Recital of the Regulation states: 'Whereas the multilateral trade negotiations concluded in 1979 have led to an agreement on implementation of Article VI of the GATT (1979 Anti-Dumping Code) and an agreement on the interpretation and application of Articles VI, XVI and XXIII of the GATT, which concerns subsidies and countervailing measures'. The 4th Recital states that 'Whereas it is therefore appropriate to amend the Community rules in the light of the 1979 agreements . . .'.

[256] Council Regulation 3017/79, above n 253, 5th Recital. The willingness (or necessity) for the EC to take into account the interpretations of its trading partners, especially the US, contrasted sharply with the US's own position during this period. See Vermulst, above n 200, at 3 and fnn 11 and 12.

United States. It thus acknowledged the fact that EC law reflected, more or less directly, the tug-of-war between the executive and the legislature that had long been a driving force in the history of US anti-dumping law. In addition, it was intended partly to protect the EC from different interpretations of the GATT Codes by other signatories, notably the United States, in the light of the objections of the US Congress to the 1967 Kennedy Round Anti-dumping Code.[257]

According to its Preamble, the new Regulation was intended to present the rules for determining normal value clearly and in sufficient detail.[258] Consequently, Article 2(5) provided that:

> In the case of imports from non-market economy countries and, in particular, those to which Regulations (EEC) No 2532/78 (fn3: OJ 31.10.78 L306/1) and (EEC) No 925/79 (fn4: OJ 29.5.79 L131/1) apply, normal value shall be determined in an appropriate and not unreasonable manner on the basis of one of the following criteria:
>
> (A) the price at which the like *product of a market economy third country* is actually sold:
>
> (I) for consumption on the *domestic market of that country*, or
> (II) to *other countries*, including the *Community*; or
>
> (B) the *constructed value* of the like product in a market economy third country; or
> (C) if neither price nor constructed value as established under (A) or (B) above provides an adequate basis, the *price actually paid or payable in the Community* for the like product, duly adjusted, if necessary, to include a reasonable profit margin . . .[259]

This merely followed verbatim the terms of its innovative predecessor.[260] Council Regulation 3017/79 thus continued to reject definitively the use of the non-market economy domestic market.

In 1984[261] and also in 1988,[262] the EC enacted new anti-dumping legislation. This was identical to Council Regulation 3017/79 so far as non-market economies were concerned.[263] In the words of the ECJ:

> [T]he aim of that provision [Article 2(5) of Council Regulation 2423/88, the successor of Council Regulation 3017/79] is to prevent account being taken of prices and costs in non-market economy countries, that is to say, which are not the normal result of market forces . . .[264]

[257] See Beseler and Williams, above n 52, at 11–13, 26–27.
[258] Council Regulation 3017/79, above n 253, 6th Recital.
[259] *Ibid*, Art 2(5).
[260] This was Council Regulation 1681/79, above n 252, Art 1, which amended Art 3 of Council Regulation 459/68, [1968] OJ L93/1.
[261] Council Regulation 2176/84, [1984] OJ L201/1. As to ECSC products, see Commission Decision 2177/84/ECSC [1984] OJ L201/17.
[262] Council Regulation 2423/88, [1988] OJ L209/17. For a discussion of Regulation 2423/88, with some references to the then current US law, see E Creally, *Judicial Review of Anti-dumping and other Safeguard Measures in the European Community* (London, Butterworths, 1992).
[263] Art 2(5) is identical in the three Regulations. On the 1984 and 1988 reforms, see Van Bael and Bellis, above n 101, at 39.
[264] Joined Cases 294/86 and 77/87 *Technointorg v Commission and Council* [1988] ECR 6077 at 6193, para 29. See also P Eeckhout, 'The Technointorg Judgment of the European Court of Justice and the Issue of Non-market Economy Dumping' (1989) 12 *World Competition* 39. See further Joined Cases C-305/86 and C-160/87 *Neotype Techmashexport v Commission and Council* [1990] ECR I-2945 at I-3000, para 26; Case C-16/90 *Nölle v Hauptzollamt Bremen-Freihafen* [1991] ECR I-5163 at I-5203, para 10. Regarding this Council Regulation, see Hu Yuanxiang, above n 6, who states (at 235) that '[i]ts core principle was to exclude totally comparisons made with the prices in the domestic markets of the State-trading countries.'

D. Legal Rule and Administrative Discretion

At first glance the 1979 Regulations might appear to have constrained the Commission's discretion more narrowly. Nevertheless, within this normative framework there remained substantial room for interpretation in daily anti-dumping practice. In fact, Council Regulation 3017/79 provided only a rough road map for the exercise of administrative discretion. It indicated some directions for the development of the highways and byways of EC anti-dumping law, and sketched in outline the normative contours of the Commission's role.

A case in point was the selection of the analogue country. The law of the EC no longer permitted the Commission to consider the possibility of establishing normal value based on the non-market economy domestic market. How was the analogue country to be chosen? Writing in 1986, two Commission officials stated that, since both the Code and EC legislation provided that the choice must be made in an appropriate and not unreasonable manner, the Community did not lay down a hierarchy of criteria. Instead the Commission's practice was 'to consider any third market-economy country which is suggested in the initial stage of the investigation, thereby ensuring that no possible analogue is excluded from examination'.[265] These authors also suggested that 'the actual choice of the surrogate country tends to have a relatively limited effect in practice'.[266] In their view, the lesser duty rule in EC anti-dumping law[267] meant that frequently the dumping margin itself did not determine the final outcome.

Nevertheless, it remained the case that the analogue country method could result in a finding of dumping that might otherwise not exist.[268] In 1987, Vermulst described the Commission as having 'extremely wide latitude' in selecting the analogue country, with the result that this crucial choice 'will largely depend on factors which are completely exogenous to a rational application of the law.'[269] Others criticised this approach as marked by such 'flexibility [that it] often turns anti-dumping actions into purely protective measures'.[270] Two leading American commentators wrote that

[265] Beseler and Williams, above n 52, at 69. Dr Beseler was then Director in the Directorate-General for External Relations of the EC, and Mr Williams was a member of the Commercial Defence Instruments Division of the same Directorate-General. For 23 products from NMEs between 1980 and 1982, the normal value was based on prices or costs in 12 different countries: see Jacobs, above n 166, at 299.

[266] Beseler and Williams, above n 52, at 72–73.

[267] EC anti-dumping law requires that the amount of the anti-dumping duty cannot exceed the dumping margin and that it must be less than the margin if such lesser duty would be adequate to remove the injury to Community industry: see now Council Regulation 384/96, Art7(2), [1996] OJ L56/1.

[268] See also Jacobs, above n 166, at 304.

[269] Vermulst, above n 200, at 434. As to the criteria then used by the Commission, see *ibid*, at 434–37. See also FL Fine, 'EEC Anti-dumping: The Problem of Imports from State Trading Countries' (1988) 20 *Law and Policy in International Business* 91 (dealing with the substantially identical Council Regulation 2423/88).

[270] N Yannopoulos, 'EC External Commercial Policies and East–West Trade in Europe' (1985) XXIV(1) *Journal of Common Market Studies* 21 at 32. The same author concluded (at 36), however, that, except for agriculture and textiles and clothing, the EC's common commercial policy had little restrictive impact on East–West trade; the main restrictive factors were internal to the CMEA and the individual economies: see *ibid*, at 37. For a contrary view, see E Piontek, 'Anti-Dumping in the EEC—Some Observations by an Outsider' (1987) 21 *Journal of World Trade Law* 67. More generally, anti-dumping measures, though perhaps having relatively little impact on overall trade flows, may have serious effects on specific sectors, as well as damaging the quality of relations between the two trading partners: see ND Palmeter, 'The Impact of the US Anti-dumping Law on China–US Trade' (1989) 23 *Journal of World Trade* 5.

> the EC anti-dumping regulations permit the administrative authority to use essentially any price as the standard for dumping by NMEs without agonizing over the level of economic development in a surrogate country or hypothetical factors of production . . .[271]

When the analogue country approach is used, the methods for selecting the country are always open to criticism. This was true in both the US and the EC, despite differences in their anti-dumping systems. What is more serious, however, is the fact that, in both settings, administrative convenience has played such a central role in the selection of the analogue country, simply because the investigating authorities depend for information on the cooperation of the analogue country producers.[272] In addition, Commission discretion in anti-dumping actions has been subject to minimal judicial review. The ECJ (later replaced in anti-dumping matters by the CFI) had to verify whether the institutions neglected to take account of essential factors for the purpose of establishing the appropriate nature of the country chosen, and whether the information contained in the documents in the case was considered with all the care required for the view to be taken that the normal value was determined in an appropriate and not unreasonable manner.[273] This concerned only compliance with procedural rules, whether the facts on which the choice was based had been accurately stated and whether there was a manifest error of appraisal or a misuse of powers.[274] One observer in the mid-1980s summarised the implications for China as increasing protectionism, to the extent to which some economic specialists wondered whether certain anti-dumping actions against China 'might be merely an early and minor manifestation of the change from the free trade to the restricted trade area'.[275]

[271] Horlick and Schuman, above n 88, at 816. However, beauty (or otherwise) is in the eye of the beholder. At the time of writing (1984), both were in private law or accounting practice. However, GN Horlick was formerly Deputy Assistant Secretary of Commerce for Import Administration, and SS Shuman was formerly Economist, Import Administration, US Department of Commerce. Their comment about EC law focused on the choice of analogue country. In contrast, DL Cuneo and CB Manuel, both from the same law firm and representing defendants, focused on EC law regarding the definition of NME, and considered EC law in this respect to be simple, straightforward and relatively rigid. With regard to US, however, they discerned in 1982 'a picture of an administering authority uncomfortable with the obvious absurdities and rigidities imposed by the governing statute and compelled to apply that statute under strict time constraints to increasingly complex economic realities. The results are (i) a series of SCE [NME] determinations reflecting limited economic analysis, and (ii) a series of hasty LTFV margin determinations that are both inequitable to the exporters and unfathomable to petitioning United States parties, thereby reducing desirable emphasis on rationality and predictability in United States anti-dumping law administration'. See Cuneo and Manuel, above n 36, at 307.

[272] For the period between 1980 and 1986, see Vermulst, above n 200, at 360 (US), 436–37 (EC), 489–93 (comparison). For EC cases involving China from 1979 to 2000, see F Snyder, 'EU Anti-dumping Actions against China, 1979–2000: Some Methodological Problems in Law and Social Science', presented at the Wissenschaftskolleg zu Berlin, Institute for Advanced Study, Berlin, 7 December 2000. On the US, see JH Bello, AF Holmer and JO Preiss, 'Searching for "Bubbles of Capitalism": Application of the US Anti-dumping and Countervailing Duty Laws to Reforming Nonmarket Economies' (1992) 25 *George Washington Journal of International Law and Economics* 665 at 679–80.

[273] See Case C-16/90 *Nölle v Hauptzollamt Bremen-Freihafen* [1991] ECR I-5163, para 13.

[274] See Case 240/84 *NTN Toyo Bearing Company Ltd and Others v Council* [1987] ECR 1809; Case 254/84 *Nippon Seiko KK v Council* [1987] ECR 1923.

[275] Kapur, above n 216, at 78–80. The quotation (at 80) is from *China Trade and Economic Newsletter* 330 (1984), p 4; see also *China Aktuell*, July 1984.

IV. Conclusion

'More and more, anti-dumping policy is trade policy'[276] but, as I have tried to show in this chapter, it is also much more. The main conclusions that can be drawn are as follows.

First, the elaboration of EC anti-dumping law, in specific historical circumstances, resulted in the creation of the legal concept of the 'non-market economy'. This legal concept was socially constructed, by means of relations among a plurality of sites of governance, as part of a changing configuration of legal ideas in specific historical circumstances and contexts of political, economic, social and symbolic power.

Secondly, a central part of modern EC anti-dumping law, the concept of 'non-market economy' had distinctive features. It formed part of a specific legal discourse if, following Foucault, we define 'discourse' as 'the group of statements that belong to a single system of formation'.[277] It was anchored tightly to EC import legislation, even though the two legislative strands had different purposes. It required the use of an analogue country and mandated the use of specific tests for determining the normal value of allegedly dumped imports. Hence it excluded completely any reference to important characteristics of the domestic economy of the exporting countries. Lastly, it reconfigured the substantial administrative discretion of the European Commission.

Thirdly, the principal factors giving rise to this new legal idea were changes in the international anti-dumping repertoire, specific European ideas about comparative economic systems and perceived new economic threats during the 1970s, including the 'opening up' of China near the end of the decade. They were combined by the European institutions, notably the Commission, in an international context marked by a substantial decline in previous US hegemony. Taken together, they legitimated a more protectionist anti-dumping policy, of which the legal concept of 'non-market economy' was an important part.

Fourthly, this legal idea emerged from the gradual elaboration of a 'cultural frame', or what I have called an international anti-dumping repertoire.[278] Building on a handful of basic principles established in the early 20th century, this involved in particular the constitution of a conceptual and normative repertoire, drawing on national legislation, multilateral negotiations and administrative decisions in several jurisdictions within a particular historical context. The most important elements were the following:

—the idea that the world was composed of two distinct types of economic systems
—changing labels for a 'non-market economy' category
—criteria for determining whether a country fit into this category
—factors to be used in determining normal value
    —'a country which has a complete or substantially complete monopoly on its trade and all domestic prices are fixed by the state'
    —'special difficulties'
    —'strict comparison may not always be appropriate'
    —'not normally appropriate'

[276] ND Palmeter, 'Editorial: The Anti-dumping Emperor' (1988) 22

[277] Foucault, above n 10, at 107.

[278] On the importance of a 'cultural frame' in the creation of the Single European Market, see N Fligstein and I Mara-Drita, 'How to Make a Market: Reflections on the Attempt to Create a Single Market in the European Union' (1996) 102 *American Journal of Sociology* 1.

—'particular market situation'
—'comparable price of the like product when exported to any third country'
—'cost of production in the country of origin'
—'absence of domestic price'
—'like product originating in another country'
—'like product of a market economy country'
—'like product of a market economy third country'
—'constructed value'
—'appropriate and not unreasonable'
—export price or cost of production
—constructed value
—appropriate and not unreasonable.

The EC legal concept drew expressly on some of these elements and marginalised others. From the standpoint of theories of international regimes,[279] the process was an evolutionary form of development, punctuated and crystallised by periodic 'contractarian moments', such as the agreement on Article VI GATT and later GATT negotiating rounds.

Fifthly, the Cold War context was absolutely decisive in the formation of this legal idea. Not only did it determine the composition of the post-World War II multilateral trade institutions, from the GATT through various working parties to the negotiating rounds that produced anti-dumping and subsidies codes; it also tended to shape relations and sharpen conflicts between the legislature and the executive. This was especially notable in relations between the Executive and Congress in the United States, which so greatly influenced the evolution of US anti-dumping law and hence its EC counterpart. The political context of the Cold War gave a specific political edge to US and EC anti-dumping law, notably by representing international trade as a fierce competition between different political and economic systems. The idea of the 'non-market economy' expressed a fundamental distinction between two different political and economic systems, capitalism and communism. In this way, among others, it also shaped ideas in the US and Western Europe about different types of economies and how they could and should be dealt with by laws on imports and anti-dumping. These ideas were based largely on (sometimes idealised) economic assumptions about the economies of the United States and post-World War II Western Europe, and how they differed from economies in Eastern Europe and the Soviet Union. Indeed, it is probable that the concept of 'non-market economy' in EC anti-dumping law would not have emerged outside the Cold War context. In other circumstances, this legal idea would not have made any sense.

Sixthly, among the most important processes were the circulation of legal ideas, norms and notions of administrative practice among different sites; the translation of concepts and norms first articulated in one site into the different institutional structure, normative language and administrative practices of another; and their continuous interpretation, reworking, integration of new ideas and reinterpretation. The most significant sites were the US, the EC and the GATT. Each had its own institutions, norms and dispute resolution processes. But if the structural features of the different sites contributed in important ways to the development of EC anti-dumping law, so

[279] See OR Young, 'International Regimes: Problems of Concept Formation' (1980) 32 *World Politics* 331 at 348–51.

too did the relations among sites. Indeed, these relations were a precondition for the process.

Seventhly, the relations between these sites involved asymmetrical power relations. By far the most important influence was the United States. Its policies, laws and their implicit assumptions, its separation of powers, and even its domestic and international politics, all played a significant role in the development of the EC legal concept of the 'non-market economy'. That the legal concept and the implicit contrast embodied in it were possible at all stemmed from the development of US hegemony in international trade after World War II. A powerful trading partner and competitor, the US was important for the EC not only as a direct normative influence or as a model of anti-dumping policy, law and administration. In addition, it was overwhelmingly US concepts and norms that were embodied in the law of the GATT and subsequently the WTO. It is not going too far to suggest that US law and policy essentially determined the direction and rate of change, though this occurred within the framework of objectives that were generally shared and deemed to be legitimate, at least in Western Europe, Canada, Australia and New Zealand.[280] As a result of these processes, a number of economic concepts, conceptions and assumptions, largely from the US though often mediated through the GATT, came to be embodied within EC anti-dumping law. This is consistent with Strange's point that

> in order to assess realistically the prospects of any international trade organization (or any set of negotiations conducted through it . . .), the important point to start with is the extent and limit of the bargaining power of the most important state or states . . .[281]

Eighthly, the GATT served not only as negotiating forum but also as a study group, mediator and interpreter of norms. Its working parties played a very significant role in proposing, synthesising and even initiating normative changes. It is self-evident that these changes originated from individual members, whose views were sometimes if not often modified during deliberations. Here it has not been possible to consider the internal discussions of GATT working parties. The focus has been instead on the working parties as a whole, their significance as norm-generating institutions, the relationship of their norms and concepts to those of other sites, and their decisive contribution to the development of EC antdumping law. The GATT negotiating rounds were the principal institutional motor of the periodic changes in EC anti-dumping law. Despite its status as a mainly diplomatic organisation, the GATT went some way toward unifying the market in the production of symbolic goods, such as the legal ideas and principles concerning State-trading country dumping.[282] It should be added that the GATT, as a diplomatic organisation, was relatively porous, and the norms that were articulated at (and perhaps between) these rounds reflected the law and practice of its contracting partners, notably the United States.

Ninthly, despite its situation as a newcomer to this dense network of relations, it was possible for the EC to innovate. To be sure, EC anti-dumping drew on many other influences, such as the GATT and US Treasury law and practice, notably the 1968 Treasury Regulation concept of a 'controlled economy country'. Nonetheless, the

[280] The complexity of the post-war liberal compromise is emphasised by Ruggie, above n 248, at 195–231. See also D Snidal, 'The Limits of Hegemonic Stability Theory' (1985) 39 *International Organization* 579.

[281] Strange, above n 107, at 188 (original emphasis omitted).

[282] See P Bourdieu, *Language and Symbolic Power* (ed JB Thompson; trans G Raymond and M Adamson) (Cambridge, Polity Press, 1991) 50.

creation of the concept of a 'non-market economy' was specific to the EC, in particular in definitively excluding the use of the non-market economy domestic price. The result of an unusual combination of circumstances, it brought together the original GATT term 'normal value', the express articulation of the analogue country approach, rejection of any detailed reference to the domestic economy or individual firms of the exporting country, cross-reference to a list of State-trading countries in legislative form and a reconfiguration of the discretionary powers of the EC Commission.

Tenthly, the concept of a 'market economy' supplied a point of reference for the idea of a 'non-market economy' in two different senses, which should be distinguished. On the one hand, the concept and features (whether they are real or idealised makes no difference for the time being) of a 'market economy' provided the starting point for defining a 'non-market economy, for example merely as different from a 'market economy', or more usually as lacking or displaying specific features. On the other hand, 'market economy' provided an objective or a goal. The direction of change was implicit in the contraposition of the terms. Conceptually speaking, and perhaps also historically, the direction of movement was from 'non-market economy' to 'market economy', not the other way around. Any movement from 'non-market economy' to 'market economy' was conceived as natural, inevitable and progressive. As a legal concept, 'non-market economy' was therefore not simply a shadow self of 'market economy'. The distinction between the two was political and teleological.

Eleventhly, the idea of the 'non-market economy' in EC anti-dumping law originated in a specific configuration of power in world politics and the international trading system, but this legal concept had power of its own. This power was productive, not merely negative, as its label might suggest.[283] In part the product of *bricolage* from a conceptual toolkit, intended originally to deal with very practical problems of international trade, it was also a discursive and political process of creating a subject, of placing particular countries within specific power relations.

Here Foucault's insights are especially useful. The concept of the 'non-market economy' was not merely a system of communication. It was a 'mode of action on actions'.[284] As a system of differentiation, it involved specific types of objectives, such as control of imports, authorisation of market access and later the creation of incentives for changes within the domestic economy of the trading party. It used certain instrumental modes, notably legal discourse, legal concepts, enforcement mechanisms and material sanctions. It also implied certain forms of institutionalisation, including specific institutions, periodic negotiation, particular legal concepts and procedures, and processes for resolving disputes. Lastly, it entailed a relatively high degree of rationalisation, partly because of the functional requirements of anti-dumping law, and partly because of the dynamics of cooperation and competition among different institutional and normative sides.[285]

The concept of the 'non-market economy' reinforced two groups of countries, within the framework of the GATT and within the broader world economy. It also

[283] On power as productive, see Foucault, above n 13.

[284] M Foucault, 'The Subject and Power', in M Foucault, *Essential Works of Foucault*, 1954–1984, vol 3: *Power* (ed JD Faubion; trans R Hurley *et al*) (Allen Lane, London, The Penguin Press, 2001) 343.

[285] The categories of differentiation, instrumental modes, institutionalisation and rationalisation are drawn from *ibid*.

helped to make this way of thinking seem entirely normal,[286] in the sense of extending its usage among other GATT contracting parties and even the non-GATT countries that fell within its ambit.[287] Moreover, it reinforced the view that prices contain only one kind of information, the signals necessary for the operation of a market economy, rather than being embedded in quite different economic and social arrangements.[288] Those inside the ambit of this concept inhabited what might be called a 'zone of politics' beyond law.[289] However, these identities were not given but socially constructed, partly by the institutions, norms, processes and asymmetrical power relations discussed here.[290] The concept of the 'non-market economy' thus consecrated opposition, not just distinction and difference. As expressed in EC anti-dumping law, it defined the terms on which insiders as a group agreed to deal with outsiders as a group. This tended to perpetuate Cold War categories and, arguably, even to imbricate the EC further in the sets of bipolar power relations that defined the period. The result of relations between sites of governance, and the concept of 'non-market economy' in EC anti-dumping law was, in Foucault's words, 'one of the forms by which our society defined subjectivity, forms of knowledge and, consequently, relations between man and truth'.[291]

[286] See M Foucalt, 'Two Lectures' in M Foucault, *Power/Knowledge: Selected Interviews and Other Writings, 1972–1977* (ed C Gordon; trans C Gordon, L Marshall, J Mepham and K Soper) (London, Harvester Press, 1980) 344–45.

[287] See also P Vandoren, 'Mise en oeuvre de la politique anti-dumping de la CEE contre les importations en provence des pays à commerce d'état' (1988) 316 *Revue du Marché Commun* 198 at 199.

[288] I am indebted to Katherine Verdery for this point.

[289] See A-M Slaughter Burley, 'Law Among Liberal States: Liberal Internationalism and the Act of State Doctrine' (1992) 92 *Columbia Law Review* 1907 at 1920–23.

[290] See also H Koh, 'Transnational Legal Process' (1996) 75 *Nebraska Law Review* 181, who gives more emphasis to process and less to the ways in which transnational legal processes are structured and impregnated by asymmetrical power relations.

[291] M Foucault, 'Truth and Juridical Forms', in Foucault, above n 286, at 5.

7

Relations between Sites and the Legalisation of Norms: Individual Treatment in EC Anti-dumping Law about China

I. Introduction

Relations between sites of governance are a form of interaction which can change the internal structural features of sites. The changes may concern any or all of the structural features of a site of governance, namely, institutions, norms or dispute settlement processes. Building on the discussion in Chapter 2 of globalisation and law, Chapter 3 showed how relations between sites of governance may involve numerous kinds of institutions, different types of norms and several forms of dispute settlement. Chapter 4 sought to illuminate the ways in which strategic actors affect relations between sites of governance and influence the choice of methods of dispute settlement, for example by administrative negotiation and by judicial decision. Chapter 5 examined some of the ways in which courts manage relations between sites of governance and the implications for relations between institutions and the development of basic legal principles within a single site. Chapter 6 demonstrated that relations between sites led to the creation of an international normative repertoire, which then was integrated, piecemeal or in its entirety, into the norms of numerous sites of governance This chapter focuses on the effects of relations between sites of governance on the norms of a single site. It analyses how changes in relations between sites of governance led to the creation of norms within a single site and to the gradual transformation of their normative character. It argues that changes in legal and economic relations between the European Union (EU) and China have led to fundamental changes in EC anti-dumping law.

Among the most striking characteristics of relations between the EU and China is the extensive use of 'soft law', that is, measures which are not legally binding but which may have practical, even legal, effects.[1] Among the many questions which have occupied scholarship on soft law are, first, how soft law is created and, secondly, whether soft law can become hard law. On the question of creation, we take soft law to be a specific type of norm or a specific type of group of norms, frequently created in the shadow of legally binding norms ('hard law'), sometimes modelled on hard law, occasionally following similar processes of normative production and often with analogous though not legally binding effects. However, these are not the only processes

[1] This definition is based on F Snyder, 'The Effectiveness of European Community Law: Institutions, Processes, Tools and Techniques' (1993) 56 *MLR* 19.

of the creation of soft law norms. Sometimes, soft law is born fully fledged, with no regard to hard law. On other occasions, it may be preceded by a period of administrative practice. On the question of transformation, soft law may sometimes become hard law. This may occur, for example, by judicial decision, or by incorporation into legislation within national or regional sites of governance, or by international agreements such as treaties in relations between sites. It is self-evident that soft law is our starting point in studying such a transformation; the opposite direction appears to be rare, though probably not unknown.

In this chapter, I begin with the earliest phases in the evolution of norms from soft law to hard law. The chapter analyses administrative practice as the origin of soft law. In this situation, there is no guarantee that such administrative practice will ever take a normative form, though we would expect that, as practice becomes routine, it would tend to produce norms. Still less is the probability that if administrative practice becomes soft law, it will ever be transformed into hard law. In other words, soft law is not necessarily a station on the way to hard law. The full process of normative transformation from administrative practice to soft law to hard law seems to occur relatively infrequently. This chapter considers a specific example of this process: the transformation of 'individual treatment' in EC anti-dumping law about China from its origins as administrative practice to soft law and finally to hard law.

Relations between the EU and China have generally been harmonious and are widely regarded as mutually beneficial,[2] at least until recently.[3] However, EC anti-dumping law applied to China remains controversial. As shown in the preceding chapter, since before 1979, the EC has usually treated China as a non-market economy. Using the analogue country method, it determines the normal value of Chinese exports by reference not to prices and production costs in China, but to those in a comparable market economy third country. Following the single duty rule, it usually applies a single anti-dumping duty to all exports of the same product from China, instead of determining a separate duty for each exporter as in anti-dumping actions involving most other trading partners. The analogue country method and the single duty rule are the main components of the EC anti-dumping law non-market economy methodology.

In EC anti-dumping law, there are two exceptions to non-market economy treatment: individual treatment and market economy treatment. Individual treatment applies when an exporter meets specified criteria laid down by EC anti-dumping law, designed to show that the exporter operates on a market basis on its export market, regardless of its operations on its domestic market. If these criteria are met, export price is determined according to the exporter's own information. However, normal value continues to be determined as under non-market economy treatment, according to the analogue country method, in which data from a market economy third country are substituted for treatment of the exporter's domestic market. As an exception to non-market economy treatment, individual treatment usually results in lower anti-dumping duties for the exporter.

[2] On EU/EC–China relations since 1949, see F Snyder, *The European Union and China, 1949–2008: Basic Documents and Commentary* (Oxford, Hart Publishing, 2009).

[3] For a recent but flawed re-assessment, see J Fox and F Godement, *A Power Audit of EU–China Relations* (London, European Council of Foreign Relations, 2009), available at http://www.ecfr.eu, which argues that the EU should adopt a more focused, pragmatic policy of reciprocal engagement.

More advantageous to the exporter is market economy treatment. It applies when an exporter meets other specified criteria in EC anti-dumping law, designed to indicate that the exporter operates on a market basis both on its domestic market and on its export market. If the exporter meets such criteria, it is treated in the same manner as any exporter from a market economy country. In these circumstances, both normal value and export price are determined according to the exporter's own information.

If the exporter cannot satisfy either the criteria for individual treatment or those for market economy treatment, it is treated on a non-market economy basis. All of these concepts are categories or classifications applied at the level of the enterprise. They differ from the more general concept of market economy status, which is a category or classification that applies at the level of the country or national economy as a whole. If a country or national economy is classified as having market economy status, all enterprises in the country automatically are treated as operating on a market basis at home and abroad, so there is no need to consider the concepts of non-market economy, individual treatment or market economy treatment.

Whether these concepts and the ways in which they are applied are compatible with WTO law is open to debate. It is useful to sketch briefly the general framework of this debate, though a detailed discussion will not be pursued here. Until China's accession to the WTO, the only legal framework for the EC's non-market economy methodology, except for EC law, was the GATT 1947 and the Interpretative Note Ad Article VI GATT. Though legally binding, as shown in Chapter 6, the Interpretative Note was an extremely general, permissive document adopted by GATT contracting parties during negotiations on the readmission to GATT of the then Czechoslovakia in 1954–55. It was applied in different ways by the EEC Member States; the EEC was never a contracting party to the GATT. Since China's accession to the WTO in 2001, GATT Article VI and the Agreement on the Interpretation of Article VI ('the Anti-dumping Agreement') apply to EU–China trade, together with the Report of the WTO Working Party on Chinese Accession[4] and the WTO Protocol on the Accession of China.[5] The Interpretative Note is often assumed to be applicable. To judge from its wording alone, however, it would appear that the Note cannot and legally does not apply to EU–China trade today. Arguably this is the case even if the Interpretative Note is defined as being part of the EC non-market economy methodology for the purposes of the WTO Chinese Accession Protocol. The Protocol permits a WTO Member to continue to apply its non-market economy methodology to China till 2016 unless China is recognised by the Member as having market economy status before then.[6] As applied to EC law, section 15 of the China Accession Protocol would appear to authorise market economy treatment. However, whether this permission includes individual treatment is open to serious question. For reasons of space, this issue cannot be pursued further here.

This chapter focuses on individual treatment. Since its origins in the early 1990s, individual treatment has been transformed from administrative practice, to soft law and then to legislation. This transformation may be characterised in either of two ways. It may be assessed as a process of juridification, according to which administrative

[4] WTO, Report of the Working Party on the Accession of China, Ministerial Conference, Fourth Session, Doha, 9–13 September 2001, WT/MIN(01)/3, 10 November 2001.

[5] WTO, Protocol on the Accession of the People's Republic of China, annexed to Accession of the People's Republic of China, Decision of 10 November 2001, WT/L/432, 23 November 2001.

[6] *Ibid*, s 15.

practice gradually assumes a normative form, at first not legally binding, and then later becomes a legally binding norm. Alternatively, it may be analysed as a process of legalisation. This process encompasses three dimensions: the existence of legal obligations, the precision with which obligations are defined and the delegation of dispute settlement to a third party.[7] Each dimension is a continuum, and each can vary independently of the others. The concept of juridification and the first dimension of the concept of legalisation both refer to the characteristic of obligation. However, the concept of legalisation recognises that obligation is a continuum, not a dichotomy. In addition, the concept of legalisation embraces not only obligation but also two other dimensions, precision and delegation. These other dimensions of legalisation are not included in the concept of juridification. However, they are useful because they enable us to appreciate the relative efficacy of obligation in practice. Consequently, this chapter employs the concept of legalisation. It enables us to present a richer, more accurate and more complete analysis of the transformation of individual treatment. In other words, it enables us to unravel some of the conceptual tangles inherent in the concept of soft law.

The legalisation of individual treatment illustrates how Europe has regulated trade with China and the extent to which it has taken account of China's economic transformation since 1979. The chapter focuses on the reasons, meaning and implications of the process of legalisation. The following sections consider the three overlapping phases. A brief conclusion summarises the discussion.

II. The Phase of Administrative Practice

The practice of granting individual treatment emerged in the case of *Tungsten Ores*.[8] In the investigation beginning in 1988, only two Chinese exporters made themselves known, one a reformed but long-standing trading corporation of the Ministry of Foreign Economic Relations and Trade, and the other attached to the Ministry of Metallurgical Industry and the result of post-1979 reforms.[9] The Commission determined different dumping margins for each, on the basis of prices actually paid or payable for the products sold for export to the Community. It did not expressly give reasons for this practice. However, in analysing the volume and price of imports into the Community, the Commission emphasised that control over Chinese export sales was increasingly decentralised, different organisations were permitted to export in order to earn foreign currency and there was 'strong internal price competition between suppliers in China'.[10] In practice, the Commission applied an individual treatment to each exporter, without using the term 'individual treatment' and without articulating criteria for allowing what in effect was an exception to general rules of EC anti-dumping law.

[7] KW Abbott, RO Keohane, A Moravcsik, AM Slaughter and D Snidal, 'The concept of legalization' (2000) 54 *International Organization* 401.

[8] *Tungsten Ores from China* [1990] OJ L83/23 (provisional), [1990] OJ L2654/1 (definitive).

[9] On these reforms, see Chen Yuan, *East–West Trade: Changing Patterns in Chinese Foreign Trade Law and Institutions* (New York, Oceana Publications, 1991) 199–244; N Lardy, *Foreign Trade and Economic Reform in China, 1978–1990* (Cambridge, Cambridge University Press, 1992) 39–41.

[10] *Tungsten Ores from China* (definitive), above n 8, para 19.

Three months later, in *Small Colour TVs*,[11] the Commission established a single dumping margin for all Chinese exporters except for two Sino-Japanese joint ventures.[12] The joint ventures sold the product in the Community under the brand name of the Japanese parents (Hitachi, Sanyo). Three other exporters belonged to the Chinese Commercial Chamber of Audio and Video Products Exporters, which acknowledged that it had strict control over members' exports. At that time, chambers of commerce in China were usually part of a specific government ministry. For the Commission, this gave rise to concerns about circumvention, meaning that in a State-controlled economy, the Government could channel exports through the company with the lowest dumping margin, and thus evade anti-dumping duties. In contrast, the two joint ventures could import components, export finished products and, subject only to certain administrative requirements, transfer profits out of China.[13] Here the Commission expressly used the term 'individual treatment'. Nevertheless, it seems to have been used as a kind of 'commonsense' expression, simply to indicate that certain companies were treated in ways which singled them out from the application of general rules. Analysis of the factors which were aggregated by the term and the logical or other steps in the process of reaching the result in the case remained a matter of administrative practice. Nonetheless, articulation of the concern regarding circumvention and the use of the term 'individual treatment' were indicators of increasing precision as part of the beginning of legalisation.

The Commission articulated further criteria in *Video Tapes in Cassettes*.[14] Several exporters, through their association, requested treatment 'on an individual basis'. This suggests that Chinese exporters, or at least governmental authorities, were aware of these developments in the Commission's anti-dumping practice. The exporters demonstrated that they were genuine joint ventures with foreign investment, and able to establish export prices freely and transfer profits out of China to foreign shareholders. The Commission granted individual treatment, without using the term. Here, as before, the criteria for doing so formed part of the Commission's ad hoc, case-by-case practice. Nevertheless, they indicated increasing precision in the determination of reasons for making decisions.

These cases showed the Commission's broad discretion. We can understand the cases as a form of interaction between sites of governance, in particular executive authorities. For parties in both Europe and China, they were part of a process of learning about each other. This was especially true of public authorities, such as the European Commission or Chinese governmental ministries, and also of the parties

[11] *Small Colour TVs from Hong Kong and China* [1991] OJ L14/31 (provisional), [1991] OJ L195/1 (definitive).

[12] The Chinese Cooperative (or Contractual) Joint Venture Law had been adopted on 13 April 1988, ending 10 years of a legal vacuum during which JVs were dealt with by analogy according to the Equity Joint Venture Law. See Kui Hua Wang, *Chinese Commercial Law* (Victoria, Australia, Oxford University Press, 2000) 115. For the legislation, see, respectively, Law of the People's Republic of China on Chinese–Foreign Contractual Joint Ventures and Law of the People's Republic of China on Chinese-Foreign Equity Joint Ventures, both in People's Republic of China, *Handbook of Foreign Economic Legislation* (Beijing, Publishing House of Law, 1997), vol I, 283, 324.

[13] See Commission of the European Communities, Proposal for a Council Regulation (EEC) extending the provisional anti-dumping duty on imports of small-screen colour television receivers originating in Hong Kong and the People's Republic of China, COM(91)139 final, Brussels, 15 April 1991, paras 19, 20; *Small Colour TVs from Hong Kong and China* (definitive), above n 11, paras 19–20.

[14] *Video Tapes in Cassettes from China* [1991] OJ L106/15 (provisional), [1991] OJ L293/2 (definitive), paras 17–20, 36.

involved in joint ventures in China. With the progress of economic reform in China, and as Chinese exporters learned more about EU anti-dumping law and procedures, the following years saw more requests for individual treatment. Indeed, sometimes individual treatment was granted without being requested. For example, an exporter in *Polyester Yarns*[15] was a China–Hong Kong joint venture. It did not request individual treatment, but the Commission determined an individual dumping margin based on actual export prices. According to the Commission, the fact that the Hong Kong partner was related to an EC group was irrelevant, though one suspects that this factor must have helped support the view that the exporter would be unlikely to engage in circumvention.[16] Here the Commission expressly used the term 'individual treatment'. As in *Small Colour TVs*, circumvention was its main concern.

Magnesium Oxide was the first case in which the Commission explicitly placed individual treatment in a more coherent normative framework.[17] At the definitive stage of the proceeding, the Commission expressly used the term 'individual treatment' and delimited its scope of application. It stated, first, that individual treatment was an exception to the general rules for non-market economy countries. Secondly, individual treatment 'must remain a strict exception to be applied solely in cases where the producer concerned has provided evidence that it is free to establish export prices without the influence of the State authorities'. The underlying rationale was circumvention, for otherwise the State could 'take advantage of the lowest dumping margin and thus undermine the effectiveness of any measures'.[18] In this case, the Commission followed the path of previous cases, continuing to elaborate criteria for granting individual treatment and continuing to emphasise its basic concern for circumvention. But *Magnesium Oxide* differed from previous cases by using a clearly normative discourse, in which there is no exception without a rule and exceptions are interpreted strictly. It transformed individual treatment from mere administrative practice into a concept in the course of legalisation. Delegation was lacking, and obligation was scarcely defined, but the concept gained considerably in precision.

Such a supply of new norms provided strategic actors with new resources. The *Magnetic Disks*[19] investigation was announced in July 1991, before *Magnesium Oxide*. All Chinese exporters requested individual treatment, claiming to be foreign investment companies, either joint ventures or with a majority foreign shareholder. Accepting one such claim at the provisional stage, the Commission reiterated its *Magnesium Oxide* view that individual treatment was a strict exception. It was to be applied solely in cases where the producer demonstrates that it is free to establish export prices without influence of the State, otherwise there was a risk of circumvention. The status of joint venture, or a majority foreign shareholding, was not sufficient. At the definitive stage, the Commission denied individual treatment. It recalled that

[15] *Polyester Yarns from Taiwan, Indonesia, India, China and Turkey* [1991] OJ L276/7 (provisional), [1992] OJ L88/1 (definitive).

[16] *Ibid* (definitive), para 26. Coats plc, the world's largest manufacturer of industrial sewing threat and consumer needlecraft products (Barbour, Viyella, etc), today holds a 50% share in Guangying Spinning Co Ltd, which was formed in 1987 as a JV with Guangzhou Cotton No 2 Co. See http://www.coats.com, and http://www.coats.com/reports/2004_annual/2004_subsidaryundertakings. pdf, last accessed 18 February 2010.

[17] *Magnesium Oxide from China* [1992] OJ L282/23 (provisional), [1993] OJ L145/1 (definitive).

[18] *Ibid* (definitive), para 13.

[19] *Magnetic Disks from Japan, Taiwan and China* [1993] OJ L95/5 (provisional), [1993] OJ L262/4 (definitive).

individual treatment was not required by the EC's basic anti-dumping Regulation, thus denying the dimension of obligation, and it noted the difficulties of establishing the legal and factual independence of companies from the State in China. The Commission affirmed that departures from the general single duty rule should be made only where it is completely satisfied that the effectiveness of the measures is not undermined by circumvention.[20] This was not yet a real step in the direction of obligation, but nevertheless it gave the concept of individual treatment much greater precision.

A sea-change in Commission practice is sometimes traced to *Bicycles*.[21] The *Bicycles* case in the European courts was part of the *Chinese Bicycles* saga, analysed in Chapter 4 of the book. Certainly the Commission's rhetoric in the case lends itself to this interpretation, and undoubtedly the case provided a platform for a more normative turn regarding individual treatment. In fact, however, *Bicycles* was closely intertwined with another case, *Photo Albums*[22] (see Table 8 below).

Table 8 Procedural Stages of Bicycles and Photo Albums

STAGE OF PROCEDURE	*Bicycles*	*Photo Albums*
Complaint	July 1991	mid-1991
Investigation	12.12.91	12.5.92
Provisional duties	5.3.93	6.9.93
Definitive duties	8.9.93	22.12.93
Application for judicial review	23.12. 93	15.4.94
Judicial review	25.9.97	18.9.96

Both cases drew heavily on previous decisions, in which most individual treatment requests were denied. The *Bicycles* case was about six months ahead of *Photo Albums*, except for judicial review. Two stages in both cases are important here. The first important stage concerns the imposition of provisional duties, because it was at this stage that the Commission clarified its individual treatment criteria, first in *Bicycles* and then in *Photo Albums*. The second important stage was that of judicial review, because for the first time in the EU–China interaction through anti-dumping cases, the normative basis of Commission practice was stated clearly in court, initially in *Photo Albums* and then in *Bicycles*.

In *Bicycles*, Chinese producers in joint ventures with non-Chinese partners, and located in an SEZ, requested individual treatment. Their legal strategies, including recourse to litigation, were discussed in Chapter 4. Though at the provisional stage of the proceedings the Commission followed previous cases,[23] at the definitive stage it articulated its rationale as a general change in administrative practice. Previously individual treatment had been given to exporters which demonstrated independence from the State in their export policy and in establishing export prices. In this action, however, the Commission stated expressly that it had 'come to the conclusion that for . . . [various] reasons the utmost prudence is required in this matter.'[24] The reasons given

[20] *Ibid* (definitive), para 8. Subsequently an investigation was opened for alleged circumvention: [1999] OJ L195/9.

[21] *Bicycles from China* [1993] OJ L58/12 (provisional), [1993] OJ L228/9 (definitive).

[22] *Photo Albums from China* [1993] OJ L228/16 (provisional), [1993] OJ L333/67 (definitive).

[23] *Bicycles from China* (provisional), above n 21, para 34.

[24] *Bicycles from China* (definitive), above n 21, para 16.

were, first, that individual treatment was appropriate only where it gave a more proportionate, more effective remedy against injurious dumping than a single, country-wide duty. Secondly, it could often lead to a distorted individual result, because it took account only of individual export prices and not necessarily of efficiency and comparative advantage. Thirdly, the Chinese economy was in transition, and it was difficult to establish whether a company was really permanently independent of the State. Fourthly, on-the-spot investigations in China were not feasible. Fifthly, individual treatment should be given only where there was no risk of circumvention. Sixthly, the fact that the State held only a minority of shares was not in itself a sufficient reason for granting individual treatment.[25] State influence thus appeared to the European Commission to be an ever-present danger, especially since on-the-spot visits were not used to ascertain the facts, and the risk of circumvention assumed central importance.[26] Though these elements were not new, this formulation brought together a wide range of criteria, including micro-economic and macro-economic, economic and political, and theoretical and practical elements. In both theory and practice, it made individual treatment more difficult to achieve, in particular because it provided a more elaborate normative justification than before for denying individual treatment. The concept of individual treatment gained greatly in precision.

In *Photo Albums* the exporter was Climax Paper Converters, a Hong Kong company that exported photo albums manufactured in Baoan, China. Climax had been subject to anti-dumping duties in an earlier case about exports from Hong Kong, so it decided to move its production facilities to mainland China. It made an agreement with the Baoan Company,[27] a cooperative undertaking with its own legal personality composed of members of the Tiegang Villagers' Committee, a consortium of landholders from Tiegang Village (where the factory was located). The aim of this Committee was to promote the development of the village through foreign investment. The Baoan Company had a licence to pursue economic activities from a Chinese government body. According to the agreement between Climax and the Baoan Company, the latter undertook to build a factory in conformity with the plans provided by the former. Climax in return undertook to supply the equipment and raw materials and the additional materials necessary for production, and to pay the rent, wages, and electricity charges and taxes. The Baoan Company was to appoint a plant manager and necessary accounting and management personnel to manage the plant jointly with staff appointed by Climax. The management and administrative personnel appointed by the Baoan Company was required to pass Climax recruitment tests. The imports and exports of the factory in China were subject to the supervision of the Baoan County Foreign Trade Company. The Baoan Company was in charge of assisting Climax in regard to import and export licence procedures. These facts reveal the emergence in China, and now on the EU market, of a new kind of Chinese enterprise, the *xiangzhen qiye* (literally 'township enterprise'), or township and village enterprise (TVE). Climax argued that its production operation in China was only a production branch, no invoice was raised for the finished product transferred between the mainland factory and the Hong Kong company, all commercial decisions with regard to production and sales policies were freely exercised in Hong Kong, and it was fully profit-orientated.

[25] *Ibid,* paras 16–27.

[26] For criticism, see Donghui Fu, 'EC Anti-dumping Law and Individual Treatment Policy in Cases involving Imports from China' (1997) 31 *Journal of World Trade* 73.

[27] Formally the Baoan County Xinan Town Tiegang Village Economic Development Company.

The Commission rejected its request for individual treatment, following its *Bicycles* rationale, and adding only that the existence of a joint venture by itself was not a sufficient reason for granting individual treatment.

Community individual treatment practice was described in Spring 1996 as consisting of 'a variety of different methodologies which follow no precise guideline but generally confirm the increasing tendency to restrict individual treatment to limited circumstances'.[28] The main criteria were ownership and control by foreign investment, freely-established export prices, transfer of profits to foreign shareholders, and real legal and factual independence from the State.[29] *Bicycles*, drawing on previous cases, put circumvention at the core of individual treatment. Individual treatment was the exception, to be granted only once a range of stringent conditions were satisfied, including but not limited to independence from the State. Applying this criterion in practice, however, resembled a search for a needle in a haystack on a dark night, especially in the absence of on-site verification. In the event, the grant of individual treatment turned on the burden of proof, which was imposed on the exporters. Whether as administrative practice or emerging 'soft law', this configuration favoured the EU, hence European industry, thus inevitably rendering EC anti-dumping law a protectionist instrument. Seen as part of a process of legalisation, the concept of individual treatment had achieved considerable precision. However, it did not embody any kind of legal obligation on the part of the EC, neither did it confer any entitlements or rights on Chinese exporters.

The disadvantages faced by Chinese exporters were accentuated by the fact that their evidence, even if accurate in Chinese terms, sometimes did not correspond to European conceptions. As *Photo Albums* illustrates, neither EC legislation nor Commission practice took sufficient account of the new enterprises resulting from China's economic transformation. *Bicycles* and *Photo Albums* showed the European institutions trying to come to grips with the emergence of Chinese capitalism, in the form of the 'socialist market economy'. But EC law and practice were based on a European (or Western) distinction between public and private, or State and market, which did not provide an appropriate means of analysing the export behaviour of Chinese companies. The European Commission did not analyse the TVE as a new type of Chinese business organisation. Neither did it consider the potential implications of the TVE for the Commission's rigid way of thinking about non-market economies in general or individual treatment in particular. Both of these concepts were premised on a sharp distinction between 'market economies' and 'non-market economies'; each was based on a different role of the State in the national economy. Perhaps still reflecting ordo-liberal ideas of relations between State and market, as sketched in Chapter 6, they contrasted sharply with now current awareness of the varieties of capitalism.[30] However, the emergence of TVEs undercut this sharp distinction and rendered its application in anti-dumping cases increasingly problematic. But even if on-site visits had been possible, it might have been difficult for the EC institutions to escape limitations of cultural perspective. In the circumstances, the real problem of assessing the legality of competition for markets was compounded by a lack of cross-cultural

[28] I Van Bael and JF Bellis, *Anti-dumping and Other Trade Protection Laws of the EC*, 3rd edn (Bicester, CCH Editions, 1996) at 229.

[29] *Ibid*, at 231.

[30] See PA Hall and D Soskice (eds), *Varieties of Capitalism: The Institutional Foundations of Comparative Advantage* (Oxford, Oxford University Press, 2001).

understanding. As long as the Commission's criteria derived from past practice, the more systematic they became, the less able they were to cope with economic changes in China. Legalisation was based on, drew upon and reflected only the European perspective. None of the three dimensions—obligation, precision or delegation—was concerned with the Chinese perspective.

III. The Phase of Soft Law

An increasing number of anti-dumping cases and of requests for individual treatment accentuated the legalisation of individual treatment. As noted earlier, we could use the term 'juridification' to denote the process of the creation of a legal concept, but this term tends to be understood as referring to the transformation of soft law into hard law. However, the changes in the concept and rules regarding individual treatment encompassed changes in the nature of obligations, the precision with which these obligations were defined and the extent of delegation of dispute settlement powers to third parties. In these circumstances, the term 'legalisation' is more appropriate.

The process of legalisation of individual treatment was driven partly by foreign investment and China's economic transformation. It was mediated through increasing interaction between the two sites of governance, the EU and China, especially between the European Commission and the Chinese Ministry of Foreign Trade and Economic Cooperation (MOFTEC), now the Ministry of Commerce (Mofcom), in a growing number of anti-dumping cases. By the mid-1990s, a dynamic non-State sector had emerged in China, sometimes under the control and influence of local governments,[31] and increasingly orientated toward export markets. Some described this as a form of 'local state corporatism',[32] or as 'a market economy with a mixed ownership basis',[33] characterised by ambiguous and poorly protected property rights,[34] which did not necessarily bear a close resemblance to the market economies that are assumed to operate in Western countries. The status of TVEs seemed especially unclear,[35] though the term was commonly used to denote a broad range of non-State enterprises, with the role of local government varying greatly.[36] One specialist suggested that

[31] See esp SB Lubman, *Bird in a Cage: Legal Reform in China after Mao* (Stanford, Stanford University Press, 1999) at 103–18; KG Lieberthal, *Governing China: Revolution through Reform* (New York, Norton, 1995) 264–65.

[32] JC Oi, 'Fiscal Reform and the Economic Foundations of Local State Corporatism in China' (1992) 45(1) *World Politics* 99; JC Oi, 'The Role of the Local State in China's Transitional Economy' (1995) 144 *China Quarterly* 1132; JC Oi, 'The Evolution of Local State Corporatism' in AG Walder (ed), *Zouping in Transition: The Process of Reform in Rural North China* (Cambridge, Mass, Harvard University Press, 1998).

[33] B Naughton, *Growing Out of the Plan: Chinese Economic Reform, 1978–1993* (Cambridge, Cambridge University Press, 1995).

[34] See DD Li, 'A Theory of Ambiguous Property Rights in Transition Economies: The Case of the Chinese Non-State Sector' (1996) 23(1) *Journal of Comparative Economics* 1.

[35] A good example is the *China: Township Enterprises Report*, a Ministry of Agriculture report on the situation in TVEs, translated in Lubman, above n 31, at 345, fn 16.

[36] See JC Oi and AG Walder (eds), *Property Rights and Economic Reform in China* (Stanford, Stanford University Press, 1999). See also AG Walder, 'Local Government as Industrial Firm: An Organizational Analysis of China's Transitional Economy' (1995) 101(2) *American Journal of Sociology* 263; Jiahua Che and Yingqi Qian, 'Institutional Environment, Community Government and Corporate Governance: Understanding China's Township-Village Enterprises' (1998) 14 *Journal of Law, Economics and Organization* 1.

> the declining attention to public and private status reflects not the increasing clarity of legal property boundaries but rather the greater legitimacy of arrangements that do not conform to the legal distinctions between public and private property . . .[37]

Recent research tends to confirm the variety of legal and property arrangements which were and are characteristic of TVEs.[38]

Other aspects of China's economic transformation also had an impact on EC anti-dumping law. European and other foreign direct investment in China increased. So too did Chinese exports to the EU. Starting in 1993, the issue of market opening took precedence in discussions about Chinese accession to the WTO.[39] On 12 May 1994, China promulgated its first Foreign Trade Law, designed to provide a legal framework for the decentralisation of foreign trade policy and the autonomy of foreign trade operators.[40] In 1996 the Chinese MOFTEC enacted Regulations to prevent exports at prices lower than the cost of production.[41] This might have stemmed from pressure by China's trading partners, and may have had effects more symbolic than material, but it expressed a concern within China about the extent to which China was targeted by anti-dumping measures, in the EU and elsewhere. It also reflected the difficulty of exercising effective control of an increasingly decentralised foreign trade system, whether through State, market, networks or other organisational forms.

The stage was set for the phase of 'soft law'. In July 1996 the Commission presented to the Anti-dumping Committee a Commission working document, later discussed with delegations from non-market economy countries. Essentially a written version of administrative practice, but phrased in more general, systematic and normative terms, it distinguished between foreign multinationals, on the one hand, and other companies, such as joint ventures or local companies, on the other hand. For the former, individual treatment was to be presumed. The latter had to meet five core criteria (discussed further below) to be granted individual treatment; three other criteria were considered on a case-by-case basis.[42]

For the first time the document presented a coherent, written set of norms concerning individual treatment. The fact that it was in writing gave a public character to these norms, the expression (though not necessarily the application) of which was removed from the realm of individual or administrative organisational discretion. This was a step towards greater specification of obligations, though they remained 'soft' rather than becoming 'hard' because the norms were not legally binding. The criteria were

[37] DL Wank, *Commodifying Chinese Communism: Business, Trust and Politics in Xiamen* (Cambridge, Cambridge University Press, 1998).

[38] Hongyi Chen, *The Institutional Transition of China's Township and Village Enterprises: Market Liberalization, Contractual Form Innovation and Privatization* (Aldershot, Ashgate, 2000); He Kang (Chief Ed), *China's Township and Village Enterprises* (Beijing, Foreign Languages Press, 2006).

[39] See Long Yongtu, 'Negotiations for China's Accession to the WTO and the Process of Market-oriented Reform' in Wang Mengkui (ed), *China: Accession to the WTO and Economic Reform* (Beijing, Foreign Languages Press, 2002) 32 at 51–52.

[40] See Wang Baoshu, 'China's Accession to the WTO and the Building of a Socialist Market Legal System', in Wang Mengkui, above n 39, 151–74, and 'Foreign Trade Law of the People's Republic of China', in *Handbook of Foreign Economic Law*, vol I, above n 12, 386.

[41] Interim Regulations of the MOFTEC on Punishment for Conduct of Exporting at a Lower-than-Normal Price, adopted on 20 March 1996: see Wang Baoshu, above n 40 at 163.

[42] E Vermulst and B Driessen, 'New Battle Lines in the Anti-Dumping War: Recent Movements on the European Front' (1997) 31(3) *Journal of World Trade* 135 at 143. The core criteria were criteria (1), (4), (6), (7) and (8) of the list published in 1997, see further below. The same factors are given, without reference to the Commission document, in E Vermulst and P Waer, *EC Anti-dumping Law and Practice* (London, Sweet & Maxwell, 1996) at 207–08.

more detailed, more precise and more orientated toward the achievement of specified objectives than earlier norms. Whether these new norms delegated dispute settlement responsibility to a third party was tested in the European courts.

This soft law was invoked on judicial review in both *Photo Albums* and *Bicycles*.[43] *Photo Albums* was decided first. Climax argued that it should be granted individual treatment because it fulfilled the necessary requirements of the Commission's internal memorandum.[44] It treated the document as conferring rights on third parties and as binding on the Commission. In contrast, the Council also recognised the existence of the document, but it claimed that the arguments about previous practice and the Commission internal memorandum were irrelevant because the Community institutions had changed their approach to individual treatment.[45] As the Commission explained at the hearing, its practice had changed because

> originally they had probably been rather naïve as to the nature of the situation in that country and . . . it was only recently that a large number of anti-dumping proceedings had been initiated in regard to Chinese products . . . [T]he original policy did not take account of the high degree of control which existed and still exists, even though that control is less than it previously was.[46]

Both Council and Commission considered the document to be simply a policy statement, with no legal effects of its own; in other words, another (albeit written) version of administrative practice which could be modified by subsequent practice. The CFI accepted this argument. The document was merely an internal working document of the Commission and could not 'give rise to justified hopes on the part of the applicant'.[47] Subsequently, in *Bicycles*, the applicant referred to 'a Commission memorandum of 1 December 1992 specifying the line of conduct it intended to adopt with regard to dumping by joint ventures in non-market economy countries'.[48] Referring to *Photo Albums*, the CFI rejected the claim for individual treatment. Both cases were entirely consistent with the 'internal instructions' case law of the European courts.[49] They demonstrated that, consistently with the European courts' case law since *ERTA*,[50] such soft law could be invoked in court. With regard to the concept of individual treatment, this was an advance towards greater legalisation along the dimension of obligation than before. *Photo Albums* and *Bicycles* also showed, however, that these norms did not confer any rights upon potential litigants, give rise to any legitimate expectations or provide the basis for any challenge to EC anti-dumping measures.

In March 1997, after *Photo Albums* but before *Bicycles*, the Commission published its criteria:

[43] Case T-155/94 *Climax Paper Converters v Council of the European Union* [1996] ECR II-873; Case T-170/94 *Shanghai Bicycle Corporation v Council of the European Union* [1997] ECR II-1383.

[44] *Climax*, above n 43, paras 69–73.

[45] *Ibid*, para 89.

[46] *Ibid*, para 91.

[47] *Ibid*, para 115.

[48] *Shanghai Bicycle Corp*, above n 43, para 94.

[49] See eg Case C-366 *France v Commission* [1991] ECR I-3579. See further A Mazuelos, *Non-binding Acts in the European Community Legal Order: Soft Law?* (PhD thesis, European University Institute, Florence, 2003), 221–28, 292–94. In this and other respects, anti-dumping cases, especially those few in which judicial review was requested, reflected broader developments in EU administrative law, though this point cannot be pursued here.

[50] Case 22/70 *Commission v Council (ERTA)* [1971] ECR 263.

(1) The majority of the shares should belong to genuinely private companies and no State officials should be on the board or in a key management position; the fact that the company is controlled by a foreign investor will be considered a relevant indication of independence.
(2) The land on which the facilities of the company are built should be rented from the State at conditions comparable to those in a market economy country or purchased (eg a proper contractual lease).
(3) The company should have the right to hire and dismiss employees and the right to fix salaries.
(4) The company should have full control over its supply of raw materials and inputs in general.
(5) The supply of utilities should be guaranteed on the basis of proper contractual terms.
(6) Proof must be given that profit can be exported and capital invested can be repatriated (only in case of foreign investment, eg joint ventures).
(7) The export prices should be determined freely; the fact that export sales are made to a related party outside the country in question will be a decisive factor.
(8) Freedom to carry out business activities should be guaranteed, in particular in respect of the following:
    (a) There should be no restrictions on selling on the domestic market.
    (b) The right to do business cannot be withdrawn outside proper contractual terms.
    (c) Quantities produced for export should be determined freely by the company in accordance with the traditional demand of its export markets.

In order for an exporter in a non-market economy country to qualify for individual treatment, it was required to meet five core criteria, namely those indicated in (1), (4), (6), (7) and (8). Some discretion was left to the Commission with regard to the remaining three criteria.

Broad in scope and diverse in nature, these criteria dealt with corporate governance, production inputs, exports and general business activities. Substantially informed by US law,[51] they seemed more a product of a brainstorming session about what a market economy company might look like than a precise analytical tool concerning exports. Some criteria betrayed a lack of knowledge about Chinese conditions, such as, for example, the fact that SEZ companies were based mainly on inward processing, were orientated toward export and were prohibited from selling on the domestic Chinese market. Only criteria (7) and (8)(c) concerned export sales directly. Probably many EC companies could not have satisfied the criteria, but this is beside the point. Anti-dumping law is designed to protect the domestic market from exogenous forces, not to regulate domestic firms. Generally, it is difficult to avoid the suspicion that the criteria were designed not merely to determine whether a company operated on a market basis with regard to its export price, but rather to achieve three broader objectives: first, to assess the market orientation of specific exporters according to an omnibus checklist; secondly, to put pressure on Chinese companies to be more orientated toward the market, as the Commission conceived it, notably by joint ventures or other links with foreign investors; and, thirdly, to put pressure on the Chinese Government to continue its economic reforms.

[51] See JA Laroski, Jr, 'NMEs: A Love Story—Nonmarket and Market Economy Status under US Antidumping Law' (1999) 30 *Law and Policy in International Business* 369.

The legal status of the criteria was ambiguous, and this ambiguity caused confusion among Chinese producers and exporters, as well as ministries. The Commission treated the criteria as guidelines for administrative practice, viewing them as a way of granting more flexibility in assessing claims. But in the future it gave special emphasis to the risk of circumvention. It also introduced on-site visits to make a 'global assessment' of exporters' independence from the State. Space prohibits giving examples, but in subsequent cases individual treatment was more often denied than granted.[52] These decisions were formally part of Commission practice. However, they were seen by all parties as being taken within a general normative, soft law framework, even though the Commission did not always review all criteria in each case and the CFI case law prevented litigants from invoking the criteria as the basis for legal claims. In other words, the criteria fell short with regard to the dimension of obligation, but they were much more precise than previous norms. Due partly to the fact that they were in writing, they also offered potential litigants at least a foot in the door of the courthouse.

IV. The Phase of Hard Law

The publication of these criteria occurred within a rapidly changing context, in the EU and elsewhere, deeply conditioned by China's impending accession to the WTO. The United States and Australia already permitted the use of domestic prices and costs in transitional economies. As the Commission noted, 'the US grants individual treatment in almost every case'.[53] In March 1997 Australia closed the leading *Glyphosate* case with no duties to be paid, announcing that China was a country in transition and in anti-dumping proceedings was a special case,[54] even though the EU refused individual treatment in its own action against China about the same product.[55] Also in March 1997, China adopted its first Anti-dumping and Anti-subsidy Regulations.[56]

In April 1998 the EC amended its basic anti-dumping Regulation. The amendment, Council Regulation 905/98, recognised the extent to which China and Russia had already established a market economy.[57] It was adopted because of international regulatory competition with the United States, pressure by the Chinese Government, and increasing EU and other foreign investment in China. Increasing foreign direct investment led to greater internationalisation of production and increased exports to the

[52] See Jianyu Wang, 'A Critique of the Application to China of the Non-market Economy Rules of Antidumping Legislation and Practice of the European Union' (1999) 33(3) *Journal of World Trade* 117.

[53] Commission of the European Communities, Communication from the Commission to the Council and the European Parliament on the treatment of former non-market economies in anti-dumping proceedings and a proposal for a Council Regulation amending Council Regulation (EC) No 384/96, COM(97)677 final, Brussels 12 December 1997, p 11 (hereafter 'Commission Communication').

[54] Australian Customs Service, Australian Customs Dumping Notice No 97/033, at http://www.customs.gov.au/site/content2790.asp, last accessed 19 February 2010; 'Glyphosate Anti-dumping Case Closed with No Duty Payment; China is Special Case—Australia decides no anti-dumping measures to be taken against glyphosate exported by China, no fines', *China Chemical Reporter*, 26 April 1997.

[55] *Glyphosate from China* [1997] OJ L243/7 (provisional), [1998] OJ L47/1 (definitive).

[56] On the evolution of Chinese anti-dumping law, see Thomas W Huang, *Trade Remedies: Laws of Dumping, Subsidies and Safeguards in China* (The Hague, Kluwer Law International, 2003); Xin Zhang, *International Trade Regulation in China: Law and Policy* (Oxford, Hart Publishing, 2006), 178–236; See Xiaochen Wu, *Anti-Dumping Law and Practice of China* (Alphen aan den Rijn, Wolters Kluwer, 2009).

[57] Council Regulation (EC) 905/98, [1998] OJ L128/19.

EU. As shown in Chapter 4, it meant that EC anti-dumping duties might potentially be imposed on products produced by partly EU companies. Chinese and Russian companies now could try to prove that they acted on a market basis and qualified for market economy treatment, so their data could be used in determining both normal value and export price.[58] The criteria for market economy treatment were:

a) decisions about prices, costs and inputs made in response to market signals and without significant State interference, with costs of inputs substantially reflecting market values;
b) one set of basic accounting records, independently audited in line with international accounting standards and applied for all purposes;
c) production costs and the financial situation of firms not being subject to significant distortions carried over from the former system;
d) firms subject to bankruptcy and property laws guaranteeing legal certainty and stability; and
e) exchange rate conversions carried out at the market rate.

Exporters did not need to submit a separate claim for individual treatment, because now market economy treatment and individual treatment would be considered together in the same examination; exporters not claiming market economy treatment were instructed to request individual treatment when returning the questionnaire.

The Commission reviewed this regime two years later. Overall, its assessment was favourable. However, the application of Regulation 905/98 had demonstrated an overlap between the market economy treatment criteria and the individual treatment criteria. In principle the market economy treatment criteria should concern a company's activities on both the domestic and the export markets, while the individual treatment criteria should concern only a company's export activities. The Chinese 'severely criticised' the confusion, particularly because it 'created the illogical situation that only those exporting producers that can fulfil the requirements for market economy status can qualify for individual treatment'. From the European Commission's standpoint, the key issue for the individual treatment criteria was whether export transactions were subject to State interference. Consequently, the Commission amended the individual treatment criteria to focus on export activities.[59]

The new individual treatment criteria were:

(1) Exporters are free to repatriate capital and profits (applicable to wholly foreign-owned firms or joint ventures).
(2) Export prices and quantities, and conditions and terms of sale are freely determined, and the majority of shares belong to genuinely private companies. State officials appearing on the board or in key management positions should be in a clear minority. The presumption is that a State-controlled company cannot guarantee its independence from State interference, and the burden rests with the exporter to prove otherwise.

[58] See Commission Communication, above n 53.

[59] Commission of the European Communities, 'Explanatory Memorandum: Review of the Anti-dumping Regime Applicable to Russia and China and a Proposal for a Council Regulation amending Council Regulation (EC) No 384/96', in Commission of the European Communities, Proposal for a Council Regulation amending Regulation (EC) No 384/96 on protection against dumped imports from countries not members of the European Community (presented by the Commission), COM(2000)363 final, Brussels, 15 June 2000 (the quotation is from p 14 of the Memorandum).

(3) Exchange rate conversions are carried out at the market rate.
(4) State interference is not such as to permit circumvention of measures if exporters are given different rates of duty.

The most novel aspect is the express reference to circumvention. This element had long been at the core of the Commission's application of individual treatment, but never before had it been made clear in writing. The amendment thus dramatically improved the precision of individual treatment. In addition, the fact that these criteria were 'considered to be relevant' in determining individual treatment expressed the Commission's intention that the criteria should not have legal force. It is likely that this was intended to remove any subsisting doubts about the possible legal effects of individual treatment and to confirm, so far as possible, the soft law character of individual treatment in the light of the European courts' evolving jurisprudence.[60] If we interpret the new individual treatment norms in their broader legal context, however, we can appreciate that the adoption of market economy treatment criteria in legal form may have amplified the possibility that, sooner or later, the individual treatment criteria which accompanied them as part of EC anti-dumping law would also come to have legal force.

It may be surprising that so many years were required to redefine the criteria for individual treatment in such a way that they were directly relevant to export activities, especially since until 1998 they were the only way in which EC anti-dumping law took account of economic changes occurring in China with direct regard to export markets. In explaining this, one could point to the Commission's ambitious, even inflated, objectives for anti-dumping law and its broad discretion in applying individual treatment, quite apart from the changeover to the Santer Commission in 1994, its resignation in disgrace in 1999, and the Commission's chronic shortage of staff and other resources. Even after 1997, the individual treatment criteria were not treated as having any legal effects, at least with regard to third parties, hence they were not invoked by litigants or subjected to judicial analysis.

The ensuing several years saw major changes in relations between the EU, China and also the WTO. The European Commission's major March 1998 policy paper on 'Building a Comprehensive Partnership with China' reflected the adoption a month later of Council Regulation 905/98. It also proposed to introduce

> a more systematic approach to the granting of individual treatment and calculation of comparative advantage. The proposal will reflect the specific behaviour and operating conditions of individual firms, whilst at the same time acting as an incentive for further reforms among Chinese companies. As such, it will interact positively with the ongoing WTO accession negotiations . . .[61]

Between 1998 and 2002, the EU and China held five summit meetings[62]; anti-dumping was discussed at least during one of them by the top leaders. Most importantly of all, China became a Member of the WTO on 11 December 2001. For many Chinese, the

[60] For example, compare the approaches of the A-G and the ECJ in Case C-443/97 *Spain v Commission* [2000] ECR I-2415.

[61] Commission of the European Communities, Communication of the Commission, 'Building a Comprehensive Partnership with China', COM(1998)181, Brussels, 25 March 1998, in Snyder, above n 2, at 380.

[62] The 1st Europe–China Summit was held in London in April 1998, the 2nd in Beijing in December 1999, the 3rd in Beijing in October 2000, the 4th in Brussels in September 2001 and the 5th in Copenhagen in September 2002. For the relevant press statements on their results, see Snyder, above n 2, at 670–77. The Joint Press Statement of the Fourth EU–China Summit, held in Brussels on 5 September 2001, referred explicitly to anti-dumping: see Snyder, *ibid*, at 674.

EC's non-market economy methodology appeared to be incompatible with China's accession to the WTO. For all parties, it gave increased impetus toward great clarity and precision in basic trade rules. Together with China's continuing economic reform, these factors contributed to a further change in EC anti-dumping law.

In November 2002, the Council adopted Council Regulation (EC) 1972/2002, which amended the basic EC anti-dumping Regulation.[63] The amendment gave legislative form and legal force to a shortened version of the 2000 individual treatment criteria. The Preamble to Council Regulation (EC) 1972/2002 noted that the basic Regulation previously lacked criteria for individual treatment, and that it was appropriate to lay down the criteria in the interests of transparency and legal certainty.[64] Since 1994, the basic Regulation had provided only that, as a general rule, the single duty rule should be used in anti-dumping measures involving non-market economy countries.[65] The 2002 Regulation added a new paragraph:

> Where Article 2(7)(a) applies, an individual duty shall, however, be specified for the exporters which can demonstrate, on the basis of properly substantiated claims that:
>
> (a) in the case of wholly or partly foreign owned firms or joint ventures, exporters are free to repatriate capital and profits;
> (b) export prices and quantities, and conditions and terms of sale are freely determined;
> (c) the majority of the shares belong to private persons. State officials appearing on the board of Directors or holding key management positions shall either be in minority or it must be demonstrated that the company is nevertheless sufficiently independent from State interference;
> (d) exchange rate conversions are carried out at the market rate;
> (e) State interference is not such as to permit circumvention of measures if individual exporters are given different rates of duty.[66]

In substance and wording, these criteria in legislative form followed exactly those in the latest revised soft law version, the only difference being a minor matter of form. In principle, however, they provide an exhaustive checklist for the benefit of all interests concerned.[67] Council Regulation (EC) 1972/2002 thus consolidated the legalisation of the concept and rules of individual treatment, rendering them legally binding, making them more precise, and providing a basis for the invocation of the criteria before the EC administration and the courts.

The last phase in the transformation of individual treatment from soft law to hard law was informed by three main factors. The first factor was the practice of the EU's main trading partners, notably the United States, which increasingly granted individual treatment to Chinese companies. Secondly, the legislative enactment of Council Regulation (EC) 905/98 served as a crucial stimulus for a hard law of individual treatment. It required the European Commission to distinguish more clearly between two sets of criteria, those for market economy treatment and those for individual treatment, which then could be used to identify three groups of Chinese enterprises:

[63] Council Regulation (EC) No 1972/2002, [2002] OJ L305/1.

[64] *Ibid*, Preamble, 7th Recital.

[65] Council Regulation (EC) No 3283/94, Art 9(5), [1994] OJ L349/1, subsequently the same article in Council Regulation (EC) No 384/96.

[66] Council Regulation (EC) No 1972/2002, above n 63, Art 1(6).

[67] All criteria should be expressly considered, along the lines of Art 3.4 of the WTO Anti-dumping Agreement, *per* the Appellate Body in *Thailand-H-Beams from Poland*, WT/DS122/AB/R, 12 March 2001, paras 121–28.

a) market-based companies;
b) companies operating on a market basis on export markets; and
c) non-market economy enterprises.

Not easy to make in theory, such distinctions proved even more difficult to apply in practice. The third and crucial factor was Chinese accession to the WTO. The process of Chinese accession informed the reform of EC anti-dumping law in the late 1990s. Accession to the WTO required China's trading partners to define the basic rules of the bilateral trade game more clearly and precisely within the new multilateral framework which would govern their activities. With the benefit of hindsight, the impact of this new site of governance on relations between the EU and China was decisive.

V. Conclusion

The legalisation of individual treatment in EC anti-dumping law about China occurred in three overlapping phases. Originating in the Commission's administrative practice, and designed initially to deal with 'bubbles of capitalism' in China, the concept then was

Table 9 Legalisation of Individual Treatment

	Phase of Development	*Administrative Practice*	*Soft Law*	*Hard Law*
Dimension of Legalisation				
Obligation		none	none	complete
Precision		little substantial	minimal to	substantial
Delegation		none	minimal	substantial

expressed as soft law and subsequently as hard law. A determining factor was the development of increasingly close relations between the EU and China, of which trade and foreign investment were crucial elements. More precisely, two sets of factors stimulated this process, though not all could be explored in detail here. Some were internal to the EU, such as the development of EC constitutional and administrative law, the case law of the European courts and increasing conflicts between Member States about the imposition of anti-dumping duties. Others were external to the EU, including changes in US anti-dumping law, Chinese economic reforms and China's accession to the WTO. All were drawn together by foreign direct investment, the development of international production networks and trade.

A constant concern of the European Commission during this period of normative transformation was circumvention. As shown in Chapter 4, this has long been a very controversial issue in international trade law. The Contracting Parties of the GATT and then Members of the WTO have never been able to agree on a definition of circumvention. In these circumstances, companies and governments have developed their own business and legal strategies to maintain and strengthen their position in the processes of competition for markets. Since 1987, EC anti-dumping law has included provisions to combat circumvention.[68]

The legalisation of individual treatment was part of a process of interaction and mutual learning, involving administrative authorities, the legislator, the judiciary, companies and even employees in both the EU and China. Furthermore, it reveals the extent to which extremely technical branches of EC law have participated in the general evolution of EU constitutional and administrative law, starting from broad administrative discretion and moving toward more transparent legislation. Viewed on an international plane, the legalisation of individual treatment in EC anti-dumping law shares a pattern of development with China's recent legal revolution and increased orientation toward the rule of law, even though the rule of law (or even the market economy) may not be understood in the same way in the legal systems and legal cultures of the two trading partners. Now the WTO transparency obligations provide a common legal framework. The legalisation of individual treatment illustrates to some extent how the EU, through EC anti-dumping law, has taken account of the transformation of the Chinese economy since the early 1990s. It also shows that the law of any single WTO Member today is conditioned not only by so-called domestic factors, but also, and fundamentally, by relations with other sites of governance.

But the reach of WTO law may extend even farther. Are the EC concept and rules about individual treatment compatible with WTO law? Individual treatment did not form part of EC law until the entry into force of Council Regulation (EC) 1972/2002 on 12 December 2002,[69] that is, after Chinese accession to the WTO. Individual treatment became EC hard law on 12 December 2002. The November 2001 WTO Protocol on the Accession of China, Article 15,[70] provides for the use of either Chinese prices or costs, or the importing country's non-market economy methodology, for a maximum of 15 years. The Protocol permits an importing WTO Member to

> use a methodology that is not based on a strict comparison with domestic prices or costs in China if the producers under investigation cannot clearly show that market economy conditions prevail in the industry producing the like product with regard to manufacture, production and sale of that product.[71]

It also provides, however, that:

> Once China has established, under the national law of the importing WTO Member, that it is a market economy, the provisions of subparagraph (a) shall be terminated provided that the importing Member's national law contains market economy criteria *as of the date of accession* . . .[72]

These two subparagraphs should be read together, so that subparagraph (d) informs the interpretation of subparagraph (a). The basic issue is whether the use of individual treatment is compatible with WTO law, even though it was not contained in EC anti-dumping law 'as of the date of accession'.[73] As this chapter demonstrates, the

[68] Art 13(10) of Council Regulation (EC) No 2176/84, as amended by Council Regulation (EC) No 1761/87, [1987] OJ L167/9.

[69] Council Regulation (EC) No 1972/2002, above n 63, Art 2.

[70] WTO, *Protocol on the Accession of China, vol 1*, (Doha, 10 November 2001) (Cambridge, Cambridge University Press, 2003) 7–8, Art 15.

[71] *Ibid*, (a)(ii).

[72] *Ibid*, (d), emphasis added.

[73] For a different analysis, see H Andersen, *EU Dumping Determinations and WTO Law* (Alphen aan den Rijn, Wolters Kluwer, 2009) 338–42.

EC's individual treatment criteria were in the form of soft law as of the date of Chinese accession to the WTO. Both the European Commission and the CFI confirmed this non legally-binding status. On this logic, one would conclude that the legalisation of individual treatment in EC anti-dumping law occurred too late to be legally applied to China after China's accession to the WTO. Individual treatment, despite its legalisation, remains a transitional category, destined, one hopes, to disappear.

8

Competing Constellations of Sites: EC Customs Law and International Production Networks

I. Introduction

Relations between sites of governance may be competitive, instead of being cooperative, tense, neutral, or characterised by mutual neglect. These different characterisations of relations apply, however, not only to relations between individual sites of governance, such as the European Union (EU) and the WTO, but also to relations between different groups, or 'constellations', of sites of governance. Today the most significant types of such relations between different constellations of sites of governance are two-fold. The first type concerns relations between regional integration and more broadly based international sites of governance. In legal terms, this usually takes the form of relations between regional integration schemes and the WTO; both are based on multilateral treaties but they differ in membership and scope. Chapter 9 of the book considers an example of this type, focusing on China's regional trade agreements within the framework of WTO law. A second type consists of relations between regional integration schemes and economic globalisation in the form of international production networks. Regional integration schemes involve a defined number of sites; international production networks concern many sites, not all of which may be known in advance. This second type of competion is the subject of this chapter.

Regional integration and economic globalisation in the form of international production networks are both friends and rivals. Each represents a different set of relations between sites of governance, or a different constellation of sites. Either can refer to economic relations or to normative relations. The extent to which they are entirely compatible with each other, as economic relations or as normative relations, is subject to debate. This tension is often creative, but sometimes it contains the seeds of contradiction. This chapter explores the tension between regional integration and globalisation, using the example of regional integration in Europe and economic globalisation in the form of international production networks (IPNs). It considers each as a specific, distinct constellation of sites of governance.

International production networks and foreign direct investment (FDI) drive foreign trade relations between the European Union and China today. Through variants of a single organisational form, IPNs link together different parts of the globe. Despite the growth of the Chinese domestic market, they remain a crucial part of EU–China relations; in fact, they contribute to and feed on domestic growth.[1] International

[1] See, eg, Zhang Qi, 'Integration proves profitable for multinationals', *China Daily*, Friday, 17 October 2008, at 15.

production networks are also the core of East Asian regional integration. Whether composed of multinational companies, small and medium-sized enterprises or both, they contribute to what is sometimes called 'fragmentation trade', that is, trade in parts and components, especially for machinery. In East Asia, fragmentation trade has expanded faster than trade in final products. Chinese domestic economic growth has enhanced these developments, creating a very complex web of business networks. The resulting current pattern of trade is comprised of intra-regional fragmentation trade in East Asia, trade between the EU and China of parts, components and products for further processing, and trade in final goods between Asia and Europe. China serves as an export platform for goods sourced from throughout Asia or in Europe but assembled or manufactured in final form in China.[2]

These trade relations rest on a foundation of intricate customs and trade legislation. With some variation, the foundation is shared by the EU, China, the United States and other trading countries. In other words, similar rules common to numerous sites of governance, including States, regional organisations and international organisations, underpin and make possible the development of these transnational economic relations. This chapter discusses this legal foundation as it exists in EC law.

The chapter has two purposes. First, it explores the interconnections between two kinds of relations among sites for governance: regional integration and globalisation. In doing so, it seeks to bring out into the open various legal arrangements that create, channel, structure or express the development of IPNs, which are among the most important economic relations involved in globalisation today. It focuses on the highly technical rules of customs and international trade law known as inward processing and outward processing arrangements. Global economic networks are well known, at least among economists and political scientists. Their legal aspects, however, have attracted relatively little attention from legal scholarship, except for private law in the form of contract law or international public law such as technical standards or intellectual property. Most such rules of national, regional or international public economic law rarely see the light of day. They are virtually unknown except within the business community, or to a handful of specialist lawyers or policy-makers in governmental institutions. This chapter tries to make such legal materials accessible and to pry open some of the broader issues they raise. It seeks to highlight the legal foundations of IPNs. It argues that EC law fosters and encourages the development of IPNs. It considers the extent to which economic globalisation in this form is compatible with regional integration.

Secondly, the chapter aims to demonstrate that these extremely technical customs rules and the international economic relations which they sustain are directly relevant to current debates about EU law. The basic argument is that globalisation and Europeanisation are both complementary and competing processes. On the one hand, globalisation reinforces and strengthens the demand for the coherence and constitutionalisation of EU decision-making. Here, 'constitutionalisation' means the

[2] See in particular chapter 9 of this book and references cited there; see also H Wai-chung Yeung, *Transnational Corporations and Business Networks: Hong Kong Firms in the ASEAN Region* (London, Routledge, 1998); M Haddad, *Trade Integration in East Asia: The Role of China and Production Networks*, World Bank Policy Research Working Paper 4160, March 2007, available at http://papers.ssrn.com/sol3/papers.cfm?abstract_id=969237, accessed 10 April 2008; B Andreosso-O'Callaghan and F Nicolas, 'Complementarity and Rivalry in EU–China Economic Relations in the Twenty-First Century' (2007) 12 *European Foreign Affairs Review* 13.

expression in a single, general legal document of the basic principles concerning the basic values and principles, institutional structure and organisation of decision-making authority. The view that the EU requires a strong, coherent and centralised foreign policy and international trade policy is a variant on this theme. On the other hand, globalisation reconfigures economic relations and undercuts potential political alliances which otherwise might encourage the constitutionalisation of Europe. For example, the different Member States have diverse and often diverging interests in the face of globalisation and the development of IPNs, and the strength of such networks is an important variable in determining the policies of Member States towards further integration. In circumstances of diverse interests among Member States, IPNs tend to enhance fragmentation.

The chapter thus seeks to contribute to our understanding of the EU legal framework regulating IPNs. At the same time, it is a plea for a re-thinking of EU constitutional law scholarship: one which takes fully into account the impact of globalisation. Far from being a negative, destructive exercise, it opens up a space for such a reorientation. The chapter deploys its argument on two different levels. Explicitly, it is concerned with the role of EU law in the creation and encouragement of IPNs as part of the processes of both globalisation and Europeanisation. Implicitly it argues that we as legal scholars and citizens need to use our constitutional imagination to envisage a new, distinctive EU constitution, which differs significantly from the traditional model of national constitutions and takes globalisation seriously. In Europe we need a new kind of constitutional imagination, which is appropriate for the current context of globalisation and global legal pluralism.

The remainder of the chapter consists of three main sections. Section II. defines the concept of globalisation, sketches the main characteristics of IPNs as a type of economic organisation and outlines the process of re-regulation known as the Europeanisation of law concerning basic customs procedures used by IPNs. Section III. analyses the resulting framework of EC legislation and a number of ECJ decisions governing these inward processing and outward processing arrangements. It also considers some aspects of the relationship between these EC customs procedures and EC anti-dumping law. A brief conclusion in section IV. summarises the argument and its implications.

II. Globalisation, IPNs and the Europeanisation of Regulation

A. Globalisation and IPNs

Globalisation, as defined in Chapter 2 of the book, refers to an aggregate of multi-faceted, uneven, often contradictory economic, political, social and cultural processes which are characteristic of our time. The most important motors of contemporary globalisation so far have been multinational firms and international financial markets.[3] Globalisation has legal, economic, political, social, cultural and other dimensions. Here I focus solely on the legal and economic dimensions.

[3] P de Senarclens, *La mondialisation: Théories, enjeux et débats*, 3rd edn (Paris, Armand Colin, 2002).

Among the most salient features of globalisation today is the development of IPNs.[4] Such networks involve 'the organization across national borders of research and development activities, procurement, distribution, product definition and design, manufacturing, and support service'.[5] This form of business organisation has developed historically from—and has further elaborated—a conjunction of related elements: the dispersion of production facilities among different countries, the technical and functional fragmentation of production, worldwide sourcing, flexibility of the production process, the fragmentation of ownership and an increase in intra-firm trade.

The development of IPNs was encouraged and stimulated by specific customs procedures. This chapter focuses on the customs operations known in EC law as the inward processing procedure and the outward processing procedure. Put simply, the inward processing procedure allows firms to import into the EU materials for processing in the EU without paying custom duties. The outward processing procedure allows materials to be exported temporarily for processing, and the resulting products to be re-imported with partial or total relief from duties. It is useful to consider these operations first from the economic standpoint. To distinguish them from the customs procedures, we can refer to the economic operations as 'inward processing traffic' (IPT) and 'outward processing traffic' (OPT), respectively. Both inward processing and outward processing are different responses to trade barriers. If there were no trade barriers, such as tariffs or quotas, there would be no demand or need for IPT or OPT, in the economic sense or in the sense of specific legal customs regimes.

Viewed as economic relationships, IPT and OPT represent one of the organisational forms of IPNs; other forms are branch plant production, contract manufacture and original equipment manufacture, and vertical integration.[6] Both in Central and Eastern Europe and in Asia, they have often been a step leading toward the development of complex, capital-intensive, cross-national production networks.[7]

B. The Europeanisation of Regulatory Law

European Community law concerning these economic networks bears a complex relationship to the processes of Europeanisation and globalisation. Regionalisation of these procedures in the form of Europeanisation of law was itself a response and a contributor to economic globalisation. In the European Union, national legislation by

[4] See eg M Borrus and J Zysman, 'Globalisation with Borders: The Rise of Wintelism as the Future of Industrial Competition' in J Zysman and A Schwartz (eds), *Enlarging Europe: The Industrial Foundations of a New Political Reality* (Berkeley, University of California at Berkeley, 1998) 27.

[5] EM Doherty (ed), *Japanese Investment in Asia: International Production Strategies in a Rapidly Changing World* (Berkeley, University of California at Berkeley, 1995), quoted in J Pellegrin, *International Business and the European Integration Process: The Example of Outward Processing Traffic between the European Union and the Central and Eastern European Countries*, unpublished PhD thesis, Department of Social and Political Sciences, European University Institute, July 1997, at 172.

[6] See T Sturgeon, *Does Manufacturing Still Matter?: The Organizational Delinking of Production from Innovation*, BRIE Working Paper 92B, Berkeley Roundtable on the International Economy, University of California at Berkeley, 1997, available at http://brie.berkeley.edu/publications/WP%2092B.pdf, last accessed 19 February 2010 and J Zysman and A Schwartz, 'Reunifying Europe in an Emerging World Economy: Economic Heterogeneity, New Industrial Options, and Political Choices' (1998) 36 *Journal of Common Market Studies* 405 at 410–11.

[7] Zysman and Schwartz, above n 6, at 417.

Member States permitting OPT preceded EC legislation. Originally OPT was 'a national response to the globalisation of production activity in certain sectors'.[8] It was stimulated by the search by firms for lower production costs, in particular for labour. Certain national governments responded to the demands of firms by creating a specific customs regime that favoured the internationalisation of production. Subsequently, the Europeanisation of the diverse OPT regimes was 'a response to the internationalisation of firms' strategies adopted by national governments in order to recapture political control over growing economic interdependence'.[9] The EC (mainly the Commission) sought to capture political control of the internationalisation of production via OPT by means of the law. By pushing for the creation of the customs categories of inward processing and outward processing in EC law, it sought to Europeanise the legal control of OPT. In other words, the Commission, as a strategic actor, aimed to shift the locus of regulation of globalising firms and the development of IPNs from the Member States to the European Community.

The Europeanisation of IPT and OPT began in the 1970s. In some cases it was a form of re-regulation of domains previously regulated by national law; in other instances it created new legal resources and opportunities. If we take the case of OPT, there have long been two types of OPT. One type, called economic OPT, provided for partial or total suspension of quotas and involved mainly textiles and clothing. The other type was known as tariff OPT. It provided for partial or total suspension of tariffs and concerned other sectors. Initially the former was managed by the Member States and the latter by the Community. A 1975 EC Directive[10] applied to both. The first Community Regulation on OPT[11] applied only to tariff OPT, and the more controversial economic OPT was first regulated by the Community only in 1982.[12] Both the 1982 Regulation and a subsequent 1994 Regulation were attempts to go beyond harmonisation through Directives and to create a uniform EC-wide law by means of Regulations.

C. Implications

A variety of subsequent studies highlighted some of the economic implications of Europeanisation of regulation of IPT and OPT, though of course this was not the only factor involved. First, firms based in the EU were (and are) involved in a wide variety of IPT and OPT operations. From the EU standpoint, such links between the EU and other industrialised countries, such as the USA, involved mainly inward processing. In 1996 the European Commission published a report on inward processing.[13] Table 10

[8] Pellegrin, above n 5, at 157.

[9] *Ibid*, at 11.

[10] Council Directive 76/119/EC of 18 December 1975 on the harmonisation of provisions laid down by law, regulation or administrative action in respect of outward processing, [1976] OJ L24/58.

[11] Council Regulation (EEC) 2473/86 of 24 July 1986 on outward processing relief arrangements and the standard exchange system [1986] OJ L212/1.

[12] Council Regulation (EEC) 636/82 of 16 March 1982 establishing economic outward processing arrangements applicable to certain textile and clothing products reimported into the Community after working or processing in certain third countries, [1982] OJ L76/1.

[13] Commission Européenne, *Rapport sur le Fonctionnement et l'Avenir du Régime Douanier Economique du Perfectionnement Actif* (Commission Européenne: DG XXI, 1996).

below indicates the increasing use of IPT between 1988 and 1994, the last year of statistics available at the time of the report.

Table 10 Inward Processing in the EU, 1988–94[14]

YEAR	*TOTAL INWARD PROCESSING in 1,000 ecu*
1988	20,959,603
1989	28,714,720
1990	27,725,170
1991	30,840,191
1992	21,467,345
1993	31,627,016
1994	36,997,799
TOTAL	198,331,845

Secondly, the development of IPT and OPT was closely related to prospects for EU enlargement. Trade between the EU and the former Central and Eastern European countries (CEECs), now EU Member States, frequently involved OPT. Most of the few existing empirical studies of EU IPT and OPT concerned the use by EU firms of OPT in the CEECs.[15] They showed that OPT represents one type of international division of labour and that it frequently provided the basis for more complex forms of IPNs. Such studies have also argued that the ways in which production facilities located in the CEECs were inserted into IPNs centred in the EU were likely to be of crucial importance to European regional integration.

Thirdly, we can add a further dimension by referring briefly to trade between the EU and China. In the early years of Chinese reform and opening up, such trade often involved links between the EU and the Chinese SEZs,[16] even though such zones were not yet standardised and apparently were not generally recognised by international law.[17] Inward processing traffic and OPT were crucial for trade between Hong Kong and mainland China, and hence for re-exports from Hong Kong to the EU, as well as for direct exports from mainland China to the EU.[18] Special economic zones and other

[14] *Ibid*, XXX/1073/96-Fr, 13.

[15] See Pellegrin, above n 5; J Zysman and A Schwartz, 'Reunifying Europe', in Zysman and Schwartz, above n 4.

[16] See eg NR Lardy, *China in the World Economy* (Washington, DC, Institute for International Economics, 1994) at 112–14; D Loesch, *Chinese Special Economic Zones at a Crossroads*, HWWA-Institut fuer Wirtschaftsforschung-Hamburg, HWWA-Diskussionspapier Nr 25, 1995. See also chapter seven in this book on individual treatment in EC anti-dumping law.

[17] See Sun Xiuping, Chen Wen and L Xianseng, *New Progress in China's Special Economic Zones* (Beijing, Foreign Languages Press, 1997) at 54. See now the basic documents concerning China's accession to the WTO in WTO, *Compilation of Legal Instruments on China's Accession to the World Trade Organization* (Beijing, Law Press China, 2002).

[18] As of the first quarter of 1997, 48% (US $6.6 billion) of Hong Kong's total exports to Chinese inland areas were for outward processing. During the same period, outward processing contributed to 75% (US $12.5 billion) of Hong Kong's imports from the inland areas. Also during this period, 85% (US $15.6 billion) of Hong Kong's re-exports of origin from Chinese inland provinces were related to outward processing (*source*: Internet, NewsFile 97).

export processing zones are not of course unique to China. They exist in many other parts of the world; there is even a World Export Processing Zones Association (WEPZA) with its own Internet website.[19]

Fourthly, IPNs increasingly involved not just inter-industry or inter-firm trade, but also intra-industry and intra-firm trade. Neither intra-industry nor intra-firm trade is wholly new, at least between industrialised countries.[20] In recent decades, however, both intra-industry trade and intra-firm trade have increased dramatically with the growth of multinational companies. According to some estimates, intra-firm trade now accounts for approximately 60 per cent of international trade. In its 1996 Communication on 'The Global Challenge of International Trade', the European Commission noted that globalisation and increased trade liberalisation imply increased networking among companies, increased intra-firm trade in manufactures, and global resourcing with regard to research, development and production facilities.[21]

Inward processing traffic and OPT are often associated with intra-industry trade (IIT). Intra-industry trade now dominates North–North trade, or trade between industrialised countries. Until recently, however, there were few studies of IIT with respect to economies in transition, and relatively little easily accessible information on China.[22] This represented a striking lacuna in view of the historical significance of OPT/IPT in EU–China trade and the fact that these economic relationships have been involved in many of the numerous EU anti-dumping actions against China.

In 1996, a study by Hellvin dealt with IIT between China and the OECD countries, including but not limited to the EU. It concluded, first, that IIT between China and OECD countries increased moderately during the 1980s and rapidly thereafter. By the late 1980s it was approximately 20 per cent of total China–OECD trade.[23] A more recent study reports that IIT accounted for more than 80 per cent of the increase in EU–China trade between 1993 and 2005.[24] Then it was reported that, '[a]ccording to Chinese statistics, 95% of the China–EU trade surplus comes from processing trade, of which 81% is generated by foreign-funded processing trade subsidiaries'.[25] Hence

[19] WEPZA is based in Flagstaff, Arizona, USA. See its website at http://www.wepza.org/, last accessed 19 February 2010.

[20] See HG Grubel and PJ Lloyd, *Intra-industry Trade: The Theory and Measurement of International Trade in Differentiated Products* (London, Macmillan, 1975).

[21] European Commission, 'The Global Challenge of International Trade: A Market Access Strategy for the European Union' (Communication to the Council, the European Parliament, the Economic and Social Committee, and the Committee of Regions), COM(96)53 final, 14.2.96, p 1 (para 4), available at http://aei.pitt.edu/view/eudocno/COM_=2896=29_53_final.html, last accessed 19 February 2010.

[22] But see, eg, CH Lee and H Reisen (eds), *From Reform to Growth: China and Other Countries in Transition in Asia and Central and Eastern Europe* (Paris, OECD Development Centre Documents, OECD, 1994); F Lemoine, *Trade Policy and Trade Patterns during Transition: A Comparison between China and the CEECs* Centre d'Etudes Prospectives et d'Informations Internationales (CEPII), Document de Travail No 96-02, February 1996. Fung *et al* argue that China and the CEECs do not compete for foreign direct investment (FDI) and instead FDI flows into the two regions are moderately complementary: Fung KC, Iikka Korhonen, Ke Li and F Ng, *China and Central and Eastern Countries: Regional Networks, Global Supply Chain, or International Competitors*, Bank of Finland BOFIT Discussion Papers 9, 2008, available at http://www.bof.fi/bofit_en/tutkimus/tutkimusjulkaisut/dp/2008/dp0908.htm, last accessed 19 February 2010.

[23] L Hellvin, *Vertical Intra-industry Trade between China and the OECD Countries*, OECD Development Centre, Technical Papers No 114, July 1996.

[24] B Andreosso-O'Callaghan and F Nicolas, 'Complementarity and Rivalry in EU–China Economic Relations in the Twenty-first Century' (2007) 12 *European Foreign Affairs Review* 13 at 21. The authors surmise (at 22) that 'much of the activities of FIEs [foreign-invested enterprises] in China are enshrined in their global production networks'.

[25] Li Gang, Director of the European Department at the Chinese Ministry of Commerce Academy, interviewed by *China Business News*: Amy Cheung, 'China–EU Trade and the Yuan Parity Rate', *China Business*

the extent of IIT is a controversial issue, because it bears directly on the reasons for China's trade surplus with the EU.

Secondly, Hellvin concluded that IIT was most important in certain product groups, such as chemicals and related products, manufactured goods, and machinery and transport equipment. It was of less importance in respect of miscellaneous manufactured goods. For this product group, it accounted for only about 4 per cent of trade,[26] even though the product group accounted for about 67 per cent of total manufacturing exports from China (but only about 5 per cent of total manufacturing imports, in part because of high tariffs).[27] More recent studies generally support these conclusions, while giving additional emphasis to professional and scientific instruments and electronics.[28] It is worth noting that the sectors most concerned by IIT are those which are also the most involved in EC anti-dumping actions against China.

Thirdly, according to Hellvin, IIT between China and OECD countries was primarily vertical in nature, while IIT among OECD countries was mainly horizontal in nature.[29] In other words, China tended to export lower-quality varieties in exchange for higher-quality varieties in a large share of the China–OECD IIT volume.[30] This was consistent with contemporary reports on the structure of traded goods between the EU and China. Figures for 1994 showed that 60 per cent of EU imports from China consisted of textiles and clothing (20 per cent), mechanical/electrical machinery (30 per cent), and toys, leather goods and footwear (20 per cent), while 60 per cent of EU exports to China consisted of mechanical/electrical machinery, transport equipment and nuclear reactors.[31] Recent studies indicate an important shift in this pattern. China's rapid development has resulted in a shift to much higher value-added products. Today the EU's main advantage lies in services, and that in itself may be short-lived.[32]

Fourthly, there is a wide variation in IIT shares among different OECD countries. If we consider only the EU Member States, the order in 1992 was UK, Italy, Germany, France, The Netherlands, Benelux, Ireland, Spain, Sweden, Austria, Denmark, Portugal and Greece.[33]

A recent study of China's integration in East Asia sheds additional light on inward and outward processing, IIT and the role of the EU.[34] The growth of foreign trade in

News, 30 November 2007, reported in *The China Perspective*, 22 April 2009, available at http://www.thechinaperspective.com/articles/chinaeutradeandtheyuanparityrate3163/index.html, last visited 22 April 2009.

[26] Hellvin, above n 23, at 28.

[27] *Ibid*, at 15.

[28] See also Andreosso-O'Callaghan and Nicolas, above n 24, at 21–22, 29, 36.

[29] 'Horizontal intra-industry trade is trade in varieties of a product characterised by different attributes, while vertical intra-industry trade is trade in varieties of a product characterised by different qualities. The former typically occurs between countries with high and similar per capita incomes, while the latter typically occurs between countries at different levels of per capita income.': Hellvin, above n 23, at 18.

[30] Note that the study used unit price as a proxy for quality differences: *ibid*, at 22. This is based, however, on the assumption of the 'open economy macroeconomic model' which presumes that international prices apply (or should apply) in China. For a critique of this assumption, see W van der Geest, 'Bringing China into the Concert of Nations: An Analysis of its Accession to the WTO' (1998) 32 *Journal of World Trade* 99 at 105–106.

[31] See the Internet homepage of the European Commission Delegation in China at http://www.ecd.org.cn.

[32] Andreosso-O'Callaghan and Nicolas, above n 24, at 36.

[33] Hellvin, above n 23, at 16, Table 2.

[34] G Gaulier, F Lemoine and D Ünal-Kesenci, *China's Integration in East Asia: Production Sharing, FDI & High-tech Trade*, Centre d'Etudes Prospectives and d'Informations Internationales (CEPII)', Paris, Document de Travail, No 2005–09, June 2005.

China since the early 1990s has relied almost entirely on processing. Inputs for processing accounted for between 40 per cent and 50 per cent of all imports.[35] However, in 2002, the EU and the USA together accounted for less than 10 per cent of imports for processing in China; Japan, Hong Kong, Singapore, Taiwan and Korea accounted for about 60 per cent. Only about 15 per cent of China's imports from the EU concerned inputs for processing. There was little change between 1993 and 2002.[36] However, about 40 per cent of China's processed exports went to the EU and the USA. This does not include exports transited through Hong Kong. Almost all of China's trade surplus with the EU and the USA consists of processing activities. In fact, if we omit processing trade, the EU has a trade surplus, not a deficit, with China.[37] With regard to types of commodities involving in processing trade, between 1993 and 2002, trade in textiles and garments, leather and shoes has declined, and trade in machinery and electrical machinery has increased.[38] As of 2004, foreign joint ventures and wholly-owned foreign firms in China accounted for almost 80 per cent of international assembly operations in China and about 45 per cent of China's total export, but less than half of China's imports from the EU and the USA. As of 2002, they accounted for about one-third of China's trade surplus.[39]

These findings suggest that, with increased market opening, increased foreign direct investment and increased per capita income, there is likely to be a continued increase in IIT, and in particular horizontal IIT, between China and the OECD countries. This would be consistent with Cantwell's presentation (see Table 11 below) of the evolution of international production and the development of intra-firm trade and IIT.

Table 11 The Evolution of International Production and the Development of Intra-firm and Intra-industry Trade

TYPE OF INTERNATIONAL PRODUCTION	*COMPOSITION OF MNC TRADE*
resource-based production	intra-firm, inter-industry trade
local market-oriented production	Some intra-firm, intra-industry trade
internationally integrated production	intra-firm and intra-industry trade

Source: J Cantwell, 'The Relationship between International Trade and International Production' in David Greenaway and L Alan Winters (eds), *Surveys in International Trade* (Oxford, Blackwell, 1994) at 308, Table 11.1.

The Europeanisation of the regulation of OPT and IPT was not of course the only reason for these developments. Indeed, the Europeanisation of regulatory law was neither straightforward nor free from conflict, whether we consider it from an institutional strategy perspective or from an economic policy perspective. For the European institutions, as for certain national governments, the creation and control of these customs procedures was an institutional and organisational response to globalisation.

35 *Ibid*, at 16.
36 *Ibid,* at 17–18.
37 *Ibid*, at 19.
38 *Ibid*, at 20–21.
39 *Ibid*, at 21–24.

For the European institutions, it also formed part of the development of the EC's common commercial policy. Frequently, the EU and the Member States (despite conflicts between Member States) were regulatory competitors. Through their respective laws, each sought to govern the global economic networks which were developing as part of (and indeed were stimulated by) the process of globalisation. Demands for these customs procedures were a response, mainly by large firms, to economic globalisation in the face of trade barriers. Conversely, the law establishing and regulating these procedures represented attempts by different, and often competing, sites of governance to regulate the economic relations and capture the political benefits of globalisation.[40]

Furthermore, the attempts to govern these economic aspects of globalisation through law involved conflicts not only between the EC and the Member States as a group, but also among the Member States themselves. Both the demand for and the use of these customs procedures varied among firms, and thus from one Member State to another. As shown in Table 12 below, between 1988 and 1994, for example, some Member States made much more use of inward processing than others. The leaders were France, the United Kingdom, Germany, The Netherlands and Italy.

Table 12 Use of Inward Processing by Member State (EC-11), 1966–94

MEMBER STATE	*TOTAL USE,*
1988–94, in 1,000 ecu	
Belgium and Luxembourg	10,538,146
Denmark	3,919,567
France	43,642,981
Germany	32,773,550
Greece	2,348,185
Ireland	6,630,856
Italy	20,374,496
Netherlands	22,872,909
Portugal	1,941,987
Spain	9,819,675
United Kingdom	43,469,493

Source: Commission Européenne, *Rapport sur le fonctionnement et l'avenir du régime douanier écconomique du perfectionnement actif*, XXX/1073/96-Fr, pp 14–15.

The use of inward processing was a rough reflection of the pattern of trade by EU Member States' imports from China at the time. The volume of trade with China, both imports and exports, varied (and still varies) widely from one EU Member State to another. Table 13 below gives statistics for January–December 1995. The leading importers of products from China were Germany, the United Kingdom, France, Italy and The Netherlands. The leading exporters of products to China were Germany, Italy

[40] See also Pellegrin, above n 5, *passim*.

and France. More detailed statistical research would be required to determine the proportion of inward processing in imports from China in each Member State and the proportion of outward processing in exports to China from each Member State.

Table 13 Trade between the EU and its Member States and China, January–December 1995 (in millions of ECU)

	Imports from China	*Exports to China*	*Balance*
France	3094	2028	–1066
Belgium and Luxembourg	1516	674	–842
Netherlands	1908	635	–1273
Germany	8966	5699	–2367
Italy	3044	2061	–943
United Kingdom	4551	957	–3594
Ireland	207	28	–179
Denmark	567	200	–367
Greece	288	13	–275
Portugal	151	26	–125
Spain	1454	658	– 796
Sweden	827	852	+25
Finland	250	440	+190
Austria	450	331	–119
EU–15	26333	14602	–11731

Source: Home Page of the European Commission Delegation in China at http://www.ecd.org.cn/ecd/trad/ as of 14 January 1999, based on Eurostat.

An even more differentiated picture emerges if we consider these relationships in terms of firms rather than in terms of territories, governments or States. For example, the Commission 1996 Report on inward processing showed that inward processing procedure was used mainly by large firms, not SMEs. This was the case even though the latter comprised 93 per cent of all EU firms and accounted for one-third of all employees. Small and medium-sized enterprises thus were (and remain) extremely important in the EU economy as compared to the USA where, at the time of the Commission Report, enterprises with fewer than 20 employees accounted for only 20 per cent of employees, and large firms employed 61 per cent of the work force and accounted for 61 per cent of business turnover.[41] Yet SMEs occupied a disproportionately small role in the global economic networks of IPT and OPT. Nonetheless, the Commission's view was that

> [o]utward processing trade using local advantages for lowering production costs or the logistics of distribution systems is turning even medium-sized companies into global players . . .[42]

[41] J Cantwell, 'The Relationship between International Trade and International Production', in D Greenaway and LA Winters (eds), *Surveys in International Trade* (Oxford, Blackwell, 1994) 303 at 308.

[42] European Commission, above n 21.

As suggested in Chapter 4 of the book, this has been a constant theme in the Commission's—and hence in the EC's—trade policy.[43]

These diverse and differentiating factors played a fundamental role in shaping conflicts regarding the creation of these customs procedures, first by national law and then by EC legislation. The conflicts regarding EC law concerned not only the process of Europeanisation of this body of law, which made uniform, often transformed and always replaced any existing national legislation. They also involved the details of legislation. Largely at the instigation of firms, Member States were able to negotiate the bits and pieces of EC OPT legislation so as largely to preserve the interests of companies situated in their territory. The process of Europeanisation in the sense of the harmonisation of national legislation thus was uneven, and the governance of OPT was not very effectively centralised.[44] As this example suggests, the Europeanisation of law is rarely straightforward. Neither is it always entirely successful, regardless of whether we measure success in terms of centralisation of regulatory law-making (the level of decision-making) or in terms of the harmonisation of law (the form of law, embodying a choice of economic policy).

Initially, it did not succeed entirely in giving the EC a large degree of effective control over IPNs, except in form. In ways other than the elaboration of uniform legislation itself, the contribution of IPT and OPT to the process of Europeanisation itself was uneven. The basic assumption, as Pellegrin emphasises with regard to OPT between the EU and the CEECs, was that territory, political competence, governance and economic activity were congruent. European Community OPT law thus represented 'an attempt to transpose the national model of market management at the Community level'.[45] In fact, however, the contribution of OPT to regional integration has varied a great deal, not only according to sector but also according to the production network involved.[46] National models of market regulation were not automatically suitable to regulation of the European market, and, as demonstrated above, the interests of Member States in OPT and IPT varied widely. There is no reason to think that IPT and OPT were any less susceptible to controversy than anti-dumping law; the Commission's 1996 Green Paper on Global Europe revealed once again the sharp differences of opinion among EU Member States concerning the latter.[47] Compared to anti-dumping law, IPT and OPT were merely less visible.

The development of European regulatory law in this instance tended to refract in a complex way the emerging internal EU constitution. European Community law on inward processing and outward processing mirrors to some extent the division of power between the Member States and the EC. Rarely, however, does law reflect politics directly. In this instance EC law was a product of a specific process of Europeanisation, occurring over a period of time and involving particular interests and specific relations between firms, States, and EC institutions. Regulation of IPNs shifted in form from the Member States to the Community. But many of the pre-

43 See the examples of the toy industry and the bicycle industry discussed elsewhere in this book.

44 Pellegrin, above n 5, *passim*.

45 *Ibid*, at 8.

46 See also Zysman and Schwartz, above n 4, at 27–59.

47 See European Commission, Communication on 'Global Europe: Europe's Trade Defence Instruments in a Changing Global Economy', A Green Paper for Public Consultation, COM (2006) 763 final, reprinted in F Snyder (ed), *The European Union and China, 1949–2008: Basic Documents and Commentary* (Oxford, Hart Publishing, 2009) 597–607.

existing conflicts remained, and they were often represented and even crystallised in the details of the legislation. The different interests of the Member States have been articulated in the terms of EC law; so too have been the interests of the firms which Member States to some extent represented in the EC legislative process. These diverse interests were partly preserved in the substance of EC law.[48]

Europeanisation of IPT and OPT law thus represented a shift in the locus of law-making and of decision-making. Opposed to this vertical logic, however, was the horizontal logic of relations between firms and States. It may be hypothesised that the Europeanisation of law tended to strengthen the ties between each Member State and the firms based or located principally within its territory. When the applicable law was national law, such ties were subject to other competing pressures within each Member State. It is likely that the Europeanisation of IPT and OPT law sharpened conflicts of interest between Member States, as each Member State sought to represent the specific interests of its own firms.

The most significant elements from the standpoint of such strategic actors are where the production process starts and whether the company intends to export the product once the product is already in the EU. From the EU standpoint, inward processing means that production starts in the third country, the product is processed further in the EU and the product then is exported to a third country, either where the production process started or another country. From the same EU standpoint, outward processing means that production starts in the EU, further processing takes place elsewhere, and the product is intended in principle for the EU market.[49] To this perspective must be added the home country of the firms concerned, either in the EU or elsewhere, because this determines many of the other interests which affect and are affected by the operations of strategic actors.

III. IPNs in EC Law and International Law

A. The EC Legislative Framework

International production networks, the fragmentation of production, the dispersion of production facilities, worldwide sourcing and intra-firm trade have developed in a symbiotic relationship with certain legal categories and concepts. The economic operations known as IPT and OPT are an effect of, first, national and, now, EC customs procedures of inward processing arrangements (or relief) and outward processing arrangements (or relief). Often the same terms (IPT and OPT) are used to refer simultaneously to economic operations and to the legal labels, pigeonholes or customs devices which denote, create and underpin them. This economic dimension of globalisation and these legal categories of customs law are symbiotic: each owes its existence to some extent to the other; and each feeds on and thrives to some extent because of the other.

[48] See F Snyder, *New Directions in European Community Law* (London, Weidenfeld & Nicolson, 1990) at 146–76, esp 171.

[49] I am grateful to Candido Garcia Molyneux for these points.

In terms of current EC law,[50] inward processing and outward processing are two of a group of procedures called 'customs procedures with economic impact'.[51] Certain basic rules are common to more than one of the procedures. They concern applications for authorisation, single authorisation, economic conditions, the decision on authorisation, other provisions on operation of the arrangements, including transfers, records, rates of yield and calculation formulae, compensatory interest and discharge, and finally administrative cooperation.[52] In 2001 the European Commission published guidelines for 'Customs procedures with economic impact', including both inward processing arrangements and outward processing arrangements.[53] The Guidelines are not legally binding and are of an explanatory nature. They are designed to help Member States to apply the modernised electronic legal procedures. In 2003, the EC enacted legislation clarifying the codes to be used on the Binding Tariff Information (BTI) notification form and the Single Administrative Document; this included IPT and OPT.[54] In addition, Member States are required to compile statistical data on trade flows, including IPT and OPT, and transmit such data to the European Commission; goods released for free circulation after being subject to inward processing are excluded.[55]

Within this framework, inward processing is the system whereby imported goods may be processed in the EC customs territory without giving rise to liability for payment of customs duties, or other commercial policy measures, if the goods are intended for export outside the customs territory of the Community in the form of compensating products.[56] This arrangement is designed to promote exports from EU

[50] After 1992, inward processing and outward processing were governed by Council Regulation (EEC) No 2913/92 establishing the Community Customs Code, [1992] OJ L302/1, in particular as amended. The implementing legislation was Commission Regulation (EEC) No 2454/93, [1993] OJ L253/1, as amended. The current implementing legislation is Commission Regulation (EEC) No 993/2001 of 4 May 2001 amending Regulation (EEC) No 2454/93 laying down provisions for the implementation of Council Regulation (EEC) No 2913/92 laying down the Community Customs Code, [2001] OJ L141/1. Arts 114–129 of the Customs Code and Arts 536–550 of the Implementing Regulation deal with inward processing. Arts 145–160 of the Customs Code and Arts 585–592 of the Implementing Regulation deal with outward processing. For further discussion, see T Lyons, *EC Customs Law*, 2nd edn (Oxford, Oxford University Press, 2008) 404–32.

[51] The other procedures are customs warehousing, processing under customs control and temporary importation.

[52] See Regulation (EEC) No 2454/93 laying down provisions for the implementation of Council Regulation (EEC) No 2913/92 laying down the Community Customs Code, [2001] OJ L141/1, as amended by Commission Regulation (EEC) No 993/2001 of 4 May 2001, Art 1.

[53] See Commission, Guidelines concerning Title III 'Customs procedures with economic impact' of Commission Regulation (EEC) No 2454/93 of 2 July 1993 laying down provisions for the implementation of Council Regulation (EEC) No 2913/92 establishing the Community Customs Code (2001/C268/01), [2001] OJ C269/1.

[54] See Commission Regulation (EC) No 2286/2003 of 18 December 2003 amending Regulation (EEC) No 2454/93 laying down provisions for the implementation of Council Regulation (EEC) No 2913/92 establishing the Community Customs Code, [2003] OJ L343/1, as amended by Commission Regulation (EC) 215/2006, [2006] OJ L38/11, and corrected by Corrigendum [2004] OJ L32/34 and Corrigendum [2004] OJ L360/33.

[55] See Commission Regulation (EC) No 1917/2000 of 7 September 2000 laying down certain provisions for the implementation of Council Regulation (EC) No 1172/95 as regards statistics on external trade, Arts 2, 6(4), 32, [2000] OJ L229/14, as amended by Commission Regulation (EC) 1669/2001, [2001] OJ L224/3, Commission Regulation (EC) No 179/2005, [2005] OJ L30/6, and Commission Regulation (EC) No 1949/2005, [2005] OJ L312/10.

[56] Council Regulation 2913/92, Art 114(1), [1992] OJ L302/1. As to the processing operations allowed under the inward processing procedure, see *ibid*, Art 114 (2)(c). Compensating products are all products resulting from processing operations: *ibid*, Art 114(2)(d). On compensating products, see *ibid*, Art 115. Certain more flexible rules were introduced by Regulation (EC) No 2700/2000 of the European Parliament

firms, permit EU firms to compete effectively on international markets and foster the international division of labour, but without adversely affecting the essential interests of Community producers.[57]

There are two basic procedures for inward processing.[58] Under the suspension system, non-EU goods intended for re-export from the EU in the form of compensating products may be imported duty-free: customs duties are suspended. Use of this system can be authorised only if the applicant actually intends to re-export the main compensating products from the EU customs territory. Under the drawback system, normal customs duties are paid but then the exporter can request their repayment or remission if the imported products are re-exported in the form of compensating products. Authorisation to use the drawback system is granted only where opportunities exist for export of the main compensating products from the EU customs territory. Export duties may be exempted under the suspension system but not under the drawback system.

The basic theme of inward processing is also subject to four more complex variations. The first variation concerns processing operations outside the Community customs territory. Imported goods in their unaltered state, or their compensating goods, can be exported temporarily for the purpose of further processing outside the customs territory of the Community.[59] This is possible, however, only after the customs authorities grant authorisation in accordance with the rules provided for outward processing.[60] Under the drawback system, the temporary exportation of compensating products will not be considered as exportation for the purposes of repayment or remission of the import duties initially paid, except where the products are not re-imported into the Community within the period prescribed.[61]

The second variation is equivalent compensation. Under special conditions, the compensating products intended to be exported may be obtained from equivalent Community goods instead of import goods.[62] As an exception to the general rules on

and of the Council of 16 November 2000 amending Council Regulation (EEC) No 2913/92 establishing the Community Customs Code [2000] OJ L311/17. Special rules apply to certain quantities of certain basic agricultural products and of intermediate goods corresponding to these basic products: see Commission Regulation (EC) No 1488/2001 of 19 July 2001 laying down rules for the application of Council Regulation (EC) No 3448/93 as regards the placement of certain quantities of certain basic products listed in Annex I to the Treaty establishing the European Community under the inward processing arrangements without prior examination of the economic conditions [2001] OJ L196/9, as amended by Commission Regulation (EC) No 1914/2003 of 30 October 2003 amending Regulation (EC) No 1488/2001 laying down rules for the application of Council Regulation (EC) No 3448/93 as regards the placement of certain quantities of certain basic products listed in Annex I to the Treaty establishing the European Community under the inward processing arrangements without prior examination of the economic conditions [2003] OJ L283/27. Following the 2004 enlargement, these rules were adapted to the new Member States by Commission Regulation (EC) No 886/2004 of 4 March 2004 adapting certain regulations and decisions in the field of free movement of goods, competition policy, agriculture, environment and external relations by reason of the accession of the Czech Republic, Estonia, Cyprus, Latvia, Lithuania, Hungary, Malta, Poland, Slovenia and Slovakia [2004] OJ L168/14. The system of prefinancing of export refunds on agricultural products was abolished by Commission Regulation (EC) No 1713/2006 of 20 November 2006 abolishing the prefinancing of export refunds in respect of agricultural products [2006] OJ L321/11.

57 See Case 260/78 *Maggi GmbH v Hauptzollamt Munster* [1979] ECR 2693 and Case C-437/93 *Hauptzollamt Heilbronn v Temic Telefunken* [1995] ECR I-1687.

58 See also Commission Regulation (EEC) No 2454/93, Arts 545–552, as inserted by Commission Regulation (EC) No 993/2001, [2001] OJ L141/1.

59 Council Regulation 2913/92, Art 123, [1992] OJ L302/1.

60 *Ibid*, Art 86; see also *ibid* Art 123. As to outward processing see further below.

61 *Ibid*, Art 127.

62 *Ibid*, Art 115(1)(a); see also *ibid*, Art 114(2)(e).

inward processing, this is interpreted restrictively.[63] Previous legislation required the equivalent goods to be of the same quality, have the same technical characteristics as the import goods and fall within the same eight-digit subheading of the combined nomenclature code.[64] Exceptionally, however, equivalent goods could be at a more advanced stage of manufacture than the import goods, provided that the essential part of the processing to which the equivalent goods are subject was carried out in the undertaking of the holder of the authorisation, or in the undertaking where the operation was being carried out on its behalf.[65] Under current legislation, the authorisation for use of the procedure is to specify whether the equivalent goods and the import goods must share the same eight-digit Combined Nomenclature code,[66] and equivalent goods may be allowed to be at a more advanced stage of manufacture than the import goods 'save in exceptional cases'.

The third variation is prior exportation.[67] The Customs Code allows compensating products obtained from goods to be exported from the Community before the importation of the import goods.[68] This is not possible, however, under the drawback system,[69] or for authorisations to be issued on the basis of certain economic conditions.[70]

The fourth variation is triangular traffic. As part of the prior exportation system the customs authorities may allow the triangular traffic system.[71] This allows the import goods to be entered for the inward processing procedure in the Community at a customs office other than the one at which the prior exportation of the compensating products took place.[72]

[63] Case C-103/96 *Directeur Général des Douanes et Droits Indirects v Eridiania Beghin-Say SA* [1997] ECR I-1453. See also Case C-156/00 *Netherlands v Commission* [2003] ECR I-2527, in which the ECJ concluded that an experienced trader such as Cargill should not have had any doubt that imported maize and wheat of EC origin were not equivalent goods.

[64] Council Regulation 2913/92, above n 56, Art 115(2). See also Commission Regulation 2454/93, Art 569(1), [1993] OJ L253/1, as amended by Commission Regulation 3665/93, [1993] OJ L335/1, which added the requirement that the goods must fall within the same eight-digit subheading of the combined nomenclature. This requirement was upheld by the Court of Justice in *Eridiania Beghin-Say*, above n 63. Special provisions laid out in Annex 78 may apply to goods included in this Annex: see Commission Regulation 2454/93, Art 569(2), [1993] OJ L253/1.

[65] Council Regulation 2913/92, Art 115(2), [1992] OJ L302/1. See also Commission Regulation 2454/93, Art 570(1), [1993] OJ L335/1.

[66] Commission Regulation (EEC) No 2454/93, Art 541(1), as inserted by Commission Regulation (EC) No 993/2001, [2001] OJ L141/1.

[67] Prior exportation is defined as 'the system whereby compensating products obtained from equivalent goods are to be exported before the import goods are entered for the arrangements using the suspension system': Commission Regulation No 2454/93, Art 536(a), as inserted by Commission Regulation (EC) No 993/2001, [2001] OJ L141/1.

[68] Council Regulation 2913/92, Art 115(1)(b), [1992] OJ L302/1. The customs authorities shall indicate the period within which the non-Community goods must be declared for the procedure taking account of the time required for the procurement and transport to the Community of the import goods. See *ibid*, Art 118(3); see also Commission Regulation 2454/93, Art 561(1), [1993] OJ L253/1. As a general rule this period must not exceed six months, but it may be extended if the holder of the authorisation submits a reasoned request, provided that the total period does not exceed 12 months. See Commission Regulation 2454/93, Art 561(2), [1993] OJ L253/1. Special rules apply to specific products, such as goods subject to a price regulating mechanism (Art 561(2)) and raw sugar (Art 561(2)).

[69] Commission Regulation 2913/92, Art 126, OJ [1992] L302/1.

[70] Commission Regulation 2454/93, Art 572(1), [1993] OJ L253/1, as amended by Commission Regulation 3665/93, [1993] OJ L335/1. As to the economic conditions which do not allow for the possibility of prior exportation under the suspension system, see Commission Regulation 2454/93, Art 552, as amended.

[71] Commission Regulation 2454/93, above n 64, Art 600. Triangular traffic system is possible only as part of the prior exportation system.

[72] *Ibid*, Art 549(i). As to the details of the triangular traffic system, see *ibid*, Art 575(3); see also *ibid*, Art 601, as amended by Commission Regulation 3665/93, above n 64. See also Commission Regulation 2454/93, above n 64, Arts 602–605. Art 603 has been amended by Commission Regulation (EC) No 2193/94, [1994] OJ L235/6.

Outward processing, as defined in EC law, is the system whereby Community goods may be exported temporarily from the customs territory of the Community in order to undergo processing operations, and the compensating products resulting from those operations may be released for free circulation with total or partial relief from import duties and non-tariff common commercial policy measures.[73] The purpose of this mechanism is to avoid the levying of customs duty on goods exported from the Community for processing.[74] This procedure may apply to all Community goods other than those whose export gives rise to repayment or remission of import duties, or which prior to export were released for free circulation with total relief from import duties by virtue of end use, for as long as the conditions from granting such relief continue to apply, or whose export gives rise to the granting of export refunds or in respect of which a financial advantage other than such refunds is granted under the common agricultural policy by virtue of the export of the said goods.[75]

B. International Treaties

Inward processing arrangements and outward processing arrangements are subject to relevant international agreements. The most important such agreements are the International Convention on the Harmonised System,[76] the WTO Agreements on rules of origin[77] and customs valuation,[78] and the International Convention on the Simplification and Harmonisation of Customs Procedures ('the Kyoto Convention'). Only the WTO Agreements and the Kyoto Convention are directly relevant here.

[73] Council Regulation (EC) 2913/92, Art145(1), [1992] OJ L302/1; see also *ibid*, Art 160. Certain more flexible rules were introduced by Regulation (EC) No 2700/2000 of the European Parliament and of the Council of 16 November 2000 amending Council Regulation (EEC) No 2913/92 establishing the Community Customs Code [2000] OJ L311/17. See also Case 49/82, *Commission of the European Communities v Kingdom of the Netherlands* [1983] ECR 1195. As to the specific conditions for the application of economic outward processing arrangements to textiles and clothing listed in chs 50 to 63 of the Combined Nomenclature and resulting from outward processing operations, see Council Regulation (EC) No 3036/94, [1994] OJ L322/1. See also Council Regulation (EC) No 1385/94, [1994] OJ L152/4 (opening and providing for the administration of Community tariff quotas for frozen hake fillets and for processing work in respect of certain textile products under Community outward processing arrangements). Allowed processing operations under the outward processing procedure are: a) the working of goods, including erecting or assembling them, or fitting them to other goods; b) the processing of goods; c) the repair of goods, including restoring them and putting them in order. See Council Regulation (EC) 2913/92, Art 145(3)(b), [1992] OJ L302/1; see also *ibid*, Art 114(2)(c). A regulatory Committee on Economic Outward Processing Arrangements for Textiles was established by Council Regulation (EC) No 806/2003 of 14 April 2003 adapting to Decision 1999/468/EC the provisions relating to committees which assist the Commission in the exercise of its implementing powers laid down in Council instruments adopted in accordance with the consultation procedure (qualified majority) [2001] OJ L122/1.

[74] See Case C-16/91, *Wacker Werke GmbH & Co KG v Hauptzollamt München-West* (*Wacker Werke I*) [1992] ECR I-6821.

[75] Council Regulation 2913/92, Art 146, [1992] OJ L302/1.

[76] International Convention on the Harmonised System, available at http://www.wcoomd.org/home_wco_topics_hsoverviewboxes_tools_and_instruments_hsconvention.htm, visited 22 April 2009.

[77] Agreement on Rules of Origin, in WTO, *The Legal Texts: The Results of the Uruguay Round of Multilateral Trade Negotiations* (Cambridge, Cambridge University Press for the WTO, 1999, 13th printing, 2007).

[78] Agreement on Implementation of Article VII of the General Agreement on Tariffs and Trade 1994, *ibid*.

Among the WTO Agreements, the plurilateral International Dairy Agreement, concluded by the EC as part of the GATT, had a direct impact on EC law.[79] As a result of the reduction in agricultural export subsidies agreed within the WTO, the EC enacted more detailed rules on the interaction between the inward processing procedure and the export refund system for agricultural products.[80] Before Chinese accession to the WTO, IPT and OPT were exempted from quotas, for example for imports into the EU of textiles from China.[81] They were also affected by bilateral international agreements adopted to implement WTO obligations. For example, the Settlement in the Form of an Exchange of Letters between the European Economic Community and the United States of America on Community exports of past products to the USA provided that certain pasta products exported following an inward processing operation were not entitled to export refunds.[82]

The Kyoto Convention was initially signed at Kyoto on 18 May 1973.[83] The Convention entered into force for the EC on 26 September 1974. Annex E.6 concerned temporary admission for inward processing. It entered into force on 6 December 1977, and, subject to certain reservations, it entered into force for the EEC on the same date.[84] Annex E.8 dealt with temporary exportation for outward processing. It entered into force for the EEC, with certain reservations, on 20 April 1978.[85] China was a signatory to the International Convention on the Simplification and Harmonisation of Customs Procedures signed at Kyoto, but did not accept the Annexes. The Convention entered into force for China on 18 March 1991.[86]

The 1973 Kyoto Convention was amended by a Protocol of Amendment on 26 June 1999.[87] The Protocol and two Appendices contain the revised Convention and a General Annex. They entered into force on 3 February 2006. The Protocol of Amendment was accepted by the EC on 17 March 2003.[88] Annex F1 and F2 concern inward processing and outward processing, respectively. Both the EC and China are

[79] Products brought into the Community under the inward processing arrangement are considered to be imported and exported for the purposes of the International Dairy Agreement (IDA) or any international trade agreement. Consequently, Community legislation does not allow authorisations for products for inward processing at a value below the minimum prices set by the IDA: see Case C-61/94 *Commission of the European Communities v Federal Republic of Germany* [1996] ECR I-3989, paras 22–27. Note that the EC was never a contracting party to the GATT.

[80] Commission Regulation (EC) No 993/2001 of 4 May 2001 amending Regulation (EEC) No 2454/93 laying down provisions for the implementation of Council Regulation (EEC) No 2912/92 establishing the Community Customs Code [2001] OJ L141/1.

[81] See Agreement on trade in textile products covered by the MFA Agreement, Arts 4(1), 4(4), [1998] OJ L380/2 (MFA textiles); Agreement on trade in textile products not covered by the MFA bilateral agreement, Arts 4(1), 4(4), [1995] OJ L104/2 (non-MFA textiles, especially silk and linen). See further F Snyder, *International Trade and Customs Law of the European Union* (London, Butterworths, 1998), 417–19, 596–99.

[82] Commission Regulation (EC) No 88/2007 of 12 December 2006 laying down special detailed rules for the application of the system of export refunds on cereals exported in the form of pasta products falling within CN codes 1902 11 00 and 1902 19, [2007] OJ L21/16.

[83] World Customs Organisation, *Handbook: International Convention on the Simplification and Harmonization of Customs Procedures* (Kyoto, 18 May 1973), 1st edn October 1975, Amend Supp No 13, January 1993.

[84] Council Decision (EEC) No 415/77, [1977] OJ L166/1.

[85] *Ibid.*

[86] http://www.intracen.org/tfs/docs/publications/ruleori4.pdf, last accessed 20 February 2010.

[87] See 'Annex II: Abstract of the International Convention on the Simplification and Harmonisation of Customs Procedure, known as Kyoto Convention, available at http://www.intracen.org/tfs/docs/publications/ruleori4.pdf, last accessed 20 February 2010.

[88] Council Decision (EC) No 2003/231/EC of 17 March 2003 concerning the accession of the European Community to the Protocol of Amendment to the International Convention on the simplification and harmonisation of customs procedures [2003] OJ L86/21.

contracting parties to the Protocol of Amendment, China having ratified on 15 June 2000 and the EC on 30 April 2004, with EC Member States having ratified on various dates for matters within their competence. However, neither the EC nor China has accepted Annex F1 on inward processing or Annex F2 on outward processing.[89] The Kyoto Convention is administered by the Permanent Technical Committee of the World Customs Organisation, based in Brussels. Both the EC and China participate actively in the Permanent Technical Committee.[90]

C. IPNs in the European Courts

International production networks transcend national or even regional legal boundaries. Consequently they often generate disputes which sometimes lead to very complex litigation. This part of the chapter considers most, if not all, cases involving IPT and OPT that have come before the European courts. The discussion is organised according to certain crucial issues in the regulation of IPNs through the inward processing and outward processing customs procedures. The first section considers cases regarding the integrity of the customs procedures. Some cases also concern the conditions for authorisation of use of the procedure, but in this first section their relation to procedural integrity is emphasised. The next section concentrates on cases that deal directly with the economic conditions which must be met before use of the procedures can be authorised. A following section examines certain issues of evidence concerning the value added by the procedures. A further section discusses cases which reveal the potential for abuse of the procedures and the ways in which the European courts have sought to regulate potential or actual abuse, in particular by transfer pricing. The discussion is intended to illustrate the most problematic aspects of IPT and OPT. It also shows how the European courts have tried to regulate IPNs on an ad hoc, case-by-case basis, by means of application and interpretation of the basic EC legislation.

1. Integrity of Customs Procedures

The first priority of the European courts in the regulation of IPNs has been to ensure so far as possible the integrity of the inward processing and outward processing procedures. The basic issue of procedural integrity has been at the heart of a number of disputes. Even before EC legislation was fully in place, the ECJ was asked to delimit the scope of inward processing.

[89] See World Customs Organisation, General Secretariat, 'Position as regards ratifications and accessions (as of 15 September 2009), International Convention on the simplification and harmonisation of customs procedures, (as amended),' available at http://www.wcoomd.org/files/1.%20Public%20files/PDFandDocuments/Conventions/PG0165E1b.pdf, last accessed 20 February 2010.

[90] On China, see General Administration of Customs of the People's Republic of China, China Customs: 2008 Annual Report, http://www1.customs.gov.cn//Portals/191/2008%20China%20Customs.doc, visited 22 April 2009.

In Case 49/82 *Commission v Netherlands*,[91] the Commission brought an Article 169 (Art 226 TEC, now Art 258 TFUE) action against The Netherlands for authorising the packing in small parcels of butter imported from third countries and stored in customs warehouses. It argued, in essence, that this kind of packing was not the simple operation of a 'usual form of handling' as required for the use of the customs warehousing procedure. The customs warehousing procedure provides for storage in a customs warehouse in the EU of goods, either from the EU or from a third country, free of customs duty. The Commission considered that the operation in this case called instead for the use of the inward processing procedure. In other words, it tried to expand the scope of IPT. Goods imported under the inward processing procedure were reserved solely for export, were subject to more stringent controls to protect Community producers and had to comply with more formal requirements. In addition, during the period in question the use of the inward processing procedure had been temporarily suspended in order to encourage EC processors of butter for export to use surplus EC butter rather than third-country butter. Even in normal circumstances, therefore, customs warehousing would have given the importer or processor greater commercial freedom of choice and would have been lower in cost. But in the specific circumstances of the case, the authorisation by The Netherlands of the customs warehousing procedure also enabled Dutch processing enterprises to avoid an agricultural levy payable on the release for consumption of butter imported from third countries.

Detailed uniform rules concerning inward processing were then not yet in force in the Community, and The Netherlands had in fact followed its previous national practice. Advocate-General Slynn pointed out, however, that

> [t]he dividing line [between customs warehousing and inward processing] is not entirely clear. None the less it seems to me that where the goods are shown to have been brought into the Community with the intention that they may be processed, and then re-exported, rather than for the essential purpose of storage with incidental handling, they ought to be dealt with under the inward processing system . . .[92]

He also identified a need for harmonisation because of the existence of different national provisions as to what operations were regarded as inward processing or as customs warehousing.[93]

The ECJ, following its Advocate-General, held that the operation in question did not come within the scope of the customs warehousing procedure and was therefore covered by the inward processing procedure, as defined in Article 2 of Council Directive 69/73 on the harmonisation of provisions laid down by law, regulation or administrative action in respect of inward processing.[94] The judgment implicitly affirmed the power of the ECJ to decide on the classification of such import transactions. Harmonisation by the judiciary could substitute at least provisionally for harmonisation by the legislator. Such judicial empowerment itself was part of the Europeanisation of law, in both the institutional and normative terms. In its judgment the ECJ also re-affirmed the pre-eminence of EC law, which then was being elaborated. Diverse national practices could not be allowed to undermine common EC policies, such as the common agricultural policy, or to impede the eventual development of

[91] [1983] ECR 1195.
[92] *Ibid*, at 1213.
[93] *Ibid*, at 1212.
[94] OJ Eng Spec Ed 1969, (I), p 75.

uniform EC customs law. In normative terms, the case also clarified the distinction between customs warehousing and inward processing. Customs warehousing could be used only for very simple procedures, whereas certain types of packaging, as well as more complex procedures, required the use of inward processing. The case thus clarified and adopted an expansive interpretation of inward processing procedure.

We can also see the case from a broader, institutional perspective. The case demonstrated that the boundary between inward processing and customs warehousing would in the last instance be policed, if necessary, by the ECJ. Patrolling this boundary represented a way of regulating the market and of managing the complex relationship between Europeanisation and globalisation. In the specific circumstances of the case, the ECJ gave priority to protecting the EC's financial interests and EC producers; these may be some meanings of Europeanisation, though certainly not the only ones. At the same time, it urged the EC legislator, that is, at the time the Member States composing the Council, to adopt uniform rules to manage on a more coherent, less ad hoc and more long-term basis the problematic relationship between Europeanisation and globalisation: in other words, to adopt a Europeanised solution to the regulation of IPNs.

The ECJ has engaged in a similar exercise of delimitation of a basic procedure regarding outward processing, again in circumstances when EC legislation was not yet consolidated. Most OPT cases involve German companies, which should not be surprising in view of the early internationalisation of German firms and the importance of OPT between Germany and Central and Eastern European countries before enlargement. An early case was Case 118/79 *Gebrüder Knauf Westdeutsche Gipswerke v Haupzollamt Hamburg-Jonas.*[95] It concerned exports of maize starch which were authorised under German OPT legislation, and which later were re-imported into the EC as compensating products manufactured from that starch and intended for the building sector. At the time there was no EC OPT legislation. For this reason, OPT was not subject to permanent customs supervision. In other words, there was no system of Community control ensuring the re-importation of the products exported under national outward processing arrangements. As pointed out by the Commission in the case, OPT was attractive for EC enterprises because of the lower production costs of third-country undertakings.[96] However, in the absence of EC control of re-imports, this could result in disturbance of the markets of third countries and lead to shortages on EC markets.

The Court of Justice was asked to interpret the concept of 'export' within the meaning of Article 7(2) of Regulation (EEC) 112/74 on production refunds in the cereals and rice sectors. It held that this concept must be interpreted to mean that any levy which may be introduced in pursuance of that provision must also be imposed on the exportation of the products in question when they are exported under outward processing arrangements and later re-imported as compensating products. In other words, products exported for OPT under national law remained subject to export levies imposed by Community law.

As a result of this judgment, not only did EC law complement national law, it also left its footprint on national law. Even in the absence of EC OPT legislation, Member States' attempts to control and capture the fruits of economic globalisation could not escape the financial consequences of Europeanisation, even though Europeanisation

[95] [1980] ECR 1183.
[96] *Ibid*, at 1187.

was not yet complete with regard to OPT. In this case, EC export levies served as an *ex ante* substitute for the *ex post* controls which would have been available under EC OPT legislation. The case illustrates the overlap and conflict of different national and EC legislation in the period before the Europeanisation of the outward processing procedure. The ECJ was the arbiter of competition between the EC and the Member States concerning by whom and to what extent economic globalisation in the form of IPNs should be regulated.

Procedural integrity was also at stake in the OPT Case C-292/91 *Gebrüder Weis GmbH v Hauptzollamt Würzburg.*[97] The case concerned the post-clearance recovery of customs duties on import. Fabrics originating, *inter alia*, in Portugal had been sent to Yugoslavia for the production of men's outer garments and then returned to the Community. Article 15 of the 1980 EEC–Yugoslavia Cooperation Agreement[98] provided, *inter alia*, that industrial products originating in Yugoslavia 'shall be imported into the Community free of quantitative restrictions and measures having equivalent effect, and of customs duties and charges having equivalent effect'. Article 30 of the Agreement provided that 'products originating in the Community' were to be considered 'products originating in Yugoslavia' on condition that they had undergone in Yugoslavia working or processing which was not 'insufficient' within the meaning of Article 3(3) of Protocol 3 to the Agreement. The defendant customs authority decided to levy customs duties on the ground that, in the context of the transitional scheme applicable to products originating in Portugal, according to which goods traded between Portugal and the other Member States were subject to residual customs duties, the fabrics in question were not to be regarded as 'originating in the Community'.

The Court of Justice held, however, that such customs duties were not recoverable where the importer had observed all the applicable provisions as regards the customs declaration and where any error as regards the categorisation as Community goods or not of goods originating in Portugal would have been far from detectable from a mere reading of the provisions in force by a normally experienced trader. In other words, the ECJ reaffirmed its institutional interpretative role, it applied a test of reasonableness, and in economic terms it gave the trader the benefit of the doubt. The ECJ favoured the market by allowing traders in these circumstances to rely on their business experience. *Lex mercatoria* prevailed, and money accrued neither to the EC as own resources, nor to the national customs administration which would otherwise have received 10 per cent of the duties to cover the cost of collection. The judgment also favoured economic globalisation by lowering the operating costs of transnational economic networks and OPT. It can also be seen, however, as a manifestation of the integrative logic of the ECJ, favouring tighter integration in the form of Europeanisation, and as a judicial effort to guarantee the integrity of the OPT procedure.

In order to ensure the integrity of these customs procedures, the ECJ has tended to interpret the authorisation conditions strictly. Case C-100/05 *ASM Lithography*[99] concerned a 1988 authorisation for inward processing, under the suspension system, of unlimited duration. ASM Lithography developed and manufactured wafer steppers used in the production of chips in the information technology industry. It bought parts

[97] [1993] ECR I-2219.
[98] [1983] OJ L41/2.
[99] Case C-100/05 *ASM Lithography BV v Inspecteur van de Belastingdienst-Douane Zuid/kantoor Roermond* [2006] ECR I-10005.

and partly assembled elements outside the EC for manufacture, as sub-assemblies or as supplies to purchasers as spare parts. It sold some compensating products outside the EC. It released other products for free circulation in the EC. After 1998, electronic components became eligible for processing under customs control. ASM's request for repayment of import duties was rejected. On a preliminary ruling, it argued that the rules for determining customs debt under the procedure for processing under customs control were a *lex specialis* with regard to the rules for inward processing, so that no prior request by the person concerned was necessary; ASM had not requested the former treatment. The ECJ rejected this argument. It interpreted Article 122(c) of the Customs Code to mean that, when it was necessary to determine the amount of customs debt due on release of compensating products for free circulation, national customs authorities were not required to apply the rules of assessment for processing under customs control, even where the import goods could have been placed under that procedure, unless the person concerned had specifically requested such treatment.

The ECJ gave a similarly strict interpretation of customs rules in Case C-19/05 *Commission v Denmark*.[100] Due to an incorrect interpretation of customs rules, Denmark authorised an undertaking to import goods under the 'end-use' scheme with suspension of duties. It sought to avoid liability for non-payment of Community own resources by asserting that the undertaking could have benefited from the inward processing scheme and not paid duties on its imports. The ECJ held that an undertaking could not be granted a licence retroactively under the inward processing scheme.

Authorisation is based on a specific rate of yield for turning the imported product into the final product. If the importer achieves a higher rate of yield, the customs authority may unilaterally alter the rate of yield that it fixed when the authorisation was issued.[101]

Case C-173/06 *Agrover*[102] concerned an Italian company that had an inward processing authorisation for paddy rice. It exported wholly-milled rice to Hungary and subsequently imported equivalent quantities of husked rice from Thailand. At the time, the EC and Hungary were parties to a Europe Agreement. No preferential agreement existed between the EC and Thailand. The Italian authorities considered that the imports were not eligible for the inward processing procedure, because compensating imports under inward processing with prior exportation applied only to countries with which the EC had a preferential agreement. On the basis of a contextual and teleological interpretation of Article 216 of the Community Customs Code, the ECJ accepted this argument. It concluded that the objective of Article 216 was to give priority to economic integration over the promotion of exports. Its express wording subjected only non-Member country goods to customs duties, but by extension it applied also to cases of prior exportation of compensating products. Here, Europeanisation trumped globalisation. Nevertheless, the ECJ also held that, if three cumulative conditions were fulfilled, the customs authorities must waive subsequent entry of import duties into the accounts where they have not contested the exemption. The conditions were that failure to levy the duty was due to an error by the customs authorities, that a person liable for duty and acting in good faith could not have reasonable detected the error and that

[100] Case C-19/05 *Commission of the European Communities v Kingdom of Denmark* [2007] ECR I-8597.

[101] Case C-187/99 *Fazenda Pública v Fábrica de Queijo Eru Portuguesa Lda* [2001] ECR I-1429; Case C-177/00 *Italian Republic v Commission of the European Communities* [2003] ECR I-233; see also Case C-156/00 *Netherlands v Commission* [2003] ECR I-2527.

[102] Case C-173/06 *Agrover Srl v Agenzia Dogane Circoscrizione Doganale di Genova* [2007] ECR I-8783.

the person concerned respected all legislation concerning the customs declaration.[103] It was for the national court to determine whether or not the conditions were fulfilled in this case.This is entirely consistent with the classic division of responsibilities between the ECJ and national courts.

Access to inward processing arrangements was at stake in Case C-103/96 *Eridania Beghin-Say*.[104] The ECJ was asked to give a preliminary ruling on the validity of a Regulation that made recourse to inward processing arrangements with equivalent compensation subject to the condition that the equivalent goods must fall within the same subheading of the Common Customs Tariff as the imported goods. The main issue was the compatibility of the Regulation with the basic EC law principles of legitimate expectations and legal certainty. The ECJ concluded that, in the circumstances of the case, a trader could not have any legitimate expectation other than being able to have recourse to equivalent compensation where the goods concerned fall within the same subheading under the nomenclature in force at the material time. This was because the availability of equivalent compensation depended on a criterion forming part of another set of rules, namely, the tariff classification of specific goods, which were liable to vary as a result of periodic changes. The possibility of such changes was foreseeable. This fact barred the creation of a legitimate expectation with regard to the inward processing procedure.

The case illustrates the interconnection and hierarchy between different sets of customs rules. Classification, origin and valuation constitute the basic skeleton of EC customs law. The inward processing procedure makes sense only within this normative framework. Its existence, as already noted, is due precisely to such normative trade barriers, whether in the EU or elsewhere. The ECJ subordinated the rules concerning inward processing to those concerning tariff classification. In more general terms, the ECJ judgment reaffirmed the primacy of Europeanisation over globalisation. In so far as inward processing may be seen to represent globalisation, the ECJ considered that, for EU-based traders, it could take place only within the normative framework of EC law. Globalisation, in other words, was subject to European integration. The activities of IPNs were constrained by the institutional demands for integrity of the inward processing procedure.

2. *Economic Conditions for Authorisation*

Authorisation to use inward processing or outward processing cannot be granted unless the applicant satisfies specified economic conditions. In principle, these conditions are designed to protect the interests of EC producers as well as to ensure administrative control over use of the procedure. The customs authorities where the application is made are required to examine whether these conditions are fulfilled, unless the conditions are deemed in advance to be satisfied. In the case of inward processing, the examination must establish the economic unviability of using Community sources, taking account of the following criteria:

[103] *Ibid,* para 34.
[104] [1997] ECR I-145.

(a) unavailability of Community-produced goods sharing the same quality and technical characteristics as the goods intended to be imported for the processing operations envisaged;
(b) differences in prices between Community-produced goods and those intended to be imported;
(c) contractual obligations.[105]

These conditions are deemed to be satisfied except where the application concerns specified import goods. These specified import goods include agricultural products covered by Annex I of the EC Treaty, goods not covered by Annex I of the Treaty resulting from the processing of agricultural products, and fishery products. In such cases, the applicant must demonstrate that the criteria are fulfilled. However, the conditions are deemed to be satisfied in the case of certain limited operations regarding these products.[106]

An unusually revealing case about these economic conditions is *Coberco Dairy Foods*,[107] even though the case concerned processing under customs control rather than inward processing. In processing under customs control, non-EC goods may be used in the EC in operations which alter their nature or state, without being subject to import duties or commercial policy measures. The resulting products, known as processed products, can be released for free circulation at an appropriate rate of import duty.[108] Authorisation cannot be granted except where certain economic conditions are fulfilled, including whether the use of non-EC sources enables processing activities to be created or maintained in the EC. Coberco applied for authorisation for processing under customs control for imported fruit juice containing sugar. It applied for the procedure because of competition from Central and Eastern European countries. It appears that, without the application, Coberco would have decided to process the products in Central or Eastern Europe.[109] The application was not supported by the Commission's Directorate-General for Agriculture, because EC sugar producers were already under pressure. The Customs Code Committee decided that the economic conditions were not fulfilled. The Dutch customs authorities based their decision on the Committee's conclusion and refused the application, leading to the reference for a preliminary ruling.

The ECJ in this case decided four important questions. First, the conclusions of the Customs Code Committee are not binding on national customs authorities, even though in some countries, such as The Netherlands, customs authorities always follow negative conclusions of the Committee.[110]

Secondly, the ECJ does not have jurisdiction to examine the validity of the conclusions of the Committee within the framework of the preliminary ruling procedure. It held that the Committee's conclusion cannot be imputed to the Commission and does not constitute an act of the institutions, as required by Article 234 EC. This does not appear to be consistent with other cases on comitology committees or analogous

[105] Regulation (EEC) No 2454/93, Art 502((2) and Part B of Annex 70, as inserted by Commission Regulation (EEC) No 993/2001 of 4 May 2001, [2001] OJ L141/1.
[106] *Ibid*, Art 539 and Annex 73.
[107] Case C-11/05 *Friesland Coberco Dairy Foods BV, trading as Friesland Supply Point Ede v Inspecteur van de Belastingdienst/Douane Noord/kantoor Groningen* [2006] ECR I-4285.
[108] Art 130 of the Customs Code.
[109] *Coberco Dairy Foods*, above n 107, para 20.
[110] *Ibid*, paras 32, 33.

bodies such as COREPER, in which the acts of such bodies have been ascribed to the Commission or the Council.[111]

Thirdly, in assessing an application for authorisation for processing under customs control, account must be taken of both the market for finished products and the market for raw materials used to produce those products. Article 133(e) of the Customs Code refers only to 'the essential interests of Community producers of similar goods'. Since the wording is not clear, the Article must be interpreted in the light of the objectives of the procedure. Processing under customs control

> was introduced to prevent processing activities being moved outside the Community because the cost of importing the raw materials was higher than the cost of exporting the finished product for which the raw materials had been used . . .[112]

It confers advantages on authorised processors which may have adverse effects on EC producers of raw materials used in the processing. The point was emphasised not only by the Commission but also by the Dutch, Greek and Italian Governments. The ECJ concluded that an examination of the economic conditions required consideration of the interests of processors of raw materials and EC producers of similar goods. This interpretation expanded the extent to which the conditions may protect EC producers. This is important because inward processing involves an increase in supply of raw materials on the EC market, so assuming stable demand it means a drop in prices for EC-sourced raw materials of the same type.

The fourth question concerned the criteria to be applied in interpreting the expression 'processing activities to be created or maintained'. Coberco's initial investment of €750,000 for a processing plant was expected to create two jobs.[113] The ECJ stated that job creation was to be taken into account but was not the only criterion. Other factors, such as the stability of the jobs, the value of the investment, the permanence of the activity and any other relevant factor should also be considered.[114] 'The criteria . . . depend on the nature of the processing activity and each examination of the economic conditions must be undertaken in the light of the specific circumstances of the situation'.[115] This formulation combines more detailed rules and case-by-case decision-making. It is intended to constrain national administrative discretion by identifying some factors to be taken into account and thus providing a more elaborate normative structure for decision-making. Its case-by-case nature and its open-ended character have the advantage of flexibility in the changing context of globalisation and delocalisation, but they do not contribute very much to legal certainty. With respect, however, these criteria do not go far enough. They present a useful checklist for national customs authorities, but they may offer little specific guidance to EC producers, applicants, national governments or foreign investors.

Authorisation to use the outward processing procedure is also subject to certain conditions. Examination of each application should establish whether:

[111] On the relationship between COREPER and the Council, see Case 25/94 *Commission v Council* [996] ECR I-1469; on the relationship between comitology committees and the Commission, see Case T-188/97 *Rothmans v Commission* [1999] ECR II-2463.

[112] Opinion of A-G Poiares Maduro, *Coberco Dairy Foods*, above n 107, para 42.

[113] *Coberco Dairy Foods*, above n 107, para 20.

[114] *Ibid*, paras 58–59.

[115] *Ibid*, para 58.

a) carrying out processing outside the Community is likely to cause serious disadvantages for Community processors; or
b) carrying out processing in the Community is economically unviable or is not feasible for technical reasons or due to contractual obligations.[116]

The basic legislation also provides, however, that 'Except where indications to the contrary exist, the essential interests of Community producers shall be deemed not to be seriously harmed'.[117] These provisions do not make clear, though, which EC producers are envisaged.

In contrast to inward processing, outward processing has a direct impact on employment in the EC, but it is not clear that this factor is given great weight in the authorisation to use outward processing. So far, it does not seem to have appeared in the case law. The main orientation of the legislation, and therefore of the case law which interprets it, is therefore to encourage outward processing.

Case C-411/01 *GEFCO* provides an example.[118] Hewlett Packard Italiana SpA obtained outward processing authorisation temporarily to export electronic cards from Italy to China or Japan for installation in printers. The printers were then re-imported into France as compensating products. On export of the goods from Italy, Hewlett Packard in error declared an incorrect tariff heading. This was established when the printers incorporating the cards were imported into France by GEFCO, acting on behalf of its customer, Hewlett Packard France, which itself was acting on behalf of Hewlett Packard Europe. GEFCO claimed to be able to deduct from its customs debt the amount of the import duties which would have been applicable to the temporary export goods according to their correct tariff heading. Following *Wacker Werke II*,[119] the ECJ interpreted the relevant provisions of the Customs Code teleologically: an objective of outward processing is to prevent customs duties from being charged on goods exported for outward processing. The Court concluded that an economic operator which had declared temporarily exported goods under an incorrect tariff heading is not prohibited from adducing proof that such a declaration had no significant effect on the operation of the procedure, but that the proof must establish, without any ambiguity, that the compensating products have resulted from processing of the temporary export goods. The ECJ also concluded that it was for the national court to determine whether the proof was sufficient. If the proof was sufficient, the amount of duty applicable to the temporary export goods could be deducted when the compensating products were released for free circulation. This result was orientated toward encouraging and facilitating outward processing. It sought to prevent fraud, yet to avoid penalising unintentional errors. While establishing the general principle, the ECJ decentralised more detailed regulation in specific cases to national courts.

[116] Commission Regulation (EEC) No 2454/93, Art 502(4), as inserted by Commission Regulation (EC) No 993/2001, [2001] OJ L141.

[117] *Ibid*, Art 585(1).

[118] Case C-411/01 *GEFCO SA v Receveur principal des douanes* [2003] ECR I-11547.

[119] See *ibid.*, para 51, referring to Case C-142/96 *Hauptzollamt München v Wacker Werke GmbH & Co KG [Wacker Werke II]* [1997] ECR IO-4649.

3. *Proof of 'import' or 'export'*

Once granted, authorisation to use inward processing or outward processing requires the import or the export of goods. At least two cases concern means of proof of import or export. These cases involve the integrity of the basic procedures, but they are treated separately from other integrity cases because they raise slightly different issues, including cooperation between national customs authorities or the potential for fraud.

Compensating goods which are exported or re-exported after inward processing may be re-imported with relief from import duties as returned goods. Relief from duties applies, however, only to the proportion of the value of the product corresponding to inward processing. In Case C-56/02 *Rebman*,[120] the plaintiff in the main action imported, between late 1994 and Spring 1995, 20 consignments containing 158 new German-origin cars from the Czech Republic. The vehicles had undergone inward processing in the EC and thus did not entirely originate there. Rebman was able to produce a declaration of returned goods and an invoice with the export stamp of the German customs authorities. As it was not the holder of the inward processing authorisation, however, it was not able to produce any documents on the basis of which the proportion of the value due to inward processing could be determined. In these circumstances, the ECJ held that the administrative cooperation procedure must be used by the customs authorities.[121]

Issues of potential fraud often arise in cases concerning outward processing. Export refunds represent a potential source of fraud. In Case C-177/00 *Italy v Commission*,[122] the ECJ held that olive oil consisting of a blend of olive oil of EC origin and olive oil imported from Tunisia under inward processing arrangements did not qualify for export refunds payable on Community products.

European Community rules provide that outward processing is not available to goods whose export gives rise to export refunds. Potential fraud was an issue in Case C-114/99 *Roquette*.[123] The case concerned non-differentiated[124] export refunds for glucose syrup which the company had exported in 1990 under an inward processing arrangement in Austria, then not an EC Member State. Roquette was unable to provide evidence that the product had been consumed in an unaltered state on the Austrian market. In fact, the glucose syrup had been used in the manufacture of penicillin and thus disappeared. The penicillin was partly exported to the EC market. The ECJ concluded that there was no question of fraud, since the export product ceased to exist as a result of manufacturing of a new product with a different tariff

[120] Case C-56/02 *IHW Rebman GmbH v Haupzollamt Weiden* [2003] ECR I-5499.

[121] At the time the administrative cooperation procedure between customs authorities was laid down in Arts 611(2)(b) and 613 of Commission Regulation (EEC) No 2454/93 of 2 July 1993 laying down provisions for the implementation of Council Regulation (EEC) No 2913/92 establishing the Community Customs Code [1993] OJ L253/1.

[122] Case C-177/00 *Italian Republic v Commission of the European Communities* [2003] ECR I-233. See also Case C-156/00 *Netherlands v Commission* [2003] ECR I-2527.

[123] Case C-114/99 *Roquette Frères SA v Office national interprofessionnel des cereals (ONIC)* [2000] ECR I-8823.

[124] Non-differentiated refunds are intended to encourage exports and are granted to cover the difference between the EC price and the international trade price. Only proof of export from the EC is required. Differentiated refunds are intended to help EC products gain access to foreign markets and the amount varies according to the target market. In this case, proof of entry into free circulation on the target market is required. See Case 89/83*Hauptsollamt Hamburg-Jonas/Dimex* [1984] ECR 2815, paras 9–10, 16, 21–22, 27, cited in the Opinion of A-G Alber, *Roquette Frères*, above n 123, para 39.

heading. Payment of the export refund could not be made conditional on the production of additional evidence showing that the glucose had actually been placed on the market in Austria.

Case C-515/03 *Eichsfelder*[125] was very similar. It involved differentiated export refunds paid on boneless beef exported from Germany to Poland (then not an EC Member State), where it underwent substantial processing to make cooked meat roulades, which then were exported to Germany. Customs clearance for release of the product for consumption in the non-EC destination country is a condition to obtaining a differentiated refund. The ECJ held that the condition is fulfilled when the product undergoes substantial processing or working in the destination country. This applies when import duties are paid in the country of destination, and it applies even if the product is then re-exported to the EC with reimbursement of duties levied in the destination country and then duties paid on import into the EC. Both *Roquette* and *Eichsfelder* potentially had the effect of facilitating outward processing arrangements.

4. *Transfer Pricing*

International production networks may seek to engage in transfer pricing in order to lower tax liability or to reduce other obligations. Transfer pricing involves shifting costs and liabilities to the unit in the chain where the financial or other liability is lowest. It is especially likely to occur in intra-firm trade, which is a form of intra-industry trade involving different units within a single company. Case C-16/91 *Wacker Werke I*[126] exemplifies the connection between inward processing and outward processing, and the potential for abuse of the system. The case was an Article 177 (later Article 234) reference for a preliminary ruling on the interpretation of Council Regulation 2473/86 on outward processing relief arrangements and the standard exchange system.[127] It concerned the value for customs purposes of certain products imported by the applicant, Wacker Werke, between 1986 and 1988. Wacker Werke had purchased the products from Wacker Corporation, established in the USA, with which it had financial links.

Wacker Werke manufactured petrol engines and purchased diesel engines from other undertakings in Germany. It then sold these two types of engine to Wacker Corporation. The engines were exported as temporary export goods under an authorisation issued on the basis of the Regulation on outward processing. When Wacker Werke sold the engines to Wacker Corporation, it added, by way of general expenses and profit margin, 25 per cent of the cost of manufacturing its petrol engines and 5 per cent of the purchase price of the diesel engines it purchased from other German undertakings. Wacker Corporation incorporated these engines into vibration plates, vibrocompacters and hydraulic pumps. It then sold these products, partly on the American and European markets directly, and partly to Wacker Werke, which re-imported them into the Community as compensating products under the outward processing arrangements. Wacker Werke bought these compensating products from Wacker Corporation

[125] Case C-515/03 *Eichsfelder Schlachtbetrieb GmbH v Hauptzollamt Hamburg-Jonas* [2005] ECR I-7355.

[126] Above n 74.

[127] [1986] OJ L212/1.

at the prices shown in the latter's price list for the American markets, less a reduction of 45 per cent.

The dispute between Wacker Werke and the German customs authority concerned the valuation of the temporary export goods. The OPT Regulation allowed compensating products in an OPT transaction to benefit on their release from free circulation in the EC from partial or total relief from customs duties. Relief was to be calculated by deducting from the amount of import duties applicable to the compensating products (here, vibration plates, vibro-compacters and hydraulic pumps) the amount of import duties that would have been applicable to the temporary export goods (petrol and diesel engines) if they were imported into the Community from the country in which they underwent the processing operation or last such operation.

The basic issue was whether the 25 per cent and 5 per cent 'uplift' or supplements added by the applicant should be taken into account. The German national court, which referred the case to the ECJ, stated that there was no evidence that the prices charged by Wacker Werke for the temporary export goods, or those charged by Wacker Corporation for the compensating products, were influenced by the links between the two companies.[128] However, the German Government argued that

> all these factors [regarding pricing] suggest a deliberate intention to set as high a value as possible for the temporary export goods in order to keep the differential duty payable at a moderate level . . .[129]

The essential problem, in its view, was the evasion of duty by transfer pricing.[130]

The ECJ held in this case that the value of the temporary export goods corresponded to the difference between the customs value of the compensating products and the processing costs determined by reasonable means, such as taking account of the transaction value of the goods in question. As in Case 118/79 *Gipswerke*,[131] it adopted a reasonableness test, gave the benefit of doubt to the company and respected the decision of the market. In other words, the applicant company won. The judgment also facilitated OPT by lowering its costs and encouraged the use of the outward processing procedure as part of the calculations of a Transatlantic economic network. Following the ECJ ruling, the *Finanzgericht* upheld Wacker Werke's application.

The German customs authority appealed the judgment. It argued that the judgment conferred unjustified customs advantages on the trader. The case was then again referred for a preliminary ruling to the ECJ as Case C-142/96 *Wacker Werke II*.[132] The ECJ, once again following Advocate-General Tesauro, held that reference to the transaction value of the temporary import goods was a reasonable means of determining processing costs. In determining the transaction value, reference could be made to the purchase price, inclusive of uplifts, even if this resulted in a higher rate of duty for the unprocessed goods than for the compensating products.[133]

With regard to the possibility of transfer pricing, the ECJ stated that the possibility of 'tariff anomalies', and the consequent financial advantages for traders, were risks

[128] *Wacker Werke I*, above n 74, at I-6839, para 6.

[129] See the Report for the Hearing, *ibid*, at I-6829.

[130] As to transfer pricing as a regulatory issue, see S Picciotto, 'Transfer Pricing and the Antinomies of Corporate Regulation' in J McCahery, S Picciotto, and C Scott (eds), *Corporate Control and Accountability: Changing Structures and the Dynamics of Regulation* (Oxford, Clarendon Press, 1993) 375.

[131] *Gipswerke,* above n 95.

[132] *Wacker Werke II*, above n 119.

[133] *Ibid*, para 22.

that were inherent in the outward processing procedure. These risks were outweighed, however, by the benefits of OPT. The ECJ held that the merits or demerits of individual cases had to be accepted, provided that there was no evidence to indicate that the inter-firm prices were influenced by their business links, or even by the fact that the 'inter-firm' prices were actually 'intra-firm' in the sense of belonging to a single, tightly-knit global economic network.[134] Such an approach might seem to give more weight to legal form than to economic reality in the sense of the practical operation of economic networks, but the ECJ judgment also entailed that the existence of transfer pricing among related enterprises was a question of fact to be decided by the national court. National judges therefore have the task of evaluating and supervising the financial arrangements of firms which litigate before them. Such a norm itself, though perhaps continuing previous national practices, is a form of Europeanisation: it represents a jurisdiction marker between different courts that is laid down by the ECJ. In the absence of any such finding, the ECJ judgment also signalled a policy preference for encouraging OPT and creating economic incentives for the development of IPNs.

D. Customs Procedures and Anti-dumping Law

Inward processing and outward processing procedures are not isolated from the legal regulation of other matters in international trade. These procedures are frequently involved in EC anti-dumping investigations and litigation concerning IPNs, for example in trade between the EU and China.[135] The resulting disputes raise extremely complex issues concerning the intersection between international law, regional law and national law, and concerning the regulation of IPNs. The following paragraphs are intended simply to indicate some of the different scenarios that have arisen in practice, and to illuminate the economic and legal strategies used by strategic actors.

In many anti-dumping cases, downstream EU users of the allegedly dumped imports argue that the imposition of anti-dumping duties will threaten their exports from the EU to third countries. Their concern is that such duties will cut off or raise the cost of worldwide sourcing, and thus interrupt the smooth operation of an IPN or similar arrangement. For this reason, they argue, such duties should not be imposed. In this way, companies appeal not only to commercial rationality, but also to virtually (in a double sense of almost and of imaginary) patriotic notions of enhancing EC trade, or at least not damaging the EC balance of payments. Such arguments, however, are rarely successful. Instead, anti-dumping duties are imposed, and the downstream users are required to source materials to produce their exports by using the more restricted inward processing procedure.

One example is the *Extramet* saga. It concerned imports of calcium metal from China and the then Soviet Union. In January 1988, the Chambre Syndicale de l'Electrométallurgie et de l'Electrochimie made a dumping complaint on behalf of the

[134] *Ibid*, para 21.

[135] For example, in Case T-87/98 *International Potash Company v Council of the European Union* [2000] ECR II-3179, it was asserted that misuse of the inward processing regime was a form of circumvention of a variable anti-dumping duty, leading the Council to impose a variable duty or a fixed duty, whichever was the higher. This assertion was implicitly accepted by the CFI.

sole Community producer, namely, Péchiney Electrométallurgie (PEM). Extramet Industrie was the main EC importer. Its activity consisted partly in granulating calcium metal. It accounted for between 62 per cent and 97 per cent of aggregate imports of calcium metal from China and Russia into the EC. The Chinese exporter was the China Nuclear Energy Industry Corporation (CNEIC), the trading arm of the sole producer of calcium metal in China, China National Nuclear Corporation (CNNC). Extramet argued that it had no source of supply other than China and Russia, because PEM, the sole EC manufacturer, either had high prices or refused to supply. PEM accounted for the entire calcium metal production in the EC.

The Commission investigation led eventually to the imposition of definitive anti-dumping duties.[136] Extramet applied for interim measures, but its application was dismissed.[137] However, its action for annulment of the anti-dumping duties was declared admissible.[138] Subsequently the ECJ declared the anti-dumping measure void.[139] Later complaints then led to a new investigation. This in turn resulted in the imposition of a new provisional anti-dumping duty[140] and then a new definitive anti-dumping duty.[141] Once again Extramet, now trading as Industrie des Poudres Sphériques (IPS), brought an application for interim measures. As before, its application for interim measures was unsuccessful.[142] It also lost on the merits, both before the CFI[143] and on appeal to the ECJ.[144]

To understand the interconnection between the inward processing procedures and anti-dumping measures, it is necessary to consider the case in more detail. In evaluating the results of its anti-dumping investigation, the Commission assessed the possible impact of eventual measures on primary users. The latter included processors such as IPS, and user industries, such as the lead and ferro-alloy industry, and the steel industry. Companies in the last groups argued that the imposition of anti-dumping duties would disrupt their exports. However, the Commission concluded, *inter alia*, that for their sales of processed calcium metal outside the EC, these firms could continue to source their inputs from Russia or China under the inward processing arrangements without paying any duty.

Similarly, when IPS applied for interim measures, the Council argued that, if interim measures were adopted, they should be conditional, *inter alia*, on the establishment of a mechanism to prevent IPS from reselling the goods imported from China and Russia without processing in the EU. This was intended to ensure that, if IPS were granted interim measures in respect of anti-dumping, it did not also circumvent the restrictions on IPT which were intended to protect EU producers. In this case, the ECJ dismissed the IPS application.

On the merits, IPS claimed that PEM, its main domestic source of supply, had abused its dominant position, partly by using the anti-dumping proceeding to strengthen its dominant position through delay and to cut off IPS's sources in China and Russia. This claim was rejected by the Commission. IPS then brought an action to

136 *Calcium Metal from China* (definitive), [1989] OJ L271/1.

137 Case C-358/89R *Extramet Industrie v Council* [1990] ECR I-431.

138 Case C-358/89 *Extramet Industrie v Council* (*Extramet I*) [1991] ECR 2501.

139 Case C-358/89 *Extramet Industrie v Council* (*Extramet II*) [1992] ECR I-3813.

140 *Calcium Metal from China* (provisional), [1994] OJ L104/5.

141 *Calcium Metal from China* (definitive), [1994] OJ L270/27.

142 Case T-2/95R *Industrie des Poudres Sphériques v Council of the European Union* [1998] ECR II-3939.

143 Case T-2/95 *Industrie des Poudres Sphériques v Council of the European Union, ibid.*

144 Case C-458/98P *Industrie des Poudres Sphériques v Council of the European* [2000] ECR I-8147.

annul the Commission's decision.[145] PEM was granted leave to intervene in support of the Commission. It invoked Eurostat data to show that it was not the only source of supply. IPS countered by arguing that PEM had added to Chinese and Russian imports the supply of calcium metal deriving from inward processing arrangements, even though such arrangements were designed for temporary importation with a view to re-exportation and not a real source of supply. The ECJ rejected the view of IPS. Without mentioning inward processing expressly, it concluded that IPS had alternative sources of supply.[146]

A second example of the intersection of inward processing and anti-dumping concerned imports of silicon metal from China.[147] China was by far the world's biggest supplier of silicon metal. The main EU users of the imports were producers of aluminium. In 1995, the Comité de Liaison des Industries de Ferro-Alliages (CLIFA) lodged a complaint on behalf of four Community producers, which allegedly represented a major proportion of the total EU silicon metal production. The Commission then initiated an expiry review of the anti-dumping measures that were then in place on silicon metal from China. Five Chinese exporters replied to the questionnaire sent as part of the Commission investigation. All were represented by the China Chamber of Commerce for Import and Export of Metals, Minerals & Chemicals (CCCMC). During the investigation it emerged that some of the main Community importers might be related to the exporters, as part of the State-controlled 'Minmetals' import and export network.

In the past more than two-thirds of China's silicon metal exports had usually gone to Japan. As Japanese and other Asian markets became saturated, Chinese production declined. With the lapse of the EC and USA anti-dumping measures then in force, or at least so EC producers argued in this case, Chinese producers could regain the previous high level of production and increase exports to the EU. On the contrary, a UK aluminium producers association argued that anti-dumping measures would damage the international competitive position of EC products. The Commission accepted the former argument. It dismissed the latter on the ground that silicon metal used for the production in the EU of aluminium for export could enter the EU without duty under the inward processing procedure. In 1997 the Council imposed a definitive anti-dumping duty.[148]

A third example concerns ferro-silico-manganese (FeSiMn) from China, used in the steel industry for deoxidisation and as an alloy. It is mainly produced from manganese ore and silicon, which are mixed together and brought to fusion temperatures in a furnace. The main downstream user is the steel industry. The original complaint came from EuroAlliages, the association representing the Community producers of ferro-silico-manganese; the latter were located in Belgium, France, Spain, and Italy. It also concerned other importing countries in addition to China. On the other side, the Commission received comments from two user associations and one user.

The users stated that the imposition of an anti-dumping duty would cause a significant increase in the cost of production of steel products. They also argued that it could endanger the competitiveness of the EC stainless steel industry on the world

[145] Case T-5/97 *Industrie des Poudres Sphériques v Commission of the European Communities* [2000] ECR II-3755.

[146] *Ibid*, para 57.

[147] [1995] OJ C193/3.

[148] *Silicon Metal from China* (definitive), [1997] OJ L345/1.

market. However, the Commission concluded that FeSiMn needed for the production of exports could enter the EU under the inward processing regime without any duty; one user was in fact using this regime to import FeSiMn from South Africa. The Council in 1998 imposed a definitive anti-dumping duty on imports of Chinese FeSiMn.[149]

In these cases, whether administrative proceedings or adjudication, the EU institutions were concerned to maintain the integrity of the two distinct but interrelated procedures: anti-dumping measures to protect certain EU producers on the one hand, and inward processing as a separate but restricted channel for imports for processing for export by other EU producers, on the other hand. The cases show that each procedure may play a different role in positioning EU companies in IPNs. The assumption underlying regular imports and anti-dumping measures is that the EU is the final destination of the products. Under IPT, however, the EU serves simply as a node or as a processing site in an IPN. These cases also illustrate the potentially contradictory roles of anti-dumping and the inward processing procedure. Inward processing may be treated by EC administrative authorities or by the courts as a sufficient source of supply for partners in IPNs when anti-dumping duties are imposed on their other imports. When anti-dumping duties are imposed on a company's imports, inward processing may provide a side door to ensure supply.

The question arises as to whether companies using these different channels for imports ever compete. The issue arose with regard to handbags from China. Large European firms control the major designs and thus access to the market. Subcontractors do the work of producing handbags, which is labour-intensive. Chinese and EU producers tend to compete for the contracts. In China handbags are produced under Chinese inward processing arrangements, and thus under outward processing arrangements as seen from the EU. These IPT/OPT arrangements involve IPNs. Large EU firms may establish a Hong Kong subsidiary, which rents factory space and hires workers for production in China. In the EU handbags are produced mainly by SMEs, especially from the southern Member States. Chinese producers dominate the EU market for plastic handbags. The fiercest competition thus concerns contracts for the production of leather handbags.

In 1997, the Commission imposed a provisional anti-dumping duty on plastic and leather handbags from China.[150] Indonesia was chosen as an analogue country. In calculating normal value, the Commission considered that, with regard to raw materials, there were no significant differences between Indonesian producers and the Chinese producers that cooperated in the investigation. Both obtained most of their raw material on the international market under inward processing arrangements. The Commission also considered that the imposition of anti-dumping duties would not harm the exports of handbags by EU firms to China, since such exports were minimal due to the high Chinese customs duties. It should be noted, however, that IPNs operated mainly outside this channel of trade and instead through OPT and IPT arrangements, in both the EU and China.

The Commission investigation revealed that a number of EC manufacturers had already moved part of their production to China. These manufacturers did not cooperate in the investigation. However, they argued that the imposition of anti-dumping

149 *Ferro-Silico-Manganese from China* (definitive), [1998] OJ L62/1.
150 *Plastic and Leather Handbags from China* (provisional), [1997] OJ L33/11.

measures would reduce employment in their EC factories. Such measures would make it impossible to cross-subsidise the manufacture of low-volume, high-priced handbags in the EC with high-volume, low-priced imports of handbags from China. Some producers, mainly in Germany and the UK, were in fact able to maintain a small EC production by achieving higher profit margins on handbags imported from China. The Commission pointed out that, even if anti-dumping duties were imposed, these firms would still be able to source handbags from China. The Commission also considered whether the imposition of anti-dumping duties would hinder EC exports of raw materials for handbags to be produced in China. It concluded, however, that the majority of Chinese manufacturers sourced the accessories in Asia, mostly in China itself, but also in Taiwan and Korea. It is worth noting that all of the sampled EC producers visited by the Commission in the anti-dumping investigation purchased their raw materials and accessories from EC suppliers.

In 1997 the Council imposed a definite anti-dumping duty on leather handbags alone.[151] This was a compromise, especially between the northern and the southern Member States. Viewed in general terms, these two groups reflected the interests of global economic networks and EU SMEs, respectively. The Council compromise recognised the dominance of global economic networks, including Chinese producers, in the EU market for plastic handbags. The compromise also served to protect the mainly SME EU producers of leather handbags, at least provisionally. This EU institutional strategy aimed to manage the conflicts and contradictions between Europeanisation and globalisation by separating domestic and international markets, and by trying to insulate them so far as possible. It remains to be seen whether and for how long such a strategy would be feasible.

IV. Conclusion

Analysing the inward processing and outward processing customs procedures, this chapter considered the ambiguous relationship between regionalisation and globalisation. Each represents a different configuration, or constellation, of sites of governance. As the discussion showed, Europeanisation and globalisation are both friends and rivals. European Union law is an expression, a means, a cause and a result of Europeanisation. At the same time certain aspects of EC law encourage the development of IPNs which cut across national and EU boundaries and are a fundamental element in economic globalisation today. European Union law thus is at war with itself. It embodies and reflects conflicting interests and thus, partly for this reason, comprises contradictory strands. This is truer of the EU than the Member States' legal systems because of the dimension of scale. Its implications are more far-reaching for the EU than for a Member State (though for Member States the implications of globalisation are also profound), in particular because the EU is relatively new, lacking in legitimacy and in search of its basic values. Certain aspects of EU law, which are orientated towards and foster globalisation, tend to undercut the influence of other aspects of EU law, which might otherwise lead to a stronger, more coherent process of

[151] *Leather Handbags from China* (definitive), [1997] OJ L208/31.

Europeanisation. This gives the relationship between Europeanisation and globalisation an especially complex character. Such assertions may seem surprising if our reading of reality is limited only to processes and consequently neglects the interests and structures which underlie them and which are manifested in the legal strategies of different strategic actors. An understanding of these interests and structures is essential, however, if we are to grasp the complex interaction of Europeanisation and globalisation. It is even more important if we wish to imagine a different way of viewing EU governance in the age of globalisation and IPNs.

International production networks have contradictory effects on relations between the EU and its Member States. They tend to strengthen, to fragment and partly to restructure these relations. In early 2004, *Le Monde* published an article entitled 'Pour relancer l'Europe, ne comptez plus sur les grandes entreprises'. It argued that large companies could no longer be the motor of European integration. Globalisation, internationalisation and delocalisation meant that, for such companies, 'Europe' was less important than 'outside Europe'. The article concluded with two rhetorical questions: 'Without large companies as a motor, how can Europe get back on the track?'; 'Does the globalisation of large companies close the door on the [neo-]functionalist method?'[152] These questions are revealing, regardless of the truth of their underlying assumptions. They indicate the extent to which Europeanisation and globalisation are seen (correctly in my view) as complementary, mutually reinforcing, but also as competing processes. Both are encouraged by EC law.

Globalisation, the development of IPNs and the Europeanisation of customs law did not erase previous differences between the interests of different Member States, or previous relations between companies and national governments in different countries. Instead, it has accentuated them. This chapter suggests that, on balance, globalisation contributes to retarding or even preventing the development of further European integration in the specific form of an EU constitution, in the sense of the elaboration of a constitutional structure analogous to that of nation States. Globalisation also restricts the constitutionalisation of EU law, in the sense of the development of constitutionalising processes or a constitutional culture, which helps to sustain and give social meaning to constitutional principles.[153] Historically it is too late for such an EU constitution of a traditional type. Globalisation based on IPNs has helped to create global legal pluralism.

The processes of Europeanisation and globalisation are both creative and destructive. The chapter has argued that EU customs laws on inward processing and outward processing arrangements are factors in these sometimes contradictory processes. In conclusion, two points should be emphasised. First, the Europeanisation of customs law during the course of European economic and legal integration has stimulated and enhanced types of global economic relations which tend to undercut classical EU constitution-making. Such economic relations are often promoted by EU Member States. Secondly, we cannot understand the interests, structures and processes involved in European integration today without taking IPNs into account. They challenge us to imagine new forms of EU governance in a world of global legal pluralism.

[152] *Le Monde*, 8–9 February 2004, at 24 ('Sans ce moteur des grandes entreprises, comment relancer l'Europe?' 'Est-ce que leur mondialisation ferme la voie "fonctionnaliste"?'[My translation: FS]).

[153] On this conception of the EU constitution, see F Snyder, 'General Course on European Community Law: Constitutional Law of the European Union: Principles, Processes and Culture' in *Collected Courses of the Academy of European Law 1995*, vol VI, no 1 (Deventer, Kluwer, 1998) 41; and F Snyder, 'The Unfinished Constitution of the European Union: Principles, Processes and Culture', in JHH Weiler and M Wind (eds), *European Constitutionalism Beyond the State* (Cambridge, Cambridge University Press, 2003) 55.

Part III

New Directions in Global Legal Pluralism

9

The Creation of New Sites of Governance: China, Regional Trade Agreements and WTO Law*

I. Introduction

Relations between sites of governance, as already seen, are often dynamic. In addition to giving rise to new legal concepts, or transforming institutions, norms or dispute resolution processes within a particular site, they may also stimulate the creation of new sites of governance. A regional trade agreement (RTA) creates a new site of governance if it constitutes a locus of decision-making with the authority to settle disputes, as it inevitably does. It results from relations between existing sites and will usually represent a more highly institutionalised form of selected aspects of these relations. Though reflecting the structural features of the sites concerned, it usually embodies new structural features of its own and enters into its own relations with other sites of governance. The creation of RTAs thus contributes to the development of global legal pluralism. An examination of China's RTAs is useful in helping us to understand why and how new sites of governance may be created. It also elucidates the ways in which structural features of a site affect, influence or determine basic structural features of the newly created site.

The chapter considers China's RTAs, proposes a typology of China's RTAs and evaluates certain significant features of these agreements in the light of WTO law.[1] China is one of the largest, most populous and most economically dynamic countries in the world today.[2] As of July 2007, it had a land mass of more than 9.3 million km[2]

* This chapter is an updated and slightly revised version of an article on 'China's Regional Trade Agreements and WTO Law', originally published in (2009) (43) 1 *Journal of World Trade* 1–57. The article has been reproduced with the permission of Wolters Kluwer Legal.

[1] Consistently with general usage in the literature, the terms 'regional trade agreement' and 'RTA' are used to encompass both agreements involving a specific region and bilateral free trade agreements (FTAs) involving two countries. See JA Crawford and RV Fiorentino, *The Changing Landscape of Regional Trade Agreements*, WTO, Geneva, Switzerland, Discussion Paper No 8, 2005, 3–4, according to whom (at 3) FTAs account for 84% of all RTAs in force, with partial scope agreements and customs unions each making up 8%. They also state (at 4, fn 12) that increasingly RTAs are concluded among countries which are not geographically contiguous, even though the term 'RTAs' is not technically correct in this situation. The preference for FTAs is due to their speed of negotiation, flexibility and selectivity: see RV Fiorentino, L Verdeja and C Toqueboeuf, *The Changing Landscape of Regional Trade Agreements: 2006 Update*, Regional Trade Agreements Section, Trade Policies Review Division, WTO, Geneva, Switzerland, Discussion Paper No 12, 2006, 6. See also, eg, R Sen, ' "New Regionalism" in Asia: A Comparative Analysis of Emerging Regional and Bilateral Trading Agreements involving ASEAN, China and India' (2006) 40(4) *Journal of World Trade* 553 at 555, fn 4.

[2] 'China is a civilization pretending to be a state,' wrote Lucian Pye 20 years ago: LW Pye, 'China: Erratic State, Frustrated Society' (1990) 69(4) *Foreign Affairs* 56, republished in LW Pye, *The Spirit of Chinese Politics* (Cambridge, Mass, Harvard University Press, 1992) ch 11 (the quotation is at 235).

and a population of more than 1.3 billion, or a population density of 141.7/km^2. Its population accounts for 20.02 per cent of the world's population. Its arable surface, however, is only 1.3 million km^2, or about 14 per cent of its total area, making a population density for arable surface of 953.8/km^2. Since the beginning of the period of 'opening up' and reform, China's growth rate has averaged about 10 per cent per year, based largely on foreign direct investment (FDI) and exports.[3] As of 2006, trade in goods accounted for 70 per cent of gross domestic product (GDP), FDI for about 40 per cent of GDP and multinational enterprises for about 60 per cent of merchandise trade.[4] In the same year, China was the world's fourth largest economy, accounting (in 2005) for 14 per cent of world GDP on a purchasing power parity (PPP) basis. Per capita income in China has grown correspondingly from US $293 in 1985 to US $2,940 in 2008.[5] Gross domestic product per capita as of 2009 was estimated at US $6,500, or in terms of PPP a national total of US $ 8,767 trillion; in PPP terms, China was second in the world behind only the USA.[6]

China 'has more contiguous neighbors than any other country in the world'.[7] Relations between China and other Asian countries are therefore long-standing and complex. Before the end of the Qing dynasty (1644–1911), China's relations with its neighbours formed a Sino-centric world order, with China at the centre, and manifested in a tributary system. According to the late Professor Wang Tieya, they did not involve State-to-State relations, but rather relations between superior and subordinates, based on cultural ascendancy, manifested in gifts, marriages and other forms of interaction, and symbolised in the kowtow.[8] After the Opium Wars, foreign powers imposed unequal treaties on China and carved up southeast Asia into States. Not surprisingly, a strong conception of national sovereignty and an overriding concern for security, social stability and protection of sovereignty are among the foundations of China's regional policy today.[9]

[3] See H Siebert, 'China: Coming to Grips with the New Global Player' (2007) 30(6) *The World Economy* 893.

[4] R Sally, *FTAs and the Prospects for Regional Integration in Asia*, European Centre for International Political Economy, Brussels, ECIPE Working Paper, 1, 2006, 1 at 3.

[5] The statistics are given by The World Bank Group, 'China Data Profile', http://ddp-ext.worldbank.org/ext/ddpreports/ViewSharedReport?&CF=1&REPORT_ID=9147&REQUEST_TYPE=VIEWADVANCED&HF=N&WSP=N, last accessed 23 Feruary 2010; The World Bank Group, 'China Data and Statistics', http://web.worldbank.org/WBSITE/EXTERNAL/DATASTATISTICS/0,,contentMDK:20535285~menuPK:1192694~pagePK:64133150~piPK:64133175~theSitePK:239419,00.html, last accessed 23 February 2010; The World Bank Group, 'China Quick Facts', http://web.worldbank.org/WBSITE/EXTERNAL/COUNTRIES/EASTASIAPACIFICEXT/CHINAEXTN/0,,contentMDK:20680895~pagePK:1497618~piPK:217854~theSitePK:318950,00.html, visited 3 April 2008.

[6] Central Intelligence Agency, *The World Factbook—China*, available at https://www.cia.gov/library/publications/the-world-factbook/geos/ch.html, last accessed 23 February 2010.

[7] HC Hinton, 'China as an Asian Power', in TW Robinson and D Shambaugh (eds), *Chinese Foreign Policy. Theory and Practice* (Oxford, Clarendon Press, 1994, reprinted 2006) 348 at 352. The CIA, above n 6, reports 22,117 km of land boundaries, including 14 countries and two regional borders (Hong Kong and Macao).

[8] See Wang Tieya, 'International Law in China: Historical and Contemporary Perspectives', *Recueil des Cours de l'Académie de Droit International de La Haye*, vol 221, (1990-II), 205. See also Li Zhaojie (James Li), 'Traditional Chinese World Order' (2002) 1 *Chinese Journal of International Law* 20.

[9] On the legacies for contemporary relations, see (on the tributary system) Wang Gungwu, 'China and Southeast Asia: The Context of a New Beginning' and (on unequal treaties) HC Hinton, 'China as an Asian Power', in Robinson and Shambaugh, above n 7,187–204 and 348–72, respectively. See also S Golden, 'Socio-cultural Aspects of the Relationship between the EU and East Asia, with particular reference to China' (2006) 4 *Asia Europe Journal* 265.

Recently, two eminent Chinese specialists on Asia summarised China's general foreign policy strategy as being 'to secure and shape a security, economic and political environment that is conducive to China concentrating on its economic, social and political development'.[10] They discerned four underlying concepts:

a) to make China a great power again;
b) to ensure China's security;
c) to practise self-restraint (*buyao dangtou*: do not seek leadership[11]); and
d) to behave as 'a responsible great power' (*fuzeren de daguo*).[12]

In their view, Chinese practice is based on maintaining 'an active great power diplomacy' (*daguo waijiao*), cultivating friendly relations with its neighbours, cooperating more in regional economic affairs than in binding regional security arrangements, and being selective in assuming international responsibilities.[13]

Both strategy and practice are profoundly informed by China's specific political and legal culture, and by its distinctive policy-making process. Concerning political culture, a leading scholar of China's foreign policy has described China's approach to regional and international relations since 1949 as being based on a focus on the specific situation and possible changes in it, the use of metaphor and simple generalisation, an orientation that is 'distinctively actor-oriented (state-centred in most cases) and relation-oriented', and moralist thinking.[14] 'Taking sides' in such relations is fundamental, but '[w]hether or not these countries' domestic political system is to China's liking or not is of little relevance', and in regional policy 'the emphasis [is] on relationships rather than regional issues themselves'.[15] Chinese political and legal culture has also been characterised by reliance 'upon ethics more than law, upon moral consensus more than judicial procedure, upon benevolent government more than checks and balances', and by a blend of pragmatism and ideology, such as nationalism.[16]

The second element is the Chinese policy process. For present purposes, its most significant characteristics may be summarised in terms of the conjunction of two features. The first is 'fragmented authoritarianism',[17] defined recently as 'the deep jurisdictional cleavages that separate functionally specific clusters of related bureaucracies (*xitong*)

[10] Zhang Yunling and Tang Shiping, 'China's Regional Strategy' in D Shambaugh (ed), *Power Shift: China and Asia's New Dynamics* (Berkeley, University of California Press, 2005) 48 at 48.

[11] Often translated as 'never seek hegemony', this originated with Deng Xiaoping, and was perhaps first expressed in his talk on 'Realize the Four Modernizations and Never Seek Hegemony', 7 May 1978, in *Selected Works of Deng Xiaoping*, vol II (1975–82), trans by The Bureau for the Compilation and Translation of the Works of Marx, Engels, Lenin and Stalin under the Central Committee of the Communist Party of China (Beijing, Foreign Languages Press, 1984, 2nd edn 1995),122 at 123.

[12] Zhang Yunling and Tang Shiping, above n 10 at 48–49 (the quotation is from p 49).

[13] *Ibid*, at 49–51 (the quotation is from p 49).

[14] Wang Jisi, 'International Relations Theory and the Study of Chinese Foreign Policy: A Chinese Perspective' in Robinson and Shambaugh, above n 9, at 492.

[15] *Ibid.*

[16] *Ibid*, at 488–91. On Chinese legal culture, see eg, Pitman B Potter, *The Chinese Legal System: Globalization and Local Legal Culture* (London, Routledge, 2001).

[17] The term 'fragmented authoritarianism' was coined by KG Lieberthal, 'Introduction: The "Fragmented Authoritarianism" Model and Its Limitations' in KG Lieberthal and DM Lampton (eds), *Bureaucracy, Politics and Decision-making in Post-Mao China* (Berkeley, University of California Press, 1992). See also K Lieberthal and M Oksenberg, *Policy Making in China: Leaders, Structures and Processes* (Princeton, Princeton University Press, 1988); AC Mertha, *The Politics of Piracy: Intellectual Property in Contemporary China* (Ithaca and London, Cornell University Press, 2005).

and the complex relationships between central and local governments'.[18] The other lies in the great importance of personal relationships, or *guanxi*,[19] both within organisations and cutting across bureaucratic lines and central-local relations. These distinctive yet interrelated elements, so crucial in Chinese domestic policy-making, continue to influence China's relations with its neighbours.[20]

Regional economic cooperation is an important part of China's current foreign economic strategy.[21] 'Global economic multilateralism and regional economic multilateralism are "the two wheels of one cart" '.[22] Applied in the Asia-Pacific region, this entails 'seeking comprehensive cooperation and partnership relationships with all regional states'; showing that China is a responsible power by 'shoulder[ing] responsibilities . . . and demonstrat[ing] its benign intentions by exercising self-restraint and displaying willingness to be restrained'; maintaining a 'peaceful rise' (*heping jueqi*) without seeking hegemony, regardless of other powers, as long as its essential interests are not threatened; opening its domestic market as part of regional integration; and participating actively in regional multilateral institutions.[23] Zhang Yunling and Tang Shiping themselves summarise China's practice of its regional strategy as '[to] participate actively, demonstrate restraint, offer reassurance, open markets, foster interdependence, create common interests, and reduce conflict'.[24]

Focusing on China's RTAs, this chapter makes three basic arguments. First, China's RTAs fall into three main categories: economic integration agreements, RTAs in the narrow sense, and bilateral free-trade agreements. This tripartite typology provides a useful way of understanding China's RTAs; by extension, it may help to make sense of the increasingly complex array of RTAs in international trade relations today.

[18] Mertha, above n 17, at 27. On the relations between 'functional systems' (*xitong)* and ministries, see A Doak Barnett (with a contribution by Ezra Vogel), *Cadres, Bureaucracy and Political Power in Community China* (New York and London, Columbia University Press, 1967) at 6–10.

[19] See eg Pye, *The Spirit of Chinese Politics*, above n 2; LW Pye, *The Dynamics of Chinese Politics* (Cambridge, Mass, Oelgeschlager, Gunn & Hain, 1981).

[20] For example, see R Foot, 'China in the ASEAN Regional Forum: Organization Process and Domestic Models of Thought' (1998) 38(5) *Asian Survey* 425. On the conjunction of hard realism and strategic culture in Chinese foreign policy, see AI Johnston, *Cultural Realism. Strategic Culture and Grand Strategy in Chinese History* (Princeton, Princeton University Press, 1995) and his 'Cultural Realism and Strategy in Maoist China' in PJ Katzenstein (ed), *The Culture of National Security: Norms and Identity in World Politics* (New York, Columbia University Press, 1996) 216. See also M Yahuda, 'How much has China learned about interdependence?', in DSG Goodman and G Segal (eds), *China Rising: Nationalism and Interdependence* (London, Routledge, 1997) 6; and, though more dated, RA Scalapino, 'China's Multiple Identities in East Asia: China as a Regional Force' in L Dittmer and SS Kim (eds), *China's Quest for National Identity* (Ithaca, Cornell University Press, 1993) 215.

[21] See Li Guanghui, 'China—ASEAN FTA necessary and beneficial', *China Daily,* 27 October 2006, at 4. The author is a researcher with the Economic Research Institute, Ministry of Commerce, People's Republic of China. For a broadly complementary view of China's relations with the WTO, see Sun Liang and Zhang Xiangchen, 'Redefining Development, Reimagining Globalization: The WTO and China's New Economic Vision' (2007) 41(6) *Journal of World Trade* 1275. For the chronological development of all Asia-Pacific FTA projects to 2005, see CM Dent, *New Free Trade Agreements in the Asia-Pacific* (London, Palgrave Macmillan, 2006), App A, at 260–77; on their thematic content, see *ibid*, App C, at 287.

[22] Jianwei Wang, 'China's Multilateral Diplomacy in the New Millennium' in Yong Deng and Fei-Ling Wang (eds), *China Rising: Power and Motivation in Chinese Foreign Policy* (Lanham, Md, Rowman & Littlefield, 2005) at 167, quoting Zhang Baili, 'Strengthening the Economic Integration between China and East Asia' in Ling Rong (ed), *The Thinking of the New Century* (Beijing, CPC Central Party School Press, 2002) 104–05. See also Cheng-Chwee Kuik, *Multilateralism in China's ASEAN Policy*, SAIS Working Paper Series, WP/05/03, Paul H Nitze School of Advanced International Studies (SIAS), Johns Hopkins University, Washington, DC, October 2003.

[23] Zhang Yunling and Tang Shiping, above n 10 at 52–54 (the quotations are from p 52).

[24] *Ibid*, at 54; they state expressly (at 64, fn 37) that '[T[his is our own description and is not in the official Chinese diplomatic lexicon'.

Secondly, China's participation in RTAs has multiple objectives.[25] They include building 'Greater China', security,[26] the search for energy and natural resources, technology transfer, investment protection and international or regional geopolitical strategy (or a combination of these reasons), which are often, if not usually, more important than trade liberalisation alone. Only selected examples can be given here for reasons of space,[27] but they should suffice to make the essential point. Thirdly, on the whole China's RTAs today are consistent with WTO law. The chapter analyses rules of origin, safeguards and dispute settlement mechanisms in each of the three types of RTAs. Though often different from WTO law, and sometimes going beyond it, China's RTAs are substantially based on WTO law, integrate WTO law to a considerable extent and for the most part are drafted with a view to WTO-consistency.

The remainder of the chapter consists of two main sections. Section II. presents several of China's most important RTAs in outline and suggests a typology of China's RTAs. While seeking to give as comprehensive a picture as possible, it focuses in detail on the Mainland–Hong Kong Closer Economic Partnership Agreement (CEPA), the ASEAN–China Free Trade Agreement (ACFTA) and the China–Chile Free Trade Agreement (CCFTA), and to some extent on the China–Pakistan Free Trade Agreement (CPFTA). Section III. compares several aspects of these RTAs and considers them in the light of WTO law. It concentrates on three significant, often distinctive features of RTAs, namely rules of origin (ROOs), safeguards and dispute settlement mechanisms. It also briefly discusses the 'noodle bowl' phenomenon potentially posed by China's RTAs. These two sections thus are typological and comparative respectively; they are also complementary in offering different perspectives which cannot be gained simultaneously from a single analysis.[28] A brief conclusion (section IV) summarises the discussion.

[25] This is not unique to China: see eg Crawford and Fiorentino, above n 1, which identifies such factors as economic, political and security considerations, deeper economic integration in areas not available under the WTO system, defensive strategies in order to avoid being left out of regional arrangements, and the creation of regional or international alliances. Some authors maintain, however, that the main purpose of RTAs is trade liberalisation: see Elma Darlini Sulaiman (Attorney-General's Chambers, Brunei Darussalam), 'WTO and Regional Trade Liberalisation: Implications on ASEAN', p 9, available at www.aseanlawassociation.org/9GAdocs/w3_Brunei.pdf, last accessed 2 March 2010. It is likely that different countries have different reasons, and in particular that those of small countries differ considerably from those of large countries.

[26] For a list of China's bilateral security partnerships in Asia and elsewhere as of 2005, see B Gill, 'China's Evolving Regional Security Strategy' in Shambaugh, above n 12, at 253, Table 24.

[27] For further discussion, see Shambaugh, above n 12; J Wong, Zou Keyuan and Zeng Huaqun (eds), *China–ASEAN Relations: Economic and Legal Dimensions* (Singapore, World Scientific Publishing Co, 2006).

[28] I use 'complementary' in the sense that 'Two descriptions of nature are said to be complementary when they are both true but cannot both be seen in the same experiment'. This sense of complementarity is drawn from the work of the physicist Niels Bohr, as discussed by Freeman Dyson, 'Working for the Revolution [Review of Gino Segrè, *Faust in Copenhagen: A Struggle for the Soul of Physics* (New York, Viking, 2007)], *The New York Review of Books*, LIV, 16, 25 October 2007, 45 at 47.

II. China's Regional Trade Agreements in Outline

A. Introduction

China so far has notified nine RTAs (with seven different partners) to the WTO (see the complete breakdown in Table 14 below[29]), has signed another concerning only goods which has entered into force, is currently involved in negotiations on seven other RTAs and is considering negotiations on at least another seven RTAs/FTAs. In all, 'the initiative, overarching strategy and negotiating motor come from Beijing'.[30] China also participates in a number of other regional arrangements. This chapter concentrates mainly on agreements which have already entered into force. They may be divided into three groups:

a) economic integration agreements, such as the agreements with Hong Kong and Macao (see section II.B. below);
b) 'standard' RTAs, such as the regional framework agreement with the Association of South East Asian Nations (ASEAN) and agreements directly related to it (see section II.C. below); and
c) bilateral free trade agreements with individual sovereign States, namely Chile and Pakistan (see section II.D. below).[31] The last section also mentions agreements now being negotiated or being considered with other sovereign States.

Table 14 RTAs Notified by China to 10 April 2009

Name of RTA	Signatories	Date of Entry into Force	Date of WTO Notification	Related WTO Provisions	Coverage	Type of Agreement	Miscellaneous
ASEAN–China	Brunei, Cambodia, Indonesia, Lao People's Democratic Republic, Malaysia, Myanmar, Philippines, Singapore, Thailand, Vietnam, China	1 July 2003	21 Dec 2004	Enabling Clause	Framework Agreement: outline the objectives and lay down the framework of ASEAN–China relationship,	EPA: Partial Agreement (Framework Agreement)	Only set out objectives in the relationship between ASEAN and China; and set out time frames for future integration

[29] This table is based on 'Regional Trade Agreements Notified to the WTO and in Force as of 15 December 2008', http://www.wto.org/english/tratop_e/region_e/a_z_e.xls, last accessed 2 March 2010, and on 'China: List of notified RTAs in force', http://rtais.wto.org/UI/PublicSearchByMemberResult.aspx?enc=BGNDAo9i1u5NEK0fWo0Yn7u86VXlYA8JFWG+eFcVR+o, visited 10 April 2009. Table 14 shows 12 agreements with eight different partners, because each agreement is counted separately, eg there are three ASEAN–China agreements on Framework Agreement, goods and services respectively, and two agreements with APTA, one concerning Accession of China and the other being the general agreement. By contrast, the WTO website as of 10 April 2009 shows nine agreements with seven different partners, with several agreements between partners being counted as a single agreement.

[30] Sally, above n 4, at 8. For other, similar assessments, see H Gao, 'The RTA Strategy of China: A Critical Visit' in R Buckley, Wai Io Lo and L Bolle (eds), *Challenges to Multilateral Trade: The Impact of Bilateral, Preferential and Regional Agreements* (Dordrecht, Kluwer Law International, 2008) 55; Dan Wei, 'China's Regional Trade Agreements: Implications and Comments' (2009) 6(1) *Manchester Journal of International Economic Law* 81.

[31] The China–Singapore Agreement is both an FTA and an economic integration agreement. The APTA, to which China is a party, is an FTA. For reasons of space, these agreements are not discussed in detail here.

Name of RTA	Signatories	Date of Entry into Force	Date of WTO Notification	Related WTO Provisions	Coverage	Type of Agreement	Miscellaneous
China–Hong Kong	China, Hong Kong	1 Jan 2004	12 Jan 2004	Art XXIV, GATT	Most tariffs eliminated; tariff quotas, NTBs, AD, CVM barred, but safeguard measure allowed; trade-investment cooperation/ promotion/ facilitation	EPA: Economic Integration Agreement	Aim to integrate mainland and Hong Kong
China–Hong Kong	China, Hong Kong	1 Jan 2004	12 Jan 2004	Art V, GATS	Enhance market access; liberalisation for service suppliers; mutual recognition of professional qualifications; financial cooperation; cooperation on tourism	EPA: Economic Integration Agreement	Aim to integrate mainland and Hong Kong
China–Macao	China, Macao	1 Jan 2004	12 Jan 2004	Art XXIV, GATT	Most tariffs eliminated; tariff quotas, NTBs, AD, CVM barred, but safeguard measure allowed; trade-investment cooperation/ promotion/ facilitation	Economic Integration Agreement	Aim to integrate mainland and Macao
China–Macao	China, Macao	1 Jan 2004	12 Jan 2004	Art V, GATS	Enhance market access; liberalisation for service suppliers; mutual recognition of professional qualifications; financial cooperation; cooperation on tourism	EPA: Economic Integration Agreement	Aim to integrate mainland and Macao

Table 14 (*cont.*)

Name of RTA	Signatories	Date of Entry into Force	Date of WTO Notification	Related WTO Provisions	Coverage	Type of Agreement	Miscellaneous
ASEAN–China	Brunei, Cambodia, Indonesia, Lao People's Democratic Republic, Malaysia, Myanmar, Philippines, Singapore, Thailand, Vietnam, China	1 Jan 2005	n/a	Art XXIV, GATT	Tariffs reduction/ elimination; ROO; allow AD, CVM, SG, GATT general exceptions	FTA	Recognition of China's market economy status
Chile–China	Chile, China	1 Oct 2006	20 June 2007	Art XXIV, GATT	Tariffs reduction/ eliminations; ROO; allow AD, CMV, SG, GATT general exceptions; agricultural export subsidies; cooperation on science and technology, education, labour and environmental standards, SMEs, IPRs, investment, mining and industrial cooperation	EPA	
China–Pakistan	China, Pakistan	24 Nov 2006 (signed, not yet in force)	n/a	Art XXIV, GATT	Tariffs reduction/ elimination; ROO; allow AD, CVM, SG; set out SPS and TBT requirements; trade-investment cooperation/ promotion/ facilitation	FTA	

Name of RTA	Signatories	Date of Entry into Force	Date of WTO Notification	Related WTO Provisions	Coverage	Type of Agreement	Miscellaneous
ASEAN–China	Brunei, Cambodia, Indonesia, Lao People's Democratic Republic, Malaysia, Myanmar, Philippines, Singapore, Thailand, Vietnam, China	1 Jul 2007	n/a	Art V, GATS	Enhance market access and national treatment; mutual recognition of standards/ criteria/ authorisation/ licensing/ certification of service suppliers; recognition of professional qualifications; allow SG, security exceptions and GATS general exceptions;	FTA	
Asia-Pacific Trade Agreement (APTA)	Bangladesh, China, India, Republic of Korea, Lao People's Democratic Report, Sri Lanka	1 Sept 2006 (for amended Agreement)	2 Nov 1976	Enabling Clause	Goods	Partial Agreement	
Asia-Pacific Trade Agreement (APTA)– Accession of China	Bangladesh, China, India, Republic of Korea, Lao People's Democratic Report, Sri Lanka	1 Jan 2002	30 Apr 2004	Enabling Clause	Goods	Accession agreement	
China–Singapore	China, Singapore	1 Jan 2009 GATT	2 Mar 2009	Art XXIV Art V, GATS	Goods and and services	FTA and Economic Integration Agreement	

B. Economic Integration Agreements with Hong Kong and Macao and Related Agreements

1. Introduction

China has concluded agreements with Hong Kong and Macao. These agreements are economic integration agreements. Compared to standard RTAs, they are designed to promote deeper integration between mainland China and its two Special Administrative Regions (SARs—see below). Initially they aimed also to strengthen the economies of Hong Kong and Macao, then suffering from a severe downturn. Their longer-term goals include the integration of Hong Kong, Macao and also Taiwan with Mainland China to establish a 'Greater China Economic Circle'.[32]

Under the principle of 'One Country, Two Systems', Hong Kong and Macao are SARs of China.[33] As agreed by the People's Republic of China and the United Kingdom in the 1984 Sino-British Joint Declaration,[34] Hong Kong reverted to Chinese sovereignty on 1 July 1997. Similarly, Macao, following the terms of the 1987 Sino-Portuguese Declaration on the Question of Macao,[35] became a SAR of the People's Republic of China on 20 December 1999. As SARs, Hong Kong and Macao retain authority over their trade, customs and other international economic relations, and are individually Members of the WTO separate from the People's Republic of China. The Mainland and Hong Kong CEPA was signed on 29 June 2003, the Annexes[36] were signed on 29 September 2003 and the CEPA came into effect on 1 January 2004. Further details were agreed on 27 August 2004 in a Record of Consultation on Further Liberalisation.[37] The Mainland and Macao CEPA[38] was signed on 18 October 2003 and entered into force on 1 January 2004. Both were notified to the WTO on 12 January 2004 under

[32] See *China News Agency*, 5 July 2003, cited in Jianyu Wang, 'China's Regional Trade Agreements: The Law, Geopolitics and Impact on the Multilateral Trading System' (2004) 8 *Singapore Year Book of International Law* 119 at 130, fn 77. In 2003 an offer of a CEPA was extended to but refused by Taiwan: see Wang, *ibid*, at 130.

[33] The first part of this paragraph is based on F Snyder, *The European Union and China, 1949–2008: Basic Documents and Commentary* (Oxford, Hart Publishing, 2009), ch 8.

[34] Joint Declaration of the United Kingdom of Great Britain and Northern Ireland and the Government of the People's Republic of China on the Question of Hong Kong, signed in Beijing on 19 December 1984, available at http://www.hkbu.edu.hk/~pchksar/JD/jd-full1.htm, visited 24 November 2007.

[35] Joint Declaration of the Government of the People's Republic of China and the Government of the Republic of Portugal on the Question of Macao, signed in Beijing on 13 April 1987, available at http://www.imprensa.Macau.gov.mo/bo/i/88/23/dc/en/, last accessed 2 March 2010.

[36] Annex 1: Arrangements for Implementation of Zero Tariff for Trade in Goods, including Table 1 List of Hong Kong Origin Products for Implementation of Zero Import Tariff by the Mainland; Annex 2: Rules of Origin for Trade in goods, including Table 1: Schedule on Rules of Origin for Hong Kong Goods Benefitting from Tariff Preference for Trade in Goods; Annex 3: Procedures for the Issuing and Verifiction of Certificates of Origin, including Form 1: Certificate of Hong Kong Origin (CEPA); Annex 4: Specific Commitments on Liberalisation of Trade in Services, including Table 1: The Mainland's Specific Commitments on Liberalisation of Trade in Services for Hong Kong, and Table 2: Hong Kong's Specific Commitments on Liberalisation of Trade in Services for the Mainland; Annex 5: Definition of 'Service Supplier' and Related Requirements; and Annex 6: Trade and Investment Facilitation.

[37] Record of Consultations on Further Liberalisation under the Mainland–Hong Kong Closer Economic Partnership Arrangement, available at http://www.ipd.gov.hk/eng/news/news/Record_of_Consultations_on_Further_Liberalization.pdf, last accessed 2 March 2010.

[38] In Portuguese, Acordo de Estreitamento das Relações Económicas e Comerciais entre o Continente Chinês e Macau.

Article XXIV GATT for goods and Article V GATS for services.[39] The following paragraphs discuss first the China–Hong Kong CEPA and then briefly the China–Macao CEPA.

2. *Mainland–Hong Kong CEPA*

The Mainland–Hong Kong CEPA covers trade in goods, trade in services, and trade and investment facilitation.[40] It aims to promote joint economic prosperity and to facilitate further development of economic links between the two regions and other countries and regions.[41] Its objectives are to strengthen trade and investment cooperation and promote joint development by progressively reducing or eliminating tariffs and non-tariff barriers (NTBs) on substantially all trade between Mainland China and Hong Kong, progressively achieving liberalisation of services trade through the reduction or elimination of substantially all discriminatory measures and promoting trade and investment facilitation.[42] The basic principles include abiding by the 'One Country, Two Systems' principle and being consistent with rules of the WTO.[43] The CEPA also recognises China as a market economy, by providing that section 15 (anti-dumping) and section 16 (countervailing measures) of China's WTO Protocol and paragraph 242 (Textiles Specific Safeguard Clause (TSSC)) of the Working Party Report on China's Accession do not apply to trade between the Mainland and Hong Kong.[44] The CEPA establishes a Joint Steering Committee composed of senior representatives or officials designated by the two sides, together with Liaison Offices and if necessary working groups.[45]

Concerning trade in goods, Hong Kong is to continue to apply zero tariffs to goods of Mainland origin. The Mainland is to apply zero tariffs to certain listed Hong Kong goods as from 1 January 2004[46] and to all other Hong Kong goods as from 1 January

[39] At least as of 2005, it was not clear, however, whether CEPA was to be classified in the Chinese legal system as an 'international agreement', as a 'regional agreement within the same country', or as another type of legal act: see Guiguo Wang, *The Law of the WTO: China and the Future of Free Trade* (Hong Kong, Sweet & Maxwell Asia, 2005) 170–71.

[40] For texts, see the official Hong Kong website for the CEPA at http://www.tid.gov.hk, visited 3 March 2008. For an early survey from Hong Kong perspectives, see E Terry (ed), *Pearl River Super Zone: Tapping into the World's Fastest Growing Economy* [by the Staff and Contributors to the *South China Morning* Post] (Hong Kong, SCMP Book Publishing, 2003). For an evaluation from the standpoint of foreign companies, focusing mainly on ROOs for goods and services, see S Thomas, N Hyacinthe and M Sadowsky, 'Accord de libre-échange entre la Chine et Hong Kong: Quelles perspectives pour les entreprises de pays tiers', *Revue de droit des affaires internationales*, 1, 2005, 77–85.

[41] Mainland–Hong Kong CEPA, Preamble.

[42] *Ibid*, Art.

[43] *Ibid*, Art 2.

[44] *Ibid*, Art 4, which states, *inter alia*, that 'The two sides recognise that through over 20 years of reform and opening up, the market economy system of the Mainland has been continuously improving, and the mode of production and operation of Mainland enterprises is in line with the requirements of a market economy . . .'

[45] *Ibid*, Art 19(1), (2).

[46] *Ibid*, Art 5(1). See Annex 1, Arrangements for Implementation of Zero Tariff on Goods, and Table 1, List of Hong Kong Origin Products for Implementation of Zero Import Tariff by the Mainland. The Annexes are an integral part of the CEPA: *ibid*, Art 21.

2006 at the latest.[47] Neither side is to apply NTBs inconsistent with the WTO to goods imported and originated from the other side.[48] Neither is to apply anti-dumping measures or countervailing measures to goods from the other.[49] Rules of origin and safeguard measures for goods are discussed in Section III. later.

Concerning trade in services, the Mainland–Hong Kong CEPA provides for the progressive reduction or elimination of restrictive measures against services and service suppliers.[50] Further liberalisation may be achieved through consultation.[51] The CEPA includes specific rules of origin for services. Services suppliers of other WTO Members that are juridical persons and established under the laws of either the Mainland or Hong Kong are entitled to preferential treatment granted by the other side under the CEPA, as long as they engage in 'substantive business operations' in the former side.[52] The GATS, notably Article V(6), does not clearly define 'substantive business operations'. Annex V of the CEPA requires, however, that '[t]he nature and scope of the services provided by a Hong Kong service supplier in Hong Kong should encompass the nature and scope of the services it intends to provide in the Mainland.'[53] The supplier must have been registered in Hong Kong and engaged in substantive business operations for three years or more; the period is five years for construction and engineering services, banking and other financial services, insurance and related services, and air transport services.[54] These restrictive rules of origin are consistent with Hoekman and Newfarmer's hypothesis that 'a country with "regionally dominant but non-globally competitive service providers" would be inclined to adopt restrictive rules of origin for services'.[55] These rules on 'substantive business operations', it has been argued, are not fully compatible with Article V(6) GATS.[56]

The CEPA grants Hong Kong service providers preferential treatment compared to that granted to other WTO Members under China's WTO timetable, or treatment going beyond China's WTO obligations.[57] Measures are adopted to strengthen cooperation in banking, securities and insurance; this includes relocation of the international treasury and foreign exchange trading centres of Mainland banks to Hong Kong, the development of their activities through acquisitions, and the 'the full utilisation of financial intermediaries in Hong Kong during the process of reform, restructuring and development of the financial sector in the Mainland'.[58] Mainland tourists from Guangdong

[47] *Ibid*, Art 5(2). On implementation, see Annex 1, Arrangements for Implementation of Zero Tariff on Goods. Such measures are extremely important in view of the high level of IIT between Mainland China and Hong Kong: a useful, though rather dated, indication is Xiaoling Hu and Yue Ma, 'International Intra-Industry Trade of China', *Review of World Economics*, 135, 1, March 1999, 82–101.

[48] Mainland–Hong Kong CEPA, Art 6(1).

[49] *Ibid*, Arts 7 (anti-dumping) and 8 (countervailing measures).

[50] *Ibid*, Art 11. The timetable is given in Annex 4, Specific Commitments on Liberalisation of Trade in Services.

[51] *Ibid*, Art 11(2).

[52] *Ibid*, Art 12(2). Qualifying business operations are stipulated in Annex 5, Definition of 'Service Supplier' and Related Requirements.

[53] *Ibid*, Annex 5, Art 3.1.2(1).

[54] *Ibid*, Annex 5, Art 3.1.2(2).

[55] The quotation is from Adrian Emch, 'Services Regionalism in the WTO: China's Trade Agreements with Hong Kong and Macao in the Light of Article V(6) GATS' (2006) 33(4) *Legal Issues of European Integration* 351 at 377, fn 99, citing B Hoekman and R Newfarmer, 'Preferential Trade Agreements, Investment Disciplines and Investment Flows' (2005) 39(5) *Journal of World Trade* 949 at 967.

[56] Emch, above n 57.

[57] For examples, see Jianyu Wang, above n 32.

[58] Mainland–Hong Kong CEPA, Art 13 (the quotation is from Art 13(3)).

Province are allowed to visit Hong Kong individually,[59] and other measures are designed to strengthen cooperation in tourism.[60] Mutual recognition of professional qualifications is encouraged.[61] The Agreement also provides for trade and investment facilitation, including customs clearance facilitation, commodity inspection and quarantine, food safety and quality and standardisation, electronic business, transparency in laws and regulation, and other matters.[62]

3. *Mainland–Macao CEPA*

The Mainland–Macao CEPA is virtually the same as the Mainland–Hong Kong CEPA, though narrower in coverage and with minor textual differences not relevant here.[63] The parties have supplemented the basic Mainland China–Macao CEPA each year to liberalise further trade in goods and services, most recently on 11 May 2009.[64]

4. *Implications*

In sponsoring the development of the two CEPAs, China has promoted both labour-intensive production and high-tech, knowledge-intensive industries, leading to a distinctive regional economy composed of extremely diverse forms of transnational economic linkages.[65] One example is the link between FDI and foreign trade in the Pearl River Delta, embracing Hong Kong, Macao and the neighbouring Mainland Chinese province of Guangzhou.[66] Building on the CEPA,[67] the Pan–Pearl River

[59] *Ibid*, Art 14(1).
[60] *Ibid*, Art 14(2), (3).
[61] *Ibid*, Art 15(1).
[62] *Ibid*, Art 17 and Annex 6, Trade and Investment Facilitation.
[63] The Mainland–Macao CEPA was signed in the Chinese language, and only the Chinese text is authentic. The full text used here is a courtesy translation, which can be found at the website of Macao Economic Services at http://www.economia.gov.mo/, visited 5 March 2008. There are minor differences concerning financial cooperation (Art 13) and areas of cooperation (Art 17). A summary of the Mainland–Macao CEPA may be found at http://www.imprensa.macau.gov.mo/edicoes/en/dse/cepa/, last accessed 2 March 2010.
[64] See the following English courtesy translations: Supplement to CEPA (signed 29 October 2004) at http://www.economia.gov.mo/web/DSE/public?_nfpb=true&_pageLabel=Pg_CEPA_CEPA_II&locale=en_US; Supplement II to CEPA (signed 21 October 2005) at http://www.economia.gov.mo/web/DSE/public?_nfpb=true&_pageLabel=Pg_CEPA_CEPA_III&locale=en_US; Supplement III to CEPA (signed 26 June 2006) at http://www.economia.gov.mo/web/DSE/public?_nfpb=true&_pageLabel=Pg_CEPA_CEPA_IV&locale=en_US; http://www.economia.gov.mo/web/DSE/public?_nfpb=true&_pageLabel=Pg_EETR_CEPA_S&locale=en_US, Supplement IV to CEPA (signed 2 July 2007) at http://www.economia.gov.mo/web/DSE/public?_nfpb=true&_pageLabel=Ln_ET_AP&locale=en_US#, all accessed 5 March 2008. Supplement V to CEPA (signed 30 July 2008) at http://www.economia.gov.mo/web/DSE/public?_nfpb=true&_pageLabel=Pg_CEPA_Index&locale=en_US, accessed 3 August 2009; Supplement VI to CEPA (signed 11 May 2009) at http://www.economia.gov.mo/web/DSE/public?_nfpb=true&_pageLabel=Pg_CEPA_Index&locale=en_US, accessed 3 August 2009. On Supplement VI, see also Wen Hui, 'Macao granted better access to Chinese mainland' (2009) 21 *China Economic News* 6–7.
[65] R Ash, 'China's Regional Economies and the Asian Region: Building Interdependent Linkages' in Shambaugh, above n 10, at 97–98.
[66] For detailed statistics on the origins of regional FDI in China in 2002, see *ibid*, at 107, Table 15.
[67] In other words, on use of the two CEPAs by manufacturing firms and service providers in Hong Kong and Macao as well as Mainland China. For firm-level priorities concerning law and public policy, see Chyau

Delta (PPRD) Regional Cooperation Framework Agreement was signed in Guangzhou on 3 June 2004 by Hong Kong, Macao and neighbouring provinces in Mainland China. It involves '9+2' members, namely, Hong Kong, Macao and nine Chinese provinces: Guangdong, Fujian, Jiangxi, Hunan, Guangxi, Hainan, Sichuan, Guizhou and Yunnan. This area accounts for 20 per cent of Chinese territory, one-third of China's population and more than 35 per cent of China's economic output.[68] The Agreement is based on voluntary participation, market orientation, openness and fairness, complementarities and joint prosperity. Cooperation is projected in 10 areas, including infrastructure, enterprise and investment, information development, tourism, commerce and trade, agriculture, labour, science, education and culture, environmental protection, and health and disease prevention.[69] So far, the parties have held four PPRD Regional Cooperation Forums. At the second session, held in Chengdu, Sichuan Province, the intellectual property rights and administration authorities of the governments of 9+2 signed the Pan–PRD Intellectual Property Cooperation Agreement.[70] Its basic principles included

> administration by law: All parties shall adhere to the principles of "one country, two systems"and "administration by law", and strive to create an ordered and structured environment for intellectual property protection.[71]

They agreed on various forms of cooperation, including economic integration and intellectual property protection:

> The nine provinces/regions shall cooperate to remove barriers of local protectionism; to enhance communication and coordination among authorities enforcing intellectual property protection within the region; to establish a uniform, effective and regulated system in intellectual property protection; and where appropriate, to step up communication and cooperation with the authorities of the SARs enforcing intellectual property protection so as to improve the overall protection of intellectual property within the region . . .[72]

The Agreement does not mention the WTO or the TRIPS Agreement.

Tuan and L Fung-Yee Ng, 'FDI and Industrial Restructuring in Post-WTO Greater PRD: Implications on Regional Growth in China' (2004) 27(10) *The World Economy* 1609, who (at 1616) found that manufacturing firms accorded more importance to industrial policy for selective industries, whereas services firms emphasised government policies to increase competition.

[68] See 'Overview of Pan–Pearl River Delta Regional Cooperation', available at the website of the Macao Special Administrative Region Economic Services, http://www.economia.gov.mo/web/DSE/public?_nfpb=true&_pageLabel=Pg_EETR_9_2_S&locale=en_US, last accessed 2 March 2010. See also Yue-man Yeung, 'The Pan–PRD and ASEAN–China FTA as Agents of Regional Integration in Pacific Asia', keynote address, Forum on *A Tale of Two Regions: China's Pan–PRD and ASEAN*, Gold Coast Hotel, Hong Kong, 4 November 2005, available at http://www.hkpri.org.hk/passagesPDF/othersSpeech/2005/Prof.%20Yeung's%20Speech.pdf, visited 20 March 2008. Yeung concludes (at 10) that currently Guangdong and Hong Kong are 'presiding' over the conjunction of Pan–PRD of 9+1 and ASEAN–China FTA of 10+1.

[69] See 'Summary of the Pan–Pearl River Delta Regional Cooperation Framework Agreement', available at the website of the Macao Special Administrative Region Economic Services, http://www.economia.gov.mo/web/DSE/public?_nfpb=true&_pageLabel=Pg_EETR_9_2_T&locale=en_US, visited 5 March 2008.

[70] Pan–PRD Intellectual Property Cooperation Agreement (Courtesy Translation), available on the website of the Hong Kong Government Intellectual Property Department at http://www.ipd.gov.hk/eng/pub_press/press_releases/agreement_eng.pdf last accessed 2 March 2010

[71] *Ibid*, Art 2(4).

[72] *Ibid*, Art 4(5).

C. Standard RTAs: ASEAN–China Framework Agreement and Related Agreements

1. Introduction

Between 1991 and 2001 world trade increased by 177 per cent, while East Asian intra-regional trade increased by 304 per cent, due mainly to the rise of China.[73] Imports and FDI from other Asian countries flowed into China, which became a major importer of intermediate goods from the Asian region and a major exporter of finished products to the world, especially the USA and the European Union.[74] This new 'triangular trade pattern'[75] resulted in the diversion of FDI to China from other countries, such as the ASEAN Member States. However, it also led to outward investment from China and, under Jiang Zemin's 'going abroad' (*zou chuqu*) strategy, to processing abroad, for example in ASEAN countries, with materials imported from China (*dailiao jiagong*).[76] Approximately 60 per cent of FDI in China between 1991 and 2001 came from other Asian countries, as compared to about 10 per cent from each of the USA, EU and Japan.[77] The resulting economic transformation had profound implications for China's domestic economy and its participation in the East Asian region. In fact, Robert Ash hypothesises that 'regional trade patterns in China reflect the emergence of transnational economic axes', and they also engage China in the broader international economy.[78] Based largely on international production networks, this is what Baldwin calls 'Factory Asia'.[79]

Regional trade agreements have structured and supported these economic changes, just as economic changes in China and its region have underpinned and legitimated RTAs. These are not economic integration agreements under the umbrella of 'One Country, Two Systems', but rather RTAs in the strict sense, focused on regional cooperation between neighbouring sovereign States and orientated towards trade and economic matters, among others. They include integration across land borders as well as overseas.

[73] H Ohashi, 'China's Regional Trade and Investment Profile' in Shambaugh, above n 10, at 72.

[74] To the extent that 'the major reason why China manages to record a [trade] surplus with the EU is because it is used as a processing platform by a number of (primarily foreign, Asian) firms. In other words, the EU trade deficit is actually a deficit vis-à-vis the whole of East Asia rather than vis-à-vis China': B Andreosso-O'Callaghan and F Nicolas, 'Complementarity and Rivalry in EU–China Economic Relations in the Twenty-first Century' (2007) 12 *European Foreign Affairs Review* 13 at 18.

[75] See G Gaulier, F Lemoine and D Ünal-Kesenci, *China's Integration into East Asia: Production Sharing, FDI & High-Tech Trade*, Centre d'Etudes Prospectives et d'Informations Internationales, Working Paper No 2005–09, June 2005, available at http://www.cepii.fr/anglaisgraph/workpap/pdf/2005/wp05-09.pdf, last accessed 22 March 2010.

[76] Ohashi, above n 73, at 76, 79–89.

[77] Andreosso-O'Callaghan and Nicolas, above n 74, at 24.

[78] Ash, above n 65, at 99.

[79] R Baldwin, *Managing the Noodle Bowl: The Fragility of East Asian Regionalism*, Centre for Economic Policy Research, Discussion Paper Series, No 5561, March 2006, available at www.cepr.org/pubs/dps/DP5561.asp, visited 12 March 2008. On the role of production networks in East Asian regional integration, see HWC Yeung, *Transnational Corporations and Business Networks: Hong Kong Firms in the ASEAN Region* (London, Routledge, 1998); and M Haddad, *Trade Integration in East Asia: The Role of China and Production Networks*, World Bank Policy Research Working Paper No 4160, 1 March 2007, available at http://papers.ssrn.com/sol3/papers.cfm?abstract_id=969237, visited 20 March 2008; Gaulier, *et al*, above n 75.

China has concluded numerous RTAs and other regional agreements. First, China is a party to the Central Asian Regional Economic Cooperation (CAREC) Programme. Initiated in 1997, CAREC focuses on transport, energy, trade policy and trade facilitation among China, Afghanistan, Azerbaijan, Kazakhstan, the Kyrgyz Republic, Mongolia, Tajikistan and Uzbekistan.[80] Secondly, China is a founder member of the Shanghai Cooperation Organisation (SCO), an intergovernmental organisation established on 15 June 2001 and comprising China, the Republic of Kazakhstan, the Kyrgyz Republic, the Russian Federation, the Republic of Tajikistan and the Republic of Uzbekistan. Though its first objective is mutual security, the SCO also includes economic and trade cooperation[81]; it thus is an example of 'functionalism upside down', in which successful cooperation concerning security 'spilled over' to other areas.[82] Thirdly, China is a party to The Strategic Framework for Action on Trade Facilitation and Investment in the Greater Mekong Sub-Region (GMS). The other countries involved in the GMS scheme are Cambodia, the Lao People's Democratic Republic (Lao PDR), Myanmar, Thailand and Vietnam.[83] Focused mainly on infrastructure, GMS has been described not as an FTA but rather 'a regional integration initiative mainly driven by market integration as opposed to formal integration'.[84] Fourthly, China, together with Bangladesh, India and Myanmar, signed on 17 August 1999 the Kunming Initiative, a Track II or non-governmental sub-regional organisation. Pioneered by the Chinese province of Yunnan, it appeals, at least rhetorically, to a pre-colonial Asian reality in which the area was 'a few centuries ago much more integrated culturally, politically, and economically' than is the case today.[85] Fifthly, China

[80] See Central Asian Regional Economic Cooperation—CAREC, on the website of the Asian Development Bank at http://www.adb.org/Carec/, visited 17 March 2008; Ministry of Commerce of the People's Republic of China, Department of International Trade and Economic Affairs [in Chinese], http:/gjx.mofcom.gov.cn/aarticle/af/ak/200610/20061003499223.html, visited 14 March 2008. For a brief overview of China's energy policy in the region, see M Jego, 'Menacé par la Chine, Gazprom veut rester maître du gaz en Asia centrale', *Le Monde*, 21 March 2008, at 14.

[81] See the SCO website at http://www.sectsco.org/EN/show.asp?id=69, last accessed 2 March 2010. For the Declaration on the Establishment of the Shanghai Cooperation Organisation, see http://www.sectsco.org/html/00088.html, visited 19 March 2008. A Framework Agreement on economic cooperation was signed on 23 September 2003, and a follow-up plan was signed on 23 September 2004. See http://www.sectsco.org/html/00030.html, visited 19 March 2008. Mongolia, Pakistan, India and Iran have observer status. India and Pakistan are potential candidates for membership, according to Wikipedia at http://en.wikipedia.org/wiki/Shanghai_Cooperation_Organization, visited 19 March 2006. For an overview of EU, Chinese and Indian policies in the region, see E Kavalski, 'Partnership or Rivalry between the European Union, China and India in Central Asia: The Normative Power of Regional Actors with Global Aspirations', in F Snyder (ed), *Europe, India and China: Strategic Partners in a Changing World* (Brussels, –Bruylant, 2009).

[82] Jianwei Wang, above n 22, at 179.

[83] See 'Strategic Framework for Action on Trade Facilitation and Investment in the Greater Mekong Sub-Region', available on the Mofcom website at http://tradeinservices.mofcom.gov.cn/en/b/2007-10-10/6577.shtml, visited 17 March 2008.

[84] S Inama, 'The Association of South East Asian Nations–People's Republic of China Free Trade Area: Negotiating Beyond Eternity With Little Trade Liberalization?' (2005) 39(3) *Journal of World Trade* 559 at 560. For a recent overview, see M Than, 'China and CLMV Countries: Relations in the Context of the Mekong Sub-region' in Saw Swee-Hock (ed), *ASEAN–China Economic Relations* (Singapore, Institute of Southeast Asian Studies Publishing, 2007) 269.

[85] See J Levesque, 'The Kunming Initiative: Going Beyond Governmental Reluctance', Article no 2473, 14 January 2008, available on the website of the Institute of Peace and Conflict Studies (IPCS), New Delhi, at http://ipcs.org/article/china/the-kunming-initiative-going-beyond-governmental-reluctance-2473.html last accessed 2 March 2010. For official documents, see Online Burma/Myanmar Library, available at http://www.burmalibrary.org/show.php?cat=2144, visited 19 March 2008. See also PV Indiresan, 'The Kunming Initiative', *Frontline*, 17, 7, 1–14 April 2000, pp 98–102, available at http://www.thehindu.com/fline/fl1707/17070980.htm, visited 19 March 2008; Ramtanu Maitra, 'Prospects Brighten for Kunming

participates in the Tumen River Area Development Programme (TADP) or Greater Tumen Initiative (GTI), involving part of Northern China. In addition to China, it comprises the Democratic People's Republic of Korea (DPRK), Mongolia, the Republic of Korea and the Russian Federation. It focuses on energy, environment, investment, transport and tourism.[86] All these agreements exemplify a pattern of RTAs as a device for increasing integration across land borders.

Sixthly, China participates in the ASEAN Regional Forum (ARF), which was established in Bangkok on 25 July 1994 and is concerned mainly with political and security matters.[87] Seventhly, together with Japan, South Korea and the ASEAN Member States, China is a member of ASEAN + 3 (APT), which was crystallised by the 1997–98 Asian financial crisis, played an important role in resolving the SARS crisis in 2003, and provides for cooperation on trade, foreign affairs, investment and finance.[88] Eighthly, as already mentioned, China is a party to the Asia Pacific Trade Agreement (APTA). Also known as the Bangkok Agreement, the APTA originally entered into force on 17 June 1976. China signed the APTA on 12 April 2001, the APTA including China entered into force on 1 January 2002 and it was notified to the WTO on 30 April 2004. Current signatories, in addition to China, are Bangladesh, India, the Republic of Korea, Lao PDR and Sri Lanka.[89]

Ninthly, among other regional arrangements, China has, since 12–14 November 1991, been a member country in Asia–Pacific Economic Cooperation (APEC).[90] Tenthly, it also plays an important role in the Asia–Europe Meeting (ASEM), consisting of ASEAN plus Three (China, Japan, Korea) and the European Union Member States.[91] Some of these regional arrangements are less directly concerned with trade.

Lastly, China is involved in other potentially overlapping arrangements. For example, the EU and China are negotiating a Partnership and Cooperation Agreement to replace the outdated 1985 EEC–China Trade and Cooperation Agreement.[92] At the

Initiative', *Asia Times*, 12 February 2003, available at http://www.atimes.com/atimes/South_Asia/EB12Df04. html, visited 19 March 2008.

[86] See the Greater Tumen Initiative website at http://www.tumenprogramme.org/index.php?id=1, visited 19 March 2008. On energy, see also S Chen, 'Plan for energy hub in Inner Mongolia', *South China Morning Post*, 3 January 2008, at A4.

[87] Other participants are Australia, Bangladesh, Brunei Darussalam, Cambodia, Canada, European Union, India, Indonesia, Japan, Democratic Peoples' Republic of Korea, Republic of Korea, Laos, Malaysia, Myanmar, Mongolia, New Zealand, Pakistan, Papua New Guinea, Philippines, Russian Federation, Singapore, Thailand, Timor Leste, United States, Vietnam. See the Asian Regional Forum website, at http://www.aseanregionalforum.org/AboutUs/tabid/57/Default.aspx, visited 19 March 2008.

[88] See R Stubbs, 'ASEAN plus Three: Emerging East Asian Regionalism?' (2002) 42(3) *Asian Survey* 440. On ASEAN+3 and SARS, see Lai Hongyi, 'Regional Cooperation in Epidemic Prevention: China and ASEAN' in Wong *et al*, above n 27, at 59. See generally the website of the US–ASEAN Business Council, at http://www.us-asean.org/ASEANOverview/asean+3.asp, visited 15 April 2008.

[89] See the WTO website www.wto.org for further details. For reasons of space, the APTA is not discussed further here.

[90] See the APEC website, http://www.apec.org/, visited 12 March 2008.

[91] See eg HE Wen Jiabao, Premier of the State Council of the People's Republic of China, 'Strengthening Partnership Through Increased Dialogue and Cooperation', Speech at the Fifth Asia–Europe Meeting, Hanoi, 8 October 2004; and HE Wen Jiabao, Premier of the State Council of the People's Republic of China, 'Strengthening ASEM Economic and Financial Cooperation to Promote Common Development', Speech at the Opening Ceremony of the Sixth ASEM Finance Ministers Meeting, 26 June 2005; both reprinted in Snyder, above n 33.

[92] See A Sautenet, 'The Current Status and Prospects of the "Strategic Partnership" between the EU and China: Towards the Conclusion of a Partnership and Cooperation Agreement' (2007) 13(6) *European Law Journal* 699; Zeng Lingliang, 'A Preliminary Perspective on Negotiations for an EU–China PCA: A New Bottle Carrying Old Wine, or New Wine in Old Bottles, or Both?' (2008) 14(5) *European Law Journal* 121.

same time, alongside the Trans-regional EU–ASEAN Trade Initiative (TREATI), its regional agreement on regulatory cooperation with ASEAN,[93] the European Union (EU) is currently negotiating an FTA with ASEAN.[94] How these agreements will be related remains to be seen.

2. *ASEAN–China FTA*

The most ambitious of China's multilateral RTAs from the standpoint of economic and trade relations is the ASEAN–China FTA (ACFTA).[95] The remainder of this section focuses on the ACFTA.

A Framework Agreement on Comprehensive Economic Cooperation between the Association of South East Asian Nations and China was signed in Phnom Penh, Cambodia, on 5 November 2002.[96] It entered into force on 1 July 2003 and was notified to the WTO under the Enabling Clause on 21 December 2004. Its signatories, in addition to China, were the ASEAN Member States: Brunei, Cambodia, Indonesia, Lao PDR, Malaysia, Myanmar, Philippines, Singapore, Thailand and Vietnam. The Framework Agreement set out the objectives, the normative and economic framework, and the timetable for future cooperation among the parties. It was the first RTA signed by China outside Greater China (the Mainland, Hong Kong, Macao, Taiwan) and also the first RTA signed by all Members of ASEAN.[97] The parties agreed to establish an ACFTA for ASEAN 6[98] and China by 2010, and for the newer ASEAN Member States[99] and China by 2015.

The ACFTA is expected to have a major impact on the Asia–Pacific region and the international trading system generally. According to the report of the experts' group which suggested its creation:

[93] See the website of the European Commission, Directorate-General for Trade, at http://ec.europa.eu/trade/issues/bilateral/regions/asem/index_en.htm, visited 18 March 2008. TREATI is concerned mainly with food safety and product standards, but includes trade facilitation as a horizontal issue.

[94] See 'Report of the ASEAN–EU Vision Group: Transregional Partnership for Shared and Sustainable Prosperity', Ha Noi, Vietnam, 10 May 2006, available at http://trade.ec.europa.eu/doclib/docs/2006/may/tradoc_128860.pdf, visited 21 March 2008. For a comparison of ASEAN and the EU, see L Henry, 'The ASEAN Way and Community Integration: Two Different Models of Regionalism' (2007) 13(6) *European Law Journal* 857.

[95] In order to avoid confusion with the Central American Free Trade Agreement (CAFTA), this chapter refers to the ASEAN–China Free Trade Agreement by the generally accepted abbreviation ACFTA, instead of the abbreviation CAFTA (China–ASEAN Free Trade Agreement) used by some authors.

[96] On the negotiations, see Lu Bo, 'ASEAN–China Free Trade Agreement: Negotiation, Implementation and Prospect', in Saw Swee-Hock, above n 84, at 86. For an overview of the general legal framework of ASEAN–China relations, see Zeng Lingliang, 'ASEAN–China Relations: An International Law Perspective' in Wong *et al*, above n 27, at 33, who, prior to the ASEAN–China Agreement on Goods and the Agreement on Dispute Settlement Mechanism (see below), argued (at 51) that 'at present, the overall legal regulation of China–ASEAN relations has not reached the stage of a legal regime'. For a case study of ACFTA from the standpoint of political economy, see Dent, above n 21, at 159–64.

[97] Jianyu Wang, above n 32, at 125; Dent, above n 21, at 159. In another article Professor Wang argued that, from the standpoint of international law, the ACFTA was not an agreement between ASEAN and China, since ASEAN does not have international legal personality, but rather a group of bilateral agreements between China and each of the 10 ASEAN Member States: see Jianyu Wang, 'The International Legal Personality of ASEAN and the Legal Nature of the China–ASEAN FTA', in Wong *et al*, above n 27, 111. The ASEAN Charter, adopted on 20 November 2007, provided in its Article 3 that ASEAN has legal personality. The Charter is available at http://www.aseansec.org/21069.pdf, last accessed 17 March 2010.

[98] Brunei Darusssalam, Indonesia, Malaysia, Philippines, Singapore and Thailand.

[99] Cambodia, Lao PDR, Myanmar and Vietnam.

> [T]he establishment of a FTA between ASEAN and China will create an economic region with 1.7 billion consumers, a regional GDP of about US $2 trillion and total trade estimated at US $1.23 trillion . . . [T]he removal of trade barriers between ASEAN and China will lower costs, increase intra-regional trade and increase economic efficiency. The establishment of an ASEAN–China FTA will create a sense of community between ASEAN Members and China. It will provide another important mechanism for supporting economic stability in East Asia and allow both ASEAN and China to have a large voice in international affairs on issues of common interest.[100]

However, the possibility of increased trade does not necessarily mean greater economic integration. China and ASEAN countries currently export similar products,[101] so they may compete in both domestic ASEAN and foreign markets in the short run, though not perhaps in the long run.[102] In addition, some economists argue that the ACFTA, like previous similar South East Asian schemes, are unlikely to achieve substantial trade liberalisation, because its rules do not provide for effective implementation of commitments.[103] Nonetheless, between mid-2005 and mid-2006, China's imports from ASEAN increased by 20.4 per cent, its exports to ASEAN increased by 23.4 per cent, and the increase in trade volume for products on which either party has a comparative advance ranged between 46.6 per cent (China's import of rubber from ASEAN) and 60.2 per cent (China's export of knitted clothes to ASEAN).[104] For ASEAN, a close link with China is designed to ensure continued economic dynamism,[105] and many economists consider that the ACFTA is based on 'a naturally integrated economy'[106] and will bring economic benefits to both ASEAN and China.[107]

[100] ASEAN–China Experts Group on Economic Cooperation, 'Forging Closer ASEAN–China Economic Relations in the Twenty-first Century', at 2 (point 11), available on the ASEAN Secretariat website at http://www.aseansec.org/asean_chi.pdf, visited 10 March 2008.

[101] For detailed analysis, see JL Tongzon, 'ASEAN–China Free Trade Area: A Bane or Boon for ASEAN Countries' (2995) 28(2) *The World Economy* 191.

[102] On the short-run/long-run distinction, see DR Holst and J Weiss, 'ASEAN and China: Export Rivals or Partners in Regional Growth' (2006) 27(8) *The World Economy* 1255. John Wong states that China and ASEAN (minus Singapore) are currently 'more competitive than complementary', even though about half of China's exports go to the Asia–Pacific region, which in turn provides about 75% of China's FDI: see J Wong, 'China–ASEAN Relations: An Economic Perspective', in Wong *et al*, above n 29, 17 at 28. See also Zhang Haibing, 'China and Southeast Asia Cooperation: New Developments and Challenges', in J Wong and Lai Hongyi (eds), *China into the Hu-Wen Era: Policy Initiatives and Challenges* (Singapore, World Scientific Publishing Company, 2006) 541, esp 553; and Chen Wen, 'ASEAN–China Trade Relations: Origins, Progress and Prospect' in Saw Swee-Hock, above n 84, 67.

[103] See Inama, above n 84, esp at 561–62, who also (at 567) emphasises that the real deadline for tariff reductions for sensitive goods is 2018. In fact, Dee argues that comprehensive regulatory reform is more important than RTAs in achieving real income gains in the region: see P Dee, 'East Asian Economic Integration and its Impact on Future Growth' (2007) 30(3) *The World Economy* 405. Sally argued in 2006 that the Asian FTAs are too weak to foster regional economic integration and need more focus on the WTO: Sally, above n 4.

[104] S Ning and Ding Liang, 'China's Free Trade Agreement (FTA) Policy and its Recent Developments', *King & Wood China Bulletin 2006*, Special Issue, October 2006, 1 at 2, available at http://www.kingandwood.com/UploadFiles/China%20Bulletin%202006%20Special%20Issue328.pdf, last visited 14 March 2008. (This document is no longer available on the Internet).

[105] See Wong, above n 102.

[106] Kawai argues that foreign trade and FDI have created a 'naturally integrated economy' in the region: M Kawai, 'East Asian Economic Regionalism: Progress and Challenges' (2005) 16(1) *Journal of Asian Economics—International Journal* 29.

[107] See, eg, Qiu *et al* who argue that, overall, ACFTA will have positive effects for both ASEAN member countries and for China: Huanguang Qiu, Jun Yang, Jikun Huang and Ruijian Chen, 'Impact of China–ASEAN Free Trade Area on China's International Agricultural Trade and its Regional Development' (2007) 15(4) *China & The World Economy* 77.

The Preamble of the ACFTA Framework Agreement reaffirmed the rights, obligations and undertakings of the parties under the WTO and other agreements, and recognised the 'catalytic role that regional trade agreements can contribute towards accelerating regional and global liberalisation and as building blocks in the framework of the multilateral trading system'.[108] The general objectives of the Framework Agreement were to:

(a) strengthen and enhance economic, trade and investment cooperation between the parties;
(b) progressively liberalise and promote trade in goods and services as well as create a transparent, liberal and facilitative investment regime;
(c) explore new areas and develop appropriate measures for closer economic cooperation between the parties; and
(d) facilitate the more effective economic integration of the newer ASEAN member States and bridge the development gap among the parties . . .[109]

The Agreement provided that the parties agreed to enter into negotiations to eliminate duties and other restrictions on substantially all trade in goods between them, except, where necessary, those restrictions permitted under Article XXIV(8)(b) GATT.[110] Article 6 established an Early Harvest Programme (EHP), under which tariffs on specific products would be eliminated according to an agreed timetable before the ACFTA was fully implemented.[111] According to the Agreement, these commitments under Articles 3 and 6 shall fulfil the WTO Agreements to eliminate tariffs on substantially all trade between the parties.[112] In fact, China made by far the most concessions, so that one author described the EHP as 'almost entirely one-sided'.[113]

Future negotiations on trade in goods were to include but not be limited to, *inter alia*, rules of origin (ROOs), modification of a party's commitments under the agreement on trade in goods based on Article XXVIII GATT, non-tariff measures including quantitative restrictions on imports or exports as well as 'scientifically unjustifiable' SPS and TBT measures, safeguards based on GATT principles, disciplines on subsidies, anti-dumping and countervailing duties based on existing GATT disciplines, and facilitation and promotion of effective and adequate IPR based on existing WTO and other relevant disciplines.[114] The WTO provisions on modification of commitments and trade remedies were to apply to products in the EHP and 'be superseded and replaced by the relevant disciplines negotiated and agreed by the Parties under Article 3(8) of this Agreement once these disciplines are implemented'.[115] Regarding services, future negotiations were to be directed to 'progressive elimination of substantially all discrimination

[108] ASEAN–China Framework Agreement, Preamble.

[109] *Ibid*, Art 1.

[110] *Ibid*, Art 3(1). Whether or not the Framework Agreement met the condition expressed in Art XXIV(8)(b) GATT would have been clearer if the Agreement had been notified to the WTO under Art XXIV GATT rather than under the Enabling Clause (Decision of 28 November 1979 on Differential and More Favourable Treatment, Reciprocity and Fuller Participation of Developing Countries (L/4903)], which does not address this issue expressly. See the Enabling Clause at http://www.wto.org/english/docs_e/legal_e/enabling_e.doc, visited 20 March 2008. I am grateful to KL Thiratayakinant for this point.

[111] See ASEAN–China Framework Agreement, Art 6, Annex 1, Annex 2.

[112] *Ibid*, Art 3(6).

[113] A Greenwald, 'The ASEAN–China Free Trade Area (ACFTA): A Legal Response to China's Rise' (2006) 16 *Duke Journal of Comparative and International Law* 193 at 198.

[114] ASEAN–China Framework Agreement, Art 3(8).

[115] *Ibid*, Art 6(3)(d).

between or among the Parties and/or prohibition of new or more discriminatory measures . . . except for measures permitted' under Article V(1)b GATS, and expansion in depth and scope of services trade liberalisation beyond those undertaken by the parties under GATS.[116]

Other provisions of the Agreement also drew on or potentially affected the rights and obligations of the parties under WTO law.[117] ASEAN as such is not a WTO Member. Nine of its Member States are WTO Members: Brunei Darussalam, Indonesia, Malaysia, Myanmar, The Philippines, Singapore and Thailand were founding Members on 1 January 1995; Cambodia joined the WTO on 13 October 2004; and Vietnam became a Member on 1 January 2007. Laos is not yet a Member of the WTO.[118] China was to accord MFN status 'consistent with WTO rules and disciplines' to all ASEAN Member States, including those not WTO Members.[119] The general exceptions to the Framework Agreement drew selectively on Article XX GATT, allowing exceptions for the protection of national security, protection of articles of artistic, historical or archaeological value, the protection of public morals or the protection of human, animal or plant life or health.[120] Within one year after entry into force, the parties were to establish appropriate formal dispute settlement procedures and mechanisms, pending which any disputes concerning the interpretation, implementation or application of the Agreement were to be settled amicably by consultations and/or mediation.[121] Article 13(2) of the Framework Agreement states that

> Except as otherwise provided in this Agreement, this Agreement or any action taken under it shall not affect or nullify the rights and obligations of a Party under existing agreements to which it is a party . . .

Several subsequent agreements amended or elaborated the Framework Agreement. First, on 6 October 2003 in Bali, Indonesia, the same parties agreed a Protocol to Amend the Framework Agreement. Though mainly concerned with the EHP, it incorporated into the Framework Agreement the ROOs applicable to products covered by the EHP.[122] It also inserted into the Framework Agreement a new Article 12A, as follows:

> Nothing in this Agreement shall prevent or prohibit any individual ASEAN Member State from entering into any bilateral or plurilateral agreement with China and/or the rest of the ASEAN member States relating to trade in goods, trade in services, investment, and/or other areas of economic cooperation outside the ambit of this Agreement. The provisions of this Agreement shall not apply to any such bilateral or plurilateral agreement.[123]

Secondly, on 29 November 2004, meeting in Vientiane, Lao PDR, the same parties signed an Agreement on Goods, as they had committed themselves to do in the

[116] *Ibid*, Art 4(a), (b).

[117] On the relationship between WTO rules and aspects of the ASEAN–China Framework Agreement concluded on 4 November 2002, see Zeng Huaqun, 'WTO Rules and China–ASEAN FTA Agreement' in Wong *et al*, above n 27.

[118] See the WTO website, at http://www.wto.org/English/thewto_e/whatis_e/tif_e/org6_e.htm, visited 3 April 2008.

[119] ASEAN–China Framework Agreement, Art 9.

[120] *Ibid*, Art 10.

[121] *Ibid*, Art 11.

[122] Protocol to Amend the Framework Agreement, Art 3.

[123] *Ibid*, Art 4.

Framework Agreement.[124] The ASEAN–China Agreement on Goods came into force on 1 January 2005. It defined more clearly relations between the Framework Agreement and WTO rules. It aligned the Framework Agreement according to WTO rules in most areas. For example, it provided for national treatment on internal taxation and regulation; Article III GATT was incorporated into and became an integral part of the Goods Agreement.[125] Similarly, Article X GATT on transparency was incorporated into and became an integral part of the Agreement.[126] The parties also agreed and reconfirmed their commitment to abide by WTO rules on, *inter alia*,[127] non-tariff measures, measures under the Agreement on Technical Barriers to Trade (TBT Agreement), measures under the Agreement on Sanitary and Phytosanitary Measures (SPS Agreement), subsidies and countervailing measures, anti-dumping measures and IPRs.[128] Similarly, they agreed not to maintain quantitative restrictions unless otherwise permitted under WTO rules.[129] With regard to each party's obligations and commitments, each party was to ensure observance by regional and local governmental bodies in its territory and by non-governmental bodies in the exercise of powers delegated by central, regional or local governments or authorities within its territory.[130] A party in serious balance of payments and external financial difficulties or threat thereof could adopt restrictive import measures in accordance with GATT 1994 and the Balance of Payments (BOP) Understanding of GATT 1994.[131] The general exceptions to free trade in goods reiterated those of Article XX GATT.[132]

In some other respects, however, the ASEAN–China Agreement on Goods diverges from WTO rules or includes provisions which modify the current treatment of China under WTO law. For example, the Agreement contains a reciprocity clause concerning tariff reductions for both normal and sensitive products.[133] It also provides specific ROOs. Trade in goods, as trade in services, is subject to a special dispute settlement mechanism. Both ROOs and the Agreement on Dispute Settlement Mechanism (ADSM) under the Agreement are discussed in Section III. Lastly, of great importance to China, each of the 10 ASEAN Member States agreed to recognise China as a full market economy (MES: market economy status). More specifically, they agreed not to apply as from the date of the signature of the Agreement sections 15 and 16 of the China WTO Protocol and paragraph 242 of the Working Party Report in relation to trade between China and each of the 10 ASEAN Member States.[134]

[124] Agreement on Trade in Goods of the Framework Agreement on Comprehensive Economic Co-operation between the Association of Southeast Asian Nations and the People's Republic of China (hereinafter 'ASEAN–China Agreement on Goods').

[125] *Ibid*, Art 2.

[126] *Ibid*, Art 4.

[127] Other provisions of WTO Agreements on goods not specifically mentioned or modified by the ASEAN–China Goods Agreement apply, *mutatis mutandis*, unless the context requires otherwise: *ibid*, Art 7(2).

[128] *Ibid*, Art 7(1).

[129] *Ibid*, Art 8(1).

[130] *Ibid*, Art 15.

[131] *Ibid*, Art 11.

[132] *Ibid*, Art 12.

[133] *Ibid*, Annex 1 (normal goods]); Annex 2, para 6 (sensitive goods]). For an assessment which concludes that 'at the present the ACFTA looks more like a bundle of bilateral deals on few tariff lines rather than an FTA', see Inama, above n 86, at 567–71 (quotation from the last page).

[134] ASEAN–China Agreement on Goods, Art 14.

Thirdly, a corresponding Agreement on Services was signed in Cebu, The Philippines, on 14 January 2007 and entered into force on 1 July 2007.[135] With certain exceptions, it closely resembled the GATS. It did not apply to government procurement.[136] Article III and Article III*bis* GATS were, *mutatis mutandis*, expressly incorporated as integral parts of the Agreement.[137] Most other provisions followed GATS provisions *verbatim*, without express reference. For example, Article 7 on monopolies and exclusive service suppliers simply reiterated Article VIII GATS. The GATS Annexes apply to the Agreement, *mutatis mutandis.*[138] The Agreement differed, however, from GATS in several respects.[139] For example, its Preamble recognised the right of the parties to regulate and introduce new regulations on services to meet national policy objectives, and their particular need to exercise this right because of differences among the parties in the development of services regulation.[140] The parties, not the WTO Services Council, were to review results of negotiations on disciplines concerning domestic regulation, pursuant to Article VI.4 GATS.[141] With regard to WTO disciplines, the parties agreed and reaffirmed their commitments to abide by the WTO agreements relevant and applicable to trade in services, but subject to any future agreements agreed by the parties.[142] The increasing participation of Cambodia, Lao PDR, Myanmar and Vietnam was to be facilitated through negotiated specific commitments, including 'appropriate flexibility for opening fewer sectors, liberalising fewer types of transactions and progressively extending market access in line with their respective development situation'.[143] In services negotiations within the ACFTA, the parties were to endeavour to achieve commitments going beyond those in the GATS.[144] On application and extension of commitments, China was to make a single schedule and apply it to all ASEAN Member Countries,[145] and each ASEAN Member Country was to make its individual schedule and apply it to China and the rest of the ASEAN Member Countries.[146] In regard to services, as with goods, the ACFTA thus resembled a bundle of bilateral agreements.

The ASEAN–China FTA Framework Agreement includes an ADSM, discussed in Section III.D.3.[147] The ADSM applies to both the ASEAN–China Goods Agreement[148] and the ASEAN–China Services Agreement.[149]

[135] Agreement on Trade in Services of the Framework Agreement on Comprehensive Economic Cooperation between the Association of Southeast Asian Nations and the People's Republic of China (hereinafter 'ASEAN–China Agreement on Services'), also available at http://gjs2.mofcom.gov.cn/accessory/200704/1176879066940.doc.

[136] *Ibid*, Art 2(2).

[137] *Ibid*, Articles 3, 4.

[138] *Ibid*, Art 28(1).

[139] See also the endnotes to the Agreement.

[140] ASEAN–China Agreement on Services, Preamble, last recital.

[141] *Ibid*, Art 5(4). The review procedure is laid down in Art 27.

[142] *Ibid*, Art 15.

[143] *Ibid*, Art 17.

[144] *Ibid*, Art 21(1).

[145] *Ibid*, Art 22(1).

[146] *Ibid*, Art 22(2).

[147] See Agreement on Dispute Settlement Mechanism of the Framework Agreement on Comprehensive Economic Cooperation between the Association of Southeast Asian Nations and the People's Republic of China.

[148] ASEAN–China Agreement on Goods, Art 21.

[149] ASEAN–China Agreement on Services, Art 30.

D. Bilateral RTAs: Free Trade Agreements with Individual Sovereign States

1. Introduction

In addition to the RTAs with its neighbours in the Asia-Pacific region discussed above, China has signed or is negotiating numerous FTAs with non-neighbouring sovereign States. According to the Chinese Ministry of Commerce dedicated website on China's FTA Network, China has signed eight FTAs with 14 FTA partners, including 31 economies.[150] The FTA between China and Chile[151] was signed on 18 November 2005, entered into force on 1 October 2006, and was notified to the WTO under Article XXIV GATT, Article V GATS and the Enabling Clause on 20 June 2007.[152] An FTA between China and Pakistan was signed on 24 November 2006, entered into force on 1 July 2007, and was notified to the WTO under Article XXIV GATT and Article V GATS on 21 January 2008. China and Singapore signed a free trade and economic integration agreement on 23 October 2008; the agreement entered into force on 1 January 2009 and was notified to the WTO under Article XXIV GATT and Article V GATS on 2 March 2009.[153] China has signed an agreement with Thailand; an early

[150] See http://fta.mofcom.gov.cn/english/index.shtml, last accessed 3 August 2009. As the various sources of information do not always coincide, this chapter aims to synthesise a number of different sources.

[151] For an overview of China–Chile relations, see General Directorate for International Economic Affairs, Ministry of Foreign Affairs, People's Republic of China, 'China–Chile', available on the website of the Chinese Ministry of Foreign Affairs, and for documents, see Ministerio de Relaciones Exteriores de Chile, Dirrección General de Relaciones Económicas Internacionales, at http://www.fmprc.gov.cn/eng/wjb/zzjg/ldmzs/gjlb/3478/default.htm, http://www.direcon.cl/index.php?accion=china_esp, both visited 20 April 2008. During the negotiations, Chile's Ambassador to China was quoted as saying that 'Chile is a good platform for Chinese firms to penetrate Latin American markets', in addition to the fact that Chile was considering granting China MES (as was done): see Zhang Jin, 'FTA talks switched to fast track', *China Daily*, 27 August 2004. Xinhua News Agency reported that 'China is Chile's second largest trading partner, with copper contributing to 30 per cent of China's imports from Chile. Statistics from the International Copper Association (China) show that 50 per cent of China's imported copper comes from Chile': 'China, Chile put free trade agreement into effect', *People's Daily Online*, 1 October 2006, available at http://english.peopledaily.com.cn/200610/01/eng20061001_308052.html, visited 17 March 2008. Among the numerous benefits for Chile is guaranteed market and prices due to strong Chinese demand: see Chinamining.org, 'China's copper demand to buoy prices in long run', *Interfax-China*, 22 February 2008, available at http://chinamining.org/News/2008-02-22/1203643602d9132.html, visited 20 March 2008. As of 2005, China had a trade deficit with Chile, so the FTA may serve to correct the imbalance and provide further market access in Latin America: see A Antkiewicz and J Whalley, 'China's New Regional Trade Agreements' (2005) 18(10) *The World Economy* 1539 at 1552. The China–Chile relationship goes beyond economics. Chile was 'the first Latin American country to establish diplomatic relations with China; the first Latin American country to support China's seat at the United Nations; the first Latin American country to finish bilateral negotiations on China's accession to the WTO; the first Latin American country to recognize the full market economy status of China; and the first Latin American country to negotiate and sign a FTA with China': Ning and Liang, above n 104, at 2, citing MOFCOM, 'Minister Bo Xilai Answering Questions of the Press on the Signing of the China–Chile Free Trade Agreement', http://boxilai2.mofcom.gov.cn/aarticle/speech/200511/20051100876121.html, last visited 25 November 2005.

[152] See WTO, WT/REG230/N/1, Committee on Regional Trade Agreements, Notification of Regional Trade Agreement, 28 June 2007.

[153] For further details, see the WTO website at http://rtais.wto.org/UI/PublicShowMemberRTAIDCard.aspx?enc=FLssqzH++2LUohH6O2wrhMeVsuJcqzoH3ijxUPYknxM=, visited 10 April 2009. For background, see 'Singapore, China agree on bilateral FTA', Singapore, 26 August 2006, available at http://news.webindia123.com/news/Articles/Asia/20060826/433126.html, visited 17 March 2008. For the feasibility study by a joint expert group, see Ministry of Commerce, China, and Ministry of Trade and Industry, Singapore, 'A Joint Study Report on a Free Trade Agreement between China and Singapore', available at http://tradeinservices.mofcom.gov.cn/en/b/2008-10-23/59036.shtml, last accessed 3 March 2010

harvest arrangement was implemented in October 2003.[154] In addition, China concluded an FTA with New Zealand on 7 April 2008[155] and an FTA with Peru on 28 April 2009.[156] It has initialled a framework agreement with Australia.[157] China and Norway have made an early announcement to the WTO that their agreement on goods and services is under negotiation.[158] In addition, China is also negotiating agreements with Bolivia,[159] Costa Rica,[160] the Gulf Cooperation Council (GCC: Saudia Arabia,

[154] For a list of Chinese bilateral agreements as of 2005, see B Gill, 'China's Evolving Regional Security Strategy', in Shambaugh, above n 10, at 247.

[155] For the text of the agreement, see the website of the New Zealand Ministry of Foreign Affairs and Trade at www.chinafta.govt.nz or the website of the Chinese Ministry of Commerce at http://gjs2.mofcom.gov.cn/aarticle/policyreleasing/200804/20080405476760.html. On the negotiations, see Ministry of Commerce, China, and Ministry of Foreign Affairs and Trade, New Zealand, 'A Joint Study Report on a Free Trade Area between China and New Zealand, available at www.mfat.nz, visited 10 March 2008; also available as 'Joint Study on the FTA between China and New Zealand', at http://www.bilaterals.org/article.php3?id_article=995&var_recherche=china, visited 3 April 2008. This also provides other relevant documents. See also 'China, New Zealand end FTA talks', *People's Daily*, 15 October 2006. New Zealand was the first developed country to agree on terms of China's accession to the WTO and the first to agree on China's MES. For China, the negotiations with New Zealand were the first such FTA negotiations with a developed country. See also 'New Zealand–China Free Trade Agreement: Frequently Asked Questions', available at http://www.mfat.govt.nz/Trade-and-Economic-Relations/Trade-Agreements/China/0-faqs.php, visited 17 March 2008.

[156] For the text of the Agreement, see http://english.mofcom.gov.cn/aarticle/newsrelease/significantnews/200905/20090506231332.html, accessed 3 August 2009. For background, see Ministry of Foreign Trade and Tourism, Peru, and Ministry of Commerce, People's Republic of China, Feasibility Report, China–Peru Free Trade Agreement (FTA), 'Peru–China Free Trade Agreement Joint Feasibility Study', available on the website of the Peru Ministry of Foreign Trade and Tourism, http://www.mincetur.gob.pe/newweb/Portals/0/Peru-China%20JFS%20Final.pdf, visited 17 March 2008.

[157] On 25 October 2003, China and Australia signed a Trade and Economic Framework Agreement establishing a basis for a feasibility study on an eventual FTA. For the text, see Bilaterals.Org, at http://www.bilaterals.org/article.php3?id_article=6894, visited 10 March 2008. It was notified to the WTO as being under negotiation on 23 May 2005 under the RTA Transparency Mechanism: see 'Regional Trade Agreements: Early Announcements made to the WTO under the RTA Transparency Mechanism', available at http://www.wto.org/english/tratop_e/region_e/early_announc_e.xls, visited 15 April 2008. On the contents of the China–Australia and China–New Zealand framework agreements, see Antkiewicz and J Whalley, above n 151, at 1546–51. *China Daily* reported that FTA negotiations started after Australia recognised China's full MES. Australia was the second developed country to do so, after New Zealand. Australia is also a major source of China's iron ore imports. As of 2005, China was 'Australia's third largest trading partner, second largest export market and second largest origin of imports'. See Hu Xiao, 'Agreements pave way for China–Australia FTA', *China Daily*, 19 April 2005, at 2. On Australia's signature of a memo recognising China's MES, see also Ning and Ding Liang, above 124 at 3. Australia also supports China's 'One China policy' and opposition to the independence of Taiwan. Strategic concerns are often considered more important than market access to both China and Australia: see T Colbatch, 'Why we want an FTA with China', *New Age* (Melbourne), 17 August 2004, reporting on a conference sponsored by the Australian Department of Foreign Affairs and Trade. From the Chinese perspective, this includes access to Australia's natural resources, such as LNG and uranium: see T Orr, *The China–Australia Free-trade Negotiations: Implications for South Africa*, Centre for Chinese Studies, University of Stellenbosch, available at http://www.ccs.org.za/downloads/The_China-Australia_Free_Trade_Negotiations_-_Implications_for_South_Africa.pdf, last accessed 3 March 2010.

[158] See http://rtais.wto.org/UI/PublicShowEARTAIDCard.aspx?enc=lPAgsQrCfuDjIX6pVdtYb3xWFlxcVjr4QlO/DhHlx2A=, last accessed 3 March 2010. Norway has recognised China's MES: see Ministry of Commerce of the People's Republic of China, Department of International Trade and Economic Affairs (in Chinese), http://gjs.mofcom.gov.cn/aarticle/af/ak/200703/20070304500802.html, accessed 14 March 2008. On the fourth round of China–Norway negotiations, see: http://english.mofcom.gov.cn/aarticle/newsrelease/significantnews/200906/20090606308744.html, accessed 3 August 2009.

[159] See General Directorate for International Economic Affairs, Ministry of Foreign Affairs, People's Republic of China, above n 151.

[160] China is Costa Rica's second trading partner after the United States. Recently it cut diplomatic relations with Taiwan in favour of the PRC. See 'Costa Rica, China begin talks on free trade', *New Post India*, 10 January 2008, available at http://www.bilaterals.org/article.php3?id_article=10918&var_recherche=china+and+costa+rica, visited 3 April 2008.

Bahrain, Kuwait, Oman, Qatar, United Arab Emirates),[161] Iceland,[162] India,[163] Malaysia[164] and the Southern African Customs Union (Botswana, Lesotho, Namibia, South Africa, Swaziland).[165] China is considering entering into agreements with South Korea[166] and possibly Brazil,[167] Taiwan[168] and Japan.[169] The following discussion

[161] In July 2004, China and the GCC signed the Framework of Economic, Trade, Investment and Technological Cooperation between China and the Gulf Cooperation Council. Aims include 'to diversify China's energy oil imports and help Gulf nations reduce US dominance in the region': see Jia Heping, 'FTA to help diversify China's energy sources', *China Business Weekly*, 15 July 2004. See also Ministry of Commerce of the People's Republic of China, Department of International Trade and Economic Affairs (in Chinese), http://gjs.mofcom.gov.cn/aarticle7af/ak/200505/20050500088391.html, visited 12 March 2008.

[162] See 'China and Iceland', *China Daily*, 26 August 2003; 'China and Iceland agree to start FTA feasibility research', *China Daily*, 18 May 2005: 'Feasibility study on the China–Iceland FTA ended', 26 July 2006 (source: Network Centre, Ministry of Commerce, People's Republic of China); 'China, Iceland Upbeat on FTA Talks', *China Daily*, 5 April 2007. China and Iceland have had diplomatic relations since 1971. Iceland supported China's bid to resume its seat on the UN Security Council. Iceland has a geographically strategic position. It was also the first European country to grant China MES. Areas of cooperation include geothermic energy and aviation. On the beginning of negotiations, see the website of the Ministry of Commerce of the People's Republic of China, Department of International Trade and Economic Affairs (in Chinese), http://gjs.mofcom.cn/aarticle/af/ak/200612/200612039457215.html, visited 12 March 2008.

[163] China is now India's main source of imports, ahead of the USA. However, it has been argued that strategic factors are equally as important as, if not more important than, trade considerations. First, an India–China FTA would help to open up US and EU-led RTAs to Chinese and India products. It could also promote an 'alternative template for FTAs', focusing on trade integration rather than on labour standards or intellectual property rights 'which are integral parts of the US FTA template that the US may want eventually to turn into the WTO template': see A Panagariya, 'An India–China Free Trade Area?, *Economic Times*, 20 April 2005. See also 'India, China plan world's largest FTA', 8 April 2005, available at http://us.rediff.com/money/2005/apr/08fta.htm, visited 17 March 2008. For further information about negotiations between China–India and China–New Zealand, see the website of bilaterals.org, at http://www.bilaterals.org/rubrique.php3?id_rubrique=100, visited 5 March 2008.

[164] Peng-Hong Cai, 'East Asian New Regionalism and China', PowerPoint presentation prepared for the Third Annual CEPII-IDB Conference, Washington DC, 9–10 February 2006, available at http://www.bid.org.uy/europe/index.php?file=news_and_events/2006/PengHong.pdf, last accessed 3 March 2010. The author is Research Professor at the Institute of Asia-Pacific Studies, Shanghai Academy of Social Sciences (SASS).

[165] See L Reddy, 'A China–SACU FTA: What's in it for SA?', *South African Foreign Policy Monitor*, August–September 2004, at 1–2, which states (at p 1) that 'The primary reasons for China's eagerness to enter into a . . . FTA with . . . SACU, particularly SA [South Africa], is to secure more predictable market access for its global exports and to obtain much-needed natural resources'. The article points out that steel and iron exports from South Africa to China increased by 173% from 2002 to 2003, and those of non-ferrous metals by 123%. See also R Sandrey, 'The SACU–China FTA', 17 March 2005, available athttp://www.tralac.org/cgi-bin/giga.cgi?cmd=cause_dir_news_item&news_id=42879&cause_id=1694, last accessed 3rd March 2010 visited 17.3.2008; G Mandigora, 'The Proposed SACU-China FTA: Opportunities and Threats for SACU's Manufacturing Sector', tralac, available at http://www.tralac.org/cgi-bin/giga.cgi?cmd=cause_dir_news_item&news_id=42898&cause_id=1694, last accessed 3 March 2010.

[166] In 2002 China became Korea's largest export market, ahead of the United States. See 'China expresses interest in FTA with Korea', *Korea Herald*, 4 August 2005. Negotiations began in 2005. However, the liberalisation of trade in agriculture, textiles and manufactured products remain sensitive issues. See 'China–ROK talks have many hurdles', *China Daily*, 13 December 2006, available at http://english.peopledaily.com.cn/200612/13/eng20061213_331954.html, visited 17 March 2008.

[167] In 2001 Brazil became China's largest export market in Latin America, and China became Brazil's largest export market in Asia. There is considerable cross-investment. In addition, Brazil has recognised a 'One-China Policy, has no official relations with Taiwan and 'does not recognise the Dalai Lama as a political representative': see 'China, Brazil strengthen relations', *Gov.cn*, Tuesday, 29 August 2006, available at http://www.gov.cn/misc/2006-08/29/content_372510.htm, visited 17 April 2008. However, there appears to be little real progress toward an FTA so far. On relations between 1974 and 2004, see 'Major events in China–Brazil relations', *China Daily*, 11 November 2004, available at http://www.chinadaily.com.cn/english/doc/2004-11/11/content_390570.htm, visited 17 April 2008. For an assessment of relations between China and Brazil between 1999 and 2006, see A de Freitas Barbosa and R Camargo Mendes, *Economic Relations between Brazil and China: A Difficult Partnership*, Dialogue on Globalisation, Briefing Papers, FES Brazil, Friedrich Ebert Stiftung, January 2006, available at http://library.fes.de/pdf-files/iez/global/ 50190.pdf, last visited 17 March 2010. A sign of various tensions is that in 2004 the President of Brazil

concentrates primarily on the China–Chile FTA, but mentions briefly the FTA between China and Pakistan.[170]

2. China–Chile FTA

The China–Chile FTA recites in its Preamble the parties' belief that the FTA will contribute to the expansion and development of trade under the WTO multilateral trading system.[171] It establishes a free trade area[172] to encourage expansion and diversification of trade, eliminate barriers to trade, promote conditions of fair competition in the FTA, create dispute resolution procedures and establish a framework for further cooperation.[173] The Agreement is to be interpreted and applied in the light of its objectives and according to customary rules of public international law.[174] Concerning relations to other agreements, the parties reaffirm their existing rights and obligations with respect to each other under the WTO Agreement and other agreements to which both countries are parties.[175] The FTA provides for national treatment in accordance with Article III GATT, including its interpretative notes, which is incorporated into and made part of the FTA, *mutatis mutandis.*[176] Geographical indications are protected consistently with the TRIPS.[177] Special provisions on suspected counterfeit trademark or pirated copyright goods are based generally on TRIPS.[178] The parties agree to work together toward an agreement in the WTO to eliminate agricultural subsidies.[179]

agreed to recognise China as a market economy for purposes of anti-dumping law, but this has yet to be approved by the Brazilian parliament.

[168] See J Chen and J Ong, 'China Seeks "Comprehensive" Trade Pact with Taiwan', Bloomberg, 5 March 2009, available at http://www.bilaterals.org/article.php3?id_article=14577, accessed 3 August 2009. A useful source for tracing developments is http://www.bilaterals.org/rubrique.php3?id_rubrique=182, accessed 3 August 2009.

[169] See 'The Report of the Joint Study Group on the Possible Trilateral Investment Arrangements among China, Japan and Korea', 23 December 2003, http://www.meti.go.jp/policy/trade_policy/jck/data/041129ifdi-e.pdf, last accessed 4 March 2010, visited 14 March 2008.

[170] The most comprehensive source of China's FTAs is the Chinese Ministry of Commerce website on China's FTA Network at http://fta.mofcom.gov.cn/english/index.shtml, last accessed 3.8.2009. To trace developments, it is useful to consult several different sources. For an overview as of China's RTAs/FTAs as of 2006, see Ning and Ding Liang, above n 104. As of March 2008, see the website of the Ministry of Commerce of the People's Republic of China, Department of International Trade and Economic Affairs (in Chinese), at http://gjs.mofcom.gov.cn/af/af.html, visited 12 March 2008, which lists the China–ASEAN Agreement on Services, China–Chile FTA, China–Pakistan FTA, China-Korea Free Trade Agreement Feasibility Survey, APEC, Strategic Framework for Action on Trade Facilitation and Investment in the Greater Mekong Sub-Region and Feasibility Study on Free Trade Agreement with Norway. For details of agreements and negotiations as of August 2009, see http://www.bilaterals.org/rubrique.php3?id_rubrique=118, accessed 3 August 2009, though this source does not always coincide with details provided by the Chinese Ministry of Commerce. See also http://sousuo.mofcom.gov.cn/query/englishQuerySearch.jsp, last accessed 3 August 2009.

[171] Free Trade Agreement between the Government of the People's Republic of China and the Government of the Republic of Chile (hereinafter 'China–Chile FTA'), Preamble.

[172] *Ibid*, Art 1.

[173] *Ibid*, Art 2(1).

[174] *Ibid*, Art 2(2). The FTA is done in Chinese, Spanish and English which are equally authentic texts, but in case of conflict the English text prevails: ibid, Art 121.

[175] *Ibid*, Art 3.

[176] *Ibid*, Art 7.

[177] *Ibid*, Art 10.

[178] Cf *ibid*, Art 11, and Arts 51–59 TRIPS.

[179] China–Chile FTA, Art 12.

The WTO SPS Agreement is considered to be an integral part of the FTA.[180] Concerning the TBT Agreement, the parties reaffirm their existing rights and obligations under the TBT Agreement, and agree to apply the principles in the WTO TBT Committee on Principles of the Development of International Standards, Guides and Recommendations with relation to Articles 2.5 and Annex 3 TBT.[181] The FTA provisions follow closely those of the TBT, and definitions of Annex I TBT apply to the FTA.[182] If a party does not accept a technical regulation of the other party as equivalent, it is required to give reasons on request.[183]

In addition to specific dispute settlement institutions (discussed in Section III.D.4), the China–Chile FTA establishes several institutions. Borrowing from the WTO model, it creates a Committee on Trade in Goods, a Committee on SPS Measures and a TBT Committee.[184] It also establishes a Free Trade Commission, consisting of representatives of the parties, to supervise implementation of the FTA, and to resolve disputes concerning the interpretation and application of the Agreement.[185] Each party is also required to establish an office to provide administrative assistance to arbitral panels and perform other functions as directed by the Commission.[186] The Trade and Economic Mixed Commission, originally created by the 1971 China–Chile Trade Agreement, is incorporated into the FTA.[187] A Supplementary Agreement on Trade in Services was signed in 2008.[188]

The FTA also establishes a framework for cooperation in numerous fields,[189] including economic cooperation,[190] research, science and technology,[191] education,[192] labour, social security and environmental cooperation,[193] SMEs,[194] culture,[195] intellectual property rights,[196] investment promotion,[197] and mining and industrial cooperation.[198] It is broader in scope than the Mainland–Hong Kong CEPA or the ACFTA. In dealing with investment, for example, it goes beyond the WTO Agreements.

A central part of the FTA is cooperation in the field of mining. The FTA aims to encourage government agencies, research organisations, private companies and other research organisations to conclude direct arrangements supporting cooperative activ-

[180] *Ibid*, Art 56(1).
[181] *Ibid*, Art 63(2).
[182] *Ibid*, Art 71(b).
[183] *Ibid*, Art 65.
[184] *Ibid*, Art 13 (Committee on Trade in Goods), Art 58 (SPS Committee) and Art 69 (TBT Committee).
[185] *Ibid*, Art 97. The representatives of the parties are the Chinese Ministry of Commerce (MOFCOM) and the Chilean General Directorate of International Economic Affairs (DIRECON).
[186] *Ibid*, Art 98(1).
[187] *Ibid*, Art 96. The full title of the 1971 Agreement is Trade Agreement between the Government of the People's Republic of China and the Government of the Republic of Chile. It was signed in Santiago on 20 April 1971.
[188] The Supplementary Agreement on Trade in Services of the Free Trade Agreement between the Government of the People's Republic of China and the Government of the Republic of Chile, available at http://gjs2.mofcom.gov.cn/aarticle/policyreleasing/200804/20080405478479.html, accessed 3 August 2009.
[189] China–Chile FTA, Art 194.
[190] *Ibid*, Art 105.
[191] *Ibid*, Art 106.
[192] *Ibid*, Art 107.
[193] *Ibid*, Art 108.
[194] *Ibid*, Art 109.
[195] *Ibid*, Art 110.
[196] *Ibid*, Art 111.
[197] *Ibid*, Art 112.
[198] *Ibid*, Art 113.

ities or joint ventures, to focus on areas of mutual and complementary interest, and to build on existing arrangements such as intergovernmental protocols or association agreements between copper companies.[199] Areas of cooperation include but are not limited to bio-mining, mining techniques and mining productivity.[200] Envisaged activities include the promotion of public/private sector partnerships and joint ventures and technology transfer,[201] an important objective in China's RTAs.[202]

These provisions suggest that the search for natural resources is a significant factor underlying China's RTAs, especially (but not only) with non-neighbouring sovereign States. As of March 2008, China was the world's largest consumer of copper.[203] Its demand was increasing because of the appreciation of the Renminbi (RMB), new investment in power grid construction, and increased demand in the air-conditioning and automobile industries.[204] However, China produced only 20 per cent of its requirements, relying for the rest on imports, including 80 per cent on spot trade, subject to fluctuations. In addition, world copper producers are increasingly being integrated, placing buyers in a difficult position,[205] when China's copper imports (in 2006) were reported to have increased by 80 per cent compared to the preceding year.[206] Chile is the largest world's largest producer of copper. In 2000, it produced about 35 per cent of the total, which in turn accounted for 40 per cent of Chilean total exports by value.[207] In such circumstances, the China–Chile FTA can perform an integrative function, 'locking in' purchaser and supplier through a trade agreement, thus replacing vertical integration through ownership or horizontal integration through intercompany contract. It serves as a hedge against price fluctuations and a guarantee of supply in an increasingly competitive market.

One aim of IPR cooperation in the China–Chile FTA is to build on the foundations of existing international agreements to which both China and Chile are parties, including the TRIPS Agreement and the principles in the Declaration on the TRIPS Agreement on Public Health, adopted at the November 2001 Doha Ministerial

199 *Ibid*, Art 113(1).

200 *Ibid*, Art 113(2).

201 *Ibid*, Art 113(3).

202 See Ning and Ding Liang, above n 104, at 6.

203 According to *The Economist*, 'China has swallowed up over four-fifths of the increase in the world's copper supply since 2000': Leader, 'The New Colonialists', *The Economist*, 15 March 2008, at 13. Nevertheless, RTAs aside, it is important to maintain perspective. *The Economist*'s recent special report on China's search for raw materials argues that '[f]or all the hue and cry, China is still just one of many countries looking for raw materials around the world': see 'A ravenous dragon: A special report on China's search for raw materials', *The Economist*, 15 March 2008, 1–18 [Special Report starting after p 60], 4. This part of the special report deals mainly with the political implications, arguing (at 4) that 'concerns about the dire consequences of China's quest for natural resources are overblown'.

204 See 'China's copper demand to buoy prices in long run', at http://www.chinamining.org/News/2008-02-22/1203643602d9132.html, updated 22 February 2008, visited 20 March 2008. It is commonly reported, in the press and by word of mouth in Beijing, that more than 1,000 new cars appear on the streets of Beijing every day: see, eg, Yongfeng Feng of the *China Guangming Daily* guest posting for the Worldwatch Institute, 23 October 2007, on the website of Envirostats!, at http://envirostats.info/2007/10/24/0511/, visited 20 March 2008.

205 See 'Resource shortage challenges China's copper industry', on the website of Chinamining.org, sponsored by the China Mining Association (CMA), updated 14 March 2008, at http://www.chinamining.org/News/2008-03-14/1205458306d12119.html, visited 20 March 2008.

206 'A ravenous dragon: A special report on China's search for raw materials', above n 203, at 6.

207 See the website of Global InfoMine, 'Chile at a glance', at http://www.infomine.com/countries/chile.asp, and of Mbendi-Information for Africa, at http://www.mbendi.co.za/indy/ming/sa/cl/p0005.htm, both visited 20 March 2008.

Conference, and the Decision on the Implementation of paragraph 6 of the Doha Declaration, adopted on 30 August 2003[208] and now incorporated into TRIPS as Article 31*bis*. Other aims of IPR cooperation include to promote technological innovation, to achieve a balance between IPR and the legitimate interests of other users and to encourage the rejection of practices which restrain competition.[209]

3. China–Pakistan FTA

The China–Pakistan FTA[210] is very similar to but more limited in scope than the China–Chile FTA. It also illustrates other important roles of RTAs in China's international and regional policy. In addition to its free trade provisions,[211] its objectives include strengthening mutual friendship between the parties.[212] The FTA is of strategic importance for both Pakistan and China concerning both their mutual neighbour India and Central Asia in general. In addition, while (unlike the China–Chile FTA) it does not envisage cooperation in a broad range of fields, it does include a specific chapter on investment. The national treatment principle applies to investors of the other party, without prejudice to domestic laws and regulations.[213] Neither party is to expropriate, nationalise or take similar measures against investments of investors of the other party except if the measures are taken in the public interest, under domestic legal procedure, without discrimination and against compensation.[214] These provisions are especially significant for China, which has invested heavily in development projects in Pakistan's Balochistan province. In addition to a lead and zinc mining project, the investments are reported to include US $230 million in the Saindak copper project and the Gwadar port.[215] The Gwadar deep-sea, year-round port is strategically located between the Middle East, Southeast Asia and Central Asia,[216] 'giving . . . [China's] westernmost regions access to the high-seas highways of the global economy'.[217] Its construction is part of a larger development plan, including international trade routes

[208] China–Chile FTA, Art 111(1)(a).

[209] *Ibid*, Art 111(1)(b), (c), (e).

[210] Free Trade Agreement between the Government of the People's Republic of China and the Government of the Islamic Republic of Pakistan (hereinafter 'China–Pakistan FTA').

[211] See 'China, Pakistan sign free trade agreement', *People's Daily Online*, 25 November 2006, available at http://english.people.com.cn/200611/24/eng20061124_324918.html, last accessed 4 March 2010.

[212] China–Pakistan FTA, Art 2(1)(a).

[213] *Ibid*, Art 48.

[214] *Ibid*, Art 49(1). Art 49(2) provides for compensation.

[215] See P Sen, 'China-Pakistan FTA', *Journalism by Other Means*, available at http://www.philip-sen.com/othermeans/2006/11/, last accessed 4 March 2010. On the Saindak project, see http://www.pakistan.gov.pk/divisions/ContentInfo.jsp?DivID=49&cPath=768_775&ContentID=4172, visited 4 April 2008. This website is no longer available. See, however,: http://www.atimes.com/atimes/South_Asia/HJ05Df01.html, last accessed 4 March 2010.

[216] See T Niazi, 'Gwadar: China's Naval Outpost on the Indian Ocean', *The Jamestown Foundation, China Brief*, on the website of the Association for Asian Research, at http://www.asianresearch.org/articles/2528.html, last accessed 4 March 2010. See also 'Gwadar Port', *Gwadar News and Business Source*, at *http://www.gwadarnews.com/gwadar-port.asp*, last accessed 4 March 2010 and 'Gwadar', *Wikipedia*, at http://www.en.wikipedia.org/wiki/Gwadar, both visited 4 April 2008.

[217] JW Garver, 'China's Influence in Central and South Asia', in Shambaugh, above n 10, at 209; see also Map 2, *ibid*, at 210.

to Xinjiang and Central Asian countries and the development of a Trade Energy, Transport and Industrial Corridor linked to Gwadar Oil City.[218]

The China–Chile and China–Pakistan FTAs exemplify the third type of RTA that China has concluded. They differ from the other types in their specific combination of legal form, general objectives and sometimes reasons for conclusion. They are bilateral agreements, as are the two CEPAs (except that Hong Kong and Macao are not States), rather than multilateral agreements (in form) such as the ACFTA agreements. They involve non-neighbouring sovereign States, thus differing from both other types of RTAs. Unlike the CEPAs or the PPRD agreements, they are not designed to promote deeper integration as part of the building of 'Greater China'. Neither are they orientated towards regional cooperation, unlike the ACFTA and similar accords. Their bilateral character sometimes means that relations between the parties are more limited, so that it may be easier to distinguish certain principal, non-trade objectives than in the case of the two other types. These bilateral agreements with non-neighbouring sovereign States are more properly designated as FTAs rather than as RTAs.

III. China's RTAs and WTO Law

A. Introduction

How are the three types of China RTAs—economic integration agreements, RTAs and FTAs—related to WTO law?[219] The law of the WTO supplies a general multilateral legal framework within which, and the normative background against which, these RTAs are concluded. In particular, Article XXIV GATT, Article V GATS and the

[218] See S Chaudhry, 'Gwadar Oil City: Pakistan, China to sign agreements in early 2008', *IntelliBriefs*, 17 October 2007, available at http://intellibriefs.blogspot.com/2007/10/gwadar-oil-city-pakistan-china-to-sign.html, visited 4 April 2008; Zafar Bhutta, 'PM's visit to China: Pakistan–China relations to be further strengthened', *Daily Times (Pakistan)*, 27 January 2008. BBC News reported that China provided much of the total funding of US $1 billion for the controversial port project, which some describe as 'China's first foothold in the Middle East', and it also reported that [t]he surrounding region is home to around two-thirds of the world's oil reserves': see 'Pakistan launches strategic port', BBC News, Tuesday, 20 March 2007, available at http://news.bbc.co.uk/2/hi/south_asia/6469725.stm, visited 4 April 2008. On the reaction of India, see eg, Abdus Sattar Ghazali, 'India Alarmed As Chinese Built Gwadar Port of Pakistan Becomes Operational', http://www.countercurrents.org/ghazali080208.htm, visited 4 April 2008; and B Raman, *Gwadar, Hambantota & Sitwe: China's Strategic Triangle*, South Asia Analysis Group, Paper no 2158, 6 March 2007, available at http://www.southasiaanalysis.org/papers22/paper2158.html, last accessed 4 March 2010.

[219] Most authors consider China's RTAs to be WTO-consistent in general. Usually they focus on one RTA, or on elements of selected RTAs. For example, Kong considers the ACFTA to be compatible with WTO law, mainly on the basis of an analysis of Art XXIV GATT and Art V GATS (cf his analysis with that of Emch, above n 57) and general consistency in terms of being orientated toward trade liberalisation and establishing a trade framework based on rules: Qingjiang Kong, 'China's WTO Accession and the ASEAN–China Free Trade Area: The Perspective of a Chinese Lawyer' (2004) 7(4) *Journal of International Economic Law* 839 at 848–51. See also Zeng Lingliang, 'ASEAN–China Relations: An International Law Perspective' in Wong *et al*, above n 27; Zeng Huaqun, 'WTO Rules and China–ASEAN FTA Agreement' in Wong *et al*, above n 27; R Sen, ' "New Regionalism" in Asia: A Comparative Analysis of Emerging Regional and Bilateral Trading Agreements involving ASEAN, China and India' (2006) 40(4) *Journal of World Trade* 553 at 568.

Enabling Clause provide ways of integrating RTAs into and subordinating RTAs to WTO law. Viewed from another perspective, RTAs may refer to these and other articles of the WTO Agreements, but their authors know that in most instances WTO law does not really have teeth, except for the politically important symbolism of reporting RTAs to the WTO, and the potential political and legal utility of the practice.

Secondly, WTO law may provide a template for specific provisions, institutions or procedures of RTAs. Most RTAs are concluded 'in the shadow of WTO law', not only in the normative sense that often WTO law supplies the criteria for evaluating their legality under international trade law, at least in principle, but also in the sense that RTAs copy, draw upon, improve upon or consciously go beyond the WTO Agreements. They are not necessarily 'based on' the WTO Agreements, in that they 'conform to' the WTO Agreements, or even that they 'bear a reasonable relationship to' the WTO Agreements, but nevertheless they frequently are drafted against the background of WTO Agreements. These new sites of governance thus are closely intertwined with the WTO site.

This does not mean that RTA provisions are the same as WTO provisions, or that they are necessarily compatible with WTO provisions. To what extent do China's RTAs differ from WTO law? To what extent are they compatible with WTO law? This section seeks to answer these questions, at least in a preliminary way.[220] In order to examine relations between China's RTAs and WTO law, it focuses on specific normative, institutional and procedural aspects of China's RTAs. With respect to each of the three types of RTAs, it concentrates on three critical issues: non-preferential ROOs,[221] safeguards and dispute settlement mechanisms.

B. Non-preferential Rules of Origin

1. Overview

Each of the three types of China's RTAs has specific ROOs (see Table 15 below). The following paragraphs discuss the Mainland–Hong Kong CEPA and the Mainland–Macao CEPA, the ASEAN–China FTA, and the FTAs between China and Chile and between China and Pakistan.

[220] There does not appear to be any comprehensive analysis of relations between East Asian RTAs and WTO law. However, on the Mainland–Hong Kong CEPA, see H Gao, 'Legal Issues under WTO Rules on the Closer Economic Partnership Agreement (CEPA) between Mainland China and Hong Kong' (2003) 2(2) *Chinese Journal of International Law* 629. On the Korea–ASEAN FTA, see Won-Mog Choi, 'Legal Analysis of Korea–ASEAN Regional Trade Inegration' (2007) 41(3) *Journal of World Trade* 581. An earlier article by the same author deals mainly with WTO rules on RTAs: see Won-Mog Choi, 'Regional Economic Integration in East Asia: Prospect and Jurisprudence' (2003) 6(1) *Journal of International Economic Law* 49. On ASEAN Member States and ASEAN relations with WTO, see Tran Thi Thuy Dong, *Aspects juridiques de la participation des Etats de l'ASEAN à l'OMC*, (Paris, L'Harmattan, 2008).

[221] For a comparative survey, see WTO, Committee on Regional Trade Agreements, 'Rules of Origin in Regional Trade Agreements: Background Survey by the Secretariat', WT/REG/W/45, 5 April 2002, available at http://docsonline.wto.org/DDFDocuments/t/WT/REG/W45.doc, visited 23 March 2008. Low symmetrical ROOs are sometimes considered to be among best practices for RTAs: see MG Plummer, '"Best Practices" in Regional Trade Agreements: An Application to Asia' (2007) 30(12) *The World Economy* 1771.

Table 15 Summary of Rules of Origin in China's RTAs

WTO (for comparison)	Transition period: disciplines, specific criteria for CTC, *ad valorem*, manufacturing or processing (Art 2(a) RO); objective of harmonisation: last substantial transformation (Article 9(1)(b) RO)
HK CEPA	Substantial transformation = manufacturing or processing operations, or CTC, or value-added content (30% + final operations), or other methods agreed by both sides, or use of two or more of above
ACFTA	40% content; full cumulation 40%; product-specific rules for sufficient transformation
Chine–Chile FTA	Cumulation 40%, except listed product-specific rules

2. *Mainland–Hong Kong and Mainland–Macao CEPAs*

The Mainland–Hong Kong CEPA contains specific ROOs.[222] Table 16 below shows the main rules for non-originating goods. Goods not wholly obtained in one side are deemed to originate in that side only if they have undergone substantial transformation in that side.[223]

The criteria for 'substantial transformation' are complex. They 'may' include manufacturing or processing operations, a change in tariff heading, 30 per cent% value-added content,[224] other criteria or mixed criteria.[225] About 73 per cent of product codes adopt processing criteria, which was the existing Hong Kong rule; about 16 per cent adopt the change of tariff heading criterion; and about 11 per cent adopt the 30 per cent value-added content rule. More flexible rules apply to piece-knitted textile garments, with different processes applying to manufacture from yarn and to manufacture from knit-to-shape panels; to favour goods from Hong Kong, China and Hong Kong 'reach[ed] a consensus to relax the origin rules for some of the goods being produced in Hong Kong'. These rules for piece-knitted garments are based on Hong Kong's bilateral agreements with the US and the EU, respectively.[226] From the standpoint of WTO law, the approach is consistent with WTO law, namely, that substantial transformation' "is a general criterion that has to be further technically defined and expressed by the adoption of different methodologies to determine origin that could be (a) the change of tariff classification, (b) *ad valorem* percentages under the revised annex K of the Kyoto convention.'[227] However, the inclusion of 'other criteria' or 'mixed criteria', to be used by agreement of the parties, renders the criteria particularly

[222] Mainland–Hong Kong CEPA, Art 10; Annex 2, Rules of Origin for Trade in Goods; and Table 1, Schedule on Rules of Origin for Hong Kong Goods Subject to Tariff Preferences for Trade in Goods. On implementation, see Annex 3, Procedures for the Issuing and Verification of Certificates of Origin.

[223] *Ibid*, Annex 2, Rules of Origin for Trade in Goods, Art 2(2).

[224] 'Total value of raw materials, component parts, labour costs and product development costs exclusively incurred in one side being greater than or equal to 30% of the FOB value of the exporting goods, and that the final manufacturing or processing operations should be completed in the area of that side': *ibid*, Annex 2, Rules of Origin for Trade in Goods, Art 5(4).

[225] *Ibid*, Annex 2, Rules of Origin for Trade in Goods, Art 5.

[226] Po-Chuen Lam, *Country Report: Hong Kong, China*, Asian Development Bank Regional Seminar on Rules of Origin, 2004, 3, available at http://www.adb.org/Documents/Events/2004/Rules_of_Origin/roo_hkg.pdf, last accessed 4 March 2010.

[227] Inama, above n 84, at 574.

Table 16 Mainland–Hong Kong CEPA ROOs

classification	products	general rule	type of criterion	specific rule	criteria	definition of criteria
non-originating		Article 4	minor processing treatment	Articles 4(1), (2), (3)	(1) processing or treatment for transportation or storage, (2) processing or treatment to facilitate packaging and delivery, (3) processing or treatment such as packaging or display for distribution and sale	
	Article 6		simple operations not sufficient to confer origin			
originating	wholly obtained	Article 2(1)	wholly obtained	Article 3	list	
	not wholly obtained	Article 2(2)	substantial transformation: Article 5	Article 5(2)	manufacturing or processing operations:	'the principal manufacturing or processing operations carried out in the area of one side which confer essential characteristics to the goods derived after the operations'
			Article 5(3)		change in tariff heading	'processing and manufacturing operations of non-originating materials carried out in the area of one side and resulting in a product of a different four-digit tariff heading . . . [under the HS system]. Moreover, no production, processing or manufacturing operations will be carried out in countries or territories other than that side which will result in a change of the four-digit tariff heading'
				Article 5(4))	value-added content	'the total value of raw materials, component parts, labour costs and product development costs exclusively incurred in one side being greater than or equal to 30% of the FOB value of the exporting goods, and that the final manufacturing or processing operations should be completed in the area of that side'
				Article 5(5)	other criteria	other methods agreed by both sides
				Article 5(6)	mixed criteria	use of two or more of the above criteria
other	specific rules	Article 7	origin of energy, factory, machinery, etc not taken into account			
		Article 8	accompanying packaging, parts, spare parts, etc classified with goods for customs purposes not taken into account			

opaque. Such a degree of uncertainty would appear to diverge from the spirit and the principles of the WTO Agreement on Rules of Origin. Article 2 of the WTO ROOs Agreement states that 'Members shall ensure that: (a) when they issue administrative determinations of general application, the requirements to be fulfilled are clearly defined'.[228] As yet there is no agreement in the WTO on harmonisation of ROOs, but one of the basic principles on which the work programme is based is that 'rules of origin should be objective, understandable and predictable'.[229]

Under the Mainland China–Macao CEPA, the parties agreed in 2005 to expand the criteria on ROOs. They supplemented 'the substantial transformation' criteria with 'other additional conditions by providing that: 'If the 'substantial transformation criteria . . . are not adequate for determining origin, additional conditions can be used (such as brand requirement, etc) upon agreement by both sides'.[230] It appears that such condition has not been added to the Mainland–Hong Kong CEPA. This change enlarges considerably the range of products originating in Macao. Though it could not be incompatible with WTO ROOs, because the latter are not yet in existence, it is not clear that it is consistent with the orientation of WTO proposals. It also moves further away from a 'substantial transformation' test or a change of tariff heading test.[231]

3. *ASEAN–China FTA*

The ASEAN–China FTA Goods Agreement also provided for ROOs.[232] Table 17 below shows the ACFTA ROOs. Products not wholly produced or obtained in a party are deemed originating and eligible for preferential treatment if they meet criteria laid down for not wholly-produced or obtained products, cumulative ROOs or product-specific criteria.[233] A product is deemed originating under the first category either if not less than 40 per cent of its content originates from any party, or if the total non-ACFTA value of materials, part or produce does not exceed 60 per cent of the FOB value of the product, provided that the final process of manufacture is performed within the territory of a party (the ACFTA content rule).[234] 'Party' refers to the individual parties to the Agreement.[235] A product is deemed as originating under cumulative ROOs if it is used in the territory of a party as materials for a finished product eligible for preferential treatment and where working or processing of the finished

228 WTO Agreement on Rules of Origin, Art 2(a).

229 *Ibid*, Art 9(1)(c).

230 See Supplement II to the Mainland and Macao Closer Economic Partnership Arrangement, amending Article 5 of Annex 2 of CEPA, Rules of Origin for Trade in Goods, 21 October 2005.

231 See also WE James, *Rules of Origin in Emerging Asia-Pacific Preferential Trade Agreements: Will PTAs Promote Trade and Development*, Asia-Pacific Research and Training Network on Trade Working Paper Series, No 19, August 2006, 33–24; a revised and edited version of this paper is published as 'Rules of Origin in Emerging Asia-Pacific Preferential Trade Agreements: Will PTAs Promote Trade and Development' in ESCAP (ed), *Trade Facilitation Beyond the Multilateral Trade Negotiations: Regional Practices, Customs Valuation and Other Emerging Issues—A Study by the Asia-Pacific Research and Training Network on Trade* (New York, United Nations, 2007).

232 ASEAN–China Agreement on Goods, Art 5. For a critique of these rules, see Inama, above n 84, at 571–78. For a comparison of ROOs in Asia-Pacific FTAs up to 2005, see Dent, above n 21, App E, at 289, which includes ACFTA and HKCCEPA.

233 ACFTA ROO, Rule 2.

234 *Ibid*, Rule 4.

235 *Ibid*, Rule 1.

product has taken place, provided that the aggregate ACFTA content of the final product is not less than 40 per cent; the ROOs allow full cumulation among the parties.[236] Lastly, a product which has undergone sufficient transformation in a party is treated as originating in the party; such product-specific rules were to be negotiated starting in January 2004,[237] and a first package was endorsed by the ASEAN–China Trade Negotiating Committee in June 2005.[238] Certain operations or processes were deemed to be minimal and not taken into account.[239]

Packing may be treated separately for ROO purposes if customs duties are assessed on the packing separately from the product[240]; otherwise no packing is to be considered as having been imported from outside the ACFTA.[241] Accessories, spare parts and tools are ignored, provided that they are classified and collected customs duties with the goods by the importing party.[242] Unless otherwise provided, the origin of power, rule, plant, equipment, or machines and tools used to obtain the product, or materials used in manufacture which do not remain in the goods, are considered neutral elements and not taken into account in determining the origin of the product.[243] These rules are clear and precise, and would not appear to raise any problems of incompatibility with WTO law.

4. *China–Chile and China–Pakistan FTAs*

The China–Chile FTA provides specific ROOs. A good is deemed to originate in China or Chile if it is produced in the territory of one or both parties, using non-originating materials that conform to a regional value content (RVC) of not less than 40 per cent, except for various listed goods which have specific rules with a higher RVC.[244] Numerous operations, including simple assembly of parts to constitute a complete article, are deemed to be insufficient working or processing to confer origin.[245] Accumulation is permitted between the two parties.[246] A set composed of originating and non-originating products is regarded as originating if the value of non-originating products does not exceed 15 per cent of the total value of the set.[247] Accessories, spare parts and tools presented as part of the good on importation are disregarded if classified and invoiced with the good.[248] Similarly, under the China–Pakistan FTA, products not wholly originating or produced in the territory of a party are deemed to be

[236] *Ibid*, Rule 5.
[237] See *ibid*, Attachment B 'Product Specific Rules'.
[238] See Association of Southeast Asian Nations, Secretariat, 'Attachment B: Product Specific Rules, Ref No BEI-Dir/SEOM/ Voi.2/04, 7 July 2005, available at http://www.thaifta.com/trade/china/seom_%20letter.pdf, visited 15 April 2008.
[239] ACTFA ROO, Rule 7.
[240] *Ibid*, Rule 9(a).
[241] *Ibid*, Rule 9(b).
[242] *Ibid*, Rule 10.
[243] *Ibid*, Rule 11.
[244] China–Chile FTA, Art 15. Annex 3 gives the product-specific requirements. On the calculation of RVC, see Art 17. See also Art 18.
[245] *Ibid*, Art 19.
[246] *Ibid*, Art20.
[247] *Ibid*, Art 22. A set is defined in General Rule 3 of the Harmonised System as goods consisting of at least two components belonging to different tariff headings.
[248] China–Chile FTA, Art 23.

Table 17 ACFTA Rules of Origin

classification	products	rule	type of criterion	criteria
non-originating	products having undergone only minimal operations or processes, or otherwise not meeting the criteria for originating products	Rule 7	minimal operations or processes	operations or processes, by themselves or in combination, considered to be minimal and not taken into account in determining whether a good has been wholly obtained in one country: ensuring preservation for purposes of transport or storage, facilitating shipment or transportation, packaging [excluding encapsulation, which is termed 'packaging' by the electronics industry] or presenting goods for sale
originating	wholly obtained or produced	Rule 3	wholly obtained products	list of products considered as wholly produced or obtained in a Party [Party means individual Members of the Agreement]
	not wholly produced or obtained, provided eligible under Rule 4, 5 or 6	Rule 4	not wholly produced or obtained	(i) not less than 40% of content originates from the Party; or (ii) if the total value of materials, part or produce originating from outside the territory of a Party (ie non-ACFTA) does not exceed 60% of the FOB value of the product so produced or obtained provided that the final process of the manufacture is performed within the territory of the Party (ie ACFTA content = at least 40%)
		Rule 5	cumulative rule of origin	used in the territory of a Party as materials for a finished product eligible for preferential treatment under the Agreement and where working or processing of the finished product has taken place, provided that the aggregate ACFTA content (ie full cumulation, applicable among all Parties) is not less than 40%
		Rule 6	product specific criteria	undergone sufficient transformation in a Party; product-specific rules determining which goods shall be considered to which sufficient transformation has been carried out were to be negotiated starting January 2004
other	specific rules	Rule 9	treatment of packing	
		Rule 10	accessories, spare parts and tools	
		Rule 11	neutral elements	

originating if not less than 40 per cent of their content originates from a party.[249] Products which have undergone sufficient transformation in a party are also considered to originate in the party.[250] Neither of these agreements raises special problems of compatibility with WTO law.

C. Safeguards

1. Overview

Safeguards constitute a second important element of RTAs which potentially raise a question of compatibility with WTO law. Table 18 below summarises safeguards for the three main China RTAs. The following paragraphs discuss the Mainland–Hong Kong CEPA, the ACFTA, and the China–Chile and China–Pakistan FTAs in more detail.

Table 18 Comparison of Safeguards in China RTAs

HK CEPA	Either party may maintain or adopt measures consistent with WTO rules
ACFTA	Parties retain Article XIX GATT and Safeguard Agreement (SG) rights; ACFTA safeguards may be taken during transitional period; ACFTA incorporates WTO SG except for various quantitative restrictions
CHINA–CHILE FTA	Bilateral safeguards in form of suspension of duty reduction or increase in duty for one year allowed during transitional period; parties retain rights and obligations under WTO SG
CHINA–PAKISTAN FTA	Bilateral safeguards allowed during transitional period (five-year period in the first phase of customs duty reduction or elimination); parties retain their rights and obligations under the WTO SG; no bilateral safeguard can be maintained if a global [WTO] safeguard is in place

2. Mainland–Hong Kong CEPA

Under the Mainland–Hong CEPA, safeguard measures may be applied if implementation of the CEPA causes a sharp increase in the import of listed products which causes, or threatens to cause, serious injury to the other side's domestic industry producing like or directly competitive products. After giving written notice, the affected side may temporarily suspend concessions and, on request, promptly begin consultations to reach an agreement.[251] In contrast to other China RTAs, no maximum duration for safeguard measures is specified. Except as otherwise provided in the CEPA,

[249] China–Pakistan FTA, Art 15.

[250] *Ibid*, Art 17. See the Annex for product-specific criteria for sufficient transformation.

[251] Mainland–Hong Kong CEPA, Art 9. In addition to references to the WTO concerning specific matters, the Mainland–Hong Kong CEPA provides that the CEPA, including Annexes, shall not affect the ability of either party to maintain or adopt 'exception measures consistent with the rules of the WTO'. This appears to refer to exceptions under Art XX GATT.

any action taken under it shall not affect or nullify the rights and obligations of either side under other existing arrangements to which it is a contracting party[252]; this includes the WTO Agreements.[253] However, the parties are 'to endeavour to refrain' from taking such restrictive measures which could affect the CEPA.[254] Compared to the WTO Safeguards Agreement, this is a skeleton text, reflecting the particularly close relations between the parties and the specific context. In general, the text is consistent with the WTO Safeguards Agreement, except that no maximum duration is specified for safeguard measures. In addition, the Mainland–Hong CEPA expressly provides that consistency with WTO rules is a basic principle of the CEPA.[255]

3. *ASEAN–China FTA*

The ASEAN–China Framework Agreement provided that WTO safeguards rules were to apply to the EHP until replaced by other disciplines agreed by the parties.[256] Under the ASEAN–China Agreement on Goods, parties which are WTO Members retain their rights under Article XIX GATT and the WTO Safeguards Agreements.[257] China has agreed to grant non-WTO ASEAN Member States the same rights.[258] During the transition period for specific products,[259] a party could initiate safeguard measures under the Goods Agreement if, as an effect of the Agreement, or 'if as a result of unforeseen developments and of the effects of the obligations incurred by the Party . . ., imports . . . increase in such quantities, absolute or relative to domestic production, and under such conditions as to cause or threaten to causeserious injury to the domestic industry . . . that produces like or directly competitive products'.[260] This follows almost *verbatim* Article 2(2) of the WTO Agreement on Safeguards. The ACFTA safeguards are limited to an increase in the tariff rate to the WTO MFN tariff rate applied to the product at the time the measures is taken[261]; this is more narrowly drafted than the WTO Safeguards Agreement[262] but nonetheless consistent with it. Such a safeguard measure could be maintained for an initial period of three years, with an eventual extension of one further year,[263] which is a shorter period than that provided in Article 7 of the WTO Safeguards Agreement. These provisions apply during the transitional period for specific products; after that, WTO rules apply.

The ACFTA safeguards thus essentially adopted the WTO Safeguards Agreement rules, which *mutatis mutandis* were incorporated into and became an integral part of the Goods Agreement, except for the quantitative restrictions in Article 5 and for

[252] Mainland–Hong Kong CEPA, Art 20(1).
[253] *Ibid*, Art 18.
[254] *Ibid*, Art 20(2).
[255] *Ibid*, Art 2(2).
[256] ASEAN–China Framework Agreement, Art 8(3)(d).
[257] ASEAN–China Agreement on Goods, Art 9(1).
[258] ASEAN–China Framework Agreement, Art 9.
[259] ASEAN–China Agreement on Goods, Art 9(2), which also provided that the transition period for a product was to begin from the date of entry into force of the Agreement (1 January 2005) and end five years from the date of completion of tariff elimination/reduction for the product.
[260] *Ibid*, Art 9(3).
[261] *Ibid*, Art 9(4).
[262] Cf WTO Agreement on Safeguards, Arts 5–7.
[263] ASEAN–China Agreement on Goods, Art 9(5).

Articles 9, 13 and 14 of the WTO Safeguards Agreement.[264] Note, however, that the ACFTA does not contain any express equivalent of the WTO Safeguards Agreement's 'substantially equivalent level of concessions' requirement[265]; this would be embraced in the general provision to the effect that parties retain their WTO rights. In addition, in seeking compensation under the WTO Agreement on Subsidies and Countervailing Measures for an ACFTA measure, the parties must seek the good offices not of the WTO Committee on Safeguards, but rather of either AEM–MOFCOM (ASEAN Economic Ministers–Ministry of Commerce of China) or SEOM–MOFCOM (ASEAN Senior Economic Officials Meeting–Ministry of Commerce of China), as appropriate, which is to be replaced by the permanent body once established.

4. *China–Chile and China–Pakistan FTAs*

The China–Chile FTA contains specific rules on trade remedies. A bilateral safeguard measure in the form of suspension of duty reduction or increase in duty may be taken during the transitional period.[266] Tariff rate quotas or quantitative restrictions are not permissible safeguard measures.[267] The measure may be applied for one year, with an extension not exceeding a further year. If the transitional period for a product is more than five years, a second safeguard measure may be imposed, provided that a period equal to the previously imposed measure has lapsed. However, no safeguard measure may be imposed under the FTA on a product that is subject to a measure under Article XIX GATT and the WTO Safeguards Agreement.[268] Investigations are to follow Article 3 of the Safeguards Agreement, which is incorporated into and made part of the FTA.[269] The party whose goods are subject to safeguards may request consultations with a view to obtaining 'mutually agreed trade liberalising compensation in the form of concessions having substantially equivalent trade effects or equivalent to the value of the additional duties expected to result from the measure'.[270] If within 45 days from the request the parties cannot agree on compensation, the exporting party may suspend the application of substantially equivalent concessions. However, the right of suspension cannot be exercised for the first year of a safeguard measure, if the measure has been taken as a result of an absolute increase in imports and conforms to the FTA provisions.[271] These provisions apply during the transitional period for specific products.

These transitional-period safeguard provisions thus track very closely those of the WTO Safeguards Agreement, which alone applies after the end of the transitional

[264] *Ibid*, Art 9(6). Art 5(1) of the WTO Safeguards Agreement provides that if a quantitative restriction is used, it shall not reduce the quantity of imports below the level of a recent period which shall be the average of imports in the last three representative years for which statistics are available, unless clear justification is given that a different level is necessary to prevent or remedy serious injury. Art 9(1) The WTO Safeguards Agreement provides special dispositions for developing country Members. Art 13 establishes and provides for the Committee on Safeguards. Art 14 provides that the provisions of Arts XXII and XXIII GATT 1994 as elaborated and applied by the DSU shall apply to consultations and settlement of disputes under the Agreement on Subsidies and Countervailing Measures.

[265] See WTO Agreement on Safeguards, Art 8.

[266] China–Chile FTA, Art 44.

[267] *Ibid*, Art 4482)(b)(ii), n 4.

[268] *Ibid*, Art 45.

[269] *Ibid*, Art 46(1).

[270] *Ibid*, Art 49(1).

[271] *Ibid*, Art 49(2). On concessions and suspension, cf Art 8 of the WTO Safeguards Agreement.

period. The China–Chile FTA safeguard provisions differ from those in the Mainland–Hong Kong CEPA and the ACFTA. The China–Chile FTA follows more closely and expressly the text of the WTO Safeguards Agreement. This is likely to be due to the fact that the objectives and the contexts of the China–Chile FTA are radically different from those of the CEPA and the ACFTA. It is notable that the latter two Agreements do not provide expressly for compensation or, failing that, for suspension of concessions, though such provisions would apply to the extent that the WTO Safeguards Agreement applies. In any event, despite these bilateral safeguard provisions, the parties under the China–Chile FTA maintain their rights and obligations under Article XIX GATT and the Safeguards Agreement, the Anti-dumping Agreement and the Agreement on Subsidies and Countervailing Measures.[272] Action taken under Article XIX GATT and the Safeguards Agreement, or anti-dumping actions under the Article VI GATT and the Anti-dumping Agreement, or countervailing actions under Article VI GATT and the Agreement on Subsidies and Countervailing Measures are not subject to FTA dispute settlement provisions.[273]

The China–Pakistan FTA contains, *mutatis mutandis*, broadly similar provisions on safeguards. Bilateral safeguard measures, consisting of suspension of duty reductions or the increase of customs duty, are permitted during the five-year transitional period for the first phase of customs duty reduction or elimination; the parties are to determine the transition period for the second phase.[274] Parties maintain their rights and obligations under Article VI GATT and the Anti-dumping Agreement, and under Article XIX GATT and the WTO Safeguards Agreement.[275] No bilateral safeguard measure can be taken against a product subject to WTO safeguards.[276] Actions taken under WTO law are not subject to the dispute settlement provisions of the FTA.[277]

D. Dispute Settlement

1. Comparing Dispute Settlement Mechanisms

Dispute settlement mechanisms (DSMs) in RTAs may be compared along several dimensions. One approach, centred on the dichotomy between diplomatic and judicial forms of dispute settlement,[278] asks to what extent the DSM is independent of governments. It focuses on elements such as whether decisions are based on consensus, the involvement

[272] See China–Chile FTA, Art 51(1) on Art XIX GATT and the Safeguards Agreement, and Art 52(1) on the the Anti-dumping Agreement and the Agreement on Subsidies and Countervailing Measures.

[273] See China–Chile FTA, Art 51(2) on Art XIX GATT and the Safeguards Agreement, and Article 52(2) on the Anti-dumping Agreement and the Agreement on Subsidies and Countervailing Measures. On dispute settlement, see the China–Chile FTA, ch X.

[274] China–Pakistan FTA, Art 27.

[275] *Ibid*, Art 25(1) (anti-dumping) and Art 26(1) (safeguards).

[276] *Ibid*, Art 27(3)(i).

[277] *Ibid*, Art 25(2) (anti-dumping) and Art 26(2) (safeguards).

[278] The classic exposition in international trade law is JH Jackson, *The World Trading System: Law and Policy of International Economic Relations*, 2nd edn (Cambridge, Mass, MIT Press, 1998) at 109–11, aspects of which are revisited in JH Jackson, *Sovereignty, the WTO and Changing Fundamentals of International Law* (Cambridge, Cambridge University Press, 2006) at 134–56. For an empirical study, see J McCall Smith, 'The Politics of Dispute Settlement Design: Explaining Legalism in Regional Trade Pacts' (2000) 54(1) *International Organization* 137.

of government officials, government control over appointments, the existence of a permanent roster of panellists, the terms of reference for panels and the extent to which the dispute-settler is empowered to give detailed proposals for resolving the specific dispute; all indicate the extent to which the DSM approaches or avoids a judicial form of dispute settlement. The distinction between inter-State dispute resolution and transnational dispute resolution is a similar but more abstract prism for capturing many of the same issues,[279] though transnational dispute resolution is, of course, not necessarily equivalent to judicial dispute resolution.

Another approach is that proposed by Schneider. In his view, the main factors to be taken into account in designing DSMs are jurisdiction, institutional features, binding effect and enforcement, standing of non-State actors, enforceability of awards in national courts and transparency of procedures.[280]

A third method concentrates on the relationship of the DSM to the WTO. It asks, for example: 'whether an RTA party may bring a matter before an RTA tribunal when the matter involves both the RTA and the WTO Agreement'; 'whether an RTA party may bring a matter before a WTO panel while the same matter is pending before an RTA tribunal'; and 'whether an RTA party may resort to a WTO panel after it receives an unfavourable award by an RTA tribunal'.[281]

These approaches overlap and are not mutually exclusive. Drawing on these approaches selectively, the following paragraphs seek to illuminate and compare the DSMs of the Mainland–Hong Kong CEPA, the ACFTA, and the China–Chile FTA and the China–Pakistan FTA.

2. *Mainland–Hong Kong CEPA*

Under the Mainland–Hong Kong CEPA, the functions of the Joint Steering Committee (JSC) include resolving disputes that may arise during the implementation of the CEPA.[282] The JSC consists of senior representatives or officials designated by the two sides,[283] hence is an intergovernmental body. The CEPA does not include detailed procedural dispute settlement procedures. It provides simply that the two sides shall resolve any problems through consultation in the spirit of friendship and cooperation, and that the Steering Committee shall make decisions by consensus.[284] There is no express reference to recourse to the WTO Dispute Settlement Understanding (DSU).

The Mainland–Hong Kong CEPA DSM thus embodies a diplomatic form of dispute settlement, based on negotiation, and is not a judicial body, even when decisions are made by the JSC. It resembles the good offices, conciliation or mediation provided

[279] See RO Keohane, A Moravcsik. and A-M Slaughter, 'Legalized Dispute Resolution: Interstate and Transnational' (2000) 54 *International Organization* 457.

[280] AK Schneider, 'Getting Along: The Evolution of Dispute Resolution Regimes in International Trade Organizations' (1998–99) 20 *Michigan Journal of International Law* 697.

[281] Seung Wha Chang, 'Regional Trade Agreements and the WTO: WTO Consistency of East Asian RTAs', 12–13 September 2005, PowerPoint presentation, available at http://project.iss.u-tokyo.ac.jp/crep/pdf/ws05/5pp.pdfm, last accessed 4 March 2010.

[282] Mainland–Hong Kong CEPA, Art 19(3), 3rd indent. .

[283] *Ibid*, Art 19(1), (2).

[284] *Ibid*, Art 19(5).

for under the WTO DSU.[285] It is characterised by a relative lack of legalism, in the sense of the existence of legal obligations, the precision with which obligations are defined and the delegation of dispute settlement to a third party.[286] The structure of the DSM reflects the close cooperation, political and economic integration, and limited social and cultural distance between the parties.

3. ASEAN–China FTA

The Agreement on Dispute Settlement Mechanism (ADSM) was agreed, together with the Goods Agreement, in Vientiane, Lao PDR, on 29 November 2004.[287] The Agreement applies to disputes arising under the Framework Agreement and its annexes; 'unless the context otherwise provides,' the expression 'Framework Agreement' includes all future instruments agreed pursuant to it.[288] The latter wording includes both the Goods Agreement and the Services Agreement, each of which also provides expressly for the application of the ADSM to disputes arising within their scope.[289] The ADSM may be invoked in respect of measures by central, regional or local governments or authorities.[290] A party may request consultations if it considers that another party's failure to carry out its obligations under the Framework Agreement results in the nullification or impairment of any benefit accruing to it directly or indirectly under the Framework Agreement, or results in the attainment of any objective of the Framework Agreement being impeded.[291] If consultations fail, the complainant may request the appointment of an arbitral tribunal.[292] The arbitral tribunal consists of three members, unless otherwise provided or agreed.[293] Each party appoints one arbitrator and 'shall endeavour to agree on an additional arbitrator who shall serves as chair'. If they cannot agree and both are WTO Members, they shall request the WTO Director-General to appoint the chair and must accept the appointment. If one party is not a WTO Member, the appointment is to be made by the President of the International Court of Justice and must be accepted by the parties.[294] Procedures under the ACFTA DSM bear a strong resemblance to those of the WTO DSU.

Dispute settlement by the arbitral tribunal combines elements of both the Panel phase and the Appellate Body phase under the WTO DSU. The function of the arbitral tribunal is to make an objective assessment of the dispute, including the facts and

[285] WTO DSU, Art 5.

[286] See KW Abbott, RO Keohane, A Moravcsik, A-M Slaughter and D Snidal, 'The concept of legalization' (2000) 54 *International Organization* 401.

[287] Agreement on Dispute Settlement Mechanism of the Framework Agreement on Comprehensive Economic Cooperation Between the Association of Southeast Asian Nations and the People's Republic of China.

[288] ADSM, Art 2(1).

[289] The inclusion of these two agreements in the Framework Agreement clarifies Art 2(5)–(7), because these articles refer to the Framework Agreement but not to the Goods Agreement or the Services Agreement.

[290] ADSM, Art 2(4).

[291] *Ibid*, Art 4(1).

[292] *Ibid*, Art 6(1).

[293] *Ibid*, Art 7(1).

[294] *Ibid*, Art 7(3).

the applicability of and conformity with the Framework Agreement.[295] The terms of reference of the arbitral tribunal are very similar to those of WTO Panels.[296] Proceedings are also similar to those of WTO Panels.[297] Unlike the WTO, all proceedings are conducted in English, and all documents submitted for use in the proceedings must be in English.[298] Provisions for third-party participation are virtually the same as in the WTO system.[299] The arbitral tribunal is to make its decision in accordance with the Framework Agreement and the rules of international law applicable between the parties to the dispute[300]; the latter would include WTO law. However, the arbitral tribunal is expressly mandated to take its decision by consensus; if this is not possible, it may decide by majority opinion.[301] Most importantly, the decision of the arbitral tribunal is final and binding on the parties to the dispute[302]; there is no appellate body.

The character of the decision of the arbitral tribunal is formulated in terms which reiterate *verbatim* Article 19 DSU.[303] Compensation and suspension of concessions or benefits are available as temporary measures in virtually the same terms as in the WTO system.[304] Throughout the proceedings, the parties are encouraged to settle the dispute themselves, either through consultation or mediation at any time,[305] or by the development of a mutually satisfactory solution within the framework of arbitral tribunal proceedings.[306] If the parties agree, conciliation or mediation may continue at the same time as the arbitral tribunal proceedings[307]; these provisions are similar to those in the WTO DSU.[308] The ADSM does not contain any specific provisions analogous to Article 25 DSU concerning resort to arbitration, as the arbitral tribunal can be considered to be a form of arbitration.

The ADSM itself provides for relations between the dispute settlement under the ADSM and dispute settlement under the WTO. In addition to the procedure for appointing a third arbitrator if the parties cannot agree, three provisions directly concern relations between the ADSM and the WTO dispute settlement system. First, Article 2(5) states expressly that, subject to Article 2(6), nothing in the Agreement shall prejudice any right of the parties to have recourse to dispute settlement procedures under any other treaty to which they are parties.[309] Secondly, Article 2(6) provides that once dispute settlement proceedings have been initiated 'under this Agreement or under any other treaty to which the parties to a dispute are parties concerning a

[295] *Ibid*, Art 8(1).

[296] Cf Art 8(2) ADSM and Art 7 DSU.

[297] Cf Art 9 ADSM and Arts 12–16 DSU.

[298] ADSM, Art 14.

[299] Cf Art 10 ADSM and Art 10 DSU.

[300] ADSM, Art 8(3)(b).

[301] *Ibid*, Art 8(5).

[302] *Ibid*, Art 8(4).

[303] Art 8(1) ADSM provides as follows: 'Where an arbitral tribunal concludes that a measure is inconsistent with a provision of the Framework Agreement, it shall recommend that the party complained against bring the measure into conformity with that provision. In addition to its recommendations, the arbitral tribunal may suggest ways in which the party complained against could implement the recommendations. In its findings and recommendations, the arbitral tribunal cannot add to or diminish the rights and obligations provided in the Framework Agreement.'

[304] Cf Art 13 ADSM and Art 22 DSU.

[305] ADSM, Art 5(1).

[306] See *ibid*, Art 8(3)(a).

[307] *Ibid*, Art 5(2).

[308] Cf Art 5 ADSM with Art 5 DSU, and compare Art 8(3)(a) ADSM with Art 11 DSU (on the function of panels; there is no analogous provision concerning the WTO Appellate Body, which is concerned only with points of law).

[309] ADSM, Art 2(5).

particular right or obligation of such parties arising under the Framework Treaty or that other treaty,' only the forum chosen by the complainant is to be used.[310] Thirdly, Article 2(7) states that these provisions do not apply where the parties to a dispute expressly agree to the use of more than one dispute settlement forum concerning the particular dispute.[311] Hence the complainant's choice of forum governs, even when the parties agree to use more than one forum in a particular dispute. If both the ADSM and the WTO DSU are chosen, there are no provisions regulating relations between the two DSMs and their eventual outcomes.

The ADSM under the current ACFTA contrasts sharply with the DSM of ASEAN itself as of late 2004. Originally, a Protocol signed in Manila on 20 November 1996 established a DSM for ASEAN.[312] In addition to consultations and good offices, conciliation or mediation, it provided for dispute resolution by panels, reporting to the Senior Economic Officials Meeting (SEOM), with an appeal to the ASEAN Economic Ministers (AEM). The basic outlines of the system were roughly inspired by the WTO DSU, but the direct involvement of national government officials meant that, unlike the WTO, it was much more diplomatic than judicial. Eight years later, the ASEAN Protocol on Enhanced Dispute Settlement Mechanism, signed in Vientiane on 29 November 2004, replaced the 1996 Protocol.[313] Modelled closely on but improving on the WTO system,[314] it established an Appellate Body to hear appeals from the already existing Panels on issues of law. The Appellate Body was to be composed of seven persons, appointed by the AEM but not affiliated with any government.[315] Appellate Body reports, as with Panel reports that were not appealed, were to be adopted by the SEOM according to a negative consensus rule.[316] However, geared toward a region which is much more heterogeneous than the EU Member States historically and in terms of culture, politics, economics and law,[317] even as late as 2004 the ASEAN's own DSM did not have implementing regulations and had never been used.[318]

[310] *Ibid*, Art 2(6). The complainant is deemed to have selected a forum when it requests the establishment of, or referred a dispute to, a dispute settlement panel or tribunal in accordance with the ADSM or any other agreement to which the parties to a dispute are parties: *ibid*, Art 2(8).

[311] *Ibid*, Art 2(7).

[312] http://www.aseansec.org/16654.htm, visited 20 March 2008.

[313] ASEAN Protocol on Enhanced Dispute Settlement Mechanism, available on the ASEAN website at http://www.aseansec.org/16754.htm, visited 20 March 2008. See also J Vander Kooi, 'The ASEAN Enhanced Dispute Settlement Mechanism: Doing It "the ASEAN Way"' (2007) *New York International Law Review* 13.

[314] For comparisons of the ASEAN DSM and WTO DSM, see Yan Luo, 'Dispute Settlement in the Proposed East Asia Free Trade Agreement: Lessons Learned from the ASEAN, the NAFTA, and the EU' in L Bartels and F Ortino, *Regional Trade Agreements and the WTO Legal System* (Oxford, Oxford University Press, 2006) 419 at 431–35; Tran Thi Thuy Dong, above n 220, at 442–67.

[315] ASEAN Protocol on Enhanced Dispute Settlement Mechanism, Art 12, available on the ASEAN website at http://www.aseansec.org/16754.htm, visited 20 March 2008.

[316] *Ibid*, Art 9(1) on Panel reports and Art 12(13) on Appellate Body reports.

[317] See Pan Zhengqiang, 'What the Asia-Pacific Can Learn from the European Integration', Online Info-Dienst Ausgabe 4/2004, Konrad-Adenauer-Stiftung eV, Länderbıro China, 20 July 2004, available at http://www.kas.de/proj/home/pub/37/1/year-2004/dokument:id-5120/index_print.html, visited 9 December 2004. See also R Barrell and A Choy, 'Economic Integration and Openness in Europe and East Asia', paper presented at the ASEM Symposium on Multilateral and Regional Economic Relations, Tokyo, 25 March 2003, 9–12, available at http://www.niesr.ac.uk/pubs/dps/dp214.pdf, last accessed 4 March 2010; P De Grauwe and Zhaoyong Zhang, 'Introduction: Monetary and Economic Integration in the East Asian Region' (2006) *The World Economy* 1643; R Chopparapu, 'The European Union: A Model for East Asia?' (2005) 3 *Asia Europe Journal* 133; W Pesek, 'Asian euro? Don't hold your breath', *International Herald Tribune*, 10–11 May 2008, at 10, 11.

[318] See A Greenwald, 'The ASEAN–China Free Trade Area (ACFTA): A Legal Response to China's Rise' (2006) 16 *Duke Journal of Comparative and International Law* 193 at 202–209.

In these circumstances, the ACFTA ADSM differs from both the 1996 and the 2004 ASEAN DSMs. It is essentially a system of arbitration, rather than a diplomatically-based system similar to the 1996 ASEAN DSM or a more judicially-based system similar to the 2004 ASEAN DSM. Overall, it is also slightly more diplomatic and less judicial in character than WTO dispute settlement. Though dispute settlement institutions were not mentioned explicitly in the ASEAN–China Experts Group Report,[319] its shape is due most likely to the preferences of China. In this particular respect, however, the ADSM is very significant. It represents, according to one author, the first trade agreement in which China has agreed 'to resolve bilateral and regional trade disputes through formal mechanisms'.[320] In addition, if it works effectively, the ADSM will also represent a novel departure from the 'ASEAN way' consensus method of settling disputes.

4. China–Chile and China–Pakistan FTAs

The China–Chile FTA establishes a distinctive dispute settlement system, which applies to the avoidance or settlement of all disputes between the parties concerning the interpretation or application of the FTA, or when a party considers that the other party's measure is inconsistent with the FTA or the other party has failed to carry out its FTA obligations.[321] Consultations form the first phase of the dispute settlement procedure.[322] If these fail, a party may request a meeting of the Free Trade Commission for recourse to good offices, conciliation or mediation.[323] The Free Trade Commission consists of representatives of the parties, namely, officials from the Chinese MOFCOM and the Chilean Directorate General for International Economic Affairs (DIRECOM).[324] Such a request may also be made following consultations on disputes concerning sanitary or phytosanitary measures and technical barriers to trade.[325] If this does not resolve the dispute, either party may request the establishment of an arbitral panel.[326]

The arbitral panel is composed of three members, one designated by each party and one by common agreement or otherwise by the WTO Director-General.[327] Panellists must be independent of the parties and not take instructions from them.[328] The chair

[319] The Experts Group Report only states (at 28) that 'the framework should create the necessary institutional mechanisms to ensure effective implementation of the framework' and calls (at 29) for the 'Establishment of appropriate institutions between ASEAN and China to carry out the framework of cooperation given its comprehensiveness and the high level of integration to be achieved between ASEAN and China': ASEAN–China Experts Group on Economic Cooperation, *Forging Closer ASEAN–China Economic Relations in the Twenty-first Century*, at 2 (point 11), available on the ASEAN Secretariat website at http://www.aseansec.org/asean_chi.pdf, last accessed 4 March 2010.

[320] Wang Jiangyu, 'ASEAN–China Free Trade Agreement: Legal and Institutional Aspects' in Saw Swee-Hock, above n 84, at 131, who appears to use the term 'formal' to mean highly institutionalised, normatively orientated, third-party dispute settlement.

[321] China–Chile FTA, Art 80.

[322] *Ibid*, Art 82.

[323] *Ibid*, Art 83. The text refers to 'Commission', which according to Art 5 of the FTA means the Free Trade Commission established under Art 97.

[324] *Ibid*, Art 97.

[325] *Ibid*, Art 83(2).

[326] *Ibid*, Art 84(1).

[327] *Ibid*, Art 85.

[328] *Ibid*, Art 85(7)(c).

of the arbitral panel must not be a national, a resident or an employee of either party, or have dealt with the matter in any capacity.[329] Members of the panel must comply with a code of conduct in conformity with the rules in WTO document WT/DSB/RC/1.[330] The China–Chile DSM thus is more independent of the parties, and consequently likely to be more legalistic and more judicial than the DSM of the CEPA or ACFTA.

The function of the arbitral panel is to make an objective assessment of the dispute, including an examination of the facts and the applicability or and conformity with the FTA.[331] If it concludes that a measure is inconsistent with the FTA, it shall recommend that the responding party bring the measure into conformity with the FTA and may suggest ways of implementing the recommendations.[332] However, it cannot add to or diminish the rights or obligations provided under the FTA.[333] On receiving the final report, the parties are to agree on the resolution of the dispute,[334] and whenever possible to eliminate the non-conformity.[335] In other words, there is no appeal. Disputes concerning the existence or consistency with the FTA of measures taken within a reasonable time are to be referred to an arbitral panel, whenever possible the original arbitral panel.[336] On request, a non-complying party must enter into negotiations with a view to reaching a mutually satisfactory agreement on any necessary compensatory adjustment.[337] In case of non-agreement, the complaining party, after giving notice, may suspend benefits of equivalent effect if the arbitral panel has decided that the respondent has not implemented the recommendation within a reasonable period of time.[338] Compensation and suspension of benefits are temporary measures[339]; the FTA follows the WTO DSU in this respect. Overall, the procedures are similar to those under the ASEAN–China ADSM.

The China–Chile FTA provides expressly, but not extensively, for relations between its DSM and that of the WTO, and also for relations between the FTA and domestic law. When a dispute arises under the China–Chile FTA, another FTA to which both countries are parties or the WTO Agreement, the complainant is entitled to select the forum.[340] Once the complainant has requested a panel under one of these agreements, the forum is to be used to the exclusion of the others.[341] The FTA does not deal specifically with possible recourse to another forum following a loss in the first forum. The FTA dispute settlement provisions do not apply to actions under Article XIX GATT and the Safeguards Agreement, Article VI GATT and the Anti-dumping Agreement, or Article VI GATT and the Agreement on Subsidies and Countervailing Measures. In contrast to the CEPA and ACFTA, the China–Chile FTA provides expressly that neither party is entitled to

[329] *Ibid*, Art 85(6).

[330] *Ibid*, Art 85(7)(d). The document is the Rules of Conduct for the Understanding on Rules and Procedures Governing the Settlement of Disputes, adopted in 1996. See WTO, *WTO Analytical Index: Guide to WTO Law and Practice*, vol 2, 2nd edn (Cambridge, Cambridge University Press for the WTO, 2007) at 1347–51.

[331] China–Chile FTA, Art 86(1).

[332] *Ibid*, Art 86(2).

[333] *Ibid*, Art 86(3).

[334] *Ibid*, Art 92(1).

[335] *Ibid*, Art 92(2).

[336] *Ibid*, Art 92(5).

[337] *Ibid*, Art 93(1).

[338] *Ibid*, Art 93(2).

[339] *Ibid*, Art 93(3).

[340] *Ibid*, Art 81(1).

[341] *Ibid*, Art 81(2).

provide for a right of action under its domestic law against the other party on the ground that a measure of the other party is inconsistent with the FTA.[342]

The China–Pakistan FTA DSM is very similar,[343] with two exceptions. The provisions concerning choice of dispute settlement forum are in substance the same as those in the China–Chile FTA.[344] One exception, however, lies in the fact that private rights can be dealt with under the FTA DSM procedures.[345] The striking exception concerns investment disputes.

Under ACFTA and the China–Chile FTA, the settlement of investment disputes follows the same procedures as other disputes. The China–Pakistan FTA, however, has special provisions for investment disputes[346] as an exception to its general dispute settlement rules.[347] Concerning investment, different procedures apply to disputes between the parties, on the one hand, and to disputes between investors and one party, on the other hand.[348] Specific provisions concern other obligations[349] and periodic consultations regarding investments.[350] Investment disputes between the parties are to be settled by consultations through diplomatic channels, if possible, otherwise by an ad hoc arbitral tribunal composed of three arbitrators, one appointed by each party and a third selected by the two arbitrators; the third must be a national of a country having diplomatic relations with both parties.[351] If the tribunal has not been constituted within four months of receipt of the request for arbitration, either party may invite the President of the International Court of Justice to make the necessary appointments.[352] The arbitral tribunal is to determine its own procedure, but it is to reach its award in accordance with the FTA provisions on investment and the principles of international law recognised by the parties.[353] Disputes between an investor and a party are, if possible, to be settled amicably through negotiations between the parties to the dispute; otherwise, they may be referred, at the option of the investor, either to the competent court of the party that is a party to the dispute, or to the International Centre for the Settlement of Investment Disputes (ICSIC).[354]

5. *Comparison of the DSMs in China's RTAs*

It may be hypothesised that the template for the DSMs in China's RTAs is the WTO DSM. A possible alternative template might be the general DSM under the North American Free Trade Agreement (NAFTA). Table 19 below compares these DSMs. It

[342] *Ibid*, Art 95.

[343] China–Pakistan FTA, ch X, Arts 57–74.

[344] *Ibid*, Art 60.

[345] *Ibid*, Art 74 provides that 'Any question regarding conformity of a measure taken by either Party under this Agreement shall be submitted and proceeded with as provided under Chapter X of this Agreement'. Chapter X concerns dispute settlement, except for investment disputes.

[346] *Ibid*, Art 53.

[347] *Ibid*, Art 58. If there is a conflict between the special provisions for investment disputes and the general dispute settlement rules, the special provisions apply: see Art 53(8).

[348] See *ibid*, Arts 53 and 54, respectively.

[349] *Ibid*, Art 55.

[350] *Ibid*, Art 56.

[351] *Ibid*, Art 53(2), (3).

[352] *Ibid*, Art 53(4).

[353] *Ibid*, Art 53(5).

[354] *Ibid*, Art 54.

indicates, first, that the ACFTA ADSM is based relatively closely on the WTO DSM. Secondly, the China–Chile FTA DSM and the China–Pakistan FTA DSM (with the exception of investment disputes) draw on the WTO DSM and also on the general NAFTA DSM. Thirdly, the Mainland–Hong Kong CEPA DSM is relatively informal, is intergovernmental and diplomatic, and does not draw directly on the WTO DSM; as already seen, however, this does not mean that it is incompatible with the WTO DSM. Fourthly, under all of the China RTAs, the choice of the complainant party determines the forum; under the ACFTA the parties may agree to use more than one forum. Fifthly, China's RTAs examined here, with two exceptions, provide that decisions may be taken by majority vote if it is not possible to reach a consensus. The exceptions are the Mainland–Hong Kong CEPA, under which disputes are to be settled by consensus, and investment disputes under the China–Pakistan FTA, which are to be settled by majority vote. Sixthly, all DSMs in China's RTAs differ from the WTO DSM in that there is no appeal. Hence they are substantially less legalistic than the WTO DSM, whose Appellate Body has developed a substantial case law, refers to previous decisions and has many aspects of an international trade court.

Table 19 Comparison of DSMs in China's RTAs, WTO and NAFTA

SUBJECT	WTO DSU	NAFTA, Section B—Dispute Settlement	ACFTA ADSM	CHINA–CHILE FTA (CCFTA)	CHINA–PAKISTAN FTA (CPFTA)	MAIN-LAND–HONG KONG CEPA (MHKCEPA)
definitions	not applic-able	not applicable	Article 1	Articles 5, 29	Article 5, 12, 28, 35, 46 [investments]	
cooperation		Article 2003: Cooperation		Article 79 CCFTA = Article 2003 NAFTA	Article 57 CPFTA = Article 79 CCFTA	
coverage and applica-tion	Article 1	Article 2004; AD and CVD excluded	Article 2(1), (2), (3), (4)	Article 80 CCFTA approximately = Article 2004 NAFTA	Article 53 and 54 [investments], Article 58; Article 58 CPFTA = Article 80 CCFTA	
administra-tion	Article 2		not applicable	Articles 97 CCFTA	Articles 75, 76, 77 CPFTA	Article 19(3) MHKCEPA
choice of forum		Article 2005 GATT Dispute Settlement: complainant party choice governs, but preference for NAFTA	Article 2(5)–(8): complainant party choice governs, unless parties expressly agree to use more than one forum	Article 81 CCFTA: complainant party choice governs	Article 53(1), (2), Article 54(1), (2) [investment disputes]; Article 60: complainant party choice governs; Article 60(1), (2) CPFTA = Article 81 CCFTA	none
service of documents		Article 2005(5)	Article 3			
general provisions	Article 3 DSU	Article 2003: Cooperation				

Table 19 (*cont.*)

SUBJECT	WTO DSU	NAFTA, Section B—Dispute Settlement	ACFTA ADSM	CHINA–CHILE FTA (CCFTA)	CHINA–PAKISTAN FTA (CPFTA)	MAIN-LAND–HONG KONG CEPA (MHKCEPA)
consulta-tions	Article 4	Article 2006: Article 2008(3) NAFTA similar to Article 4(11) DSU	Article 4: Article 4(1) chapeau ADSM = Article 4(2) DSU; Article 4(2) ADSM similar to Article 4(4) DSU; Article 4(3) ADSM based on Article 4(3) DSU; Article 4(4) ADSM virtually = Article 2006/4) NAFTA; Article 4(5) ADSM = Article 4(6) DSU; Article 4(6) ADSM follows Article 4(11) DSU; Article 4(6) ADSM = Article 4(8) DSU; Article 4(8) ADSM = Article 4(9) DSU	Article 82 FTA = Article 4(1)–(5) DSU	Article 56 [investments]; Article 59; Article 59 CPFTA = Article 82 CCFTA	Article 19(5), 1st sentence
good offices, conciliation and mediation	Article 5	Article 2007	Article 5: Article 5(1) ADSM = Article 5(2), first two sentences DSU; Article 5(2) ADSM = Article 5(5) DSU; Article 5(3) ADSM = Article 5(2) DSU	Article 83(1) similar to Article 5(4) DSU	Article 61; Article 61 CPFTA = Article 5(1), (2) ACFTA	
establish-ment of Panels	Article 6	Article 2008	Article 6: Article 6(1), (2) similar to Article 6(1), (2) DSU	Article 83(2)–(4) FTA = Article 2007(1)–(5) NAFTA (FTA Commission has no analo-gue in ADSM); Article 84 FTA approx-imately = Article 2008(1)–(2) NAFTA	Articles 62, 63; Article 62 CPFTA = Article 84 CCFTA [except longer deadlines]; meetings]	Article 19(4) [Steering Article 8: Committee
terms of reference for Panels	Article 7	Article 2012(3), (4), (5)	Article 8(2) ADSM similar to Article 7(1) DSU	Article 87(4) CCFTA similar to Article 7(1) DSU	Article 64: Article 64(1) CPFTA = Article 86(1) CCFTA; Article) 64(2) CPFTA = Article 87(4) CCFTA; Article 64(3), (4) CPFTA = Article 86(2), (3) CCFTA	Article 19(5), 2nd sentence

SUBJECT	WTO DSU	NAFTA, Section B—Dispute Settlement	ACFTA ADSM	CHINA–CHILE FTA (CCFTA)	CHINA–PAKISTAN FTA (CPFTA)	MAIN-LAND–HONG KONG CEPA (MHKCEPA)
composition of Panels	Article 8	Article 2009, Article 2010	Article 7: Article 7(1) ADSM similar to Article 8(5) DSU; Article 7(3) generally similar to Article 8(7) DSU	Article 85 CCFTA similar to Article 7 ADSM and correspond-ingly to DSU; Article 85(7) = Article 2009 (2) NAFTA	Article 63: Article 63(1)–(6), (8) CPFTA = Article 85(1)–(7), (9) CCFTA	
procedures for multiple commit-ments	Article 9		Article 6: Article 6(3), (4), (5) based on Article 9 DSU			
third parties	Article 10	Article 2008(3), (4), Article 2013	Article 10 ADSM = Article 10 DSU			
function of Panels	Article 11		Article 8: Article 8(1) similar to Article 11 DSU; Article 8(3)(a) ADSM = Article 11, last sentence DSU	Article 86(1) CCFTA similar to Article 11(DSU), Article 86(2) CCFTA = Article 19(2) DSU	Article 64: Article 64(1) CPFTA = Article 86(1) CCFTA; Article 64(3), (4) CPFTA = Article 86(2), (3) CCFTA	
Panel procedures	Article 12, Appendix 3	Article 2012(1), (2)	Article 9(5), Annex 1: Article 9(2) = Article 12(4), (5) DSU; Article 9(4); Annex 1 ADSM similar to Annex 3 DSU; Article 11 ADSM analogous to Article 12(12) DSU but explicit emphasis on finding mutually satisfactory solution and settling dispute amicably	Article 87, Annex 7 CCFTA based on Article 12 DSU; express provision for decisions by consensus whenever possible (Article 87(3)); Article 88 CCFTA = Article 11(1), (2) ADSM	Article 65, Annex III: Article 65(1), (2) CPFTA = Article 87(1), (2); Article 65(3) CPFTA almost = Article 87(3) CCFTA	
right to seek information	Article 13	Article 2014, Article	Annex 1 (8)	Article 89 2015 CC FTA analogous to Article 13 DSU and similar to Article 2015 NAFTA	Article 68: Article 68 CCPTA = Article 87 CCFTA	

Table 19 (*cont.*)

SUBJECT	**WTO DSU**	**NAFTA, Section B—Dispute Settlement**	**ACFTA ADSM**	**CHINA–CHILE FTA (CCFTA)**	**CHINA–PAKISTAN FTA (CPFTA)**	**MAIN-LAND–HONG KONG CEPA (MHKCEPA)**
confiden-tiality	Article 14		Article 9(1), (4) first sentence ADSM similar to Article 14(1), (2) DSU			
interim review stage	Article 15	Article 2016	Article 9(7) similar to Article 15(2) DSU	Article 90 FTA = Article 2016 NAFTA and broadly similar to Article 15 DSU	Article 69: Article 69 CPFTA = Article 90 CCFTA	
adoption of Panel reports	Article 16	Article 2017	Article 8(4) and Article 9(8), (9) ADSM differ from DSU articles on panels, AB and DSB	Article 91 FTA = Article 2017(1), (2) NAFTA	Article 70 CPFTA = Article 2017 NAFTA	
appellate review	Article 17	no appeal	no appeal	no appeal	no appeal	
communi-cations with the Panel or Appellate Body	Article 18	not applicable	Article 9(4) DSM broadly similar to Article 18 DSU			
Panel and Appellate Body recom-mendations	Article 19	Article 2018 [implemen-tation of the final report]	Article 1, 2nd and 3rd sentences ADSM = Article 19 DSU	Article 92(2) CCFTA = Article 91(1) DSU	Article 71 CPFTA almost = Article 92 CCFTA	
time-frame for DSB decisions	Article 20	not applicable; no appeal	not applicable; no appeal	not applicable; no appeal: Article 93(6), 2nd sentence CCFTA	not applicable: no appeal	not applicable: no appeal beyond Steering Committee
surveillance of imple-mentation of recom-mendations and rulings	Article 21	not applicable	Article 12(1), (2) ADSM = much of Article 21(3) DSU; Article 12(3) ADSM = Article 21(5) DSU	Article 92(1) CCFTA no analogue in DSU; Article 92(3), (4) similar to Article 21(3) (b), (c) DSU; Article 92(5), (6) similar to Article 21(5) DSU	Article 71 CPFTA = Article 92(1),(2) CCFTA	

SUBJECT	WTO DSU	NAFTA, Section B—Dispute Settlement	ACFTA ADSM	CHINA–CHILE FTA (CCFTA)	CHINA–PAKISTAN FTA (CPFTA)	MAIN-LAND–HONG KONG CEPA (MHKCEPA)
compensa-tion and suspension of conces-sions	Article 22	Article 2019	Article 13(1) ADSM = Article 22(1) DSU; Article 13(2) = Article 22(2), 1st sentence; Article 13(3) partly = Article 22(2), 2nd sentence, and partly analogous to Article 22(6) DSU; Article 13(4) no analogue in DSU; Article 13(5) = Article 22(3)(a), (b); Article 13(6) = Article 22(8), first sentence DSU	Article 93: Article 93(1), (2) CCFTA approximately = Article 22(2); Article 93(3), first two sentences FTA = Article 22(1) DSU; Article 93(3), 3rd sentence CCFTA = Article 22(8) 1st sentence DSU; Article 93(4) CCFTA = Article 22(3)(a), (b) DSU; Article 94 FTA analogous to Article 21(5) DSU	Article 72 CPFTA approximately = Article 93(2) CCFTA; Article 72(2), (3), (4) CPFTA virtually = Article 93(4), (5), (6) CCFTA; Article 73 CPFTA virtually = Article 94 CCFTA	none
strengthen-ing of the multilateral system	Article 23	not applicable	not applicable	not applicable	not applicable	
special procedures involving LDCs	Article 24	not applicable	not applicable	not applicable	not applicable	
arbitration	Article 25		not applicable, as ADSM highest instance is arbitration	not applic-able, as FTA highest instance is arbitration	not applicable, as CPFTA highest instance is arbitration	
non-violation complaints	Article 26	Article 2012(4)	Article 4(1)(a) ADSM	Article 80(a) CCFTA but not expressed as such		
responsibil-ities of the secretariat	Article 27	not applicable	not applicable	Article 97 [Free Trade Commission], Article 98 [administra-tion of dispute settlement proceedings]	Articles 75, 76, 77 [Free Trade Commission]	

SUBJECT	**WTO DSU**	**NAFTA, Section B—Dispute Settlement**	**ACFTA ADSM**	**CHINA–CHILE FTA (CCFTA)**	**CHINA–PAKISTAN FTA (CPFTA)**	**MAIN-LAND–HONG KONG CEPA (MHKCEPA)**
referrals of matters from judicial or admin-istrative - proceedings	not applic-able	Article 2020	not applicable	not applicable	not applicable	
private rights	not applic-able	Article 2021	not applicable	Article 95 CCFTA = Article 2022 NAFTA	Article 74	
alternative dispute resolution	Article 3(7)	Article 2022	see Articles 4, 5, 8(3)(a), weak provisions on implementation	see Articles 82, 83 CCFTA	see Articles 53(1), 54(1) [investment], 59, 61,	
language			Article 14 ADSM	Article 121 CCFTA		

IV. Conclusion

China's RTAs are new sites of governance, which have been created relatively recently. They reflect to some extent the structural dimension and the relational dimension of the sites of governance on which they are based. For example, they often mirror institutional, normative or dispute resolution processes of China and its trading partners. In other words, China's RTAs may share certain features with RTAs everywhere, but they also have specific characteristics deriving from their specific context, in particular certain features of the dominant site of governance, namely China, to which they owe their existence.

The RTAs so far concluded by China fall into three broad categories: economic integration agreements, traditional regional trade agreements (RTAs) and bilateral free trade agreements (FTAs). This tripartite typology helps us to understand the range of China's RTAs already concluded, in negotiation or currently being contemplated. Only selected examples of each type could be given in this chapter. Once a broader range of RTAs can be taken into account, however, this typology is likely to be useful in analysing China's RTAs in the future, and also in understanding their objectives, organisation, operation and relations to China's domestic structures, policy processes, legal and political culture, and international and regional policies.

These RTAs are a manifestation of China's changing perceptions of external affairs and multilateral trade institutions.[355] They reflect a multiplicity of specific motives.

[355] See eg Cheng-Chwee Kuik, *Multilateralism in China's ASEAN Policy*, SAIS Working Paper Series, WP/05/03, Paul H Nitze School of Advanced International Studies (SIAS), Johns Hopkins University, Washington, DC, October 2003.

Economic rationale, in the sense of access to export markets and providing a legal framework for a dense web of IPNs, especially in Asia, plays a significant role, but geopolitical reasons are more important.[356] The latter include building 'Greater China', enhancing political trust,[357] using regional integration to strengthen China's position in the Asia-Pacific[358] and as a platform for broader political alliances and increased leverage in international institutions, achieving international recognition as a 'market economy' for anti-dumping purposes, the search for economic and military security, and access to energy and raw materials.[359] Even on the basis of the small sample of China's RTAs analysed here, one may hypothesise that, in addition to demonstrating a multiplicity of motives, distinct configurations of motives and different priorities are characteristic of different agreements. For example, the CEPA combines economic integration, a 'gift to Hong Kong', or a possible model for Mainland–Taiwan relations. The ACFTA joins regional trade, technology transfer, political influence and security. Access to raw materials is a central element in the China–Chile FTA, while investment, energy, raw materials and border security play an important role in the China–Pakistan FTA. Analysis of future RTAs should help to complete and, if necessary, modify these hypotheses. In other words, it is necessary to situate each RTA in its broader context, and to analyse what is at stake in the RTA as a whole and in each specific legal provision.

Is there a single template for China's RTAs? Various authors have advanced different models. In 2006, Penghong Cai suggested a 'China pattern', with the following characteristics: 'China does not have a clear strategy', 'domestic regulatory system is in transition', the 'rise of China is regarded as an indefinite factor' and 'unstable geopolitical environment is hard for China'.[360] These are general parameters for Chinese policy-making about RTAs, potentially denying the existence of a single RTA template or logic.[361] A second perspective, which seems to be especially appropriate for

[356] See also Jianyu Wang, above n 32, at 129–32. This echoes Sen's remarks about the 'new regionalism' in Asia: see Sen, above n 1, at 554–55, 566.

[357] See Jianyu Wang, above n 32, at 140, who emphasises the contribution of China's RTAs to 'peaceful existence and enhanced security' in the region.

[358] Note that, despite China's increasingly important economic and political role in the region, Garver concludes that 'India remains the overwhelmingly dominant power in the region' and that 'while China's capabilities in Central and South Asia are growing, that growth is taking place in the shadow of the far more vigorous growth of United States and Western influence': JW Garver, 'China's Influence in Central and South Asia' in Shambaugh, above n 10, at 224, 225. Similarly, in terms of security, the United States 'remains predominant': M Yahuda, 'The Evolving Asian Order: The Accommodation of Rising Chinese Power' in Shambaugh, above n 10, at 359.

[359] On energy as a rationale, see eg, D Zweig and Bi Jianhai, 'China's Global Hunt for Energy' (2005) 25 *Foreign Affairs* 25; RN Cooper, 'China's Coming Demand for Energy' in B Eichengren, C Wyplosz and Yung Chul Park (eds), *China, Asia, and the New World Economy* (Oxford, Oxford University Press, 2008). On energy security as part of China's energy policy, see People's Republic of China, Development Research Center of the State Council, 'National Energy Strategies and Policies', in China Development Forum, 'China's National Energy Strategy and Reform: Background Reports', (15–17 November 2003) [Development Research Center, State Council, 'China's National Energy Strategy and Policy, 2000–2020', November 2003, draft national plan], pp 3–46 at http://www.efchina.org/FReports.do?act=detail&id=112, visited 30 April 2008; J Sinton, RE Stern, NT Aden and MT Levine, *Evaluation of China's Energy Strategy Options*, prepared for and with the support of the China Sustainable Energy Programme (China Energy Group, Lawrence Berkeley National Laboratory, Berkeley, 2005), available at http://china.lbl.gov/publications/nesp.pdf, visited 30 April 2008.

[360] Peng-Hong Cai, *East Asian New Regionalism and China*, PowerPoint presentation prepared for the Third Annual CEPII–IDB Conference, Washington DC, 9–10 February 2006, available at http://www.cepii.fr/anglaisgraph/communications/pdf/2006/09100206/PengHong.pdf, last accessed 18 March 2010

[361] Dent, above n 21, at 237–38.

present purposes, is advanced by Antkiewicz and Whalley. They note that a striking feature of China's RTAs is the speed at which they are agreed and their variation in structure. In their view:

> [T]he approach seems to be one of pragmatic management of a series of bilateral relationships in a customised manner, in which conventional economic and trade agreements, such as tariff-based free trade areas of [sic] customs unions, are merged into broader more encompassing relationship-building rather than precise narrower texts . . .[362]

Focusing on a range of East Asian RTAs, Christopher Dent has proposed that China's RTAs follow the 'emerging developing country FTA model'. In his view, this model reflects the main characteristics of China's political economy. Its features are a 'relatively simple FTA framework with a narrow policy and regulatory focus', 'simple, regime-wide only rules of origin normally based on a value content modality', trade liberalisation concerned mainly with goods with some inclusion of services, sensitivity to national sovereignty in areas such as infrastructure, culture or strategic industry sectors, 'relatively simple liberalisation phase-in schedules' including an EHP for goods, and adherence to WTO rules on anti-dumping duties and countervailing duties.[363] Each of these perspectives operates at a different level of abstraction, and each focuses on different elements, ranging from the content of legal texts through policy parameters to general strategy. They are not necessarily incompatible, thus calling again for careful analysis of each agreement. Their diversity suggests, however, that, at least at this stage, the distinction proposed here between economic integration agreements, RTAs and bilateral FTAs provides a useful typology for analysing China's RTAs.[364]

China's RTAs are negotiated and drafted in the shadow of WTO law. This is not to say that WTO law really provides a detailed template or model for China's RTAs. Depending on the type of RTA, it may do so for different provisions, but not for the RTA as a whole. Dispute settlement is a good example. The WTO DSU provides the basic template for the DSMs in China's RTAs, with NAFTA as a much more limited model drawn upon in bilateral FTAs. However, it appears more useful to focus separately on each of the three categories of China's RTAs. This is the case even though not all RTA DSMs provide expressly for relations between the RTA DSM and the WTO DSU.

Neither ASEAN nor enhanced ASEAN provides a template for DSMs in China's RTAs. Even when the WTO DSU is the model, however, the RTAs are much less detailed than the WTO analogue. More emphasis is given to amicable or mutually satisfactory solutions. Implementation relies more on diplomacy and informal pressures. For example, the ACFTA ADSM does not have any institution specifically entrusted with implementation comparable to the WTO DSB.[365] This is consistent with much of Chinese legal culture, which until now has usually cut against the letter and spirit of Article 3(10) DSU, according to which 'requests for . . . the use of the dispute settle-

[362] Antkiewicz and Whalley, above n 151, at 1554.

[363] Dent, above n 21, at 237–38.

[364] In their useful review of agreements by the BRICSAM countries, including but not limited to China, Antkiewicz and Whalley suggest three types of agreements: those with large OECD countries, those with small entities in the same region, and agreements with other BRICSAM countries: A Antkiewicz and J Whalley, 'BRICSAM and the non-WTO' (2006) 1 *Review of International Organizations* 237 at 239. This typology adopts the perspective of the BRICSAM country concluding an agreement and is based on the identity of the trading partner. It differs from the typology proposed here which aims to take account of the perspectives of all parties to the agreement and is based on the general objectives of the agreement.

[365] Cf ADSM Art 12 and Art 21(6) DSU.

ment procedures should not be intended or considered as contentious acts'.[366] In contrast, some lawyers have argued that ACFTA's long-term success depends on ASEAN's adoption of a more legalised dispute settlement mechanism.[367] Whether this hypothesis is borne out by the facts, and whether such a form of dispute settlement is ever adopted in fact, depends very much on China. To date, there is little, if any, indication that China would prefer to settle ACFTA or other RTA disputes in a legalistic way.

The multiplicity and diversity of China's present (and doubtless future) RTAs pose the 'spaghetti bowl' or 'noodle bowl' problem, in which RTAs are overlapping and possibly contradictory.[368] Figure 3 below shows the East Asian 'noodle bowl' as of January 2006.

The 'noodle bowl' phenomenon is usually most acute with regard to ROOs; product-specific rather than content-based ROOs magnify the problem.[369] It also has an important impact on foreign investment, exports, and regional economic and trade governance. On the basis of an economic model based on the increased exports which would result from a bilateral FTA, Baldwin recently concluded that currently Japan is

Figure 3 The East Asian 'Noodle Bowl' Syndrome

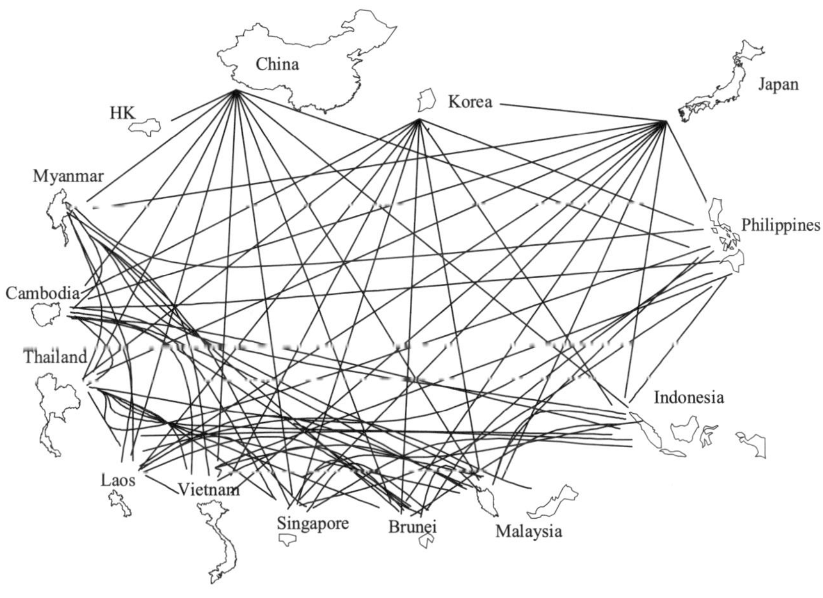

Source: R Baldwin, *Managing the Noodle Bowl: The Fragility of East Asian Regionalism*, Centre for Economic Policy Research, Discussion Paper Series, No 5561, March 2006, at 3. The figure is based on Baldwin's calculations. East Asia means ASEAN, China, Japan and Korea.

366 WTO DSU Art 3(10).

367 Greenwald, above n 318, at 216. In 2001 Dobson argued that, given the diversity of Asia and its preference for consensus as a means of resolving problems. The success of ASEAN+3 would depend on strong political leadership and effective administration: see W Dobson, 'Deeper Integration in East Asia: Regional Institutions and the International Economic System' (2001) 24(8) *The World Economy* 995 at 1014.

368 In general, see R Baldwin, *Managing the Noodle Bowl: The Fragility of East Asian Regionalism*, Centre for Economic Policy Research, Discussion Paper Series, No 5561, March 2006, available at www.cepr.org/pubs/DP5561.asp, visited 12 March 2008.

369 To the extent that it may be less expensive for business to pay MFN tariffs instead of taking advantage of preferential ROOs, with the result that the RTA does not lead to trade creation among members: see Sen, above n 1, at 579.

the principal hub in East Asia, but that 10 years from now East Asian regional integration would most likely be characterised by two hubs, China and Japan.[370] Currently, in his view, there is no real regionalism in Asia, if 'regionalism means preferential tariff liberalisation', and East Asian regionalism is fragile, because 'there is no "top-level management" '.[371] Sen also concludes there is little convergence among RTAs in Asian 'new regionalism', due to differences in income levels and development strategies.[372] The great diversity of Asia, for example in contrast to the European Union, plays a very important part.[373] China's policies will be among the crucial determinants of any convergence among Asia-Pacific RTAs.

By virtue of China's size, population, history and culture, economic dynamism and importance in world trade, its policy toward RTAs is certain to have a major impact on the international trading system, the future role of the WTO in managing RTAs, and the continuing debate about relations between multilateralism and regionalism.[374] China's accession to the WTO has enhanced the possibilities of China's regional and international cooperation.[375] From a regional perspective, the main Asia-Pacific economies are now within the multilateral trading system. These elements provide a solid foundation for China's development in the context of Asia-Pacific regional integration and also farther afield.[376] From an international perspective, Chinese theory and practice of RTAs, including FTAs, are destined to play an important part in the debate about multilateralism and regionalism. Overall, China's RTAs are compatible with WTO law, though they diverge in some respects and go beyond WTO law in others. In any event, the only real WTO-law obligation is to notify RTAs; even in this respect WTO rules are not well-defined, and most RTAs are notified once they are already in force.[377] China now has the potential, challenge and opportunity to contribute to the development of a new role for the WTO in managing RTAs. It thus can shape and develop further relations between the WTO and these new sites of governance. Conversely, it can, and doubtless will, play a very significant role in determining relations between the new sites of governance in Asia and the WTO.

[370] RE Baldwin, 'The Spoke Trap: Hub-and-Spoke Bilateralism in East Asia' in Eichengreen *et al*, above n 365, at 70.

[371] Baldwin, above n 368, at 4 and 2 respectively.

[372] Sen, above n 1, at 581.

[373] See Pan Zhengqiang, above n 317.

[374] See also Jianyu Wang, above n 32, at 121. Jong-Wha Lee and Innwon Park, 'Free Trade Areas in East Asia' (2005) 28(1) *The World Economy* 21 argue that East Asian RTAs are more likely to be non-discriminatory than discriminatory vis-à-vis other countries because they are likely to apply lower tariff levels for outsiders than those applied to members, relying on trade facilitation and investment liberalisation to benefit members.

[375] Socialisation through participation in the WTO is also likely to influence Chinese policy-making and practice in international relations. See AI Johnston, *Social States: China in International Relations, 1980–2000* (Princeton, Princeton University Press, 2008); M Pearson, 'China in Geneva: Lessons from China's Early Years in the World Trade Organization' in AI Johnston and RS Ross (eds), *New Directions in the Study of China's Foreign Policy* (Stanford, Stanford University Press, 2006) 242.

[376] See also Qingjiang Kong, 'China's WTO Accession and the ASEAN–China Free Trade Area: The Perspective of a Chinese Lawyer' (2004) 7(4) *Journal of International Economic Law* 839 at 848.

[377] Wang concludes that 'the real implication seems to be that almost no RTA can ever be declared unlawful under the current WTO regime and that the process of CRTA [Committee on Regional Trade Agreements] examination can, in practice, be ignored': see Wang, above n 32, at 138. On reasons for the weakness of the CRTA, see Crawford and Fiorentino, above n 1, at 19. For suggestions to strengthen CRTA procedure, see Industrial Structure Council, METI, Japan, *2007 Report on Compliance by Major Trading Partners with Trade Agreements—WTO, FTA/EPA and BIT* (Industrial Structure Council, METI, Tokyo, Japan, 2007), at 507–509, also available at www.meti.go.jp/english/report/index.html; Y Devuyst and A Serdarevevic, 'The World Trade Organization and Regional Trade Agreements: Bridging the Constitutional Credibility Gap' (2007) 18(1) *Duke Journal of Comparative and International Law* 1.

10

Social Solidarity Ethics and the WTO: Toward Closer Relations between Sites of Governance

I. Theoretical Framework

A. Foundations

This final chapter builds on the preceding chapters to consider the role of ethical issues in international trade regulation and global governance. Both international trade regulation and global governance raises numerous ethical issues, if we take ethics to mean the moral values of individuals or groups, values pertinent to specific societies, and transnational or international ideals. Ethics states 'the values, virtues and responsibilities that help . . . us to distinguish behaviours or policies that are legitimate from those that are unacceptable'.[1] Here I focus on international trade regulation. The core of ethical concerns with regard to international trade is usually taken to comprise human rights, labour standards and environmental protection.[2] It must be expanded, however, to include the right to food, water, shelter and health, which in certain circumstances may conceivably be as important as, or even more important than, other human rights such as free speech, assembly and others. A broader conception might also include social justice, the distribution of wealth, the right of human dignity and social solidarity.

[1] R Martin, 'Public Health Ethics and SARS: Seeking an Ethical Framework to Global Public Health Practice', 2004 (1) *Law, Social Justice & Global Development Journal* at http://elj.warwick.ac.uk/global/issue/2004-1/martin.html.

[2] For example, see 'Ethics in International Economics: The WTO, NAFTA, the IMF and the World Bank', interview of Professor Michael Kevane, conducted by David Perry, Director of Ethics Programmes at the Markkula Centre for Applied Ethics, Santa Clara University, broadcast 30 April 2001 on 'Ethics Today', KSCU Radio, 103.3 FM, available on the Internet at http://www.scu.edu/ethics/publications/iie/wtotext.html, [text version] and http://itrs.scu.edu/realvideo/004/EthicsToday-04-30-01.html [for broadcast], last accessed 4 March 2010. See also R Howse and M Mutua, 'Protection des droits humains et mondialisation de l'economie: Un defi pour l'OMC', *Droits et Democratie*, 2000, available on the Internet at http://www.dd-rd.ca/site/_PDF/publications/globalization/wto/protection_des_DH_ OMC.pdf, last accessed 4 March 2010; UN Commission on Human Rights, 'Globalization and Its Impact on the Full Enjoyment of Human Rights' available on the Internet at http://www.tradeobservatory.org/, visited 23 May 2002; International Federation for Human Rights, *The WTO and Human Rights*, Report no 320/2, November 2001, available on the Internet at http://www.wtowatch.org/library, visited 23 May 2002; International Institute for Sustainable Development, 'What's It All For: Setting Clear Goals for the World Trade Organization (WTO),' IISD Viewpoint, World Trade Organization Fourth Ministerial Conference, 9/13 November 2001 (August 2001), available at http://www.wtowatch.org/library, visited 23 May 2002; MS Swaminathan, 'Towards a world conservation ethics', *The Courier*, May 2000, available on the UNESCO website at http://www.unesco.org/courier/ 2001_12/uk/science4.htm, visited 19 June 2002.

This chapter is particularly concerned with ethical values such as development,[3] respect for the environment and social justice. Each of these values has several meanings, and the values may conflict. They pose crucial challenges to global governance, not only by the ways in which they are expressed or articulated, but also, and more controversially, in the extent to which they are politically or socially accepted as desirable and the means by which they are put into practice (or not) in various countries. In this chapter, the values of development, respect for the environment and social justice are referred to collectively as 'social solidarity ethics'. They are, in my view, among the most important (if not the most important) ethical values for the future. Realising them in practice would require, would enhance and would entail widespread social solidarity. This chapter uses the concept of sites of governance and the theory of global legal pluralism to address this challenge. It argues that an important way of ensuring that social solidarity ethics are taken into account in institutional decisions about international trade regulation is to strengthen institutional relations between sites of governance.

Each of the preceding chapters provided part of the foundation for this discussion. Chapter one sketched the argument, main themes and organisation of the book. Chapter two then presented a broad survey of research on globalisation and law. It introduced the processes of globalisation, the unequal distribution of its benefits and risks, the partial internationalisation of law, the creation of new types of institutions and norms, new fields of research, and a variety of theoretical approaches to the governance of globalisation and global governance.

Chapter three then sought to answer the question: How is economic globalisation governed? It analysed the specific example of the global commodity chain in toys, involving the EU, the USA, China, the WTO and other sites of governance. It suggested that economic globalisation, as other forms of globalisation, is governed by global legal pluralism, which can be defined as the multiplicity of sites of governance throughout the world that are activated and brought into relation with each other by strategic actors in specific instances.

Chapter four focused on relations between sites as a dynamic social process. It concentrated on the role of strategic actors in constructing, sustaining and transforming these relations. On the basis of the *Chinese Bicycles* saga, it showed how strategic actors contributed to changes in institutions, norms and dispute settlement processes, and to the transformation of relations between sites. Its basic hypothesis was that there is a correlation between international economic integration and the rise of global legal pluralism. Globalisation, international competition, legal strategies and their consequences, both intended and unintended, are among the main foundations of global legal pluralism.

The following chapters then concentrated mainly on relations between three sites of governance: the EU, the WTO and China. Chapter five was devoted to relations between the EU and the WTO. It analysed in detail how the ECJ has managed these relations. Exercising and expanding its judicial role, the ECJ has established a detailed normative framework for, and thus literally created and constructed, relations between the EC and the WTO.

[3] For present purposes, development means sufficient food, water, shelter and health. A broader yet consistent definition of development is given by Ismail as consisting of fair trade, capacity building, balanced rules and good governance: F Ismail, 'Mainstreaming Development in the World Trade Organization' (2005) 39(1) *Journal of World Trade* 11 at 12.

Chapter six examined the processes through which relations between sites of governance can give rise to new legal concepts. It analysed the ways in which interactions among three sites of governance in particular—namely the USA, the EC and the GATT—generated an international normative repertoire concerning anti-dumping law, culminating in the creation of the concept of 'non-market economy'. It showed how the legal concept of 'non-market economy' in EC anti-dumping law was socially constructed by means of relations among a multiplicity of sites in specific historical circumstances. In this story, China cast a long shadow, but it was a relatively passive player.

China was an active player in the following chapter. Chapter seven considered ways in which relations between the EC and China contributed to a transformation in the normative character of rules concerning the treatment of Chinese exporting companies in EC anti-dumping law. It traced the legalisation of the concept of individual treatment from administrative practice, to soft law to legally binding norms, mirroring the changes in EC–China relations in conjunction with the transformation of Chinese economy and society.

Relations between the EU and China were also the subject of chapter eight. This chapter considered the ways in which EC customs law helped to foster and sustain the development of IPNs. Basic concepts of customs law, such as inward processing and outward processing, have been among the most important sets of norms for the development of the building blocks of economic globalisation and for the articulation of particular types of relations between sites. They are used extensively not only in international economic relations, but also in the construction of regional integration schemes and free trade areas. Regionalisation and international economic integration are two different types of relations between sites of governance, to which the chapter referred as different constellations of sites.

Another example of specific constellations among sites are China's RTAs. Chapter nine analysed the legal aspects of these RTAs as new sites of governance. It proposed that China's RTAs may be classified by means of a three-fold typology of economic integration agreements, standard regional trade agreements and bilateral free trade agreements. It also discussed in some detail normative relations between these new sites of governance and the WTO, for example with regard to safeguards, rules of origin and dispute settlement mechanisms. It argued that, on the whole, China's RTAs are compatible with WTO law.

These earlier chapters provide a number of building blocks for thinking about global governance, and for potentially linking together sites of governance to enhance and develop social solidarity ethics. They include new social contracts,[4] further development of specific normative instruments[5] and constitutional tools,[6] and other concepts and mechanisms for managing legal pluralism.[7] In this final chapter, I aim to elaborate the suggestion made earlier that we need to build on the existing diversity of

[4] See JN Rosenau, *Distant Proximities: Dynamics Beyond Globalization* (Princeton, Princeton University Press, 2003) 300–14.

[5] See M Delmas-Marty, *Les forces imaginaires du droit (II): Le pluralisme ordonné* (Paris, Editions du Seuil, 2006).

[6] See M Rosenfeld, 'Rethinking Constitutional Ordering in an Era of Legal and Ideological Pluralism' (2008) 6(3)–(4) *International Journal of Constitutional Law: I-CON* 415.

[7] See PS Berman, 'Global Legal Pluralism' (2007) 80 *Southern California Law Review* 1155; D Halberstam and E Stein, 'The United Nations, the European Union, and the King of Sweden: Economic Sanctions and Individual Rights in a Plural World Order' (2009) 46 *CML Rev* 13.

institutions, legal forms and legal cultures, but to strengthen coordination between sites of governance from the standpoint of institutions, norms and dispute resolution processes. I focus here on the potential role of the WTO in elaborating and promoting social solidarity ethics in international trade regulation and global governance. The chapter thus seeks to contribute, in a modest way, to a re-thinking of the meaning of international trade, and to a redefinition of international trade regulation and global governance.

B. The WTO and Ethics

Ethics, organisational design and our conception of the objectives and means of international trade regulation are intimately intertwined. The WTO is central to international trade regulation today. It is at one and the same time an expression, a result, a cause and an instrument of globalisation. To what extent does the WTO take account of ethical issues? Should it do so? If so, how might it do so?

At first sight, WTO law does not give much attention to the core ethical issues in international trade. The WTO Agreements do not expressly mention ethics.[8] Moreover, certain relevant terms hardly appear in the WTO database: a preliminary search in 2002 revealed that ethics received 45 mentions,[9] child labour 35 mentions, morality 22 mentions,[10] and ethical trade three mentions out of a total of 14,938 documents. Neither were these usually policy documents. With regard to ethics, for example, the documents were almost without exception speeches or presentations at seminars.[11] There appears to be a notable absence of legal texts with an express reference to what has been identified as a core of ethical concerns. By 2009, the situation had improved, to the extent that a general search on the WTO website produced 135 mentions, concerning such matters as the environment, corporate ethics, ethics of civil society, access to medicines and animal welfare.[12]

It would be misleading, however, to conclude that WTO law is not concerned with ethics, for three reasons. First, international trade is embedded in specific social and moral contexts; this includes both trade flows and patterns, and the ways we think

[8] According to R Howse at the Forum on 'Ethics and International Trade', Academy of International Trade Law, Macao, 10 July 2002.

[9] See the speech by former WTO Director-General Ruggiero, *A Shared Responsibility: Global Policy Coherence for our Global Age*, 1998, http://www.wto.org/english/news_e/sprr_e/bonn_e.htm.

[10] Patents were excluded because of the identification of *ordre public* with morality.

[11] For example, a Consumer Union, USA, speaker at a Non Governmental Organisations symposium at the WTO in Geneva in 2001 on issues confronting the world trading system noted, with regard to food safety and the SPS Agreement, that 'the debate about GMOs is a multi-dimensional debate, including ethical, trade and economic issues', and pointed out that 'The most difficult part of the debate was not over facts but values—ethical, religious, etc'. See Non Governmental Organisations Symposium, *Symposium on issues confronting the world trading system—summary reports by the moderators*, 6 and 7 July 2001, WTO, Geneva, Session I: Food Safety and the SPS Agreement, Saturday 7 July 2001, available at http://www.wto.org/english/forums_e/ngo-e/ngo_symp2001_repsps_e.htm, visited 25 May 2002.

[12] http://search.wto.org/search?entqr=0&access=p&as_dt=i&sort=date%3AD%3AL%3Ad1&output=xml_no_dtd&ie=UTF-8&as_filetype=&as_sitesearch=&btnG=Search&as_lq=&client=english_frontend&as_epq=&as_oq=&as_eq=&num=10&ud=1&site=English_website&as_q=ethics&oe=UTF-8&proxystylesheet=english_frontend&ip=80.11.168.249&as_occt=any&as_ft=i&start=20, visited 15 May 2009.

about them or construct them in theoretical terms. Similarly, specific values are inevitably crystallised in international trade rules,[13] and in our ideas about the meaning and purposes of international trade regulation. Examples are principles of non-discrimination such as MFN treatment or national treatment, the protection of intellectual property rights, or special and differential treatment for developing countries. The second paragraph of the Preamble to the WTO Agreement refers specifically to the

> need for positive efforts designed to ensure that developing countries, and especially the least developed among them, secure a share in the growth in international trade commensurate with the needs of their economic development.[14]

Much depends upon how such principles are interpreted and to what extent they are implemented in practice. We may approve of such values or not, but it is difficult not to admit that current international trade rules embody certain ethical values.

Secondly, Article XX (a) GATT 1994 provides that, within specified limits, contracting parties may adopt or enforce measures necessary to protect public morals.[15] A similar provision is contained in Article XIV(a) GATS, though here 'public morals' and 'public order' are alternatives. Public morals and ethics are not identical, and in specific cases public morals may differ substantially from ethics as already defined. Nevertheless, it is striking that so far there have been no dispute cases concerning Article XX(a) GATT and that *US-Gambling*[16] is the only case concerning Article XIV(a) GATS.[17]

Thirdly, even admitting, for the sake of argument, that free trade itself may be an ethical value, as some would contend, it is important to recall that, under the WTO Agreements, free trade is not an end in itself but rather a means of achieving other objectives. The Marrakesh Agreement establishing the WTO provides that

> relations in the field of international trade and economic endeavour should be conducted with a view to raising standards of living, ensuring full employment and a large and steadily growing volume of real income and effective demand, and expanding the production of and trade in goods and services, while allowing for the optimal use of the world's resources in accordance with the objective of sustainable development, seeking both to protect and preserve the environment and to enhance the means for doing so in a manner consistent with their respective needs and concerns at different levels of economic development . . .[18]

[13] See also M Poiares Maduro, 'Is There Any Such Thing as Free or Fair Trade? A Constitutional Analysis of the Impact of International Trade on the European Social Model' in G de Búrca and J Scott (eds), *The EU and the WTO: Legal and Constitutional Issues* (Oxford, Hart Publishing, 2001) 257.

[14] Marrakesh Agreement Establishing the World Trade Organisation, in WTO, *The Results of the Uruguay Round of Multilateral Trade Negotiations: The Legal Texts* (Geneva, WTO, 1995; originally published by the GATT Secretariat, 1994).

[15] See S Charnowitz, 'The Moral Exception in Trade Policy' in S Charnowitz, *Trade Law and Global Governance* (London, Cameron May, 2002) 325.

[16] *United States—Measures Affecting the Cross-Border Supply of Gambling and Betting Services*, Report of the Panel, WT/DS285/R, 10 November 2004, para 286; *United States—Measures Affecting the Cross-Border Supply of Gambling and Betting Services*, AB-2005-1, Report of the Appellate Body, 7 April 2005, paras 297–98. The Appellate Body mentions public order but not public morals.

[17] See also WTO, *WTO Analytical Index: Guide to WTO Law and Practice*, vol 1 (GATT), vol 2 (including GATS), 2nd edn (Cambridge, Cambridge University Press, 2007); Appellate Body Secretariat (compiler), *WTO Appellate Body: Repertory of Reports and Awards 1995–2006*, 3rd edn (Cambridge, Cambridge University Press, 2007).

[18] Marrakesh Agreement establishing the World Trade Organisation, above n 14, Preamble, 1st Recital, at 6.

Clearly, giving priority to free trade and open markets over sustainable development, protection of the environment or respect for the needs of developing countries is a choice about which of the ethical values that are expressed in the Marrakesh Agreement have or should have priority. More controversial issues are raised when trade concerns are balanced against social solidarity, protection of human rights, labour standards, respect for a country's social and economic organisation or preservation of local culture. These matters are dealt with less directly or not at all in the texts of the WTO Agreements. Consequently, the interpretation of WTO law and other public international law to deal with such matters within the WTO framework raises more complex issues.

The crucial point, therefore, is not a distinction between 'ethics' and 'no ethics', but rather how to reconcile or choose between different—even competing—values, standards or ethical positions. Seen from this vantage point, the WTO necessarily takes account of ethics. Its institutional structure, norms and dispute settlement outcomes inevitably reflect, express and crystallise certain values and conceptions about the nature and beneficiaries of international trade, as well as ideas about how individual choices should be structured and ideas about how society should be organised, whether nationally, regionally or internationally. These values necessarily embody ethical choices, whether they correspond to one's own *desiderata* or not. The WTO is based on certain ethical values, which originated in specific historical circumstances and specific social, political and economic contexts. In other words, the WTO takes account of ethics and posits values, even though one might think that they are the wrong ones, or that they need to be balanced by recourse to other, potentially competing values, or that our present conception of international trade has developed in a specific historical context and needs to be revised. As outlined earlier in this book, it is crucial that the WTO opens up to ethical values which reflect the diversity of its Members. Such values include social solidarity ethics.

C. Relations between Sites of Governance

Using the theory of global legal pluralism, this chapter makes a case for the development of a more intricate, more complex institutional web of international trade regulation and global governance, involving closer relations between the WTO and other sites of governance. Employing an institutional approach, it focuses primarily on institutional matters, and less directly on substantive issues. It is based on two premises. First, institutions matter. Secondly, institutional cooperation can be an appropriate form of deliberation and contribution to decision-making. These themes are developed here with more than a slight nod to Neil Komesar's point that policy choices are often, if not essentially, choices about institutions.[19] The chapter thus aims to suggest a different way of thinking not only about the ethical aspects of international trade, but also about the issue of trade linkages.[20] Intentionally, it does not focus mainly on

[19] N Komesar, *Imperfect Alternatives: Choosing Institutions in Law, Economics and Public Policy* (Chicago, University of Chicago Press, 1994).

[20] On linkages, see Charnowitz, *Trade Law and Global Governance*, above n 15; 'Symposium: The Boundaries of the WTO' (2002) 96(1) *American Journal of International Law* 1, Garcia, 'Symposium: Linkage as Phenomenon: An Interdisciplinary Approach: Introduction: Pointing the Way to the Trade Law

defining 'free trade', on asking how so-called 'free trade' norms can be combined or reconciled with so-called 'non-trade values', or more generally on relations between the norms produced by different international organisations or embodied in different multilateral agreements. Such an approach would merely replicate the well-worn and so far unproductive discourse of the 'trade linkage' debate.[21]

In the published literature so far, relatively little attention has been given to inter-institutional relations. There are, however, some notable exceptions. Joel Trachtman emphasises the importance of cooperation as well as competition between international organisations, and Andrew Lang identifies institutional design as an important task for lawyers.[22] However, the former focuses on institutional relations through the lens of the allocation of jurisdiction, and transforms the issue of cooperation into an issue of 'a search for the optimal jurisdictional area'.[23] The latter focuses primarily on what I have called the structural dimension of sites of governance, and gives less attention to the relational dimension. However useful each may be in its own terms, their contribution to the present chapter lies mainly in identifying the necessity of a study of institutional relations between the WTO and other sites of governance.

Two other sources take an institutional analysis further. Frederick Abbott provides a detailed case study of relations between the WTO and the World Intellectual Property Organisation (WIPO). He starts from the view that producer interests have been the drivers of the international trading system until recently, when it has become urgent to take account of a wider spectrum of interests. He proposes the WTO–WIPO relationship as a new model of multilateral governance, or 'distributed governance', involving

> the distribution of governance responsibilities to the institution best adapted to the particular subject matter or goal-attainment, but within an integrated decision-making and enforcement structure . . .[24]

This is an idea which, as Abbott suggests, can be applied to relations of the WTO and other institutions, as well as in other settings.

Another step forward in an institutional analysis of relations between sites of governance is the second published volume of a major research project on the relationship of human rights policies and norms to the WTO.[25] It is useful here because it provides a relatively systematic survey of ways of defining and connecting human rights and trade, and it also offers a number of case studies of related issues. For the present purposes, however, its strengths are mirrored in its limitations. First, it is concerned with human rights rather than social solidarity ethics. Though the two sometimes overlap,

and Global Social Policy of the 21st Century" (1998) 19 *University of Pennsylvania Journal of International Economic Law* 201. A useful survey and critique up to 2007 may be found in ATF Lang, 'Reflecting on "Linkage": Cognitive and Institutional Change in the International Trading System' (2007) 70(4) *MLR* 523. See also S Picciotto, 'The WTO as a Node of Global Governance: Economic Regulation and Human Rights Discourses' (2007) 1 *Social Justice & Global Development Journal/LGD*, at http://go.warwick.ac.uk/lgd/2007_1/picciotto, which focuses mainly on principles, rules and discourse.

21 As demonstrated by Lang, above n 20.

22 *Ibid*, at 548.

23 JP Trachtman, 'Institutional Linkage: Transcending "Trade and . . ."' (2002) 96(1) *The American Journal of International Law* 77 at 92.

24 FM Abbott, 'Distributed Governance at the WTO–WIPO: An Evolving Model for Open-Architecture Integrated Governance' (2000) 3 *Journal of International Economic Law* 63 at 65.

25 T Cottier, J Pauwelyn and E Bürgi (eds), *Human Rights and International Trade* (Oxford, Oxford University Press, 2005).

they diverge in many respects. For example, the former are orientated mainly toward the individual, while the latter are also (and perhaps more) concerned with groups. Not all aspects of social solidarity ethics have been or can best be expressed in terms of human rights. Secondly, it is premised on a sharp distinction between trade and human rights. This is reminiscent of the traditional 'trade and . . .' literature. It thus is limited in the extent to which it can contribute to re-thinking the ideas of international trade, international trade regulation and global governance so that social solidarity ethics are an integral part of the concept of international trade, an essential component of international trade regulation and a natural objective of global governance. Nevertheless, the focus of the project on institutional issues means that it is a valuable resource for this chapter.

This chapter argues that increasing the salience of social solidarity ethics in international trade regulation (and revising our conception of international trade) requires strengthening relations between sites of governance. To what extent is this feasible in the case of the WTO? To answer this question, the chapter presents its arguments in two main sections. Section II. below considers in some detail current relations between the WTO and other sites of governance. Section III. then analyses a number of selected examples for increasing the salience of social solidarity ethics in international trade regulation. In other words, section II. provides a snapshot of the present, while section III. seeks to chart some directions for the future. A brief conclusion (section IV.) summarises the main points.

II. Current Relations between the WTO and Other Sites of Governance

A. Introduction

Currently the WTO has institutional relationships with a large number of other international organisations. These relationships differ in form, normative character, scope and substance. They range on a spectrum from ad hoc invitations to attend meetings on a case-by-case basis to long-standing formal agreements. They are more diffuse and variegated, however, than might be suggested by a spectrum based on any single formal criterion. As a whole, they bear witness to a uneven, halting, gradual transformation of the mandate of the WTO. Initially, the focus of the WTO, as of the GATT, was on trade, financial and economic matters narrowly defined. Over time, and very slowly, the WTO has opened up to other subject matters and other interests. This gradual transformation, which is still underway, testifies to a cognitive evolution[26] on the part of the WTO, and perhaps to the beginning of a change in our idea of the nature and purposes of international trade and international trade regulation. While it is important not to over-estimate the extent of the changes so far, they do indicate the possibility of the development of a new, broader conception of international trade regulation, embracing social solidarity ethics.

[26] On collective learning in international organisations and its consequences, see E Adler, 'Cognitive Evolution: A Dynamic Approach for the Study of International Relations and Their Progress' in E Adler and B Crawford (eds), *Progress in Postwar International Relations* (New York, Columbia University Press, 1991) 43.

The WTO Agreement grants an explicit mandate to the Director-General concerning coherence among the WTO, the International Monetary Fund (IMF) and the World Bank.[27] The Doha Round of Multilateral Trade Negotiations (MTNs) is to some extent premised on coherence. Types of inter-agency cooperation on technical assistance and capacity-building exist with several international organisations. The 'Aid-for-Trade programme' brings together several multilateral organisations and regional development banks to assist developing countries in trying to reap the benefits of trade opening.[28] The WTO also has formal cooperation agreements with other international organisations. For example, in the area of standard-setting, there is now a mechanism—the Standards and Trade Development Facility—involving the WTO, World Bank, Food and Agriculture Organisation (FAO), World Health Organisation (WHO) and the World Organisation for Animal Health. As of 2006, some 75 international organisations had regular or ad hoc observer status in WTO bodies.[29] The WTO also participates as an observer in many international organisations. The WTO Secretariat maintains working relations with almost 200 international organisations in activities ranging from statistics, to research, standard-setting and technical assistance training.[30]

Over time, the development of informal consultations and working linkages have eventually led to the conclusion of formal agreements and informal working arrangements not only with the IMF and the World Bank, but also with the WIPO, the WHO, the FAO and other organisations. While there is broad consensus on the desirability of increased coherence and coordination of the WTO with other international organisations, there is no consensus on which bodies the WTO should cooperate with, or what form that coordination should take.

The following paragraphs are intended to provide a brief, but relatively comprehensive outline of these arrangements. They deal with these arrangements roughly in chronological order. They discuss, first, the GATT legacy of relations with the IMF, the World Bank and the UN; secondly, other intergovernmental organisations in the period 1995–2000; thirdly, a wider range of organisations after 2000; and, lastly, more recent developments. More specific examples of institutional relations, for instance concerning the production of norms or dispute settlement, are given later in the chapter.

B. The GATT Legacy: IMF, World Bank and the UN

Before the establishment of the WTO, the relationships between the GATT 1947 and other international organisations were mostly informal. Relations with the IMF, the

[27] Art III:5, Marrakesh Agreement Establishing the World Trade Organisation, above n 14. For detailed analysis, see GP Sampson, 'Greater Coherence in Global Economic Policymaking: A WTO Perspective', in AO Krueger (ed), *The WTO as an International Organization* (Chicago, University of Chicago Press, 1998) 257, and J Baneth, 'Comment on the Paper by Gary P Sampson' in Krueger, *ibid*, at 271–77.

[28] See the WTO website at http://www.wto.org/english/tratop_e/devel_e/a4t_e/aid4trade_e.htm, accessed 18 July 2009.

[29] P Lamy, D-G of the WTO, 'The Place of the WTO and its Law in the International Legal Order', Address before the European Society of International Law, Paris, May 2006, (2006) 17(5) *European Journal of International Law* 969.

[30] *Ibid*.

World Bank and the United Nations (UN) were exceptions. This section gives a number of specific examples.

A close relationship between the GATT and the World Bank was implicit in Part IV of the GATT, specifically in Article XXXVI:6, 7 and Article XXXVIII:2(b), (c). Concerning the IMF Article XV of GATT 1947 (and 1994) on 'exchange arrangements' deals specifically with relations between the GATT and the IMF. The basic principle is that

> The Contracting Parties shall seek co-operation with the International Monetary Fund to the end that the Contracting Parties and the Fund may pursue a co-ordinated policy with regard to exchange questions within the jurisdiction of the Fund and questions of quantitative restrictions and other trade measures within the jurisdiction of the Contracting Parties.'[31]

Article XV GATT also provides that 'exchange questions' fall within the competence of the IMF and that nothing in the GATT prevents recourse to exchange controls consistent with the Statute of the IMF.[32] From the onset of the GATT, the Articles of Agreement of the IMF and the provisions of the GATT were designed to complement each other by introducing a coherent set of rules aimed at the progressive liberalisation of trade and payments.

Other provisions translate these general obligations into more specific terms. For example, Article II:3 GATT prohibits Members from altering their method of converting currencies so as to impair the value of their tariff concessions. Article VII GATT requires Members normally to use exchange rates recognised by the IMF when valuing goods for customs purposes. Article VI:2 and 3 (Ad Note) treat multiple currency practices in certain circumstances as constituting a subsidy to exports. Article XVI GATT (Ad Note) permits the use of multiple exchange rates strictly in accordance with the IMF Articles of Agreement. Formal institutional cooperation in the form of consultation and coordination between the GATT and the IMF was established by an exchange of letters in 1948.[33]

The advent of the WTO led to the conclusion of formal arrangements between the WTO and numerous international organisations,[34] thus providing a normative basis for different forms of partnership. The five core functions of the WTO, as defined by Article III.5 of the WTO Agreement, include contributing to more coherent global economic policy-making. Article XV GATT seeks partly to provide for such linkages. WTO Members are required not to frustrate the intent of the GATT provisions by exchange actions, or the provisions of the IMF Articles of Agreement through trade action. The importance of a disciplined use of exchange restrictions as well as close institutional cooperation with the IMF (in particular in the case of restrictions for balance-of-payments purposes or restrictions on capital movements) has also been carried into the GATS.

[31] Art XV:1 GATT.

[32] Art XV:2 GATT.

[33] F Roessler, *La relation entre l'ordre commercial mondial et le système monétaire international*, Conférences d'Actualité, CERIC, Faculté de Droit et de Science Politique d'Aix-Marseille, 1987, at 25. For a thorough recent study, see Dukgeun Ahn, 'Linkages between International Financial and Trade Institutions: IMF, World Bank and WTO' (2000) 34(4) *Journal of World Trade* 1.

[34] BM Hoekman and MM Kostecki, *The Political Economy of the World Trading System: The WTO and Beyond*, 2nd edn (Oxford, Oxford University Press, 2001) at 68–69. See also AO Krueger (ed), *The WTO as an International Organization* (Chicago and London, University of Chicago Press, 1998).

A key area for cooperation between the WTO and the IMF is based on the statutory requirements of Articles XIV and XV GATT (GATT Article XV sets out the role of the IMF in relation to Members' use of these balance-of payments provisions[35]) and Article XI GATS. These underpin, in particular, the GATT and GATS provisions and procedures that apply to IMF participation in consultations of the Committee on Balance-of-Payments Restrictions (BOPs), and on any related IMF involvement in dispute settlement proceedings under the BOPs provisions of Article XVIII:B GATT. The staff of the IMF cooperate closely with the WTO Secretariat in preparing background material for the BOPs Committee's consideration of this issue.

Conditions attached to invocation of these provisions are intended to avoid abuse. They also seek to avoid the risk that the measures taken under Article XII might be inconsistent with the obligations contained in Articles VI and VIII of the IMF Agreement (freedom of current account payments). This mandate was elaborated further in a Ministerial Declaration and a Decision on Least Developed Countries, which led to the establishment of formal relations between the WTO, on the one hand, and the IMF and the World Bank separately, on the other hand.[36]

In November 1996, acting under Article III:5 of the WTO Agreement, the WTO General Council adopted a decision approving the agreements with the IMF and the World Bank.[37] The Agreement between the WTO and the IMF[38] provided for exchange of information, mutual observer status and other forms of cooperation. Exceptions to observer status for the IMF concerned the WTO Committee on Budget, Finance and Administration, the DSB and dispute settlement panels. However, the WTO could invite the IMF as an observer to the DSB 'where matters of jurisdictional relevance to the Fund' were considered. The Agreement between the WTO and the World Bank was in similar terms, except that the provision for World Bank observer status in the WTO DSB is slightly more indirect and applies when the parties 'expect that particular matters of common interest to both organisations' are likely to be at issue.[39]

Even before the formal agreements with the IMF and the World Bank, a global arrangement between the WTO Secretariat and the UN as a whole was agreed in an exchange of letters between the Director-General of the WTO and the UN Secretary General on 29 September 1995.[40] It was based on the previous arrangement between the GATT and the UN.[41] The GATT–UN arrangement included the exchange of

[35] M Auboin, *Fulfilling the Marrakesh Mandate on Coherence: Ten Years of Cooperation between the WTO, IMF and World Bank* (Geneva, WTO, 2007).

[36] See 'WTO and IMF sign cooperation agreement' Press/62, 9 December 1996; 'WTO and World Bank sign cooperation agreement', Press/72, 28 April 1997; 'WTO Agreements with the Fund and the Bank', World Trade WT/GC/W/43, 4 November 1996 (96-4680): available on the WTO website at http://www.wto.org.

[37] WTO General Council, Minutes of Meeting held in the Centre William Rappard on 7, 8 and 13 November 1996, point 7, WT/GC/M/16, 6 December 1996.

[38] WTO, WTO Agreements with the Fund and the Bank, approved by the General Council at its meeting on the 7, 8 and 13 November 1996, Annex I: Agreement between the International Monetary Fund and the World Trade Organisation, WT/L/95, 18 November 1996.

[39] *Ibid*, Annex II: Agreement between the International Bank for Reconstruction and Development, the International Development Association and the World Trade Organisation.

[40] WTO, General Council, 15 November 1995, Arrangements for Effective Cooperation with Other Intergovernmental Organisations, Relations between the WTO and the United Nations, Communication from the Director-General, WT/GC/W/10, 3 November 1995.

[41] See UN General Assembly Document of 9 March 1976 (A/AC.179/5), Ad Hoc Committee on the Restructuring of the Economic and Social Sectors of the United Nations System, Relations of the General Agreement on Tariffs and Trade with the United Nations, Note by the Secretariat, attached to Letter dated

information and documents, resolutions of the UN, reciprocal representation, coordination, cooperation between secretariats, statistical services, personnel arrangements, administrative cooperation, affiliation of GATT to the UN Pension Fund, UN regional commissions, the International Trade Centre (ITC), commercial policy courses and relations with the IMF. Taking account of the differences between the GATT and the WTO, the WTO–UN arrangement included information exchange, reciprocal representation, cooperation between secretariats, including with regard to statistics, and administrative matters.

The United Nations Economic and Social Council (ECOSOC) and its regional commissions for Africa, Asia and Latin America also undertake regular training programmes in collaboration with the WTO for developing countries. The Committee on Trade and Environment of the WTO and the WTO Secretariat cooperate with the UN Environment Programme (UNEP) and UNCTAD, as well as the secretariats of multilateral environmental agreements, in organising information sessions, regional seminars and high-level meetings on trade and the environment.[42]

To give one example, the WTO Secretariat and the Secretariat of the UN Environment UNEP collaborate 'in the context of our respective mandates and within our respective resources'. Such cooperation poentially embraces working relations at all levels, including with regard to technical cooperation and research initiatives. It includes the provision and exchange of non-confidential information, such as access to trade-related environmental databases, and reciprocal representation at meetings of a non-confidential nature, in accordance with the decisions of the competent bodies of the respective organisations. The WTO Secretariat is an observer of the Governing Council of the UNEP. Conversely, the UNEP is an observer of the WTO Committee on Trade and Environment.[43] The two also have informal staff meetings and information sessions; where feasible, the Secretariats of Multilateral Environmental Agreements are invited to participate in these meetings.[44]

C. 1995–2000: Agreements with WIPO, OIE and ITU

Following its establishment on 1 January 1995, the WTO not only built on the GATT legacy; it also entered into arrangements with other intergovernmental organisations. In December 1995, the WTO and the WIPO reached an agreement, with a desire 'to establish a mutually supportive relationship between them, and with a view to estab-

29 September 1995 from the United Nations Secretary-General to the Director-General of the WTO, in the Annex to WTO General Council, 15 November 1995, Arrangements for Effective Cooperation with Other Intergovernmental Organisations, Relations between the WTO and the United Nations, Communication from the Director-General, WT/GC/W/10, 3 November 1995.

[42] See 'Cooperation avec d'autres organisations internationales', available on the WTO website http://www.wto.org/french/thewto_f/coher_f/coher_f.htm, Last Accessed 4 March 2010.

[43] *Ibid.*

[44] See 'Elements of Cooperation between the WTO and UNEP', WTO News: 1999 Press Releases, Press/1`54, 29 November 1999, available on the WTO website at http://www.wto.org/english/news_e/pres99_e/pr154_e.htm, visited 24 May 2002.

lishing appropriate arrangements for cooperation between them'.[45] It entered into force on 1 January 1996. It provided for the accessibility to WTO Members and their nationals of laws and regulations in the WIPO collection, and to any computerised database of WIPO containing laws and regulations. The WTO Secretariat and the TRIPS Council were to have access to laws, regulations or translations of such measures already communicated to WIPO under Article 63.2 TRIPS. This Article deals with the notification by WTO Members to the TRIPS Council of laws, regulations, final judicial decisions and administrative rulings of general application concerning intellectual property rights. The WIPO was to give assistance as regards translations to WTO developing-country Members which were not Members of WIPO. Special provisions concerned the implementation, for the purposes of the TRIPS Agreement, of Article 6 of the Paris Convention for the Protection of Industrial Property; Article 6 deals with the conditions of registration of marks and the independence of the protection of the same mark in different countries. The WIPO also undertook to make available to developing-country WTO Members the same legal–technical assistance relating to the TRIPS Agreement that it makes available to developing-country WIPO Member States. The WIPO and the WTO Secretariat undertook to enhance cooperation regarding legal–technical assistance and technical cooperation concerning TRIPS, to keep in regular contact and to exchange non-confidential information. The WTO–WIPO Agreement has been hailed as a model for relations between the WTO and other international organisations.[46]

The WTO General Council on 22 October 1997 approved an Agreement on cooperation between the WTO and the Office International des Epizooties (OIE).[47] Now known as the World Organisation for Animal Health, the OIE is an intergovernmental organisation created by an International Agreement on 25 January 1924. Since then it has grown from 24 to 174 Member Countries in April 2009. It changed its name to World Organisation for Animal Health in May 2003 but retained its previous acronym. The OIE has agreements with UN specialised organisations such as the WHO and the FAO. The SPS Agreement of the WTO recognises the OIE as the leading international standards-setting organisation for animal health and animal diseases that are transmissible to humans.[48] Together with the WHO, it has played an important role in managing the recent swine flu epidemic, for example in providing information and in setting standards for diagnostic testing and requirements for vaccines.[49] The norms of the OIE thus may complement those of the WTO in managing trade in goods and services, especially those involving animal and human mobility.

[45] The Agreement Between the World Intellectual Property Organization and the World Trade Organisation (of 22 December 1995), at http://www.wipo.int/treaties/en/agreement/trtdocs_wo030.html, visited 22 January 2008. See also WTO, Council for Trade-related Aspects of Intellectual Property Rights, Text of Proposed 'Agreement between the World Intellectual Property Organisation and the World Trade Organisation', IP/C/6, 13 December 1995.

[46] See Abbott, above n 24.

[47] WTO, Committee on Sanitary and Phytosanitary Measures, Draft Agreement between the World Trade Organisation and the Office International des Epizooties (OIE), Note by the Secretariat, G/SPS/W/61, 22 May 1996.

[48] See Art 3(4) and Art 12(3) SPS.

[49] See the OIE website at http://www.oie.int/fr/normes/mmanual/2008/pdf/2.08.08_SWINE_INFLUENZA.pdf, last accessed 4 March 2010 .

The WTO General Council approved an agreement with the International Telecommunications Union (ITU) on 10 October 2000.[50] The ITU is the leading international standardisation body in the telecommunications sector. The Agreement provides for cooperation within the scope of the mandate of each organisation, reciprocal observer status (with the usual exceptions on the WTO side), exchange of information, and technical and administrative cooperation.

D. 2000–present: Agreements with UNCTAD, ITC, FAO and Codex Alimentarius

The WTO and the United Nations Conference on Trade and Development (UNCTAD) are parties in a strategic partnership for the purpose of implementing the Doha Development Agenda (DDA), cooperating to ensure that trade serves development goals, and assisting the beneficial integration of the developing and least developed countries (LDCs) into the global economy and the multilateral trading system. In order to deepen and give practical effect to this strategic partnership, the WTO and the UNCTAD on 16 April 2003 signed a Memorandum of Understanding. This Memorandum provides a legal framework that identifies more clearly the partners' fields of cooperation and facilitates their joint activities. It should also be noted that in 2000 the UNCTAD published a very useful study of the various WTO Agreements to support developing countries in multilateral trade negotiations.[51] It also offers a Programme on Dispute Settlement in International Trade, Investment and Intellectual Property, which includes WTO law.[52]

The Integrated Framework for Trade-related Technical Assistance (TRTA) and the Joint Integrated Technical Assistance Programme (JITAP) are just two of the examples of partnership initiatives where the WTO and the UNCTAD are core partner agencies working together with a view to increasing the participation of less-developed countries in the multilateral trading system. The UNCTAD is also an observer to the Standards and Trade Development Facility (STDF) Working Group and Policy Committee as of March 2007. It further serves as executing agency for selected STDF projects.[53] Conversely, the WTO is represented at the UNCTAD's Trade and Development Board, as well as at the Commission on Trade in Goods and Services, and Commodities.

The International Trade Centre (ITC) is the joint technical cooperation agency of the UNCTAD and the WTO for business aspects of trade development. It was established in 1964 and was jointly operated by GATT (now the WTO) and the UNCTAD after 1968.[54] The three Geneva-based organisations play a complementary role in close

[50] WTO, Council for Trade in Services, Agreement between the International Telecommunications Union and the World Trade Organisation, S/C/11, 21 September 2000.

[51] UNCTAD, *Positive Agenda and Future Trade Negotiations* (New York and Geneva, United Nations, 2000).

[52] See http://www.unctad.org/Templates/WebFlyer.asp?intItemID=4403&lang=1, visited 17 May 2009.

[53] See http://www.wto.org/english/thewto_e/coher_e/wto_unctad_e.htm visited 23 January 2008.

[54] For a brief history, see UN General Assembly Document of 9 March 1976 (A/AC.179/5), Ad Hoc Committee on the Restructuring of the Economic and Social Sectors of the United Nations System, Relations of the General Agreement on Tariffs and Trade with the United Nations, Note by the Secretariat, Attached to the Letter dated 29 September 1995 from the United Nations Secretary-General to

cooperation for trade development from developing countries. While the UNCTAD and the WTO work principally with governments, the ITC works with the business community. It handles strategic and operational aspects of trade development and focuses on exports. The ITC in Geneva is the largest multilateral team dedicated entirely to TRTA.[55] The Hong Kong Ministerial Declaration in 2005 acknowledged the work done by the ITC. It reaffirmed

> the priorities established in paragraph 38 of the Doha Ministerial Declaration for the delivery of technical assistance and urge[d] the Director-General to ensure that programmes focus accordingly on the needs of beneficiary countries and reflect the priorities and mandates adopted by members . . .

The Ministerial Declaration continued by stating that

> In particular, we encourage all Members to cooperate with the International Trade Centre, which complements WTO work by providing a platform for business to interact with trade negotiators, and practical advice for small and medium-sized enterprises (SMEs) to benefit from the multilateral trading system.[56]

The WTO has observer status in the meetings of the Codex Alimentarius Commission, which was created in 1963 by the FAO and the WHO to develop food standards, guidelines and related texts such as codes of practice under the Joint FAO/WHO Food Standards Programme.[57] Relations between the WTO, FAO and Codex Alimentarius are discussed in more detail in Section III of this chapter.

E. 1997–present: Informal Working Arrangements with WHO, ILO and OECD

The period from 1997 to the present has been characterised also by the development of informal working arrangements with other organisations. The WTO and the WHO collaborate in matters of public health. In 1997 the WHO, in collaboration with the WTO, prepared a document on food safety and globalisation of trade in goods to assist developing countries in complying with the WTO SPS Agreement.[58] Subsequently in 2002 they carried out a joint study on the WTO Agreements and public health.[59]

Another example is the International Labour Organisation (ILO). The ILO Constitution provides that the ILO shall cooperate within the terms of the Constitution with public international organisations having specialised responsibilities in related

the Director-General of the World Trade Organisation, annexed to World Trade Organisation, General Council, 15 November 1995, Arrangements for Effective Cooperation with Other Intergovernmental Organisations, Relations between the WTO and the United Nations, Communication from the Director-General, WT/GC/W/10, 3 November 1995.

[55] http://www.intracen.org/AidforTrade/?mn=0&sm=0?13 last accessed 4 March 2010.

[56] WTO Ministerial Declaration, Hong Kong, 2005.

[57] See http://www.codexalimentarius.net.

[58] WHO, *Food Safety and Globalization of Trade in Food: A Challenge to the Public Health Sector*, Food Safety Unit, Programme of Food Safety and Food Aid, World Health Organization, WHO/FSF/FOS/97.8.Rev 1 (1997).

[59] WHO and WTO, *WTO Agreements and Public Health: A Joint Study by the WHO and the WTO Secretariat*, 2002.

fields,[60] and that the ILO may also make appropriate arrangements for the representatives of public international organisations to participate without vote in its deliberations.[61] The WTO and the ILO have informal working relationships, notably with regard to the highly controversial matter of labour standards. Collaboration includes participation by the WTO in meetings of ILO bodies, exchange of documentation and informal cooperation between the two secretariats, as well as regular meetings between the two Directors-General.[62] In June 2001 the ILO Working Party on the Social Dimension of Globalisation agreed that a permanent forum for the exchange of views should be established.[63] Subsequently the ILO set up a World Commission on the Social Consequences of Globalisation, headed by the Presidents of Finland and of Tanzania.[64] In 2007, the WTO and the ILO published their first joint report.[65] As a follow-up, at the request of the High-Level Committee on Programmes (HLCP) of the UN system Chief Executives Board (CEB), the ILO then undertook a mapping exercise of the ILO's trade-related activities. It also agreed with the WTO Secretariat to continue their collaboration by carrying out a joint study on the links between globalisation, trade and informal employment.[66]

The WTO and the Organisation for Economic Cooperation and Development (OECD) cooperate in numerous activities.[67] The Doha Development Agenda Trade Capacity Building Database (TCBDB) has been established by the WTO jointly with the OECD to provide information on trade-related technical assistance and capacity building projects. The database covers national as well as regional projects, and is an on-going activity. The 2006 Joint WTO/OECD Report on Trade-related Technical Assistance and Capacity Building was circulated at the end of April 2007.[68] The OECD and the WTO have also collaborated closely to develop a framework for monitoring aid for trade. This framework has three levels: global monitoring of aid for trade flows, based on the OECD Creditor Reporting System; donor monitoring in the form of self-assessments; and in-country monitoring, also in the form of self-assessments. A recent joint OECD/WTO report, *Aid for Trade at a Glance 2007: 1st Global Review*, gave the first comprehensive global picture of aid for trade, and should enable the international community to assess what is being achieved, what is not and where improvements are needed.[69]

[60] ILO Constitution, Art 12(1), at http://www.ilo.org.

[61] *Ibid*, Art 12(2).

[62] See 'Trade and Labour Standards: A Difficult Issue for Many WTO Member Governments', Doha WTO Ministerial 2001: Briefing Notes, available on the WTO website at http://www.wto.org/english/thewto_e/minist_e/min01_e/brief_e/brief16_e.htm, visited 25 May 2002.

[63] ILO Constitution, Art 12(2).

[64] See 'ILO tackles social consequences of globalisation', available on the ILO website at http://www.ilo/org/public/english/wcsdg/entry1.htm, visited 8 June 2002.

[65] E Lee and M Jansen (eds), *Trade and Employment: Challenges for Policy Research* (Geneva, ILO and WTO, 2007).

[66] International Labour Organisation Governing Body, Working Party on the Social Dimension of Globalisation, 'Trade and Employment: Follow-Up to the Joint ILO/WTO Secretariat Study', WP/SDG, GB.300/WP/SDG/, 300th Session, Geneva, November 2007, available at http://www.ilo.org/wcmsp5/groups/public/-ed_norm/-relconf/documents/meetingdocument/wcms_084891.pdf, visited 14 May 2009.

[67] On the relationship between the WTO Subsidies Agreement and OECD arrangements on export credits, see J Pauwelyn, *Conflict of Norms in Public International Law: How WTO Law Relates to Other Rules of International Law* (Cambridge, Cambridge University Press, 2003) at 348–49.

[68] See http://tcbdb.wto.org/ visited 23 January 2008.

[69] See http://www.oecd.org/document/46/0,3343.en_2649_34665_39619566_1_1_1_1,00.html, visited 23 January 2008.

F. The Future: Relations with UNESCO, MEAs, NGOs and Private Standards Bodies

Most recently, the WTO has undertaken relations with a wider group of organisations, which in the past might have been considered to have relatively little to do with trade. Even today, the WTO does not have any direct institutional relationships with the United Nations Education, Scientific and Cultural Organisation (UNESCO). The potential impact of the UNESCO Convention on Cultural Diversity in WTO law is considered in section II.C.ii of the chapter.

More than 250 multilateral environmental agreements (MEAs) dealing with various environmental issues are currently in force.[70] About 20 of these include provisions that can affect trade.[71] Closer cooperation between MEA Secretariats and WTO Committees is essential to ensure that the activities of these organisations develop coherently to the extent possible. This objective was recognised in the Plan of Implementation of the 2002 World Summit on Sustainable Development (WSSD) in Johannesburg, which called for efforts to 'strengthen cooperation among UNEP and other United Nations bodies and specialized agencies, the Bretton Woods institutions and WTO, within their mandates.'[72] In addition to looking at the relationship between specific trade obligations in the environmental agreements and WTO rules, the negotiations have covered procedures for MEA Secretariats and relevant WTO Committees to exchange information on a regular basis. The WTO attends the main meetings of MEAs which contain trade-related measures. The Committee on Trade and Environment (CTE) of the WTO has invited a number of MEA Secretariats to participate in a total of eight Information Sessions from 1997 till 2007. The MEA Secretariats presented background notes on their respective MEAs and responded to questions from Members on the trade-related aspects of their agreements.[73] Most MEAs also address the issue of the observership of international organisations in their statutes, and allow international organisations who have expressed an interest to attend meetings as observers.[74] Observer status is discussed in more detail in section III.D. below.

Non-governmental organisations (NGOs) play an extremely important role in the regulation of international trade and in global governance today. Consequently, it is crucial to consider relations between the WTO and NGOs. The Marrakesh Agreement of 1994 includes a specific reference to NGOs in Article V:2. On 18 July 1996, the General Council further clarified the framework for relations with NGOs by adopting a set of guidelines[75] which 'recognize . . . the role NGOs can play to increase the awareness of

[70] On the relationship between norms in the WTO Agreements and in MEAs, see Pauwelyn, above n 67, at 350–51.

[71] See www.wto.org visited 21 January 2008.

[72] *Ibid.*

[73] WTO, Note by the Secretariat Committee on Trade and Environment Special Session, *Existing forms of cooperation and information exchange between UNEP/MEAs and the WTO*, Document No: TN/TE/S/2/Rev.2_16 January 2007.

[74] WTO, Note by the Secretariat Committee on Trade and Environment Special Session, *Matrix on trade measures pursuant to selected, multilateral environmental agreements*, Document No: WT/CTE/W/160/ Rev.4, TN/TE/S/5/Rev.2 14 March 2007.

[75] WTO, 'Guidelines for arrangements on relations with Non-Governmental Organizations', Decision adopted by the General Council on 18 July 1996, WT/L/162, 23 July 1996, available on the WTO website at http://www.wto.org/english/forums_e/ngo_e/guide_e.htm, visited 3 July 2002.

the public in respect of WTO activities'. These guidelines are instrumental for both Members and the WTO Secretariat in maintaining an informal and positive dialogue with the various components of civil society. Since 1996, arrangements for NGOs have essentially focused on attendance at Ministerial Conferences, participation in issue-specific symposia, and the day-to-day contact between the WTO Secretariat and NGOs. An on-line computer network was to be accessible to the public and was to be used for this process. In fact, however, it was only on 14 May 2002 that the WTO began to take steps towards openness and accountability by accelerating derestriction of official WTO documents.

Private standardisation bodies are extremely important in international trade. The standards which they produce raise difficult issues of compliance and market access for producers in developing countries. As shown in Chapter 3, they complement and sometimes replace technical regulations or governmental standards. Technical regulations, standards and conformity assessment procedures are governed by the WTO Agreement on Technical Barriers to Trade ('TBT Agreement'), except for measures concerning sanitary and phytosanitary measures, such as food standards, which fall under the WTO Agreement on Sanitary and Phytosanitary Measures ('SPS Agreement'). In the terms of the TBT Agreement, technical regulations are legally binding, while standards are not. The disciplines of the WTO are much more stringent and more effective with regard to technical regulations than with regard to standards. In turn, governmental standards are more effectively regulated than private standards. For example, under the TBT Agreement, central government standardising bodies are required to accept and comply with the Code of Good Practice for the Preparation, Adoption and Application of Standards. Members of the WTO are also required to take such reasonable measures as may be available to them to ensure that their local government and non-governmental standardising bodies accept the Code.[76] However, the governance of private standards remains problematic.

Currently, the WTO does not have effective links with private standards bodies. Overall, private standards bodies may participate in WTO deliberations indirectly through national governmental organisations, but the WTO does not have any official relations with these organisations. The TBT Code of Good Practice does not apply automatically to private standards bodies, which can decide whether or not to join. It does not cover international standardisation organisations, though governmental or non-governmental standardising bodies one or more of whose members are Members of the WTO may accept the Code. Neither are private standards bodies or international standardising organisations bound by the emerging normative framework for the governance of standards-setting, which is composed of principles for the development of international standards, a standards information system and a code for specifying the stage of development of a standard.[77]

[76] Agreement on Technical Barriers to Trade, Art 4, in, *The Legal Texts: The Results of the Uruguay Round of Multilateral Trade Negotiations* (Cambridge, Cambridge University Press, 13th printing 2007; first published in 1994 by the GATT Secretariat). The Code of Good Practice may be found *ibid*, at 139–42.

[77] See WTO, Committee on Technical Barriers to Trade, 'Problems Faced by Developing Countries in International Standards and Conformity Assessment', Discussions of the TBT Committee in the context of the Second Triennial Review of the TBT Agreement, Report by the Chairman, G/L/422, 29 November 2000, available at http://209.85.229.132/search?q=cache:xNmmc-141v8J:www.wtocenter.org.tw/SmartKMS/fileviewer%3Fid%3D47160+%22Problems+Faced+by+Developing+Countries+in+International+Standards+and+Conformity+Assessment%22&cd=1&hl=fr&ct=clnk&gl=fr;, last accessed 4 March 2010 'Decision on Proposed Understanding on WTO–ISO Standards Information System', available at http://www.wto. org/english/docs_e/legal_e/37-dtbt1_e.htm, visited 14 May 2009.

So far, there does not seem to have been any authoritative determination as to whether private standards fall within the scope of the SPS Agreement or the TBT Agreement using the same criteria as governmental standards.[78] In some cases, other WTO Agreements may also be relevant. For example, GlobalGAP (formerly EurepGAP) is a private sector body that sets voluntary standards for the certification of agricultural products, and its standards deal with numerous topics, including worker health and safety, and waste and pollution management.[79] In the past several years, developing countries have continually raised the issue of private standards such as those of GlobalGAP in the WTO SPS Committee.[80] In December 2008, the SPS Committee circulated a fact-finding questionnaire about experience with private sector standards. Replies were circulated, and a document compiling all relies was prepared. [81] An *ad hoc* working group was created. In late September 2009, the Mercosur delegations (Argentina, Brazil, Paraguay and Uruguay) submitted a proposal for a legal framework for private standards.[82] As of the time of writing, this is still being discussed.

III. Developing Social Solidarity Ethics in International Trade Regulation

A. The Matrix of Relations between Sites of Governance

The preceding discussion shows clearly that the WTO has institutional relations with numerous other sites of governance. These relations are of different types and concern many topics. The most frequently used legal techniques for these relationships are formal agreements, mutual observership and memoranda of understanding. Often they are supplemented by relations among top officials and transparency norms.[83] Taking these features into account, how can we increase the salience of social solidarity ethics in international trade regulation? The theory of sites of governance provides a useful perspective for thinking about this question. Institutions, norms and dispute resolution

[78] In the SPS Agreement, the basic rights and obligations in Art 2 explicitly refer to the rights and obligations of 'Members', but simultaneously Art 1.1 states that the Agreement applies to 'all sanitary and phytosanitary measures which may, directly or indirectly, affect international trade', without explicitly limiting this application to SPS measures taken by governmental authorities. In the case of TBT, the legal definitions given for standards, conformity assessment procedures and non-governmental bodies within Annex 1 to the TBT Agreement would appear of particular relevance in this regard.

[79] See the GlobalGAP website at http://www.globalgap.org/cms/front_content.php?idart=3&idcat=9&lang=1, visited 17 May 2009; and WTO, Committee on Sanitary and Phytosanitary Measures, 'Private Standards and the SPS Agreement', Note by the Secretariat, G/SPS/GEN/746, 24 January 2007.

[80] See, eg, GH Stanton and C Wolf, 'Private Voluntary Standards and the World Trade Organisation (WTO) Committee on Sanitary and Phytosanitary Measures', available at http://www.agrifoodstandards.net/en/filemanager/active?fid=134, visited 17 May 2009.

[81] WTO, 'Work on Private Food Health and Safety Standards Moves to New Phase', WTO 2009 New Items, 25–26 February 2009, available at http://www.wto.org/english/news_e/news09_e/sps_25feb09_e.htm, visited 17 May 2009.

[82] WTO, Committee on Sanitary and Phytosanitary Measures, 'Legal Framework for Private Standards in the WTO', Communication from Mercosur (Argentina, Brazil, Paraguay and Uruguay), G/SPS/W/246, 30 September 2009.

[83] See also V Mosoti, 'Institutional Cooperation and Norm Creation', and LR Helfer, 'Mediating Interactions in an Expanding International Intellectual Property Regime (Comment on Victor Moscoti)' in Cottier *et al*, above n 25, at 165–79 and 180–90, respectively.

processes are the three aspects of the structural dimension of sites. Relations among sites may concern any or all of these aspects.

We can use these ideas to elaborate an institutionalist perspective on relations between sites of governance. The literature on corporate governance provides a helpful starting point. Bratton and McCahery construct a corporate government matrix, based on the idea that comparative corporate governance 'may be seen as a two-course menu that offers two choices in each course'. The first course is a choice of convergence model, either strong or weak. In the former, global competitive forces dominate, while in the latter national institutions are predominant. The second course is a choice with regard to divisibility: to what extent are national governance systems open to outside elements by cross-reference to the components of other systems?[84] The resulting matrix is as shown in Table 20 below.[85]

Table 20 The Corporate Governance Matrix

	Divisible	**Indivisible**
Strong Convergence	(1) Global cross-reference	(2) Chicago School
Weak Convergence	(3) National-cross reference	(4) National embeddedness

Box 1 combines strong convergence with divisibility. It implies a hybrid but unitary system of corporate governance worldwide. Box 2, combining strong convergence and indivisibility, 'implies competitive struggle between entire systems, with one system winning in the end'.[86] In Box 3, which combines weak convergence and divisibility, cross-reference is used only to improve national systems, but there is no international convergence. Box 4, combining weak convergence with indivisibility tends to preserve national systems, with little cross-reference and little international convergence. According to Bratton and McCahery, Box 1 is 'virtually absent from the legal literature', while Box 3 represents the 'international mainstream approach'.[87] On the basis of their analysis, these authors argue that corporate governance institutions are indivisible, deeply embedded in national political and social contexts, and part of a system with specific complex incentive structures. Consequently, in their view, global cross-reference in the domain of corporate governance is not likely or desirable.[88]

Borrowing from the analysis by Bratton and McCahery, but rearranging the order of presentation, we can construct a matrix of sites of governance. It focuses on selected international organisations concerning international trade regulation, rather than on systems of corporate governance. Table 21 below presents such a matrix of relations between these sites of governance.

Box 1 brings together weak convergence and the strong embeddedness of a specific site in its particular context. It implies that there is little, if any, convergence in the structural dimension (institutions, norms, dispute resolution processes) among sites of

[84] WW Bratton and JA McCahery, 'Comparative Corporate Governance and the Theory of the Firm: The Case against Global Cross Reference' (1999) 38(2) *Columbia Journal of Transnational Law* 214 at 255.

[85] Table 20 reproduces 'Table 3—The Comparative Governance Matrix', *ibid.*

[86] *Ibid*, at 256.

[87] *Ibid.*

[88] *Ibid.*

governance. Each preserves its own characteristics and remains confined to its own particular tasks. Box 2 combines weak convergence and divisibility. It implies limited cross-reference among sites, with the result that a specific site of governance uses cross-reference to other sites primarily to improve its own institutions, norms or dispute resolution processes. Box 3, which combines strong convergence with indivisibility, is a position that is best represented by proposals that the WTO should act as a global trade constitution, integrating, where necessary, elements, such as norms, from other sites of governance in order to strengthen itself as an institution and increase its global reach.[89] Box 4 combines strong convergence and divisibility. It means that every site can potentially refer to and integrate into its functioning elements of the structural dimension (institutions, norms, dispute resolution processes) originating from any other site.

Table 21 Matrix of International Organisations in International Trade Regulation

	Indivisible	**Divisible**
Weak Convergence	(1) Strong embeddedness of a specific site of governance	(2) Limited cross-reference among sites of governance
Strong Convergence	(3) Strong constitutionalisation of the institution, eg WTO	(4) Global cross-reference

Compared to corporate governance systems, the WTO and other international institutions might seem to be less deeply embedded in various national political, social, economic and legal contexts. To some extent this may be true, but two points need to be kept in mind. First, the WTO is embedded to different degrees and in different ways in the distinctive legal and institutional contexts of each WTO Member. Chapter three demonstrated the specific features of relations between the EU and the WTO as constructed by the ECJ. China, the USA or each other WTO Member has its own specific contexts—legal, institutional and other—in which the WTO is to some extent embedded. Secondly, the context of the WTO is international as well as national or regional. International organisations such as the WTO, the WCO, the ILO, the WHO, the OIE and the UN operate in separate spheres, as least in principle. A strong version of this viewpoint concerning the WTO is presented by Abbott and Snidal in their analysis of why the WTO has not taken action on bribery and corruption, unlike most other major international organisations.[90] In their view, the WTO is characterised by a focus on hard law; it 'remains mired in the obsessive quid pro quo thinking that has dominated tariff negotiations for fifty years'; it is a Member-driven organisation so that delegates, Secretariat officials and the heads of working groups are kept on a short leash; and it focuses on technical issues with little reference to their broader normative dimension, let alone ethics.[91] While this characterisation may be justified from the

[89] For an exposition and critique of this position, see esp DZ Cass, *The Constitutionalization of the WTO; Legitimacy, Democracy and Community in the International Trading System* (Oxford, Oxford University Press, 2005). See also J Trachtman, 'The Constitutions of the WTO' (2006) 17(3) *European Journal of International Law* 623.

[90] KW Abbott and D Snidal, 'International Action on Bribery and Corruption: Why the Dog Didn't Bark in the WTO' in DLM Kennedy and JD Southwick (eds), *The Political Economy of International Trade Law: Essays in Honor of Robert E Hudec* (Cambridge, Cambridge University Press, 2002).

[91] *Ibid*, at 179, 180, 196, 197, 199 and 200 (the source of the quotation).

standpoint of combating bribery and corruption, each of these points is subject to debate and discussion.[92]

So far, convergence of the WTO with many sites of governance orientated toward social solidarity ethics would appear to be relatively weak. The WTO would seem, therefore, to be a relatively indivisible institution. Nevertheless, as the preceding discussion in this chapter shows, the WTO today has relations with a wide range of sites of governance, and these relations have changed a good deal in the past decade. Much depends on the self-conception of the WTO, its relations with other sites of governance and the contribution of these other sites to their relations with the WTO. In addition, not all of the organisations with which the WTO currently has or is developing relations are equally indivisible. Both elements are important aspects of our conceptions of international trade and of international trade regulation.

Indeed, on the basis of the historical review of WTO relations with other sites of governance so far, it may be suggested that each institution is to some extent divisible, in that some of its components can be adopted for use in other institutions without serious adverse or destabilising effects. This is consistent with Trachtman's argument that specific institutions differ in their 'primary coverage' or 'core competence', but nonetheless an institution may recognise norms developed by another within its core field, institutions may develop 'more subtle and variegated mechanisms [of relationship] than across-the-board deference or across-the-board ignorance', and functional integration between institutions may progressively become more intricate and complex.[93] In developing and deepening relations between the WTO and other sites of governance, it is essential to go beyond a conception of international institutions that sees each institution as responding to a specific set of clients and demands, and as limited to a specific function.[94] In both theory and practice, cross-reference is possible between the WTO and other sites of governance.[95] In the present context, increased cross-reference means stronger inter-institutional relations.

Increasing the salience of social solidarity ethics in international trade regulation requires a stronger convergence between the WTO and other sites of governance. The argument here is that the WTO should aim for strong convergence and divisibility with international institutions which have a mandate to represent, or which in practice tend to promote, social solidarity ethics. This means maximising Box 4 (global cross-reference) and if necessary Box 2 (limited cross-reference), but avoiding Box 1 (strong embeddedness) and Box 3 (strong constitutionalisation of the WTO). Seen in terms of sites of governance, this entails creating and managing effective relations between the WTO and other sites of governance concerning institutions, norms and dispute settlement processes.

Drawing on the theory of global legal pluralism, and building on this institutionalist perspective on relations between sites, we can identify several ways to increase the

[92] For a useful critique of this 'legal centralism' view of the WTO, see ATF Lang, 'Re-thinking Trade and Human Rights' (2007) 15(2) *Tulane Journal of International and Comparative Law* 335.

[93] Trachtman, above n 23, at 90.

[94] See also Lang, above n 91, at 378, citing PA Hall and RCR Taylor, 'Political Science and the Three New Institutionalisms' (1966) 44 *Political Studies* 936.

[95] For a statement of a similar position by an ex D-G of the WTO, which was not however fully carried through in practice, see R Ruggiero, 'A Shared Responsibility: Global Policy Coherence for Our Global Age', Address to the Conference on *Globalisation as a Challenge for German Business: Export Opportunities for Small and Medium-Sized Companies in the Environmental Field*, Bonn, 9 December 1997, available on the WTO website at http://www.wto.org/english/news_e/sprr_e/bonn_e.htm, visited 18 June 2002.

salience of social solidarity ethics in WTO decision-making. The first consists of strengthening existing institutional relations. The second concerns increasing inter-site cooperation in the production of norms. A third method is to expand the use of observer status in WTO bodies; it is treated separately here because it involves both strengthening inter-institutional relations and potential cooperation in the production of norms. A fourth method is increased cross-reference in the settlement of disputes. These ideas are explored in the following paragraphs.

B. Institutional Relations between Sites

The first way to increase the salience of social solidarity ethics in international trade governance is to strengthen existing institutional relations between sites of governance concerned with such matters. Currently the WTO has strong institutional relations with other sites mainly in economic domains. One example consists of links with the World Bank and the IMF concerning the development of a coherent economic policy at the international level.[96] The WTO also cooperates with the UN in the field of technical cooperation for economic development. This is a commercial objective, which includes training, seminars and workshops for officials from developing countries and countries in transition, with regard to trade policy and effective negotiation.[97] It also includes the Integrated Framework for TRTA, which deals entirely with trade policy, obstacles or impediments to developing countries' efforts to expand trade, and technical assistance.[98] Furthermore, the WTO works with the OIE and the FAO in the creation and application of standards.

Today, however, it is no longer credible to pretend that the WTO has an impact solely on trade. Neither is it possible to separate the economy distinctly from other aspects of social life. Consider the environment. The WTO cooperates with UN agencies regarding environmental protection, but it does not have any specific agreement concerning the environment. Nevertheless, references to the environment may be found, for example, in Article XX GATT, Article XIV GATT, the TBT Agreement and the SPS Agreement, as well as in WTO case law.[99] Within the WTO, the Committee on Trade and Environment (CTE) has the task of studying the relationship between trade and the environment, and of making recommendations for any changes needed in trade agreements.[100] The work of the CTE is based on two principles. First, the WTO is competent to deal only with trade, and it deals with environmental issues only when

[96] See generally AO Krueger (ed), *The WTO as an International Organization* (Chicago and London, University of Chicago Press, 1998).

[97] See 'WTO technical cooperation', available on the WTO website http://www.wto.org/english/thewto_e/whatis_e/tif_e/dev3_e.htm, visited 25 May 2002.

[98] See 'An Integrated Framework for Trade Related Technical Assistance, including for Human and Institutional Capacity-Building, to Support Least-Developed Countries in Their Trade and Trade-Related Activities: Revision', WT/LDS/HL/1/Rev.1, 23 October 1997 (97-4650), available on the WTO website http://www.wto.org/english/trratop_d/devel-e/framework.htm, visited 25 May 2002.

[99] Among recent studies, see J Wiers, *Trade and Environment in the EC and the WTO: A Legal Analysis* (Groningen, Europa Law Publishing, 2002); F Francioni (ed), *Environment, Human Rights and International Trade* (Oxford, Hart Publishing, 2001).

[100] On the CTE, see GC Shaffer, 'The World Trade Organization Under Challenge: Democracy and the Law and Politics of the WTO's Treatment of Trade and Environment Matters' (2001) 25(1) *Harvard Environmental Law Review* 1.

they have a significant effect on trade. Secondly, if the CTE does identify problems, its solutions must uphold the principles of the WTO trading system. The formal position of the CTE is that clauses in the WTO Agreements, for example concerning goods, services and intellectual property, allow governments to give priority to their domestic environmental policies. States should preferably use international environmental agreements, not the WTO, to deal with other countries' environmental policies.[101]

Strengthening links between the WTO and other organisations, together with the articulation of a more coherent and convincing normative framework, may improve the extent to which environmental issues are to be taken into account by the WTO. They may take the form of formal or informal partnerships, or mechanisms for sharing information, including ad hoc requests to review the implications of a measure being considered or to consider a broad subject area. Helfer gives the example of the invitation to the WTO by the Conference of the Parties to the Convention on Biological Diversity (CBD) to 'take into account the fact that the provisions of [TRIPS and the CBD] are interrelated and to further explore this relationship'.[102]

As these examples demonstrate, institutional relations are often intimately intertwined with cooperation in the production of norms. It is notable that the WTO does not take part in the UN Global Compact. First proposed by UN Secretary-General Kofi Annan on 31 January 1999 and launched on 26 July 2000, the Global Compact aims to disseminate good practices based on nine principles drawn from the Universal Declaration on Human Rights, the ILO's Fundamental Principles on Rights at Work, and the Rio Principles on Environment and Development. It involves governments, companies, civil society organisations and the UN, but the WTO does not participate.[103]

Multifaceted cooperation among sites of governance may involve the creation of new institutions, mechanisms or networks. For example, the WTO Director-General invited the Deputy Directors-General of the FAO, OIE, World Bank and WTO to informal meetings in 2001 to examine the financial and technical means for encouraging the participation of developing countries in international standard-setting. They agreed, among other things, on the necessity of establishing a permanent mechanism to coordinate their resources in order to avoid overlap, and to prepare a formal statement of common objectives.[104] Subsequent meetings were planned on these topics,

[101] Based on 'Trading into the Future: The Introduction to the WTO: Beyond the agreements: The environment—a new high profile' at http://www.wto.org/english/res_e/doload_e/tif.pdf, last accesseed 4 March 2010.

[102] Convention on Biological Diversity, Conference of the Parties, Decision V/26 on Access to Genetic Resources, www.biodiv.org/decisions/default.asp?lg=08&dec=V/26,last accessed 4 March 2010, §B,2, quoted in Helfer, above n 83, at 189.

[103] See the Global Compact website at http://www.unglobalcompact.org. The UN Secretary-General asks world business to observe nine principles: (1) support and respect the protection of international human rights within their sphere of influence; (2) make sure their own corporations are not complicit in human rights abuses; (3) uphold freedom of association and the effective recognition of the right to collective bargaining; (4) uphold the elimination of all forms of forced and compulsory labour; (5) uphold the effective abolition of child labour; (6) uphold the elimination of discrimination in respect of employment and occupation; (7) support a precautionary approach to environmental challenges; (8) undertake initiatives to promote greater environmental responsibility; and (9) encourage the development and diffusion of environmentally friendly techniques.

[104] See Troisième rapport du Directeur général, Organisation Mondiale du Commerce: Conseil général, Session extraordinaire sur la mise en œuvre, Mesures visant à accroitre la participation des pays en développement membres aux travaux des organisations internationales de normalisation compétentes dans le domaine des mesures sanitaires et phytosanitaires, Organisation Mondiale du Commerce, WT/GC/54, 7 novembre 2001 (01-5490), available on the WTO website at http://docsonline.wto.org/GEN_viewerwindow.asp?D:/DDFDOCUMENTS/U/WT/GC/54, visited 10 June 2002.

and the WTO Director-General asked each organisation to provide information concerning the type of technical assistance it furnished to developing countries to facilitate their participation in international standard-setting bodies and whether they were able to increase their assistance.[105] At the WTO Ministerial Conference in Doha, the WTO issued a joint statement with the World Bank and the 'three sisters', the FAO, the OIE, and the WHO,[106] on the participation of developing countries in the development and application of international standards. They confirmed their intention to undertake technical assistance activities and investment in infrastructure to assist developing countries in the establishment of appropriate food safety and animal and plant health measures.[107]

The strategy of strengthening relations between sites of governance is not, however, free from controversy. The WTO–IMF Agreement, signed on 9 December 1996 in Singapore on the opening of the First WTO Ministerial Conference, was intended to provide a basis for greater coherence, provide channels of communication 'to ensure that the rights and obligations of Members are integral to the thinking of each organisation', and grant observer status to staff of the IMF and the WTO in certain decision-making bodies of the other.[108] In addition to new formal relations, the WTO envisaged global coherence and consistency of recommendations, and strengthened cooperation between the WTO, the IMF and the World Bank at staff level.[109]

These proposals for further formal and informal agreements proved, however, to be politically sensitive. They led to certain concerns among WTO members. The WTO Director-General then issued a statement on the subject confirming, first, that the only point of reference in these relations would be the WTO Agreements and Decisions. Secondly, he stated that the formulation of national policies was within the sovereign domain of governments, and the agreements with other institutions were designed to provide a mechanism for the WTO to address the IMF and the WB in order to protect the interests of WTO Members consistently with their rights and obligations under the WTO Agreements. Thirdly, however, he pointed out that the novel feature of the proposed agreements concerned the matter of Global Coherence, according to which,

[105] See Rapport du Directeur Général, Organisation Mondiale du Commerce, Conseil général, Session extraordinaire sur la mise en œuvre: Mesures visant a accroitre la participation des pays en développement membres aux travaux des organisations de normalisation compétentes, available on the WTO website at http://docsonline.wto.org/GEN_viewerwindow.asp?D:DDFDOCUMENTS/U/WT/GC/42, visited 10 June 2002.

[106] These three organisations are responsible for international standards, guidelines and recommendations relevant to the SPS Agreement. The OIE deals with animal health; the FAO and the WHO jointly provide the Secretariat of the Codex Alimentarius, which deals with food safety; and the FAO provides the Secretariat of the International Plant Protection Convention (IPPC), which deals with plant health.

[107] See 'Participation of Developing Countries in the Development and Application of International Standards, Guidelines and Recommendations on Food Safety, Animal and Plant Health: A Joint Statement by the Directors-General of the Food and Agricultural Organisation of the United Nations, the Office International des Epizooties, the World Health Organisation, the World Trade Organisation and the World Bank', in 'Agencies to boost developing countries' participation in setting food safety and related norms', WTO News: 2001 Press Releases, Press/254, 11 November 2001, available on the WTO website at http://www.wto.org/english/news_e/pres01_e/pr254_e.htm, visited 24 May 2002.

[108] See 'WTO and IMF sign cooperation agreement', WTO News: 1996 Press Releases, Press/62, 9 December 1996, available on the WTO website http://www.wto.org/english/news_e/pres96_e/pr062_e.htm, visited 24 May 2002.

[109] See Note by the Secretariat, 'WTO Cooperation with the IMF and the World Bank and Greater Coherence in Global Economic Policy-Making', World Trade Organisation (94-2226), Sub-Committee on Institutional, Procedural and Legal Matters, Preparatory Committee PC/IPL/W/10, 31 October 1994, available on the WTO website at http://docsonline.wto.org/GEN_viewerwindow.asp?D:/DDFDOCUMENTS/T/WT/PCIP, visited 18 June 2002.

under each agreement, consultations and reports at least twice each year were to deal with a wide range of matters on the coherence of polices of the WTO, the IMF and the WB.[110] This was consistent with paragraph 10 of the IMF Agreement and paragraph 8 of the WB Agreement. The consultations on coherence were based on paragraph 2 of each Agreement, within the framework of Article III:5 of the Marrakesh Agreement and the mandate in the Declaration on the Contribution of the WTO to Achieving Greater Coherence in Global Economy Policy-Making.[111]

Subsequent cooperation has focused mainly on trade, especially mainstreaming trade into development strategies.[112] However, these efforts have unfortunately been based almost entirely on the fundamental postulate that, above all, 'Trade reform and liberalisation are powerful factors for economic growth, and can contribute to poverty reduction and sustainable development'.[113]

Another controversial example concerns relations between the WTO and NGOs. The 1996 WTO Guidelines provided that the WTO Secretariat was to play a more active role in relations with NGOs, for example by organising ad hoc symposia or making informal arrangements. They also stated, however, that

> there is currently a broadly held view that it would not be possible for NGOs to be directly involved in the work of the WTO or its meetings. Close consultation and cooperation with NGOs can also be met constructively through appropriate processes at the national level where lies primary responsibility for taking into account the different elements of public interest which are brought to bear on trade policy-making . . .[114]

Thus the WTO CTE considers that, as a matter of principle, it would be inappropriate to allow NGOs to participate directly as observers in CTE proceedings. Nevertheless, following the WTO General Council Decision of 18 July 1996 on 'Guidelines for observer status for international intergovernmental organisations in the WTO', it allows intergovernmental organisations to participate in CTE meetings as permanent observers; this includes the secretariats of many multilateral environmental agreements.[115]

More generally, however, the WTO practice regarding NGOs has been severely criticised. According to two leading scholars witing ten years ago, it was not the absence

[110] See 'Statement by the Director-General on Consultations and Coherence' Addendum to the Agreement between the WTO and the IMF and the World Bank, World Trade Organisation WT/L/194/Add.1, 18 November 1996 (96-4879), available on the WTO website http://docsonline.wto.org/GEN_viewerwindow.asp?D:/DDFDOCUMENTS/T/WT/L/194, visited 18 June 2002.

[111] The basic documents are listed in 'Coherence—closer cooperation between multilateral institutions', available on the WTO website http://www.wto.org/english/thewto_e/coher_e/coher_e.htm, visited 25 May 2002.

[112] See 'Report by the Director-General on Implementation of the Agreements', Agreements between the WTO and the IMF and the World Bank, World Trade Organisation WT/GC/W/68, 13 November 1967 (97-5040), and 'Annotated Checklist of Issues Raised by Delegations', Agreements between the WTO and the IMF and the World Bank, World Trade Organisation Restricted WT/GC/W/140, 3 February 1999 (99/0400), both available on the WTO website http://docsonline.wto.org/GEN_viewerwindow.asp?D:DDFDOCUMENTS/T/WT/GC/W, visited 18 June 2002; Report (2000) by the Director-General, Coherence in Global Policy-Making: WTO Cooperation with the IMF and the World Bank, World Trade Organisation Restricted WT/TF/COH/S/4, 14 December 2000 (00-5474), available on the WTO website at http://docsonline.wto.org/GEN_viewerwindow.asp?D:DDFDOCUMENTS/T/WT/TF/C, visited 18 June 2002.

[113] Integrated Framework Steering Committee, 'Joint Communiqué by the Six Core Agencies of the Integrated Framework—IMF, ITC, UNCTAD, UNDP, World Bank and WTO', World Trade Organisation WT/IFSC/1, 28 February 2002 (02-1004), available on the WTO website at http://docsonline.wto.org/GEN_viewerwindow.asp?D:DDFDOCUMENTS/T/WT/IFSC, visited 18 June 2002.

[114] Guidelines, point VI.

[115] See 'Environment: CTE Agenda Part 9: CTE on: other organisations', available at http://www.wtop.org/english/tratop_e/envir_e/cte09_e.htm, visited 10 June 2002.

of legal texts but rather a deeply-rooted culture of secrecy which prevents outside groups and organisations from participating in WTO activities.[116] The role of civil society in the WTO is still controversial and ambiguous. Despite the wording of Article V(2) of the Agreement Establishing the WTO authorising the consultation of NGOs, it was not until the *Hormones* case that the WTO Appellate Body concluded that the Panel was entitled to permit a party to the dispute to annex to its own pleadings documents from NGOs.[117] The NGOs are still not given access to the DSB, but they have now been allowed a role in the proceedings through *amicus curiae* briefs since the report of the Appellate Body in *United States—Shrimps.*[118] The Appellate Body, in *US-CVD on Hot rolled steel*, held the view that Article 17.9 of the DSU gives it the 'legal authority to accept . . . *amicus curiae* briefs'.[119]

More recently, the Director-General of the WTO has announced a number of new initiatives designed to improve dialogue with civil society. A first series of issue-specific dialogues was organised by the WTO Secretariat on Friday 27 April 2007. It addressed 'The Development Component of the DDA [Doha Develoment Agenda]' from different perspectives, including that of an NGO representative. However, the Director-General still considers that 'it is in fact necessary to preserve the inter-state framework of the WTO while keeping an ear open to the non-state actors that represent civil society'.[120] Opening up the WTO dispute resolution process more to *amicus curiae* briefs may be a move in the right direction, assuming that conditions of fairness, access, transparency and accountability are satisfied. This should go hand in hand with capacity building and technical assistance to foster the development of more NGOs in developing countries.

Institutional cooperation thus can be extremely controversial, especially when it goes beyond consultation and involves participation in the production of norms. With regard to the division of functions in global governance, it has been argued that

> the separation of monitoring tasks across agencies stems from the fact that international agencies are controlled by multiple principals . . . [Thus p]artitioning the labour and trade monitoring tasks between two agencies allows each standard and the associated punishment for deviations to be set at the highest level to which the principals are able to agree.[121]

This also means that the specific tasks and terrain of each international institution tend to be defended by that institution's most powerful clients. More generally, the lack of coordination among international institutions frequently reflects the fragmentation of domestic policy-making and the lack of such coordination within governments.[122] Consequently, relations among the array of international institutions tend merely to reflect the distribution of power among and within individual States or groups of States. Increased cooperation then may be contested in terms that it threatens to tread

[116] R Howse and M Mutua, 'Protection des droits humains et mondialisation de l'economie: Un defi pour l'OMC', *Droits et Democratie*, 2000, at 13, available on the Internet at http://www.dd-rd.ca/site/publications/index.php?id=1271&lang=fr&page=9&subsection=catalogue last accessed 4 March 2010.

[117] *European Communities—Measures concerning Meat and Meat Products (Hormones)*, Report of the Appellate Body, 16 January 1998, adopted 13 February 1998 (WT/DS26/AB/R), para 110.

[118] *United States–Import Prohibition of Shrimp and Certain Shrimp Products*, Report of the Appellate Body, 12 October 1998, adopted 21 November 2001 (WT/DS58/AB/R), paras 79–91.

[119] WTO document WT/DS138/AB/R (2000).

[120] Lamy, above n 29, at 974.

[121] AV Deardorff and RM Stern, 'Introduction and Overview' in AV Deardorff and RM Stern (eds), *Social Dimensions of US Trade Policies* (Ann Arbor, Mich, University of Michigan Press, 2001) 12–13.

[122] See also T Cottier, J Pauwelyn and E Bürgi, 'Linking Trade Regulation and Human Rights in International Law: An Overview' in Cottier *et al*, above n 25, at 10–11.

on what WTO Members consider to be their sovereign interests, or to impinge on the character of the WTO as an organisation driven by governments, when what is actually at stake are substantive conflicts.

C. Increasing Cooperation in Norm Production

1. Introduction

A second way of heightening the salience of social solidarity ethics is by increasing cooperation in norm production.[123] As the proposal for closer relations between the WTO and the IMF demonstrates, participation in meetings is one thing—whether this means simply being present, or being able to participate in discussion—but participating in making rules is quite another. Nevertheless, in addition to its institutional partnerships, which are multiple and extremely diverse, the WTO already cooperates to some extent with other sites in the creation of norms. With regard to the cooperation between the WTO and other sites in norm creation, we can distinguish two different processes. The first type consists of processes of borrowing or re-institutionalisation. In this type, the WTO draws directly on norms developed by other sites of governance and integrates or applies them in its own autonomous norm-generating processes. The second type concerns processes of cooperative deliberation. In this type, both WTO institutions and institutions from another site of governance are involved in the processes of deliberation leading to the creation of norms, though the institutions from the two sites are not necessarily on an equal footing. These two processes of re-institutionalisation and cooperative deliberation are combined in practice. They are discussed further below.

2. Processes of Re-institutionalisation

Processes of re-institutionalisation of norms occur when one site of governance borrows norms from another site and then integrates them into its own normative repertoire.[124] This includes statements by the governing bodies of one organisation

[123] For a brief survey from the standpoint of public international law, see Victor Moscoti, 'Institutional Cooperation and Norm Creation in International Organizations', in Cottier *et al*, above n 25, at 165–79.

[124] The idea of re-institutionalisation is based on an analogy with Bohannan's idea of the 'double institutionalisation' of African so-called customary law by colonial State courts. He wrote that: 'All social institutions are marked by "customs" and these "customs" exhibit most of the stigmata cited by any definition of law. But there is one salient difference. Whereas custom continues to inhere in, and only in, these institutions which it governs (and which in turn govern it), law is specifically recreated by agents of society, in a narrower and recognisable context—that is, in the context of the institutions that are legal in character and, to some degree at least, discrete from all others.' See P Bohannan, 'The Differing Realms of the Law' in P Bohannan (ed), *Law and Warfare: Studies in the Anthropology of Conflict* (New York, American Museum of Natural History, 1967) 43 at 45, reprinted from *American Anthropologist*, Special Publication, *The Ethnography of Law* (ed L Nader), vol 67, no 6, pt 2, 1965, 33–42.

concerning the impact of norms developed in other organisations.[125] The WTO Agreements contain numerous references to norms produced in other sites of governance. First, consider plant and animal health and food safety. Three organisations—the OIE, the FAO and the WHO—are responsible for international standards, guidelines and recommendations relevant to the WTO SPS Agreement: the OIE deals with animal health; the FAO and the WHO jointly provide the Secretariat of the Codex Alimentarius, which deals with food safety; the FAO also provides the Secretariat for the IPPC, which deals with plant health.[126] The SPS Agreement states that Members' measures based on standards developed in the Codex Alimentarius, the IOE and the IPPC are presumed to be compatible with the WTO. So, while the Codex and others do not by any means legislate in the normal sense, the norms that they produce have legal effects in creating a presumption of WTO compatibility when such international standards are respected. The SPS Agreement provisions thus provide important incentives for States to base their national standards on, or bring their national standards into conformity with, international standards, stemming originally from other organisations.

A second example is public health. The WTO Agreements recognise that there are cases where Members may wish to subordinate trade-related considerations to other legitimate policy objectives and constraints, such as health. Article XX(b) GATT guarantees Members' right to take measures to restrict imports and export of products when those measures are necessary to protect the health of humans, animals and plants. Jurisprudence of the WTO has confirmed that WTO Members have the right to determine the level of health protection they deem appropriate. Human health has been recognised by the WTO Appellate Body as being 'important in the highest degree'.[127]

The rights and obligations entailed by the SPS and the TBT Agreements are somewhat different, for instance with regard to the assessment of health risks. Of the two, the SPS Agreement deals with specific risks to health. It contains specific rules for countries that want to restrict trade to ensure food safety and the protection of human life from plant- or animal-carried diseases. The TBT Agreement has a broader scope of application, but only requires taking available scientific information into account, whereas in the SPS Agreement it is a fundamental requirement that Members have a scientific basis to justify trade measures aimed at mitigating a health risk. If available scientific evidence is not sufficient, the SPS Agreement permits the adoption of provisional measures.

The TRIPS Agreement also covers some areas that are relevant to health. The issue of patent protection for pharmaceutical products is particularly critical. The TRIPS Agreement contains several provisions that enable governments to implement their intellectual property regimes in a manner which takes account of immediate and longer-term public health considerations. It also provides for some flexibility in the implementation of the Agreement by allowing countries to limit patent owners' exclusive rights, for instance by granting compulsory licenses and allowing parallel importation of patented products. This flexibility was reaffirmed by the WTO Members at the

125 As proposed by Cotter *et al*, above n 25, at 23.

126 See http://www.wto.org/english/news_e/pres01_e/pr254_e.htm, visited 22 January 2008.

127 *European Communities—Measures Affecting Asbestos and Asbestos-Containing Products*, Report of the Appellate Body, AB-2000-11, WT/DS/135/AB/R, 12 March 2001, para 172.

Doha Ministerial Conference and is now crystallised by an amendment of the TRIPS Agreement in Article 31*bis*.[128]

In the case of trade in services, examples relating to health services concern the four modes of supply.[129] The GATS imposes only very limited general obligations on Members, who are free to choose which service sectors to open up and which modes of service to liberalise. Exempt from the GATS are any services supplied in the exercise of governmental authority. This possibility and the right to regulate for domestic policy purposes provide substantial scope for national policy-making with regard to health regulations.[130]

A third example is cultural diversity. A new UNESCO Convention on Cultural Diversity was signed by 148 countries meeting in Paris in October 2005 to protect cultural diversity.[131] The Convention recognises that cultural diversity is a dynamic concept that depends upon the free flow of ideas, 'nurtured by constant exchanges and interaction between cultures'.[132] As for the regulation of conflicts with other treaties, Article 20 of the Convention suggests that, in case of direct conflicts between the Convention and the WTO, the latter should have the upper hand in any forum. The Article 20(1)(b) requirement to take the Convention 'into account' in the application and interpretation of other treaties can be discharged through good faith contextual reference to the Convention. The language of Article 20(2), 'whereby *nothing* in the Convention (including the obligation to take the Convention into account) can modify concurrent treaty rights and obligations' [emphasis added], is significantly stronger in favour of the WTO Agreements.[133] However, this is not inconsistent with existing WTO Appellate Body jurisprudence. Since the WTO Agreements do not include a general cultural exception, the scope for recourse to the UNESCO Convention is arguably *a priori* limited.

A fourth example of re-institutionalisation in norm-making in the WTO concerns biodiversity and plant genetic resources. Despite the lack of progress so far, this example is considered in some detail here because of its particular significance for developing countries. It also illustrates the extent to which improvement is needed in relations between the WTO and other sites of governance if social solidarity ethics are to be realised in practice. Of great importance are the Convention on Biological Diversity (CBD)[134] and the International Treaty on Plant Genetic Resources for Food and Agriculture (ITPGR).[135] The CBD came into force on 29 December 1993. The ITPGR was approved by the FAO Conference in November 2001 and entered into force on 29 June 2004.

The objectives of the CBD are conservation and the sustainable use of biological diversity, fair and equitable sharing of the benefits from the use of, *inter alia*, plant

[128] Council for TRIPS, Decision of 30 August 2003, 'Implementation of paragraph 6 of the Doha Declaration on the TRIPS Agreement and public health', WT/L/540, available at http://www.wto.org/english/tratop_e/trips_e/implem_para6_e.htm; WTO, Amendment of the TRIPS Agreement, Decision of 6 December 2005, WT/L/641, 8 December 2005, at http://docsonline.wto.org/DDFDocuments/t/WT/L/641.doc.

[129] Art I:2 GATS.

[130] *WTO Agreements and Public Health*, A Joint Study by WHO and WTO Secretariat, WHO and WTO, 2002.

[131] See http://www.asil.org/insights/2005/11/insights051115.html#_edn1, visited 23 January 2008.

[132] *Ibid*, Preamble, para 11.

[133] See http://www.asil.org/insights/2005/11/insightcomment051121_000.html, visited 23 January 2008.

[134] Convention on Biological Diversity, concluded at Rio de Janeiro on 5 June 1992.

[135] See http://www.intracen.org/AidforTrade/?mn=0&sm=0?13, last accessed 4 March 2010.

genetic resources, including by appropriate access, technology transfer and funding.[136] The CBD, in accordance with the UN Charter and international law principles, affirms the sovereign right of countries concerning exploitation of their own resources.[137] It provides that national governments have the authority to determine access to plant genetic resources subject to national legislation.[138] Access, where granted, is to be on mutually agreed terms.[139] It is subject to the principle of prior informed consent of the party providing the resources, unless that party decides otherwise.[140] The sharing of the benefits of plant genetic resources is to take place on a fair and equitable basis, and to be determined by mutually agreed terms.[141] The CBD contains special provisions on dispute settlement.[142]

The objectives of the ITPGR are

> the conservation and sustainable use of plant genetic resources for food and agriculture and the fair and equitable sharing of the benefits arising out of their use . . .[143]

It is closely linked to the FAO and to the CBD.[144] It provides expressly for farmers' rights, including the protection of traditional knowledge, the right to participate equitably in benefit-sharing and the right to participate in making decisions.[145] Most notably, it provides that, while States agree to establish a multilateral system,[146]

> the Contracting Parties recognise the sovereign rights of States over their own plant genetic resources for food and agriculture, including that the authority to determine access to those resources rests with national governments and is subject to national legislation . . .[147]

Access to plant genetic resources is to be provided solely

> for the purpose of utilisation and conservation for research, breeding and training for food and agriculture, provided that such purpose does not include chemical, pharmaceutical and/or other non-food/feed industrial uses . . .[148]

Recipients are not permitted to claim any intellectual property rights or other rights that limit facilitated access to the resources.[149] Access is to take place consistently with relevant international agreements and with national laws.[150] The contracting parties agree that access will be provided according to national legislation or, if there is none, according to specific standards.[151] The ITPGR sets down specific rules for benefit-sharing,

[136] CBD, Art 1. The CBD also covers marine animals.
[137] *Ibid*, Art 3.
[138] *Ibid*, Art 15(1).
[139] *Ibid*, Art 15(4).
[140] *Ibid*, Art 15(5).
[141] *Ibid*, Art 15(7).
[142] *Ibid*, Art 27 and Annex II.
[143] ITPGR, Art 1.1. 'Plant genetic resources for food and agriculture' means 'any genetic material of plant origin of actual or potential value for food and agriculture'. 'Genetic material' means 'any material of plant origin, including reproductive and vegetative propagating material, containing functional units of heredity'. 'Variety' means 'a plant grouping, within a single botanical taxon of the lowest known rank, defined by the reproductible expression of its distinguishing and other genetic characteristics'. See ITPGR, Art 2.
[144] *Ibid*, Art 1.2.
[145] *Ibid*, Pt III, Art 9.
[146] *Ibid*, Arts 10.2, 11–13.6.
[147] *Ibid*, Art 10.1.
[148] *Ibid*, Art 12.3(a).
[149] *Ibid*, Art 12.3(d).
[150] *Ibid*, Art 12.3(f).
[151] *Ibid*, Art 12.3(h).

including exchange of information, technology transfer, capacity-building and sharing of commercial benefits.[152] It also lays down detailed provisions for dispute settlement.[153]

Other instruments adopted under the auspices of the CBD or the ITPGR contribute further to the development of an adequate regulatory framework for plant genetic resources. In February 2004, the Conference of the Parties (COP) of the CBD adopted Decision VII/19 on access and benefit-sharing related to genetic resources.[154] It foresaw the development of an international regime on the matter. The COP also adopted an Action Plan on Capacity-building for Access and Benefit-sharing.[155] In June 2006, the Governing Body of the ITPGR adopted a Standard Material Transfer Agreement.[156] It regulates the transfer of genetic material from the provider to the recipient. In May 2008, the COP instructed a Working Group to complete the international regime and set up expert groups on:

a) compliance;
b) concepts, terms, working definitions and sectoral approaches; and
c) traditional knowledge on genetic resources.

It adopted a roadmap for the negotiation of an international Access and Benefit-sharing (ABS) regime.[157] The main features of such an international regime, now under discussion, are:

a) it is 'essentially . . . based on the notion of comity under international law';
b) it is 'applicable to a signatory party when a patent involving claims over genetic materials and associated traditional knowledge accessed in another signatory party has been applied or granted';
c) it requires a party to recognise a final determination made by a competent authority of the party where such resources and knowledge have been accessed in violation of the national law';
d) there is no requirement for substantive harmonisation of national access or patent law; and
e) it could be based on an independent international convention or on a protocol to existing one, such as the CBD.[158]

The WTO has taken note of and has drawn on these developments, because they potentially have a direct impact on international trade in plant genetic resources. A proposal was submitted within the WTO to amend the TRIPS Agreement so that all patent applications would be required to disclose the country that provides or is the source of genetic resources and/or traditional knowledge associated with the product

[152] *Ibid*, Art 13.

[153] *Ibid*, Art 22 and Annex II.

[154] Available on the website of the Convention on Biological Diversity, at http://www.cbd.int/decision/cop/?id=7756, accessed 10 June 2009.

[155] See Action Plan on Capacity-building for Access to Genetic Resources and Benefit-sharing, available at http://www.cbd.int/programmes/socio-eco/benefit/action.shtml.

[156] This was provided in ITPGR, Art 13(2)(d)(ii). See now the Standard Material Transfer Agreement adopted by the Governing Body of the ITPGR in its Resolution 1/2006 of 16 June 2008.

[157] CBD, COP Decision IX/12, Bonn, 13–20 May 2008, available at http://www.cbd.int/decisions/?dec=IX/12. An outline of the international regime is included in Annex I to the Decision. The terms of reference for the International Regime for Access and Benefit-sharing were set out in COP Decision VII/19D.

[158] C Correa, 'Elements of an International Regime for the Recognition of National Regulations on Access to Genetic Resources', UNCTAD/DITC/TED/2007/9 (New York and Geneva, UNCTAD, 2008) at viii.

concerned. However, the proposal was not accepted, and discussions are continuing.[159] In the short run, an agreement is unlikely. In such circumstances, a better option may be a process of cooperative deliberation.

3. Processes of Cooperative Deliberation

By 'processes of cooperative deliberation', I mean processes in which representatives of two or more sites of governance participate in discussion and deliberation, leading potentially to the creation and adoption of new norms. The WTO Agreements contain express references to new norms to be elaborated outside of, as well as within, the WTO. Articles 3.5 and 12.4 of the SPS Agreement are examples which combine processes of re-institutionalisation with cooperative processes. They provide that the SPS Committee should elaborate a procedure for monitoring the processes of international harmonisation and the use of norms, directives or international recommendations. Article 3.3 of the SPS Agreement provides that Members may introduce SPS measures resulting in a higher level of protection than would be achieved by measures based on international standards, if there is a scientific justification, or as a consequence of the level of protection a Member determines to be appropriate, in accordance with Article 5.1–5.8 of the Agreement.

At its meeting of 15–16 October 1997, the SPS Committee adopted a provisional procedure to monitor the process of international harmonisation and the use of international standards, guidelines or recommendations having an important effect on international trade. It decided to draw up a list of such norms. It also decided that the Committee could invite any standardisation organisation concerned to present information, either in writing or by oral presentation at an ordinary meeting of the Committee, concerning any norm, directive or recommendation, including modifications or revision in progress.[160] The monitoring procedure was renewed at least until July 2001.[161]

The status of international organisations in the SPS Agreement and TBT Agreement leads to a further important point. Relevant standard-setting bodies are identified in the SPS Agreement as the Codex Alimentarius Commission, the IPPC and the OIE, although further international bodies may be identified through the SPS Committee provided they are open for membership to all WTO Members.[162]

Inter-organisational cooperation also concerns the procedure of identification of norms. Article 4 SPS requires governments to accept the sanitary or phytosanitary

[159] WIPO, Intergovernmental Committee on Intellectual Property and Genetic Resources, Traditional Knowledge and Folklore, 13th Session, Geneva, 13–17 October 2008, 'Genetic Resources: Factual Update of International Developments', WIPO/GRTKF/IC/13/8(b), 8 September 2008, para 39, at 11.

[160] See Décision du Comité, Procédure pour la surveillance du processus d'harmonisation internationale, Comité des measures sanitaires et phytosanitaires, Organisation Mondiale du Commerce G/SPS/11, 22 octobre 1997 (97-4606), available on the WTO website http://docsonline.wto.org/GEN_viewerwindow.asp?D:/DDFDOCUMENTS/U/G/SPS/11.W, visited 10 June 2002.

[161] See *Procedure to monitor the progress of international harmonisation*, Third Annual Report, Committee on Sanitary and Phytosanitary Measures, WTO (G/SPS/18), 19 September 2001 (01-4453), available on the WTO website at http://docsonline.wto.org/GEN_viewerwindow.asp?D:/DDFDOCUMENTS/T/G/SPS/18.D, visited 10 June 2002.

[162] SPS Agreement, Annex A, para 3.

measures of other members as equivalent, even if these measures differ from their own or from those used by other Members trading in the same product, assuming certain conditions are satisfied. In Autumn 2001 the SPS Committee adopted a Decision on equivalence, effective from 24 October 2001, outlining steps to make it easier for WTO Members to make use of the 'equivalence' provisions in Article 4 SPS.[163] It provides, *inter alia*, that WTO Members should participate actively in the ongoing work of the Codex Alimentarius on the issue of equivalence, and in any work related to equivalence undertaken by the OIE and in the framework of the IPPC.[164] The report of the SPS Committee meeting on 31 October–1 November 2001 recorded that

> The Equivalence Decision says the work of the Codex Alimentarius, the OIE and the IPPC on equivalence needs to be encouraged. The chairman said he would write a letter to the three organizations to bring this to their attention. The committee agreed to invite the three observer organizations to future informal meetings on the subject—observers do not normally attend informal meetings.[165]

The TBT Agreement goes further and endorses standards developed by any international body that is open to the relevant bodies of all WTO Members. There is no need for consensus in the development of the standards for them to be relevant. However, the standard-setting bodies are encouraged to operate with open, impartial and transparent procedures. Moreover, international bodies may apply for observer status to the relevant committees.[166] Article 1.1 of the TBT Agreement provides that

> general terms for standardization and procedures for assessment of conformity shall normally have the meaning given to them by definitions adopted within the United Nations system and by international standardizing bodies taking into account their context and in the light of the object and purpose of this Agreement.

Article 2.4 of the Agreement provides that Members must use international standards as a basis for their measures, except where these would be an ineffective or inappropriate means of fulfilling the legitimate objective pursued.

There are numerous other examples of deliberative cooperation between the WTO and other sites of governance. For instance, it is generally considered that the 1996 WTO Declaration on core labour standards helped to achieve consensus in the ILO to adopt, on 18 June 1998, the Declaration on Fundamental Principles and Rights at Work.[167] To give another example, in 1998 the WTO and WIPO agreed on a joint initiative to provide technical cooperation to help developing countries meet the 1 January 2000 deadline for conforming with TRIPS.[168] Thirdly, the OECD and the

[163] Decision on the Implementation of Article 4 of the Agreement on the Application of Sanitary and Phytosanitary Measures (G/SPS/19), available on the WTO website at http://www.wto.org/english/tratop_e/sps_e/equivalence2001_e.htm, visited 18 June 2002.

[164] *Ibid*, Art 9.

[165] 'Committee looks at equivalence, transparency, diseases and GMOs', WTO News: 2001 News Items, Sanitary and Phytosanitary Measures Committee, 31 October–1 November 2001, available on the WTO website at http://www.wto.org/english/news_e/news01_e/sps_nov2001_e.htm, visited 10 June 2002.

[166] MA Young, 'The WTO's use of relevant rules of international law: an analysis of the Biotech case' (2007) 56(4) *ICLQ* 907.

[167] EU Petersmann, 'The "human rights approach" advocated by the UN High Commissioner for Human Rights and by the International Labour Organization: is it relevant for WTO law and policy?' (2004) 7(3) *JIEL* 605.

[168] See 'WTO and WIPO join forces to help developing countries meet year-2000 commitments on intellectual property', WTO News: 1998 Press Releases, Press/1`08, 21 July 1998, available on the WTO website at http://www.wto.org/english/news_e?pres98_e/pr108_e.htm, visited 24 May 2002.

WTO have collaborated closely to develop a framework for monitoring aid for trade. This framework has three levels:

a) global monitoring of aid-for-trade flows, based on the OECD Creditor Reporting System;
b) donor monitoring, in the form of self-assessments; and
c) in-country monitoring, also in the form of self-assessments.

A joint OECD/WTO Report, 'Aid for Trade at a Glance 2007: 1st Global Review', subsequently provided the first comprehensive global picture of aid for trade and will enable the international community to assess what is being achieved, what is not, and where improvements are needed.[169] The WTO thus engages in numerous processes of cooperation deliberation with other sites of governance. These processes need to be expanded, however, and social solidarity ethics should be basic criteria for justifying and evaluating their work.

D. Expanding Observer Status

Reciprocal observer status is one way of enhancing relations between sites, increasing mutual learning, and contributing to the redefinition of the objectives of international trade and a rethinking of the objectives and means of international trade regulation. For international intergovernmental organisations, observer status is intended to enable them to follow WTO discussions on matters which interest them directly. It is conferred either:

a) on request by organisations with competence and direct interest in trade policy, on a case-by-case basis, to specific WTO bodies; or
b) by specific invitation to organisations to attend meetings of the Ministerial Conference, the General Council or subsidiary bodies, or, on a case-by-case basis, to specific organisations to follow particular issues in a WTO body.

Observer status is specific to the particular WTO body for which it is granted and does not automatically extend to other WTO bodies. It entails the right to receive copies of main WTO documents and other documents of the specific body which the observer attends. Observer organisations may be invited to speak after WTO Members have spoken. Observer status does not include the right to circulate papers or to make proposals, unless there is a specific invitation to do so, and it does not include the right to participate in decision-making.[170] The Committee on Budget, Finance and Administration and the DSB are excluded, except as noted earlier in this chapter, but otherwise observer status may be granted to one or more (including all) of the full range of WTO bodies, including committees, working groups and special sessions of

[169] See http://www.oecd.org/document/46/0,3343,en_2649_34665_39619566_1_1_1_1,00.html, visited 23 January 2008.

[170] WTO, 'Rules of Procedure for Sessions of the Ministerial Conference and Meetings of the General Council', WT/L/161, 25 July 1996, Annex 3: Observer Status for International Intergovernmental Organisations in the WTO. Guidelines for Observer Status for Governments in the WTO are found in Annex 2.

committees.[171] It may also apply to WTO negotiating bodies, for example concerning special sessions of the Committee on Agriculture or the Council for Trade in Services, or other negotiating bodies established following the Doha Mandate. For example, numerous multilateral environmental agreements have been granted or have requested observer status in the special session of the CTE.[172]

Negotiating Bodies of the WTO, such as the Trade Negotiations Committee established at the Doha Ministerial, may decide on arrangements concerning observer status for international intergovernmental organisations.[173] As of June 2009, the Committee on Trade and Development had invited 27 organisations as observers and 13 international intergovernmental organisations as ad hoc observers on a meeting-by-meeting basis. Virtually all of the observers were international intergovernmental organisations; the ad hoc observers included only one well-known NGO. The CTE included among its 23 observers the CBD, the Convention on International Trade in Endangered Species of Wild Fauna and Flora (CITES) and the Pacific Islands Forum; the Southeast Asian Fisheries Development Centre (SEAFDEC) was one of the two international intergovernmental organisations which had ad hoc observer status. The requests of numerous other organisations were pending. In contrast, the CTE Special Session had invited 11 organizations on an ad hoc/meeting-by-meeting basis: the Basel Convention on the Transboundary Movements of Hazardous Waste and their Disposal (Basel Convention), the CBD, the CITES, Montreal Protocol on Substances that Deplete the Ozone Layer (Montreal Protocol), the OECD, the Rotterdam Convention on the Prior Informed Consent Procedure for Certain Hazardous Chemicals and Pesticides in International Trade (Rotterdam Convention), the Stockholm Convention on Persistent Organic Pollutants (Stockholm Convention), the UNCTAD, the UNEP, the United Nations Framework Convention on Climate Change (UNFCCC) and the WCO. Requests from several other organisations were pending.

If we view observer status from the perspective of the other organisations, the UNCTAD, the International Trade Centre (ITC) and South Centre may serve as examples. The UNCTAD had observer status on all permitted WTO Councils, committees and bodies, except for the Committee of Participants on the Expansion of Trade in Information Technology Products. The ITC is not required to submit a formal request for observer status and is invited to attend those meetings which it wishes to attend. As of June 2009, it had observer status in the General Council, the Council for Trade in Services, the SPS Committee, the Committee on Trade and Development, the CTE, the TBT Committee, the Working Group on Transparency in Government Procurement, the Working Group on Trade, Debt and Finance, the Committee on Government Procurement, the Committee of Participants on the Expansion of Trade in Information Technology Products and the Council for Trade in Services, Special Sessions. South Centre had observer status only on the Committee on Trade and Development.

[171] For the current list of observers (as of 4 June 2009), see WTO, 'International intergovernmental organisations granted observer status to WTO bodies', http.//www.wto.org/English/theWTO_e/igo_obs_e.htm, accessed 4 June 2009.

[172] For an overview as of 2003, see WTO, Committee on Trade and Environment, Special Session, 'Observer Status: Note by the Secretariat', TN/TE/S/4, 31 January 2003.

[173] This paragraph is based on WTO, 'International intergovernmental organisations granted observer status to WTO bodies', available at http://www.wto.org/english/theWTO_e/igo_obs_e.htm, accessed 4 June 2009.

Other international organisations also participate as observers in WTO meetings. An example of multifaceted cooperation concerns the WTO and the OIE. On 4 May 1998, the Director-General of the OIE and the Director-General of the WTO exchanged letters of cooperation. The letters formalised cooperation already taking place between the two organisations with regard to participation as observers in each others' meetings, sharing information and exchanging documents, technical advice from the OIE for the WTO SPS Committee, technical advice for use in dispute settlement cases, and jointly organised seminars, conferences and training activities, especially for developing countries.[174] To give a specific example, the OIE provided written guidance to the SPS Committee on national standards on BSE and foot-and-mouth disease.[175] In addition, the SPS Committee grants ad hoc observer status on a meeting-by-meeting basis to the European Free Trade Association (EFTA), the Latin American Economic System (SELA), the Inter-American Institute for Cooperation on Agriculture (IICA), the Regional International Agricultural Health Organisation (OIRSA), the ACP Group and the OECD. At its March 2001 meeting it continued consideration of requests for observer status from the Office international de la vigne et du vin (OIV) and the Asian Pacific Coconut Community (APCC).[176]

Granting observer status can be controversial. One example is that of NGOs, already discussed. To give another example, in the TRIPS Council, the FAO and the WHO have observer status and ad hoc observer status, respectively. However, the United States has consistently opposed granting observer status in the TRIPS Council to the CBD, on the ground that its Secretariat does 'not have a broad interest in TRIPS issues'.[177] Helfer remarks that the WTO has stricter criteria for observer status than does the WIPO, and these criteria are interpreted and applied more strictly. The WTO requires the applicant organisation to 'have competence and a direct interest in trade policy matters or . . . have responsibilities related to those of the WTO'.[178] The WTO criteria include

> taking into account such factors as the nature of the work of the organization concerned, the nature of its membership, the number of WTO Members in the organization, reciprocity with respect to access to proceedings, documents and other aspects of observership, and whether the organization has been associated in the past with the work of the CONTRACTING PARTIES to GATT 1947 . . .[179]

In contrast, under the WIPO criteria,

> each body [in WIPO] shall decide, in a general way, or for a particular session or meeting, which other States and [intergovernmental] organizations shall be invited to be represented by observers . . .[180]

[174] See 'Joint release: WTO and OIE, WTO and the Office International des Epizooties sign cooperation agreement', WTO News: 1998 Press Releases, Press/99, 4 May 1998, available on the WTO website at http://www.wto.org/english/news_e/pres98_/pr99_e.htm, visited on 25 May 2002.

[175] Report (2001) on the Activities of the Committee on Sanitary and Phytosanitary Measures', point 9, WTO, G/L/485, 4 October 2001 (01-4796), available on the WTO website at http://docsonline.wto.org/GEN_viewerwindow.asp?D:/DDFDOCUMENTS/T/G/L/485.DO, visited on 10 June 2002.

[176] *Ibid*, point 8.

[177] International Center for Trade and Sustainable Development (ICTSD), 'Trips Council Sets Agenda for June Meeting', *Bridges*, at 6, n 19 (22 May 2002), quoted in Helfer, above n 83, at 187.

[178] WTO, Rules of Procedure for Sessions of the Ministerial Conference and Meetings of the General Council, Annex 3: Observer Status for International Intergovernmental Organisations in the WTO, WT§/I/161, 25 July 1996.

[179] *Ibid.*

[180] WIPO, *General Rules of Procedure*, WIPO Publication No 399 (FE) Rev 3, Rule 8(2) (Geneva, WIPO, 1990).

Many current views of WTO observer status are based on the idea that most international institutions are indivisible, regardless of the extent of convergence which they demonstrate with regard to other institutions. To return to Table 21 above, they accord with the ideas in Box 1 (weak convergence, indivisibility) or in Box 3 (strong convergence, indivisibility). Currently the WTO emphasises strong convergence and divisibility with regard to the IMF and the World Bank in particular. We need to promote the ideas that the WTO in particular should seek to maximise weak convergence plus divisibility (Box 2) or strong convergence plus divisibility (Box 4) with those sites of governance which emphasise social solidarity ethics. For example, a basic minimum threshold should be that each institution in the partnership, including the WTO, should automatically permit other partner institutions to be observers at all relevant meetings, with the right to speak and (possibly) eventually the right to vote; to receive all documents; to enjoy participation rights as nearly as possible equal to those of members of the host institution (ie the WTO) itself; and to be entitled to procedures and rules of justification designed to ensure accountability. Observer status thus may concern a wide variety of institutional relations, without necessarily involving direct participation in the production of norms or participation in dispute resolution processes.

E. Dispute Settlement Processes

The WTO dispute settlement institutions frequently refer to norms originating outside the WTO. Here this is considered only briefly, because it is already the subject of a voluminous literature.[181]

One of the WTO's distinctive features is its sophisticated dispute settlement mechanism. Under Article 56 of the text of the International Law Commission on 'Responsibility of States for Internationally Wrongful Acts', which appears as an annex to UN General Assembly Resolution 56/83, the WTO dispute settlement mechanism is a special system, or *lex specialis.*[182] Consequently, the DSB can go beyond general international law in consolidating the WTO legal system. The WTO Panels and the Appellate Body have jurisdiction only over matters as specified in the WTO Agreements, namely, Article 1 of the DSU. However, they regularly have recourse to non-WTO international law rules in interpreting the WTO Agreements.[183]

Case law interpreting the basic WTO Agreements is a primary device for deciding what relations between sites of governance actually mean in practice. For example, Article XV:9(a) GATT 1947 exempted from all GATT obligations the recourse to exchange control measures in conformity with the IMF Statute. In practice, the contracting parties agreed that the definition of this boundary would be addressed on

[181] A useful review is J Pauwelyn, *Conflict of Norms in Public International Law: How WTO Law Relates to Other Rules of International Law* (Cambridge, Cambridge University Press, 2003) 440–86.

[182] United Nations General Assembly, 56th Session, Agenda Item 162, Resolution adopted by the General Assembly, 56/83 Responsibility of States for Internationally Wrongful Acts, 28 January 2002, available at http://www.lcil.cam.ac.uk/Media/ILCSR/A_56_83(e).pdf, visited 17 May 2009.

[183] For useful reviews, see J Pauwelyn, 'How to Win a WTO Dispute Based on Non-WTO Law' (2003) 37(6) *Journal of World Trade* 997; J Pauwelyn, 'Human Rights in WTO Dispute Settlement', in Cottier *et al*, above n 25, at 204.

a case-by-case basis. In the only case between 1947 and 1987, Italy consulted with other contracting parties in the framework of the Comité des restrictions à l'importation (balance des paiements) before having recourse to IMF exchange control measures. Though not a judicial authority, the GATT contracting parties operated on a case-by-case basis.[184]

The WTO dispute settlement institutions also draw upon norms produced in other sites. For example, in the *LAN* case, the Appellate Body held that, in interpreting the tariff concessions in Schedule LXXX GATT, the Panel should have considered the Harmonised System of Coding and Product Classification and its Explanatory Notes of the WCO as supplementary means of interpretation within the meaning of Article 31 of the Vienna Convention.[185] In the *EC—Hormones* case, the Appellate Body consolidated the position of the Codex Alimentarius as the international institutional source of food safety standards.[186] In *India—Agricultural Products*, the Appellate Body concluded that, in dealing with the conclusions of IMF experts, the Panel did not fail in its duty to evaluate the facts because it was simply consulting experts, not delegating its powers.[187] In *EC—Tariff Preferences*, the Panel, in examining the context of the Enabling Clause, reviewed the drafting history of GSP arrangements in the UNCTAD and referred to the Agreed Conclusions from the UNCTAD's Special Committee on Preferences and the UNCTAD Resolution setting up this Committee.[188]

As the treaties proliferate, so do dispute settlement systems, as well as the potential for clashes with the WTO's compulsory and binding dispute settlement mechanism. Chapter eight discussed relations between the dispute settlement mechanisms in China's regional agreements and the WTO dispute settlement system. Another example is the *EC—Swordfish* dispute.[189] In 1999, Chile enacted swordfish conservation measures, by regulating gear and limiting the level of fishing through the denial of new permits. Chile effectively prohibited the utilisation of its ports for landing and service to EC factory ships that disregarded minimum conservation standards. The EC challenged those measures as being contrary to its WTO rights to have access to Chilean ports for landing or transshipment. Chile demanded that the EC enact and enforce conservation measures for its fishing operations on the high seas, in accordance with the United Nations Convention on the Law of the Sea (UNCLOS). Chile responded to the EC's WTO challenge by initiating the dispute settlement provisions of the UNCLOS, and invited the EC to the International Tribunal on the Law of the Sea (ITLOS). The substantive issues before the WTO included the right of Chile to benefit from the application of Article XX GATT on the conservation of natural resources, when acting pursuant to the UNCLOS.[190] The issue before the ITLOS could have

[184] F Roessler, *La relation entre l'ordre commercial mondial et le système monétaire international*, Conférences d'Actualité, CERIC, Faculté de Droit et de Science Politique d'Aix-Marseille, 1987, 7–9.

[185] *European Communities—Customs Classification of Certain Computer Equipment*, Report of the Appellate Body, WT/DS62/AB/R, adopted 5 June 1998, paras 89–90.

[186] *European Communities—Measures concerning Meat and Meat Products (Hormones)*, Report of the Appellate Body, WT/DS26/AB/R, adopted 13 February 1998.

[187] *India—Quantitative Restrictions on Imports of Agricultural, Textile and Industrial Products*, Report of the Appellate Body, AB-1999-3, WTO/DS90/AB/R, 23 August 1999, paras 146–52. See also D Ahn, 'Linkages between International Financial and Trade Institutions' (2000) 34(4) *Journal of World Trade* 1.

[188] *European Communities—Conditions for the Granting of Tariff Preferences to Developing Countries*, WT/DES246/R, adopted as modified by the Appellate Body report on 20 April 2004, paras 7.64, 7.79–7.116, 7.128, 7.135–7.145, 7.158. For comment, see J Bradley, 'The Enabling Clause and the Applied Rules of Interpretation (Comment on Lorand Bartels)' in Cottier *et al*, above n 25, at 504–506.

[189] *Chile—Measures Affecting the Transit and Importing of Swordfish*, WT/DS193/1.

[190] Lamy, above n 29, at 983.

included whether or not Chile was entitled to regulate and limit access to swordfish as part of a conservation programme. In such a situation, it is conceivable that both instances would have examined whether the UNCLOS effectively requires, authorises or tolerates Chile's measures, and whether the Chilean measures were compatible with the UNCLOS, an element that could influence a WTO Panel in its decision as to whether or not Chile might benefit from the application of Article XX(g) GATT. It was, therefore, conceivable that the two forums might reach different conclusions on the same facts or on the interpretation of the applicable law. In the event, the parties reached an agreement to suspend both their disputes before the ITLOS and before the WTO. But in the absence of a mutual agreement, the WTO Panel would have proceeded much faster than the ITLOS.

Short of any agreement between the parties, and in the absence of any international rule as to how these two different mechanisms should interact, many scenarios might conceivably emerge. In light of the quasi-automaticity of the compulsory and binding WTO dispute mechanism, it is unlikely that a WTO Panel would decline jurisdiction because another dispute process—albeit more relevant and better equipped—has been seized for a similar or related dispute. If both processes were triggered at the same time, it is quite probable that the WTO Panel process would proceed more quickly. This is a potential source of imbalance in relations between sites of governance. Although the WTO, through its dispute settlement system, can show that it does take into account the norms of other sites of governance, it will be for the WTO Panels, Appellate Body and DSB to determine the balance between conflicting norms. In assessing the invocation of such WTO exceptions, the WTO may in fact be deciding on the relative hierarchical value between two sets of norms. Similarly, if a WTO Member invokes the environmental exception to justify a trade restriction adopted pursuant to an MEA, in practice it is likely to be the WTO which will determine whether, and the extent to which, compliance with such an MEA can provide a WTO justification for trade restriction.[191] If, in support of its invocation of the WTO exception for public morals, a Member points to an ILO resolution condemning a specific State for violation of core labour standards, it is the WTO which will finally decide on the legal value and impact of such an ILO resolution on international trade and its opposability to trade rules. Not surprisingly, negotiators in a variety of international forums have felt compelled to address the question as to whether norms created outside the WTO are inferior to WTO norms.[192] These examples indicate that further cooperative deliberation in the creation of norms is required, as well as greater attention to non-WTO norms in WTO dispute settlement processes.

So far the WTO has been careful to preserve its terrain and its integrity, notably, for understandable reasons, in matters such as dispute resolution. In November 1996, the WTO General Council adopted a Decision on *Agreements between the WTO and the IMF and the World Bank*. This provided for the IMF to send a member of its staff as an observer to meetings of the WTO DSB where matters of jurisdictional relevance to the IMF were to be considered, or with the same status at particular meetings or in respect of particular agenda items; similar status was granted to World Bank staff at

[191] See eg *European Communities—Measures Affecting the Approval and Marketing of Biotech Products*, Report of the Appellate Body, WTO/DS291/AB/R, WTO/DS292/AB/R, WTO/DS293/WTO/R, adopted 21 November 2006.

[192] See JL Dunoff, Constitutional Conceits: The WTO's "Constitution" and the Discipline of International Law' (2006) 17(3) *European Journal of International Law* 647.

meetings where particular matters of common interest were under discussion. The IMF was to be permitted to submit its views to a WTO Panel on whether an exchange measure within its jurisdiction was consistent with its Articles of Agreement; this was to be done by letter directed to the Chairman of the DSB, who was to inform the Chair of the Panel of the availability of the communication. Documents to be provided to the IMF or the World Bank in respect of Panels included only Panels' final reports submitted to the DSB, not documents submitted or prepared in the course of the work of Panels.[193] Such access should be extended to other sites of governance such as the FAO, ILO and UNCTAD.

The lack of coherence among competing sites of international trade regulation today is amplified by the relative power of the WTO, and in particular its dispute settlement mechanism. This shows the discrepancy between the WTO's very powerful enforcement mechanism and the traditional decentralised system of countermeasures still used in other sites of governance. According to the current Director-General of the WTO,

> the solution lies not in weakening our dispute system . . . The solution to the potential imbalance lies in strengthening the enforcement (the effectiveness) of other legal orders so as to rebalance the relative power of the WTO in the international legal order . . .[194]

However, this needs to go hand-in-hand with greater use by the WTO of the re-institutionalisation of norms, increased participation in processes of cooperative deliberation, expansion of observer status and partial restructuring of the WTO dispute settlement process.

IV. Conclusion

Overall, one can distinguish three general strategies by which the WTO could take greater account of social solidarity ethics. The first strategy is constitutionalisation, in the sense of enlarging the scope of the current WTO and incorporating new norms directly within the WTO itself. This strategy is premised on strong convergence and indivisibility (Table 21 above, Box 3). It preserves the current understanding of concepts such as 'trade', 'free trade' and 'non-trade issues', as well as the distinction between separate, functionally specific international institutions. Based on traditional notions of trade linkage and expansion of the WTO mandate, this strategy is in my view not politically feasible. Neither is it a satisfactory way to integrate social solidarity ethics into our ideas of international trade and its regulation.

A second option is regulatory competition. In this scenario, the WTO would compete with other international organisations in the regulation of international trade. In terms of Table 21 above, it is based on the idea of weak convergence and indivisibility (Box 1). Strategic actors, such as governments, companies or NGOs, would choose

[193] See *Agreements between the WTO and the IMF and the World Bank*, Decision adopted by the General Council at its meeting on 7,8 and 13 November 1996, WTO WT/L/194, 19 November 1996 (96-4878), available on the WTO website at http://docsonline.wto.org/GEN_viewerwindow.asp?D:/DDFDOCUMENTS/T/WT/L/194, visited 18 June 2002. See also 'WTO and World Bank sign cooperation agreement', WTO News: 1997 Press Releases, Press/72, 28 April 1997, available on the WTO website at http://www.wto.org/english/news_e/pres97_e/pr72_e.htm, visited 25 May 2002.

[194] Lamy, above n 29.

which site to invoke in specific circumstances. This option describes, more or less accurately, current relations among sites of governance, or at least our common understandings of how they work and how they should work. Its shortcomings are too well known to require further discussion.

The third strategy is coordination. It is premised on the idea that both the WTO and those international institutions concerned or potentially concerned with social solidarity ethics are divisible and capable of at least weak convergence (Table 21 above, Box 2) and in some relations of strong convergence (Table 21 above, Box 4). In this case, the relations between the plurality of sites of governance concerned with international trade would be strengthened, so that the WTO would be able to draw more effectively on the institutions, norms and dispute resolution processes of other sites of governance.[195]

In reality, we need to recognise that the boxes in Table 21 can be best understood not as separate and fixed categories. Instead, each should be unpacked and considered to be a bundle of elements involving several parameters. The first parameter concerns their content. Relations between sites may potentially concern any or all of the structural features of a site, namely institutions, norms or dispute settlement processes. The traditional debate on trade linkages, as already seen, has focused mainly on cross-reference in terms of norms. A second parameter refers to the decisional basis of such relations. They can be based either on prior agreement, or on ad hoc decisions. Relations between sites may result from agreement, though of course the term 'agreement' covers a wide spectrum, ranging from absolute contracts of adhesion to entirely voluntary undertakings. Alternatively they can be created by ad hoc decisions, such as case law. The term 'case law' as used here includes not only judicial decisions or 'jurisprudence', but also encompasses a potentially wide range of decisions in individual cases by other decision-makers, such as WTO working parties or other bodies. In other words, relations between sites, which either were previously linked by agreement or were not linked at all, may be established by decisions taken to resolve conflicts on an individual, case-by-case basis. Thirdly, relations may vary in normative form or in the extent to which they are 'legalised', for example with regard to the types of obligations imposed, the precision of the agreements and whether disputes between the sites are settled by a third party.[196]

This chapter argues in favour of coordination. It suggests that the WTO can best take account of social solidarity ethics in the governance of international trade by strengthening its relations with other sites of governance. Viewed from the standpoint of the theory of global legal pluralism, the WTO is a specific site in the governance of globalisation. It is a divisible institution that is characterised by relatively strong convergence with other international sites of governance. Such a characterisation of the WTO involves to some extent a re-thinking of ideas about trade and global governance. Consequently, the best strategy for increasing the extent to which the WTO takes account of ethical issues is to strengthen its relations with other sites in the context of global legal pluralism. Relations between the WTO and other sites of governance can be strengthened by building closer relations involving institutions,

[195] For different perspectives on the same issues, see EU Petersmann, 'How to Constitutionalize International Law and Foreign Policy for the Benefit of Civil Society' (1998) 20(1) *Michigan Journal of International Law* 1; JP Trachtman, 'International Regulatory Competition, Externalization, and Jurisdiction' (1993) 34(1) *Harvard International Law Journal* 47.

[196] See KW Abbott, RO Keohane, A Moravcsik, AM Slaughter and D Snidal, 'The Concept of Legalization' (2000) 54 *International Organization* 401.

norms or dispute resolution processes of the sites concerned; on the basis of prior agreement or of ad hoc decisions; and according to legally binding measures or by means of soft law. A useful and realistic strategy would favour the development of wide-ranging relations, based on prior agreement and using soft law.[197]

With this mind, this chapter aimed to establish a baseline by providing an introductory survey of some of the main links between the WTO and other sites. It showed that, despite its many links with other international institutions, the WTO currently has relatively few, or in any event weaker, relations with other sites which are directly concerned with social solidarity ethics.[198] Further improvement requires a WTO institutional strategy, not simply a strategy based on linkages between different international normative regimes. This chapter argues that the WTO can deal with these issues best by an institutional strategy consisting of four elements:

a) strengthening existing relations with other sites of governance;
b) increasing cooperation in the production of norms;
c) expanding the use of observer status; and
d) increased cross-reference to non-WTO norms in WTO dispute settlement.

This is an institutional strategy orientated toward relations with other sites, instead of an institutional strategy orientated only toward internal structures. Greater coordination between sites is required if the objective is regular and sustained cooperation to help achieve social solidarity ethics in the regulation of international trade.

Clearly, however, this strategy is not unproblematic or free from controversy. Relations between sites usually reflect underlying power relations, not only transnationally and between countries but also within countries. For example, just as post-World War II regimes were essentially the projection of the United States regulatory system on to the rest of the world,[199] so the priority of the IMF over GATT rules in cases of conflict reflected the division of powers in the United States between the Treasury and the State Department.[200] Today, relations between the WTO, successor of the GATT, and other sites of governance are unbalanced and unevenly developed. Changes are necessary if the WTO is to deal adequately with ethical aspects of international trade. The WTO needs to establish stronger institutional relations with those sites of governance which are concerned most directly with social solidarity ethics. It needs to integrate social solidarity ethics into our thinking about international trade and our conception of international trade regulation. We should expect that such changes in the relational dimension as well as of the structural dimension of the WTO and other sites of governance would be strongly contested. However, this transformation is necessary if international trade regulation is to reflect the changing relations between WTO Members, including but not only the EU and China, to reflect the diversity of societies and cultures in the world today, and to embody social solidarity ethics.

197 For a different proposal, focusing only on rule-making, see Abbott and Snidal, above n 89, at 204. See also E Kwakwa, 'Some Comments on Rulemaking at the World Intellectual Property Organization' (2002) 12 *Duke Journal of Comparative & International Law* 179.

198 See also Howse and Mutua, above n 116.

199 See AM Burley-Slaughter, 'Regulating the World: Multilateralism, International Law, and the Projection of the New Deal Regulatory State' in J Ruggie (ed), *Multilateralism Matters: The Theory and Praxis of an Institutional Form* (New York, Columbia University Press, 1993) 125. See also GJ Ikenberry, 'A World Economy Restored: Expert Consensus and the Anglo-American Postwar Settlement' (1992) 46(1) *International Organization* 289.

200 Roessler, above n 184, at 2.

Bibliography

Abbott, FM, 'The WTO Medicines Decision: World Pharmaceutical Trade and the Protection of Public Health' (2005) 99 *The American Journal of International Law* 317.

—— (ed), *China in the World Trading System: Defining the Principles of Engagement* (London, Kluwer Law International, 1998).

Abbott, KW and Snidal, D, 'Hard Law and Soft Law in International Governance' (2000) 54 *International Organization* 421.

—— 'International Action on Bribery and Corruption: Why the Dog Didn't Bark in the WTO', in DLM Kennedy and JD Southwick (eds), *The Political Economy of International Trade Law: Essays in Honor of Robert E Hudec* (Cambridge, Cambridge University Press, 2002).

Abbott, KW, Keohane, RO, Moravcsik, A, Slaughter, AM and Snidal, D, 'The Concept of Legalization' (2000) 54 *International Organization* 401.

Abdelgawad, W (ed), *Mondialisation et droit de la concurrence: Les réactions normatives des états face à la mondialisation des pratiques anticoncurrentielles et des opérations de concentration*, Actes du Colloque des 14–15 juin 2007, Université de Bourgogne, CNRS, Travaux du Centre de recherche sur le droit des marchés et des investissements internationaux (Paris, Litec, 2008).

Abel, RL, 'Transnational Legal Practice' (1994) 44 *Case Western Reserve Law Review* 737.

Adaraoegbe, A, 'Energy, Economic Development, the Environment and Effective Global Governance: An Introduction' (2005) 5 *International Energy Law & Taxation Review* 185.

Adler, E, 'Cognitive Evolution: A Dynamic Approach for the Study of International Relations and Their Progress' in E Adler and B Crawford (eds), *Progress in Postwar International Relations* (New York, Columbia University Press, 1991).

Adler, E and Crawford, B (eds), *Progress in Postwar International Relations* (New York, Columbia University Press, 1991).

Agence France-Presse, 'No end of a dog's life for robot pets', *South China Morning Post*, Wednesday, 12 May 1999, at 10.

Ahn, D, 'Linkages between International Financial and Trade Institutions' (2000) 34(4) *Journal of World Trade* 1.

Alston, P (ed), *People's Rights* (Collected Courses of the Academy of European Law) (Oxford, Oxford University Press, 2001).

—— (ed), *Labour Rights as Human Rights* (Collected Courses of the Academy of European Law) (Oxford, Oxford University Press, 2005).

—— 'Resisting the Merger and Acquisition of Human Rights by Trade Law: A Reply to Petersmann' (2002) 13(4) *European Journal of International Law* 815.

Alter, KJ, *Establishing the Supremacy of European Law: The Making of an International Rule of Law in Europe* (Oxford, Oxford University Press, 2001).

Alter, KJ and Meunier, S, 'Nested and Overlapping Regimes in the Transatlantic Banana Trade Dispute' (2006) 13(3) *Journal of European Public Policy* 362–82.

Aman, AC Jr, 'The Globalizing State: A Future-oriented Perspective on the Public/Private Distinction, Federalism, and Democracy' (1998) 31 *Vanderbilt Journal of Transnational Law* 769.

Ancuceanu, R, 'Maximum Residue Limits of Veterinary Medicinal Products and Their Regulation in European Community Law' (2003) 9(2) *European Law Journal* 215.

Anders, G and Bannon, L, 'EToys to Join Web-Retailer Parade with IPO', *The Wall Street Journal*, Tuesday, 6 April 1999, at B1.

Andersen, H, *EU Dumping Determinations and the WTO Law* (Alphen aan den Rijn, Wolters Kluwer, 2009).

Andreosso-O'Callaghan, B and Nicolas, F, 'Complementarity and Rivalry in EU–China Economic Relations in the Twenty-first Century' (2007) 12 *European Foreign Affairs Review* 13.

Anghie, T, Chimni, BS, Mickelson, K and Okafor, O (eds), *The Third World and International Legal Order: Law, Politics and Globalization* (Leiden: Martinus Nijhoff, 2003).

Anheier, H, Glasius, M and Kaldor, M (eds), *Global Civil Society 2001* (Oxford, Oxford University Press, 2001).

Anthony, RA, 'The American Response to Dumping from Capitalist and Socialist Economies—Substantive Premises and Restructured Procedures after the 1967 GATT Code' (1969) 54 *Cornell Law Review* 159.

Antkiewicz, A and Whalley, J, 'BRICSAM and the non-WTO' (2006) 1(3) *Review of International Organizations* 237.

—— 'China's New Regional Trade Agreements' (2005) 28(10) *The World Economy* 1539.

Antoniadis, A, 'The European Union and WTO Law: A Nexus of Reactive, Coactive and Proactive Approaches' (2007) 6(1) *World Trade Review* 45.

Appelbaum, RP, 'The Future of Law in a Global Economy' (1998) 7(2) *Social and Legal Studies* 171.

Appelbaum, RP, Felstiner, W and Gessner, V (eds), *Rules and Networks: The Legal Culture of Global Business Transactions* (Oxford, Hart Publishing, 2001).

Archibugi, D, 'The Global Governance of Communicable Diseases: The Case for Vaccine R&D' (2005) 27(1) *Law and Policy* 33.

Arai-Takahashi, Y, 'The World Health Organisation and the Challenges of Globalisation' (2004) 1 *Law, Social Justice and Global Development*, available at http://www2.warwick.ac.uk/fac/soc/law/elj/lgd/2004_1/arai/ last accessed 4 March 4 2010.

Arnaud, AJ, *Entre modernité et mondialisation. Cinq leçons d'histoire de la philosophie du droit* (Paris, Librairie Générale de Droit et de Jurisprudence, 1998).

—— *Critique de la raison juridique, 2. Gouvernants sans frontières: Entre mondialisation et post-mondialisation* (Paris, Librairie Générale de Droit et de Jurisprudence, 2003).

Arturo, L, 'Impact of Globalisation on Law Enforcement Institutions' (2006) 7(1) *Human Rights and UK Practice* 10.

Arup, CJ, *The New World Trade Organization Agreements: Globalizing Law Through Services and Intellectual Property* (Cambridge, Cambridge University Press, 2000).

ASEAN–China Experts Group on Economic Cooperation, 'Forging Closer ASEAN–China Economic Relations in the Twenty-First Century', available on the ASEAN Secretariat website at http://www.aseansec.org/asean_chi.pdf.

Ash, R, 'China's Regional Economies and the Asian Region: Building Interdependent Linkages' in D Shambaugh (ed), *Power Shift: China and Asia's New Dynamics* (University of California Press, Berkeley, 2005).

Auboin, M, 'Fulfilling the Marrakesh Mandate on Coherence: Ten Years of Cooperation between the WTO, IMF and World Bank' (Geneva, WTO, 2007).

Audouard, R. 'Trade without Diplomatic Relations—The Experience of the Federal Republic of Germany' in D Kim and W Gumpel (eds), *New Directions in East–West Relations: German and Korean Perspectives* (Seoul, Korea, Institute of East and West Studies, Yonsei University, 1987).

Bai, Lin, 'Improving the Non-governmental System of Outsourcing Labour Regulation in China' (2007) 13(6) *European Law Journal* 772.

Bail, C, Falkner, R and Marquard, H (eds), *The Cartagena Protocol on Biosafety: Reconciling Trade in Biotechnology with Environment and Development?* (London, Earthscan, 2001).

Baldwin, R, *Managing the Noodle Bowl: The Fragility of East Asian Regionalism*, Centre for Economic Policy Research, Discussion Paper Series, No 5561, March 2006, available at www.cepr.org/pubs/dps/DP5561.asp.

Baldwin, RE, 'The Spoke Trap: Hub-and-Spoke Bilateralism in East Asia' in B Eichengreen, C Wyplosz and YC Park (eds), *China, Asia and the New World Economy* (Oxford University Press, 2008).

Balog, J. 'The untold toy success story: Elmo's evolution is a surprise to those involved', *USA Today*, Wednesday, 11 December 1996, at 1B.

Baneth, J, 'Comment on the Paper by Gary P Sampson' in AO Krueger (ed), *The WTO as an International Organization* (Chicago, University of Chicago Press, 1998).

Barcellona, P, Oral intervention at the Conference on 'Quelle culture pour l'Europe? Ordres juridiques et cultures dans le processus de globalisation', Réseau Européen de Droit et Société (REDS) and Istituto di Ricerca sui Problemi dello Stato e delle Istitutionzi (IRSI), Rome, 2–3 November 1998.

Barceló, JJ, 'Antidumping Laws as Barriers to Trade—The United States and the International Antidumping Code' (1972) 57 *Cornell Law Review* 491.

—— 'A History of GATT Unfair Trade Remedy Law—Confusion of Purposes' (1991) 14 *The World Economy* 311.

Barnett, AD (with a contribution by E Vogel), *Cadres, Bureaucracy and Political Power in Community China* (New York and London, Columbia University Press, 1967).

Barnett, MN and Duvall, R (eds), *Power in Global Governance* (Cambridge, Cambridge University Press, 2005).

Barnett, T and Whiteside, A, *AIDS in the Twenty-First Century: Disease and Globalization*, 2nd rev edn (London, St Martins Press, 2006).

Baroncini, E, 'The European Community and the Diplomatic Phase of the WTO Dispute Settlement Understanding' (1998) 18 *Yearbook of European Law* 157.

Barr, MS and Miller, GP, 'Global Administrative Law: The View from Basel' (2006) 17(1) *European Journal of International Law* 15.

Barrell, R and Choy, A, 'Economic Integration and Openness in Europe and East Asia', paper presented at the ASEM Symposium on Multilateral and Regional Economic Relations, Tokyo, 25 March 2003, 9–12, available at http://www.niesr.ac.uk/pubs/dps/dp214.pdf, last accessed 4 March 2010.

Bates, G, 'China's Evolving Regional Security Strategy', in D Shambaugh (ed), *Power Shift: China and Asia's New Dynamics* (Berkeley, University of California Press, 2005).

Baumer, M and Jacobsen, HD, 'Institutional Aspects of East–West Economic Relations' (1976) 10 *Journal of World Trade* 434.

Baxi, U, *Human Rights in a Posthuman World* (New Delhi, Oxford University Press, 2007).

BBC News, 'Pakistan launches strategic port', Tuesday, 20 March 2007, available at http://news.bbc.co.uk/2/hi/south_asia/6469725.stm, last accessed 4 March 2010.

Beber, G, 'Agreements concluded by the Community and Their Possible Direct Effect: From International Fruit to Kupferberg' (1983) 20 *CML Rev* 35.

Bello, JH, Holmer, AF and Preiss, JO, 'Searching for "Bubbles of Capitalism": Application of the US Anti-dumping and Countervailing Duty Laws to Reforming Nonmarket Economies' (1992) 25 *George Washington Journal of International Law and Economics* 665.

Bender, P, 'The European Parliament and the WTO: Positions and Initiatives' (2002) 7 *European Foreign Affairs Review* 193.

Benjamin, W, 'The Task of the Translator: An Introduction to the Translation of Baudelaire's *Tableaux Parisiens*' in W Benjamin, *Illuminations* (ed H Arendt, trans H Zohn (New York, Schocken Books, 1985).

Benton, LA, *Law and Colonial Cultures: Legal Regimes in World History, 1400–1900* (Cambridge, Cambridge University Press, 2002).

Benvenisti, E and Barak-Erez, D, *The Welfare State, Globalization and International Law* (Berlin, Springer, 2003).

Bercusson, B and Estlund, C, *Regulating Labour in the Wake of Globalisation: New Challenges, New Institutions* (Oxford, Hart Publishing, 2008).

Berkey, JO, 'The European Court of Justice and Direct Effect for the GATT: A Question Worth Revisiting' (1998) 9 *European Journal of International Law* 626.

Berman, PS, 'The Globalization of Jurisdiction' (2002) 151 *University of Pennsylvania Law Review* 311.

—— *From International Law to Law and Globalization*, ExpressO Preprint Series, Working Paper 665, 5 July 2005, http:/law.bepress.com/espresso/eps/665.

—— 'Global Legal Pluralism' (2007) 80 *Southern California Law Review* 1155.

Bermann, GA, Herdegen, M and Lindseth, PL (eds), *Transatlantic Regulatory Cooperation: Legal Problems and Political Prospects* (Oxford, Oxford University Press, 2001).

Bernstein, E, *Temporarily Yours: Intimacy, Authenticity and the Commerce of Sex* (Chicago, University of Chicago Press, 2007).

Berrod, F, 'La Cour de Justice refuse l'invocabilité des accords OMC: essai de régulation de la mondialisation—A propos de l'arrêt de la Cour de Justice du 23 novembre 1999, *Portugal c/ Conseil* (accords textiles avec le Pakistan et l'Inde)' (2000) 36(3) *Revue Trimestrielle de Droit Européen* 419.

Bertezzolo, G, 'The European Union Facing the Global Arena: Standard-setting Bodies and Financial Regulation' (2009) 34(2) *EL Rev* 247.

Beseler, JF and Williams, AN, *Anti-dumping and Anti-subsidy Law: The European Communities* (London, Sweet & Maxwell, 1986).

Bettcher, D and Lee, K, 'Glossary on Globalisation and Public Health' (2002) 56(8) *Journal of Epidemiology and Community Health* 8.

Bhagwati, JN, *In Defense of Globalization* (New York, Oxford University Press, 2004).

Bhala, R, *International Trade Law: Cases and Materials* (Charlottesville, Michie Law Publishers, 1996).

Bhutta, Z, 'PM's visit to China: Pakistan–China relations to be further strengthened', *Daily Times* (Pakistan), Sunday, 27 January 2008.

Bierwagen, RW, *GATT Article VI and the Protectionist Bias in Anti-dumping Laws* (Deventer, Kluwer, 1990).

BikeBiz, 'Lies, damn lies and statistics', available at http://www.bikebiz.com/infozone/stats.php, last accessed 4 March 2010 .

Billette, A, 'Les terres agricoles, de plus en plus convoitées', *Le Monde*, Wednesday, 15 April 2009, at 4.

—— 'Après un offensive discrète au Kazakstan, la Chine lorne les terres russes inexploitées', *Le Monde*, Tuesday, 21 April 2009, at 4.

Bitonio Benedicto, ER Jr, 'Toward a Code of Conduct in the Textile, Clothing and Footwear Industries: Laws and Possibilities' (ILO, Sectoral Activities Programme, Workshop Background Paper 1998), available at http://www.ilo.org./public/english/100secto/papers/tcfcode/index.htm.

Black, J, *Constructing and Contesting Legitimacy and Accountability in Polycentric Regulatory Regimes*, IILJ Working Paper 2007/12, Global Administrative Law Series, Institute for International Law and Justice, New York University School of Law, available at http://www.iilj.org.

Blomley, N, Delaney, D and Ford, RT, *The Legal Geographies Reader* (Oxford, Blackwell, 2001).

Bo, Lu, 'ASEAN–China Free Trade Agreement: Negotiation, Implementation and Prospect' in S-H Saw (ed), *ASEAN–China Economic Relations* (Singapore, ISEAS Publishing, 2007).

Bobin, F., 'Face à la montée des eaux, les Maldives cherchent des terres d'accueil', *Le Monde*, Friday, 17 April 2009, at 4.

Bohannan, P, 'The Differing Realms of the Law' in P Bohannan (ed), *Law and Warfare: Studies in the Anthropology of Conflict* (Texas Press, Sourcebooks in Anthropology, 1967), reprinted from American Anthropologist, Special Publication, *The Ethnography of Law* (ed L Nader), vol 67, no 6, pt 2, 33.

Bonacich, E, Cheng, L, Chinchilla, N, Hamilton, N and Ong, P (eds), *Global Production: The Apparel Industry in the Pacific Rim* (Philadelphia, Temple University Press, 1994).

Bonell, MJ, *An International Restatement of Contract Law: The UNIDROIT Principles of International Commercial Contracts* (New York, Transnational Juris Publications, Inc, 1994).
Bontinck, G, *The TRIPs Agreement and the ECJ: A New Dawn? Some Comments about Joined Cases C-300/98 and C-392/98* Parfums Dior *and* Assco Gerüste, Jean Monnet Working Paper 16/01, Jean Monnet Program, New York University School of Law, available at <http://www.jeanmonnetprogram.org/papers/01/013901.html.
Bontrager Unzicker, AD, 'From Corruption to Cooperation: Globalization Brings a Multilateral Agreement against Foreign Bribery' (2000) 7 *Indiana Journal of Global Legal Studies* 655.
Borrus, M and Zysman, J, 'Globalisation with Borders: The Rise of Wintelism as the Future of Industrial Competition' in Zysmanand, J, Schwartz, A (eds), *Enlarging Europe: The Industrial Foundations of a New Political Reality* (University of California at Berkeley, 1998).
Boudant, J, *L'Anti-Dumping communautaire* (Paris, Economica, 1991).
Bourdieu, P, *Outline of a Theory of Practice* (trans R Nice) (Cambridge, Cambridge University Press, 1977).
—— 'The Force of Law: Toward a Sociology of the Juridical Field' (1987) 38 *The Hastings Law Journal* 814.
—— *Language and Symbolic Power* (ed JB Thompson, trans G Raymond and M Adamson) (Cambridge, Polity Press, 1991).
Bourgeois, JHJ, 'Effects of International Agreements in European Community Law: Are the Dice Cast?' (1984) 82 *Michigan Law Review* 1250.
—— 'The European Court of Justice and the WTO: Problems and Challenges' in JHH Weiler (ed), *The EU, the WTO and the NAFTA: Towards a Common Law of International Trade?* (Oxford, Oxford University Press, 2000).
Bourgeois, JHJ and Lynskey, O, 'The Extent to which the EC Legislature takes account of WTO Obligations: Jousting lessons from the European Parliament' in A Dashwood and M Maresceau (eds), *Law and Practice of EU External Relations: Salient Features of a Changing Landscape* (Cambridge University Press, Cambridge, 2008).
Bourrinet, J and Maljean-Dubois, S (eds), *Le commerce international des organismes génétiquement modifiés* (Paris, La documentation française, 2002).
Braithwaite, J and Drahos, P, *Global Business Regulation* (Cambridge, Cambridge University Press, 2000).
Brand, RA, 'Direct Effect of International Economic Law in the United States and the European Union' (1996–97) 17 *Northwestern Journal of International Law and Business* 556.
Bratton, WW and McCahery, JA, 'Comparative Corporate Governance and the Theory of the Firm: The Case against Global Cross Reference' (1999) 38(2) *Columbia Journal of Transnational Law* 214.
Bratton, W, McCahery, J, Picciotto, S and Scott, C (eds), *International Regulatory Competition and Coordination: Perspectives on Economic Regulation in Europe and the United States* (Oxford, Clarendon Press, 1996).
Bronckers, M, 'The Relationship of the EC Courts with Other International Tribunals: Non-committal, Respectful or Submissive?' (2007) 44 *CM L Rev* 610.
—— 'Editorial: La jurisprudence des juridictions communautaires relatives à l'OMC demande réparation: plaidoyer pour les droits des Etats membres' (2001) 37 *Cahiers de Droit Européen* 3.
Brosset, E and Truilhé-Marengo, E (eds), *Les enjeux de la normalisation technique internationale: Entre environnement, santé et commerce international* (Paris, La documentation française, 2006).
Brown, SS, 'The People's Republic of China and the US Unfair Trade Laws' (1988) 22 *Journal of World Trade* 79.
Brütsch, C and Lehmkuhl, D (eds), *Law and Legalization in International Relations* (London, Routledge Cavendish, 2007).
Burke-White, W, 'International Legal Pluralism' (2004) 25 *Michigan Journal of International Law* 963.

Burley-Slaughter, AM, 'Regulating the World: Multilateralism, International Law, and the Projection of the New Deal Regulatory State' in J Ruggie (ed), *Multilateralism Matters: The Theory and Praxis of an Institutional Form* (New York, Columbia University Press, 1993).

'By the Sweat and Toil of Children: A Report to Congress' (Bureau of International Affairs, US Department of Labor, 15 July 1994), available at http://www.dol.gov/dol/ilab/public/media/reports/sweat/main.htm.

Cai, Peng-Hong, 'East Asian New Regionalism and China', PowerPoint presentation prepared for the Third Annual CEPII–IDB Conference, Washington DC, 9–10 February 2006, available at http://www.bid.org.uy/europe/index.php?file=news_and_events/2006/PengHong.pdf, last accessed 4 March 2010

Canelas de Castro, P, *Recent Developments in Water Law: Principles and Comparative Cases* (Lisbon, Luso-American Foundation, 2005).

Cantwell, J, 'The Relationship between International Trade and International Production', in D Greenaway and LA Winters (eds), *Surveys in International Trade* (Oxford, Blackwell, 1994).

Capaldo, GZ, *The Pillars of Global Law* (Aldershot, Ashgate, 2008).

—— (ed), *The Global Community: Yearbook of International Law and Jurisprudence 2001–Present* (Oxford, Oxford University Press, 2002).

Capeller, W, 'Not Such a Neat Net: Some Comments on Virtual Criminality' (2001) 10 *Social & Legal Studies* 229.

Carfantan, JY, *Le choc alimentaire mondial: ce qui nous attend demain* (Paris, Albin Michel, 2009).

Casella, A, 'On Market Integration and the Development of Institutions: The Case of International Commercial Arbitration' (1996) 40 *European Economic Review* 155.

Cass, DZ, *The Constitutionalisation of the WTO: Legitimacy, Democracy and Community in the International Trading System* (Oxford, Oxford University Press, 2005).

Central Intelligence Agency, *The World Factbook—China*, available at https://www.cia.gov/library/publications/the-world-factbook/geos/ch.html.

Chalmers, D, 'New Protectionism and the European Communities—A question of Constitutionality?' in BS Jackson and D McGoldrick (eds), *Legal Visions of the New Europe* (London, Graham and Trotman, 1993) 259.

Chang, Seung Wha, 'Regional Trade Agreements and the WTO: WTO Consistency of East Asian RTAs', 12–13 September 2005, PowerPoint presentation, available at http://project.iss.u-tokyo.ac.jp/crep/pdf/ws05/5pp.pdf.

Charnowitz, S, 'Opening the WTO to Nongovernmental Interests' (2000) 24 *Fordham International Law Journal* 173.

Charnowitz, S, 'The Moral Exception in Trade Policy' in S Charnowitz, *Trade Law and Global Governance* (London, Cameron May, 2002).

—— *Trade Law and Global Governance* (London, Cameron May, 2002).

Charlesworth, H, Chinkin, C and Wright, S, 'Feminist Approaches to International Law' (1991) 85(4) *American Journal of International Law* 613.

Chaudhry, Sajid, 'Gwadar Oil City: Pakistan, China to sign agreements in early 2008, IntelliBriefs, 17 October 2007, available at http://intellibriefs.blogspot.com/2007/10/gwadar-oil-city-pakistan-china-to-sign.html.

Chayes, A and Chayes, AH, *The New Sovereignty: Compliance with International Regulatory Agreements* (Cambridge, Mass, Harvard University Press, 1995).

Che, Jihua and Qian,Yingyi, 'Institutional Environment, Community Government and Corporate Governance: Understanding China's Township-Village Enterprises' (1998) 14 *Journal of Law, Economics and Organization* 1.

Chemillier-Gendreau, M and Moulier Boutang, Y (eds), *Le droit dans la mondialisation* (Actes du congrès Marx International II) (Paris, Presses Universitaires de France, 2001).

Chen, H, *The Institutional Transition of China's Township and Village Enterprises: Market Liberalization, Contractual Form Innovation and Privatization* (Aldershot, Ashgate, 2000).

Chen, J and Ong, J, 'China Seeks "Comprehensive" Trade Pact with Taiwan', Bloomberg, 5 March 2009, available at http://www.bilaterals.org/article.php3?id_article=14577, accessed 3 August 2009.

Chen, S, 'Plan for Energy Hub in Inner Mongolia', *South China Morning Post*, Thursday, 3 January 2008, at A4.

Cheng-Chwee, Kuik, *Multilateralism in China's ASEAN Policy*, SAIS Working Paper Series, WP/05/03, Paul H Nitze School of Advanced International Studies (SIAS), Johns Hopkins University, Washington, DC, October 2003.

Cheung, A, 'China–EU Trade and the Yuan Parity Rate' (Interview of Li Gang, Director of the European Department, Chinese Ministry of Commerce Academy), *China Business News*, 30 November 2007, reported in *The China Perspective*, 22 April 2009, available at http://www.thechinaperspective.com/articles/chinaeutradeandtheyuanparityrate3163/index.html, last accessed 4 March 2010

Cheyne, I, 'International Agreements and the European Community Legal System' (1994) 19 *EL Rev* 581.

Chiba, Masaji, *Legal Pluralism: Toward a General Theory through Japanese Legal Culture* (Tokyo, Tokai University Press, 1989).

Chimni, BS, 'International Institutions Today: An Imperial Global State in the Making' (2004) 15(1) *European Journal of International Law* 1.

China Bicycle Yearbook 2005 (Tokyo, Cycle Press, 2004).

'China 2008 : Exports Levelling Off', *Bike Europe*, Facts and Figures, Market Reports, China 2008, published 23 March 2009.

'China and Iceland agree to start FTA feasibility research', *China Daily*, 26 August 2003.

'China, Pakistan sign free trade agreement', *People's Daily Online*, 25 November 2006, available at http://english.people.com.cn/200611/24/eng20061124_324918.html, last accessed 4 March 2010- .

'China, Brazil strengthen relations', *Gov.cn*, Tuesday, 29 August 2006, available at http://www.gov.cn/misc/2006-08/29/content_372510.htm.

'China–ROK talks have many hurdles', *China Daily*, 13 December 2006, available at http://english.peopledaily.com.cn/200612/13/eng20061213_331954.html, last accessed 4 March 2010

Chinamining.org, 'China's copper demand to buoy prices in long run', Interfax-China, 22 February 2008, available at http://chinamining.org/News/2008-02-22/1203643602d9132.html.

—— 'Resource shortage challenges China's copper industry', on the website of Chinamining.org, sponsored by the China Mining Association (CMA), updated 14 March 2008, at http://www.chinamining.org/News/2008-03-14/1205458306d12119.html.

'Chinese Toy Making: Where the Furbies come from', *The Economist*, 19 December 1998, 95.

Chinkin, C, Wright, S. and Charlesworth, H, 'Feminist Approaches to International Law: Reflections from Another Century,' available at http://cigj.anu.edu.au/cigj/link_documents/Charlesworthpubs/Charlesworth%20Book%20Chapters/Feminist_Approaches_2005.pdf.

Choi, Won-Mog, 'Regional Economic Integration in East Asia: Prospect and Jurisprudence' (2003) 6(1) *Journal of International Economic Law* 49.

—— 'Legal Analysis of Korea–ASEAN Regional Trade Integration' (2007) 41(3) *Journal of World Trade* 581.

Chopparapu, R, 'The European Union: A Model for East Asia?' (2005) 3 *Asia Europe Journal* 133.

Chu, Tianshu and Prusa, TJ, *The Reasons for and the Impact of Antidumping Protection: The Case of People's Republic of China*, East-West Center Working Papers, University of Hawai'i, Economics Series, No 69, April 2004.

Chu, Wan-wen, 'Causes of Growth: A Study of Taiwan's Bicycle Industry' (1997) 21 *Cambridge Journal of Economics* 55.

Chu, W and Tung, AC, *The Impact of Currency Appreciation on Taiwan's Industries* (Taipei, Council for Economic Planning and Development, 1990).

Clarke, DC, 'Methodologies for Research in Chinese Law' (1996) 30 *University of British Columbia Law Review* 201.

Cohen, J and Sabel, C, 'Extra Rempublicam Nulla Justitia?' (2006) 34 *Philosophy and Public Affairs* 147.

Colbatch, T, 'Why we want an FTA with China', *New Age* (Melbourne), 17 August 2004.

Coleman, A and Maogoto, J, 'After the party, is there any cure for the hangover? The Challenges of the Global Economy to Westphalian Sovereignty' (2003) 30(1) *Legal Issues of European Integration* 35.

Comaroff , J and Comaroff, JL (eds), *Law and Disorder in the Postcolony* (Chicago, University of Chicago Press, 2006).

Commission Européenne, *Rapport sur le Fonctionnement et l'Avenir du Régime Douanier Economique du Perfectionnement Actif* (Commission Européenne: DG XXI, Bruxelles, 1996).

Commission of the European Communities, *Report from the Commission to the Council on the Surveillance Measures and Quantitative Quotas Applicable to Certain Non-textile Products Originating in the People's Republic of China*, COM(95)614 final, Brussels, 6 December 1995.

—— 'The Global Challenge of International Trade: A Market Access Strategy for the European Union' (Communication to the Council, the European Parliament, the Economic and Social Committee, and the Committee of Regions), COM(96)53 final, 14 February 1996.

—— *Second Report from the Commission to the Council on the Surveillance Measures and Quantitative Quotas Applicable to Certain Non-textile Products Originating in the People's Republic of China*, COM(97)11 final, Brussels, 29 January 1997.

—— 'Communication from the Commission to the Council and the European Parliament on the Treatment of Former Non-market Economies in Anti-dumping Proceedings and a Proposal for a Council Regulation amending Council Regulation (EC) No. 384/96', COM(97)677 final, Brussels, 12 December 1997.

—— *Third Report from the Commission on the Quantitative Quotas and Surveillance Measures Applicable to Certain Non-textile Products Originating in the People's Republic of China*, COM(1998)128 final, Brussels, 9 March 1998.

—— 'Explanatory Memorandum: Review of the Anti-dumping Regime Applicable to Russia and China and a Proposal for a Council Regulation amending Council Regulation (EC) No 384/96', in Commission of the European Communities, *Proposal for a Council Regulation amending Regulation (EC) No 384/96 on protection against dumped imports from countries not members of the European Community (presented by the Commission)*, COM(2000)363 final, Brussels, 15 June 2000.

—— Communication on 'Global Europe: Europe's Trade Defence Instruments in a Changing Global Economy', A Green Paper for Public Consultation, COM (2006) 763 final, Brussels, 6 December 2006.

Conaghan, J, Fischl, R and Klare, K, *Labour Law in an Era of Globalization: Transformative Practices and Possibilities* (Oxford, Oxford University Press, 2002).

Congress of the United States, Congressional Budget Office, *How the GATT Affects US Anti-dumping and Countervailing Duty Policy* (Washington, DC, Congressional Budget Office, September 1994).

Convention on Biological Diversity, 'Action Plan on Capacity-building for Access to Genetic Resources and Benefit-Sharing, available at http://www.cbd.int/programmes/socio-eco/benefit/action.shtml.

Cook, W, 'Judicial review of the EPO and the direct effect of TRIPS in the European Community' (1997) 7 *European Intellectual Property Review* 367.

Coombe, RJ, 'Anthropological Approaches to Law and Society in Conditions of Globalization', in N Blomley, D Delaney and RT Ford (eds), *The Legal Geographies Reader* (Oxford, Blackwell Publishers, 2001).

Cooper, RN, 'China's Coming Demand for Energy' in B Eichengren, C Wyplosz, and YC Park (eds), *China, Asia, and the New World Economy* (Oxford, Oxford University Press, 2008).

Corne, PH, *Foreign Investment in China: The Administrative Legal System* (Hong Kong, Hong Kong University Press, 1997).

Correa, C, *Elements of an International Regime for the Recognition of National Regulations on Access to Genetic Resources*, UNCTAD/DITC/TED/2007/9 (New York and Geneva, UNCTAD, 2008).

'Costa Rica, China begin talks on free trade', *New Post India*, Thursday, 10 January 2008, available at http://www.bilaterals.org/article.php3?id_article=10918&var_recherche=china+and+costa+rica.

Cottier, T, 'Dispute Settlement in the World Trade Organization: Characteristics and Structural Implications for the European Union' (1998) 35 *CML Rev* 325.

Cottier, T and Germann, G, 'The WTO and EU distributive policy: the case of regional promotion and assistance' in G de Búrca and J Scott (eds), *The EU and the WTO: Legal and Constitutional Issues* (Oxford, Oxford University Press, 2001).

Cottier, T and Schefer, KN, 'The relationship between World Trade Organization, national and regional law' (1998) 1 *Journal of International Economic Law* 83.

Cottrell, J, 'Product Liability', in S Nossal (ed), *Law Lectures for Practitioners 1993* (Hong Kong, Hong Kong Law Journal Limited 1993).

Crane, GT, 'Reform and Retrenchment in China's Special Economic Zones', in Joint Economic Committee, Congress of the United States (ed), *China's Dilemma's in the 1990s: The Problems of Reforms, Modernization, and Interdependence* (Armonk, NY, ME Sharpe, 1993) 841.

Crawford, JA and Fiorentino, RV, *The Changing Landscape of Regional Trade Agreements*, WTO, Geneva, Switzerland, Discussion Paper No 8, 2005.

Creally, E, *Judicial Review of Anti-dumping and Other Safeguard Measures in the European Community* (London, Butterworths, 1992).

CREDIMI, Université de Grenoble, France, *Souveraineté étatique et marches internationaux à la fin du XXè siècle, A propos de 30 ans de recherché du CREDIMI, Mélanges offerts à Philippe Kahn* (Paris, Litec, 2000).

Cruz, Bacquero, J, 'Disintegration of the Law of Integration in the External Economic Relations of the European Community' (1997) 3 *Columbia Journal of European Law* 257.

Cummings, SL, *The Internationalization of Public Interest Law*, UCLA School of Law, UCLA Public Law Series, Paper 6-11, 13 November 2006.

Cuneo, DL and Manuel, CB Jr, 'Roadblock to Trade: The State-controlled Economy Issue in Antidumping Law Administration' (1982) 5 *Fordham International Law Journal* 277.

Cutler, AC, *Private Power and Global Authority: Transnational Merchant Law in the Global Political Economy* (Cambridge, Cambridge University Press, 2003).

—— 'Globalization, the Rule of Law, and the Modern Law Merchant: Medieval or Late capitalist Associations?' (2001) 8 *Constellations* 480.

Cutler, AC, Haufler, V and Porter, T (eds), *Private Authority and International Affairs* (Albany, State University of New York Press, 1999).

Dale, E, *Anti-dumping Law in a Liberal Trade Order* (London, Macmillan for the Trade Policy Research Centre, 1980).

Darian-Smith, E, 'Power in Paradise: The Political Implications of Santos's Utopia' (1998) 23 *Law & Social Enquiry* 81.

—— *Bridging Divides: The Channel Tunnel and English Legal Identity in the New Europe* (Berkeley, University of California Press, 1999).

—— 'Structural Inequalities in the Global Legal System' (Review Essay), (2000) 34 *Law & Society Review* 809.

Davidson, P, 'Net retailer eToys faces big risks as its star rises', *USA Today*, Thursday, 8 April 1999, at B.1.

Dawar, K, 'Global Governance and Its Implications for Consumers' (2006) 16(1) *Consumer Policy Review* 2.

Deardorff, AV and Stern, RM, 'Introduction and Overview' in Deardorff, AV and Stern, RM (eds), *Social Dimensions of US Trade Policies* (Ann Arbor, University of Michigan Press, 2001).
De Bièvre, D, *International Institutions and Domestic Coalitions: The Differential Effects of Negotiations and Judicialisation in European Trade Policy*, EUI Working Paper SPS No 2003/17, Department of Political and Social Sciences, European University Institute, Florence, 2003.
De Búrca, G and Craig, P (eds), *EU Law: Text, Cases, and Materials*, 2nd edn (Oxford, Oxford University Press, 1998).
De Búrca, G and Scott, J, 'The Impact of the WTO on EU decision-making', in G de Búrca and J Scott (eds), *The EU and the WTO: Legal and Constitutional Issues* (Oxford, Oxford University Press, 2001).
Dee, P, 'East Asian Economic Integration and its Impact on Future Growth' (2007) 30(3) *The World Economy* 405.
De Grauwe, P and Zhang, Zhaoyong, 'Introduction: Monetary and Economic Integration in the East Asian Region' (2006) 29(12) *The World Economy* 1643.
Delmas-Marty, M, *Trois défis pour un droit mondial* (Paris, Editions du Seuil, 1998).
—— *Towards a Truly Common Law: Europe as a Laboratory for Legal Pluralism* (trans N Norberg) (Cambridge, Cambridge University Press, 2002).
—— 'Global Crime Calls for Global Justice' (2002) 10(4) *European Journal of Crime, Criminal Law and Criminal Justice* 286.
—— 'The Contribution of Comparative Law to a Pluralist Conception of International Criminal Law' (2003) 1(1) *Journal of International Crime and Justice* 13.
—— *Les forces imaginaires du droit (II): Le pluralisme ordonné* (Paris, Editions du Seuil, 2006).
Del Vecchio, A, 'Globalisation and Its Effect on International Courts and Tribunals' (2006) 5(1) *Law and Practice of International Courts and Tribunals* 1.
De Ly, F, *International Business Law and Lex Mercatoria* (Dordrecht, North Holland, 1992).
Deng, Xiaoping, 'Realize the Four Modernizations and Never Seek Hegemony', 7 May 1978, in *Selected Works of Deng Xiaoping*, vol II (1975–82), trans by The Bureau for the Compilation and Translation of the Works of Marx, Engels, Lenin and Stalin under the Central Committee of the Communist Party of China (Foreign Languages Press, Beijing, 1984, 2nd edn 1995).
Dent, CM, *New Free Trade Agreements in the Asia-Pacific* (London, Palgrave Macmillan, 2006).
Denton, R, 'The Non-market Economy Rules of the European Community's Anti-dumping and Countervailing Duties Legislation' (1987) 36 *International and Comparative Law Quarterly* 198.
Detlof, H and Fridh, H, 'The EU Treatment of Non-Market Economy Countries in Antidumping Proceedings'(Kommerskollegium/Swedish National Board of Trade, Stockholm), 5 May 2006.
De Senarclens, P, *La mondialisation: Théories, enjeux et débats*, 3rd edn (Paris, Armand Colin, 2002).
De Sousa Santos, B, 'Law: A Map of Misreading. Toward a Post-Modern Conception of Law' (1987) 14(3) *Journal of Law and Society* 279.
—— *Toward a New Common Sense: Law, Globalization and Emancipation* (London, Butterworths LexisNexis, 2002), 1st edn published as *Toward a New Common Sense: Law, Science and Politics in the Paradigmatic Transition* (New York, Routledge, 1995).
De Sousa Santos, B and Rodríguez-Garavita, CA (eds), *Law and Globalization from Below: Towards a Cosmopolitan Legality* (Cambridge, Cambridge University Press, 2005).
Devuyst, Y and Serdarevevic, A, 'The World Trade Organization and Regional Trade Agreements: Bridging the Constitutional Credibility Gap' (2007) 18(1) *Duke Journal of Comparative and International Law* 1.
Dewing, I and Russell, PO, 'Financial Integration in the EU: the First Phase of EU Endorsement of International Accounting Standards' (2008) 46(2) *Journal of Common Market Studies* 243.

Dezalay, Y and Garth, BG, *The Internationalization of Palace Wars: Lawyers, Economists, and the Contest to Transform Latin America* (Chicago, University of Chicago Press, 2002).

Didier, P, *Les principaux accords de l'OMC et leur transposition dans la Communauté européenne* (Bruxelles, Bruylant, 1997).

Diebold, W Jr, 'The End of the ITO' (October 1952) 16 *Essays in International Finance* (Princeton, NJ, International Finance Section, Department of Economics and Social Institutions, Princeton University).

Dillon, S, *International Trade and Economic Law and the European Union* (Oxford, Hart Publishing, 2002).

Directeur général, Organisation Mondiale du Commerce, Troisième rapport. Conseil général, Session extraordinaire sur la mise en œuvre, Mesures visant à accroitre la participation des pays en développement membres aux travaux des organisations internationales de normalisation compétentes dans le domaine des mesures sanitaires et phytosanitaires, Organisation Mondiale du Commerce, WT/GC/54, 7 novembre 2001 (01-5490), available on the WTO website at http://docsonline.wto.org/GEN_viewerwindow.asp?D:/DDFDOCUMENTS/U/WT/GC/54, last accessed 10 June 2002.

Dobson, W, 'Deeper Integration in East Asia: Regional Institutions and the International Economic System' (2001) 24(8) *The World Economy* 995.

Doherty, EM (ed), *Japanese Investment in Asia: International Production Strategies in a Rapidly Changing World* (Berkeley, University of California at Berkeley, BRIE, 1995).

Downey, A and Graham, J, 'The Regulation of Dumping from State-Controlled Economics: Where Next?' in D Wallace and DA Flores (eds), *Interface Two: Conference Proceedings on the Legal Framework of East-West Trade* (Washington, DC, The International Law Institute, Georgetown University Law Center, 1982).

Drexl, J, 'The TRIPS Agreement and the EC: What comes next after joint competence?' in FK Beier and G Schricker (eds), *From GATT to TRIPS—The Agreement on Trade-related Aspects of Intellectual Property Rights* (Munich, Max Planck Institute, 1996).

Drummonds, HH, 'Transnational Small and Emerging Business in a World of Nikes and Microsofts' (2000) 4 *Journal of Small and Emerging Business Law* 249.

Dunbabin, JPD, *The Cold War: The Great Powers and Their Allies* (London and New York, Longman, 1994).

Dunoff, JL, 'Constitutional Conceits: The WTO's "Constitution" and the Discipline of International Law' (2006) 17(3) *European Journal of International Law* 647.

Earnest, DC, and Rosenau, JN, 'Signifying Nothing? What Complex Systems Theory Can and Cannot Tell Us about World Politics' in NE Harrison (ed), *Complexity in World Politics: Concepts and Methods of a New Paradigm* (Buffalo, SUNY Press, 2006).

Eberhard, C, *Le Droit au miroir des cultures. Pour une autre mondialisation* (Paris, Librairie Générale de Droit et de Jurisprudence, 2006).

—— (ed), *Traduire nos responsabilités planétaires: Recomposer nos paysages juridiques* (Brussels, Bruylant, 2008).

The Economist,'A Ravenous Dragon: A Special Report on China's Search for Raw Materials', 15 March 2008, 1–18 [after p 60]

Economy, E and M Oksenberg, M (eds), *China Joins the World: Progress and Prospects* (New York, Council on Foreign Relations, 1999).

Eden, L and Hampson, FO, 'Clubs are Trump: The Formation of International Regimes in the Absence of a Hegemon' in JR Hollingsworth and R Boyer (eds), *Contemporary Capitalism: The Embeddedness of Institutions* (Cambridge University Press, Cambridge, 1997).

Edgecliffe-Johnson, A,'Net gains take precedence over bricks and mortar', *Financial Times*, 28–29 August 1999, at 25.

Eeckhout, P, 'The Technointorg Judgment of the European Court of Justice and the Issue of Non-market Economy Dumping' (1989) 12 *World Competition* 39.

—— 'Judicial Enforcement of WTO Law in the European Union—Some Further Reflections' (2002) 5(1) *Journal of International Economic Law* 91.
—— *External Relations of the European Union: Legal and Constitutional Foundations* (Oxford, Oxford University Press, 2004).
—— 'The domestic legal status of the WTO Agreement: Interconnecting legal systems' (2005) 34 *CML Rev* 11.
Egli, P and Kokott, J, 'International Decision: *Portuguese Republic v Council of the European Union*' (2000) 94 *American Journal of International Law* 740.
Ehlermann, CD, *Some personal experiences as member of the Appellate Body of the WTO*, Policy Paper RSC No 02/9, Robert Schuman Centre for Advanced Studies, European University Institute, Florence.
Ehlermann, CD, Kupper, S, Lambrecht, H and Ollig, G. *Handelspartner DDR: Innerdeutsche Wittschaftsbeziehungen* (Baden Baden, Nomos Verlag, 1975).
Ehrenhaft, PD, 'The Treasury's Approach to Imports for State-controlled Economy Countries under the Antidumping and Countervailing Duty Laws' in D Wallace, GC Spina, RM Rawson and B McGill (eds), *Interface One: Conference Proceedings on the Application of U. Antidumping and Countervailing Duty Laws to Imports from State-Controlled Economies and State-Owned Enterprises* (Washington, DC, The Institute for International and Foreign Trade Law, Georgetown University Law Center, 1980).
—— 'The Application of Antidumping Duties to Imports from "Non-market Economies" ', in JH Jackson, and EA Vermulst (eds), *Antidumping Law and Practice: A Comparative Study* (New York, Harvester Wheatsheaf, 1990).
—— 'US Policy on Imports from Economies in Transition' in PD Ehrenhaft, BV Hindley, C Michalopoulos, and LA Winters (eds), *Policies on Imports from Economies in Transition: Two Case Studies* (Washington, DC, The World Bank, 1997).
Ehrlich, E, *Fundamental Principles of the Sociology of Law*, originally published 1936 (trans WL Moll) (New Brunswick, Transaction Publishers, reprint 2002).
Einhorn, T, 'The Impact of the WTO Agreement on TRIPS (Trade-Related Aspects of Intellectual Property Rights) on EC Law: A Challenge to Regionalism' (1998) 35 *CML Rev* (1998) 1069.
Emch, A, 'Services Regionalism in the WTO: China's Trade Agreements with Hong Kong and Macao in the Light of Article V(6) GATS' (2006) 33 (4) *Legal Issues of European Integration* 351.
Espósito, C, 'International trade and national legal orders: The problem of direct applicability of WTO law' in P Mengozzi (ed), *International Trade Law on the 50th Anniversary of the Multilateral Trade System* (Milano, Giuffrè, 1999).
'EU 2005: Production Shifts from Asia to Eastern Europe', *Bike Europe*, Facts and Figures, Market Reports, EU 2005, published 8 August 2007, available at http://www.bike-eu.com.
'Europe 2006: Shift from Imports to Production in Eastern Europe Continues', *Bike Europe*, Facts and Figures, Market Reports, EU 2006, published 4 January 2008, available at http://www.bike-eu.com.
Evenett, SJ and Vermulst, E, 'The Politicisation of EC Anti-dumping Policy: Member States, Their Votes and the European Commission', paper presented at the Symposium on a Centennial of Anti-Dumping Legislation and Implementation, University of Michigan, 12 March 2004 (on file with the author).
Everling, U, 'Will Europe slip on bananas? The Bananas Judgment of the Court of Justice and national courts' (1996) 33 *CML Rev* 401.
Eucken, W, *Grundsätze der Wirtschaftspolitik* (Tıbingen,JB Mohr, 1940), published in English as *The Foundations of Economics: History and Theory in the Analysis of Economic Reality* (trans TW Hutchinson) (Chicago, University of Chicago Press, 1951).
Falk Moore, S, 'Law and Social Change: The Semi-autonomous Social Field as an Appropriate Subject of Study' (1973) 7(4) *Law and Society Review* 719.

—— *Law as Process: An Anthropological Approach* (London, Routledge & Kegan Paul, 1978).

Falkner, R, *Business Power and Conflict in International Environmental Politics* (London, Palgrave Macmillan, 2008).

—— (ed), *The International Politics of Genetically Modified Food* (London, Palgrave Macmillan, 2007).

'Feasibility study on the China–Iceland FTA ended', *China Daily*, 18 May 2005.

Feenstra, R, 'Integration of Trade and Disintegration of Production in the Global Economy' (1998) 12(4) *Journal of Economic Perspectives* 31.

Feller, PB, 'The Antidumping Act and the Future of East–West Trade' (1967) 66(1) *Michigan Law Review* 115.

Ferrarese, MR, *Le istituzioni della globalizzazione: Diritto et diritti nella società transnazionale* (Bolgogna, Il Mulino, 2000).

Festschrift for Professor Upendra Baxi, (2007) 1 *Law, Social Justice & Global Development Journal* at http://www2.warwick.ac.uk/fac/soc/law/elj/lgd/2007_1, last accessed 4 March 2010;

Fidler, DP, 'Globalization, International Law and Emerging Infectious Diseases' (1996) 2(2) *Emerging Infectious Diseases* 77.

—— 'The globalization of public health: Emerging infectious diseases and international relations' (1997) 5 *Indiana Journal of Global Legal Studies* 11.

—— *International Law and Infectious Diseases* (Oxford, Oxford University Press, 1999).

—— 'Emerging Trends in International Law concerning Global Infectious Disease Control' (2003) 9(3) *Emerging Infectious Diseases* 285.

Fine, FL, 'EEC Antidumping: The Problem of Imports from State Trading Countries' (1988) 20 *Law and Policy in International Business* 91.

Finlayson, JA and Zacher, MW, 'The GATT and the Regulation of Trade Barriers: Regime Dynamics and Functions' in SD Krasner (ed), *International Regimes* (Ithaca, Cornell University Press, 1983).

Finnemore, M and Toope, SJ, 'Alternatives to "Legalisation": Richer Views of Law and Politics' (2000) 54(3) *International Organization* 385.

Fiorentino, RV, Verdeja, L and Toqueboeuf, C, *The Changing Landscape of Regional Trade Agreements. 2006 Update*, Regional Trade Agreements Section, Trade Policies Review Division, WTO, Geneva, Switzerland, Discussion Paper No 12, 2006.

Fischer-Lescano, A and Teubner, G, 'Regime Collisions: The Vain Search for Legal Unity in the Fragmentation of Global Law' (2004) 25(4) *Michigan Journal of International Law* 999.

De Fiumel, H, 'Problems of Implementing EEC General Trade Policy toward Socialist Countries' (1981–82) 17(4) *Soviet and Eastern European Foreign Trade* 50.

Fitzpatrick, P, 'Law and Societies' (1984) 22 *Osgoode Hall Law Journal* 115.

Fitzpatrick, P, *Modernism and the Grounds of Law* (Cambridge, Cambridge University Press, 2001).

Fligstein, N, *The Architecture of Markets: An Economic Sociology of Twenty-first Century Capitalist Societies* (Princeton, Princeton University Press, 2001).

Fligstein, N and Mara-Drita, I, 'How to Make a Market: Reflections on the Attempt to Create a Single Market in the European Union' (1996) 102(1) *American Journal of Sociology* 1.

Foot, R, 'China in the ASEAN Regional Forum: Organization Process and Domestic Models of Thought' (1998) 38(5) *Asian Survey* 425.

'Former Tyco Toys lines sold to Calif. firm', *Philadelphia Inquirer*, 4 February 1998, at C.1.

Foucault, M, *The Archaeology of Knowledge* (trans AM Sheridan Smith) (London, Routledge, 1972, rep 1989).

—— *Discipline and Punish: The Birth of the Prison* (trans A Sheridan) (London, Penguin Books, 1979).

Foucault, M, *Essential Works of Foucault, 1954–1984, Volume 3 Power* (ed JD Faubion, trans R Hurley *et al*), (London, Allen Lane, The Penguin Press, 1994).

—— 'Two Lectures', in M Foucault, *Power/Knowledge: Selected Interviews and Other Writings, 1972–1977* (ed C Gordon, trans C Gordon, L Marshall, J Mepham and K Soper) (London, Harvester Press, 1980).

—— *Power/Knowledge: Selected Interviews and Other Writings, 1972–1977* (ed C Gordon, trans C Gordon, L Marshall, J Mepham and K Soper) (New York, Pantheon Books, 1980).

—— *The History of Sexuality, Volume I: The Will to Knowledge* (trans R Hurley) (London, Penguin, 1990) originally published in French as *La Volonté de savoir* (Paris, Editions Gallimard, 1976); first trans as *The History of Sexuality: Volume I. An Introduction* (New York, Vintage, 1978).

—— 'The Subject and Power', in M Foucault, *Essential Works of Foucault, 1954–1984, Volume 3: Power* (ed JD Faubion, trans R *Hurley et* al) (London, Allen Lane, The Penguin Press, 2001).

—— 'Truth and Juridical Forms', in M Foucault, *Essential Works of Foucault, 1954–1984, Volume* 3: *Power* (ed JD Faubion, trans R *Hurley et* al) (Allen Lane, The Penguin Press, London, 2001).

—— 'Society Must Be Defended', in P Rabinow and N Rose (eds), *The Essential Foucault: Selections from Essential Works of Foucault 1954–1984* (London, The New Press, 2003).

Fox, J and Godement, F, *A Power Audit of EU–China Relations* (London, European Council of Foreign Relations, 2009), available at http:/www.ecfr.eu.

Francioni, F (ed), *Environment, Human Rights and International Trade* (Oxford, Hart Publishing, 2001).

Freeman, LC, *The Development of Social Network Analysis: A Study in the Sociology of Science* (Vancouver, Empirical Press, 2004).

Freeman, D, 'Working for the Revolution [Review of Gino Segrè, *Faust in Copenhagen: A Struggle for the Soul of Physics* (Viking, New York, 2007)]', *The New York Review of Books*, LIV, 16, 25 October 2007, 45–47.

Freidberg, S, *French Beans and Food Scares: Culture and Commerce in an Anxious Age* (Oxford, Oxford University Press, 2004).

Freitas Barbosa, De, A and Camargo Mendes, R, 'Economic Relations between Brazil and China: A Difficult Partnership', Dialogue on Globalisation, Briefing Papers, FES Brazil, Friedrich Ebert Stiftung, January 2006, available at http://library.fes.de/pdf-files/iez/global/50190.pdf.

Friedman, LM, 'Erewhon: The coming global legal order' (2001) 37 *Stanford Journal of International Law* 347.

Friedman, TL, *The Lexus and the Olive Tree* (New York, Farrar, Strauss and Griroux, 1999).

Froebel, F, Heinrichs, J and Kreye, O, *The New International Division of Labour: Structural Unemployment in Industrialised Countries and Industrialisation in Developing Countries* (trans P Burgress) (Cambridge, Cambridge University Press; Editions de la Maison des Sciences de l'Homme, 1980).

Fu, Donghui, 'EC Anti-dumping Law and Individual Treatment Policy in Cases involving Imports from China' (1997) 31 *Journal of World Trade* 73.

Fung KC, Korhonen, Iikka, Li, Ke and Ng, F, *China and Central and Eastern Countries: Regional Networks, Global Supply Chain, or International Competitors*, Bank of Finland BOFIT Discussion Papers 9, 2008, available at http://www.bof.fi/NR/rdonlyres/D470E696-C845-4FFD-88E3-BFC90C26B1F3/0/dp0908.pdf, last accessed 4 March 2010.

Galvin, P and Morkel, A, 'The Effect of Product Modularity on Industry Structure: The Case of the World Bicycle Industry' (2001) 8(1) *Industry and Innovation* 31.

Gao, H, 'Legal Issues under WTO Rules on the Closer Economic Partnership Agreement (CEPA) between Mainland China and Hong Kong' (2003)2(2) *Chinese Journal of International Law* 629.

—— 'The RTA Strategy of China: A Critical Visit', in R Buckley, WI Lo and L Bolle (eds), *Challenges to Multilateral Trade: The Impact of Bilateral, Preferential and Regional Agreements* (Dordrecht, Kluwer Law International, 2008).

Garapon, A, 'La place paradoxale de la culture juridique américaine dans la mondialisation', in V Gessner and D Nelken (eds), *European Ways of Law: Towards a European Sociology of Law* (Oxford, Hart Publishing, 2007).
Garcia Molyneux, C, *Domestic Structures and International Trade: The Unfair Trade Policy Instruments of the United States and the European Union* (Oxford, Hart Publishing, 2001).
Garth, B and Dezalay, Y, *Dealing in Virtue: International Commercial Arbitration and the Construction of a Transnational Legal Order* (Chicago, University of Chicago Press, 1996).
Garver, JW, 'China's Influence in Central and South Asia', in D Shambaugh (ed), *Power Shift: China and Asia's New Dynamics* (Berkeley, University of California Press, 2006).
General Agreement on Tariffs and Trade, Anti-Dumping and Countervailing Duties (Geneva, GATT, 1958) (GATT Sales No GATT/1958.2).
—— *Analytical Index of the General Agreement (Revised)* (Geneva, The Contracting Parties to the GATT, April 1959).
—— 'Anti-dumping and Countervailing Duties, Report of Group of Experts', GATT Sales No GATT/1961-62 (1961).
—— 'Reports Adopted by the Contracting Parties, Accession, Special Relations, Etc, Relations with Poland, Report on First Annual Review, adopted on 7 November 1962 (L/1785), in General Agreement on Tariffs and Trade, *Basic Instruments and Selected Documents, Eleventh Supplement (Decisions, Reports, etc, of the Twentieth Session)* (Geneva, The Contracting Parties to the GATT, March 1963).
—— 'Notes on the drafting, interpretation and application of the Articles of the General Agreement' (Geneva, GATT, 3rd rev, 1970).
—— 'Report by the Committee on Anti-dumping Practices adopted on 12 February 1970', GATT Doc No L/3333, art 2, reprinted in GATT, *Basic Instruments and Selected Documents*, 17th Supplement (1970), 43.
—— 'Seventh Report by the Committee on Anti-Dumping Practices adopted on 21 November 1975' (L/4241), GATT, BISD, 22nd Supplement (Geneva, February 1976), 21–27.
—— *Analytical Index*: *Status of Legal Instruments* (Geneva, The Contracting Parties to the GATT, December 1993).
—— *Analytical Index: Guide to GATT Law and* Practice, updated 6th edn (Geneva, WTO, 1995).
Gaulier, G, Lemoine, F and Ùnal-Kesenci, D, *China's Integration into East Asia: Production Sharing, FDI & High-Tech Trade*, Working Paper, Centre d'Etudes Prospectives et d'Informations Internationales, No 2005-09, June 2005, available at http://www.cepii.fr/anglaisgraph/workpap/pdf/2005/wp05-09.pdf.
Gerber, DJ, 'Constitutionalizing the Economy: German Neo-liberalism, Competition Law and the "New" Europe' (1994) 42 *American Journal of Comparative Law* 25.
—— 'Competition Law and International Trade: The European Union and the Neo-Liberal Factor' (1995) 4 *Pacific Rim Law & Policy Journal* 37.
Gereffi, G, 'New Realities of Industrial Development in East Asia and Latin America: Global, Regional and National Trends' in RP Appelbaum and J Henderson (eds), *States and Development in the Pacific Rim* (London, Sage, 1992).
—— 'The Organization of Buyer-driven Global Commodity Chains: How US Retailers Shape Overseas Production Networks' in G Gereffi and M Korzeniewicz (eds), *Commodity Chains and Global Capitalism* (Westport, Ct, Greenwood, 1994).
—— 'Commodity Chains and Regional Divisions of Labor in East Asia' (1996) 12 *Journal of Asian Business* 75.
—— 'Global Commodity Chains: New Forms of Coordination and Control among Nations and Firms in International Industries' (1996) 4 *Competition & Change* 427.
Gereffi, G, Humphrey, J and Sturgeon, T, 'The Governance of Global Value Chains' (2005) 12(1) *Review of International Political Economy* 78.
Gessner, V 'Global Legal Interaction and Legal Cultures' (2007) 7(2) *Ratio Juris* 132.

—— (ed), *Contractual Certainty in International Trade: Empirical Studies and Theoretical Debates on Institutional Support for Global Economic Exchanges* (Oxford, Hart Publishing, 2009).

Gessner, V and Budak, AC (eds), *Emerging Legal Certainty: Empirical Studies on the Globalization of Law* (Dartmouth, Ashgate, for the Oñati International Institute for the Sociology of Law, 1998).

Gessner, V and Nelken, D (eds), *European Ways of Law: Towards a European Sociology of Law* (Oxford, Hart Publishing, 2007).

Ghai, Y (ed), *Autonomy and Ethnicity: Negotiating Competing Claims in Multi-Ethnic States* (Cambridge, Cambridge University Press, 2000).

Ghai, Y and Cottrell, J (eds), *Economic, Social and Cultural Rights in Practice: The Role of Judges in Implementing Economic, Social and Cultural Rights* (London, Interrights, 2004).

Ghai, Y, Luckham, R and Snyder, F (eds), *The Political Economy of Law: A Third World Reader* (Delhi, Oxford University Press, 1987).

Ghazali, Abdus Sattar, 'India Alarmed as Chinese Built Gwadar Port of Pakistan Becomes Operational', http://www.countercurrents.org/ghazali080208.htm.

Giddens, A, 'A Reply to My Critics' in D Held and JB Thompson (eds), *Social Theory of Modern Societies: Anthony Giddens and His Critics* (Cambridge, Cambridge University Press 1989).

—— *The Consequences of Modernity* (Cambridge, Polity Press, 1990).

Gilson, R, 'Globalizing Corporate Governance: Convergence of Form or Function' (2001) 49 *American Journal of Comparative Law* 329.

Giorgi, F, *La constitution du pluralisme constitutionnel à la constitutionnalisation de l'Union européenne : Plaidoyer pour un renouveau théorique*, Thèse pour la Doctorat en Droit, Faculté de Droit, Université du Luxembourg, 17 June 2009.

'Glyphosate Anti-dumping Case Closed with No Duty Payment; China: Is Special Case—Australia decides no anti-dumping measures to be taken against glyphosate exported by China, no fines', *China Chemical Reporter*, 26 April 1997.

Golden, S, 'Socio-cultural Aspects of the Relationship between the EU and East Asia, with particular reference to China' (2006) 4 *Asia Europe Journal* 265.

Goldmann, B, 'La lex mercatoria dans les contrats et l'arbitrage international' (1994) *Journal du Droit International*, juillet-août-septembre, 195.

Goldstein, J, 'Creating the GATT Rules: Politics, Institutions, and American Policy' in JG Ruggie (ed), *Multilateralism Matters: The Theory and Praxis of an Institutional Form* (New York, Columbia University Press, 1993).

Goldstein, J, Kahler, M, Keohane, RO and Slaughter, AM, 'Response to Finnemore and Toope' (2001) 55(3) *International Organization* 759.

Goodale, M and Merry, S, *Practice of Human Rights: Tracking Law between the Global and the Local* (Cambridge, Cambridge University Press, 2007).

Gostin, LO, 'World Health Law: Toward a New Conception of Global Health Law Governance for the 21st Century' (2005) 5(1) *Yale Journal of Health Policy Law* 413.

Govaere, I, 'The Reception of the WTO Agreement in the European Union: The Legacy of GATT' in P Demaret, JF Bellis and G García Jimenéz (eds), *Regionalism and Multilateralism after the Uruguay Round: Convergence, Divergence and Interaction* (Brussels, European Interuniversity Press, 1997).

Gowan, R and Brantner, F, *A Global Force for Human Rights? An Audit of European Power at the UN*, London, European Council on Foreign Relations Policy Paper, 2008.

Graham, EM and Richardson, JD (eds), *Global Competition Policy* (Washington, DC, Institute for International Economics, 1997).

Graf Vitzthum, W, Mehdi, R and Prieto, C (eds), *Europe et mondialisation—Europa und die Globalisierung* (Aix-en-Provence, Presses Universitaires d'Aix-Marseille, 2006).

Granovetter, M, 'Economic Action and Social Structure: The Problem of Embeddedness' (1985) 91(3) *The American Journal of Sociology* 481.

Greenwald, A, 'The ASEAN–China Free Trade Area (ACFTA): A Legal Response to China's Rise' (2006) 16 *Duke Journal of Comparative and International Law* 193.

Gregory, S, 'Mattel plans to buy Pleasant for $700 million: El Segundo firm would acquire the nation's no. 2 doll marker as part of a strategy to cash in on foreign markets', *Los Angeles Times*, Tuesday, 16 June 1998, at D.1.

Griller, S, 'Judicial enforceability of WTO law in the European Union: Annotation to Case C-149/96, *Portugal v Council*' (2000) *Journal of International Economic Law* 441.

Griffiths, J, 'What is Legal Pluralism?' (1986) 24 *Journal of Legal Pluralism* 1.

Grubel, HG and Lloyd, PJ, *Intra-Industry Trade: The Theory and Measurement of International Trade in Differentiated Products* (London, Macmillan, 1975).

Gu, Weixia, and Zhang, Xianchu, 'The China Style "Commission-Oriented" Competence on Arbitral Jurisdiction: Analysis of Chinese Adaptation into Globalisation' (2006) 9(6) *International Arbitration Law Review* 185.

Haddad, M, *Trade Integration in East Asia: The Role of China and Production Networks*, World Bank Policy Research Working Paper 4160, March 2007, available at http://papers.ssrn.com/so13/papers.cfm?abstract_id=969237.

Haibing, Zhang, 'China and Southeast Asia Cooperation: New Developments and Challenges', in J Wong and Lai Hongyi (eds), *China into the Hu-Wen Era: Policy Initiatives and Challenges* (Singapore, World Scientific Publishing Company, 2006).

Hall, PA and Soskice, D, *Varieties of Capitalism: The Institutional Foundations of Comparative Advantage* (Oxford, Oxford University Press, 2001).

Hall, PA and Taylor, RCR, 'Political Science and the Three New Institutionalisms' (1966) 44 *Political Studies* 936.

Halberstam, D and Stein, E, 'The United Nations, the European Union, and the King of Sweden: Economic Sanctions and Individual Rights in a Plural World Order' (2009) 46 *CML Rev* 13.

Halpérin, JL, *Profils des mondialisations du droit* (Paris, Dalloz-Sirey, 2009).

Han, Xiaowei, *Study of the Antidumping Cases in the European Court of Justice: The Special Regulations Regarding China 'Non-Market Economy' State*, Working Paper 2006/3, Centre for European Studies, Peking University (in Chinese).

Hardt, M and Negri, A, *Empire* (Cambridge, Mass, Harvard University Press, 2000).

Harris, RL and Seid, MJ, *Critical Perspectives on Globalization and Neoliberalism in the Developing Countries* (Leiden, Brill, 2000).

Harrison, J, *Human Rights Impact of the World Trade Organisation* (Oxford, Hart Publishing, 2007).

Hartogh, M (ed), *Living Law: Reconsidering Eugen Ehrlich* (Oxford, Hart Publishing, 2008).

Haufler, V, 'Self-regulation and Business Norms: Political Risk, Political Activism' in AC Cutler, V Haufler and T Porter (eds), *Private Authority and International Affairs* (Buffalo, State University of New York Press, 1999).

Held, D, McGrew, A, Goldblatt, D and Perraton, J, *Global Transformations: Politics, Economics and Culture* (Cambridge, Polity Press, 1999).

Helfer, LR, 'Mediating Interactions in an Expanding International Intellectual Property Regime (Comment on Victor Moscoti)' in T Cottier, J Pauwelyn and E Bırgi (eds), *Human Rights and International Trade* (Oxford, Oxford University Press, 2005).

Hellvin, L, *Vertical Intra-Industry Trade between China and the OECD Countries*, OECD Development Centre, Technical Papers No 114, July 1996.

Hellwig, JF, 'The Retreat of the State? The Massachusetts Burma Law and Local Empowerment in the Context of Globalization(s)' (2000) 18 *Wisconsin International Law Journal* 477.

Henry, L, 'The ASEAN Way and Community Integration: Two Different Models of Regionalism' (2007) 13(6) *European Law Journal* 857.

Hepple, B, 'A Race to the Top? International Investment Guidelines and Corporate Codes of Conduct' (1999) 20 *Comparative Labor Law and Policy Journal* 347.

—— *Labour Laws and Global Trade* (Oxford, Hart Publishing, 2005).

Hestermeyer, H, *Human Rights and the WTO: The Case of Patents and Access to Medicines* (Oxford, Oxford University Press, 2007).

Heydebrand, W, 'Globalisation and the Rise of Procedural Informalism in American and European Law' in V Gessner and D Nelken (eds), *European Ways of Law: Towards a European Sociology of Law* (Oxford, Hart Publishing, 2007).

Higgott, R, 'Contested Globalization: The Changing Context and Normative Challenges' (2000) 26 *Review of International Studies* 131.

—— 'The Theory and Practice of Global and Regional Governance: Accommodating American Exceptionalism and European Pluralism' (2005) 10(4) *European Foreign Affairs Review* 575.

Hilf, M, 'The Application of GATT within the Member States of the European Community, with Special Reference to the Federal Republic of Germany' in M Hilf, F Jacobs and EU Petersmann (eds), *The European Community and GATT* (Deventer, Kluwer, 1986).

—— 'The Role of National Courts in International Trade Relations' (1997) 18 *Michigan Journal of International Law* 321.

Hinton, HC, 'China as an Asian Power' in TW Robinson and D Shambaugh (eds), *Chinese Foreign Policy. Theory and Practice* (Oxford, Clarendon Press, 1994, rep 2006).

Hippler Bello, J, 'The WTO Dispute Settlement Understanding: Less is More' (1996) 90 *American Journal of International Law* 416.

Hippler Bello, J, Holmer, AF and Preiss, JO, 'Searching for "Bubbles of Capitalism": Application of the US Antidumping and Countervailing Duty Laws to Reforming Nonmarket Economies' (1992) 25 *George Washington Journal of International Law and Economics* 665.

Hirshmann, AO, *National Power and the Structure of Foreign Trade* (Berkeley, University of California Press, 1945, expanded edn 1980).

Hirst, P and Thompson, G, *Globalization in Question: The International Economy and the Possibilities of Governance* (Cambridge, Polity Press, 1996).

Hobe, S, 'Global Challenges to Statehood: The Increasing Important Role of Nongovernmental Organizations' (1997) 5 *Indiana Journal of Global Legal Studies* 191.

Hoekman, B and Newfarmer, R, 'Preferential Trade Agreements, Investment Disciplines and Investment Flows' (2005) 39(5) *Journal of World Trade* 949.

Hoekman, BM and Kostecki, MM, *The Political Economy of the World Trading System: The WTO and Beyond*, 2nd edn (Oxford, Oxford University Press, 2001).

Hoekman, BM and Mavroidis, PC, 'Dumping, Antidumping and Antitrust' (1996) 30 *Journal of World Trade* 27.

Holzmeyer, C, 'Human Rights in an Era of Neoliberal Globalization: The Alien Tort Claims Act and Grassroots Mobilization in *Doe v Unocal*' (2009) 43(2) *Law and Society Review* 271.

Holst, DR and Weiss, J, 'ASEAN and China: Export Rivals or Partners in Regional Growth' (2006) 27(8) *The World Economy* 1255.

Hong Kong Industry Department, Quality Services Division, 'Health and Safety Standards Circular No 1/97: International: Toy Safety Standards', 20 January 1997, available at http://www.info.gov.hk/id/psis/hssc/hssc0197.htm.

Hong Kong Trade Development Council, 'Hong Kong's Toy Industry', *Hong Kong & China Economics*, on the Internet homepage of the Hong Kong Trade Development Council at http://www.tdc.org.hk/main/industries/t2_2_39.htm.

—— *Practical Guide to Exporting Toys for Hong Kong Traders* (Hong Kong Trade Development Council, Research Department, March 1999).

—— Research Department, 'Review and Outlook of Hong Kong's Toy Exports', *Trade Watch*, April 1999, at 6.

Hook, W, 'China Rocks Global Bike Industry' in *Sustainable Transport e-update, Bulletin of the Institute for Transportation & Develoment Policy (ITDP)*, No 3, January 2003, available at http://www.itdp.org/index.php/news_events/news_detail/china_global_bike_industry/, last accessed 4 March 2010 .

Hopkins, TK and Wallerstein, I, 'Commodity Chains in the World Economy Prior to 1800' (1986) 10(1) *Review* 157.

—— 'Commodity Chains: Construct and Research' in G Gereffiand M Korzeniewicz (eds), *Commodity Chains and Global Capitalism* (Westport, Ct, Greenwood Press, 1994).

Hopt, KJ, Kanda, H, Roe, M, Wymeersch, E and Prigge, S (eds), *Comparative Corporate Governance: The State of the Art and Emerging Research* (Oxford, Clarendon Press, 1998).

Horlick, GN, 'The United States Antidumping System' in JH Jackson and EA Vermulst (eds), *Antidumping Law and Practice: A Comparative Study* (New York and London, Harvester Wheatsheaf, 1990).

Horlick, GN and Schuman, SS, 'Non-market Economy Trade and US Antidumping/ Countervailing Duty Laws' (1984) 18(4) *The International Lawyer* 807.

Howse, R, 'Human Rights in the WTO: Whose Rights? What Humanity? Comment on Petersmann' (2002) 13(3) *European Journal of International Law* 651.

—— 'From Politics to Technocracy—and Back Again: The Fate of the Multilateral Trading Regime' (2002) 96 *American Journal of Comparative Law* 94.

Howse, R and Mutua, M, 'Protection des droits humains et mondialisation de l'economie: Un defi pour l'OMC' (2000) *Droits et Democratie*, available on the Internet at http://www.ichrdd.ca/francais/commdoc/publications/mondialisation/omcDroitsMon.ht.

Howse, R and Nicolaidis, K, 'Legitimacy and Global Governance: Why Constitutionalizing the WTO is a Step Too Far' in RB Porter, P Sauvé, A Subramanian, and A Beviglia-Zampetti (eds), *Efficiency, Equity, and Legitimacy: The Multilateral Trading System at the Millennium* (Washington, DC, Brookings Institution Press, 2001).

Hoye, D, 'Tickle-Me Elmo Hottest Yule Toy', *The Arizona Republic*, Wednesday, 4 December 1996.

Hu, Yuanxiang, *Legal and Policy Issues of the Trade and Economic Relations between China and the EEC: A Comparative Study* (Kluwer, Deventer, 1991),

Hu, Xiao, 'Agreements pave way for China-Australia FTA', *China Daily*, 19 April 2005, at 2.

Hu, Xiaoling and Ma, Yue, 'International Intra-Industry Trade of China' (1999) 135(1) *Review of World Economics* 82.

Hudec, RE, 'The Legal Status of GATT in the Domestic Law of the United States' in M Hilf, F Jacobs and EU Petersmann (eds), *The European Community and GATT* (Deventer, Kluwer, 1986).

Hudec, R, *Adjudication of International Trade Disputes*, Thames Essay No 16 (London, Trade Policy Research Centre, 1978).

Hunt, A and Wickham, G, *Foucault and Law: Towards a Sociology of Law as Governance* (London, Pluto Press, 1994).

Ianni, EM, 'The International Treatment of State Trading' (1982) 16 (6) *Journal of World Trade Law* 480.

Ickenbery, J, 'A World Economy Restored: Expert Consensus and the Anglo-American Postwar Settlement' (1992) 46(1) *International Organization* 289.

IERR, 'International: Collective Bargaining—Two New Global Accords on CSR and Labour Standards' (2005) 382 *European Industrial Relations Review* 26.

Inama, S, 'The Association of South East Asian Nations—People's Republic of China Free Trade Area: Negotiating Beyond Eternity With Little Trade Liberalization?' (2005) 39(3) *Journal of World Trade* 559.

'India, China plan world's largest FTA', 8 April 2005, available at http://us.rediff.com/money/ 2005/apr/08fta.htm.

Indiresan, PV, 'The Kunming Initiative' (April 2000) 17(7) *Frontline*, 1–14, 98–102, available at http://www.thehindu.com/fline/fl1707/17070980.htm.

Ingram, A, 'Global Leadership and Global Health: Contending Meta-narratives, Divergent Responses, Fatal Consequences' (2005) 19(4) *International Relations* 381.

International Federation for Human Rights, *The WTO and Human Rights*, Report no 320/2, November 2001, available on the Internet at http://www.wtowatch.org/library.

International Institute for Sustainable Development, 'What's It All For: Setting Clear Goals for the World Trade Organization (WTO)', IISD Viewpoint, World Trade Organization Fourth Ministerial Conference, 9/13 November2001 (August 2001), available at http://www.wtowatch.org/library.

International Labour Office, Governing Body, Working Party on the Social Dimension of Globalisation. 'Trade and Employment: Follow-Up to the Joint ILO/WTO Secretariat Study', WP/SDG, GB.300/WP/SDG/, 300th Session, Geneva, November 2007, available at http://www.ilo.org/wcmsp5/groups/public/-ed_norm/-relconf/documents/meetingdocument/wcms_084891.pdf.

—— 'ILO Tackles Social Consequences of Globalisation', available on the ILO website http://www.ilo/org/public/english/wcsdg/entry1.htm.

—— Working Party on the Social Dimensions of the Liberalization of International Trade, 'Overview of Global Developments and Office Activities concerning Codes of Conduct, Social Labelling and Other Private Sector Initiatives Addressing Labour Issues' (GB.273/WP/SDL/1(Add.1) and GB.273/WP/SDL/1(Rev.1), both 273rd session, Geneva, November 1998, available on the Internet at http://www.ilo.org/public/english/20gb/docs/gb273/sdl-1a1.htm and http://www.ilo.org/public/english/20bg/docs/gb273/sdl-1.htm, respectively.

Irwin, DA, Mavroidis, PC and Sykes, AO, *The Genesis of the GATT* (Cambridge, Cambridge University Press, 2008).

Ismail, F, 'Mainstreaming Development in the World Trade Organization' (2005) 39(1) *Journal of World Trade* 11.

Jackson, JH, *World Trade and the Law of GATT* (New York, Bobbs-Merrill, 1969).

—— 'State Trading and Nonmarket Economies' (1989) 23 *The International Lawyer* 891.

—— 'Dumping in International Trade: Its Meaning and Context' in JH Jackson and E Vermulst (eds), *Antidumping Law and Practice: A Comparative Study* (London, Harvester Wheatsheaf, 1990).

—— 'Status of Treaties in Domestic Legal Systems: A Policy Analysis' (1992) 86 *American Journal of International Law* 310.

—— *The World Trading System: Law and Policy of International Economic Relations* (Cambridge, Mass, MIT Press, 1997).

—— *The World Trading System: Law and Policy of International Economic Relations*, 2nd edn (Cambridge Mass, MIT Press, 1997).

—— *The World Trade Organization: Constitution and Jurisprudence* (London, The Royal Institute of International Affairs 1998).

—— *The Jurisprudence of GATT and the WTO; Insights on Treaty Law and Economic Relations* (Cambridge University Press, Cambridge, 2000).

—— 'International Law Status of WTO Dispute Settlement Reports: Obligation to Comply or Option to "Buy Out"?' (2004) 98(1) *The American Journal of International Law* 109.

—— *Sovereignty, the WTO and Changing Fundamentals of International Law* (Cambridge, Cambridge University Press, 2006).

—— 'Direct Effect of Treaties in the US and the EU, the Case of the WTO: Some Perceptions and Proposals' in A Arnull, P Eeckhout, and T Tridimas (eds), *Change and Continuity in EU Law: Essays in Honour of Sir Francis Jacobs* (Oxford, Oxford University Press, 2008).

Jackson, JH, Davey, WJ and Sykes, AO, *Legal Problems of International Economic Relations: Cases, Materials and Text on the National and International Regulation of Transnational Economic Relations*, 3rd edn (St Paul, Minn, West Publishing Company, 1995).

Jacobs, F, 'Anti-dumping Procedures with regard to Imports from Eastern Europe' in M Maresceau (ed), *The Political and Legal Framework of Trade Relations between the European Community and Eastern Europe* (Kluwer, Deventer, 1989).

Jacques, M, *When China Rules the World: The Rise of the Middle Kingdom and the End of the Western World* (London, Allen Lane, 2009).

Jaffé, D, *The History of Toys: From Spinning Tops to Robots* (Stroud, Sutton Publishing Ltd., 2006).

James, WE, *Rules of Origin in Emerging Asia-Pacific Preferential Trade Agreements: Will PTAs Promote Trade and Development*, Asia-Pacific Research and Training Network on Trade Working Paper Series, No 19, August 2006.

—— 'Rules of Origin in Emerging Asia-Pacific Preferential Trade Agreements: Will PTAs Promote Trade and Development' in ESCAP (ed), *Trade Facilitation Beyond the Multilateral Trade Negotiations: Regional Practices, Customs Valuation and Other Emerging Issues—A Study by the Asia-Pacific Research and Training Network on Trade* (New York, United Nations, 2007).

Janicke, M, 'Trend-Setters in Environmental Policy: The Character and Role of Pioneer Countries' (2005) 15(2) *European Environment* 129.

Japan, Ministry of Economy, Trade and Industry, Industrial Structure Council, *2007 Report on Compliance by Major Trading Partners with Trade Agreements—WTO, FTA/EPA and BIT* (Tokyo, Industrial Structure Council, METI, 2007), also available at www.meti.go.jp/english/report/index.html.

Jayasuriya, K, 'Globalization, Law and the Transformation of Sovereignty: The Emergence of Global Regulatory Governance' (1999) 6 *Indiana Journal of Global Legal Studies* 425.

—— 'Globalization, Sovereignty, and the Rule of Law: From Political to Economic Constitutionalism?' (2001) 8 *Constellations* 442.

Jego, M, 'Menacé par la Chine, Gazprom veut rester maître du gaz en Asia centrale', *Le Monde*, 21 March 2008, at 14.

Jemielniak, J, 'Legitimization Arguments in the Lex Mercatoria Cases' (2005) 18(2) *International Journal for the Semiotics of Law* 175.

Jia, Heping, 'FTA to help diversify China's energy sources', *China Business Weekly*, 15 July 2004.

Joerges, C, 'The Science of Private Law and the Nation-State' in F Snyder (ed), *The Europeanisation of Law. The Legal Effects of European Integration* (Oxford, Hart Publishing, 2000).

Joerges, C and Vos, E (eds), *EU Committees* (Oxford, Hart Publishing, 1999).

Jones, CAG, 'Capitalism, Globalization and Rule of Law: An Alternative Trajectory of Legal Change in China' (1994) 3 *Social and Legal Studies* 195.

Joint Declaration of the Government of the People's Republic of China and the Government of the Republic of Portugal on the Question of Macao, signed in Beijing on 134.1987, available at http://www.Macau99.org/mo/e_doc_declaracao.html, or http://www.imprensa.Macau.gov.mo/bo/i/88/23/dc/en/ .

Joint Declaration of the United Kingdom of Great Britain and Northern Ireland and the Government of the People's Republic of China on the Question of Hong Kong, signed in Beijing on 19 December 1984, available at http://www.hkbu.edu.hk/~pchksar/JD/jd-full1.htm.

Johnston, AI, *Cultural Realism, Strategic Culture and Grand Strategy in Chinese History* (Princeton, Princeton University Press, 1995).

—— 'Cultural Realism and Strategy in Maoist China' in PJ Katzenstein (ed), *The Culture of National Security: Norms and Identity in World Politics* (New York, Columbia University Press, 1996).

—— *Social States: China in International Relations, 1980–2000* (Princeton, Princeton University Press, 2008).

Jost, TS, 'The Globalization of Health Law: The Case of Permissibility of Placebo-based Research' (2000) 26 *American Journal of Law and Medicine* 175.

Kahler, M, 'Conclusion: The Causes and Consequences of Legalization' (2000) 54 *International Organization* 661.

Kahn, P, 'Les principes généraux de droit devant les arbitres du commerce international' (1989) *Journal du droit international* 305.

Kang, H, (Chief Editor). *China's Township and Village Enterprises* (Beijing, Foreign Languages Press, 2006).

Kapur, H, *China and the European Economic Community: The New Connection* (Dordrecht, Martinus Nijhoff, 1986).

Kavalski, E, 'Partnership or Rivalry between the European Union, China and India in Central Asia: The Normative Power of Regional Actors with Global Aspirations' in F Snyder (ed), *Europe, India and China: Strategic Partners in a Changing World* (Brussels, Bruylant, 2008).

Keck, ME and Sikkink, K, *Activists Beyond Borders: Advocacy Networks in International Politics* (Ithaca, Cornell University Press, 1998).

Kennedy, D, *The Dark Sides of Virtue: Reassessing International Humanitarianism* (Princeton, Princeton University Press, 2005).

—— 'The Mystery of Global Governance', Kormendy Lecture, Ohio Northern University, Pettit College of Law, 25 January 2008, available at http://www.watsoninstitute.org/blss.

Kent, B,'Maintaining the Model Train Tradition in a Digital World', *The New York Times*, Sunday, 7 December 1997, at 6.

Keohane, RO, 'The Theory of Hegemonic Stability and Changes in International Economic Regimes, 1967–1977' in OR Holsti, RM Siverson and AL George (eds), *Change in the International System* (Boulder, Westview Press, 1980).

Keohane, RO, Moravcsik, A and Slaughter, AM, 'Legalized Dispute Resolution: Interstate and Transnational' (2000) 54 *International Organization* 457.

Kessler, JL, 'The Antidumping Act of 1916: Antitrust Analogue or Anathema?', 35th Annual Meeting, Section of Antitrust Law, American Bar Association, San Francisco, California, 10–12 August 1987, in (1987) 56 *Antitrust Law Journal* 485.

Killmann, B, 'The access of individuals to international trade dispute settlement' (1996) 13(3) *Journal of International Arbitration* 143.

Kingsbury, B; Krisch, N and Stewart, RB. 'The Emergence of Global Administrative Law', New York University School of Law, New York University Public Law and Legal Theory Working Papers, Paper 17, 1 October 2005, available at http://lsr.nellco.org/nyu/èplltwp/papers/17.

Kiss, A, Shelton, D and Ishibashi, K (eds), *Economic Globalization and Compliance with International Environmental Agreements* (Dordrecht, Kluwer Law International, 2003).

Klabbers, J, 'International Law in Community Law: The Law and Politics of Direct Effect' (2002) 21 *Yearbook of European Law* 262.

Klein, M, *No Logo* (London, Flamingo, 2000).

Kloten, N, 'Zur Typenlehre der Wirtschafts—und Gesellschaftsordnungen' (1955) 7 *Ordo* 123.

Kneebone, S (ed), *The Refugees Convention 50 Years On: Globalisation and International Law* (London, Sweet & Maxwell, 2004).

Koch, CH Jr, 'Envisaging a Global Legal Culture' (2004) 25 *Michigan Journal of International Law* 1.

Koenig, M, 'Mondialisation des droits de l'homme et transformation de l'îtat-nation. Une analyse néo-institutionnaliste' (2006) 67 *Droit et Société* 673.

Kogut, B, 'Designing Global Strategies: Comparative and Competitive Value-added Chains' (1985) 26(4) *Sloan Management Review* 15.

Koh, H, 'Transnational Legal Process' (1996) 75 *Nebraska Law Review* 181.

Komesar, N, *Imperfect Alternatives: Choosing Institutions in Law, Economics and Public Policy* (Chicago, University of Chicago Press, 1994).

Kommerskollegium/National Board of Trade, 'Treatment of "the Community Interest" in EU Antidumping Investigations', 14 June 2005, Stockholm, Sweden, available at http://www.kommers.sw/binaries/attachments/5152_Community_interest_in_EU_Antidumping _ Investigations-National_Board_of_Trade_Sweden.pdf.

Kong, Qingjiang. 'China's WTO Accession and the ASEAN-China Free Trade Area: The Perspective of a Chinese Lawyer', 2004 7 4 *Journal of International Economic Law*, 839–861.

Kostecki, NM, *East–West Trade and the GATT System* (New York, St Martin's Press, for the Trade Policy Research Centre, London, 1978).

Koutrakos, P, *EU International Relations Law* (Oxford, Hart Publishing, 2006).

Krasner, S, 'State Power and the Structure of International Trade' (1976) 28(3) *World Politics* 317.

—— (ed), *International Regimes* (Ithaca and London, Cornell University Press, 1983).

—— 'Global Communications and National Power: Life on the Pareto Frontier' (1991) 43(3) *World Politics* 336.

—— *Sovereignty: Organized Hypocrisy* (Princeton, Princeton University Press, 1999).

Krisch, N, 'The Pluralism of Global Administrative Law' (2006) 17(1) *European Journal of International Law* 247.

Krisch, N and Kingsbury, B, 'Introduction: Global Governance and Global Administrative Law in the International Legal Order' (2006) 17(1) *European Journal of International Law* 1.

Krueger, AO (ed), *The WTO as an International Organization* (Chicago and London, University of Chicago Press, 1998).

Kuijper, PJ, 'The New WTO Dispute Settlement System: The Impact on the European Community' (1995) 29 *Journal of World Trade* 49.

Kuijper, PJ and Bronckers, M, 'WTO Law in the European Court of Justice' (2005) 42 *CM L Rev* 1313.

Kuik, Cheng-Chwee, *Multilateralism in China's ASEAN Policy*, SAIS Working Paper Series, WP/05/03, Paul H Nitze School of Advanced International Studies (SIAS), Johns Hopkins University, Washington, DC, October 2003.

Kuilwijk, KJ, *The European Court of Justice and the GATT Dilemma: Public Interest v Individual Rights* (Beuningen, The Netherlands, Nexed Editions Academic Publishers, 1996).

Kurtenbach, E, 'In the Cycling Kingdom, Ever More Two-wheelers Are Battery-powered', *International Herald Tribune*, Monday, 27 July 2009, at 16.

Kuyper, P, 'The new WTO Dispute Settlement system: The Impact on the Community' in J Bourgeois, F Berrod, and E Gippini-Fournier (eds), *The Uruguay Round Results: A European Lawyer's Perspective* (Brussels, European Interuniversity Press, 1995).

Kwakwa, E, 'Some Comments on Rulemaking at the World Intellectual Property Organization' (2002) 12 *Duke Journal of Comparative & International Law* 179.

Ladeur, KH, 'Towards a Legal Theory of Supranationality: The Viability of the Network Concept' (1997) 3(1) *European Law Journal* 33.

—— *The Theory of Autopoesis as an Approach to a Better Understanding of Postmodern Law—From the Hierarchy of Norms to the Heterarchy of Changing Patterns of Legal Relationships*, EUI Working Paper LAW no 2003/4 (Florence, European University Institute, 2003).

—— (ed), *Public Governance in the Age of Globalization* (Aldershot, Ashgate, 2004).

Laget-Annamayer, A, 'Le statut des accords OMC dans l'ordre juridique communautaire: en attendant la consécration de l'invocabilité' (2006) 42(2) *Revue trimestrielle de droit européen* 249.

Lai, Hongyi, 'Regional Cooperation in Epidemic Prevention: China and ASEAN' in J Wong, K Zou and H Zeng (eds), *China–ASEAN Relations: Economic and Legal Dimensions* (Singapore, World Scientific, 2006).

Lam, Po-Chuen. 'Country Report: Hong Kong, China', Asian Development Bank Regional Seminar on Rules of Origin, 2004, available at http://www.adb.org/Documents/Events/2004/Rules_of_Origin/roo_hkg.pdf.

Lamy, P, 'The Place of the WTO and its Law in the International Legal Order'. Address before the European Society of International Law, Paris, May 2006, (2006) 17(5) *European Journal of International Law* 969.

Lang, ATF, 'Re-thinking Trade and Human Rights' (2007) 15(2) *Tulane Journal of International and Comparative Law* 335.

—— 'Reflecting on "Linkage": Cognitive and Institutional Change in the International Trading System' (2007) 70(4) *MLR* 523.

Lantz, RH, 'The Search for Consistency: Treatment of Nonmarket Economies in Transition under United States Antidumping and Countervailing Duty Laws' (1995) 10 *American University Journal of International Law and Policy* 993.

Lardy, NR, *Foreign Trade and Economic Reform in China, 1978–1990* (Cambridge, Cambridge University Press, 1992).

—— *China in the World Economy* (Washington DC, Institute for International Economics, 1994).

Laroski, JA Jr, 'NMEs: A Love Story—Nonmarket and Market Economy Status under US Antidumping Law' (1999) 30 *Law and Policy in International Business* 369.

Lasok, D, *The Trade and Customs Law of the European Union* (London, Kluwer, 1998).

Laurent, A, 'The Impact of Globalization on Law Enforcement Institutions' (2006) 7(1) *Human Rights and UK Practice* 10.

Lechner, JF and Boli, J (eds), *The Globalization Reader* (Oxford, Blackwell Publishing, 2003).

Lee, CH and Reisen, H (eds), *From Reform to Growth: China and Other Countries in Transition in Asia and Central and Eastern Europe* (Paris, OECD, 1994).

Lee, CK, 'Factory Regimes of Chinese Capitalism: Different Cultural Logics in Labor Control' in A Ong and DM Nonini(eds), *Ungrounded Empires: The Cultural Politics of Modern Chinese Transnationalism* (New York, Routledge, 1997).

Lee, E and Jansen, M (eds), *Trade and Employment: Challenges for Policy Research* (A Joint Study of the International Labour Office and the World Trade Organization) (Geneva, ILO and WTO, 2007).

Lee, Jong-Wha and Innwon Park, 'Free Trade Areas in East Asia' (2005) 28(1) *The World Economy* 21.

Lee, P and Kennedy, B, 'The Potential Direct Effect of GATT 1994 in European Community Law' (1996) 30(1) *Journal of World Trade* 67.

Leebron, D, 'Implementation of the Uruguay Round results in the United States' in JH Jackson and AO Sykes (eds), *Implementing the Uruguay Round* (Oxford, Oxford University Press, 1997).

Lefevre, S, *Les actes communautaires atypiques* (Brussels, Bruylant, 2006).

Leibovich, M and Stoughton, S, 'When keeping up isn't child's play; Mattel to acquire Learning Co as industry pursues digitally savvy children', *The Washington Post*, Tuesday, December 1998, at D01.

Lemoine, F, *Trade Policy and Trade Patterns during Transition: A Comparison between China and the CEECs*, Centre d'Etudes Prospectives et d'Informations Internationales (CEPII), Document de Travail No 96-02, Paris, February 1996.

Leng, J, 'China's Banking Reform in the Context of Globalization and Transition' (2006) 17(5) *European Business Law Review* 1271.

Leonard, S, *The Dragon Awakes: China's Long March to Geneva* (Cameron May 1999).

Leptin, G, 'Economic Relations between the Federal Republic of Germany and the German Democratic Republic' in D Kim and W Gumpel (eds), *New Directions in East–West Relations: German and Korean Perspectives* (Seoul, Korea, Institute of East and West Studies, Yonsei University, 1987).

—— 'The Economic Relations between the Federal Republic of Germany and the German Democratic Republic, Giving Special Consideration to their Relationship with the European Communities' in D Kim and W Gumpel (eds), *New Directions in East–West Relations: German and Korean Perspectives* (Seoul, Korea, Institute of East and West Studies, Yonsei University, 1987).

Le Roy, E, *Le jeu des lois: Une anthropologie 'dynamique' du Droit* (Paris, LGDJ, 1999).

—— (ed), *Les pluralismes juridiques, Cahiers d'Anthropologie du Droit* (Paris, Karthala, 2003).
Lessig, L, *Code and Other Laws of Cyberspace* (New York, Basic Books, 1999).
Levesque, J, 'The Kunming Initiative: Going Beyond Governmental Reluctance', Article no 2473, 14 January 2008, available on the website of the Institute of Peace and Conflict Studies (IPCS), New Delhi, at http://www.ipcs.org/printWhatsnew.jsp?action=showView&kValue=2473&status=article.
Lewin, K, *Field Theory in Social Science: Selected Theoretical Papers* (ed D Cartwright) (New York, Harper and Row, 1951).
Li, DD, 'A Theory of Ambiguous Property Rights in Transition Economies: The Case of the Chinese Non-State Sector' (1996) 23(1) *Journal of Comparative Economics* 1.
Li, Guanghui, 'China–ASEAN FTA necessary and beneficial', *China Daily*, 27 October 2006, at 4.
Li, Zhaojie (James Li), 'Traditional Chinese World Order' (2002) 1 *Chinese Journal of International Law* 20.
Lieberthal, KG, 'Introduction: The "Fragmented Authoritarianism" Model and Its Limitations' in KG Lieberthal and DM Lampton (eds), *Bureaucracy, Politics and Decision-making in Post-Mao China* (Berkeley, University of California Press, 1992).
—— *Governing China: Revolution through Reform* (New York, Norton, 1995).
Lieberthal, K and Oksenberg, M, *Policy Making in China: Leaders, Structures and Processes* (Princeton, Princeton University Press, 1988).
LIEI, 'Globalisation through WTO Integration: Neither Friend Nor Foe' (2003) 30(2) *Legal Issues of European Integration* 95.
Likosky, M (ed), *Transnational Legal Processes: Globalisation and Power Disparities* (London, Butterworths LexisNexis, 2002).
—— *The Silicon Empire. Law, Culture and Commerce* (Aldershot, Ashgate, 2005).
Lipschutz, RD and Rowe, JK, *Globalization, Governmentality and Global Politics: Regulation for the Rest of Us?* (London, Routledge, 2005).
Lipson, C, 'Why are Some International Agreements Informal?' (1991) 45(4) *International Organization* 495.
Lipson, C, 'The Transformation of Trade: The Source and Effects of Regime Change' in SD Krasner (ed), *International Regimes* (Ithaca, Cornell University Press, 1983).
Lisiecki, J, 'Financial and Material Transfers between East and West Germany' (1990) 42 *Soviet Studies* 51.
Liu, LH, *Translingual Practice: Literature, National Culture and Translated Modernity—China, 1900–1937* (Stanford, Stanford University Press, 1995).
Liu, Xiang and Vandenbussche, H, 'European Union Antidumping Cases against China: An Overview and Future Prospects with Respect to China's World Trade Organisation Membership' (2002) 36(6) *Journal of World Trade* 1125.
Loesch, D, *Chinese Special Economic Zones at a Crossroads*, HWWA-Institut fuer Wirtschaftsforschung-Hamburg, HWWA-Diskussionspapier Nr 25, 1995.
Long, Yongtu, 'Negotiations for China's Accession to the WTO and the Process of Market-Oriented Reform' in Wang, Mengkui (ed), *China: Acession to the WTO and Economic Reform* (Beijing, Foreign Languages Press, 2002).
Lovell, T, 'Nancy Fraser's Integrated Theory of Justice: A "Sociologically Rich" Model for a Global Capitalist Era?' 2007 (1) *Law, Social Justice & Global Development Journal (LGD)*, available at http://www.go.warwick.ac.uk/elj/lgd/2007_1/lovell.
'Lowered Export Subsidies Hits Chinese Industry', *Bike Europe*, News, published 10 July 2007, available at http://www.bike-eu.com.
Lubman, S, 'The Legal and Policy Environment for Foreign Direct Investment in China: Past Accomplishments, Future Uncertainties', in *Private Investments Abroad* (Mathew Bender & Co, 1998).
—— *Bird in a Cage: Legal Reform in China after Mao* (Stanford, Stanford University Press, 1999).

Luhmann, N, *Essays on Self-Reference* (New York, Columbia University Press, 1990).

Luo, Yan, 'Dispute Settlement in the Proposed East Asia Free Trade Agreement: Lessons Learned from the ASEAN, the NAFTA, and the EU' in L Bartels and F Ortino (eds), *Regional Trade Agreements and the WTO Legal System* (Oxford, Oxford University Press, 2006).

Lukas, M, 'The role of private parties in the enforcement of the Uruguay Round Agreements' (1995) 29(5) *Journal of World Trade* 181.

Lynch, K, *The Forces of Economic Globalization: Challenges to the Regime of International Commercial Arbitration* (Dordrecht, Kluwer Law International, 2003).

Lyons, T, *EC Customs Law*, 2nd edn (Oxford, Oxford University Press, 2008).

Macmillan, F, 'International Economic Law and Public International Law: Strangers in the Night' (2004) 10(6) *International Trade Law and Regulation* 115.

Macrory, PFJ, Appleton, AE and Plummer, MG (eds), *The World Trade Organization: Legal, Economic and Political Analysis* (New York, Springer, 2005).

Madore, J, 'Mattel confident Tyco deal will pass antitrust scrutiny', *The Buffalo News*, Tuesday, 19 November 1996, at 3D.

Maduro, MP, 'Is There Any Such Thing as Free or Fair Trade? A Constitutional Analysis of the Impact of International Trade on the European Social Model' in G de Búrca and J Scott (eds), *The EU and the WTO: Legal and Constitutional Issues* (Oxford, Hart Publishing, 2001).

—— 'Contrapunctual Law: Europe's Constitutional Pluralism in Action' in N Walker (ed), *Sovereignty in Transition* (Oxford, Hart Publishing, 2003).

—— 'Interpreting European Law: Judicial Adjudication in a Context of Constitutional Pluralism' (2007) 2(1) *European Journal of Legal Studies*, available at http://www.ejls.eu.

—— 'L'interprétation du droit communautaire: la fonction juridictionnelle dans le contexte du pluralisme constitutionnel', speech to the French Court of Cassation, available at http://www.networks-presidents.eu/spip.php?rubrique89&lang=fr.

Mahiou, A and Snyder, F (eds), *La sécurité alimentaire/Food Security and Food Safety* (Leiden, Martinus Nijhoff for The Hague Academy of International Law, 2006).

Maitra, Ramtanu, 'Prospects Brighten for Kunming Initiative', *Asia Times*, 12 February 2003, available at http://www.atimes.com/atimes/South_Asia/EB12Df04.html.

Majone, G (ed), *Deregulation or Re-regulation? Regulatory Reform in Europe and the United States* (London, Pinter Press, and New York, St Martin's Press, 1990).

Maljean-Dubois, S, Mehdi, R et Collectif (eds), *La société internationale et les grandes pandémies*, 14ème Rencontres internationales d'Aix-en-Provence, 8 et 9 décembre 2006 (Paris, Pédone, 2007).

'Major events in China-Brazil relations', *China Daily*, 11 November2004, available at http://www.chinadaily.com.cn/english/doc/2004-11/11/content_390570.htm.

Mandigora, G, 'The Proposed SACU–China FTA: Opportunities and Threats for SACU's Manufacturing Sector', tralac, available at http://rta.tralac.org/scripts/content.php?id=4924.

Manin, P, 'A propos de l'invocabilité de l'accord instituant l'Organisation mondiale du commerce et de l'accord sur les marches publics: la question de l'invocabilité des accords internationaux conclus par la Communauté européenne' (1997) 33 *Revue Trimestrielle de Droit Européen* 399.

Mann, J, *About Face: A History of America's Curious Relationship with China, from Nixon to Clinton* (New York, Knopf, 1999).

Mansfield, E (ed), *International Conflict and the Global Economy* (Cheltenham, Edward Elgar, 2004).

Marchetti, R, 'Toward a World Migratory Regime' (2008) 15(2) *Indiana Journal of Global Legal Studies* 471.

Maresceau, M (ed), *The Political and Legal Framework of Trade Relations between the European Community and Eastern Europe* (Deventer, Kluwer, 1989).

Maresceau, M, 'The GATT in the case-law of the European Court of Justice' in M Hilf, FG Jacobs and EU Petersmann (eds), *The European Community and GATT* (Deventer, Kluwer, 1983).

Marks, G, *Multi-level Governance and European Integration* (Boulder, Rowman & Littlefield, 2001).
Martin, LL (ed), *International Institutions in the Global Economy* (Cheltenham, Edward Elgar Publishing, 2005).
Martin, R, 'Public Health Ethics and SARS: Seeking an Ethical Framework to Global Public Health Practice' 2004 (1) *Law, Social Justice & Global Development Journal (LGD)*, at http://elj.warwick.ac.uk/global/issue/2004-1/martin.html.
Masahiro, Kawai. 'East Asian Economic Regionalism: Progress and Challenges', (2005) 16 1 *Journal of Asian Economics—International Journal*, 29.
Maslen, J, 'The European Community's Relations with the State-Trading Countries 1981–1983' (1983) 3 *Yearbook of European Law* 323.
Mastropasqua, A, *Le Marché commun et la défense contre le dumping—De la nécessité d'une législation anti-dumping communautaire* (Rome, Guido Pastena Editore, 1965).
Mattli, W and Woods, N (eds), *The Politics of Global Regulation* (Princeton, Princeton University Press, 2009).
Maturana, H and Varela, F, *Autopoesis and Cognition: The Realisation of the Living* (Dordrecht, D Reidel Publishing Co, 1980; 1st edn 1973).
Matzer, M, 'Advertising and Marketing: Holiday '97', *The Los Angeles Times*, Thursday, 6 December 1997, at 4.
Mazuelos, A, *Non-binding Acts in the European Community Legal Order: Soft Law?*, PhD thesis (Florence, European University Institute, 2003).
McCahery, J, Picciotto, S and Scott, C, *Corporate Control and Accountability: Changing Structures and the Dynamics of Regulation* (Oxford, Clarendon Press, 199
McCall Smith, J, 'The Politics of Dispute Settlement Design: Explaining Legalism in Regional Trade Pacts' (2000) 54(1) *International Organization* 137.
McGovern, E, *International Trade Regulation: GATT, the United States and the European Community*, 2nd edn (Exeter, Globefield Press, 1986).
McMurray, C and Smith, R, *Diseases of Globalisation: Socioeconomic Transitions and Health* (London, Earthscan, 2001).
'Media blackout on bicycle suit', *South China Morning Post* (Hong Kong), Wednesday, 10 January 2007, at A4.
Meidinger, E, 'Emerging Trans-Sectoral Regulatory Structures in Global Civil Society: The Case of ISEAL (the International Social and Environmental Accreditation and Labelling Alliance)', paper prepared for the 'Tools for Regulation' Panel, Joint Annual Meetings of the Law and Society Association and the Research Committee for the Sociology of Law, 4–7 July 2001, Budapest, Hungary; revised Draft 1.2 available at http://law.buffalo.edu/homepage/eemeid/scholarship/ISEAL.pdf.
—— 'The Administrative Law of Global Private–Public Regulation: The Case of Forestry' (2006) 17 *European Journal of International Law* 47.
Melissaris, E, *Ubiquitous Law: Legal Theory and the Space for Legal Pluralism* (Farnham, Ashgate, 2009).
Mengozzi, P, 'La Cour de justice et l'applicabilité des règles de l'OMC en droit communautaire à la lumière de l'affaire *Portugal c. Conseil*' (2000) 3 *Revue du Droit de l'Union Européenne* 509.
Merry, SE, 'Legal Pluralism' (1988) 22 *Law & Society Review* 869.
—— *Human Rights and Gender Violence: Translating International Law into Local Justice* (Chicago, University of Chicago Press, 2006).
Mertha, AC, *The Politics of Piracy: Intellectual Property in Contemporary China* (Ithaca and London, Cornell University Press, 2005).
Meuser, RL, 'Note: Dumping from "Controlled Economy" Countries: The Polish Golf Cart Case' (1979) 11 *Law and Policy in International Business*, 777.
Michaels, R, *The Re-Statement of Non-State Law: The State, Choice of Law and the Challenge from Global Legal Pluralism*, Duke Law School Working Paper Series, Duke Law School Faculty Scholarship Series, Paper 21, 1 October 2005.

Miller, M, 'The TRIPS Agreement and direct effect in European Community law: You can look . . . but can you touch?' (1999) 74 *Notre Dame Law Review* 597.

Mockle, D (ed), *Mondialisation et Etat de Droit* (Brussels, Bruylant, 2002).

Montaña-Mora, M, 'Equilibrium: A rediscovered basis for the Court of Justice of the European Communities to refuse direct effect to the Uruguay Round Agreements?' (1966) 30 *Journal of World Trade* 43.

Montgomery, B, President of the European Bicycle Manufacturers Association, in 'Des clauses de sauvegarde arrêteront-elles la Chine?' *Usinenouvelle.com*, 28 April 2005, available at http://www.usinenouvelle.com/article/des-clauses-de-sauvegarde-arreteront-elles-la-chine.52314, last accessed 4 March 2010

Mosoti, V, 'Institutional Cooperation and Norm Creation' in T Cottier, J Pauwelyn and E Bırgi (eds), *Human Rights and International Trade* (Oxford, Oxford University Press, 2005).

Muchlinski, PT, ' "Global Bukowina" Examined: Viewing the Multinational Enterprise as a Transnational Law-making Community' in G Teubner (ed), *Global Law Without a State* (Dartmouth, Aldershot, 1997).

—— 'Human Rights, Social Responsibility and the Regulation of International Business: The Development of International Standards by Intergovernmental Organisations' (2003) 3(1) *Non-State Actors in International Law* 123.

Müller, W, Khan, N and Neumann, H-A. *EC Antidumping Law—A Commentary on* Regulation 384/96 (New York, John Wiley & Sons, 1998).

Murray, J, *Corporate Codes of Conduct and Labour Standards*, International Labour Organization, Bureau for Workers' Activities, Working Paper 1996, available at http://actrav.itcilo.org/actrav-english/telearn/global/ilo/guide/jill.html, last accessed 4 March 2010

Murshed, SM, *Globalization, Marginalization and Development* (London, Routledge, 2002).

Mytelka, LK and Delapierre, M, 'Strategic Partnerships, Knowledge-based Network Oligopolies, and the State', in AC Cutler, V Haufler and T Porter (eds), *Private Authority and International Affairs* (Buffalo, State University of New York Press, 1999).

Nagel, T, 'The Problem of Global Justice' (2005) 33 *Philosophy and Public Affairs* 113.

Nariman, F, 'East Meets West: Tradition, Globalization and the Future of Arbitration' (2004) 20(2) *Arbitration International* 123.

Naughton, B, *Growing Out of the Plan: Chinese Economic Reform, 1978–1993* (Cambridge, Cambridge University Press, 1995).

Neeley, JS, 'Non-market economy Import Regulation: From Bad to Worse' (1989) 20 *Law & Policy in International Business* 529.

Neville, MA, 'The Antidumping Act of 1916: A War-time Legacy' (1981) 26 *New York Law School Law Review* 535.

Neville, P, 'The Development of International Regulatory Associations' (2005) 12(3) *Journal of Financial Crime* 264.

Neuwahl, N, 'Individuals and the GATT: Direct effect and the General Agreement on Tariffs and Trade in Community Law' in N Emiliou and D O'Keeffe (eds), *The European Union and World Trade Law after the Uruguay Round* (Chichester, Wiley, 1996).

Newton, J and Tse, Lai-hing, 'Kids' Stuff: The Organisation and Politics of the China–EU Trade in Toys', in R Strange, J Slater and L Wang (eds), *Trade and Investment in China: The European Experience* (London, Routledge 1998).

New Zealand, Ministry of Foreign Affairs and Trade, 'New Zealand–China Free Trade Agreement: Frequently Asked Questions', available at http://www.mfat.govt.nz/Trade-and-Economic-Relations/Trade-Agreements/China/0-faqs.php.

Niazi, T, 'Gwadar: China's Naval Outpost on the Indian Ocean', The Jamestown Foundation, China Brief, on the website of the Association for Asian Research, http://www.asianresearch.org7articles/2528.html.

Nicolaidis, K and Shaffer, G, 'Transnational Mutual Recognition Regimes: Governance without Global Government' (2005) 68 *Law and Contemporary Problems* 267.

Niels, G, 'What Is Anti-dumping Policy Really About?' (2000) 14(4) *Journal of Economic Surveys* 467.

Ning, Susan and Ding, Liang, , 'China's Free Trade Agreement (FTA) Policy and its Recent Developments' *King & Wood China Bulletin 2006*, Special Issue, October, 2006, at 1–7,

Ni, Ping, and Wang, Wenlan, *Life with Bicycles* (Beijing, Zhong Guo Wen Lian [China Association of Artists] Publishers, 2004).

Nitz, J, 'Probleme und Perspektiven der Wirtschaftsbeziehungen DDR-BRD' (1989) 10 *IPW Berichte* [Institut für Internationale Politik und Wirtschaft der DDR, Berlin] 8.

Nixon, F, 'Controlling the Transnationals? The UN Code of Conduct' in Y Ghai, R Luckham and F Snyder (eds), *The Political Economy of Law: A Third World Reader* (Delhi, Oxford University Press, 1987).

Nörr, KW 'Franz Böhm and the Theory of the Private Law Society' in P Koslowski (ed), *The Theory of Capitalism in the German Economic Tradition: Historicism, Ordo-Liberalism, Critical Theory, Solidarism* (Berlin, Springer-Verlag, 2000).

Nowrot, K, 'Legal Consequences of Globalization: The Status of Non-governmental Organizations under International Law' (1999) 6 *Indiana Journal of Global Legal Studies* 579.

Obijiofor, A, *Global Health Governance: International Law and Public Health in a Divided World* (Toronto, University of Toronto Press, 2005).

—— 'International Law and Communicable Diseases' (2002) 80(12) *Bulletin of the World Health Organization*, 946.

—— 'Salvaging Our Global Neighbourhood: Critical Reflections on the G8 Summit and Global Health Governance in an Interdependent World' (2004) 1 *Law, Social Justice and Global Development [LJD]*, http://www2.warwick.ac.uk/fac/soc/law/elj/lgd/2004_1/aginam/.

O'Brien, R, Goetz, AM, Scholte, JA and Williams, M, *Contesting Global Governance: Multilateral Economic Institutions and Global Social Movements* (Cambridge, Cambridge University Press, 2000).

Odell, JS, *Negotiating the World Economy* (Ithaca, Cornell University Press, 2001).

Ohashi, H, 'China's Regional Trade and Investment Profile' in D Shambaugh (ed), *Power Shift: China and Asia's New Dynamics* (Berkeley, University of California Press, 2005).

Oi, JC, 'Fiscal Reform and the Economic Foundations of Local State Corporatism in China', (1992) 45(1) *World Politics* 99.

'The Role of the Local State in China's Transitional Economy' (1995) 144 *The China Quarterly* 1132.

—— 'The Evolution of Local State Corporatism' in AG Walder (ed), *Zouping in Transition: The Process of Reform in Rural North China* (Cambridge, Mass, Harvard University Press, 1998).

Oi, JC and Walder, AG (eds), *Property Rights and Economic Reform in China* (Stanford, Stanford University Press, 1999).

Okafor, OC, 'The Global Process of Legitimation and the Legitimacy of Global Governance' (1997) 14 *Arizona Journal of International and Comparative Law* 117.

—— *The African Human Rights System, Activist Forces and International Institutions* (Cambridge, Cambridge University Press, 2007).

O'Keeffe, D and Bavasso, A (eds), *Liber Amicorum for Gordon Slynn: Judicial Review in European Law* (London, Chancery, 2000).

Organisation mondiale du commerce, Comité des mesures sanitaires et phytosanitaire, Décision du Comité, Procédure pour la surveillance du processus d'harmonisation internationale, Comité des mesures sanitaires et phytosanitaires, Organisation Mondiale du Commerce G/SPS/11, 22 octobre 1997 (97-4606), available on the WTO website http://docsonline.wto.org/GEN_viewerwindow.asp?D:/DDFDOCUMENTS/U/G/SPS/11.W.

—— Troisième rapport du Directeur général: Conseil général, Session extraordinaire sur la mise en œuvre, Mesures visant à accroître la participation des pays en développement membres aux travaux des organisations internationales de normalisation compétentes dans le domaine des mesures sanitaires et phytosanitaires, Organisation Mondiale du Commerce, WT/GC/54,

7 novembre 2001 (01-5490), available on the WTO website at http://docsonline.wto.org/GEN_viewerwindow.asp?D:/DDFDOCUMENTS/U/WT/GC/54.

Orr, T, 'The China–Australia Free-Trade Negotiations: Implications for South Africa', Centre for Chinese Studies, University of Stellenbosch, available at http://www.ccs.org.za/downloads7ACFTA%20Exec%20Summary.pdf.

Paliwala, A, 'Free Culture, Global Commons and Social Justice in Information Technology Diffusion' 2007 (1) *Law, Social Justice & Global Development Journal (LGD)*, at http://www.go.warwick.ac.uk/elj/lgd/2007_1/paliwala.

Palmeter, ND, 'Editorial: The Antidumping Emperor' (1988) 22 *Journal of World Trade* 5.

—— 'The Impact of the US Antidumping Law on China–US Trade' (1989) 23 *Journal of World Trade* 5.

Pan, Zhengqiang, 'What the Asia-Pacific Can Learn from the European Integration', Online Info-Dienst Ausgabe 4/2004, Konrad-Adenauer-Stiftung eV, Länderbıro China, 20.7.2004, available at http://www.kas.de/proj/home/pub/37/1/year-2004/dokument:id-5120/index_print.html.

Panagariya, A, 'An India–China Free Trade Area?, *Economic Times*, 20 April 2005.

Pape, W, 'Socio-Cultural Differences and International Competition Law' (2002) 5(4) *European Law Journal* 438.

Park, JD, *The Special Economic Zones of China and Their Impact on Its Economic Development* (Westport, Conn, Praeger, 1997).

Patten, C, 'Globalisation and the Law' (2004) 1 *European Human Rights Law Review* 6.

Patterson, ER, 'Improving GATT Rules for Nonmarket Economies' (1986) 20 *Journal of World Trade Law* 185.

Pattison, JE, *Antidumping and Countervailing Duty Laws* (New York, Clark Boardman Co Ltd, 1984).

Pauly, LW and Reich, S, 'National Structures and Multinational Corporate Behaviour: Enduring Differences in the Age of Globalization' (1997) 5 *International Organization* 1.

Pauwels, W, Vandenbussche, H and Weverbergh, M, 'Strategic Behaviour under European Antidumping Duties' (2001) 8(1) *International Journal of the Economics of Business* 75.

Pauwelyn, J, *The Nature of WTO Obligations*, Jean Monnet Working Paper 1/02, Jean Monnet Program, New York University Law School, available at http://www.jeanmonnetprogram.org/papers/02/020101.rtf.

—— *Conflict of Norms in Public International Law: How WTO Law Relates to Other Rules of International Law* (Cambridge, Cambridge University Press, 2003).

—— 'How to Win a WTO Dispute Based on Non-WTO Law' (2003) 37(6) *Journal of World Trade* 997.

—— 'Human Rights in WTO Dispute Settlement' in T Cottier, J Pauwelyn and E Bürgi (eds), *Human Rights and International Trade* (Oxford, Oxford University Press, 2005).

Peacock, A and Willgerodt, H (eds), *Germany's Social Market Economy: Origins and Evolution* (London, Macmillan for the Trade Policy Research Centre, 1989).

Pearson, M, 'China in Geneva: Lessons from China's Early Years in the World Trade Organization' in AI Johnston and RS Ross (eds), *New Directions in the Study of China's Foreign Policy* (Stanford, Stanford University Press, 2006).

Peerenboom, R, *China Modernizes: Threat to the West or Model for the Rest?* (Oxford, Oxford University Press, 2007).

—— (ed), *Judicial Independence in China: Lessons for Global Rule of Law Promotion* (Cambridge, Cambridge University Press, 2009)

Peers, S, 'Fundamental right or political whim? WTO law and the European Court of Justice' in G de Burca and J Scott (eds), *The EU and the WTO: Legal and Constitutional Issues* (Oxford, Oxford University Press, 2001).

Pegg, J, 'Ikea faces threat of illegal toy charges', *South China Morning Post*, Wednesday, 12 May 1999, at 3.

Pellegrin, J, *International Business and the European Integration Process: The Example of Outward Processing Traffic between the European Union and the Central and Eastern European Countries*, PhD Thesis, Department of Social and Political Sciences, European University Institute, July 1997.

Peng, SY, 'The WTO Legalistic Approach and East Asia: From the Legal Culture Perspective' (2000) 1 *Asian-Pacific Law & Policy Journal* 13.

People's Republic of China, *Handbook of Foreign Economic Law*, 2 vols (Beijing, Publishing House of Law, 1997).

People's Republic of China, General Administration of Customs, *China Customs: 2008 Annual Report*, http://www1.customs.gov.cn//Portals/191/2008%20China%20Customs.doc.

People's Republic of China, Macao Special Administrative Region, Economic Services, 'Overview of Pan—Pearl River Delta Regional Cooperation', http://www.economia.gov.mo/web/DSE/public?_nfpb=true&_pageLabel=Pg_EETR_9_2_S&locale=en_US.

—— Macao Special Administrative Region, Economic Services, 'Summary of the Pan–Pearl River Delta Regional Cooperation Framework Agreement', http://www.economia.gov.mo/web/DSE/public?_nfpb=true&_pageLabel=Pg_EETR_9_2_T&locale=en_US.

—— Ministry of Commerce, 'Strategic Framework for Action on Trade Facilitation and Investment in the Greater Mekong Sub-Region', at http://tradeinservices.mofcom.gov.cn/en/b/2007-10-10/6577.shtml.

People's Republic of China, Ministry of Commerce, and New Zealand, Ministry of Foreign Affairs and Trade, 'A Joint Study Report on a Free Trade Area between China and New Zealand, available at www.mfat.nz.

People's Republic of China, Ministry of Commerce, and Ministry of Trade and Industry, Singapore, 'A Joint Study Report on a Free Trade Agreement between China and Singapore', available at http://www.iesingapore.gov.sg/wps/wcm/connect/resources/file/ebf07d479d475cf/Joint_Study_Rpt_on_a_CSFTA.pdf?MOD=AJPERES.

People's Republic of China, State Council, Development Research Center, 'National Energy Strategies and Policies' in China Development Forum, *China's National Energy Strategy and Reform: Background Reports* (15–17 November 2003) (Development Research Center, State Council, 'China's National Energy Strategy and Policy, 2000–2020', November 2003, draft national plan, Beijing), 3–46, available at http://www.efchina.org/FReports.do?act=detail&id=112.

Perez, O, 'Normative Creativitiy and Global Legal Pluralism: Reflections on the Democratic Critique of Transnational Law' (2003) 10(2) *Indiana Journal of Global Legal Studies* 25.

—— *Ecological Sensitivity and Global Legal Pluralism: Rethinking the Trade and Environment Conflict* (Oxford, Hart Publishing, 2004).

Perry, D, 'Ethics in International Economics: The WTO, NAFTA, the IMF and the World Bank' (Interview of Professor Michael Kevane, conducted by David Perry, Director of Ethics Programmes at the Markkula Centre for Applied Ethics, Santa Clara University, broadcast 30 April 2001 on 'Ethics Today' KSCU Radio, 103.3 FM), available on the Internet at http://www.scu.edu.Ethics.

Peru, Ministry of Foreign Trade and Tourism, and People's Republic of China, Ministry of Commerce, Feasibility Report, China–Peru Free Trade Agreement (FTA), 'Peru–China Free Trade Agreement Joint Feasibility Study', available on the website of the Peru Ministry of Foreign Trade and Tourism, http://www.mincetur.gob.pe/newweb/Portals/0/Peru-China%20JFS%20Final.pdf.

Pescatore, P, Davey, WJ and Lowenfeld, A (eds), *Handbook of GATT Dispute Settlement* (Irvington-on-Hudson, NY, Transnational, 1997).

Petersmann, EU, 'Application of GATT by the Court of Justice of the European Communities' (1983) 20 *CML Rev* 397.

—— *Constitutional Functions and Problems of International Economic Law* (Fribourg, University of Fribourg Press, 1991).

—— 'GATT Dispute Settlement Proceedings in the Field of Antidumping Law' (1991) 28(1) *CML Rev* 69.

—— 'National Constitutions and International Economic Law', in M Hilf and EU Petersmann (eds), *National Constitutions and International Economic Law* (Deventer, Kluwer, 1993).

—— 'How to Constitutionalize International Law and Foreign Policy for the Benefit of Civil Society?' (1998) 20 *Michigan Journal of International Law* 1.

—— 'How to Promote the International Rule of Law? Contributions by the WTO Appellate Review System' in J Cameron and K Campbell (eds), *Dispute Resolution in the World Trade Organisation* (London, Cameron May, 1998).

—— 'Time for a United Nations "Global Compact" for Integrating Human Rights into the Law of Worldwide Organizations: Lessons from European Integration' (2002) 13(3) *European Journal of International Law* 621.

—— 'Taking Human Dignity, Poverty and Empowerment of Individuals More Seriously, Rejoinder to Alston' (2002) 13(4) *European Journal of International Law* 845.

—— 'The "Human Rights Approach" Advocated by the UN High Commissioner for Human Rights and by the International Labour Organization: Is It Relevant for WTO Law and Policy?' (2004) 7(3) *Journal of International Economic Law* 605.

Peterson, VS, *A Critical Rewriting of Global Political Economy: Integrating Reproductive, Productive and Virtual Economies* (London, Routledge, 2003).

Pesek, W, 'Asian Euro? Don't Hold Your Breath', *International Herald Tribune*, Saturday–Sunday, 10–11 May 2008.

Peukert, H,'Walter Eucken (1891–1950) and the Historical School' in P Koslowski (ed), *The Theory of Capitalism in the German Economic Tradition: Historicism, Ordo-Liberalism, Critical Theory, Solidarism* (Berlin, Springer-Verlag, 2000).

Phelan, DR, *The Application of United States and European Community Domestic Trade Laws to the Imports of Non-market economy GATT Contracting Parties—A Time for Change*, EUI Working Paper LAW No 92/28 (Florence, Department of Law, European University Institute, 1992).

Picciotto, S, *International Business Taxation: A Study in the Internationalization of Business Regulation* (London, Weidenfeld & Nicolson, 1992).

—— 'Transfer Pricing and the Antinomies of Corporate Regulation' in J McCahery, S Picciotto and C Scott (eds), *Corporate Control and Accountability: Changing Structures and the Dynamics of Regulation* (Oxford, Clarendon Press, 1993).

—— 'The Regulatory Criss-Cross: Interaction between Jurisdictions and The Construction of Global Regulatory Networks' in W Bratton, N McCahery, S Picciotto and C Scott (eds), *International Regulatory Competition and Coordination* (Oxford, Clarendon Press, 1996).

—— 'Networks in International Economic Integration: Fragmented States and the Dilemmas of Neo-liberalism' (1996–97) 17 *Northwestern Journal of International Law & Business* 1014.

—— 'North Atlantic Cooperation and Democratizing Globalism' in GA Bermann, M Herdegen and PL Lindseth (eds), *Transatlantic Regulatory Cooperation: Legal Problems and Political Prospects* (Oxford, Oxford University Press, 2000).

—— 'Democratizing Globalism' in D Drache (ed), *The Market or the Public Domain: Global Governance and the Asymmetry of Power* (London, Routledge, 2001).

—— 'The WTO as a Node of Global Governance: Economic Regulation and Human Rights Discourses' (2007) 1 *Social Justice & Global Development Journal/LGD*, http://go.warwick.ac.uk/lgd/2007_1/picciotto.

Piontek, E, 'Anti-Dumping in the EEC—Some Observations by an Outsider' (1987) 21 *Journal of World Trade Law* 67.

Pischel, G, 'Trade, Treaties and Treason: Some Underlying Aspects of the Difficult Relationship between the EU and the WTO' (2001) 6 *European Foreign Affairs Review* 103.

Plummer, MG, ' "Best Practices" in Regional Trade Agreements: An Application to Asia' (2007) 30(12) *The World Economy* 1771.

Pollack, MA and Shaffer, G (eds), *Transatlantic Governance in the Global Economy* (Lanham, Md, Rowman & Littlefield, 2001).

Pollack, 'Makeover at Barbie's: Mattel Sheds Jobs and Looks to the Internet', *International Herald Tribune*, Saturday–Sunday, 17–18 April 1999, at 9.

Polouektov, A, 'Non-market Economy Issues in the WTO Anti-dumping Law and Accession Negotiations: Revival of a Two-tier Membership' (2002) 36(1) *Journal of World Trade* 1.

Pomerantz, K, *The Great Divergence: China, Europe, and the Making of the Modern World Economy* (Princeton, Princeton University Press, 2000).

Porges, J, 'Codes of Conduct', Asian Labour Update at http://www.freeway.org/

Potter, PB, *The Chinese Legal System: Globalization and Local Legal Culture* (London, Routledge, 2001).

Pradhan, R, von Benda-Beckmann, F and von Benda-Beckmann, K (eds), *Water, Land and Law: Changing Rights to Land and Water in Nepal*, Proceedings of a workshop held in Kathmandu, 18–20 March 1998 (Kathmandu, Wageningen, Rotterdam, Legal Research and Development Forum [FREEDEAL], Wageningen Agricultural University [WAU] and Erasmus University Rotterdam [EUR], 2000).

Preston, LE, 'The Evolution of Multinational Public Policy towards Business' in CR Lehman, and RM Moore (eds), *Multinational Culture: Social Impacts of a Global Economy* (Westport, Conn, Greenwood, 1992).

Pye, LW, *The Dynamics of Chinese Politics* (Cambridge, Mass, Oelgeschlager, Gunn & Hain, 1981).

—— 'China: Erratic State, Frustrated Society' (1990) 69(4) *Foreign Affairs* 56.

—— *The Spirit of Chinese Politics* (Cambridge, Mass, Harvard University Press, 1992).

Question no 103 de Mme Ernst de la Graete (H-0986/92) [Objet: L'importation de bicycles en provenance de la Chine et des pays bénéficiaires du système de préférences généralisées] and Question no 104 de M. Gil-Robles Gil-Delgado (H.1025/92) [Objet: Bicyclettes], Débats du Parlement européen, No 3-423/303, 28.10.92.

Qiu, Huanguang, Yang, Jun, Huang, Jikun and Chen, Ruijian, 'Impact of China–ASEAN Free Trade Area on China's International Agricultural Trade and Its Regional Development' (2007) 15(4) *China & The World Economy* 77.

Quiggin, J. 'Globalization and Economic Sovereignty', (2001) 9 *The Journal of Political Philosophy,* 56–80.

Rabach, E and Kim, EM, 'Where is the Chain in Commodity Chains? The Service Sector Nexus' in G Gereffiand M Korzcnicwicz (eds). *Commodity Chains and Global Capitalism* (Westport, Conn, Greenwood, 1994) 137.

Raman, B, *Gwadar, Hambantota & Sitwe: China's Strategic Triangle*, South Asia Analysis Group, Paper no 2158, 6 March 2007, available at http://www.southasiaanalysis.org/%5Cpapers22%5paperCpaper2158.html.

Ravaloson, J, 'Les organisations non gouvernementales et la sécurité alimentaire: vers un modèle de gouvernance globale?' in A Mahiou and F Snyder (eds), *La sécurité alimentaire/Food Security and Food Safety* (Leiden, Martinus Nijhoff for The Hague Academy of International Law, 2006).

Record of Consultations on Further Liberalisation under the Mainland–Hong Kong Closer Economic Partnership Arrangement, available at http://www.ipd.gov.hk/eng/news/news/Record_of_Consultations_on_Further_Liberalization.pdf.

Reddy, L. 'A China—SACU FTA: What's in it for SA?', *South African Foreign Policy Monitor*, August-September 2004, 1–2.

Redfern, A and Hunter, M, *Law and Practice of International Commercial Arbitration*, 3rd edn (London, Sweet & Maxwell, 1999).

Reid, AS, 'The Internationalisation of Corporate Codes of Conduct' (2003) 24(10) *Business Law Review* 233.

'Report of the ASEAN–EU Vision Group: Transregional Partnership for Shared and Sustainable Prosperity', Ha Noi, Vietnam, 10 May 2006, available at http://trade.ec.europa.eu/doclib/docs/2006/may/tradoc_128860.pdf.

Richards, PM, *Political Primacy in Economic Laws: A Comparison of British and American Anti-dumping Legislation, 1921*, Working Paper No 13/93, Department of Economic History, London School of Economics, July 1993.

Riha, T, 'Ordo—The German Neoliberal Model of Economic Order' (1986) 39 *Economia Internazionale* 31.

Riles, A, *The Network Inside Out* (Ann Arbor, University of Michigan Press, 2000).

—— 'The virtual sociality of rights: the case of "women's rights are human rights"' in M Likosky (ed), *Transnational Legal Processes: Globalisation and Power Disparties* (London, Butterworths LexisNexis, 2002).

Risse, T, Ropp, S and Sikkink, K (eds), *The Power of Human Rights: International Norms and Domestic Change* (Cambridge, Cambridge University Press, 1999).

Risse-Kappen, T, 'Exploring the Nature of the Beast: International Relations Theory and Comparative Policy Analysis Meet the European Union' (1996) 34 *Journal of Common Market Studies* 53.

Rittberger, V (ed), *International Regimes in East–West Politics* (London and New York, Pinter Publishers, 1990).

Rittberger, V and Zürn, M, 'Towards Regulated Anarchy in East-West Relations: Causes and Consequences of East-West Regimes' in V Rittberger (ed). *International Regimes in East–West* Politics (London and New York, Pinter Publishers,1990).

Robé, JP, 'Multinational Enterprises: The Constitution of a Pluralistic Legal Order' in G Teubner (ed), *Global Law Without a State* (Dartmouth, Aldershot, 1997).

Roberts, S. 'After Government? On Representing Law Without the. State' (2005) 68(1) *MLR* 1.

Robertson*, R, Globalization: Social Theory and Global Culture* (London, Sage, 1992).

Robinson, D and Stuart, TE, 'Network Effects in the Governance of Strategic Alliances' (2007) 23(1) *Journal of Law, Economics and Organization* 242.

Roessler, F, *La relation entre l'ordre commercial mondial et le système monétaire international*, Conférences d'Actualité, Centre d'Etudes et de Recherches Internationales et Communautaires (CERIC), Faculté de Droit et de Science Politique d'Aix-Marseille, 1987.

Romano, C, 'The proliferation of international judicial bodies: The pieces of the puzzle' (1999) 31(4) *New York University Journal of International Law and Politics* 709.

Rosas, A, 'The European Union and Mixed Agreements' in A Dashwood and C Hillion (eds), *The General Law of EC External Relations* (London, Sweet &. Maxwell, 2000).

Rosenau, JN, 'Toward an Ontology for Global Governance' in M Hewson and TJ Sinclair (eds), *Approaches to Global Governance Theory* (Albany, State University of New York Press, 1999).

—— *Distant Proximities: Dynamics Beyond Globalization* (Princeton, Princeton University Press, 2003).

—— 'Many Damn Things Simultaneously—At Least for a While: Complexity Theory and World Affairs' in JN Rosenau, *The Study of World Politics: Theoretical and Methodological Challenges* (London, Routledge, 2006).

Rosenfeld, M, 'Rethinking Constitutional Ordering in an Era of Legal and Ideological Pluralism' (2008) 6(3)–(4) *International Journal of Constitutional Law: I-CON* 415.

Ruggie, J, 'International Regimes, Transactions, and Change: Embedded Liberalism in the Postwar Economic Order' in S Krasner (ed), *International Regimes* (Ithaca, Cornell University Press, 1983).

Ruggiero, R, 'A Shared Responsibility: Global Policy Coherence for Our Global Age', Address to the Conference on *Globalisation as a Challenge for German Business: Export Opportunities for Small and Medium-Sized Companies in the Environmental Field*, Bonn, 9 December 1997, available on the WTO website at http://www.wto.org/english/news_e/sprr_e/bonn_e.htm.

Ruttley, P, 'The Effect of WTO Agreements in EC law: How Private Parties Can Use WTO Agreements in Litigation before the EC Courts and the National Courts of EC Member States' in P Ruttley, I Macvay and C George (eds), *The WTO and International Trade Regulation* (London, Cameron May, 1998).

Said, E, *The World,the Text and the Critic* (Cambridge, Mass, Harvard University Press, 1983).

Sajhau, JP, *Business Ethics in the Textile, Clothing and Footwear (TCF) Industries: Codes of Conduct*, International Labour Organization, Sectoral Activities Programme, Working Paper SAP 2.60/WP.110 1998, available on the Internet at http://www.ilo.org/public/english/100secto/papers/bzethics/index.htm.

Sally, R, *FTAs and the Prospects for Regional Integration in Asia*, European Centre for International Political Economy, Brussels, ECIPE Working Paper, 1, 2006.

Salter, L, 'The Standards Regime for Communication and Information Technologies' in AC Cutler, V Haufler, and T Porter (eds), *Private Authority and International Affairs* (Buffalo, State University of New York Press, 1999).

Sampson, GP, 'Greater Coherence in Global Economic Policymaking: A WTO Perspective' in AO Krueger (ed), *The WTO as an International Organization* (Chicago, University of Chicago Press, 1998).

Sanchez, R, 'Towards a Science of Strategic Product Design: System Design, Component Modularity, and Product Leveraging Strategies', Proceedings of the Second International Product Development Conference on New Approaches to Development and Engineering, 30–31 May 1994, European Institute for Advanced Studies in Management, Brussels, Belgium.

—— 'Product and Process Architectures in the Management of Knowledge Resources' in PI Robertson and NJ Foss (eds), *Resources, Technology and Strategy: Explorations in the Resource-Based Perspective* (London, Routledge, 2000).

Sanchez, R and Mahoney, JT, 'Modularity, Flexibility and Knowledge Management in Product and Organisation Design' (1996) 17 (Winter Special Issue) *Strategic Management Journal* 63.

—— 'Modularity and Dynamic Capabilities' in HW Voberda and T Elfring (eds), *Rethinking Strategy* (London, Sage, 2000).

Sandrey, R, 'The SACU–China FTA', 17 March 2005, available at http://www.tralac.org/scripts/content.php?id=4917.

Sands, P, Mackenzie, R and Shany, Y, *The Manual of International Courts and Tribunals* (London, Butterworths, 1999).

Sassen, S, *Losing Control? Sovereignty in an Age of Globalization* (New York, Columbia University Press, 1996).

—— 'The locational and institutional embeddedness of the global economy' in GA Bermann, M Herdegen, and PL Lindseth (eds), *Transatlantic Regulatory Cooperation: Legal Problems and Political Prospects* (New York, Oxford University Press, 2000).

—— 'Opening remarks: Producing the Transnational Inside the National' in M Likosky (ed), *Transnational Legal Processes: Globalisation and Power Disparities* (London, Butterworths LexisNexis, 2002).

Sautenet, A, 'The Current Status and Prospects of the "Strategic Partnership" between the EU and China: Towards the Conclusion of a Partnership and Cooperation Agreement' (2007) 13(6) *European Law Journal* 699.

Scalapino, RA, 'China's Multiple Identities in East Asia: China as a Regional Force' in L Dittmer and SS Kim (eds), *China's Quest for National Identity* (Ithaca, Cornell University Press, 1993).

Scharpf, F, *Governing in Europe: Effective and Democratic?* (Oxford, Oxford University Press, 1999).

Schepel, H, *The Constitution of Private Governance: Product Standards in the Regulation of Integrating Markets* (Oxford, Hart Publishing, 2005).

Schiff Berman, P, 'The Globalization of Jurisdiction' (2002) 151 *University of Pennsylvania Law Review* 311.

—— 'Global Legal Pluralism' (2007) 80 *Southern California Law Review* 1155.
Schmid, C, *A theoretical reconstruction of WTO constitutionalism and its implications for the relationship with the EU*, EUI Working Paper No 2001/5, Department of Law, European University Institute, Florence.
Schmidt, K, 'The Public Sector in a Market Economy' in A Peacock and H Willgerodt (eds), *Germany's Social Market Economy: Origins and Evolution* (London, Macmillan for the Trade Policy Research Centre, 1989).
Schmidtchen, D and Schmidt-Trenz, H-J, *Territoriality of Law and the International Trade Game: Towards a New Institutional Economics of International Transactions*, German Working Papers in Law and Economics, vol 2006, art 25, available at http://www.bepress.com/gwp/default/vol2006/iss1/art25.
Schneider, AK, 'Getting Along: The Evolution of Dispute Resolution Regimes in International Trade Organizations' (1998–99) 20 *Michigan Journal of International Law* 697.
Schroeder, FC, 'The Two Legal Levels of East-West Trade' in D. Kim and W Gumpel (eds), *New Directions in East–West Relations: German and Korean Perspectives* (Seoul, Korea, Institute of East and West Studies, Yonsei University, 1987).
Scott, C (ed), *Torture as Tort: Comparative Perspectives on the Development of Transnational Human Rights Litigation* (Oxford, Hart Publishing, 2001).
Scott, J, 'GATT and Community Law: Rethinking the "Regulatory Gap"' in J Shaw and G More (eds), *New Legal Dynamics of the European Union* (Oxford, Oxford University Press, 1995).
Sell, SK, 'Multinational corporations as agents of change: The globalization of intellectual property rights' in AC Cutler, V Haufler and T Porter (eds), *Private Authority and International Affairs* (Buffalo, State University of New York Press,1999).
Sen, A, *Poverty and Famines: An Essay on Entitlement and Deprivation* (Oxford, Oxford University Press, 1981).
Sen, P, 'China–Pakistan FTA', *Journalism by Other Means*, available at http://philip-sen.com/othermeans/the_peoples_republic/, last accessed 17 March 2010.
Sen, R, '"New Regionalism" in Asia: A Comparative Analysis of Emerging Regional and Bilateral Trading Agreements involving ASEAN, China and India' (2006) 40(4) *Journal of World Trade* 553.
Senden, L, *Soft Law in European Community Law* (Oxford, Hart Publishing, 2004).
Sengenberger, W and Campbell, D, *International Labour Standards and Economic Interdependence* (Essays in commemoration of the 75th anniversary of the International Labour Organisation and the 50th anniversary of the Declaration of Philadelphia) (Geneva, ILO, 1994).
Sepulveda, JF, Gomez-Dantes, O, McGuinness, MJ and Knaul, F, 'The New World Order and International Health' (1997) May 10: 314 *British Medical Journal* 1404.
Shaffer, G, *Defending Interests: Public-Private Partnerships in WTO Litigation* (Washington, DC, Brookings Institution Press, 2003).
—— 'Globalization and Social Protection: The Impact of EU and International Rules in the Ratcheting Up of US Privacy Standards' (2000) 25 *Yale Journal of International Law* 1.
—— 'The Blurring of the Intergovernmental: Public–Private Partnerships behind US and EC Trade Claims' in MA Pollack and G Shaffer (eds), *Transatlantic Governance in the Global Economy* (Lanham Md, Rowman & Littlefield, 2001).
—— 'The World Trade Organization under Challenge: Democracy and the Law and Politics of the WTO's Treatment of Trade and Environment Matters' (2001) 25 *Harvard Environmental Law Review* 1.
Shambaugh, D (ed), *Power Shift: China and Asia's New Dynamics* (Berkeley, University of California Press, 2005).
Shapiro, M, 'The Globalization of Law' (1993) 37 *Indiana Journal of Global Legal Studies* 37.
Sharman, JC, *Havens in a Storm: The Struggle for Global Tax Regulation* (Ithaca, Cornell University Press, 2006).

Shelton, D (ed), *Commitment and Compliance: The Role of Non-binding Norms in the International Legal System* (Oxford, Oxford University Press, 2000).
Siebert, H, *Global Governance: An Architecture for the World Economy* (New York, Springer, 2003).
—— 'China: Coming to Grips with the New Global Player' (2007) 30(6) *The World Economy* 893.
Silbey, SS, ' "Let them eat cake": Globalization, Postmodern colonialism, and the possibilities of justice' (1997) 31 *Law and Society Review* 207.
Sinclair, TJ, 'Passing judgment: Credit rating processes as regulatory mechanisms of governance in the emerging world order' (1994) 1 *Review of International Political Economy* 133.
'Singapore, China agree on bilateral FTA', Singapore, 26 August 2006, available at http://news.webindia123.com/news/Articles/Asia/20060826/433126.html.
Singh Juss, S, *International Migration and Global Justice* (Aldershot, Ashgate, 2006).
Sinton, J, Stern, RE, Aden, NT and Levine, MT, 'Evaluation of China's Energy Strategy Options', Prepared for and with the support of the China Sustainable Energy Programme (China Energy Group, Lawrence Berkeley National Laboratory, Berkeley, Ca, 2005), available at http://china.lbl.gov/publications/nesp.pdf.
Slaughter, A-M, 'International Law in a World of Liberal States' (1995) 6 *European Journal of International Law* 503.
—— 'The Real New World Order' (1997) 75(5) *Foreign Affairs* 183.
—— 'Agencies on the loose? Holding government networks accountable' in GA Bermann, M Herdegen and PL Lindseth (eds), *Transatlantic Regulatory Cooperation: Legal Problems and Political Prospects* (New York, Oxford University Press, 2000).
—— *A New World Order* (Princeton, Princeton University Press, 2004).
Slaughter-Burley, AM, 'Law among Liberal States: Liberal Internationalism and the Act of State Doctrine' (1992) 92 *Columbia Law Review* 1907.
—— 'International Law and International Relations Theory: A Dual Agenda' (1993) 87 *American Journal of International Law* 205.
Smart, J and Smart, A, 'Personal Relations and Divergent Economies: A Case Study of Hong Kong Investment in South China' (1991) 15 *International Journal of Urban and Regional Research* 216.
Smith, R, Woodward, D, Acharya, A, Beaglehole, R and Drager, N, 'Communicable Disease Control: A "Global Public Good" Perspective' (2004) 19(5) *Health Policy and Planning* 271.
Smith, T, Sonnenfeld, DA and Naguib, D (eds), *Challenging the Chip: Labor Rights and Environmental Justice in the Global Electronic Industry* (Philadelphia, Temple University Press, 2006).
Snidal, D, 'The Limits of Hegemonic Stability Theory' (1985) 39 *International Organization* 579.
Snyder, F, *Capitalism and Legal Change: An African Transformation* (New York, Academic Press, 1981).
—— 'Anthropology, Dispute Processes and Law: A Critical Introduction' (1981) 8 *British Journal of Law and Society* 141; slightly revised version published in P Sack (ed), *Law and Anthropology* (Aldershot, Dartmouth Publishing Co, 1992); reprinted in PA Thomas (ed), *Legal Frontiers* (Aldershot, Dartmouth, 1996).
—— *New Directions in European Community Law* (London, Weidenfeld & Nicolson, 1990).
—— 'The Effectiveness of European Community Law: Institutions, Processes, Tools and Techniques' (1993) 56 *MLR* 19.
—— 'Legal Aspects of Trade between the European Union and China: Preliminary Reflections' in N Emiliou and D O'Keeffe (eds), *The European Union and World Trade Law after the GATT Uruguay Round* (Chichester, John Wiley & Sons, 1996).
—— 'General Course on European Community Law: Constitutional Law of the European Union: Principles, Processes and Culture' in *Collected Courses of the Academy of European Law 1995*, vol. VI no. 1 (Deventer, Klewer, 1998)

—— *International Trade and Customs Law of the European Union* (London, Butterworths, 1998; repub London, Tolley, 2007).

—— 'Europeanisation and Globalisation as Friends and Rivals: European Union Law in Global Economic Networks' in F Snyder (ed), *The Europeanisation of Law: The Legal Effects of European Integration* (Oxford, Hart Publishing, 2000).

—— 'Judicial Review in the Age of Globalization: Chinese Toys in the European Court of Justice' in D O'Keeffe and A Bavasso (eds), *Liber Amicorum for Gordon Slynn: Judicial Review in European Law* (London, Chancery, 2000).

—— (ed), *The Europeanisation of Law: The Legal Effects of European Integration* (Oxford, Hart Publishing, 2000).

—— 'Sites of Criminality and Sites of Governance' (2001) 10(2) *Social and Legal Studies* 251.

—— 'The Origins of the "Nonmarket Economy": Ideas, Pluralism and Power in EC Antidumping Law about China' (2001) 7 *European Law Journal* 369.

—— 'Ethique, OMC et pluralisme juridique mondial: Reflexions sur la gouvernance de la mondialisation' in JC Naudet (ed), *Mondialisation et éthique des échanges* (Marseille, Librairies de l'Université d'Aix, 2003).

—— ' The Unfinished Constitution of the European Union: Principles, Processes and Culture' in JHH Weiler and M Wind (eds), *European Constitutionalism Beyond the State* (Cambridge, Cambridge University Press, 2003).

—— 'Governing Economic Globalisation: Global Legal Pluralism and European Law' (1999) 5(4) *European Law Journal* 334; slightly shorter version published as 'Governing Globalisation', in M Likosky (ed), *Transnational Legal Processes: Globalisation and Power Disparities* (London, Butterworths LexisNexis, 2002); partly reprinted as 'Governing Economic Globalisation: Global Legal Pluralism and European Law' in S Falk Moore (ed), *Law and Anthropology: A Reader* (New York, Blackwell Publishers, 2004).

—— (ed) *International Food Security and Global Legal Pluralism/Sécurité alimentaire international et pluralisme juridique mondial* (Brussels, Bruylant, 2004).

—— 'Les sites de gouvernance' in R Mehdi and L Boisson de Chazournes (eds), *Une société internationale en mutation: quels acteurs pour une nouvelle gouvernance* (Brussels, Bruylant, 2005).

—— 'Antidumping Law and Cross-cultural Encounters: Toward a Legal Anthropology of International Economic Relations' in C Eberhard and G Vernicos (eds), *La quête anthropologique du droit: Autour de la demarche d'Etienne Le Roy* (Paris, Editions Karthala, 2006).

—— 'Toward an International Law for Adequate Food', in A Mahiou and F Snyder (eds), *La sécurité alimentaire/Food Security and Food Safety* (Leiden, Martinus Nijhoff for The Hague Academy of International Law, 2006).

—— (ed), *The European Union and China, 1949–2008: Basic Documents and Commentary* (Oxford, Hart Publishing, 2009).

Sobczak, A, *Réseaux de sociétés et codes de conduite: Un nouveau modèle de régulation des relations de travail pour les entreprises européennes*, PhD Thesis (Florence, European University Institute, 2001).

Sohn, C, 'Treatment of Non-market Economy Countries under the World Trade Organization Anti-dumping Regime' (2005) 39(4) *Journal of World Trade* 763.

Sohn, M, Sapsin, J and Gibson, E, 'Globalization, Public Health and International Law' (2004) 32(4) *Journal of Law and Medical Ethics* 87.

Stanton, GH and Wolf, C, 'Private Voluntary Standards and the World Trade Organisation (WTO) Committee on Sanitary and Phytosanitary Measures', available at http://www.agrifoodstandards.net/en/filemanager/active?fid=134.

Stein, E, 'International integration and democracy: No love at first sight' (2001) 95 *The American Journal of International Law* 489.

Steinberg, RH, 'Direct Application of Multilateral Trade Agreements in the United States' in P Demaret, JF Bellis and G García Jiménez (eds), *Regionalism and Multilateralism after the*

Uruguay Round: Convergence, Divergence and Interaction (Brussels, European Interuniversity Press, 1997).

Steiner, HJ, Alston, P and Goodman, R, *International Human Rights in Context: Law, Politics, Morals*, 3rd edn (Oxford, Oxford University Press, 2007).

Stern, B, 'Vers la mondialisation juridique?' (1996) 4 *Revue générale de droit international public* 979

Stewart, TP (ed), *The GATT Uruguay Round: A Negotiating History (1986–1992), Volume II: Commentary* (Deventer and Boston, Kluwer, 1993).

Strange, S, *States and Markets*, 2nd edn (London and Washington, Pinter, 1988).

Strange, R, Slater, J and Wang, L (eds), *Trade and Investment in China: The European Experience* (London, Routledge, 1998).

Streit, M, 'Economic Order, Private Law and Public Policy: The Freiburg School of Law and Economics in Perspective' (1992) 148 *Zeitschrift für die gesamten Staatswissenschaften/ Journal of Theoretical and Institutional Economics* 675.

Streit, M and Wohlgemuth, M, 'The Market Economy and the State: Hayekian and Ordoliberal Conceptions' in P Koslowski (ed), *The Theory of Capitalism in the German Economic Tradition: Historicism, Ordo-Liberalism, Critical Theory, Solidarism* (Berlin, Springer-Verlag, 2000).

Strzelecki, M, 'Bike Maker Shifts Gears to Exports', *The Wall Street Journal Europe*, Friday/Saturday/Sunday, 11–13 April 2003, at A5.

Stubbs, R, 'ASEAN plus Three: Emerging East Asian Regionalism?' (2002) 42(3) *Asian Survey* 440.

Sturgeon, T, *Does Manufacturing Still Matter?: The Organizational Delinking of Production from Innovation*, BRIE Working Paper 92B, Berkeley Roundtable on the International Economy, University of California at Berkeley, 1997.

Sulaiman, Elma Darlini (Attorney-General's Chambers, Brunei Darussalam), 'WTO and Regional Trade Liberalisation: Implications on ASEAN', p 9, available at www.aseanlawassociation.org/9GAdocs/w3_Brunei.pdf.

Sun, Liang and Zhang, Xiangchen, 'Redefining Development, Reimagining Globalization: The WTO and China's New Economic Vision' (2007) 41(6) *Journal of World Trade* 1275.

Sun, Xiuping, Wen, Chen and Xiansheng, Lei, *New Progress in China's Special Economic Zones* (Beijing, Foreign Languages Press, 1997).

Swaminathan, MS, 'Towards a world conservation ethics', *The Courier*, May 2000, available on the UNESCO website at http://www.unesco.org/courier/2001_12/uk/science4.htm.

'Symposium Issue: The Inaugural Engelberg Conference on the Culture and Economics of Participation in an International Intellectual Property Regime' (1996–97) 29 *New York University Journal of International Law and Economics*.

Szablowski, D, *Transnational Law and Local Struggles: Mining Communities and the World Bank* (Oxford, Hart Publishing, 2007).

Tagaras, H. 'L'effet direct des accords internationaux de la Communauté' (1984) 19 *Cahiers de Droit Européens* 15.

Tamanaha, BZ, '"The Folly of the "Social Scientific" Theory of Legal Pluralism' (Summer 1993) 20(2) *Journal of Law and Society* 192.

—— 'A Non-essentialist Version of Legal Pluralism' (2000) 27(2) *Journal of Law and Society* 296.

—— 'Understanding Legal Pluralism: Past to Present, Local to Global' (2007) 29 *Sydney Law Review* 375.

Tao, Jingzhu, *Arbitration Law and Practice in China.* (New York, Wolters Kluwer, 2008).

Taylor, AL, 'Global Governance, International Health Law and WHO: Looking towards the Future' (2002) 80(12) *Bulletin of the World Health Organization* 975.

Tempest, R, 'Barbie and the World Economy', *Los Angeles Times World Report* [A Special Section Produced in Cooperation with *The Korea Times*], Sunday, 13 October 1996, at 3.

Terry, E (ed), *Pearl River Super Zone: Tapping into the World's Fastest Growing Economy* (by the Staff and Contributors to the *South China Morning Post*) (Hong Kong, SCMP Book Publishing, 2003).

Teubner, G, 'Substantive and Reflexive Elements in Modern Law' (1983) 17 *Law & Society Review* 239.

—— (ed), *Autopietic Law: A New Approach to Law and Society* (Berlin, De Gruyter, 1988).

—— *Law as an Autopoietic System* (Oxford, Blackwell Publishers, 1993; orig pub as *Recht als autopoietisches System* (Frankfurt, Surkampf, 1989)).

—— 'The Two Faces of Janus: Rethinking Legal Pluralism' (1992) 13 *Cardozo Law Review* 1443.

—— 'The Many-headed Hydras: Networks as Higher-order Collective Actors' in J McCahery, S Picciotto and C Scott (eds), *Corporate Control and Accountability: Changing Structures and the Dynamics of Regulation* (Oxford, Clarendon Press, 1993).

—— 'Breaking Frames: The Global Interplay of Legal and Social Systems' (1997) XLV *American Journal of Comparative Law* 149.

—— (ed), *Global Law Without a State* (Dartmouth, Aldershot, 1997).

—— 'Foreword: Legal Regimes of Global Non-state Actors' in G Teubner (ed), *Global Law Without a State* (Dartmouth, Aldershot, 1997).

—— 'Global Bukowina: Legal Pluralism in the World Society' in G Teubner (ed), *Global Law Without a State* (Dartmouth, Aldershot, 1997).

—— 'Legal Irritants: Good Faith in British Law or How Unifying Law Ends Up in New Divergences' in F Snyder (ed), *The Europeanisation of Law: The Legal Effects of European Integration* (Oxford, Hart Publishing, 2000).

—— 'The Anonymous Matrix: Human Rights Violations by "Private" Transnational Actors' (2006) 69(3) *MLR* 327.

Than, M, 'China and CLMV Countries: Relations in the Context of the Mekong Sub-region' in Swee-Hock Saw (ed), *ASEAN–China Economic Relations* (Singapore, ISEAS Publishing, 2007).

The Group of Lisbon, *Limits to Competition* (Lisbon, Gulbenkian Foundation, 1993).

'The Report of the Joint Study Group on the Possible Trilateral Investment Arrangements among China, Japan and Korea', 23 December 2003, http://www.meti.go.jp/policy/trade_policy/jck/data/041129ifdi-e.pdf.

Thomas, C. 'Globalization and the Reproduction of Hierarchy' (2000) 33 *University of California at Davis Law Review* 1451.

Thomas, S, Hyacinthe, N and Sadowsky, M, 'Accord de libre-échange entre la Chine et Hong Kong: Quelles perspectives pour les entreprises de pays tiers' (2005) 1 *Revue de droit des affaires internationales* 77.

Thomas, PA (ed), *Legal Frontiers* (Aldershot, Dartmouth, 1996).

Timmermans, CA,, 'The Implementation of the Uruguay Round by the EC' in JHJ Bourgeois, JF Berrod and E Gippini Fournier (eds), *The Uruguay Round Results: A European Lawyers' Perspective* (Brussels, European Interuniversity Press, 1995).

Tomsa, Branko, *La politique commerciale commune de la CEE et les pays de l'Europe de l'Est* (Brussels, Etablissements Emile Bruylant, 1977).

Tongzon, JL, 'ASEAN–China Free Trade Area: A Bane or Boon for ASEAN Countries' (2005) 28(2) *The World Economy* 191.

Trachtman, J, 'Institutional Linkage: Transcending Trade and . . .' (2002) 96(1) The *American Journal of International Law* 77.

—— 'The Constitutions of the WTO' (2006) 17(3) *European Journal of International Law* 623.

—— 'International Regulatory Competition, Externalization, and Jurisdiction' (1993) 34(1) *Harvard International Law Journal* 47.

—— 'Bananas, Direct Effect and Compliance' (1999) 10 *European Journal of International Law* 655.

Tran, Dong, Thi Thuy, *Aspects juridiques de la participation des Etats de l'ASEAN à l'OMC*, (Paris, L'Harmattan, 2008).

Trebilcock, MJ, 'Competition Policy and Trade Policy: Mediating the Interface' (1996) 30 *Journal of World Trade* 71.

Trebilcock, MJ and Howse, R, *The Regulation of International Trade*, 2nd edn (New York, Routledge, 1999).

Triart, N, *Le role de la CJCE dans les relations entre l'ordre juridique communautaire et les traits internationaux, entre preservation de l'autonomie et respect de la communauté de droit*, Thèse de Doctorat en droit, Faculté de Droit et de Science Politique, Université Paul Cézanne Aix-Marseille III, 21 January 2009.

Trocaire, 'Conditions for Toy Workers', available at http://www.trocaire.org/toy3.html.

Trubek, DM, Mosher, J and Rothstein, JS, *Transnationalism in the Regulation of Labor Relations: International Regimes and Transnational Advocacy Networks* (Labor and the Global Economy Research Circle, The International Institute, University of Wisconsin-Madison, January 1999).

Trubek, DM, Dezalay, Y, Buchanan, R and Davis, JR, 'Global Restructuring and the Law: Studies of the Internationalization of Legal Fields and the Creation of Transnational Arenas' (1994) 44 *Case Western Reserve Law Review* 407.

Tshuma, L, 'Hierarchies and Government versus Networks and Governance, Competing Regulatory Paradigms in Global Economic Regulation' (2000) 1 *Law, Social Justice and Global Development Journal/LGD*, available at http://elj.warwick.ac.uk/global/issue/2000-1/tshuma.html.

Tsui, E, *Marketing Strategies of the Toy Industry in Hong Kong*, unpublished MBA dissertation, University of Hong Kong, 1988.

Tuan, Chyau and LFung-Yee Ng, 'FDI and Industrial Restructuring in Post-WTO Greater PRD: Implications on Regional Growth in China' (2004) 27(10) *The World Economy* 1609.

Tuchtfeldt, E, 'Will Communism and Capitalism Become Similar Economic Systems?' in A Peacock and H Willgerodt (eds), *Germany's Social Market Economy: Origins and Evolution* (London, Macmillan for the Trade Policy Research Centre, 1989).

Tumlir, J, 'International economic order and democratic constitutionalism' (1983) 34 *ORDO* 71.

Turner, M, 'The Fading Tradition of Tang the Toymaker', *International Herald Tribune*, Friday, 8 January 1999, at 8.

Twining, W, *Globalisation and Legal Theory* (London, Butterworths, 2000).

—— 'Human Rights: Southern Voices—Francis Deng, Abdullahi An-Na'im, Yash Ghai and Upendra Baxi' 2007 (1) *Law, Social Justice & Global Development Journal/LGD*, at http://www.go.warwick.ac.uk/elj/lgd/2007_1/twining; also substantially published as W Twining, ' Human Rights: Southern Voices—Francis Deng, Abdullahi An-Na'im, Yash Ghai and Upendra Baxi' (2006) 11 *Review of Constitutional Studies* 203.

United Nations, Commission on Human Rights, 'Globalization and Its Impact on the Full Enjoyment of Human Rights' available on the Internet at http://www.wtowatch.org/library.

United Nations, General Assembly, 'Resolution adopted by the General Assembly, 56/83 Responsibility of States for Internationally Wrongful Acts', Agenda Item 162, 56th Session, 28 January 2002, available at http://www.lcil.cam.ac.uk/Media/ILCSR/A_56_83(e).pdf.

—— Ad Hoc Committee on the Restructuring of the Economic and Social Sectors of the United Nations System, 'Relations of the General Agreement on Tariffs and Trade with the United Nations', Document of 9 March 1976 (A/AC.179/5), Note by the Secretariat, attached to Letter dated 29 September 1995 from the United Nations Secretary-General to the Director-General of the World Trade Organisation, in the Annex to: World Trade Organisation, General Council, 15 November 1995, 'Arrangements for Effective Cooperation with Other Intergovernmental Organisations, Relations between the WTO and the United Nations', Communication from the Director-General, WT/GC/W/10, 3 November 1995.

United States, Department of Labor, Bureau of International Affairs, 'By the Sweat and Toil of Children: A Report to Congress' (15 July 1994), available at http://www.dol.gov/dol/ilab/public/media/reports/sweat/main.htm.

United States, Department of Labor, Bureau of International Affairs, 'The Apparel Industry and Codes of Conduct: A Solution to the International Child Labor Problem?' (1996), available at http://www.dol.gov/ialb/public/media/reports/apparel/main.htm.

Van Bael, I and Bellis, JF, *Anti-Dumping and Other Trade Protection Laws of the EC*, 3rd edn (Bicester, CCH Editions, 1996).

Van de Broek, N, 'Legal Persuasion, Political Realism, and Legitimacy: The European Court's Recent Treatment of the Effect of WTO Agreements in the EC Legal Order' (2001) *Journal of International Economic Law* 411.

Van den Bossche, P, 'The European Community and the Uruguay Round Agreements' in JH Jackson and AO Sykes (eds), *Implementing the Uruguay Round* (Oxford, Oxford University Press, 1997).

Van Den Bossche, P and Alexovicova, I, 'Effective Global Economic Governance by the World Trade Organisation' (2005) 8(3) *Journal of International Economic Law* 667.

Vandenbussche, H and Wauthy, X, 'Inflicting Injury through Product Quality: How European Antidumping Policy Disadvantages European Producers' (2001) 17 *European Journal of Political Economy* 101.

Van der Geest, W, 'Bringing China into the Concert of Nations: An Analysis of its Accession to the WTO' (1998) 32 *Journal of World Trade* 99.

Van Der Grijp, N, *Regulating Pesticide Risk Reduction: The Practice and Dynamics of Legal Pluralism*, PhD thesis, University of Amsterdam (Amsterdam, VU Drukkerij, 2008).

Vander Kooi, J, 'The ASEAN Enhanced Dispute Settlement Mechanism: Doing It "the ASEAN Way"' (2007) 20 *New York International Law Review* 13.

Vandoren, P, 'Mise en oeuvre de la politique anti-dumping de la CEE contre les importations en provence des pays à commerce d'état' (1988) 316 *Revue du Marché Commun* 198.

van Kemenade, W, *China, Hong Kong, Taiwan, Inc* (trans D Webb) (New York, Alfred A Knopf, 1997).

Vermulst, EA, *Antidumping Law and Practice in the United States and the European Communities: A Comparative Analysis* (Amsterdam, Elsevier North Holland, 1987).

Vermulst, E and Driessen, B, 'New Battle Lines in the Anti-dumping War: Recent Movements on the European Front' (1997) 31(3) *Journal of World Trade* 135.

Vermulst, E and Graafsma, F, 'A Decade of European Community Anti-dumping Law and Practice Applicable to Imports from China' (1992) 26(3) *Journal of World Trade Law* 5.

Vermulst, E and Waer, P, *EC Anti-dumping Law and Practice* (London, Sweet & Maxwell, 1996).

Viner, J, *Dumping: A Problem in International Trade* (Chicago, Chicago University Press, 1923).

—— 'Conflicts of Principle in Drafting a Trade Charter' (1947) 25 *Foreign Affairs* 612.

Völker, ELM, 'Importing from East-Bloc Countries: Common Rules and Remedies for the Parties Concerned' (1985) *Legal Issues of European Integration* 99.

von Benda-Beckmann, F, 'Who's Afraid of Legal Pluralism?' (2002) 47 *Journal of Legal Pluralism and Unofficial Law* 37.

von Benda-Beckmann, K, 'Globalisation and Legal Pluralism', (2002) 4(1) *International Law Forum* 19.

von Benda-Beckmann, F, von Benda-Beckmann, K and Griffiths, A (eds), *Mobile People, Mobile Law: Expanding Legal Relations in a Contracting World* (Aldershot, Ashgate, 2005).

Von Bogdandy, A, 'Globalization and Europe: How to Square Democracy, Globalization and International Law' (2004) 15(5) *European Journal of International Law* 885.

—— 'Pluralism, direct effect and the ultimate say: On the Relationship between International and Domestic Constitutional Law' (2008) 6(3)–(4) *International Journal of Constitutional Law* 397.

Von Bogdandy, A and Makatsch, T, 'Collision, Co-existence or Co-operation? Prospects for the Relationship between WTO Law and European Union Law' in G de Búrca and J Scott (eds), *The EU and the WTO: Legal and Constitutional Issues* (Oxford, Hart Publishing, 2001).

Von Struensee, V, 'Sex Trafficking: A Plea for Action' (2002) 6 *European Law Journal* 379.

Wagner, R, 'ORDO Liberalism and the Social Market Economy' in HG Berman and AMC Waterman (eds), *Economics and Religion: Are They Distinct?* (Dordrecht, Kluwer, 1994).

Wahab, M, 'Globalisaton and ODR: Dynamics of Change in E-Commerce Dispute Settlement' (2004) 12(1) *International Journal of Law & Information Technology* 123.

Wai, CK, 'Child Labor in China (Change HKCIC-June 1996)', at http://www.citinv.it/associazioni/CNMS/archivio/lavoro/childlab.html, last visited 17 March 2010.

Wai-chung Yeung, H, *Transnational Corporations and Business Networks: Hong Kong Firms in the ASEAN Region* (London, Routledge, 1998).

Walder, AG, 'Local Government as Industrial Firm: An Organizational Analysis of China's Transitional Economy' (1995) 101(2) *American Journal of Sociology* 263.

Walker, N, 'The EU and the WTO: Constitutionalism in a New Key' in G de Búrca and J Scott (eds), *The EU and the WTO: Legal and Constitutional Issues* (Oxford, Hart Publishing, 2001).

—— 'The Idea of Constitutional Pluralism' (2002) 65(3) *MLR* 317.

—— 'Beyond Boundary Disputes and Basic Grids: Mapping the Global Disorder of Normative Orders' (2008) 6 *International Journal of Constitutional Law: I-CON* 373.

Walt, G, 'Globalisation of International Health', 7 February 1998 351(9100), *Lancet*, 434.

Wang, Guiguo, *The Law of the WTO: China and the Future of Free Trade* (Hong Kong, Sweet & Maxwell Asia, 2005).

Wang, Bashu, 'China's Accession to the WTO and the Building of a Socialist Market Economy Legal System' in Wang Mengkui (ed), *China: Accession to the WTO and Economic Reform* (Beijing, Foreign Languages Press, 2002).

Wang, Gungwu, 'China and Southeast Asia: The Context of a New Beginning' in TW Robinson and D Shambaugh (eds), *Chinese Foreign Policy, Theory and Practice* (Oxford, Clarendon Press, 1994).

Wang, Jianwei, 'China's Multilateral Diplomacy in the New Millennium' in Yong Deng and Fei-Ling Wang (eds), *China Rising: Power and Motivation in Chinese Foreign Policy* (Lanham, Md, Rowman & Littlefield, 2005).

Wang, Jianyu, 'A Critique of the Application to China of the Non-market Economy Rules of Antidumping Legislation and Practice of the European Union' (1999) 33(3) *Journal of World Trade* 117.

—— 'China's Regional Trade Agreements: The Law, Geopolitics and Impact on the Multilateral Trading System' (2004) 8 *Singapore Year Book of International Law* 119.

—— 'The International Legal Personality of ASEAN and the Legal Nature of the China–ASEAN FTA' in J Wong, Zou Keyuan and Zeng Huaqun (eds), *China–ASEAN Relations: Economic and Legal Dimensions* (Singapore, World Scientific, 2006).

—— 'ASEAN–China Free Trade Agreement: Legal and Institutional Aspects' in Swee-Hock, Saw (ed), *ASEAN–China Economic Relations* (Singapore, ISEAS Publishing, 2007).

Wang, Jisi, 'International Relations Theory and the Study of Chinese Foreign Policy: A Chinese Perspective' in TW Robinson and D Shambaugh (eds), *Chinese Foreign Policy. Theory and Practice* (Oxford, Clarendon Press, 1994; reprint 2006).

Wang, Kui Hua, *Chinese Commercial Law* (Victoria, Australia, Oxford University Press, 2000).

Wang, Lei, 'China's Difficulties and Concerns as a Respondent to Antidumping Proceedings' (1996) 19 *World Competition* 55.

Wang, Tieya, 'International Law in China: Historical and Contemporary Perspectives' *Recueil des Cours de l'Académie de Droit International de La Haye*, vol 221 (1990-II) 205.

Wank, DL, *Commodifying Chinese Communism: Business, Trust and Politics in Xiamen* (Cambridge, Cambridge University Press, 1998).

Wares, WA, *The Theory and Practice of American Commercial Policy* (Lexington, Mass, Lexington Books, 1977).

Watrin, C, 'Alfred Mıller-Armack—Economic Policy Marker and Sociologist of Religion' in P Koslowski (ed), *The Theory of Capitalism in the German Economic Tradition: Historicism, Ordo-Liberalism, Critical Theory, Solidarism* (Berlin, Springer-Verlag, 2000).

Weber, M, *Max Weber on Law in Economy and Society* (ed M Rheinstein, trans E Shils and M Rheinstein) (Cambridge, Mass, Harvard University Press, 1966).

Wei, Dan, 'China's Regional Trade Agreements: Implications and Comments' (2009) 6(1) *Manchester Journal of International Economic Law* 81.

Weiler, JHH, ' In Defence of the Status Quo: Europe's Constitutonal *Sonderweg*' in J Weiler, and M Wind (eds), *European Constitutonalism Beyond the State* (Cambridge, Cambridge University Press, 2003).

Weiss, F, 'From World Trade Law to World Competition Law' (2000) 23 *Fordham International Law Journal* S250.

—— 'Globalisation through WTO Integration: Neither Friend Nor Foe' (2003) 30(2) *Legal Issues of European Integration* 95.

Wellenstein, E, 'The Relations of the European Communities with Eastern Europe' in D O'Keeffe and HG Schermers (eds), *Essays in European Law and Integration* (Deventer, Kluwer, 1982).

Wen, Chen 'ASEAN–China Trade Relations: Origins, Progress and Prospect' in Swee-Hock Saw (ed), *ASEAN–China Economic Relations* (Singapore, ISEAS Publishing, 2007).

Wen, Hui, 'Macao granted better access to Chinese mainland', *China Economic News*, 8 June 2009, at 6.

Wen, Jiabao, Premier of the State Council of the People's Republic of China, 'Strengthening Partnership Through Increased Dialogue and Cooperation', Speech at the Fifth Asia-Europe Meeting, Hanoi, 8 October 2004, reprinted in F Snyder (ed), *The European Union and China, 1949–2008: Basic Documents and Commentary* (Oxford, Hart Publishing, 2009).

—— 'Strengthening ASEM Economic and Financial Cooperation to Promote Common Development', Speech at the Opening Ceremony of the Sixth ASEM Finance Ministers Meeting, 26 June 2005; reprinted in F Snyder, *The European Union and China, 1949–2008: Basic Documents and Commentary* (Oxford, Hart Publishing, 2009).

Wieacker, F, 'Foundations of European Legal Culture' (1990) 38 *American Journal of Comparative Law* 1.

Wiener, JB, 'Something Borrowed or Something Blue: Legal Transplants and the Evolution of Global Environmental Law' (2001) 27 *Ecology Law Quarterly* 1295.

Wiers, J, *Trade and Environment in the EC and the WTO: A Legal Analysis* (Groningen, Europa Law Publishing, 2002).

Wilcynski, J, 'Dumping and Central Planning' (1996) 74 *Political Economy* 250.

Wilson, RA (ed), *Human Rights, Culture and Context: Anthropological Perspectives* (London, Pluto Press, 1997).

Wolf, RC, *Trade, Aid and Arbitrate: The Globalization of Western Law* (Aldershot, Ashgate/Dartmouth, 2004).

Wong, J, Zou Keyuan and Zeng Huaqun (eds), *China–ASEAN Relations: Economic and Legal Dimensions* (Singapore, World Scientific Publishing Company, 2006).

Woodman, GR, 'Ideological Combat and Social Observation: Recent Debate about Legal Pluralism' (1998) 42 *Journal of Legal Pluralism* 21.

World Bank Group, 'China Data and Statistics', at http://web.worldbank.org/WBSITE/EXTERNAL/COUNTRIES/EASTASIPADIFICHN.

—— 'China Data Profile', at http://devdta.worldbank.org/external/CPProfile.asp?PTYPE=CP&CCODE=CHN., accessed 2 April 2008.

—— 'China Quick Facts', at http://web.worldbank.org/WBSITE/EXTERNAL/COUNTRIES/EASTASIAPACIFICEXT/CHINAEXTN/0,,contentMDK:20680895~pagePK:1497618~piPK:217854~theSitePK:318950,00.html, accessed 3 April 2008.

World Commission on the Social Dimensions of Globalisation, *A Fair Globalisation: Creating Opportunities for All* (Geneva, ILO, 2004), available http://www.ilo.org/public/english/wcsdg/docs/report.pdf, last accessed 4 March 2010

World Customs Organisation, *Handbook: International Convention on the Simplification and Harmonization of Customs Procedures* (Kyoto, 18 May 1973), 1st edn October 1975, Amending Supplement No 13, January 1993.

—— General Secretariat, 'Position as regards ratifications and accessions (as of 30 June 2008)', International Convention on the simplification and harmonisation of customs procedures (as amended), available at http://www.wcoomd.org/files/1.%20Public%20files/PDFandDocuments/Conventions/PG0156E1.pdf.

World Health Organisation, 'Food Safety and Globalization of Trade in Food: A Challenge to the Public Health Sector', Food Safety Unit, Programme of Food Safety and Food Aid, World Health Organization, WHO/FSF/FOS/97.8.Rev 1 (1997).

World Health Organisation and World Trade Organisation, 'WTO Agreements and Public Health: A Joint Study by the WHO and the WTO Secretariat', 2002.

World Intellectual Property Organisation (WIPO), *General Rules of Procedure*, WIPO Publication No 399 (FE) Rev 3, Rule 8(2) (Geneva, WIPO, 1990).

World Trade Organisation, 'An Integrated Framework for Trade Related Technical Assistance, including for Human and Institutional Capacity-Building, to Support Least-developed Countries in Their Trade and Trade-Related Activities: Revision', WT/LDS/HL/1/Rev.1, 23 October 1997 (97-4650), available on the WTO website at http://www.wto.org/english/trratop_d/devel-e/framework.htm.

—— 'Annotated Checklist of Issues Raised by Delegations', Agreements between the WTO and the IMF and the World Bank, World Trade Organisation Restricted WT/GC/W/140, 3 February 1999 (99/0400), both available on the WTO website at http://docsonline.wto.org/GEN_viewerwindow.asp?D:DDFDOCUMENTS/T/WT/GC/W.

—— Appellate Body Secretariat (compiler), *WTO Appellate Body: Repertory of Reports and Awards 1995–2006* 3rd edn (Cambridge, Cambridge University Press, 2007).

'Coherence—closer cooperation between multilateral institutions', available on the WTO website at http://www.wto.org/english/thewto_e/coher_e/coher_e.htm.

—— Committee on Regional Trade Agreements, 'Rules of Origin in Regional Trade Agreements: Background Survey by the Secretariat', WT/REG/W/45, 5 April 2002, available at http://docsonline.wto.org/DDFDocuments/t/WT/REG/W45.doc.

—— Committee on Sanitary and Phytosanitary Measures, 'Committee looks at equivalence, transparency, diseases and GMOs', WTO News: 2001 News Items, Sanitary and Phytosanitary Measures Committee 31 October–1 November 2001, available on the WTO website at http://www.wto.org/english/news_e/news01_e/sps_nov2001_e.htm.

—— Committee on Sanitary and Phytosanitary Measures, Decision on the Implementation of Article 4 of the Agreement on the Application of Sanitary and Phytosanitary Measures (G/SPS/19), available on the WTO website at http://www.wto.org/english/tratop_e/sps_e/equivalence2001_e.htm.

—— Committee on Sanitary and Phytosanitary Measures, Draft Agreement between the World Trade Organisation and the Office International des Epizooties (OIE), Note by the Secretariat, G/SPS/W/61, 22 May 1996.

—— Committee on Sanitary and Phytosanitary Measures. Procedure to monitor the progress of international harmonisation, Third Annual Report, Committee on Sanitary and Phytosanitary Measures, World Trade Organisation (G/SPS/18), 19 September 2001 (01-4453), available on the WTO website at http://docsonline.wto.org/GEN_viewerwindow.asp?D:/DDFDOCUMENTS/T/G/SPS/18.D.

—— Committee on Sanitary and Phytosanitary Measures, 'Report (2001) on the Activities of the Committee on Sanitary and Phytosanitary Measures', point 9, World Trade Organization, G/L/485, 4 October 2001 (01-4796), available on the WTO website at http://docsonline.wto.org/GEN_viewerwindow.asp?D:/DDFDOCUMENTS/T/G/L/485.DO.

—— Committee on Technical Barriers to Trade, 'Problems Faced by Developing Countries in International Standards and Conformity Assessment', Discussions of the TBT Committee in

the context of the Second Triennial Review of the TBT Agreement, Report by the Chairman, G/L/422, 29 November 2000, available at http://www.wtocenter. org.tw/SMARTKMS/file-viewer?id=47720.
—— Committee on Trade and Environment, Special Session, 'Existing forms of cooperation and Information exchange Between UNEP/MEAs and the WTO', Note by the Secretariat of the Committee, Document No: TN/TE/S/2/Rev.2_16 January 2007.
—— Committee on Trade and Environment, Special Session, 'Matrix on Trade Measures pursuant to Selected Multilateral Environmental Agreements', Note by the Secretariat of the Committee, Document No: WT/CTE/W/160/Rev.4, TN/TE/S/5/Rev.2 14 March 2007.
—— Committee on Trade and Environment, Special Session, 'Observer Status: Note by the Secretariat', TN/TE/S/4, 31 January 2003.
—— Council for Trade-Related Aspects of Intellectual Property Rights. Text of Proposed 'Agreement between the World Intellectual Property Organisation and the World Trade Organisation', IP/C/6, 13 December 1995.
—— 'Cooperation avec d'autres organisations internationales', available on the WTO website at http://www.wto.org/french/tratop_f/envir_f/envir_coop_with-other-inter_org_f.htm.
—— Director General, Renato Ruggiero, 'A Shared Responsibility: Global Policy Coherence for our Global Age', 1998, Speech by the Director General of the World Trade Organisatoin, at http://www.wto.org/english/news_e/sprr_e/bonn_e.htm.
—— 'Elements of Cooperation between the WTO and UNEP', WTO News: 1999 Press Releases, Press/1`54, 29 November 1999, available on the WTO website at http://www.wto.org/english/news_e/pres99_e/pr154_e.htm.
—— General Council, Arrangements for Effective Cooperation with Other Intergovernmental Organisations, Relations between the WTO and the United Nations, Communication from the Director-General, WT/GC/W/10, 3 November 1995, WTO General Council, 15 November 1995.
—— General Council, Minutes of Meeting held in the Centre William Rappard on 7, 8 and 13 November 1996, point 7, WT/GC/M/16, 6 December 1996.
—— 'Guidelines for Arrangements on Relations with Non-Governmental Organizations', Decision adopted by the General Council on 18 July 1996, WT/L/162, 23 July 1996, available on the WTO website at http://www.wto.org/english/forums_e/ngo-e/guide_e.htm.
—— Integrated Framework Steering Committee, 'Joint Communique by the Six Core Agencies of the Integrated Framework—IMF, ITC, UNCTAD, UNDP, World Bank and WTO', World Trade Organisation WT/IFSC/1, 28 February 2002 (02-1004), available on the WTO website at http://docsonline.wto.org/GEN_viewerwindow.asp?D:DDFDOCUMENTS/T/WT/IFSC.
—— 'International intergovernmental organisations granted observer status to WTO bodies', available at http://www.wto.org/english/theWTO_e/igo_obs_e.htm.
—— 'Joint release: WTO and OIE, WTO and the Office International des Epizooties sign cooperation agreement', WTO News: 1998 Press Releases, Press/99, 4 May 1998, available on the WTO website at http://www.wto.org/english/news_e/pres98_/pr99_e.htm.
—— Non Governmental Organisations (NGOs) Symposium: 'Symposium on issues confronting the world trading system—summary reports by the moderators', 6 and 7 July 2001, World Trade Organisation, Geneva, Session I: Food Safety and the SPS Agreement, Saturday 7 July 2001, available at http://www.wto.org/english/forums_e/ngo-e/ngo_symp2001_repsps_e.htm.
—— 'Participation of Developing Countries in the Development and Application of International Standards, Guidelines and Recommendations on Food Safety, Animal and Plant Health: A Joint Statement by the Directors-General of the Food and Agricultural Organisation of the United Nations, the Office International des Epizooties, the World Health Organisation, the World Trade Organisation and the World Bank', in 'Agencies to boost developing countries' participation in setting food safety and related norms', WTO News: 2001 Press Releases, Press/254, 11 November 2001, available on the WTO website at http://www.wto.org/english/news_e/pres01_e/pr254_e.htm.

—— 'Regional Trade Agreements: Early Announcements made to the WTO under the RTA Transparency Mechanism', available at http://www.wto.org/english/tratop_e/region_e/early_announc_e.xls,.

—— 'Report by the Director-General on Implementation of the Agreements', Agreements between the WTO and the IMF and the World Bank, World Trade Organisation WT/GC/W/68, 13 November 1967 (97-5040), available on the WTO website at http://docsonline.wto.org/GEN_viewerwindow.asp?D:DDFDOCUMENTS/T/WT/GC/W.

—— Report (2000) by the Director-General, Coherence in Global Policy-Making: WTO Cooperation with the IMF and the World Bank, World Trade Organisation Restricted WT/TF/COH/S/4, 14 December 2000 (00-5474), available on the WTO website at http://docsonline.wto.org/GEN_viewerwindow.asp?D:DDFDOCUMENTS/T/WT/TF/C.

—— Report of the Working Party on the Accession of China, Ministerial Conference, Fourth Session, Doha, 9–13 September 2001, WT/MIN(01)/3, 10 November 2001.

—— 'Rules of Procedure for Sessions of the Ministerial Conference and Meetings of the General Council', Annex 2: Guidelines for Observer Status for Governments in the WTO, Annex 3: Observer Status for International Intergovernmental Organisations in the WTO, WT/L/161, 25 July 1996.

—— Secretariat, Note by the Secretariat, 'WTO Cooperation with the IMF and the World Bank and Greater Coherence in Global Economic Policy-Making', World Trade Organisation (94-2226), Sub-Committee on Institutional, Procedural and Legal Matters, Preparatory Committee PC/IPL/W/10, 31 October 1994, available on the WTO website at http://docsonline.wto.org/GEN_viewerwindow.asp?D:/DDFDOCUMENTS/T/WT/PCIP.

—— 'Statement by the Director-General on Consultations and Coherence' Addendum to the Agreement between the WTO and the IMF and the World Bank, World Trade Organisation WT/L/194/Add.1, 18 November 1996 (96-4879), available on the WTO website at http://docsonline.wto.org/GEN_viewerwindow.asp?D:/DDFDOCUMENTS/T/WT/L/194.

—— *The Results of the Uruguay Round of Multilateral Trade Negotiations: The Legal Texts* (WTO, Geneva, 1995).

—— 'Trade and Labour Standards: A Difficult Issue for Many WTO Member Governments', Doha WTO Ministerial 2001: Briefing Notes, available on the WTO website at http://www.wto.org/english/thewto_e/minist_e/min01_e/brief_e/brief16_e.htm

—— 'Trading into the Future: The Introduction to the WTO: Beyond the agreements: The environment—a new high profile' at http://www.wto.org/english/thewto_e/whatis_e/tif_e/bey4_e,htm.

'Work on Private Food Health and Safety Standards Moves to New Phase', WTO 2009 New Items, 25–26 February 2009, available at http://www.wto.org/english/news_e/news09_e/sps_25feb09_e.htm.

—— 'WTO Agreements with the Fund and the Bank', World Trade WT/GC/W/43, 4 November 1996 (96-4680), available on the WTO website at http://www.wto.org.

—— WTO Agreements with the Fund and the Bank, approved by the General Council at its meeting on the 7, 8 and 13 November 1996, Annex I: Agreement between the International Monetary Fund and the World Trade Organisation, WT/L/95, 18 November 1996.

—— *WTO Analytical Index: Guide to WTO Law and Practice*, 2 vols, 2nd edn (Cambridge, Cambridge University Press, 2007).

—— 'WTO and IMF sign cooperation agreement', WTO News: 1996 Press Releases, Press/62, 9 December 1996, available on the WTO website at http://www.wto.org/english/news_e/pres96_e/pr062_e.htm.

—— 'WTO and WIPO join forces to help developing countries meet year-2000 commitments on intellectual property', WTO News: 1998 Press Releases, Press/1`08, 21 July 1998, available on the WTO website at http://www.wto.org/english/news_e?pres98_e/ pr108_e.htm.

—— 'WTO and World Bank sign cooperation agreement', Press/72, 28 April 1997, available on the WTO website at http://www.wto.org/english/news_e/pres97_e/pr72_e.htm.

—— 'WTO technical cooperation', available on the WTO website at http://www.wto.org/english/thewto_e/whatis_e/tif_e/dev3_e.htm.

Wilcynski, J, 'Dumping and Central Planning' (1996) 74 *Political Economy* 250.

Wong, J, 'China–ASEAN Relations: An Economic Perspective' in J Wong, Zou Keyuan and Zeng Huaqun (eds), *China–ASEAN Relations: Economic and Legal Dimensions* (Singapore, World Scientific Publishing Co, 2006).

Wu, Chong, 'Folding bikes perfect answer to traffic jams', *China Daily*, Saturday, 3 December 2005, at 4.

Wu, Xiaochen, *Anti-dumping Law and Practice of China* (Alphen aan den Rijn, Wolters Kluwer, 2009).

Xinhua News Agency, 'China, Chile put free trade agreement into effect', *People's Daily Online*, 1 October 2006, available at http://english.peopledaily.com.cn/200610/01/eng20061001_308052.html.

Yach, D and Bettcher, D, 'The Globalization of Public Health, II: The Convergence of Self-interest and Altruism' (1998) 88(5) *American Journal of Public Health* 738.

Yahuda, M, 'The Evolving Asian Order: The Accommodation of Rising Chinese Power' in D Shambaugh (ed), *Power Shift: China and Asia's New Dynamics* (Berkeley, University of California Press, 2006).

—— 'How Much Has China Learned about Interdependence?' in DSG Goodman and G Segal (eds), *China Rising: Nationalism and Interdependence* (London, Routledge, 1997).

Yannopoulos, N, 'EC External Commercial Policies and East–West Trade in Europe' (1985) 24(1) *Journal of Common Market Studies* 21.

Yasuaki, O, 'A Transcivilizational Perspective on Global Legal Order in the Twenty-first Century: A Way to Overcome West-Centric and Judiciary-Centric Deficits in International Legal Thoughts' (2006) 8(1) *International Community Law Review* 29.

Yeung, Henry, WC, *Transnational Corporations and Business Networks: Hong Kong Firms in the ASEAN Region* (London, Routledge, 1998).

Yeung, Yue-man, 'The Pan-PRD and ASEAN–China FTA as Agents of Regional Integration in Pacific Asia', Keynote address, Forum on A Tale of Two Regions: China's Pan-PRD and ASEAN, Gold Coast Hotel, Hong Kong, 4 November 2005, available at http://www.hkpri.org.hk/passagesPDF/othersSpeech/2005/Prof.%20Yeung's%20Speech.pdf, visited 20 March 2008.

Young, MA, The WTO's Use of Relevant Rules of International Law: An Analysis of the Biotech Case' (2007) 56(4) *International and Comparative Law Quarterly* 907.

Young, OR, 'International Regimes: Problems of Concept Formation' (1980) 32 *World Politics* 331.

Yuan, Cheng, *East–West Trade: Changing Patterns in Chinese Foreign Trade Law and Institutions* (New York, Oceana, 1991).

Zacher, M (with Sutton, BA), *Governing Global Networks: International Regimes for Transportation and Communications* (Cambridge, Cambridge University Press, 1996).

Zeng, Huaqun, 'WTO Rules and China–ASEAN FTA Agreement', in J Wong, Zou Keyuan and Zeng Huaqun (eds), *China–ASEAN Relations: Economic and Legal Dimensions* (Singapore, World Scientific, 2006).

Zeng Lingliang, 'A Preliminary Perspective on Negotiations for an EU–China PCA: A New Bottle Carrying Old Wine, or New Wine in Old Bottles, or Both?' (2008) 14(5) *European Law Journal* 121.

—— 'ASEAN–China Relations: An International Law Perspective', in J Wong, Zou Keyuan and Zeng Huaqun (eds), *China–ASEAN Relations: Economic and Legal Dimensions* (Singapore, World Scientific, 2006).

Zhang, Jin, 'FTA talks switched to fast track', *China Daily*, 27 August 2004.

Zhang, Qi, 'Integration proves profitable for multinationals', *China Daily*, Friday, 17 October 2008, at 15.

Zhang, Yunling and Tang, Shiping, 'China's Regional Strategy' in D Shambaugh (ed), *Power Shift: China and Asia's New Dynamics* (Berkeley, University of California Press, 2005).
Zhang, Xin, 'Where Angels Dare to Tread' (trans JA Mathews), in *Contemporary Chinese Women Writers VI: Four Novellas by Zhang Xin* (Panda Books and Chinese Literature Press, 1998).
Ziegler, C, *Favored Flowers: Culture and Economy in the Global System* (Durham, Duke University Press, 2007).
Zifcak, S (ed), *Globalisation and the Rule of Law* (London, Routledge, 2005).
Zonnekeyn, G, 'The Legal Status of WTO Panel Reports in the EC Legal Order: Some Reflections on the Opinion of Advocate General Mischo in the Atlanta Case' (1999) *Journal of International Economic Law* 713.
—— 'The Latest on Indirect Effect of WTO law in the EC Legal Order: The Nakajima Case Law Misjudged?' (2001) 4(3) *Journal of International Economic Law* 597.
—— 'The status of adopted panel and Appellate Body reports in the European Court of Justice and the Court of First Instance' (2000) 34 *Journal of World Trade* 93.
—— 'The Status of WTO Law in the EC Legal Order: The Final Curtain?' (2000) 34 *Journal of World Trade* 111.
Zumbansen, P, 'Piercing the Legal Veil: Commercial Arbitration and Transnational Law' (2002) 8 *European Law Journal* 400.
—— ' "New Governance" in European Corporate Law Regulation as Transnational Legal Pluralism' (2009) 15(2) *European Law Journal* 246.
Zürn, M, *Interessen und Institutionen in der internationalen Politik: Grundlegung und Anwendungen des situationsstrukturellen Ansatzes* (Opladen, Leske & Budrich, 1992).
—— 'Intra-German Trade: An Early East–West Regime' in V Rittberger (ed), *International Regimes in East–West Politics* (London and New York, Frances Pinter Publishers, 1990).
Zweig, D and Bi, Jianhai, 'China's Global Hunt for Energy', *Foreign Affairs*, 25 September–October 2005, at 25.
Zysman, J and Schwartz, A, 'Reunifying Europe in an Emerging World Economy: Economic Heterogeneity, New Industrial Options, and Political Choices' (1998) 36 *Journal of Common Market Studies* 405.
—— (eds), *Enlarging Europe: The Industrial Foundations of a New Political Reality* (Berkeley, University of California at Berkeley, 1998).

Index

Abbott, F 387
Abbott, KW 18, 401
Accell Group NV 124
accounting, international standards agencies 16–17
ACFTA *see* ASEAN-China FTA
Agreement on Trade-related Aspects of Intellectual Property (TRIPS) 16
Agrover case 307–8
Alston, P 39
Aman, AC 37
Americanisation 15–16
analogue country approach 241–2, 243, 258–9
animal health and food safety 409
Annan, Koffi 39, 404
Anti-dumping Code (1979) 244
anti-dumping law
  Cold War divisions 218–19, 229
  and customs procedures 315–19
  as economic buffer 91
  economic regulation and 115–19
  effectiveness 134–7
  European *see* EU law; European Commission
  in European courts 157–8, 160–2
  Europeanisation 236–8
  Exemption Regulation development 115–19, 127–9 *Table*, 136–7
  and global legal pluralism 214–15
  meaning of dumping 5
  as policy instrument 90–1
  politicisation 141 *Table*
  pre-WWII origins 215–18
  as protectionism 90
  regulating international competition 91
  scenarios 138–41
  significant sites for 261–2
antitrust law 14
Antkiewicz, A 378
APEC (Asia-Pacific Economic Cooperation) 339
appellate body reports (WTO) 175–8
arbitration, international commercial 31
ASEAN Regional Forum (ARF) 339, 367–8
ASEAN-China Agreement on Goods 343–4
ASEAN-China Agreement on Services 345–6
ASEAN-China FTA (ACFTA) 340–5
  dispute resolution mechanisms 365–8
  economic benefits 341
  objectives 342–3
  rationales 377
  ROOs 357–8, 359 *Table*
  safeguards 361–2
  signatories 340
  subsequent agreements 343–5
ASEM (Asia-Europe Meeting) 339
Ash, R 337
Asia-Europe Meeting (ASEM) 339
Asia-Pacific Economic Cooperation (APEC) 339
ASM Lithography case 306–7
Association of the European Two-wheeler Parts and Accessories Association (COLIPED) 133
autopoesis 30–1

Bai Lin 21
Baldwin, R 337, 379–80
banking supervision 17, 37
Barbie doll production 44–5
Basel Committee for Banking Supervision 17, 37
Berman, PS 41
bicycle industry *see* European bicycle industry; world bicycle industry
Bicycles from China case 3, 271–3, 276
Bicycles from Czechoslovakia case 224–5, 229, 243
Bike Europe (website) 131
biodiversity/plant genetic resources 410–13
Bourdieu, P 13
Bourgeois, J 201
Braithwaite, J 28–9
Bratton, WW 400
BRICSAM countries 16, 37
Brittan, Sir Leon 115
Bronckers, M 33
Büchel & Co 118
business contracts, international 14

Cassis de Dijon case 255–6
Central Asian Regional Economic Cooperation (CAREC) Programme 338
Central and Eastern European Countries (CEECs) 132
centrally administered economy 254
China
  domestic market 135–6
  economic integration agreements *see* Hong Kong; Macao
  as economic power 323–4
  economic/legal transformation 14
  foreign policy 325
  government role 104–5
  IIT with OECD countries 291–2
  interaction with EU 274–5
  labour control 72
  as non-market economy 210–11, 266
  personal relationships 326
  policy process 325–6
  regional policy 324, 326
  regional trade agreements
    basic arguments 326–7
    bilateral 346–9
    categories 376
    with Chile *see* China-Chile FTA
    China-Pakistan FTA 352–3

China (*cont.*):
regional trade agreements (*cont.*):
conclusion 376–80
DSMs *see* dispute resolution mechanisms (DSMs)
economic integration agreements *see* Hong Kong; Macao
FTAs *see* ASEAN-China FTA; China-Chile FTA; China-Pakistan FTA
models 377–8
multilateral 337–40
'noodle bowl' syndrome 379–80
notified to April 2009 328–31
Pearl River Delta 335–6
rationales 376–7
ROOs *see* rules of origin
safety *see* safety
relations with EU 278–82, 339–40
relations with West 249–50, 256
special economic zones (SEZS) 68–9, 277
trade with EU 290–1, 294–5
China Bicycle Association 135
China Bicycle Company 111–12, 136
see also Shanghai Bicycle Corporation
China-Chile FTA 349–52, 353
co-operation framework 350–1
DSM 368–70
ROOs 358
safeguards 362–3
and TRIPS 351–2
and WTO agreements 349–50
China-Pakistan FTA 352–3
DSM 369–70
ROOs 358, 359
safeguards 363
Chinese Bicycles case 89–90, 94, 271–3
analysis *see* European bicycle industry; European Commission
chronology of saga 142–50
EBMA protection search 95–7, 109–10, 118–19, 120
globalisation effects 140, 141
phases 123–9, 138
results 134–7
see also European bicycle industry; world bicycle industry
Coberco Dairy Foods case 309
Codex Alimentarius Commission 395
Cold War divisions
anti-dumping law 218–19, 229
and non-market economies 261, 264
COLIBI 133
COLIPED (Association of the European Two-wheeler Parts and Accessories Association) 133
commercial arbitration, international 31
Commission v Denmark 307
Commission v Netherlands 304
commodity chains 5
competition policy, antitrust law and 14
constitutional sites 52–3
constitutionalisation 421
contracts
and globalisation 26
international business 14
controlled economy country 262
Coombe, RJ 13
cooperative deliberation 413–15
coordination role 422–3
corporate government matrix 400
criminal law 14–15
criminal tribunals, international 15
cultural diversity 410
customs procedures
and anti-dumping law 315–19
see also under inward/outward processing traffic
cybercrime 14
Cycles Mercier 131
Czechoslovakia 224–5, 232, 234

de-nationalisation 13–14
debt security rating agencies 16–17
Decathlon 130
Delmas-Marty, M 33, 40
Deng Xiaoping 95
Denmark, bicycle quotas 95–6
Dent, C 378
development issues 382
Dezalay, Y 31, 38, 87
direct effect (EU), and WTO law 165–78
agreements (WTO) 166–74
background 165–6
dispute settlement processes (WTO), outcomes 174–8
interpretative obligation 195–9, 204–5
jurisprudence constante 167–74
dispute resolution mechanisms (DSMs)
and China's RTAs 363–76
ACFTA 365–8
China-Chile FTA 368–70
China-Pakistan FTA 369–70
comparison summary 363–4
Mainland-Hong Kong CEPA 364–5
WTO/NAFTA comparisons 370–6
WTO dispute settlement processes 418–21
distributed governance 387
distribution of powers 191–9
Doha Round of Multilateral Trade Negotiations 389
domestic sovereignty 15
Drahos, P 28–9
DSMs *see* dispute resolution mechanisms
dumping *see* anti-dumping law

economic liberalisation 34–5, 36
Eichsfelder case 313
environmental issues 397, 403–4
environmental law, international 14, 24–5
Eridania Beghin-Say case 308
ethics *see* social solidarity ethics
ETRA (European Twowheel Retailers' Association 133
EU
institutions, and WTO law 156–65
IPT *see* inward/outward processing traffic
relations with China 278–82
trade with China 290–1, 294–5, 339–40

EU law
anti-dumping law
administrative discretion 239, 241
analogue country approach 241–2, 243
EC circumventions 109–11, 114, 126–7, 133, 282–3
EC legislation 98–9
first legislation 238–9
innovation 262–3
normative mistranslation 239 41
breaches of WTO law *see* World Trade Organisation law, EU breaches
compatibility with WTO law 156
direct effect *see* direct effect (EU), and WTO law
foreign trade in goods law 234–6
foundational period 234–5
impact on WTO law 153–5, 203–8
and IPNs 286–7
legality criteria from WTO law 178–88
clear reference exception 181–2
general principle 178–80
necessity principle 180–1
transposition exception 182–8, 205–6
member states
monitoring/enforcement of WTO obligations 201–3, 207–8
powers 192–5
and national courts, interpretative obligations 195–9, 204–5
national law harmonisation, WTO basis 199–201, 206–8
EU legal order, WTO law and 155–6
Eucken, W 254
European bicycle industry
bicycle quotas (Denmark) 95–6
dumping
established 100
export price 102
injury determination 102–3
margin 102
normal values 100–2
public interest test 103
imports 111–12, 119–20, 131–2, 134–5
market sources 99–100
restructuring 130–2, 134
structure 116, 118–19, 120–2
see also world bicycle industry
European Bicycle Manufacturers Association (EBMA) 92
decline 132–4, 140
protection search 95–7, 109–10, 118–19, 120, 137
European Commission 93
Chinese bicycles analysis 97–103
confirmation 104–5
Exemption Regulation development 115–19, 127–9 *Table*, 136–7
interpretation of WTO law 158–9
legal strategy 137
market economy treatment (MET) 122, 125–6
see also anti-dumping law
European Council, interpretation of WTO law 159–60
European courts
interpretation of WTO law 157–8
post-Lisbon Treaty 153
use of WTO law 160–5
European Twowheel Retailers' Association (ETRA) 133
Exemption Regulation development 115–19, 127–9 *Table*, 136–7

Falk Moore, S 29, 49–50, 52
Falkner, R 24
family law 14
FAO, plant/animal health and food safety 409
Financial Action Task Force on Money Laundering (FATF) 17
financial markets 14
Fischer-Lescano, A 40
food safety 409
foreign trade in goods law, Europeanisation 234–6
Foucault, M 31–2, 260, 263, 264
fragmented authoritarianism 325–6
France 236–7
fundamental rights (EU) 164
Fur Felt Hoods, Bodies and Caps from Czechoslovakia case 225

Galvin, P 93, 112–13
Garth, B 31, 38, 87
GATT *see* General Agreement on Tariffs and Trade
Gebrüder Knauf WestdeutscheGipswerke case 305
Gebrüder Weis case 306
GEFCO case 311
General Agreement on Tariffs and Trade (GATT) 16, 153
Art VI 219–20, 225–8, 230, 232, 241–2, 256
Interpretative Note 220–4, 227, 232, 241, 244
Cold War divisions 218–19, 229
Europeanisation 237–8
Experts Report 226
and global legal pluralism 214–15
international context (1970s) 255
legacy of relationships 389–92
UN relationships 391–2
and US (1960s) 224–34
working parties 232–4
World Bank relationship 389–90
Gereffi, G 46
Germany
intra-German trade 236
Ordoliberal school 254–5
Giant (China) Co Ltd 92–3, 123, 124, 125, 131, 136
global commodity chains 5
Global Compact 39
global governance 34–41, 42
contract and 26
debate 35–6
demands 36
economic liberalisation 34–5, 36
hierarchy 26–7
networks *see* transnational networks
and NGOs 38–9
participants 37–8

global governance (*cont.*):
pluralism *see* legal pluralism
role of law 39–41
sites of governance 31-4, 84-8
global legal pluralism 29–34
definitions 29–30, 49, 214
as economic network 48–9
elements 48–54
private international trade law 30–1
sites of governance 31–4, 84–8
see also toy industry
global toy industry *see* toy industry
globalisation
definition 11, 42–3
exporters, effects on ownership structure 138–9
factors 11–12
features 43–4
governance *see* global governance
importers, effects on ownership structure 139
institutions/norms 16–20
and IPNs 285–6, 287–8
legal fields, internationalisation 12–16
legislation framework 18–20
producers, effects on ownership structure 139–41
regulatory 28–9
research fields 20–5
thin globalisation 15
governance *see* global governance
Greater Mekong Sub-Region (GMS) 338
Group of Lisbon 36
guanxi 326

Halberstam, D 41
hard law
definition 2–3
and individual treatment 278–82
Hardt, M 32
Harrison, J 20
health issues 409–10
health law, international 22–3
Hellvin, L 291–2
Hestermayer, H 20
Higgott, R 36
Holzmeyer, C 38
Hong Kong, economic integration agreements
details 332–3
Mainland-Hong Kong CEPA 333–5
Hong Kong Toys Council (HKTC), Code of Practice 75
Hopkins, TK 55, 64
Howse, R 39
human rights
fundamental rights (EU) 164
internationalisation 33
scholarship 20–1
and social solidarity ethics 387–8

IAIS (International Association of Insurance Supervisors) 17
IASC (International Accounting Standards Committee) 16–17
ICTI (International Council of Toy Industries), Code of Conduct 73
IIT *see* intra-industry trade
ILO 395–6
IMF 390–1
indirect effect principle 192
individual treatment
administrative discretion cases 268–74
background 4–5, 265–6
conclusion 282–4
hard law criteria 278–82
legalisation process 267–8, 282–4
soft law
criteria 271–3, 277–8
phase 274–8
informal agreements 17–18
insurance supervision 17
intellectual property 14
interdependence sovereignty 15
interlegality 33
International Accounting Standards Committee (IASC) 16–17
international agreements (EU) 164–5
International Association of Insurance Supervisors (IAIS) 17
international business contracts 14
international commercial arbitration 31
International Convention on the Simplification and Harmonisation of Customs Procedures (Kyoto Convention) 64–8, 301, 302–3
International Council of Toy Industries (ICTI), Code of Conduct 73
international criminal tribunals 15
international environmental law 24
international health law 22–3
International Labour Organisation (ILO) 395–6
international legal sovereignty 15
International Monetary Fund (IMF) 390–1
International Organisation of Securities Commissions (IOSCO) 17
international production networks (IPNs)
background 285–7
conclusion 319–20
customs procedures *see under* inward/outward processing traffic
and EU law 286–7
EU legislative framework 297–301
in European courts 303
and globalisation 285–6, 287–8
IPT/OPT *see* inward/outward processing traffic
transfer pricing 313–15
international standards organisations 16–17
International Trade Centre (ITC) 394–5
internationalisation 12–16
Internet, new technology and 14
interpretation of WTO law, European courts 157–8
intra-industry trade (IIT) 291–3
inward/outward processing traffic (IPT/OPT)
as customs procedures 298–301
integrity of 303–8
economic conditions for authorisation 308–11
Europeanisation 288–9
implications 289–97
import/export proof 312–13

international treaties 301–3
meaning 288
IOSCO (International Organisation of Securities Commissions) 17
IPNs *see* international production networks
IPT *see* inward/outward processing traffic (IPT/OPT)
Italy v Commission 312
ITC (International Trade Centre) 394–5

Jacques, M 16
Jiang Zemin 337
joint ventures (JVs) 100, 106
juridification process 267–8, 274
Juss, S Singh 21

Kahler, M 19
Kennedy, D 21, 40
Kennedy Round Anti-dumping Code 227–30, 233, 237, 241
US effect 230–1
Keohane, RO 18
Kiss, A 24
Kissinger, Henry 249
Kneebone, S 21
Koenig, M 22
Komesar, N 386
Kostecki, MM 232
Krasner, S 15
Krisch, N 33
Kross Ltd 130
Kruschchev Ultimatum 224–6
Kunming Initiative 338
Kyoto Convention 64–8, 301, 302–3

labour law/regulation 14
Ladeur, K-H 31
legal fields, internationalisation 12–16
legal pluralism *see* global legal pluralism
legal sovereignty, international 15
legislation framework 18–20
Lehne, Klaus-Heiner 115
lex mercatoria 30–1, 50–2
Likosky, M 20
Luxembourg Compromise 234

Macao, economic integration agreements
details 332–3
Mainland-Macao CEPA 335
MacCahery, JA 400
Maduro, MP 33, 40
Magnesium Oxide case 270–1
Mainland-Hong Kong CEPA 333–5
DSMs 364–5
ROOs 355–7
safeguards 360–1
Mainland-Macao CEPA 335
ROOs 357
Marchetti, R 21–2
market economy treatment 4–5, 122, 125–6
advantages 267
non-market economy, distinction 209–10
Maturana, H 30
Merry, SE 21
Michaels, R 33
MOFTEC 123–4
money laundering 17
Moody's agency 16
Morkel, A 93, 112–13
Muchlinski, P 21
multilateral environmental agreements (MEAs) 397

national security 14
Negri, A 32
neoliberal economic policies 15
NGOs *see* non-governmental organisations
Nixon, Richard 249
non-governmental organisations (NGOs) 397–8, 406–7
and global governance 38–9
non-market economies 4–5, 248–59
and Cold War *see* Cold War divisions
conceptual/normative elements 260–1
effects 263–4
definition 248
determination factors 248
international context 255–6
as legal category 252
legal framework 267
market economy, distinction 209–10, 211–12
issues 212–14, 263
normal value calculation 251, 253, 254, 257, 263
Regulations
administrative discretion 258 9
consolidation 256–7
first 250–3
reasons for 253–6
see also State-trading countries
non-preferential rules of origin *see* rules of origin (ROOSs), and China's RTAs
'noodle bowl' syndrome 379–80
norm production, cooperation 408–15
background 408
cooperative deliberation 413–15
re-institutionalisation 408–13
Nuclear Non-proliferation Treaty (1968) 229

observer status expansion 415–18
Office International des Epizooties (OIE), WTO agreements 393
plant/animal health and food safety 409
OPT *see* inward/outward processing traffic (IPT/OPT)
Ordoliberal school 254–5
Organisation for Economic Cooperation and Development (OECD)
countries 291–3
and WTO 396
outward processing traffic *see* inward/outward processing traffic

panel reports (WTO) 174–5
Pauwelyn, J 40
Pearl River Delta Agreement 335–6
Penghong, Cai 377
Perez, O 33
Petersmann, EU 39

Photo Albums case 271, 272–3, 276
plant/animal health and food safety 409
Poland 130
Poland, accession Report 232–4, 242
Polish Golf Case case 243
private standardisation bodies 398–9
production networks *see* international production networks
property law 14
prostitution 15
public interest law 14

Quiggin, J 15

re-institutionalisation 408–13
Rebman case 312
regional trade agreements (RTAs) 323
  see also under China
regulatory competition 421–2
Riles, A 21
ROOs *see* rules of origin
Roqette case 312–13
Rosenau, JN 32, 40, 49–50
Rosenfeld, M 40
RTAs *see* regional trade agreements
rules of origin (ROOSs), and China's RTAs 342, 343, 354–60
  ACFTA 357–8
  CEPAs *see* Mainland-Hong Kong CEPA; Mainland-Macao CEPA
  China-Chile FTA 358
  China-Pakistan FTA 358, 359
  types summary 354–5

S&P agency 16
safeguards, and China's RTAs 360–3
  ACFTA 361–2
  China-Chile FTA 362–3
  China-Pakistan FTA 363
  comparison summary 360
  Mainland-Hong Kong CEPA 360–1
Santos, B de Sousa 15–16, 33
Schneider, AK 364
secondary legislation (EU), and WTO law 160–4
securities commissions 17
semi-autonomous social fields 29, 52
Sen, R 380
sex trafficking 15
Shaffer, G 16, 24
Shanghai Bicycle Corporation 92–3, 94
  litigation experience 106–9, 111
  see also China Bicycle Company
Shanghai Cooperation Organisation (SCO) 338
Shapiro, M 15
Silbey, SS 37–8
sites of governance 31–4, 84–8, 89–90
  institutional relations between 403–8
  matrix of relationships 399–401
  relations between 386–8
  WTO and other 388–9, 401–3
Small Colour TVs case 269
Snidal, D 401
Snyder, F 13
social fields 13
social law 14
social solidarity ethics
  background 382–4
  conclusion 421–3
  constitutionalisation 421
  coordination 422–3
  core issues 381–2
  definition 381
  dispute settlement processes 418–21
  and human rights 387–8
  norms *see* norm production, cooperation
  observer status expansion 415–18
  regulatory competition 421–2
  sites *see* sites of governance
  and WTO 384–6, 402–3
SOE status 100, 108
soft law
  definition 3, 265–6
  and individual treatment 274–8
  juridification process 267–8, 274
  meaning 17–18
sovereignty concepts 15
special economic zones (SEZS) 68–9, 277–8
spheres of authority 32, 40, 49–50
standards 21
Starway SA 93, 111–12, 117–18, 131
State-trading countries 235–6, 246
  as legal category 248–50
  see also non-market economies
Stein, E 41
Strange, S 262
Subsidies Code 244–6, 256
Szablowski, D 34

terrorism 15
Teubner, G 20, 30, 40, 50
TME (Toy Manufacturers of Europe) 58
Tokyo Round Codes 244–6, 247, 253, 256
Toy Coalition 74
toy industry
  specific sites/segments 54–5
    connections between 69–72, 78–83
  and WTO 82–3
Toy Manufacturers of Europe (TME) 58
Trachtman, J 387
Trade Agreements Act (1979) (US) 247–8
Trans-regional EU-ASEAN Trade Initiative (TREATI) 340
transaction economy 254
transfer pricing 313–15
transnational networks 27–9
  governmental 27
  hybrid 28–9
  private 27–8
TREATI (Trans-regional EU-ASEAN Trade Initiative) 340
TRIPS Agreement
  as basis for national law (EU) harmonisation 199
  and China-Chile FTA 351–2
  EU and member states, respective powers 192–9
  in European courts 158
  geographical indications 192–3
  health issues 409–10

interpretative obligations 196–8
time limits 192, 195
and US hegemony 16
Tumen River area Development Programme (TADP) 339
TVEs 274–5
Tyco Toys 69–72

UNESCO 397
United Kingdom, anti-dumping approach 241
United Nations Conference on Trade and Development (UNCTAD), WTO agreement 394–5
United Nations, GATT/WTO relationships 391–2
United States
anti-dumping laws 215–17
and GATT (1960s) 224–34
and Kennedy Round Code effect 230–1
subsidies/countervailing duties 245–6
Trade Agreements Act (1979) 247–8
Treasury Dept
and Congress 242–4
and Kennedy Round Code 229–30, 231
and market economy surrogate 243–4
normative innovation 224–6
normative mistranslation 240–1
Uruguay Round Agreements 82–3
US hegemony 15–16, 262

van der Grijp, N 33, 52
Varela, F 30
Vermulst, EA 247
Video Tapes in Cassettes case 269–70
von Benda-Beckmann, F 22

Wacker Werke I case 313–14
Wacker Werke II case 311, 314
Wahab, M 33
Walker, N 33, 40, 41, 52–3
Wall Street Journal Europe 130
Wallerstein, I 55, 64
Washington Consensus 36
Weber, M 34
Westphalian sovereignty 15
Whalley, J 378
WHO
plant/animal health and food safety 409
WTO collaboration 395
work, new forms of 14
World Bank, GATT relationship 389–90
world bicycle industry
competing legal strategies 109–12
global value chain 93–4
industrial context 112–14
strategic actors 92–3
see also Chinese Bicycles case; European bicycle industry
World Customs Organisation (WCO) 65–6
World Intellectual Property Organisation (WIPO) 387
World Social Forum (WSF) 36
World Trade Organisation (WTO)
agreements 301–2
appellate body reports 175–8
biodiversity/plant genetic resources 410–13
coordination role 422–3
cultural diversity 410
development 16, 35–6
environmental issues 397, 403–4
health issues 409–10
ILO cooperation 395–6
and IMF 391–2
institutional relations with other sites 388–9, 401–8
ITU agreement 394
multifaceted cooperation 404–5
and multilateral environmental agreements 397
negotiating bodies 416
and non-governmental organisations 397–8, 406–7
norms *see* norm production, cooperation
observer status expansion 415–18
OECD cooperation 396
OIE agreements 393
panel reports 174–5
plant/animal health and food safety 409
and private standardisation bodies 398–9
and public health 409
and social solidarity *see* social solidarity ethics
toy industry and 82–3
UN relationships 391–2
UNCTAD agreement 394–5
UNESCO relations 397
WHO collaboration 395
WIPO agreements 387, 392–3
World Trade Organisation (WTO) law
as basis for national law (EU) harmonisation 199–201
and China's RTAs 353–76
DSMS *see* dispute resolution mechanisms
relevant provisions/role 353–4, 378–80
ROOs *see* rules of origin
safety *see* safety
compatibility with EU law 156
direct effect *see* direct effect (EU), and WTO law
dispute settlement processes 418–21
see also dispute resolution mechanisms
and distribution of powers 191–9
ethical issues 384–6
EU breaches 188–91
duty to state reasons 188–9
non-contractual liability 189–91
and EU institutions 156–65
and EU legal order 155–6
impact on EU law 153–5, 203–8
indirect effect principle 192

Ziegler, C 28
Zumbansen, P 31